THE CHINA STATION
WAR AND DIPLOMACY
1830–1860

THE CHINA STATION
WAR AND DIPLOMACY
1830–1860

BY
GERALD S. GRAHAM

*Rhodes Professor of Imperial History
Emeritus at the University of London*

CLARENDON PRESS · OXFORD
1978

Oxford University Press, Walton Street, Oxford OX2 6DP

OXFORD LONDON GLASGOW
NEW YORK TORONTO MELBOURNE WELLINGTON
IBADAN NAIROBI DAR ES SALAAM LUSAKA CAPE TOWN
KUALA LUMPUR SINGAPORE JAKARTA HONG KONG TOKYO
DELHI BOMBAY CALCUTTA MADRAS KARACHI

British Library Cataloguing in Publication Data
Graham, Gerald Sandford
  The China station.
  1. Great Britain – Royal Navy – History
  2. China – History – 19th century
  3. Great Britain – History, Naval – 19th century
  I. Title
  951'.03   DS757   78–40070

ISBN 0–19–822472–9

*Phototypeset in V.I.P. Bembo by
Western Printing Services Ltd, Bristol*

*Printed in Great Britain by
The Pitman Press, Bath*

To
Constance Mary Graham

PREFACE

SIXTY years ago, as a High School boy, I delivered a halting speech at the annual county oratorical contest held in the town hall of Markham, Ontario. It was entitled 'China, World Power of the Future', and was based on a score of books and pamphlets provided by missionary aunts and merchant uncles in Canton and Foochow. I had of course little notion at the time that my borrowed forecast, uttered with so much confidence would become half a century later an accepted fact of modern history.

Twenty-five years ago, at the Institute for Advanced Study at Princeton, I began work on *Great Britain in the Indian Ocean, 1810–50*, and in the course of preliminary investigations started to collect material on the operations of the Royal Navy in the China seas, a vaguely defined area within the limits of the East Indies station. It soon became clear that the combined subject was too vast for one volume. The desultory gathering of relevant China records continued, but not until the manuscript of the Indian Ocean book went to the printer in 1966 was it possible to concentrate wholeheartedly on Far Eastern waters.

The long-delayed encounter between industrial Britain and traditional, isolationist China has received extended treatment, especially within recent decades, from Chinese and Western scholars who have made use of indigenous sources. Not only has the first Anglo-Chinese, or Opium war been studied from the Chinese perspective, the whole of the conflict, cultural, diplomatic, and economic, that dragged on between the 1830s and the end of the 1850s, has benefited enormously from the work of historians, whose specialized investigations have brought into better focus the misty panoramas of an oriental empire.

The military aspects of three China wars that occupied much of this period have not been neglected.[1] Civilian and

---

[1] Although it is customary to designate the second Anglo-Chinese war as covering the years 1856–60, I have preferred to describe the 1860 campaign as a *third* war.

service officers' journals, logs, diaries, memoirs, and official reports in European languages provide a huge body of source material. Possibly, however, because of the unequal nature of the conflict, this kind of documentation has not been given the same attention as that reflecting the multifold consequences following Chinese defeats and the opening of 'doors' to the West. This book is mainly concerned with the part played by the Royal Navy in propelling a highly reluctant China into the concert of nations.

But as I have said more than once elsewhere, naval strategy cannot be separated from diplomacy and politics. Governments and their agents inevitably set the stage for the long-delayed contest that was intended to end Chinese isolation from the rest of the world. Because I do not read Chinese, this study is limited to the European effort in peace and war, and the response of the British naval commander, plenipotentiary, or governor to the words and actions of the 'inscrutable Chinaman'. It would be presumptuous to do more than seek to understand the conflict through European eyes. It is not for me to attempt an analysis of the Chinese mind, more particularly, the official mind, which baffled and infuriated British contemporaries, and which is scarcely comprehensible today. Leaning over backwards to compensate for ignorance—often a pretence suggesting the balanced consideration of both sides of a question—produces a spurious objectivity.

At the end of the first war, (1841–2), that percipient governor of Hong Kong, Sir John Davis (who normally eschewed purple prose) remarked that the British campaign was 'the farthest military enterprise, of the same extent, in the history of the world, surpassing, in that respect, the expeditions of Alexander and Caesar in one hemisphere, and those of Cortes and Pizarro in the other. . . .' No commander-in-chief on the China station was ever tempted to make such comparisons; indeed, there were times when a series of easy victories seemed to attract more public shame than credit. Soldiers and sailors never saw themselves as heroic figures in any epoch-making dramas. Except as professional tacticians in time of war, naval officers were rarely in the area long enough to make or to receive much impact. They knew no more about China beyond the confines of the Canton estuary, or back of the

Treaty ports, than did their contemporaries trading on the Niger know of central Africa. Admiral Sir Edward Owen, commander-in-chief of the East Indies station between 1828 and 1832, was probably exceptional in political awareness; he was one of the first to experience the tensions of *cold* war. His successor in 1841, Sir William Parker, was equally astute, but his time was largely occupied in capturing enemy ports, and finally, far up the Yangtse at Nanking, bringing hostilities to an end. There were brilliant navigators and surveyors like the crusty and egocentric Captain Edward Belcher, whose published accounts of his varied voyages provide the historian with useful first-hand, though highly biased source materials. But few shone like Captain William Hall of the steamship *Nemesis*, whose accomplishments give a Nelsonic glow to otherwise dreary one-sided engagements.

On the other hand, these men of action were in frequent touch with civilians of outstanding character and dedication in many different spheres—men who developed a marked sympathy for the Asian way of life. There were pioneering missionaries like Dr. Robert Morrison and his son, John; there was the eccentric and enterprising Reverend Karl Friedrich August Gutzlaff from Pomerania, who entered China as an interpreter on board an opium carrier, and subsequently managed to combine zealous evangelical work with official tasks under the British government, not to mention the publication of scores of articles and books in five different languages; and the first of a distinguished family line, George Tradescant Lay, agent of the British and Foreign Bible Society, a naturalist of rare initiative, and her Majesty's Consul at Canton, Foochow, and Amoy. There were courageous and sensitive diplomats like Sir Rutherford Alcock, who began his career as an army surgeon, served as Consul in Foochow and Shanghai, and who ultimately became first Consul-General in Japan; and Sir Harry Parkes, severely practical, yet not without imagination, intense, relentless in his efforts to demonstrate the superiority of Western values and civilization. There were scholar-administrators like Sir John Davis, and that notable linguist, Thomas Francis Wade. Even governors with no special claim to scholarship or literary authority seemed to grow larger than life in response to the Eastern ethos. Men such as these bear testimony to the aptness of an old Chinese proverb: 'The China Sea salts all rivers that flow into it.'

If not all great men, the times and place did seem to produce an unusual number of exceedingly able men of thought and action. Yet, in recording their efforts to open China by diplomatic persuasion and force of arms, it is almost impossible to avoid taking a moral stance, or, at the least, hinting that a moral issue exists. Mercantile cupidity, commercial expansion, military violence, missionary proselytizing, have always been topics capable of evoking personal prejudice, if not righteous indignation. Like the slave trade or the opium trade, condemnation is inherent in the iniquitous quality of either. But while the Chinese effort to suppress the opium traffic was incidentally responsible for the start of the first Anglo–Chinese war, the main argument, emphasized almost ceaselessly since the middle of the nineteenth century, has been that the fundamental wrong committed against China was the premeditated assault on a defenceless country which wanted no truck with the rapacious West. An apprehensive China, it was contended, would gladly have drawn back into her shell, and dispensed with a mutually profitable trade that had been going on for some two centuries. In short, like the Spanish conquistador in America, the European had forced an entrance by brute exercise of the sword.

It is important to remember, however, that British commercial and territorial expansion was the result of accepted policies pursued by every European power, or more specifically, by every maritime power. The distinguished historian of Japan, Sir George Sansom, recognized the unavoidable consequences of the *Zeitgeist*. 'In the circumstances of the age, expansion was the law of their being. . . . Although it may be condemned on moral grounds to-day, it was historically inevitable.'[2] It is, therefore, futile to argue that China should have been left to her own resources. In view of the expansionist or imperialist ethos of the age, such immunity was an impossibility. The lack of some kind of diplomatic relationship was bound sooner or later to precipitate a collision, whether or not the opium trade had been legalized, or the smuggler eradicated. So long as China was determined to

[2] *The Western World and Japan* (London, 1950), p. 69.

regard the foreign visitor as of inferior status and consequently undeserving of equitable treatment, the instability of the British position continued to be not only unintelligible to frustrated merchants and anxious officials, but increasingly intolerable. By 1839 procrastination, evasion, insult, and recrimination had raised emotions to the flash-point. Two utterly contrasting civilizations—so different as to be incomprehensible one to another—came into conflict. With the peace settlement of 1860, a reconciliation seemed in sight; the political seclusion of the most ancient of existing empires appeared to have been broken. Yet, the fundamental differences remained unresolved; a traditional Chinese wariness of the West had not been exorcized. Today, more than a hundred years later, the contour has changed, but the separating gulf has scarcely narrowed.

This study is based on official correspondence in Admirality, Colonial Office, and Foreign Office files contained in the Public Record Office, on letters to and from the Board of Control in the archive of the East India Library, and in the National Archives of India in New Delhi. There is, of course, some repetition of correspondence vis-à-vis London and New Delhi, but, in jig-saw fashion, Company records most opportunely filled many gaps. Similarly, a good deal of Admiralty correspondence is repeated in Foreign Office files, usually as copies. In the case of drafts which I have been unable to check with the final dispatch, the word draft is added to the reference in brackets.

Private papers formed an indispensable buttress, in particular the Russell, Pottinger, and Ellenborough Papers in the Public Record Office, and the Aberdeen, Broughton, and Auckland Papers in the British Library. The Duke of Wellington kindly allowed me to consult the Wellington Papers, and a similar privilege was accorded me by the Trustees of the Broadlands Archives in regard to the Palmerston Papers, designated in the text as Broadlands MSS. Both files are in the keeping of the Royal Commission on Historical Manuscripts, Quality Court, Chancery Lane, W.C. 2. With equal generosity, Jardine, Matheson, and Company gave me access to the Company archive, removed some years ago from Hong Kong to the University Library in Cambridge. The Private Letter Books contained much revealing comment, especially on the Canton imbroglio. I am deeply indebted to the directors and custodians of these institutions as well as to the librarians and their departmental associates in the National Maritime Museum, Greenwich, the Royal Commonwealth Society, King's College, London (in particular Mr. Anthony Shadrake), and the School of Oriental and African Studies.

In Macao, the Biblioteca Nacional offered a considerable collection of books on China written in English, but most of my Far Eastern searches were conducted in the University Library of Hong Kong, possessors of the invaluable Hankow Collection, including a set of the *Chinese Repository*, published between 1832 and 1851. Thanks to an Emeritus Fellowship award from the Leverhulme Trust, and a grant from the University of London's Hayter Travel Fund, I was able to make two expeditions to the South China Sea, and, although certain projected journeys up the coast had to be abandoned, it was possible to visit Canton, and to live in a hotel almost precisely on the site of the old English Factory. A circuitous trip to Fatshan gave me an opportunity to see something of the ever-changing network of the upper delta, just as visits to Macao brought life to the Typa anchorage, Kum-sing-mun, and the islands of Lintin, Lantau, and the Great Ladrones. From Taiwan, where the hospitable Academia Sinaica offered every kindness and extended every facility, it was only possible to gaze, perhaps a little wistfully, across the misty channel in the direction of the Forbidden Coast that contained Amoy and Foochow.

During two happy years of teaching at the University of Western Ontario, following my retirement from London in 1970, it was an unexpected stroke of good fortune to find a large cache of mainly contemporary printed material in the University Library, the gift of a far from wealthy railway employee, Mr. John Davis Barnett, who over the years had made it his hobby to built up an almost unique collection. Harvard University was not too far away from London, Ontario, and a generous departmental grant made a visit possible. In my personal experience, only the Widener Library can compete with the British Library in providing the book or the pamphlet that has all but disappeared from the face of the earth. At Harvard and 'Western' as in Hong Kong, no effort was spared to satisfy my professional greed and curiosity.

I am grateful for much useful advice to Professor L. K. Young of the Department of History, Professor D. J. Dwyer of the Geography Department [now at Keele University], and Mr. H. A. Rydings, librarian—all of the University of Hong Kong. There too, the Master of Robert Black College, Dr. Cheong Weng Eang, gave me every assistance and much hospitality. The specialized knowledge of Mr. Alan Pearsall of the National Maritime Museum has been constantly available, and, looking backwards to my last years at King's College, I recall how much is owing to the scholarly zeal and judgement of my assistant, Mr. Gordon Dodds, now on the staff of the Ontario Archives in Toronto. My old friend and colleague, Professor R. W. Beachey, was unselfish enough to read a manuscript execrably typed with two fingers. I am particularly indebted to Professor J. J. Gerson, whose sensitive and cogent criticisms and comments were supported by a wide understanding of the period as well as by a knowledge of the Chinese language.

On its long and arduous journeys, as it developed from archival jottings in Chancery Lane and Blackfriars, to rough drafts in Delhi, Macao, and Hong Kong, and finally to page proofs in East Sussex, this book was accompanied by my wife—all the way.

Hobbs Cottage,
Beckley, Rye,
Sussex.
3 July 1977.

G.S.G.

CONTENTS

LIST OF MAPS

ABBREVIATIONS USED IN FOOTNOTE REFERENCES

Adm.   Admiralty records in the Public Record Office.
Add. MSS.   Additional Manuscripts in the British Library Manu-
            script Room.
B.L.   British Library
C.O.   Colonial Office records in the Public Record Office.
F.O.   Foreign Office records in the Public Record Office.
I.O.A.   India Office Library and Archive.
J.M.A.   Jardine Matheson archive in the University Library,
            Cambridge.
N.A.I.   National Archives of India, New Delhi.
Nemesis   *The Nemesis in China*, comprising A History of
            the late War in that Country; with an account of the
            Colony of Hong Kong, from Notes of Captain W. H.
            Hall, R.N. and Personal Observations by W. D. Ber-
            nard Esq., M.A. Oxon. 3rd edn. (New York, 1969).
P.R.O.   Public Record Office, London.
S.(N.)O.   Senior (Naval) Officer.

The names of warships are italicized, and on first mention are followed by the number of guns carried, e.g. *Blenheim* (72). Just as a
captain might vary the rig in detail, so also he could determine within
limits the number of guns carried. Consequently, a *74* may appear
occasionally as a *72*, a *48* as a *46*, or a *28* as a *26*.

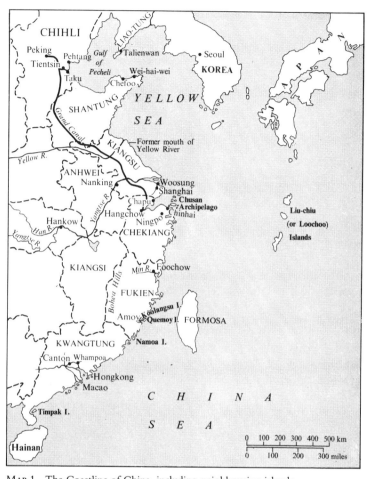

MAP 1   The Coastline of China, including neighbouring islands

INTRODUCTION

THE opening of the all-sea route to India by Vasco da Gama at the end of the fifteenth century ushered in the modern era of trade relations between Europe and China. Both Spain and Portugal in the course of their adventuring had established empires in the Americas, but doubtless encouraged by papal dispensation, the Portuguese were the first to penetrate eastern seas, and establish trading posts on the Chinese coast. Superseded in the seventeenth century by the expanding empire of the Dutch, Portugal managed, none the less, to hang on to the little peninsula of Macao on the south-west side of the Canton estuary. Possibly in return for help in suppressing pirates, she was allowed to lease this foothold from the Chinese in 1557, subject to Chinese supervisory jurisdiction.[1] And there, by agreement with the Portuguese, the East India Company was allowed to set up and maintain its own mercantile establishment. But like their hosts, the British and other foreign traders and their families were visitors on sufferance. Until the middle of the nineteenth century, Macao was a European base; it was not a true European colony.

Although strategically situated for the China trade, Macao was obviously little more than a precarious refuge for British merchants. Whatever good-will the Portuguese governor might exhibit, whatever his sympathies, in a crisis he was helpless against determined intervention on the part of the Chinese. In the long run, as the Superintendent of Trade, Captain Charles Elliot was to suggest in 1840, either Macao would have to be seized and held, with or without Portuguese concurrence, or a more comfortable and secure retreat acquired in the vicinity of the Canton estuary, say, an island like Hong Kong. As it happened, until the first Anglo-Chinese war brought matters to a head, the rather cramped peninsula

[1] Macao's separate identity had been tacitly accepted as early as 1573, when a barrier wall was built across the isthmus separating the peninsula from the mainland. Not until 1849, however, did the Portuguese manage to assert their independence by shaking off the Chinese share of administration, leaving the Emperor's officials with no more privileges than those properly belonging to the representatives of other foreign nations.

had to make do. However brittle a base from which to operate, it remained, until the dramatic emergence of Hong Kong, the sole British entrepôt in the Far East.

Macao was a curiously hybrid outpost of Europe—a fragment of seventeenth-century Portugal grafted loosely on the flank of China. Weary British officials found the town 'as picturesque as a scene from an opera', with its pink, blue, and whitewashed houses, some with doorways carved in the Gothic manner, its cathedral, Governor's palace, ornate churches, public fountains, and an imposing promenade, the Praya Grande, running along the east side of the peninsula. Consul Harry Parkes spent a blissful week in Macao, away from the 'cabin'd, cribb'd, confin'd' Factory life of Canton. 'The stillness that remains there,' he wrote to his sister in July 1852, 'although it denotes decay, is very pleasant, and incites the memory to recall old associations. . . .'[2]

From the top of Penha Hill, not far above the grotto containing the bronze bust of Camoens, the visitor has an almost limitless view of sky and sea and islands, with, on clear days, the dark grey outlines of Lintin and sometimes Lantau looming faintly in the far distance. Off the south-west tip of the peninsula is the Typa anchorage, leading to the Inner Harbour, today still clamorous and crowded with junks and fishing craft of all sizes, jostling the passenger steamers that journey back and forth to Hong Kong, forty miles to the east. Across the Inner Harbour lie the gaunt and ominously silent hills of China. Turning to the north, the rough-hewn promontory shrinks in the distance to a thin isthmus, cut by 'the barrier', 'that memento of celestial jealousy' as Commander Bingham called it, which still separates Chinese from Portuguese-leased territory.[3] Across the barrier, the Chinese kept (and probably still keep) a watchful eye on their tiny neighbour, a surveillance which Captain Loch found 'highly degrading', the more

---

[2] Stanley Lane-Poole, *Life of Sir Harry Parkes, Vol. 1, Consul in China* (London, 1894), 173–4. Parkes made his visit not long after the death of the now celebrated portrait and landscape painter, George Chinnery. 'Poor old Chinnery is gone at last,' he remarked in the same letter, 'the oldest resident in China, I believe; he and Macao were inseparable. His pictures are to be sold in a day or two.'

[3] J. Elliot Bingham, R.N. (late First Lieutenant on H.M.S. *Modeste*), *Narrative of the Expedition to China from the Commencement of the War to the Present Period . . .* , 2 vols. (London, 1842), ii. 270.

so since the Portuguese force was, by order, restricted to 300 troops, usually, as events seem to confirm, of indifferent quality.[4] None the less, he and every other naval or consular officer who kept a journal and published it, while lamenting the fate of a 'dwindling, dying city' with all the appearances of past greatness and 'power departed', found Macao, with its shady gardens, pleasant walks, and cooling sea breezes, a heaven-sent refuge after the tensions of Canton Factory existence, the boredom of the 'stationed' ship, or the semi-torpor of veranda life in Hong Kong.

Like eighteenth-century Newfoundland moored off the Banks, Macao could be compared to a 'stationed' or 'receiving' ship, anchored in the estuary for the benefit of a trade conducted through Canton, some eighty miles to the northward. Although connections had been made with Amoy, Taiwan, and subsequently Ningpo during the reign of Charles II, Canton, the most southerly of Chinese cities, had early become the favoured operating port for East India Company ships, and such privately-owned British vessels as traded under Company licence. In 1715, a permanent Factory was established on the river front, outside the city walls, where merchants could live and do business during the trading season that ordinarily opened in October and ended early in April. In due course other nations such as Holland, Sweden, France, and the United States followed suit. In 1757, Peking designated Canton as the sole Chinese port open to European traders.

Situated some forty miles up the Canton or Pearl River,[5] with a good harbour, Whampoa, only twelve miles away, Canton was in easy reach of Macao. But compared with Macao, it provided a suffocating existence for the foreigner. Before 1830, the Company community rarely exceeded thirty, along with an equal number of representatives of British private firms; probably less than half the British total was made up of other Europeans and Americans. By 1840, the six principal Factories had a resident population of about 300,

---

[4] G. G. Loch, R.N., *The Closing Events of the Campaign in China* (London, 1843), p. 25.

[5] The Canton estuary was fed by many branches that frequently changed shape and direction. There was no one Canton river in the nineteenth century; but British merchants of the time continued to describe the main channel in use as *the* Canton River, and not infrequently after 1840 as the Pearl or the Chu Kiang.

packed into an area less than 400 yards long and with an average depth of 700 feet.[6] Outside this cloistered enclave, there was little room for physical manoeuvre. The city gates were firmly closed to would-be tourists, and although the surrounding countryside was not barred, it was approachable only by way of a dense suburb through which it was always disagreeable and sometimes dangerous to pass. An oblong square, which lay between the Factories and the river, scarcely provided strolling room. However, three times a year, groups were allowed to cross over the water to the Fati gardens—but without wives; in deference to Chinese sensibilities, European women were not allowed to share the monotony of Factory life. The only stimulating recreation was to be obtained on the river, which at this point was about 500 yards wide. Here boating enthusiasts could exercise their muscles and their skills with single-pair wherries, or in regatta competition with six-oared gigs or cutters. But apart from such pastimes life could be irksome, especially for the younger men who quickly developed the habit of breaking regulations. Some of the so-called 'incidents'—hand-to-hand encounters, which sometimes resulted in serious injuries and occasionally in fatalities—were indirectly the product of community boredom. Except in times of crises, there were no warships tied to the quay, whose officers might provide an evening's entertainment; no naval guns to ensure security from insult and disorder.

To reach the Canton market on time, the well-armed East India carriers of around 800 to 1,000 tons burden forsook their customary Thames habitat in the early spring to begin the long haul around the Cape, and across the Indian Ocean to the South China Sea. A few might strike northward past Madagascar to rendezvous at Bombay or Madras, but all were intent on reaching their goal before the withering of the south-west monsoon that blows with pendulum-regularity between May and September.

By the mid-forties, the development of the steam-engine made possible the opening of what might be called 'express' services, which operated on either side of that sandy barrier,

---

[6] The community included a few Parsees, who by 1840 seem to have been classified as British residents.

the isthmus of Suez. The journey to the China seas was thus cut by more than a month, sometimes by two. But it was an awkward route, especially for the cargo carrier,[7] and the sailing track around the Cape was scarcely affected by competition from what was known as the Overland route. Even the compound engine of the fifties, capable of providing seven knots or more, could not offset the contrary power of gale winds at the height of the monsoon, which compelled sensible masters to tack as though they were navigating a true sailing ship. Hence, the often considerable differences in time taken for a dispatch to reach London from Macao, or Calcutta and Trincomalee from Hong Kong, and vice versa. So much depended on the season of the year. In the early forties, five weeks was regarded as a very quick passage from Hong Kong to Calcutta, even with favouring winds. Against the monsoon, one could count on two months or more. Sometimes six months elapsed before the Governor of Hong Kong received a reply to a dispatch forwarded to the Supreme Council at Calcutta, and probably marked urgent.[8] Similarly, even after steam came to the assistance of sail on the Cape route, the round trip—London to Hong Kong and back—might still take as much as nine months, and very occasionally a year.

But whatever the length and hazards of the journey, year upon year, lighters from the newly-arrived Indiamen at Whampoa continued to unload their cargoes at Canton —woollens, lead, Cornish tin, raw cotton from Bombay (later on, calicoes), and the usual array of clocks and musical boxes. Generally in April, the restless Company ships weighed anchor, cleared the river and departed for home on the failing wings of north-east monsoon winds that bore them towards the Sunda Straits and the Cape. Most of them carried raw silk and nankeens, porcelain ware, lacquered cabinets, rhubarb root, and, above all else, tea. By the late 1820s, Britain was

---

[7] At Alexandria, goods and persons were transferred to canal boats or barges, which took them to Cairo; thence across eighty miles of desert to Suez on the Red Sea, where waiting steamers resumed the journey to Bombay, Madras, or Calcutta, or more directly, around Pointe de Galle (Ceylon) on through the Straits of Malacca towards the Canton markets. See G. S. Graham, 'By Steam to India', *History Today*, May 1964, pp. 301–12.

[8] By comparison, 'express' deliveries from Canton to Peking could be made in twenty days, and the reply received within seven weeks of the original dispatch.

drinking some thirty million pounds of tea a year.[9] Unfortunately, as the British people consumed more and more tea, British exports failed to balance the cost, and with painful reluctance silver had to be paid into Chinese exchequers to meet the broadening trade gap. It has been calculated that by 1817, China had received about £150 million worth of bullion from Europe.[10] Then, in spectacular fashion, opium came to dominate the scene, reversing completely the balance of trade in favour of the West.

Before the late eighteenth century, opium smoking in China was not commonplace, and the cultivation of the poppy had been largely ignored. Consequently, as the Chinese demand for the drug increased by leaps and bounds, Company merchants and administrators soon realized that Bengal opium fields represented unique gold-mines of national and private profit. By the end of the first quarter of the nineteenth century, the production of opium had become an extensive and expanding enterprise, on which the Government of India relied increasingly for revenue. By 1832, the opium duty was providing one-eighteenth of British India's gross revenue, a proportion which eventually rose to nearly one-seventh. Understandably, no doubt, the British government at home was appreciative of the manner in which the balance of trade had been so nicely reversed, and, like the Government of India, was by no means anxious to discard so profitable a business.

Although the Company controlled the sales and encouraged the export of opium to China, the Company played no part in its distribution. East India ships (in response to the Chinese ban on imports) were forbidden to carry the drug, and the British traffic was thus confined to private traders, who were licensed by the Company, and remained under its control until the Company monopoly was revoked by legislation in 1833. Until that time, the private trader had been barred from participating in the long haul around the Cape; but over the years, and especially in the last quarter of the eighteenth century, firms like Jardine, Matheson, Thomas Dent, and the American

[9] The British duty on tea amounted annually to at least £3000,000, which, it has been estimated, came to approximately half the cost of the Royal Nay. See P. W. Fay, *The Opium War 1840–1842* (Chapel Hill, N.C., 1975), pp. 17–18.
[10] Edgar Hold, *The Opium Wars in China* (London, 1964), p. 36.

Russell & Co., had practically monopolized the 'country trade' between eastern ports. Indian cotton had been the principal cargo in the past, and remained an important export, but by the 1830s the hitherto neglected island of Lintin, strategically placed in the estuary, twenty-five miles south of the Bocca Tigris narrows that led up river to Canton, had become the smuggling haven of a host of private entrepreneurs, British and foreign. There, the innumerable chests of Indian opium were transferred chiefly to small, fast Chinese craft, whose rewarding task was to circumvent by devious routes the laws of Imperial China. Like the Company representatives, the private firms had their legitimate connections in Canton and Macao, but the bulk of their opium business was transacted at or around Lintin.

The private trader was a vital cog in the machinery of distribution; at the same time, he was but a subordinate partner in a formidable alliance that included not only Calcutta, but the British government in London. Apart from periods of war, trade was the nexus binding India to China, and China to the remote corridors of Whitehall. Tea remained always an essential element in the chain of circumstance, but the cementing constituent that gave strength to this curiously close, triangular relationship was opium.

But even before the opium traffic became a serious problem, and ultimately a *casus belli*, British relations with China were uneasy and occasionally tense. The ugly breaches which opened up in times of angry British resistance to unpredictable and arbitrary demands were indications that an association that left scant room for mutual accommodation might collapse entirely if the crisis were sufficiently grave. The machinery for the negotiation of ticklish commercial issues was apparently available. In Canton, routine trade was supervised by an Imperial Commissioner of Customs, known to the British as the Hoppo. Under his authority, a loosely organized guild of Chinese business men, the Hong merchants (or Cohong), held the exclusive right to conduct commercial and ultimately all external relations with the 'barbarians'.[11] Unfor-

---

[11] In 1828, an edict was issued from Peking commanding that all dealings, including written correspondence with government officials, should be conducted through the

tunately, if satisfaction were not forthcoming, there was in the circumstances, no means of direct access to the local mandarins of Canton, or beyond to the Governor of Kwantung province, or higher still to the Viceroy of the dual provincial jurisdiction of Kwantung and Kwangsi. The only acceptable method of communication with higher authority was indirectly by petition through the Hong merchants, a long-drawn process that was exasperating, and usually futile.

In the absence of any diplomatic connections, either with Peking or Canton, Company officials had little chance to settle really serious disputes by arbitration. Of necessity, it became customary to bend the knee and accept such terms as the Chinese had decided, unless, of course, the threat of excessive exactions or restraints seemed likely to presage ruin. Then, and only then, was the Company tempted to call on the home government for intervention. Until the 1830s, the risk of such confrontations was rare. Most of the Hong merchants were amiable souls who wanted the trade to prosper on sensible business lines; and apart from interludes of depression, and the occasional efforts of officious imperial commissioners or local inspectors to break the calm with penal impositions, the system was made to work, but at a price.

Appeasement in terms of extravagant fees, bribes, and constant self-abnegation proved to be a largely effective, if sometimes humiliating, British operating policy. There was a good deal of behind-the-scenes bargaining. Covert deals were made, and suitable presents delivered, not only to the Hoppo, but to the members of the Hong, sometimes for conniving at the evasion of their own Imperial laws. In retrospect, trade relations seem to have been largely a matter of 'muddling along', and the wonder is that the clumsy machinery, however well-greased by corruption, worked as well as it did. 'Take it or leave it' was the official Chinese attitude, that offered little room for negotiation. Trade with the 'barbarians'[12] remained a

---

Hong merchants, a process that was intended to emphasize the subordinate status of the foreign trader.

[12] The Chinese authorities regarded all Europeans as 'barbarians', outside the pale of what they deemed civilization. But there were various categories. Professor J. J. Gerson informs me that the differentiation (based in part on the relative level of sophistication) was rarely defined, yet could be recognized and was acknowledged by

favour granted on Chinese terms. Yet, the seasonal freights moved back and forth, growing in volume as the years went by. The Company's Select Committee of Supercargoes (generally known as the Select Committee) who were responsible for making the import and export arrangements, were determined to keep the Canton River open to traffic, and, with the support of their directors in London, had shown themselves ready—until their patience gave way in 1829—to placate Chinese authority in the interest of a highway that led to increasing riches.[13]

Whether mandarins, governors, and viceroys were much influenced or softened by the apologetic demeanour and conciliatory surrenders of Company agents may be doubted; their reactions were unpredictable; their minds unamenable to Western logic. In the fifties, it was to take Lord Elgin more than a year to appreciate 'the inconsistence which characterized everything in China'. Few British officials at home or abroad ever understood the bland bureaucrat whose mask remained impenetrable except, perhaps, to the most sensitive linguist-cum-psychologist. When he was starting to learn about China during Melbourne's second administration (1835–41), Palmerston was quite certain that he was capable of understanding and dealing with the most obtuse Chinese administrator, whether in Canton or Peking. People, he asserted with characteristic jauntiness, were the same the world over. 'As long as those who deal with the Chinese choose to allow themselves to be stopped at these outposts of artfully assumed Etiquette, and of cunningly invented Peculiarity, such Persons will be baffled and repulsed, but those who march on with Determination . . . will find the Chinese just as reasonable as the Rest of the world; and just as open to Conviction, when they find themselves the weakest.'[14]

---

the specific written Chinese characters employed. The East India Company 'Old Hand' might be one kind of 'barbarian'; the swashbuckling 'free-trader' quite another, and far less savoury.

[13] Originally carried back and forth in Company ships, the supercargoes were ordered, in 1770, to stay ashore, and take up permanent quarters, according to the season, in Macao and Canton. Five supercargoes normally constituted the Select (or managing) Committee of the Company.

[14] Palmerston to Captain Charles Elliot, 24 Jan. 1840, Broadlands MSS., GC/EL/29/2.

'Dresses vary, but strip them off, and you will find the same animal Form when you come to the naked man, with very little Diversity of Structure.'[15] Within three years of his earlier pronouncement, he was to eat his words.

Few naval officers before Admiral Sir John Fisher's time were possessed of Palmerston's self-confidence and *savoir-faire*. Neither by training nor, usually, by inclination, were they likely to be close students of human nature. Without exception, they were to be baffled by the contradictions and anomalies that contributed to the China enigma. Although frequently thawed by gentle courtesy and genuine hospitality, the naval officer was almost totally unprepared to deal with the 'inscrutable Oriental' as described by the press. In South America, on the east coast of Africa, and in the Pacific, he had shown himself to be a highly successful diplomat. But very few of his breed felt qualified to deal with the mandarin politicians, 'that hidebound body of pedantic literati, the grist of an irrational examination mill', so utterly impregnable to Western argument, so indifferent to Western notions of justice, so devious in negotiation, and yet at times so extraordinarily warm and disarming.

Indeed, a broad ignorance of China and the Chinese continued to hang like a black shadow over every conference table. Neither Admiralty nor Foreign Office could provide elementary directives, because no detailed knowledge of the people, the geography of the interior, the economy, and above all else, customs and traditions, was available. Only Sir John Barrow, Secretary to the Admiralty, seems to have been aware that Formosa was larger than Ireland, and, more that that, he knew the position of the island in relation to the mainland. At the time of the dissolution of the East India Company in 1834, only a handful of English residents could speak the language; and whether in war, during trade negotiations, or in the course of exploration, the scarcity of capable interpreters was too often reflected in personal misunderstandings and the obscurity of official statments. None the less, Admiralty instructions to commanders-in-chief and captains continued to emphasize 'the indispensable necessity of respecting their usages and institutions, and of studying their wishes and feelings for the

[15] Palmerston to Admiral George Elliot, 16 Jan. 1841, ibid., GC/EL/38/1.

purpose of preserving amicable relations with so peculiar a
Country as China, where actions indifferent in themselves and
which among European Nations would lead to little or no
inconvenience might produce an impression highly unfavourable to the British character and destructive of that wholesome
influence which is so important should attach in China to
anything connected with Great Britain'.[16]

Sometimes, however, curious imponderables helped to
bridge the language and culture gap. There was poor old
Admiral Kuan, inefficient and not especially bright, but a
brave man with a good and generous heart, who, in the midst
of battle, worried less about his life than about the loss of his
red status button and then, refusing surrender, died needlessly
at his post. In the manner of his death he showed a kind of
nobility that the Royal Navy understood and respected, and he
was given a hero's salute as his body was carried away for
burial. There was sympathy, but less deference for the Tartar
general who sought to retrieve his honour by immolating
himself in the hour of his defeat. Dramatic suicide carried
military tradition beyond Western concepts of duty. The
action was not comprehensible to the British serviceman, but
it was awesome.

In general, the most useful observations on the life and
customs of the country were made by soldiers. They had, after
all, better opportunities, because they marched upon and frequently lived off the land. A good few of both Services kept
diaries or journals, some of which were published for the
benefit of a British public eager for tales of travel and adventure. Obviously, they vary considerably in quality and interest, but whether the scene was viewed from shipboard or from
the shore, whether in northern latitudes or southern, the visitor gazed on a land of anomalies and contradictions—mysterious even to Company greybeards—where fearful squalor
might provide the background for objects of exquisite beauty,
where poverty could go hand in hand with touching hospitality, and where, of a sudden, deep humanity might reveal itself
alongside barbarous cruelty and treachery. All told, the soldier
and the sailor were being constantly presented with a sublime
puzzle that the most astute observer could never satisfactorily

[16] Instructions to Admiral Inglefield, 3 Aug. 1846, Adm. 13/3/149.

complete. The missing piece was a true knowledge of the Chinese character, and that unknown quantity, that 'inscrutable' quality, was more than once to upset careful British calculations.

Yet one strong thread of understanding runs through the pages of almost every diary and travelogue: the traditional courtesy to the stranger, which was, by and large, a part of the Chinese way of life. With the exception of Canton and its environs, and some of the coastal areas south of Foochow, in general, unless ordered to express hostility, people showed themselves either shyly friendly or indifferent in the presence of the barbarian. The consequences of power politics did not greatly interest them, so long as they were allowed to grow and sell their rice in peace, and their fields were not made the scene of destructive struggle. The ordinary people as distinct from the administrative class, so it was stated in an official report by the Select Committee of Supercargoes, were 'very far from being adverse to British Intercourse or connection, and possess a character of energy, industry and intelligence we believe superior to any other of the Inhabitants of Asia'.[17]

Meanwhile, uncomprehending, complacent, and apparently secure China looked down in contempt on the bustling intruders from across the seas. Inexorably, however, the pressures were accumulating. The first fateful sign that China could not cut herself off from the world became evident in 1808, when Napoleon revealed his intentions of incorporating Spain and Portugal within his European system. In such an event, British trade to China was bound to suffer, not least because British merchants would probably find themselves dislodged from their settlement at Macao. In consequence, a squadron was dispatched under Admiral Drury, commander-in-chief of the East Indies station, to protect the peninsula against a possible attack by a French force known to be in the neighbourhood. Unaware of the gravity of the European upheaval, and of the repercussions likely to affect trading operations as far away as the China seas, Peking refused to recognize or tolerate this or any other foreign effort at self-

---

[17] To Sir Charles T. Metcalfe, President in Council at Fort William, Macao, 3 Aug. 1831, Foreign Department, Consultation No. 7–8, 14 Oct. 1831 (N.A.I.).

protection which might infringe Chinese neutrality or threaten territorial integrity. In the eyes of the Imperial Court, the presence of British warships in the estuary, and the landing of troops at Macao, were acts of insolence, direct and indecent deeds of trespass; and the Governor at Canton was ordered to issue an ultimatum to the effect that Chinese forces were prepared to fight, but military action would be suspended provided the British squadron withdrew from Chinese waters. The squadron did withdraw. No doubt it was a wise decision, but the resident merchants inevitably 'lost face', and more than that, they paid the penalty of increased tax exactions and tighter trading restrictions.

This 'hands off' gesture was but a prologue to the stirring drama to come. The entry of the United States into the war in June of 1812 provided, in retrospect, the Western 'writing on the wall'. For the first time in modern history, the South China Sea became a significant theatre of operations. Americans traded with Canton in considerable numbers, and the United States government was prepared to send privateers to wreak as much injury as possible on their principal trade rival and enemy. In response to this threat, the Admiralty extended their convoy system eastward for the sake of the tea trade and, if possible, to cut American connections with Canton. The senior British naval officer in Chinese waters at the time was Captain Robert O'Brien, who commanded the cruiser *Doris*. O'Brien was a man of strong opinions, and when the Irish in him was aroused (which was not infrequent) a man of precipitate action. He believed that the Chinese were favouring the Americans, and although well aware of Chinese regulations and susceptibilities, and not unmindful of the fiasco of 1808, he had his armed convoy escorts anchor in Macao harbour, and in May of 1814 encouraged the pursuit of an American merchantman up river as far as Whampoa.

Under Chinese regulations, foreign warships were permitted to anchor off the coast *outside* the islands at the mouth of the Canton River; in short, they were forbidden to enter the estuary, which of course included the Bogue, that narrow entry to the main water route leading to Whampoa and Canton. In the reproving words of the Viceroy, the Celestial Empire had established laws which were venerable, just, explicit, and liberal. Hitherto, foreign merchants had regarded them with respect. The uncivilized wrangling and contending outside the gates was of no concern to him. But the 'barbarians' should not, under any circumstances, enter 'our inner seas' with their cruisers 'to violate our Regulations, and render useless the vast benevolence of the Celestial Empire'.[18]

Various proclamations followed this lofty communication, prohibiting the sale of provisions or supplies of any sort to British ships and Factory residents, and forbidding British men-of-war boats from passing the Bogue should sympathetic captains wish to send sustenance to their harassed countrymen at Whampoa or Canton. Such actions struck O'Brien as an outrageous abandonment of neutrality in the interests of armed American merchant ships 'some of which are laden with the plunder of British ships'.[19] In the meantime, the Admiralty had learned of O'Brien's violation of Macao's harbour waters, and of the concern of the Foreign Office. No satisfactory explanation of his conduct being forthcoming, he was summoned back to Indian waters by his commander-in-chief, court-martialled in April 1816, and dismissed the service.[20] Twenty years later, he might well have been congratulated, if not promoted, for showing so much initiative.

The sacrifice of O'Brien may have been intended as a burnt offering to the Celestial Gods in the hope that success might attend Lord Amherst's mission in Peking. Whatever the intent, this famous and ill-considered pilgrimage failed to reach the outskirts of the throne.[21] The deliberate humilation of the embassy undoubtedly led to a temporary hardening of Foreign Office and consequently of Admiralty attitudes. Early in 1818, when Canton officials began searching Company ships for contraband, a British warship sailed up to Whampoa and showed her guns as well as the flag. This unusual and

---

[18] Viceroy to O'Brien, encl. No. 4 [May 1814] in Commodore George Sayer to Croker, Malabar Coast, 20 Feb. 1815, Adm. 1/188.

[19] O'Brien to Captain B. Hodgson, H.M.S. *Glendower*, Chuenpi, 2 Oct. 1814, encl. in Sayer to Croker, 20 Feb. 1815, Adm. 1/188.

[20] Rear-Admiral George Burlton to Croker, 28 July 1815, and Commodore George Sayer to Croker, Trincomalee, 12 May 1816, transmitting the original sentence received from the acting Judge-Advocate at the court martial held in April 1816, Adm. 1/189.

[21] The mission reached Peking on 29 August 1816, and left again the same day.

challenging demonstration had good effect.[22] The presence of two English frigates, wrote the Captain of the *Liverpool*, 'operated most powerfully in the late re-opening of the Trade' that had been so much disturbed by Cantonese interventions. The key to a continued 'good understanding' was obviously a man-of-war. The commander-in-chief of the station, Rear-Admiral Sir Henry Blackwood, was clearly impressed, and promised to keep a frigate 'if I can possibly afford one, constantly cruising in those Seas'.[23]

But the 'iron hand' of logic was not to the liking of Company hands, who believed they understood the sinuosities of the Chinese mind far better than the commander-in-chief, or indeed any civil servant in Whitehall. Fearful that the use of force might mean a confrontation, and the loss of all privileges and profits to their trading rivals, they preferred to keep on wearing the hairshirt of Chinese capriciousness. As it happened, however, this painful role of acquiescence and appeasement was soon to be rudely interrupted. Without any assistance from the traders, the Navy was quite capable of creating its own diplomatic 'incidents'; and the Navy carried the national flag and the national honour.

On 15 December 1821, a boat party from the frigate *Topaze*, anchored off Lintin Island, was sent ashore for the daily supply of water. Chinese villagers armed with spears and bamboo rods met them in considerable force, and attempted to take possession of hoses and spouts. The duty officer of the *Topaze*, noticing the critical situation of the watering party, hastily dispatched reinforcements. After using blank cartridges with little or no effect, the rescuers fired ball, and in the course of the struggle two Chinese were killed.[24] In conformance with

---

[22] Correspondence connected with the 'gunboat diplomacy' of March 1818, is contained in Adm. 1/190.

[23] Blackwood to Croker, *Leander*, off S.E. end of Ceylon, 15 Mar. 1821, encl. letter from Captain Collier Adm. 1/191.

[24] Blackwood to Croker, 1 Feb. 1822, enclosing letter from Cmdr. Price Blackwood of the *Curlew*, 31 Jan. 1822, Adm. 1/191.

The first reaction of the Select Committee was to disclaim responsibility in the hope of saving their brittle trading connections, and on 29 December they appealed to the Viceroy at Canton for understanding and leniency. (In this connection, see letter to Captain Richardson of the *Topaze*, off Lintin, 3 Jan. 1822, signed by Committee members J. B. Urmston, J. Molony, and W. Fraser, enclosed in Blackwood to Croker, *Leander* at Bombay, 9 Apr. 1822, ibid.).

traditional practice, the Viceroy, when he learned of the affair, asked for the delivery of two of the *Topaze*'s crew. The recent fate of the American sailor Terranova of the Baltimore brig, *Emily*, doubtless encouraged him in his demand, and equally affected the decision of Captain Richardson to make no surrenders. A few months earlier, in attempting to get rid of an importunate fruit seller, Terranova accidentally struck the woman with some loose object which happened to be lying on the deck. She fell out of her bum-boat and was drowned. When the Hong merchants promised a fair trial, despite the lessons of the past, the culprit was handed over to the Chinese authorities, who subsequently after farcical trial had him strangled on the common execution ground. With this tragedy fresh in mind, even the hitherto appeasing Select Committeemen supported the Captain in his defiance of Canton. As a result, early in January 1822, all Company trade was suspended, and all British warships were ordered to leave Chinese territorial waters. In the circumstances, there was no alternative but to haul down the flag from the Factory roof; in a matter of hours, the entire British Canton establishment, including goods and cash, was removed to waiting ships at Whampoa. In close line-ahead, they managed to pass the Bogue forts without drawing fire, and joined the *Topaze* off Lintin.

The days of 'muddling through' seemed to be over; the mood of the merchant community, as represented by the Select Committee, appeared to have hardened. Both Company and private traders were no longer confident that they could maintain the old relationship with judicial mixtures of concessions and bribes. It was impossible that business could continue under existing conditions, wrote the Company's Factory chief, J. B. Urmston. 'I consider,' he concluded, 'that the East India Company and the British Government are solemnly and imperatively called upon the place the trade with China on a distinct and honorable footing. . . .'[25] Once again, Admiral Blackwood came out in support of a more active policy in the face of 'crude intimidation'. He was certain that the Government of India would support the Company, and he

[25] On board H.C.S. *Waterloo* at Chuenpi, to Rear-Admiral Blackwood, 4 Feb. 1822, Adm. 1/191.

ordered Captain Boyle of the *Glasgow* to convey his views post-haste to Calcutta, along with the suggestion that the commander-in-chief himself might visit the China coast, as the Supreme Government saw fit.[26]

The *Topaze* affair blew over, and within the year trading relations were resumed. Then followed a period of uneasy calm as the merchant community waited nervously for a judgement from London. It came with decisive bluntness on 11 June 1822. On that day, the Company's Court of Directors decided unanimously to abandon the threat of force as a means of protecting or forwarding British interests in China. The policy of concession and conciliation was to be resumed; and in a most positive manner, the Court advised the First Lord of the Admiralty to stop all peace-time visits by H.M. ships to the China coast unless assistance was urgently requested by the Governor-General of India. It was highly desirable, the recommendation continued, 'to prevent as far as possible the recurrence of events similar to that which has put to imminent hazard a branch of commerce so important to the East India Company, and to the interests of the British nation'.[27] The Admiralty complied, and with ministerial approval instructed the commander of the East Indies station to avoid the China seas, unless dire emergency warranted special intervention by ships of the Royal Navy.[28]

For the next decade, this unambiguous command remained part of standing Admiralty instructions. No explanation was offered; there was no appeal for patience and forbearance in the interests of Anglo-Chinese accord and steady commerce. Ships' commanders were simply informed that British commerce with China stood in no need of armed protection.[29]

So the old problem of unequal association remained unresolved. For the sake of constant and relatively stable trade

[26] Blackwood to Croker, *Leander* at Trincomalee, 16 Feb. 1822, Adm. 1/191.

[27] Secretary of Court of Directors to Lord Melville, East India House, 11 June 1822, Adm. 1/3919.

[28] Croker to Commodore Grant, 12 June 1822, Adm. 2/1328. The extension of the eastern boundary of the East Indies station in 1820 to 170° west longitude had made it clear that China was not necessarily excluded from the attentions of the squadron based on Bombay and Trincomalee.

[29] See Instructions to Sir James Brisbane, Captain, H.M.S. *Boadicea*, 4 Feb. 1825, Adm. 2/1329; also instructions to Admiral Gage in 1826, to Admiral Owen in 1829 (Adm. 2/1329), and to Admiral Gore in 1832, Adm. 13/2.

relations, Company representatives on the spot were asked to accept Chinese standards of law, and, (unless they involved matters of life and death), Chinese standards of justice. Inability to negotiate with the Hong merchants on equal terms, and to claim equal treatment for British nationals, with the right of diplomatic access to the highest authority in Canton, left them in a particularly vulnerable, if not cruel position. Retreat was out of the question, since this would involve the abandonment of a profitable commerce for the benefit of rivals like the Americans. There was no alternative, but to accept. This was the view of the Company's supreme tribunal in London, and it was, subsequently, to have the support of James Stuart Mill, who more than thirty years later warned the Foreign Office of the stupidity of punching a huge feather pillow like China. Diplomacy stood for nothing when there was no fleet to back it. In the interests of commerce, Britain should confine her attentions strictly to 'certain points of the coast, which the trading propensities of both nations will keep under any circumstance'.[30]

But would the situation have been radically altered had there been a squadron 'to back' Company diplomacy? Would the problem have been simpler, if not soluble, had the Chinese been aware of the extent and quality of British power? Certainly—and for more than two decades to come—the Royal Navy did not count as an instrument of diplomacy, because Peking had no notion of its true capability. Even when ships' gunnery did reveal the shattering effects of shell fire on strong forts, reports to the capital were so distorted by obsequious officials as to transform costly defeats into victories. In the circumstances, there was little or no hope in the 1820s that the Emperor and his Court could be made to see reason, and come to terms. If a final settlement were to be reached, it became gradually clear to Foreign Office officials that Peking would have to learn, through 'imposing demonstrations of force', the immense and devastating power that lay in the hands of the Mistress of the Seas.

No other Western power was so well endowed as Britain to rend the darkness that surrounded the Emperor's Court. Neither France, nor the United States, not to speak of Russia,

[30] *Edinburgh Review*, Jan. 1860, pp. 103–4.

had the ships or the bases necessary to lever open Chinese coastal doors. Although more than 3,000 miles away, India could supply men, guns, munitions, and stores to nourish expeditionary forces during three China campaigns. And in Singapore Britain possessed an indispensable half-way house, controlling the Malacca Strait and the main route to the East. By 1842, she held Hong Kong with its Victoria harbour, adjoining the convenient anchorage at Kowloon. In addition, no other European power commanded the commercial *savoir-faire* that Britain was capable of apportioning around the globe.

Yet, it was not until the beginning of the 1840s that the process of demonstrating power, of 'showing the flag' beyond coastal boundaries, became a practicable operation. The coming of steam, by making possible the penetration of Chinese rivers, opened up the interior to British warships. By 1842, steamers lke the *Nemesis* could guide or pull battleships as far as Nanking on the Yangtse-kiang, more than 200 miles from the sea. By the end of the 1850s, they were capable, on their own, of reaching Hankow some 400 miles further on. But for the moment, hearing was not believing. Before the truth could penetrate the cloistered walls of the Manchu Court, the capital itself, so it appeared, would have to feel the compulsive power of modern instruments of war. For Oriental peoples, wrote a shrewd French observer, not without irony, 'the fear of the English is the beginning of wisdom'.[31]

---

[31] Henri de Ponchalon, *Indo-China, Souvenirs de voyage et de campagne, 1858–1860* (Tours, 1896), quoted J. F. Cady, *The Roots of French Imperialism in Eastern Asia* (Ithaca, N.Y., new edn. 1967), p. 139 n. 7.

I

COMPANY TRADE AND TRIBULATIONS

In 1822 the Royal Navy had been barred from visiting the China Sea, and for nearly a decade both private and Company Englishmen and Scots had suffered nasty blows to pride as well as purse. Late in 1829, when renewed efforts at negotiation failed utterly to eradicate the injustices associated with Chinese rules of commercial dealing, the Select Committee rebelled against their predecessors' policy of appeasement, supported, as it had been, by the Court of Directors in London. By a majority vote, the Committee resolved to suspend all commercial intercourse at Canton, and to redirect the Company's China ships to Manilla. At the same time, they called upon the Supreme Government in India to back up their action by a direct address to the Emperor of China, stiffened if possible by the dispatch of four warships, two to be stationed in the Canton estuary, and two in the Gulf of Pecheli at the entrance to the Pei River leading towards Peking.

Like his Company masters in England, the Governor-General of Bengal, Lord Bentinck, was unconvinced by the power-play, and not a little shocked by the Committee's disregard for instructions.[1] Obviously unable to keep up with day-by-day affairs in Canton and Macao, and scarcely aware of the fast accumulating and combustible resentments, he had some difficulty in understanding why a sudden breakdown in Anglo-Chinese relations (which had occurred only once previously in 1814, at the behest of the Navy) should justify a complete suspension of Company trade and the huge financial losses which such action would entail.[2] 'On what grounds', he wondered, was it assumed 'that the cautious policy of not

---

[1] Lord William Cavendish Bentinck, Governor-General of Bengal since 1828, became the first Governor-General of India in 1833.

[2] To the Secret Committee, East India Company, 7 May 1830 (No. 5), Foreign Dept., Consultation No. 7, 7 May 1830 (N.A.I.).

admitting Ships of War, and of excluding all possible chance of collision or cause of offence, hitherto so successfully pursued and in a very recent instance, strongly recommended by a preceding Select Committee, is erroneous and unnecessary?' Since full information was lacking, clearly 'so radical a change of the peaceful policy hitherto invariably and successfully followed', and one which 'carefully abstained from all displays of power' could not be undertaken without the sanction of the authorities in London.[3]

Lord Bentinck's cautious rebuke reached Macao at the end of July 1830. In the eyes of the Select Committee, it seemed to suggest that the merchant community, as the result of an isolated existence, were suffering from nerves, an assumption that was bitterly resented by members who claimed to have been misunderstood. The Committee was not, they replied, trying to intimidate Canton with the prospect of awful devastation at the hands of the British fleet. They were simply intent on showing the Chinese authorities that the repeated harassments of British trade and damages to British property could not take place 'without attracting the attention of the Governor of India. . . .' If the commander-in-chief of the East Indies station could be immediately instructed to 'show the flag', such emergency action would do far more to check extortionate and rapacious practices 'than any measure which the Committee might have in their power to adopt.'[4]

Except in the event of a recognizable emergency, Admiral Sir Edward Campbell Rich Owen dared not act without an order from the Governor-General. But did the Committee's apparent panic, as so reported, indicate a real emergency? Was there, in fact, an urgent need for immediate naval help in defence of British interests? Otherwise, he was bound by his standing instructions to stay away from Chinese waters. It was unlikely that the Committee would breach the Company's traditional policy of conciliation and appeasement without good reason, in which case he could only pray that His

---

[3] Minute, 3 April 1830, encl. No. 5 in Bentinck to Court of Directors, 3 Apr. 1830, L/P & S/5 (I.O.A.).

[4] R. Huddleston, secretary to the Select Committee, to George Swinton, secretary to the Supreme Government at Fort William, 30 July 1830, Foreign Dept., Consultation No. 9, 14 Oct. 1830 (N.A.I.).

Majesty's government would reconsider the risks involved in barring British warships absolutely, and in the light of the Committee's protestations allow 'occasional visits to the ports of China', a prestige exercise performed regularly by French and American vessels of war.[5]

Bentinck had avoided direct action, partly because he mistrusted what he regarded as the over-shrill representations of the Select Committee, and partly because of a reluctance to breach the Company's long-standing code of conduct in regard to Chinese relations. Hence it was left to the Court of Directors in London to make the final decision. Late in May 1830, the Court met to consider the unwarranted, indeed, insubordinate conduct of the Committee in breaking with established policy. There was no discussion of the provocations leading to unprecedented rebellion. Angry and shaken by the unexpected flouting of their orders (a reaction which was fully shared by the Chinese authorities in Canton, when they learned of the situation), the Committee was dismissed, and in November 1830, a new membership was given the awkward task of combining customary gentle diplomacy with profitable trade relations.

Much depended on the character of the president of the re-created Committee, whose main task was to calm the troubled waters that threatened to engulf the British trade. The new appointee, Charles Marjoribanks, was a man of discretion, common sense, and strong fibre, but beyond such personal qualifications, he had scant armour to rely on. The Court refused to concede that recent events, as described to them, justified any dramatic military gesture, and at their behest Admiral Owen was instructed by the Admiralty to stick to standing orders until alterations appeared to be warranted. In short, like every other commander-in-chief since 1822, he was told that the Chinese were not to be disturbed by the threatening presence of British ships of war in Chinese waters, unless circumstances dictated urgent need.[6]

---

[5] Owen to Croker (Secretary to the Admiralty), *Southampton* at Kedgeree, 7 May 1830, Adm. 1/196; also Owen to Bentinck, same date, encl. No. 1, in Bentinck to Court of Directors, L/P & S/1 (I.O.A.).

[6] See Barrow (Admiralty) to Owen, 13 Nov. 1830, Adm. 2/1590; and Owen to Elliot (Admiralty), 9 May 1831 (No. 142), repeating the content of Barrow's letter of 13 November, Adm. 1/202.

As it happened, scarcely had the old Committee been replaced when their successors were confronted in 1831 with 'fresh aggressions' by the Canton government. Although charged with the task of peace-making, they, in turn, had no choice but to call on the Governor-General for aid, and on the commander-in-chief 'for the countenance which [he] could give them with the squadron'. On this occasion, they insisted the emergency was very real; human lives and property were in danger, as the result of an organized campaign of hysterical violence. On 12 May 1831, the British Factory had been attacked by a mob, encouraged, so it was rumoured, by the Hoppo. The King's picture had been mutilated, the senior Hong merchants, assumed to be over-friendly with British traders, threatened with death, and the senior Linguist thrust into chains and committed to prison.[7] More than that, the Factory gates and the quay had been destroyed; most of the walls had been demolished, trees had been uprooted, and the surrounding grounds and gardens laid waste.[8]

Whatever the origins of the ferment, it was now clear that the age of one-sided negotiations—of turning the other cheek—was coming to an end. In the words of the Committee's president, ' . . . a blow had been inflicted of most serious nature on the credit and security of our Company'. The British government had either to take a firm stand on behalf of its nationals, or order them to withdraw 'bag and baggage' from Macao and Canton: ' . . . firmness, resistance and even Acts of violence', read the Committee's resolution, 'have always

---

[7] A further rupture might have been anticipated following the arrest and imprisonment of one of the most prosperous Hong merchants in the course of the previous trading season. His alleged crime was his 'traitorous connection with the English'. 'In placing the strictest restraints upon our feelings by passing over this occurrence in silence, we were conscious at the same time,' wrote Marjoribanks, 'that a blow had been inflicted of a most serious nature on the credit and security of our Company.' Charles Marjoribanks and members of the Select Committee to C. T. Metcalfe, Vice-President in Council at Fort William, Macao Factory, 26 May 1831, Foreign Dept., Chinese Receipts and Issues (1831–2) (N.A.I.). This communication was received in Calcutta on 24 August. See also, Canton Register, vol. iv, No. 15, 2 Aug. 1831, containing correspondence in protest against the merchants' failure to vindicate their own and the Hong merchant's innocence. Happily for the victim, he died in prison.

[8] See Resolutions of the Select Committee, Macao, 30 May 1831 [in print] with a copy of the report on the destructive attack, addressed to the Supreme Government of India, in Owen to Elliot, Trincomalee, 29 Aug. 1831 (No. 280), Adm. 1/204.

succeeded in producing a Spirit of conciliation, while tame submission has only had the effect of inducing still further oppression.'[9] The Chinese authorities were intent on reducing foreigners 'to the lowest and most restricted possible condition'. In response to this malevolent persecution, British merchants could either tacitly acquiesce or show 'temperate yet firm remonstrance and resistance'. Obviously, there was only one choice. On 10 June, the Committee issued a proclamation suspending all trade in the Canton River after 1 August 1831.

In the hope of making diplomatic contact with Peking, Britain had in the past sent two embassies to China, one led by Lord Macartney in 1793, and the second by Lord Amherst in 1816. Both had failed lamentably, and rather than continue this suppliant manner of approach the Committee now recommended that a high-ranking naval officer, accompanied by a strong detachment from the East Indies squadron, should set out for the Gulf of Pecheli, and thence deliver a strong remonstrance to the Emperor in Peking. 'We are decidely of opinion,' the resolution went on, 'that with little sacrifice of Commercial Interests and without any acts of aggression on the unoffending Natives of the Country it [the Chinese Empire] could be readily brought to a sense of its own comparative weakness, and an intercourse infinitely more favourable be established to any which Foreigners have hitherto enjoyed. This we believe could be accomplished either with or without the acquisition of an independent settlement.' This was the first mild suggestion that Britain might seize an island off the Chinese coast.

As a matter of fact, an extraterritorial establishment was already in existence north-east of Macao on an island in the Canton estuary. Lintin had no official existence, but until 1839 it remained the centre of the opium trade. Even during the winter months store ships kept their anchorage off the 'lonely' island, whence a lucrative business was conducted with the mainland, usually with the connivance of the Canton authorities. It must have appeared to eager supercargoes but a short and easy step from unofficial *de facto* presence to permanent occupation. The possession of a coastal island, declared the Committee, 'would enable us to intercept the whole of the

[9] Ibid.

Asiatic Trade and to carry terror to the Neighbourhood of Peking itself'. Such a stroke, by ending the false and foolish policy of appeasement, would clear the air by negotiation on equal terms.[10]

The petition of the private merchants in July (1831) supported the Company Committee's judgement, and thus indicated a new unity of purpose between the British rivals. The private firms were at last ready to agree that 'extreme measures of resistance' were preferable to peace at the price of increasing exactions and precarious trade.[11] Shaped by William Jardine and James Innes, a pungent address to the Canton authorities underlined with heat the lack of equality that marked all Anglo-Chinese business dealings, and the 'unjust and offensive Regulations' that muddied a mutually profitable relationship. The recent attack on the Factories, hitherto regarded as inviolate sanctuaries by the foreign trader (and for which an annual rent was paid), had shattered all confidence, not only in the good faith of the Canton government, but in the ability of the Hong merchants to protect foreign visitors. Unless there were a change of mood, permitting redress of grievances and guarantees of life and property, it might be necessary, as a purely defensive measure, to bring up an armed detachment from Whampoa.[12]

The reaction of the Canton authorities to this blunt challenge reflected, in a mixture of reason and fantasy, the embittered Chinese point of view. The foreign Factories, it was

[10] Ibid. A copy of the document is contained in I.O.A., R/10/9. See also, Select Committee (Marjoribanks, Davis, Daniell, and Smith) to Court of Directors, 18 June 1831, implying rather than stating the need for armed naval support, Adm. 125/92.

[11] See Owen to Elliot, 20 Aug. 1831 (No. 280), Adm. 1/204.

[12] Printed address in Foreign Dept., Chinese Receipts and Issues (1831–2) (N.A.I.); also, enclosed in Owen to Elliot, 13 Nov. 1831, Adm. 1/205. See, in addition, Memorial of private merchants to House of Commons, 28 Dec. 1830, quoted in H. B. Morse, *The Chronicles of the East India Company trading to China, 1635–1834* (Oxford, 1926), iv. 244–5.

None the less, William Jardine privately confessed his astonishment at the Committee's sudden change of temper. In his view, the Viceroy in Canton might have been handled successfully with customary care and finesse. By precipitate boldness, the Committee had lost the opportunity of obtaining redress, which would in all probability have been accorded. 'The Chief [of the Select Committee] still talks of resistance, but when or how, no one knows, while the Chinese authorities increase in insolence every day, from entertaining an opinion that the Committee are probably supported from England. . . .' To W. T. Copeland, Canton, 22 July 1831, Private Letter Books (B 9), vol. 1, 1830–2 (J.M.A.).

pointed out, rested on Chinese soil under the jurisdiction of the provincial city. The regulations for the conduct of the inhabitants of such Factories were rightly the product of Chinese authority. Why should barbarian merchants presume to say that the Chinese could not make and enforce their own rules. 'Those who knock head at the gate of the market and solicit commercial intercourse must obediently keep the royal regulations.'

The Celestial Empire in cherishing tenderness to distant foreigners, has constantly stooped to show compassion, but between the flowery Chinese and Barbarians, there doubtless is a settled distinction; between those within and without, there must be established a grand barrier. The dignity of the Great Emperor requires obedience and severity. How can the foreign merchants of every nation be suffered to indulge their own wishes in opposition to and contempt of the laws!

But there were 'barbarians' and 'barbarians' and the Chinese with characteristic shrewdness sought to divide their adversaries. Canton had suspected for some time that the days of the Company monopoly were numbered, and leading officials made no bones about their preference for disciplined Company servants as opposed to the rude and aggressive private traders. After all, it was Jardine and his colleagues, not the Select Committee, who had had the audacity to present them with an offensive address. 'At present,' declared the Hoppo in July 1831, 'the said Chief Marjoribanks is profoundly intelligent and acts with great propriety.' He was a gentleman. On the contrary, 'the said Jardine, Innes and others, are merely private English merchants, and are not at all comparable to the Company.' The Company agents were accustomed, by tradition and training, to show obedience; the representatives of private firms were uncontrolled barbarians, voracious, uninhibited in their ambitions, cunning in their audacity and their perversity.[13]

Not until August 1831, did Lord Bentinck receive in India the Select Committee's report of the assault on the Factory

<hr>

[13] The printed Chinese replies (12 and 13 July) to the private merchants' petition are contained in Adm. 1/205, and in Foreign Dept., Receipts and Issues (1831–2) (N.A.I.), and in the *Canton Register*, iv. No. 15, 2 Aug. 1831, a copy of which is enclosed in Receipts and Issues (1831–2) as above.

which had occurred in the previous May. Whereupon his doubts vanished. 'I am disposed to place great reliance in the wisdom, discretion and experience of the Select Committee who now preside over the affairs of the Company at Canton,' he informed Admiral Owen on 27 August, 'and more particularly of Mr. Marjoribanks, the Chief of the Factory.' In view of the British community's precarious situation, he hoped that the commander-in-chief would find it convenient to visit Macao with his flagship, *Southampton*, and any other available vessels of the squadron, as soon as possible. He himself was perfectly willing to write a strong letter of protest to the Viceroy in Canton, but in view of previous humilations, a similar memorial to the Emperor would be considered only in last resort.[14]

The ensuing proceedings reflect the uncertainties of communication between Calcutta, Macao, and the East Indies squadron. Apart from the accident of storms, predictable monsoons allied to capricious currents played havoc with mail service. Since the connection was intermittent to say the least, Bentinck had sensibly suggested to the commander-on-chief that he open any official mail from Canton or Calcutta that his cruisers might intercept on the high seas. As it happened, in mid-September the *Southampton*, en route to Calcutta, intercepted Captain Fremantle's *Challenger* (28), carrying Indian mails. Owen opened Bentinck's dispatch, and learned that an expected confrontation with the Chinese made his presence on the Chinese coast infinitely desirable. Happily, a second lucky interception gave him a Select Committee dispatch of 3 August, addressed to Bentinck, which indicated that the emergency had ended, and that the decision to suspend all trade in the Canton River after 1 August had been cancelled.

Consequently, while the *Challenger* sailed for Macao in mid-October as a precaution against renewed violence, Owen remained for a month on the Malayan coast, before returning to Trincomalee to prepare his diminutive squadron for action should a new emergency arise in the Chinese Sea.[15] Although

[14] Bentinck to Owen, 27 Aug. 1831, encl. Bentinck to Court of Directors, same date (No. 5), and Bentinck to Marjoribanks, same date (No. 4), L/P & S/5/1.

[15] Owen to Marjoribanks *et al.*, Penang, 10 Nov. 1831, Adm. 125/92. Owen planned to visit Singapore in December, and thence to Trincomalee by early March of 1832. Owen to Metcalfe, 14 Nov. 1831, L/P & S/5/1 (I.O.A.).

the situation had appeared to improve there could be no certainty that further eruptions would not occur during the trading season. So the *Wolf* (18) was detached with orders to follow in the wake of the *Challenger*, not only to provide added military support, but to deliver personal letters from the Governor-General, one to the Viceroy in Canton and the second to the Emperor himself. These communications, with rather portentous civility, requested reparations for damages committed, and further protection for British lives and property. The *Challenger* carried only copies of the same.[16]

Meanwhile, the British merchant community suspected that no more than an armistice was likely to ensue. Successive declarations from Canton echoed the same raucous note of intimidation towards the 'barbarian', and members of the Select Committee were little comforted by the flattering distinction drawn by the Hoppo between Company officials and private firms like Jardine, Dent, and Innes. They did not necessarily count on more physical violence; they simply accepted as a fact of living, the 'continuance of that unfriendly disposition which is too deeply ingrafted in the Government mind to be readily removed'.[17] At the same time, they had learned to appreciate the melancholy truth that more advantage was to be gained 'from the apprehensions than from the friendly disposition of the Chinese government.[18]

In retrospect, it is understandable that fears of continued restrictions and capricious exactions should have driven the newly appointed Committee to seek the armed support that appeared vital to self-respect as well as survival. Although one crisis had petered out, the prospect of further humiliations leading conceivably to the abandonment of the Canton Factory could scarcely have left their minds. During past days and nights of alarm and tension, the Company servants had shown

[16] Owen to Capt. the Hon. George Elliot, 13 Nov. 1831, Adm. 1/205. See also, Memorandum relative to the East Indies Station and its Duties, encl. Owen to Elliot, 12 June 1832 (No. 139), Adm. 1/209; Owen to Metcalfe (Vice-President of Council, Fort William), 29 Aug. 1831 (No. 280), Adm. 1/204; and the Supreme Government's correspondence with the Court of Directors, Sept.–Oct. 1831, L/P & S/5/1 (I.O.A.).

[17] Marjoribanks *et al.*, Macao, to Metcalfe at Fort William, 3 Aug. 1831, Foreign Dept., Consultation No. 7–8, 14 Oct. 1831 (N.A.I.).

[18] Same to same, 3 Oct. 1831, Foreign Dept., Consultation No. 15, 23 Dec. 1831 (N.A.I.).

dignity, strength, and, in the circumstances, uncommon patience. Immediate anxiety had been relieved, but they had little doubt that the same troubles would recur. The private merchants were equally worried about the future, but less confident that the issues could be resolved by gestures of strength. William Jardine seems to have been fully informed of the Governor-General's views, and of his instructions to Admiral Owen, but he was at a loss to understand how the commander-in-chief could reveal the power of ships' guns, unless he could manage to provoke the forts and junks into firing first. 'Time must determine,' he wrote to a friend in India, 'but I cannot bring myself to contemplate seriously an open rupture . . .'[19]

Heartened by the goodwill of Lord Bentinck, while sensibly fearful of thunderbolts from the 'All-highest' in Leadenhall Street, towards the end of October 1831, the Select Committee set down for the Governor-General's benefit their views on the problem of reconciling British demands with Chinese intransigence. Unfortunately, in an effort to win Company support, a document that began in a clumsily restrained fashion was expanded into a treatise of extreme prolixity. They appreciated how much 'the best interests of England' militated against 'any extension of territorial dominion', and that advocacy of any such policy would be rightly condemned. An island or two off the coast could of course be obtained by a handful of seamen and troops, but they were well aware that forcibly acquired territories had a habit of expanding *ad infinitum* as in India. That subcontinent had disintegrated after the collapse of the Moguls; in similar manner, the 'Tartar dominion' might fall apart as secret societies took advantage of British intervention to foment rebellion.

On the other hand, there was always the hope that all problems could be resolved if the Emperor could be reached in person, and his eyes opened to the truth. In such an event, the corrupt, the capricious, the despotic, and the imbecilic authorities in Canton might be replaced or silenced. In short, one way of salvation lay with the Oz-like wizard who dwelt in the mysterious palace in the Forbidden City of Peking.

[19] Jardine to Lt.-General Kyd, Canton, 23 Nov. 1831, Private Letter Books (B9), vol. 1, 1830–2 (J.M.A.).

Perhaps such a hypothesis over-simplifies the Select Committee's argument, and suggests an unwarranted *naïveté*. Like their predecessors of a century earlier, the British merchants were both bemused and baffled by the magical ethos of China. Yet, they were sensible enough to recognize that the Chinese claim of self-sufficiency was real enough to justify their determined aloofness from the rest of mankind. The egocentric stance of the Oriental was not based entirely on ignorance of the world about him. In the words of a Committee memorial: ' . . . possessing within the limits of the empire nearly every variety of climate, and the necessaries and luxuries of life arising from successful agriculture and an extensive inland Commerce, there is perhaps no nation in the world, so independent as China of communication with the rest of mankind.'[20]

This statement, included in an address to the Governor-General, was followed two weeks later by a lengthy communication to the Court in London. The argument was much the same as that presented to Lord Bentinck, whom the Committee extolled as the wise and understanding guardian of their interests. Once again they protested, but hardly convincingly, their opposition to any territorial acquisition 'while it can be avoided'. But barring a confrontation which could mean war, the time had arrived for a 'decided stand'. British interests in China must be placed on a firm and secure footing, with guarantees against acts of violent aggression. Preliminary to this end, the trade should be exempted from the multiple exactions hitherto imposed, port duties should be reduced, and authenticated lists of all governmental duties on imports should be published—nearly all, it is worth noticing, the objects contemplated earlier by the Macartney and Amherst missions.

In one instance only did the Select Committee exhibit diplomatic restraint. Had Lord Amherst been accorded suitable conditions for negotiation at Peking, he was authorized to seek

[20] Marjoribanks *et al.*, British Factory, China, to Lord Bentinck, Governor-General in Council, 25 Oct. 1831, Foreign Dept., Consultation No. 16, 23 Dec. 1831 (N.A.I.). The same enormous document, including twenty-four handwritten pages containing illustrations of Chinese relations with the foreigner, dating from the eighteenth century, is contained in a dispatch to Admiral Owen, who enclosed it with a letter to Elliot [of the Admiralty], 24 Jan. 1832 (No. 21), Adm. 1/206.

the right of diplomatic representation, chiefly as a means of presenting grievances that originated with such frequency in Canton. The Committee, while they would have welcomed such an ambassadorial appointment, felt certain that, even under the shadow of men-of-war, the request would be turned down. 'Softly, softly' was an approach to be preferred if trading relations were to be safeguarded, the more so, in view of the newly established machinery of propaganda. 'By our Printing Press, we can throw off in a few hours any number of Copies of any Document in the Chinese language, and with the enemies among their own countrymen, that officers of Government ever have, it would be extraordinary if one Copy should not find its way within the walls of the Imperial Palace.' In short, the power of incontrovertible misrepresentation would no longer be in the hands of the Canton authorities.[21]

It was characteristic of an ingenuous Committee to trust in the efficacy of 'leaflet raids', and at the same time argue the necessity of a 'decided stand'. They did not, however, on this occasion, offer an opinion as to whether flag displays or guns, the velvet glove or the iron fist, should operate to achieve the ends they regarded as indispensable. The Governor-General was equally averse to giving specific advice, for the very good reason that any recommendation would be based on information at least two months old, and probably no longer relevant. In any event, as he was in the habit of repeating, when it became a matter of deciding major problems of policy, it was not for the Indian government to anticipate the judgement of their rulers. The ultimate assessment would have to be made by the Court of Directors with the blessing of the Cabinet in England. In the meantime, he too stressed the advantages of caution. Any active demonstration of military power could only be justified in an emergency, involving, say, the lives and properties of British subjects. Since the Chinese government had adopted a more pacific tone of voice, it was surely inexpedient to send a British squadron to the coast, when its very presence would be subject 'to an injurious interpretation'.[22]

---

[21] Marjoribanks et al., British Factory, Canton, to Court of Directors, 7 Nov. 1831, Foreign Dept., Consultation No. 17–18, 23 Dec. 1831 (N.A.I.).

[22] Bentinck to Owen, 2 Nov. 1831, Foreign Dept., Consultation No. 51–2, 25 Nov. 1831 (N.A.I.).

None the less, as has been noted, Lord Bentinck was himself responsible for sending written warnings to both Viceroy and Emperor, urging an amicable settlement of grievances. Although the diminutive *Wolf* and the *Challenger* departed as 'doves of peace', they were also ships of war. As it happened, four days before Lord Bentinck wrote his cautionary letter to Owen, the *Challenger*, *en route* to Macao, had encountered the schooner *Cochin*, recently in Macao, bearing the disturbing news of an affray at Dane's Island, near Whampoa, between a party of Company ships' officers and a group of Chinese. A few lives had been lost, including one of the Company's surgeons.[23] Captain Fremantle immediately ordered the *Cochin* to sail directly for Penang, to warn the commander-in-chief. Owen was naturally disquieted when the news reached him, but since no mention was made of a political crisis resulting from the incident, once again he felt obliged to hold his hand in patience. Unhappily for his peace of mind, November and December were the worst months for passages eastward of Singapore. The *Challenger* could not possibly reach the China coast until early in December, and the *Wolf* not until the end of the month. The only comforting factor in the whole situation concerned the return of the Viceroy to Canton. His presence, it was hoped, would ease the tensions existing between British merchants and unfriendly local functionaries.[24]

Owen's hopes of a more amicable, or at least a less belligerent, attitude on the part of the returning Viceroy were not to be sustained. The *Challenger* and the Company's *Clive* joined forces at Macao on 4 December, and on the 8th the Select Committee sent a deputation to Canton requesting an audience for the reception of a translated copy of the Governor-General's letter.[25] The Viceroy refused to receive the document, which, according to custom, he insisted on calling a

[23] This information was generally confirmed by the commander of a trading vessel, the *John Bannerman*, which also reported the arrival at Macao of the Indian Navy's cruiser *Clive*.

[24] Owen to Bentinck, Penang, 21 Nov. 1831, encl. Fremantle's letter to Owen, Singapore, 2 Nov. 1831, Foreign Dept., Consultation No. 19–20, 23 Dec. 1831 (N.A.I.).

[25] The *Wolf* arrived about ten days later with the original letters, dated Simla, 27 Aug. 1831. No attempt was made to deliver the letter addressed to the Emperor.

petition, and petitions were only forwarded through the normal channel of communication, namely the Hong merchants. The proposal that a communication from the Governor-General of India should be made to follow this circuitous course, Mr. Marjoribanks rejected with scorn. Ultimately, a compromise was worked out. The letter would be delivered through the medium of a mandarin of high official rank, but only if the British delegation made the journey from Macao in their boats, the warships remaining at anchor below the Bogue forts. Accordingly, on the morning of 31 December 1831, boats from the *Challenger* and *Clive* and from one or two of the Company's merchant vessels, fully officered and manned, arrived at the stairs leading to the Factory garden, where the ceremony was performed with all formality.[26]

But the Viceroy did not reply directly to the Governor-General. Instead, he put his answer in the form of a judgement, ordering it to be transmitted to the Select Committee by his middle man agency, the Hong merchants. This document the Committee refused to receive, whereupon he directed that the Hong merchants should deliver a copy to Captain Fremantle 'for the information of the British authorities', meaning the Governor-General. The Viceroy admitted that there had been violence, and a certain amount of property destruction, but he justified the transgression on the grounds that the embankment and the quay had been enlarged without the consent of the leasing authority. The Imperial government had, therefore, a perfect right to destroy them, and have them rebuilt to the original dimensions.[27]

The key to the Viceroy's partial and none too courteous response lay simply in the traditional assumption of absolute supremacy. 'The Emperor could do no wrong'. Foreign merchants trading with the Empire had no rights. They functioned on privilege, and the privilege could be withdrawn from all or any one of the barbarian nations competing for Chinese trade. It is worthwhile noting, in the course of the exchange, that not once did the opium traffic appear as a

---

[26] Owen to Elliot, Singapore, 28 Jan. 1832 (No. 22), enclosing Captain Fremantle's report, Adm. 1/206. See also, C. R. Low, *History of the Indian Navy* (2 vols., London, 1877), ii. 1–2.
[27] Owen to Elliot, 28 Jan. 1832, doc. cit., above.

serious cause of concern and a potential *casus belli*. The main issue was not smuggling, which was a problem for the Chinese authorities to resolve in their own way; it was a matter of absolute sovereignty, involving, in effect, the countenancing of commercial intercourse, by dispensation, among inferiors, both native and foreign. As inferiors, the foreign merchants could not, as has been mentioned, communicate directly with any of the higher authorities in the system, whether at Canton or Peking, however substantial the grievance. They could correspond only through intermediaries—the Hong merchants. Unhappily, these intermediaries as inferiors in their native environment, were in the painful position of being pressed between upper and nether millstones. Subject on the one hand to exorbitant exactions levied by higher officials in Canton, which brought some of them to bankruptcy, they were at the same time under constant pressures from the foreign traders, equally in danger of suffering losses and possible bankruptcy in the event of extortionate demands.

Because they were a profit-making group, the Hong merchants were naturally unwilling to antagonize their British patrons. Yet the more wealth they managed to amass, the more vulnerable was their situation *vis-à-vis* the Canton authorities, whose greedy interventions could mean the loss of their possessions, their freedom, and even their heads. Such a luckless middle man status was bound, as Admiral Owen put it, to lead 'to an obliquity in their intercourse'. In short, the Hong merchants were diffident about reporting the truth to either side, just, as the future was to reveal so lamentably, the governing authorities at Canton were fearful of telling the truth to Peking.

For the moment, the naval commander-in-chief accepted the Governor-General's opinion that, if threats were made, unsupported by adequate forces, a mere parade of intimidation would simply result in even greater failure and humiliation. Indeed, the exercise of obviously predominant force could jeopardize valuable trade. Rarely reticent about his achievements, Owen was, none the less, one of the most astute sailor-diplomats the East Indies squadron ever possessed;[28]

[28] Owen had served with distinction during the Napoleonic War, taking an active

and the navy was not unnoted for officers of balance and intelligence. In subtlety and intellectual quality, he was the superior of Lord Bentinck, who admired his talent and possessed the good sense to give him his head. Like the Governor-General, Owen had to make most of his judgements on the basis of second-hand information from men on the spot, and the accumulating load of correspondence was immense. Frequently afloat, he had been allowed, as has been noted, to intercept official dispatches, and within a congested stern cabin he laboriously culled the masses of evidence and comment.

Owen recognized the difficulties of the Canton merchants, who had borne the brunt of intimidation and violence, and he appreciated their dilemma. While admitting that the harassed men on the spot were far more knowledgeable on matters of trade negotiation, and far more understanding of native idiosyncrasies than distant observers like himself, he was also aware that their judgement could be warped under constant stress. There was, he wrote to Lord Bentinck on 24 January 1832 (in a letter which was forwarded to the Court of Directors late in February), 'so much ardour in the feelings which surround them that it will require more firmness on the part of the Committee to resist urgency than to press on the Chinese authorities for what in fair consideration may be right.' Judging by Captain Fremantle's reports, the temperate remonstrances of the Committee had had good effect in regaining the goodwill of the Viceroy. The Danes Island affair had blown over, and Owen had become sanguine in his hopes for a peaceful settlement, provided the Committee had 'the firmness to resist the false impression prevalent in those around them, who not in friendship to the Honble. Company or in respect for the British Government, but in mistaken feelings or in the pursuit of other and probably more selfish objects, are goading them to measures which it would be difficult to justify.'[29]

---

part in the Walcheren expedition of 1809. Before taking up his appointment on the East Indies station, he had been successively commander-in-chief in the West Indies (1822–5), and Surveyor-General of Ordnance (1827). Created G.C.B. in 1845, and a full admiral a year later, he died at the age of 78.

[29] Encl. B, contained in Owen to Elliot, 24 Jan. 1832 (No. 21), Adm. 1/206.

The Committee in their elaborate reports had shown a proper wariness of the dangers of territorial expansion, but had nevertheless pointed out that if circumstances were compulsive, the occupation of an 'Insular position' would require only a very moderate striking force. Whatever their reservations, it was clear that the merchants were more and more conscious of the advantages of possessing a British base of operations. Such an acquisition would obviously mean less reliance on the highly vulnerable Portuguese Macao; it would relieve the merchants from the trammels of Chinese law and custom, from the perpetually recurring quarrels that disrupted trade, and 'from the contempt of Foreigners which is so studiously expressed by the authorities on every occasion which presents itself'.

Owen had much sympathy for this point of view. But a good deal of capital had been invested in the Lintin entrepôt, and its surrender, he believed, would mean considerable loss. Admittedly, the island lacked a decent harbour. On the other hand, not more than twelve miles away to the west, on the eastern shore of Macao Island, was Kum-sing-mun Harbour. This deep and well-sheltered bight offered not only that rare commodity—good water—in abundance, but a good measure of security for both lawful and unlawful traders. Apparently unaffected by either Mandarin or Portuguese law, it provided the perfect anchorage for the opium receiving ships of both British and American firms. Of course, if every effort to find a compromise acceptable to Canton or Peking failed, armed conflict might be unavoidable. But in Owen's opinion, desultory clashes were not likely to develop into an outright war. The Committee had more than once suggested that Canton might be pressed into negotiation by a blockade of the River, and at one time this plan had come close to being implemented. Unfortunately, a complete embargo was likely to involve the British government in acrimonious exchanges with other European states. Moreover, as Owen was quick to realize from his study of the Kwantung delta, the Chinese, as well as the foreigner not subject to Company fiat, could circumvent the blockade, if necessary, by circuitous inland water carriage. He himself was inclined to prefer a punitive operation against Canton 'with a sufficient force', following of course the evacuation of the Factory staff. But apart from wiping out war junks and frightening the city by a few well-placed shells, it is difficult to guess what he hoped to gain by a gesture which, as events later were to show, would simply stiffen the resolve and harden the hearts of the authorities. The Committee had never recommended the capture of the city, but they had claimed that 200 seamen brought up from the anchorage at Whampoa could hold the Factory against any enemy attack. Such a calculation, Owen observed sardonically, seemed to place 'a great reliance on the forbearance of a numerous population, the individuals of which in other Countries are by no means found deficient in the Active energies of Common life . . .'.

Of course, if the worst came to the worst, and large-scale hostilities began, these could scarcely be limited to the Canton area. Britain would inevitably find herself at war with the Chinese Empire. Success could well depend on exploiting local jealousies and antagonisms, northward along the entire coast-line, at the expense of the Celestial Court in Peking. The province of Fukien, for example, offered an attractive base of operations for an invading force, chiefly because its people were acquainted with Europeans, and therefore less likely to share the general prejudice against strangers. But such an alternative as all-out war, with its threat of internal chaos and the demise of long-standing commercial connections, could only be considered in last resort. Owen himself did not believe that circumstances, however painful to pride and person, should or could lead to so tragic a dénouement. He believed, wrongly as it turned out, that the Committee were unduly alarmist in their approach to the problem of Anglo-Chinese relations; that they held 'false notions' of the precise danger that overhung British interests. He was willing to accept that the days of appeasement—of abasement for the sake of continuing trade returns—were over, but until all hope of compromise had died, he was opposed to using gun power as the decisive argument. Moreover, he was confident that the government of India would not commit the navy to an undertaking that carried with it so much risk and so much danger for the future.[30]

<hr />

[30] See encl. B, Owen to Bentinck, 24 Jan. 1832, doc. cit.

Meanwhile, all the varied correspondence connected with the recent imbroglio, which Owen had tried to assimilate in his cabin on the *Southampton*, was on its way to London, where the Court of Directors would ponder the conflicting issues before advising the British government whether or not the only solution was a resort to force. The Admiral himself made ready to depart from Singapore. Either at Madras or Trincomalee his squadron would wait 'in readiness to act on the decision taken by the General Government', should, perchance, events in the neighbourhood of Canton call for prompt intervention.[31]

However sombre the prospects (conceivably because the future was so clouded), the Select Committee celebrated New Year's day 1832 at the Canton Factory 'in a style that could hardly be surpassed'. Some hundred 'gentlemen of the foreign community' were invited, and the number of toasts to competitive rivals suggested the wisdom of business men hanging together, if they were not to hang separately. On proposing the health of the Governor-General, Charles Marjoribanks as chairman expatiated on the debt owed to his Lordship who had warned the Chinese authorities that he would interpose the full weight of his own authority should it be necessary to shield Britannia's subjects from wrong and oppression. In a farewell compliment to the British private merchants,[32] he congratulated them on their liberal business methods, and thanked them for assistance, so readily offered in time of need. Lancelot Dent of Thomas Dent & Co., expressed the gratitude of the private firms for the friendly support provided by the Company's Select Committee, and eulogized their President. Friendly relations with France and the United States were not forgotten, and 'The prosperity of the American government' was on this occasion drunk with exceptional enthusiasm. Even the Emperor of China was included, although the toast was more in the nature of prayer than a compliment. The proposer expressed the deep hopes of the gathering that 'the period was not far distant when our communication with the government

---

[31] Owen to Elliot, 28 Jan. 1832 (No. 22), doc. cit.

[32] Marjoribanks retired on grounds of ill health. He sailed for England in January 1832, and was succeeded as President by the experienced John Francis Davis.

and people, would assume the same freedom as prevails in civilized states'. Despite the enormous amount of spirits consumed, 'the great harmony prevailed throughout the evening, and the party separated at an early hour.'[33]

During the rest of the month, the Select Committee, in letters to the Court of Directors, to the Governor-General, and to the naval commander-in-chief, continued to press for naval reinforcements. Within the factory, tension had not decreased, and there was a feeling in the air that an explosion might occur at any moment. Hence, the Committee urged that Admiral Owen should visit the China coast at the beginning of the south-west monsoon in May, with as many ships as could be spared. In the event of trouble, the present detachment was sufficient to contain the meagre native forces, but not large enough, nor commanded by an officer of sufficient authority, to justify a downright challenge to the Canton government: 'We make these reasonable Requisitions; if they are refused we demand them.'[34] In short, the Committee were convinced that without the presence of 'a more imposing force', further efforts at negotiation would be quite ineffectual.[35]

Owen was more than willing to proceed to Canton in May if circumstances so ordered, and both he and the Governor-General waited impatiently for further news from Canton.

---

[33] 'Retrospection of Public Occurrences during the past ten years', excerpt from the *Canton Register*, in *Chinese Repository*, xi. Jan. 1842 (No. 1), pp. 1–2.

[34] Select Committee to Owen, 9 Jan. 1832, Foreign Dept., Consultation No. 32–5, 20 Feb. 1832 (N.A.I.). See also, Select Committee to Court of Directors, 4 Jan. and 15 Jan. 1832, Adm. 125/92.

[35] The Squadron available to Owen on the East Indies station in January 1832 was as follows:
Southampton (52) Captain Laws. (Flagship).
Crocodile (28) Captain Montagu. Refitting in Trinco.
Challenger (28) Captain Fremantle—in China till about the end of February.
Cruizer (18) Commander Parker. Gone to Macao with despatches; will rejoin (at Trinco) early part of April.
H.B.M. Wolf (18) sloop-of-war. Commander Hamley has proceeded to Calcutta; if not required by General Gov.'t expected at Trinco early in March.
Comet (18) Commander Sandilands—arrived at Madras from N.S.W. 29 November; and now said to be conveying troops from thence to Malacca.
These constituted the whole effective force Owen could count upon, with the exception of the *Zebra* (18) Commander De Saumaurez, temporarily detached for duties in the vicinity of New South Wales.
Owen to Bentinck, 31 Jan. 1832, Foreign Dept., Consultation No. 10–11, 5 Mar. 1832 (N.A.I.).

Meanwhile, Captain Fremantle was again deputed to visit the British Factory to garner the latest intelligence and offer additional protection. This gesture hardly satisfied the anxious merchants. Marjoribanks wanted the Admiral to come in person, along with at least a thousand men.[36] As it happened, Owen was in no position to act much longer as a buttress of British morale. He had already become aware from newspaper reports that this tour of duty was coming to an end, and that he was likely to be succeeded in the late spring of 1832 by Vice-Admiral Sir John Gore. Although he saw the need to calm and comfort frustrated and beleaguered Company representatives, whose very isolation encouraged fear, he sensed that the men on the spot had exaggerated the imminent danger of a collision. Already, the Viceroy had accepted a share of responsibility for the recent unfortunate incidents (which Owen felt 'must certainly be gratifying to the Committee'), and had admitted that the Hong merchants were chiefly to blame for allowing events to reach an impasse. 'I should hope,' Owen told the Select Committee, 'that a perseverance in that firm but temperate course which hitherto has been the guide of your proceedings, will ultimately obtain from the conciliatory disposition which you find more manifest at present, than on other similar occasions which have formerly occurred, an arrangement if not satisfactory as the Committee may desire that will at least secure to them every reasonable facility in carrying on their Trade.'[37]

Meanwhile, with the arrival of spring and the approach of the south-west monsoon, the trading season came to a gradual close. The Company colours as well as those of the Dutch and French were hauled down; the Americans made ready to shut their doors. Owen's prediction seemed to have been based on a correct assessment. On the surface, Anglo–Chinese relations seemed to be back on the old footing, as though menacing thunders had been based on no more than short-lived misunderstandings. The Chinese authorities had clearly 'mani-

---

[36] See Jas. Matheson to Chas. Thomas at Singapore, Canton, 9 Feb. 1832, Private Letter Books (B9), vol 1, 1831–4 (J.M.A.).
[37] Owen to Select Committee, *Southampton* at Singapore, 27 Jan. 1832, encl. B in Owen's letter to the Governor-General, of 27 Jan. 1832 (No. 18), Foreign Dept., Consultation No. 12, 5 Mar. 1832 (N.A.I.).

fested a disposition to conciliate if not to make atonement'. This was just as well, since the Company was in no way prepared to undertake a punitive expeditionary force. Both Owen and the Governor-General of India were agreed that the temporary occupation of the Bogue forts was hardly likely to bring the Canton government to terms. 'I should consider my position as one of infinite embarrassment', Bentinck remarked with characteristic caution in April 1832, 'had any fresh aggressions on the part of the Chinese occasioned the exigency for acting on my own responsibility, unprepared as I am with any distinct plan of operations and definite suggestions as to the means which should be employed for carrying them into effect. . . .'[38]

In short, the Governor-General was in no mood to consider even the prospect of 'fire and sword'. The very thought might beget the deed. Even before he received confirmation that relations with the Canton authorities had returned to prim normalcy, he refused to believe that the presence of a naval squadron in the South China Sea could bring any lasting benefits. With all the optimism and cheer of the skilled arbitrator, he maintained that the situation, however grim, had not degenerated beyond hope of negotiation and compromise. Unless it was intended to exercise *force majeure*, to adopt a belligerent attitude would be the height of absurdity.

With reliable grape-vine connections in both camps, James Matheson had already written to his Indian correspondent to tell him that there was now no probability of a collision accompanied by physical violence. No offensive edicts had issued from Canton in recent weeks, and Chinese war junks had been expressly directed not to interrupt the carriage of supplies to the British Factory. There was, therefore, no further need to worry about sending ships to China. Moreover, the majority of the Select Committee had become 'pacifically inclined', and unlikely to call upon the Admiral for

[38] To Owen, Delhi, 9 Apr. 1832, enclosed in Owen to Elliot, 11 May 1832 (No. 124), Adm. 1/208. See also, Foreign Dept., Consultation No. 1–3, 30 Apr. 1832 (N.A.I.).

Captain Fremantle thought that any operation against Canton would require eight warships, a flotilla of gunboats and 3,000 troops. See his letter to Owen, 9 June 1832, L/P & S/5/7 (I.O.A.). For Owen's comment in approval, see Owen to Elliot (Adm.), 13 June 1832, L/P & S/9/7 (I.O.A.).

military aid.[39] Six months later, he was able to report that all was quiet on the eastern front, the merchant community being 'exempt from any aggravated persecution on the part of our Celestial Masters, for the present. . . .'[40]

This Indian summer of respite continued into late 1833. In October of the same year, during an armed collision between opium ships and local authorities at the western entrance to Hong Kong harbour, a Chinese lost his life, and a threatening confrontation seemed inevitable. Happily, the *Magicienne* (36) was in the offing; the Canton authorities drew in their horns, and the matter was allowed to drop.[41]

[39] Letters of 1 Jan. and 9 Feb. 1832, Private Letter Books (B9), vol. 1, 1831–4 (J.M.A.).

[40] Jas. Matheson to Thos. Williamson of Bombay, Canton, 13 July 1832, Private Letter Books, (B9), vol. 1, 1831–4 (J.M.A.).

[41] See Select Committee (W. H. C. Plowden, J. F. Davis, J. N. Daniell) to Captain Plumridge of the *Magicienne*, 5 Dec., Plowden to Admiral Gore, 14 Dec., and Plumridge to Gore, 10 Dec. 1833, encl. in Gore to Elliot, 14 Feb. 1834 (No. 19), Adm. 1/213.

It may be worth noticing that in consequence of Chinese law and custom in regard to homicide, it had become impossible to hand over admittedly guilty British subjects to Chinese criminal tribunals. At this time, no Briton had been executed under the 'life for a life' ruling for fifty-five years.

II

THE NAPIER FIASCO 1833–1834

WITH the increasing demand for tea in Britain, the East India Company had disciplined itself to prefer a role of passive submission, within bounds, rather than risk confrontation, with the prospect of hostilities and the loss of lucrative trade. In short, an anomalous relationship had been allowed to continue. Let the Court at Peking keep on asserting supremacy over mankind, and reject all overtures that implied negotiation between equals! For the sake of swelling commerce, patience should remain the watchword of every Company agent. National honour at the risk of profit had not yet acquired Palmerstonian glamour. Admittedly, the undeveloped state of Chinese defences suggested that guns might accomplish what diplomatic mission had so far failed to achieve, and during the next two or three years, the use of force became increasingly a topic of discussion and the subject of official memorials. But for the present, it was considered only as a distant means of last resort. The Honourable Company never forgot to weigh the consequences.

'Individual Chinese may be, and often are afraid of Europeans, but the government is not', the Select Committee had reported in 1789; and certainly since that time perfunctory exhibitions of power, if intended to test the resolution of China's rulers, had induced no wind of change. Legitimate commercial dealings were still limited to Canton. Elsewhere on the coast, Europeans were forbidden to buy or sell, or to receive any supplies of rice or water. On the other hand, they were neither to be fired upon without cause, nor subjected to search. In 1832 the Governor at Canton, as though proclaiming the end of a 'cold war', declared himself anxious to respond to his Emperor's wishes; to facilitate foreign trade, he was prepared 'to show tenderness to strangers from distant parts of the world'.[1] None the less, it seemed doubtful whether 'ten-

[1] *Chinese Repository*, Journal of Occurrences, Feb. 1833, i. 423.

derness' played any substantial part in Chinese long-term policy. Before sailing for home in January 1832, Charles Marjoribanks had sensed a growing sensitivity and apprehension on the part of the Imperial government. The high-handed, even vicious conduct of the more rascally opium-runners, and especially their corrupting influence on many of the local coastal authorities, had begun seriously to ruffle peacock feathers in Peking. With the approaching demise of the East India Company trade monopoly, the situation was likely to worsen. With no Select Committee in control, who would be responsible for good order, the Hong merchants reported anxiously to their Viceroy? 'If no such Chief [as Marjoribanks] come to Canton, there will be no concentrated responsibility, and, if that Nation's Country Ships and foreign Merchants come to Canton to trade, the ships being many and the men not few, in the event of any silly foolish ignorant opposition to and violation of the Commands of Government, after all who will be responsible?'[2]

For the moment, this problem was of no great concern to Westminster. Neither Cabinet nor Parliament had ever considered the question of charter abolition within the diplomatic and political context. Judging by parliamentary debates, the death of monopolies was something ordained by Holy Writ. The cry for unrestrained trade expansion drowned out the arguments of opposition interests. Weakened by the Reform Act of 1832, and under constant attack from merchant legions clamouring for wider markets, the East India Company could offer only feeble defence against their hungry assailants. In 1833 the China trade monopoly was revoked by an indifferent House of Commons.[3] The Act of 1833 was a victory for general principles, anticipating the day when Free Trade should become a cherished dogma and a sacrosanct symbol of peace on earth. No one was bold enough to suggest—and in any event he would not have been listened to—that the Act meant a radical change in Britain's political relations with China, a change that conceivably could lead to a head-on collision involving, over the years, large-scale hostilities.

With the rapid growth of the tea trade, and the expansion of

[2] Quoted, Morse, *Chronicles of the East India Company*, iv. 246.
[3] 3 & 4 Geo. IV, cap. xciii.

the opium trade, the fragile pattern of Anglo-Chinese relations was breaking up. Friction between autocratic Chinese authorities and resentful British merchants had led to an increasing number of incidents and reprisals. Even had the Company's charter remained intact, the day of reckoning could not long be postponed. The Hong merchants, after a long and generally friendly association, naturally preferred to maintain the old connection rather than face the unpredictable but more aggressive private trader. Certainly, the departure of the Select Committee was to destroy their efficacy as a cushion between conflicting forces, East and West. Important personal links were lost. Heretofore a *modus vivendi* had survived a succession of crises, and, with occasional interruptions, trade had continued to flow to and from Canton. The laws of the Empire had been frequently broken, but pretence was a cement that kept the basic relationship intact, and bribery a lubricant that made the wheels of obsolete machinery revolve however stridently. The Duke of Wellington expressed essential government policy when he bluntly declared: 'That which we now require is not to lose the enjoyment of what we have.'

Lulled over past years by the servility and the frequent conciliatory approaches of Company representatives, the Chinese Imperial government had awakened but slowly to 'the white peril', represented by increasing numbers of European and American merchant ships. Scarcely apparent at the beginning of the thirties, China was beginning to alternate in mood, if not in policies, between an awareness of the traditional inferiority of other nations and a dread of their growing strength. At one moment, concessions and submissions prolonged the dream of superiority; at the next, the dream appeared about to disintegrate as the barbarian gave evidence of his military power.[4]

But in 1833, the problem of when and how to use force was of less concern to residents of the British Factory in Canton than the threat of free trade. The abandonment of the Company cast a shadow quite as ominous for the future as the portentous threats of the Viceroy. Judging by the number of memorials, a great many of the private merchants, whose

---

[4] See *Remarks on British Relations and Intercourse with China*, by an American Merchant (London, 1834), reviewed in *Chinese Repository*, iii. Jan. 1835, pp. 406 et seq.

special trading privileges were subject to Company authority, were quite as fearful as Company servants. The signatories represented firms of stability. They were professionals, and, however unconventional their business practices, they possessed some sense of responsibility, as well as a measure of diplomatic and commercial *savoir-faire*. They anticipated a flood of newcomers, and they knew that a majority of them would be adventurers—the hawks and vultures of free enterprise—'men unconnected by any bond of union', whose motto was 'trade and be damned'. The record of swindling and absconding British traders, if not lengthy, was already impressive. 'Under what is called Free Trade, such instances would no longer be rare occurrences.' As for the Select Committee, long aware that their days were numbered, they foresaw not only the mischief certain to be wrought on their own fortunes, but the dangers that a free-for-all would bring to a highly vulnerable British community. Inevitably, Free Trade would mean the end of the old order, the conclusion of an undignified, yet profitable and, on the whole, peaceable relationship between superior and inferior on the China coast.[5]

The transfer of power was not long delayed. By April 1834, British trade on the China coast ceased to be under the authority of the Select Committee of Supercargoes. In its stead, the government, in consultation with Company advisers, arranged for the appointment of a Superintendent of Trade, who should possess consular as well as commercial authority. He would be assisted, as under the Company system, by a commission of experienced men, preferably, in the beginning, old Company hands. In December 1833, the new post was offered to one of the famous Napier family, William John, the eighth baron, a descendant of John Napier of Merchiston, the Scottish inventor of logarithms.

Like others of his lineage, the new Superintendent, although lacking the more lustrous military laurels, had by no means an undistinguished service record. Born in 1786, he had joined the navy at the age of sixteen, took part in the battle of Trafalgar three years later, and after considerable active ser-

---

[5] Marjoribanks *et al.*, British Factory, Canton, to Court of Directors, 7 Nov. 1831, Foreign Dept., Consultation No. 17–18, 23 Dec. 1831 (N.A.I.).

vice, chiefly in the Mediterranean, retired with the rank of captain to his Selkirkshire estate, where he turned to sheep farming. However, on succeeding to the title in 1823, he returned to the navy, and remained on the active list until the age of forty-seven, when Palmerston, for reasons difficult to assess, appointed him Chief Superintendent of Trade. It is possible that the Foreign Secretary thought that the appointment of a peer of illustrious family would impress the Chinese. Unfortunately, traders as a class were not held in as high esteem as mathematicians, and Canton refused to recognize him as other than a superior supercargo.

But if Napier lacked both administrative and commercial qualifications for the job, the same might be said for a score of British colonial governors in other parts of the world. Whether a consequence of the patronage system or a dearth of suitable candidates, the British government in the nineteenth century leaned heavily on the Services, and not infrequently with these appointments, discretion was not the companion of valour. But even had Napier possessed the necessary diplomatic and business acumen, he was scarcely the man to undertake consular duties in a country whose laws, customs, eccentricities, and sensitivities were quite unknown to him. As a Superintendent of Trade he was to prove both naïve and obstinate in rejecting outright the conciliatory proposals of the British community and the tactful remonstrances of the Hong merchants. As representative of the British government, he showed himself unduly sensitive to, and resentful of, the inevitable Chinese pinpricks, restrictions, and verbal bludgeonings which he construed as insults to the Crown.[6]

Napier's task was not made easier by the ambiguous quality of his instructions. In a personal dispatch of 26 January 1834, Lord Palmerston urged the new Superintendent to take every opportunity to extend the trade to other parts of the Chinese dominions. To attain this object, it was obviously desirable to establish direct communication with the Court of Peking, 'bearing in mind, however, that peculiar caution and circumspection will be indispensable on this point, lest you should awaken the fears, or offend the prejudices of the Chinese

---

[6] See Robert Mudie, *China, and its Resources and Peculiarities* (London, 1840), p. 174; also, for an estimate of Lord Napier, Edgar Holt, *The Opium Wars in China*, pp. 46–8.

government; and thus put to hazard even the existing oppor-tunities of intercourse, by a precipitate attempt to extend them'. The first aim of the British government was to keep the peace. As far as trade was concerned, victory in war could be as dangerous as defeat. The day might come when guns would have to be used, but only as a last resort.[7]

Similar instructions had already been issued to the new commander-in-chief, Vice-Admiral Sir John Gore. On arrival at Calcutta in June of 1832, he had been told never to adopt any course of policy likely to involve hostilities with the Chinese, unless given 'the most distinct and positive' orders by the authorities in England.[8] Two years later, at the time of Lord Napier's arrival in the China Sea, the Admiralty reminded him that, in dealing with local Chinese officials, 'every demonstra-tion of deference ought to be observed towards them'. For example, commanding officers should make certain that their vessels anchored well outside the Canton River; on no account were they to pass the Bocca Tigris.[9]

It was Gore who was responsible for driving the 'edge of the wedge' into standing Admiralty instructions, a modifica-tion for which Lord Napier subsequently had reason to be grateful. The commander-in-chief was a cool, dependable, and thoughtful officer, the right man (so it appeared to the British government, who put great trust in him) to calm the outraged, restrain the impetuous, and impress the unfriendly. Gore had a nose for atmosphere, and by the beginning of 1834 had begun to smell trouble in the offing. He sensed that the projected change from Company to state control of the China trade was already testing what had always been a highly brittle

[7] See 'Heads for a private letter to Lord Napier', prepared on 25 Jan. 1834, and dispatched the next day, F.O. 17/4. Included in this F.O. volume is a copy of the Act 3 & 4 Geo. IV, cap. xciii, establishing the new trade system following the end of the China monopoly. It also contains James Stephen's memorandum, and a Treasury minute on the working of the Act, as well as copies of the Orders-in-Council necessary to implement the Act. Further details on arrangements are included in F.O. 17/5. A substantial extract from the Palmerston letter to Napier of 26 Jan. 1834, was published in *Chinese Repository*, xi. Jan. 1842, pp. 22–3.

[8] Metcalfe *et al*. to Gore, Fort William, 11 June 1832, encl. in Gore to Elliot, 12 June 1832, Adm. 1/208. Gore's acknowledgement of the same date is contained in Foreign Dept., Consultation No. 15–18, 11 June 1832 (N.A.I.).

[9] Barrow to Gore, 11 July 1834, Adm. 2/1592. A draft of this letter, signed by Lord Auckland, the new First Lord in Melbourne's first Cabinet (July–Nov. 1834) is contained in Adm. 1/213.

relationship. In mid-February, with becoming diffidence, he urged the Admiralty to arrange for the stationing of 'a rated ship' at Singapore, which should be available to visit Lintin regularly during the favourable season. Such an arrangement, in his opinion, would give much needed confidence to the trade, and 'keep evil minded men in awe'.[10] With uncharacteristic benevolence, their Lordships accepted the recommendation, with the proviso, however, that such visits should be conducted with great caution and discretion, 'the ostensible object being the purchase of Stores and Provisions'. At the same time, however, he was told that, in the event of an emergency, reinforcements might be summoned from the Indian Ocean, with, circumstances permitting, the consent of the Governor-General of India.[11] In like fashion, while sternly warned by the Foreign Secretary to deal gently and circumspectly with the Chinese government, Napier was reminded that Macao was within Chinese provincial boundaries, and it might be well worthwhile to discover 'whether there be any, and what, places at which ships might find requisite protection in the event of hostilities in the China seas'.[12] An early crisis was not anticipated, but Palmerston had become aware that the balance between appeasement and profit was increasingly unstable. It is not inconceivable that on the eve of Lord Napier's departure for the Far East, he was pondering the matter of an island base as an alternative to the Macao entrepôt.

Accompanied by his wife and family, Lord Napier left Portsmouth in the frigate H.M.S. *Andromache* (Capt. Chads) on 7 February 1834. He arrived at Macao on 15 July, where he was joined by John F. Davis and Sir George B. Robinson, experienced members of the defunct Select Committee and now associated with Napier as second and third Superintendents. The commission also included Captain Charles Elliot R.N. as Master-Attendant,[13] and that remarkable missionary scholar, the Reverend Robert Morrison, who held the office of

---

[10] Gore to Elliot, 14 Feb. 1834 (No. 19), Adm. 1/213.
[11] Barrow to Gore, 11 July 1834, Adm. 2/1592.
[12] See 'Heads for a private letter, 26 Jan. 1834, doc. cit.
[13] Elliot was to become Chief Superintendent of Trade in 1837; he was promoted Admiral in 1865.

Chinese Secretary and interpreter. Already infirm by reason of age and repeated illness, the first British missionary to enter China barely survived his last trip to Canton in July 1834; he died there in August, and Napier lost the help of an adviser whose knowledge of the language as well as the people might conceivably have influenced his manner of negotiation.[14]

As a representative of His Majesty's government, Palmerston expected the new Superintendent to announce his arrival at Canton by letter to the Viceroy. The event had been anticipated, not without some anxiety, by both the British merchant community and the local Chinese authorities. Hardly had the *Andromache* dropped anchor, when watchful messengers hastened to warn the Viceroy that the long-awaited barbarian 'Eye' or chief had arrived and proposed to ascend the Canton River. Such an action was without precedent, and the Viceroy was at a loss to understand the purpose of the visit. Should the new 'headman' wish to come to Canton, he must first, according to law and tradition, make petition through the Hong merchants, and then await the mandate of the Emperor. This official warning was dated 21 July, but by that time Napier was preparing to step ceremoniously ashore at Chuenpi, below the entrance to the Bocca Tigris. He assumed apparently that 'being disembarked from a Man of War in the presence of Chinese might have a good effect with that Government.'[15]

Napier was more than a merchants' 'headman'; he was a government envoy, who thought of himself as the representative of a British king, which, strictly speaking, he was not. A more adept and imaginative officer would have listened more

[14] Appointed Chinese translator to the East India Company in 1809, Morrison completed a Chinese–English dictionary in 1814, and under his supervision the entire Bible was printed in Chinese in 1824, Morrison himself translating the New Testament. His linguistic services certainly took precedence over the missionary; after more than a quarter of a century his converts numbered ten. His burial place, close beside many soldiers and seamen of the period, lies in the peaceful, if somewhat untidy, English cemetery of Macao.

[15] Captain Chads (*Andromache*) to Vice-Admiral Gore, 25 July 1834, encl. No. 8 in Gore to George Elliot, 27 Nov. 1834 (No. 85), Adm. 1/214. The second son of Gilbert, first Earl of Minto, George Elliot, promoted Admiral in 1853, acted as Secretary to the Admiralty for nearly a year, 1834–5. He commanded the expeditionary force to China in 1840, and served as joint plenipotentiary with his cousin, Charles Elliot.

carefully to the cautions of his advisers and the pleadings of the Hong merchants, who urged patience. But Napier had no intention of cooling his heels on the Macao promenade while awaiting the pleasure of an oriental potentate. The Foreign Secretary had commanded him to present his credentials to the Viceroy in Canton; and, setting a precedent for Lord Cardigan, the Superintendent prepared to charge headlong into the unknown. Palmerston had instructed him to proceed directly to Canton; this order he would carry out, 'come hell or high water'.

Moving carefully by cutter through the Bocca Tigris (frequently called the Bogue) and up the sinuous and uncharted river, Napier reached Canton on the morning of 25 July. With the coming of daylight the British colours were hoisted on the flagstaff of the Factory, so recently occupied by representatives of the Select Committee of Supercargoes.[16] His arrival was apparently witnessed by the Hoppo, whose routine declaration of daily proceedings was brightened by one excited comment:

In examining, we perceived during the night of the 18th of the present moon, about midnight, the arrival of a barbarian ship's boat at Canton, bringing four English devils, who went into the English factories to reside. After having searched and examined, we could find no permit or pass; and having heard by report, that there is at present a Ship of War of the said nation anchored in the outer sea, but not having been able to learn for what purpose, we think that such coming as this is manifestly a clandestine stealing into Canton. . . . This is a list of the four barbarians' names: Lord Napier, who, we hear, is a War Commander; Davis, Morrison, Robinson.[17]

Consequently, the day after his arrival, when Napier's private secretary presented his Lordship's letter of authority at the city gate (a document which described the nature and object of the mission), it was refused on the customary ground that petitions could be directed only through the Hong merchants. To address the Viceroy in terms of equality was unprecedented arrogance. As His Excellency charitably reported to the Emperor:

[16] See 'A Sketch of Lord Napier's Negotiations With the Authorities at Canton', *Asiatic Journal* (London, 1837), Aug. 1837, p. 4.
[17] Ibid.

. . . although the English barbarians are beyond the bounds of civilization, yet having come to the Inner Country to trade, they should immediately give implicit obedience to the established laws. If even England has its laws, how much more the Celestial Empire! How flaming bright are her great laws and ordinances! More terrible than the awful thunderbolt! Under the whole Heaven, none dares to disobey them! Under her shelter are four seas! Subject to her soothing care are ten thousand kingdoms! That a barbarian should rush up to Canton, without even requesting a *Red Permit* is a great infringement of the established laws! But, in tender consideration of his being a newcomer, strict investigation will not be made. It being inexpedient, however, that he should remain at Canton, it must be required that, as soon as the commercial business, regarding which he has to enquire and hold jurisdiction, is finished, he shall lose no time in returning to Macao. . . .[18]

Meanwhile, the Chinese senior naval officer at the Bogue was making every effort to persuade Captain Chads to leave the estuary, and hinted that if the Superintendent's cutter continued its shuttle service to Canton, it would be fired upon. The *Andromache* was already preparing to leave for India, but in view of the ungracious challenge, and on Napier's entreaty, Chads delayed his final departure. He sailed away on a week's cruise, in order, as he remarked a little facetiously, 'to feel the pulse of the Chinese'.[19]

However forbidding the atmosphere of Canton, Napier was still hopeful of getting the ear of Peking. If not, as he wrote to Palmerston on 14 August, in a long, discursive letter, force would have to be used to bring the Emperor to reason. Memories of Macartney's and Amherst's humiliations, added to his own cold reception, had made him doubly sensitive to edicts which rejected Britain's claim to equality. 'I believe', he wrote, 'the very mention of an Army or a fleet of Ships to the Emperor would bring him to his senses.' On the other hand, he would utterly disclaim

any thought of conquest, even of partial occupation beyond a certain time . . . [He would not] disturb . . . the passage of their vessels, or the tranquility of their towns—[only] destroy their Forts and Bat-

---

[18] Ibid. A detailed account of the negotiations is contained in Hsin-pao Chang, *Commissioner Lin and the Opium War* (Cambridge, Mass., 1964), pp. 52–8.

[19] See Chads's correspondence with Gore and Napier, 3, 5, and 10 Aug. 1834, encl. in Gore to Elliot (No. 85), doc. cit., Adm. 1/214.

teries along the Coast and the riversides without interfering with the people. . . . Three or four Frigates and Brigs with a few steady British troops not *Sepoys*—would settle the thing in a space of time inconceivably short.

Napier appreciated that without the presence of a frigate, trade might be stopped at any moment, and he was correct in his forecast. The temperory departure of the *Andromache* from the head of the estuary in no way mollified the Chinese. If the situation worsened, he might have to retire to Macao. 'Then has the Viceroy gained his point—and the Commission is degraded.'[20]

Four days later, the Hong merchants, at the bidding of the Viceroy, stopped the delivery of cargoes to British ships. The gentlemen of Canton were 'now beginning to show their teeth'.[21] As a result, the *Andromache* was asked to delay her final departure, perchance negotiations failed to avert a crisis. Meanwhile, the frigate *Imogene* had arrived in the estuary, and Captain Blackwood took over command of naval operations. Blackwood was inclined to believe that both vessels could pass the Bogue forts 'in half an hour's notice', but was reluctant to pursue so drastic a course. In view of the instructions from his commander-in-chief, Admiral Gore, he was insistent that the *Andromache* should return to India as soon as possible. Napier fully appreciated Blackwood's dilemma (as Superintendent of Trade he had no direct authority over the movements of H.M. ships, apart from the rarely invoked emergency powers), but he took pains to point out that his appeal for two frigates was simply to insure against sudden accidents. Subsequently on 3 September, his request for the *Andromache* became an order.

. . . I shall feel it my duty as the first representative of the King ever appointed to this place—and as responsible for all the evil consequences of untimely concession, to act with vigour and determination, being persuaded in my own mind from numerous examples of former occurrences that an opposite course would be attended with very fatal consequences to the general Trade, the personal respectability of the merchants, and the dignity of the British Empire.[22]

[20] Napier to Palmerston, 14 Aug. 1834, F.O. 17/6.
[21] Napier to Chads, 18 Aug. 1834, encl. 9 in No. 85, doc. cit., Adm. 1/214.
[22] See Napier correspondence with Chads, Gore, and Blackwood, 18 Aug. to 3 Sept. 1834, encl. in Gore to Elliot (No. 85), doc. cit., Adm. 1/214.

As his convictions hardened under the stress of frustration, Napier found himself more and more at odds not only with the Viceroy, but with most of the old Company merchants, who looked with disfavour on the impetuousness of an over-confident tenderfoot, totally unacquainted with the convolutions of the Chinese mind. Veterans like Charles Marjoribanks foresaw the day when a chronic state of goading affronts, and shameful humiliations, would have to be remedied by the use of force; on the other hand, at this particular time of transition from Company to government supervision, they believed that a gesture—say, a demonstration, suggesting the threat of armed intervention—might be sufficient to tide things over until the new establishment had revealed its strength and stability to the Canton authorities. Rattled by unfamiliar responsibilities, suffering from lack of sleep and very angry, Napier saw no alternative to immediate, military action. He had made up his mind at last that equal diplomatic status, meaning equitable trading terms, could only be extorted 'at the point of the bayonet', meaning a complete military defeat. At the moment, unfortunately, both warships and bayonets were lacking. Too late in the day, he was to urge the British government to send a small expeditionary force, with the first south-west monsoon, 'which on arriving should take possession of the island of Hong Kong in the Eastern entrance of the Canton River. . . .'[23] Lord Napier was the first high-ranking British official to point the finger at the island of Hong Kong, which he thought 'admirably adapted for every purpose. . . .'

In Canton, Napier's condition deteriorated rapidly. Indeed, a far more robust *détenu* must have suffered from the sense of close confinement, and yearned for those salutary 'whiffs of grape', that would bring the Chinese to their senses. Separated by some eighty miles of difficult water-way from Macao, and twelve miles from the head of navigation at Whampoa, the Chief Superintendent had been under oppressive surveillance since his arrival on 25 July. Every action of his daily existence

---

[23] The substance of these recommendations was contained in two private letters addressed to Grey and Palmerston respectively. They were read to Captain Chads in Macao by Lady Napier on 14 October, shortly after her husband's death. See Chads to Gore, *Andromache* at sea, 18 Nov. 1834, encl. 7 in No. 85, doc. cit.; see also, report of the surgeon, T. R. Colledge, ibid.

was watched; he was virtually a prisoner, without the normal prisoner's privacy. At dinner on the evening of 24 August, he and his suite suddenly found their residence surrounded by clamorous soldiers, some of whom broke through the gates to nail an offensive edict on the Factory wall. This was the first indication that the Viceroy intended to cut off trading relations. But even more ominous was the nightly presence of shadowy figures that skulked about the grounds, watching and waiting. Fearful of becoming the victims of mob violence, the Chinese servants fled the Factory at daybreak, leaving the Europeans to barricade themselves as best they could.

Advised by Lord Napier of the critical situation, Captain Blackwood had already made preparations to relieve the besieged Britons. In advance of the two frigates, which had been summoned to Whampoa, he dispatched a small party consisting of a sergeant and twelve marines to give heart and at least symbolic protection to their fellow-countrymen.[24] Should they find the British position on the river bank at Canton untenable, they were ordered to withdraw, along with the Factory staff, to Whampoa, and there await the arrival of the *Imogene* and the *Andromache*.

The passage of the Bocca Tigris by the frigates on 7 September was not without drama. It was well known that substantial resources had been employed to strengthen the defences at the entrance to the river. When the *Alceste* had forced her way close to Canton in 1816, the opposition had been insignificant. But since then, walls had been reinforced and batteries added. On the starboard approach, past Chuenpi, lay the new Anunghoy fort with 40 guns; the old fort still functioned with 16 guns. On the port side, were the double-tiered batteries of Tycocktow—in all, 39 guns. Further along, close to mid-stream was Tiger Island, recently fortified with 18 guns. Blackwood had insisted that there was to be no bombardment of the forts unless either the war junks or the land batteries fired first. This, the Captain prayed, they might be provoked into doing.[25]

---

[24] Blackwood to Gore, 6 Sept. 1834, encl. No. 1 in Gore to Elliot (No. 85), doc. cit., Adm. 1/214; see also Napier's letter to Blackwood (received 5 Sept.) encls. 8 and 9 in No. 85.

[25] Captain Blackwood's account of the engagement is contained in his corres-

The Chinese junks began the engagement by firing blanks. Happily for the peace of mind of British gunners, these were soon followed by solid shot, most of which fell short. The din was terrific, but the direct consequences scarcely more lethal than the fall-out from a fireworks display. Steadily the two frigates moved towards the entrance of the river, no more than a quarter mile in width. Within range of the yet untried defences, the wind suddenly shifted to the north, halting the ships momentarily in their tracks. Fortunately, the tide was running strongly up stream. The *Imogene* was thus able to advance obliquely towards the Taikoktow battery on the port side, while Chads in the *Andromache* nudged his way towards the Anunghoy forts on the other tack. The *Imogene*, waiting until enemy ranging shots appeared to be closing on target, replied with thirty-two pound ball, two guns firing in quick succession. The *Andromache* followed suit. Both were successful in shattering parapets and embrasures, but lower down, owing to the thickness of the walls, little was accomplished beyond the scaling of the stone work.

Although plentiful and vigorous in the opening rounds, Chinese gunnery continued to be wild, and as the battle proceeded, became increasingly so. There was little or no methodical reloading and training of the pieces; the gunners simply let fly when the frigates came anywhere near the line of fire. Had they been skilled in gun-laying and disciplined in drill, more than a hundred mounted cannon should have demolished both ships during their laborious tacking back and forth in the difficult passage. But there was neither annihilation nor decimation. The casualties by the evening of 8 September amounted to two men killed and a half a dozen wounded. The Emperor was shocked when he learned of the unexpected disaster, which the Viceroy's camouflaged report could not entirely disguise. 'It seems that all our forts are erected in vain; they cannot beat back two barbarian ships. It is ridiculous—detestable.'[26]

---

pondence with Napier, enclosed with Gore to Elliot (Admiralty), 27 Nov. 1834 (No. 85), Adm. 1/214. Details in regard to fortifications and gun-power were obtained following the battle.

[26] *Asiatic Journal* Aug. 1837, op. cit., p. 11. See also, Sir John Francis Davis, *The Chinese; A General Description of the Empire of China and its Inhabitants* (2 vols. London,

Ever since 7 September, the beleaguered little garrison in their Canton Factory had awaited the arrival of the two frigates. Not until the morning of the 12th did an excited lookout descry English sails in the roadstead at Whampoa. It was assumed, certainly by the Chinese, that the ships would find their way up to Canton by the next tide, and almost immediately overtures were forthcoming, including the withdrawal of all offensive vice-regal proclamations, such as the embargo on trade, provided the invading frigates returned to Macao. This sudden turn of fortune gave a momentary fillip to the exhausted Superintendent. 'I beg to congratulate you on living in a sound skin after the Chinese War,' he wrote to Captain Chads on the 12th. 'The whole thing has succeeded so far admirably and the enemy begins to cry for Quarter. I hope the trade will now be open in a day or two and the Honor of the Country saved in spite of some who urged me to adopt a different line of conduct. Thanks however to your 32 pdrs. which are more efficacious than other arguments.'[27]

Napier's elation might have been justified had the two frigates been sufficiently lightened, and warped up the river close to the Factory. But no such orders came from Canton, conceivably because Napier thought it unnecessary, or more probably because he believed navigational difficulties would make the journey too hazardous. On the other hand, with the thermometer indoors as high as 90°, the ailing Plenipotentiary may well have lacked the resolution to press Blackwood to come to the rescue. Since neither ships nor boats made their appearance—the marines had returned to Whampoa—the Viceroy and his counsellors regained their courage along with renewed truculence. The trade which Napier believed would soon be resumed remained at a standstill, while recent ingratiating suggestions of possible negotiations were replaced by new prohibitions. Soldiers were called out to surround the Factory, and to exercise with menacing gestures in neighbouring streets. A good many were stationed on the

---

1840), ii. 34–8, 308. Davis's account of the engagement was based on a report printed in the *Canton Register*. Nos. 34–40, vol. vii, of the *Canton Register* are contained in Adm. 1/214, as enclosures with No. 85.

[27] 12 Sept. 1834, encl. No. 8 in No. 85, doc. cit., Adm. 1/214; also, Napier to Blackwood, 12 and 13 Sept., encl. No. 3 in No. 85, doc. cit.

hills overlooking Whampoa. The Viceroy had begun, as he announced in a special proclamation, to enforce 'the machinery of expulsion and destruction'. In retrospect, there is little doubt that had the *Imogene* and the *Andromache* been able to move the remaining twelve or more miles to Canton, Napier would not only have departed with dignity, but might even have succeeded in coming to terms with the intransigent Viceroy.

Meanwhile, the surgeon, T. R. Colledge, alarmed by the condition of his patient, advised immediate evacuation and removal to Macao. Unsupported by his deputies Davis and Robertson, who had joined the frigates at Whampoa, Napier made up his mind to leave the Factory and board the *Andromache* which had carried him from England two months earlier.[28] Addressing the local British Chamber of Commerce on the 15th, he acknowledged a personal defeat. It was no longer expedient for him to persist in a course which was so obviously harmful to the merchants' interests. Since the subject in dispute was no longer a commercial matter, 'but altogether personal in reference to myself, I can retire with the satisfaction of knowing that your interests are not compromised thereby, indulging the hope that the day will yet arrive when I shall be placed in my proper position of authority which nothing can withstand'. It had been his duty, he went on, 'to use every effort to carry his Majesty's instructions into execution; and having done so thus far without effect, though nearly accomplished on two occasions, I cannot feel myself authorized any longer to call upon your forbearance'.[29]

Too weak to fight what was bound to be a losing battle of missives, Napier entrusted to his surgeon the task of negotiating the terms of surrender. In the end, the two frigates were asked to turn tail and leave Whampoa, without the Superintendent. In return, the Viceroy promised his guest a safe passage to Macao. 'The presence of H.M. ships *Imogene* and

---

[28] Johnston to Blackwood, Canton, 13 Sept. 1834, encl. 3 in No. 85, doc. cit. See also, letters of Napier to Blackwood, and to a Hong merchant, Hwang-chow-Foo, 15 Sept. 1834, ibid.

[29] Quoted in 'Sketch of Lord Napier's Negotiations', *Asiatic Journal*, Aug. 1837, p. 13.

Andromache being no longer required at Whampoa,' Napier wrote to Captain Blackwood on the 21st, 'in consequence of an undertaking come to with the Chinese authorities, I have to request you will, on receipt of this, proceed with both ships to the Anchorage at Lintin. The Chinese authorities have provided for the conveyance of myself and suite to Macao.'[30] Blackwood was shrewd enough to read tragedy between the lines. Napier was being carried as a hostage, a guarantee that the frigates would pass the Bocca Tigris without again attacking the forts.

On the evening of the same day that this letter was written, the Superintendent walked unsteadily to the wharf, to board the boat which was to carry him by slow degrees down river. A beaten man, and yet a brave one, he had quit the post which, he had previously boasted, would only be abandoned at the point of the bayonet.

Amid the taunts of citizens and soldiery, the slow retreat began. It took seven days to reach Macao. Harassed night and day by the incessant beating of gongs and the explosion of firecrackers and muskets, detained for long periods at intermediary posts, Napier's condition steadily worsened. Even had the journey been shorter and less arduous, a far deeper wound than that meted by official and mob insolence—the sense of failure—had already doomed a highly sensitive man. He reached Macao on 26 September, and two weeks later, he was dead. It may have been Napier's misfortune, as James Matheson put it in retrospect, that he was not under anyone's influence. Suspecting the judgement of experienced hands whom he saw as traditional pussyfooters and appeasers, he refused to listen to members of his Commission, like John Francis Davis, his second in command, who strongly objected to a militant approach without sufficient force to sustain it. He did indeed, as he confessed, stick to the letter of his instructions, which was a mistake. But he died as a Napier should, with dignity and without defiance.

Charged by the *Canton Register*[31] for his failure to support Napier in Canton, Blackwood argued that the agreed object

[30] Encl. 3 in No. 85, doc. cit.

[31] The relevant copies of vol. vii (26 Aug. to 7 Oct.) are enclosed with Gore to Elliot, 27 Nov. 1834 (No. 85), Adm. 1/214.

was Whampoa and the protection of British shipping in that harbour—not to threaten Canton with destruction. That the Captain had certain qualms of conscience is clear, however, from his remarks on navigational perils. 'Odd to say, no one knew the depth of water from Whampoa to Canton,' and, according to old Company Hands, no one had ever thought of sounding the river. 'I have ascertained with tolerable accuracy,' wrote Blackwood, 'that a little above Whampoa there is not much more than twelve or thirteen feet of water—much too little for either of our ships.'[32] At a later date, ships of similar draught to the *Andromache* were to make the journey, but even when the passage was buoyed, not without risk of grounding. Owing to shifting mud and sand, channels were quite unpredictable from one year to the next. In a single season, typhoons or a heavy monsoon could alter their courses substantially. In the circumstances, Blackwood's caution may have been justified,[33] but with so much at stake, a Nelsonian gamble should not have been beyond the capacities of a sufficiently resolute seaman.

The Napier rescue expedition had failed in its purpose, but in the opinion of Captain Chads of the *Andromache*, it had at least revealed to Chinese authorities the vulnerability of Canton.[34] James Matheson's reaction was more to the point. In a letter to a correspondent in Singapore, he agreed that 'in drubbing the Chinese', a lesson had been taught which would not easily be forgotten, but what was much more important, 'he [Napier] has placed us in a better position than if we had quietly yielded to them in the first instance'. It was now obvious to Matheson and most of his business colleagues that the assault on the forts of the Bocca Tigris, and the ascent of the Canton River represented the preliminary round in a con-

[32] To Vice-Admiral Gore, Macao, 9 Oct. 1834, encl. No. 5 in No. 85, doc. cit, Adm. 1/214.
[33] See Blackwood to Gore, 8 and 14 Oct. 1834, encl. 4, in No. 85, doc. cit. The second dispatch, including the surgeon's report of the withdrawal of the Commission from Canton to Macao, provides a concise summary of events.
[34] Chads to the First Lord of the Admiralty, Sir James Graham, Lintin, 1 Oct. 1834, encl. No. 5 in Gore to Elliot, 27 Nov. 1834 No. 85, doc. cit. Copies of the Elliot, Gore, Chads, Blackwood correspondence relating to the events in Canton during Napier's sojourn, and the naval operation in his support (Sept. 1834–Jan. 1835) are contained in Adm. 125/92.

flict that could no longer be postponed.[35] Direct communication between the British Superintendent and the Viceroy at Canton, without the intervention of the Hong merchants, had gradually become recognized as essential to harmonious trading relations. From now on, it was clear that Whitehall was no longer in a position to rest on its oars, patiently awaiting the dawn of reason. A continued policy of drift could be more damaging in its consequences than the armed confrontation, which the Company over many years had been so zealous in avoiding. Unless strong action were taken in retaliation for Napier's humiliation, the attitude of the Chinese would certainly become 'imperious in the extreme, and the situation of the Europeans insupportable'.

In a petition addressed to His Majesty in Council on 9 December 1834, the merchants resident in Canton asked for the appointment of a plenipotentiary possessing sufficient authority and backed by sufficient force to exact reparation. It was their firm conviction

founded on the invariable tenor of the whole history of foreign intercourse with China, as well as of its policy on occasions of internal commotion, down to the present moment, that the most unsafe of all courses that can be followed in treating with the Chinese government, or any of its functionaries, is that of quiet submission to insult, or such unresisting endurance of contemptuous or wrongful treatment, as may compromise the honour, or bring into question the power of our country.[36]

Recent experience had demonstrated that two frigates could demolish without difficulty the entire Chinese navy and such forts as were within reach. The addition of a steamboat along with three or four light-draught sailing vessels would be sufficient to ensure the round up of most of the Chinese shipping. Five steamers were already in active use in India—four at

---

[35] James Matheson to John Purvis, Canton, 25 Sept. 1834, Private Letter Books (B9), vol. 2, 1834–8; also, William Jardine to Gladstones of London, Canton, 27 Sept. 1835, ibid., vol. 4, 1835–6 (J.M.A.).

[36] The petition was signed by 35 of the 40 British traders living in Canton at the time, by all the commanders of Company vessels then in harbour at Whampoa and by other ships' captains and traders stationed outside the river. See Harvard Pamphlets (fourteen in number) on the 'Commercial Relations of Great Britain with China', Widener Library, Harvard University.

Calcutta, including the famous *Enterprize*[37] and one at Bombay. Why should not similar shallow-draught vessels be used in Chinese rivers and estuaries? Each could be fitted with two 10-inch howitzers capable of firing grape, canister or shells. 'As it would be a novel arm of warfare, it would create astonishment and terror. . . .'[38] A steamboat, accompanied by a frigate and three or four light-draught sloops, could rendezvous at the entrance of the Peiho 'as near to the capital, as may be found most expedient', whence, in the words of the merchant petition, they would be in a position, to demand with 'the mouths of their cannon' reparation for the humiliations suffered by Lord Napier, and—even more—the opening of other ports besides Canton to British shipping.[39]

Not until March 1835 did the British government have full details of the collapse of the Napier Commission.[40] Until then they appeared to be intent on maintaining at least the spirit of East India Company procedure—'suffer in patience for the sake of trade'. It was not by force and violence that His Majesty intended to preserve a commercial intercourse between his subjects and China, wrote the Foreign Secretary, the Duke of Wellington, to Napier, early in February 1835, but 'by conciliatory measures'.[41] Scarcely a month later, the Duke learned that fate had intervened to extinguish such amicable sentiments in circumstances of peculiar personal tragedy and national humiliation.[42]

[37] In 1825, *Enterprize* was the first steam vessel (464 tons) to round the Cape and reach Calcutta. The journey from Falmouth took nearly four months. The Indian government bought the ship for £40,000, and sent her to Burma, where she played a modest part in the closing stages of the first Burmese War.

[38] See Gore to Elliot (Admirality), Bombay, 31 Dec. 1834 (No. 94), Adm. 1/214.

[39] John F. Davis, who had succeeded Napier as Chief Superintendent, described the merchants' petition as both 'crude and ill-digested'. Davis had served with the Company since 1813, and since 1827 had been a member of the Select Committee. As one of the Old Guard, he found himself quite out of sympathy with the free traders, and his growing isolation doubtless accounted for his resignation in favour of Sir George Robinson in January 1835, after scarcely three months in office. In this connection, see Chang, op. cit., pp. 62-3.

[40] The Admiralty received Gore's letter of 27 November on 12 March 1835.

[41] Wellington to Napier, 2 Feb. 1835, quoted in Edgar Holt, op. cit., p. 38. The Duke held office in Peel's short-lived Ministry from December 1834 to April 1835. See also, S. Wells Williams, *The Middle Kingdom* (2 vols., revised edn., New York, 1883), ii. 476.

[42] First news of an impending crisis did not reach Admiral Gore until the second week of November 1834. The communication had been forwarded from Macao in the

The uneventful stalemate that characterized Anglo-Chinese relations during the spring and summer of 1835 may have appeared to suggest a continued 'reverent submission' to the Imperial ruler in Peking. But whatever the goodwill exuded by pacifist members of the House of Commons, surface appearances could not have been more deceptive. With the coming of free trade, the days of appeasement and diplomatic *laissez-faire* were bound to be numbered. As it happend, however, the walls of the Middle Kingdom were about to be shattered, not by the trumpetings of vice-regal plenipotentiaries, or the shells of versatile steamboats, but by the dogged persistence of clipper owners like Jardine Matheson and their enterprising rivals. Opium was to be the charge that burst the gates of Canton, to symbolize the opening of a new era in Anglo-Chinese relations. Not that the implications of an 'opium war' were to be fully recognized in Peking. British gunboats might frighten Canton into temporary submission, but the further frontiers of the Empire remained closed to questing developers from Europe and the United States. China continued to be resentful of, and aloof from, an outer world of alien states, whose kings were still regarded as subordinate tributaries. Forty years were to elapse before the ambassadors of five foreign nations stood before the Imperial throne to present their ribboned credentials.

---

middle of August. Two weeks later, spurred by north-east monsoon winds, the *Andromache*, which had set out in early October, brought him a full account of the débâcle, concluding with the death of Lord Napier. His two dispatches to the Admiralty were dated 11 November (No. 78), and (in company with several enclosures, which have been noted) 27 November 1834 (No. 85), both contained in Adm. 1/214.

III

THE ENDEAVOURS OF CAPTAIN ELLIOT: THE PROBING OF CANTON

THE late autumn months of 1834 saw a considerable increase of British shipping on the Canton River, as the free traders began their first season under the new Act. Relations with the Chinese authorities in Canton were correct rather than cordial. None the less, there seemed to be a mutual effort to ignore the unhappy clashes of July–September 1834, and to let sleeping dogs lie. Sir George Robinson, who took over from Davis as Chief Superintendent on 19 January 1835, seems to have had little to do but sign ships' manifests, promising himself that he would never 'wilfully incur any hazard or danger to the important trade confided to my care'.

However, scarcely had Robinson assumed the tasks of administrator and peacemaker than there occurred an incident which for a moment threatened to set ablaze the greying embers of the Napier disaster. While standing over from Manilla, the merchant ship *Argyle* had run into a violent north-east gale. She lost nearly all her sails, and was fortunate to find shelter for the night off the China coast. In the morning, the second officer and eleven hands were sent in a cutter to seek out a pilot. Scarcely ashore, they were seized, and placed in detention by the local authorities. As soon as the news reached Macao, some forty miles away, Captain Charles Elliot, accompanied by the Reverend Charles Gutzlaff as interpreter, and the *Argyle*'s captain, pushed up to Canton with all speed. At about 8.00 a.m. on 1 February, they entered the city. A few minutes later, they were stopped, and unceremoniously bundled outside the walls. Despite the splendour of his post captain's uniform and decorations, Elliot was twice struck over the head. The authorities refused all communication with officers of the British mission, tension mounted, and a crisis was only avoided when the cutter's crew were surrendered without an apology some three weeks later.[1]

Once again, British officials had acted precipitately and unconstitutionally. When Captain Fremantle had finally delivered the Governor-General' letter to the Viceroy in December 1831, notice had been given of his approach, and a time and place for the reception had been fixed. The meeting had been conducted without much warmth, but with proper decorum. In the cautionary words of the *Canton Register* of 17 February 1835, it should have set a precedent for future presentations of importance. As it happened, the *Argyle* incident merely served to strengthen the resolve of those who saw no lasting solution to the problem of Anglo-Chinese relations except through the use of force. Nearing the end of his barely four months' spell as Foreign Secretary, the Duke of Wellington lent his weighty authority in support of the same view, viz., that nothing could be gained without adequate means to enforce compliance. 'I would recommend', he wrote in March 1835, 'that till the trade has taken its regular course, particularly considering what has passed recently [the Napier imbroglio], there should always be within the Superintendent's reach a stout Frigate and a smaller vessel of war.'[2]

Such a proposal had often been mooted and, out of deference to Chinese sensibilities, regularly rejected. Robinson himself believed that Canton would never tolerate the permanent stationing of a man-of-war even in the estuary, 'at least for some time to come until they [the Chinese] became assured no ulterior views were in contemplation'. As for bringing a warship past the Bocca Tigris, that would inevitably be resisted.[3] Meanwhile, British diplomatic leverage suffered additional weakness owing to the fact that British merchant ships and trading personnel were so readily available as hostages. In the event of a crisis, Robinson pointed out, both men and ships could be removed from the Canton River and, as nearby Macao would be vulnerable, the only satisfactory alternative was 'the embarkation of all British Families and

[1] *Asiatic Journal*, 2nd series, xviii. part ii, Sept. 1835, pp. 22–3. The account is based on the report in the *Canton Register*, 3 Feb. 1835. See also encl. in No. 16, Robinson to Bentinck, 21 Feb. 1835, Adm. 1/215.

[2] Memorandum, 24 March 1835, F.O. 17/8.

[3] Robinson to Palmerston, 29 Jan, 1836 (No. 6), F.O. 17/14.

Subjects resident in that place . . . on board the Merchant Ships, which might then take their Station in some of the beautiful harbours in the neighbourhood of Lantao or Hong Kong.'[4]

In November 1835, Robinson moved his headquarters to the cutter *Louisa* off Lintin, in order to escape (as he informed the Foreign Office) the restraints and hazards of Macao. Although the Chinese were hardly likely to approve his choice of an opium entrepôt, he enjoyed the serenity and security of his floating office, a 'seat of authority' safe from the interference of Chinese officers, yet not 'divorced' from the supervision of merchant shipping.[5] But with rolling seas and the extra agitations provided by the occasional typhoon, Lintin was not a comfortable all-season anchorage, and Robinson's staff were to object strenuously to the new arrangements. As it happened, Palmerston's belated decision to end the experiment arrived scarcely more than a month after the Chief Superintendent surrendered to constant nagging, and recommended removal to the island of Hong Kong.[6]

As a matter of fact, an awareness of Macao's vulnerability in the event of a serious confrontation had been steadily gaining ground. Lord Napier had appreciated the danger, and had suggested the occupation of a neighbouring island, possibly Hong Kong, not only as a trading depot, but as a more defensible refuge for British merchants and their families than the exposed peninsula on the Chinese mainland. Charles Elliot, the deputy Superintendent, had made a similar suggestion. In his view, the occupation of the Bonin Islands off the coast of Japan would not only mean the elimination of notorious pirate haunts, but could provide a base for trading 'with the richest part of the Chinese Empire and with the South Coast of Japan'.[7]

Individual private firms as well as Company employees also took a hand in lobbying the government. James Matheson

---

[4] Robinson to Palmerston, Macao, 13 Apr. 1835 (No. 2), F.O. 17/9.

[5] Robinson to Palmerston, 11 Dec. 1835 (No. 14), F.O. 17/10. Robinson moved aboard the *Louisa* on 25 November without waiting for permission from Whitehall. There he spent the remainder of his two years as Superintendent.

[6] See Palmerston to Robinson, 28 May and 7 June 1836 (draft), F.O. 17/13; and Robinson to Palmerston, 11 Apr. 1836, F.O. 17/14.

[7] Elliot to Robinson, 9 Feb. 1835, F.O. 17/16.

wrote directly to Palmerston, elaborating merchant objections to having but one precarious seat of operations. British traders wanted access to Amoy, Ningpo, and Chusan, and Matheson specially recommended Amoy as possessing an eminently suitable anchorage for warships. More than that, Amoy was nicely placed as a sentry post to watch over the coastal trade.[8] His views, or rather his uneasiness, were also reflected in a vigorous declaration of difficulties drawn up by the British Chamber of Commerce at Canton, which drew attention to the lack of military support, and the complete inability of British representatives in China to negotiate from strength.[9]

In his anxiety to inject a little iron in British policy, Matheson had either overlooked or ignored the important step that had already been taken in positive defence of British interests. Provided they remained well out in the estuary, Admiralty vessles were now permitted to visit Chinese waters, as long as they came singly; and shortly after taking over from Admiral Gore in the spring of 1835, Rear-Admiral Thomas Bladen Capel proposed sending a 16-gun sloop to Macao to 'show the flag' and bolster drooping merchant spirits.[10] Capel's action simply confirmed the reversal of traditional standing orders which Gore had initiated, and which the Admiralty had accepted. But in Gore's view, one ship at a time was not enough, and he had objected strongly to the proviso allowing the dispatch from India of a larger emergency force, *only* if the consent of the Governor-General was forthcoming. Such a procedure could involve a delay of possibly four to six

[8] 21 Dec. 1835, F.O. 17/12.

[9] Memorial of 8 Dec. 1835, forwarded by Robinson to Palmerston on 11 Dec. 1835, F.O. 17/10.

James Matheson had been the first president of the British Chamber of Commerce in Canton. Following the death of Lord Napier, he accompanied the widow back to England, where he intended to use his many connections to the full, and press for stronger action in China. As it happened, he had hardly settled down when, on the fall of Melbourne's first Cabinet in late November 1834, his friend Lord Palmerston was replaced as Foreign Secretary by the Duke of Wellington, 'a cold-blooded fellow . . . a strenuous advocate of submissiveness and servility'. Quoted, Chang, pp. 83–4. But the Duke had barely time to recant his faith in the virtues of conciliation, when Peel's first Cabinet resigned, and Palmerston returned to his old office and his old friends in April 1835.

[10] See Capel to George R. Dawson (Admiralty), 23 May 1835 (No. 16), Adm. 1/215. Capel's instructions were dated 6 Oct. 1834.

months, which made a nonsense of emergency safeguards. Moreover, as Gore made bold to point out for the benefit of the Admiralty, Lord Bentinck had demonstrated a growing reluctance to reach a decision on such questions as naval intervention in support of British interests; he preferred to await final orders from home, however prolonged the delay. This had not always been so. During his early period of office, the Governor-General had shown himself much more independent and self-confident. He had not hesitated to lean heavily on Admiral Owen, and frequently offered him a free hand. Gore had not been so fortunate, and he was anxious that his successor should have at least the same freedom to make decisions as had Admiral Owen, in the event, or threat of, an emergency. In one of his last letters to the Admiraly, Gore urged that 'a greater degree of latitude' and 'a fuller degree of confidence' be given to the commanding officer on the spot. 'The Governor-General of India has of late in three instances declined to give an opinion on the affairs of China, so that my successor must act for himself. . . .'[11]

Despite the multitude of cares that pressed on him, it seems probable that Palmerston, on his return to office in April 1835, was pondering the vexed problem of 'force' in the China seas. Certainly, the great number of private petitions and official memoranda weighed heavily on his desk, if not his mind. On the extent of his reading, it is idle to speculate, but it may be that he paid some attention to the views of the Reverend Charles Gutzlaff, that adventurous German-born missionary, whom, it was somewhat erroneously assumed, had an unrivalled understanding of the Chinese mind and character. Robinson had sent him Gutzlaff's 'Essay on the present State of Our Relations with China', which called for strong punitive action should the Canton trade again be disrupted, and British merchants humiliated. Gutzlaff suggested, for instance, a naval expedition to the Chusan islands. 'The force used for this purpose must be so respectable as to give a death-blow to Chinese arrogance.[12] But the most persistent propagandist among the civilian 'war hawks' was Mr. Hamilton Lindsay. In company with Gutzlaff, he had taken the *Amherst*, a trading

[11] To Sir George Elliot (Admiralty), 23 Jan. 1835 (No. 7), Adm. 1/214.
[12] Encl. in Robinson to Palmerston, Macao, 26 Mar. 1835, F.O. 17/9.

vessel of some 350 tons, on an unprofitable reconnoitring voyage up the China coast in the spring of 1832. The expedition reached as far north as Weihaiwei, and included visits to the Loochoo Islands and Korea, but accomplished little in the way of fostering new trade connections. Until diplomatic relations between Britain and China were placed on an acceptable basis, Lindsay subsequently acknowledged in his report, 'the only chance of pushing English manufactures on this Coast is by carrying them [as] a small item in an Opium cargo. . . .'[13]

With many years of service as a supercargo behind him, Lindsay, like Gutzlaff, had considerable experience of Chinese customs, manners, and language, and in a trading world where even limited expertise was a rarity, his advocacy carried some weight. His letter to Lord Palmerston, later published as a pamphlet, was unfortunately written with the bellicosity of a Crown attorney who believes in the remedial effects of capital punishment. In brief, he recommended that Peking be told that Great Britain had no plans for territorial aggrandizement; she wanted simply 'a commercial treaty on a liberal basis', which could be secured by a naval force of eleven vessels, including one battleship, capable of wiping up Chinese forces and thus winning from the Emperor the desired commercial agreement. Lindsay made no bones about the need for active intervention. Threats had hitherto been of no avail; Britain must be prepared 'to coerce by a direct armed interference the Chinese empire, with its countless millions of inhabitants. . . . Nothing, however, is further from my wish', he concluded, 'than that we should oppress them because we are the stronger. Our entire demands should be no more than a com-

---

[13] Morse, iv. 335. Lindsay could not have been a very subtle commercial ambassador, and it would appear that his fumbling and unauthorized efforts to filter British cottons and calicoes into northern China did little but exacerbate sensitive opinion in Peking and Canton. Chinese reactions to the expedition's fortunes varied from the severely critical to the contemptuous. When news reached Canton that Lindsay had pasted up placards in public places setting forth the greatness of the British Empire, the pacific intentions of the British government, and the earnest desire of British agents to cultivate a friendly commerce, James Matheson was both amused and pained. 'The Chinese of Canton,' he informed a colleague in Bombay, 'observe laughingly that we are now our own trumpeters on the occasion, and it is probably the case that the document is somewhat bombastical. . . .' To Thomas Williamson, Canton, 13 July 1832, Private Letter Books (B 9), vol. 1, 1831–4 (J.M.A.).

mercial treaty, giving us the liberty of trade at two or more of the northern ports.'[14] It seemed obvious to far less contentious men than Lindsay, that Britain could, with a modest naval force, compel Canton, and ultimately Peking, to come to terms. But not even Palmerston—and no one felt more deeply about the humiliations suffered by British merchants and officials—wanted to take the final step. None the less, the amendment of Admiralty instructions on Gore's advice indicated that Whitehall's restraining bonds were weakening. The reasoning was intentionally ambiguous, but the message was clear. The Foreign Office recognized the need for a naval presence in the China Sea. '. . . it is Viscount Palmerston's opinion, with reference both to the protection of British ships and property from plunder, and to the necessity of sometimes enforcing subordination among the merchant seamen, that a Ship of War should be constantly employed on the China Station, and that the Commander of such a ship should be instructed to communicate with the British authorities in China. . . .'[15]

Throughout 1836, the Chief Superintendent persevered with his experimental 'velvet glove' policy, intended (as he expressed it) to place British trade and political relations with the Chinese Empire on 'a respectable, safe and becoming footing'. But to the irritation and gathering resentment of his fellow commissioners, especially Captain Charles Elliot, Robinson preferred to act alone. He had, in the words of one of the discomfited, 'virtually suspended the functions of his colleagues'. Confident of his ability to fathom the Chinese character, he was not averse to writing lengthy letters of advice to the Foreign Secretary. In the end, their boring prolixity, besides encouraging Palmerston's growing preference for his ambitious rival, Captain Elliot, paved the way for his

---

[14] The letter, dated 24 July 1835, is contained in F.O. 17/12, and, curiously enough, precisely the same, also addressed to Palmerston, dated Jan. 1835, in F.O. 17/16. See reply of Sir George Staunton, Bart., *Remarks on the British Relations with China and the Proposed Plans for improving them* (London, 1836), 43 pp.

[15] J. Backhouse (F.O.) to Chas. Wood (Adm.), 23 Mar. 1836 (draft), F.O. 17/16.

In the purely formal sense, there was no 'China station', unless Macao could be regarded, like Valparaiso, as a British *dépôt de convenance*. Until 1844, following the cession of Hong Kong, any detachment or squadron in the China seas was under the authority of the commander-in-chief of the East Indies Station.

undoing. In a dispatch of 18 April 1836, he warned the Foreign Secretary that there was no alternative to friendly *laissez-faire*, 'to a continuance in my present quiescent line of policy'. This course, he felt bound to pursue 'simply because all has proceeded well and successfully during its operation; and I consider that so long as that is the case, I am best fulfilling the duties of my office'.[16] But even Robinson was sensible enough not to regard the 'flower of conciliation' as a hardy perennial. He did not really trust the governors of Canton; otherwise, he would not have urged Whitehall to keep his Lintin ship as floating headquarters for the Superintendent and his staff. To make Canton the administrative centre would mean placing British residents at the mercy of local whims and pressures, with the added risk of violent collisions.

Elliot took the opposite view. He favoured Canton as business headquarters, on the ground that policies of conciliation should go hand in hand with demonstrations of trust in Chinese good faith. In March 1836, he had made bold to advise the Foreign Office:

Being at Canton, and conforming heartily to the spirit of our cautious and conciliatory instructions, I see every day more reason to believe, that without much address upon our parts, and in short, by the mere force of circumstances, we should soon come to make ourselves so useful to the native authorities, as to lead them (gradually and silently indeed, but surely) not only to admit, but to court direct communication with us. In China, to keep things quiet is the best evidence as well as the whole end of successful administration: as soon as the viceroy found out that we were sincere allies with them in that object, he would sedulously cultivate our friendliness.[17]

But long before this naïve admonition reached London, Palmerston had made up his mind to sack Robinson. In mid-June 1836, he wrote to Elliot, informing him that he could consider himself as Superintendent-elect. Not until mid-December did the letter of confirmation reach China; and it arrived at a critical moment in the history of Anglo-Chinese relations. The Emperor and his counsellors had at long last awakened to the political as well as the moral consequences of the opium traffic, and with uncommon abruptness had

[16] *Chinese Repository*, xi. Apr. 1842, No. 4, p. 188.
[17] Ibid.

decided that steps should be taken not to legalize the trade, but to prohibit it with drastic penalties. The new Superintendent was to face a crisis even more significant for the future than that encountered by Lord Napier.

Like Napier, Charles Elliot was not lacking in self-confidence and natural independence, qualities that might have been expected from the offspring of a distinguished and energetic family. His father, Sir Hugh Elliot, brother of Gilbert, first Earl of Minto, had been a career diplomat, who had transferred to the colonial service, eventually becoming Governor of Madras. Undoubtedly, the Minto connection helped both father and son. Both were men of intelligence, but, in the case of Charles, the son, a better than average brain did not justify the self-assurance that seems to have impressed Palmerston, nor warrant his unkind denigration of Robinson. For some time past, Elliot had been developing private channels of communication with the Foreign Office, and, even as a junior commissioner, the nephew of the first Earl of Minto did not hesitate on occasion to tell Palmerston of his dissatisfaction with the practices and proposals of his chief.

Born in 1801, Elliot had joined the peacetime navy in 1815 as a first-class volunteer. He was present at the bombardment of Algiers in 1816, and subsequently served in the Persian Gulf, on the African coast, and briefly in the West Indies. He retired on half-pay in 1828 with the rank of captain. Two years later, he became Protector of Slaves in British Guiana, returning home in 1833 for consultations on legislation for the abolition of slavery. In the following year, largely, it appears, on the recommendation of J. F. Davis, he accepted an invitation to accompany Lord Napier to China, and within two years, from the very modest post of 'master attendant', he had risen to the headship of the Commission.

Although Palmerston provided Elliot with the customary official admonition, 'every effort must be made to avoid giving offense to the Chinese authorities', he added a piece of advice that he had absorbed from Robinson over the previous year, viz., 'you must not, in the manner of the old Company merchants, deal subserviently with the local Chinese authorities'. In brief, courtesy and firmness should go hand in hand. No doubt a 'quiescent policy' smoothed the paths of trade, but the Canton government had to be taught the western fashion of correspondence between equals, and learn that the Celestial Emperor did not hold power over all wordly mortals. 'His Majesty's government do not "deem it expedient" that you should give to your written communications with the Chinese government, the name of Petitions.'[18]

Palmerston was, of course, asking the impossible in demanding that the Canton authorities breach their traditional system of communication without disturbing a workable relationship based on *laissez-faire*. It was a challenge, which if insisted upon, could mean no communication at all. Elliot recognized the dilemma, but took it for granted that the Foreign Secretary, once he appreciated the true situation, would prefer a reluctant acquiescence to a brusque affirmation of principle. Hence, he proposed, on grounds of simple commercial expediency, a temporary return to the old system, involving, as it did, a tacit recognition of inequality. For the moment, direct official communication with Canton was impossible of attainment; of this, Elliot was certain. Consequently, in the interests of a stable trade, it was imperative that no one should 'rock the boat' until he had presented his credentials, and, as he hoped, initiated fresh negotiations.

Already, on the very day of receiving notice of appointment, he had written to the Foreign Office emphasizing the need for 'a conciliatory disposition to respect the usages, and above all, to refrain from shocking the prejudices of this government', a course at once 'most consonant with the magnanimity of the British nation, and with the substantial interests at stake, in the maintenance of peaceful commercial relations with this empire'. In view of the risks involved, he trusted that his refusal to challenge the Cantonese authorities would neither surprise nor displease Lord Palmerston. And he added: '. . . the very remarkable movements of this government in respect to the foreign trade actually in agitation, and the critical state of uncertainty in which the results still remain, furnish me a strong additional motive for desiring to place myself at Canton as soon as possible.'[19] In brief, why make a fuss about non-essentials? The Chinese insistence on methods

---

[18] 22 July 1836, *Chinese Repository*, xi. No. 4, p. 189.
[19] Ibid., pp. 195–6.

of address, such as the insistence on petitions through the Hong merchants rather than formal correspondence between equals, struck him as childish, scarcely deserving to be made an issue of principle, especially at the expense of trade. As future events were to reveal, Elliot's policy of conciliation was not less, and, in one sense, was more 'quiescent' or 'pacific' than that of his predecessor, because he was willing to pocket his own and his country's pride on matters of protocol. The recently installed Viceroy was only too happy to continue the mutually profitable trade on the old Company basis.[20] However, to safeguard himself against the Emperor's displeasure should events misfire, he sent a deputy to Macao, along with representatives of the Hong merchants, to inquire about the credentials of the 'barbarian headman', and the credibility to be attached to his mission. On the whole, the impressions seems to have been favourable, and the Emperor was informed that Elliot appeared to be a decent kind of Englishman, who, it could be assumed, would profit from his predecessor's disgrace, and be up to no tricks. The Emperor was pleased to accept this recommendation; the British commission received their 'red permit' from the Collector of Customs, the Hoppo, and on 12 April 1837, after an interval of thirty months, the Union flag was once more raised on the flagstaff in front of the British Factory.

Meanwhile, the conflict over the opium traffic had been joined. Because he saw the evil effects of smuggling on Anglo-Chinese commercial life—and in particular, because the noxious drug was distributed from British ships—Elliot had long hoped that the trade might be legalized, and thereby controlled. Such a step appears to have been debated in Peking, but by the middle of 1837 it was clear that the Imperial government preferred to harry, and, if possible, disable the smuggler. 'The legalization of the trade is no longer thought of,' wrote James Matheson in October 1837, 'and Government is evidently making a strong effort for its entire suppression. In this, of course, they will be unable to succeed, but some time

---

[20] Tang-ching was successor to Lu K'un, whose succinct advice to British merchants, delivered shortly before his death in 1835, was crystal clear: 'Obey and remain, disobey and depart; there are no two ways.'

may elapse before they will be convinced of this, and then perhaps the idea of legalization may again come on the *tapis*.'[21]

In February 1837, Elliot had written nearly identical letters to the First Lord of the Admiralty and to the commander-in-chief of the East Indies station requesting one or more warships 'to afford such countenance to the general Trade as may be practicable without inconveniently committing His Majesty's Government upon any delicate question'.[22] Since Peking had decided to exterminate the smuggler, he went on, the interruption of the opium trade was bound, not merely to cripple British purchasing power, 'but of placing us, in respect to the prices of export staples, completely in the power of a copartnership of native dealers'. Already, the failure of opium deliveries had meant an almost entire cessation of transactions in Canton. Buoyed up with the hope that the trade would be legalized, wrote Matheson in November 1837, the merchant community were shocked by the Chinese government's recently adopted policy of 'entire suppression', a policy which they were pursuing 'with a pertinacity and success of which we have no previous example'. Practically all the native smuggling craft had been destroyed, and what little trade remained was carried ashore by foreign passage-boats. Hitherto, 'mandarin boats' in and about the Canton estuary had been paid to turn a blind eye on furtive opium runners; they were now compelled under the heaviest penalties to arrest the offenders.[23]

In confessing his distaste for the opium trade, Elliot was in all probability quite honest, but the threat to British trade forced him into awkward rationalization. Legalization had been rejected by Peking; there was, therefore, no alternative to the old system of connivance. Without an opium market, the entire tea business would collapse. Hence, devious means might be necessary 'consistent with safety and discretion' to preserve a commerce, now put at risk by Peking's drastic

[21] To Alexander Grant, c/o Messrs. Magniac, Smith & Co., Canton, 20 Oct. 1837, Private Letter Books (B 9), vol. 2, 1834–8 (J.M.A.).

[22] Macao, 2 Feb. 1837, F.O. 17/19. See also, Backhouse (F.O.) to Wood, 30 June 1837 (draft), asking the Admiralty to support Elliot's plea for occasional visits by H.M. warships, F.O. 17/23.

[23] To James Pearson of Calcutta, Canton, 27 Nov. 1837; see also, his letter to Robt. Smith of Bombay, 9 Jan. 1838, Private Letter Books (B 9), vol. 2, 1834–8 (J.M.A.).

assault on the smuggler. Apart from the moral implications of such reasoning, Elliot's proposal to pursue 'the lesser evil' reflected the naïveté of the amateur. Whatever the threatened loss, no British government could support contraband activities which were illegal under the laws of China, and which, indeed, China's rulers hoped could be extinguished by joint effort. Whatever his private views, Palmerston had no choice but to declare that his government could not interfere 'for the purpose of enabling British subjects to violate the laws of the country to which they trade'. Consequently, any losses suffered by persons as a result of the more effectual execution of laws would have to be borne by the parties who brought the loss on themselves by their own acts.[24]

Conditions were changing fast on the China coast, and very perceptibly the cautionary policy adopted by the Foreign Office, and recommended to the Admiralty, was being eroded by Elliot's fears and by events. Capel was not the man to 'jump the gun'; as a disciplined sailor-diplomat he was likely to be prudent. For this reason, the Admiralty wondered whether it might not be wise to suggest to the commander-in-chief that he visit Macao in person, and have a talk with the Superintendent.[25] In response to this diffident query, the Foreign Office warned their Lordships against supporting 'any proceeding' which might suggest to the Chinese that the Royal Navy was being employed in 'unprovoked hostility' against them. This ambiguous declaration of pacific intentions was followed by a blunt and unqualified confirmation of the new policy earlier adumbrated by Palmerston. The Admiralty were told that all existing instructions on the use of the East Indies squadron had been cancelled. In the future, one or more ships should visit the China coast *as often as convenient*, and for this purpose frigates were to be preferred to sloops or brigs. The object was, firstly, 'to afford protection to British interests', and to give weight to any representations by British subjects should they have just cause for complaint against the Chinese authorities; and sec-

---

[24] See items of correspondence between Elliot and Palmerston (Nov. 1837–June 1838) in 'Review of Public Occurrences during the last ten years, from 1832 to 1841', *Chinese Repository*, xi. May 1842 No. 5, pp. 265–6.

A similar judgement had been given earlier by the Governor-General of India. See H. Prinsep to Elliot, 20 Apr. 1837 (No. 11), Adm. 125/93.

[25] See Barrow to Fox-Strangeways (F.O.), 6 Sept. 1837, F.O. 17/23.

ondly, to assist the Superintendent in maintaining order among the crews of the British merchantmen in the port of Canton.[26]

Meanwhile, back in England, an event had occurred far more significant in retrospect than any sudden change in British naval policy. Unbeknown to Elliot, Capel, and the Emperor of China, a new age had dawned. It was marked by nothing so ominous as opium trails that led unswervingly towards war and the collapse of the old and arrogant Middle Kingdom, but by the death of a British king, William IV, on 20 June 1837. The news did not reach Bombay and Trincomalee until October, when the formal announcement offered seamen of the Royal Navy a welcome break from shipboard routine. Not that the interruption was unaccompanied by distress. For those engaged in slapping black paint on rough hulls, there was always the disturbing thought that within a few days most of it would have to be scraped off again. The funeral ceremony 'to mark the Public Grief for this great National deprivation' was but a short-lived prelude to celebrations amid the rum casks which signalled the start of the Victorian age. Ships in port 'topped' their yards, and hoisted their colours half-staff high, the Royal Standard at the main, and the Union Jack at the mizzen. At 8 a.m., the *Winchester*, Capel's flagship, began firing her seventy-two guns in minute time, proclaiming, salvo by salvo, with reverberating response the years of the late King's life. At 12.45 colours were hoisted, yards were squared, and, following the further proclamation announcing the accession of a Queen, the rigging was manned by the assembled ships' companies, and three cheers were hurled across the waters in attempted unison. After the Royal Salute of twenty-one guns, the ships again 'topped' their yards, and lowered their colours to half-mast, 'subdued in their mourning'.[27]

At Macao there was less attention to ceremony. Superinten-

---

[26] 20 Sept. 1837 (draft), F.O. 17/23; and Instructions to Rear-Admiral Sir Frederick Maitland, 9 Oct. 1837, Adm. 13/2. The same instructions were repeated to Rear-Admiral Sir William Parker, when he became commander-in-chief, 27 May 1841, Adm. 2/1330.

[27] See Capel to Wood, 21 Oct. 1837 (No. 45), Adm. 1/218.

dent Elliot carried worries comparable to those of a wartime commander. Native smuggling had been curbed to the point of extinction, as James Matheson had pointed out, but now armed British 'fast boats' ran the gauntlet to Whampoa, or carried their cargoes to secret rendezvous up the coast. Occasionally, shots were exchanged with Chinese preventive craft, and the danger of a serious and bloody clash became an alarming possiblity as Canton's efforts to block the traffic by force increased in ardour and effectiveness. In August, Elliot received through the Hong merchants the first of a series of Imperial orders to drive away the opium store ships, most of them anchored off Lintin. He was also requested to pass on the Emperor's commands to his new sovereign. Quite properly, Elliot replied that he could in no circumstances transmit orders to the British monarch that did not come directly from Peking. Moreover, his commission extended only to the supervision of the normal legal trade with the Chinese Empire. He had no authority to seek out and banish ships and crews for alleged contravention of the laws of China.

It would, in any event, have been a hopeless task. With so much profit at stake, it was hardly likely that smugglers would give up their trade. The threat of death by strangulation might temporarily discourage operations from the Chinese side, but no Emperor's edicts or Viceroy's commands could prevent 'barbarian' smugglers from fighting for survival, especially when their efforts went unchallenged by Her Majesty's representatives in the China Sea. As he looked ahead, Elliot could envisage bloody chaos should Great Britain decide to co-operate with the Viceroy at Canton. None the less, it was a dilemma that called for the 'active interposition' of the British government. Thanks to untrustworthy correspondents in Canton, the Emperor was obviously ignorant of the true state of British relations with the local authorities. Direct contact with Peking was vital if some kind of solution was to be reached, and Elliot suggested to the Foreign Office that a special commission might make the effort to fix a rendezvous in Chusan with delegates of the Imperial Court.[28]

During the rest of November, the discussion on methods of

[28] See Elliot to Palmerston, 19 Nov. 1837, *Chinese Repository*, xi. May 1842, No. 5, pp. 263–4.

communication to resolve the imbroglio continued. But on the specific question of the opium traffic, there was clearly no middle way leading to reconciliation. With legalization removed from discussion, there was clearly no possibility of papering the cracks with compromises and courteous retreats, even if the contestants met around the negotiating table. Ignorant of the military capacities of the Western intruder, the Emperor continued to threaten his Viceroy with all the extremities of Chinese law unless he forced submission on the British Superintendent. In the circumstances, as the condemnatory edicts continued to flow, any British demand for direct communication between equals was little more than an academic gesture. The Foreign Office still talked about, and supported Elliot in his pursuit of the principle of reciprocal equality, but paradoxically there was no condemnation of those British subjects who violated the laws of the country with which they traded. An impasse had been reached. On the opium question, there was no room for manoeuvre, no possibility of detour to a common meeting ground. On the morning of 2 December, the flag which had been hoisted so confidently over the British Factory in April 1836, was once more hauled down.

The last warnings from Peking were probably obscured by translation. Nevertheless, from the evidence of reliable Cantonese sources, Elliot had little doubt that the entire trade of the River would be stopped within a month unless the British opium ships anchored off Lintin were dispersed. Refusal to prohibit the private trade meant confrontation, and eventual settlement only by arms. A storm was brewing, he wrote to Palmerston, that might sweep them all—legitimate traders and opium traders—out to sea. Amid the encircling gloom, it seemed to him 'highly necessary' for the protection of British interests that an effective naval force should be ordered immediately to take up station in the South China Sea.[29]

The destiny of the British merchant community, especially

[29] To Palmerston, 7 Dec. 1837, F.O. 17/22. Nine hundred and thirty seven pages of correspondence relating chiefly to the opium trade in the Canton area, including reports and letters from Capel, Maitland, and subordinate naval commanders, the Viceroy at Canton, and the Foreign Secretary, are contained in Adm. 125/93. Beginning with 18 Jan. 1837, the volume concludes in Feb. 1840.

in Canton, was indeed an uncertain one. With the Viceroy's administration, Elliot had tried appeasement and failed. In spite of Whitehall's ambiguous pleas for mixing caution with boldness he had lacked the visible power to make his threats felt. And while British policy vacillated, and the flag of Britain rose and fell over the Factory at Canton, the pressures to eradicate the opium traffic, resulting at times in violence and death, continued to mount. Although Foreign Office attitudes by the end of 1837 were obviously hardening, the navy was still being urged to handle the inevitably recurring incidents with restraint. Undoubtedly, Admiral Sir Thomas Maitland, the new commander-in-chief, was voicing standard Whitehall misgivings when he remarked that too many visits by war-ships might aggravate suspicions and accentuate hostility. It would be necessary, he wrote to Elliot from Madras, to reassure the authorities that the presence of British ships of war was simply a demonstration of national solicitude. Since the China Trade was now a British as well as a Company responsibility, the Government 'considered itself bound to see that the Ships and Persons of Her Majesty's Subjects are duly protected from injury of insult, as is the case in all other portions of the Globe'.[30]

The Superintendent must have accepted this comforting intelligence a little wryly. For some time now, he would have been grateful for a substantial token of protection against injury and insult. He would also have appreciated such an addition to his powers as might have enabled him to keep 'due order amongst the seafaring class of Her Majesty's subjects, who visit this part of the Empire.'[31] But this suggestion which would have given Elliot control over all British merchant shipping in the China seas was vetoed by the Admiralty.[32]

On 12 July 1838, the *Wellesley* (72), The Admiral's flagship, accompanied by the brig *Algerine* (10), passed through Macao Roads, and proceeded to Tong-ku (or, as it was frequently to be called, Urmston) Harbour, a few miles to the south-eastward of Lintin. Following the customary rude welcome

[30] Maitland to Elliot, *Wellesley* at Madras, 21 Apr. 1838 (No. 1), F.O. 17/27.
[31] To Backhouse (F.O.), 2 Mar. 1838 (No. 10), F.O. 17/26.
[32] Wood to Strangeways, 1 Aug. 1838, F.O. 17/28.

expressing official Canton's wish that the Admiral clear out as soon as possible, Maitland landed his family at Macao. There, he learned to his surprise that Captain Elliot was returning to Canton to make one final effort at restoring the *status quo*. Elliot reached Canton on 25 July, and on the following day the flag was once again hoisted over the British Factory. 'The object [of the visit] is of course not known', wrote James Matheson to his London agent (and Palmerston's confidante) John Abel Smith, M.P., 'but report says he is making an effort to open a *direct communication with the Viceroy*, without the interruption of the Hong merchants.'[33] Inevitably the effort failed. On the 29th, Elliot's secretary delivered a letter at the city gate, addressed to the Viceroy. The contents, which offered an explanation of Admiral Maitland's visit, were intended to remove any fears that another invasion up the river might be attempted. The letter was returned to the Superintendent unopened on the same day; only petitions forwarded in the orthodox manner were acceptable. Elliot returned to Macao on 31 July.

In order to avoid the same embarrassing problem of protocol, Maitland himself made no effort to communicate with the Viceroy. Following Palmerston's reiterated advice, he was intent on avoiding any violation of Chinese customs and prejudices. At the same time, like any good policeman, he could hardly shield himself from the consequences of agitations, however provoked. Scores of small craft under British or American flags were now plying openly between Lintin and Whampoa, most of them well armed against interference by preventive patrols. Collisions, involving exchange of fire, were becoming more frequent. The crisis came at the end of July, when by ill chance a small British vessel, the *Bombay*, was boarded on the assumption that she was an opium carrier. Whether or not the pretext was genuine, it was strongly suspected that the Chinese were looking for Admiral Maitland. Such an insult to the flag could not be allowed to pass.

The *Wellesley*, at the Superintendent's behest, made sail for the Bocca Tigris, in company with the *Larne* (16), the *Algerine* and the cutter *Louisa*. On 4 August, the little squadron anchored off Chuenpi. The appearance of ship of the line with

[33] Canton, 27 July 1838, Private Letter Books (B 9), vol. 3, 1836–9 (J.M.A.).

gun-ports open had an immediate effect. Apologies were offered for the insult to the captain of the *Bombay*, and for the time being there was an end to rude messages and provocative trade harassment. The flag rose once again over the British Factory, and although Elliot's second letter, similarly delivered at one of the city gates, was, as usual, returned, Maitland managed to establish most friendly relations with the Chinese naval officers. Admiral Kuan, in grace and charm the equal of any courtier in the *salons* of Europe, paid complimentary visits to the *Wellesley*, suffered ships' cooking with oriental equanimity, and listened with becoming gravity and patience as the commander-in-chief elaborated on the peaceful purpose of his mission. No aggressions were intended; and, in well-memorized words (with which he had described his mission to Elliot), Maitland explained that the British government, not the Company, was now in command of British interests in the China seas, and it was 'in accordance with the genius of the English government to look after the interests of its subjects in foreign countries', to see that they suffered no injustice, and to ensure that they conducted themselves peaceably.[34]

The *Wellesley* returned to the Tong-ku anchorage in August, where Maitland waited for the end of the south-west monsoon. It was a peaceful and relaxing interlude. Clearly neither squadron wanted a fight, and judging by the repeated bestowal of gifts and other tokens of goodwill, Admiral Kuan enjoyed the company of his brother officer. On one occasion, Kuan wrote him a note of condolence on the death of his niece, and, before his departure, Maitland presented his friend with a case of wine. Maitland's conduct, both as a strategist and a host, was approved by the Admiralty. On 5 October 1838, with the blessings and good wishes of her honourable opponents, the *Wellesley* set sail for India.

Happy as were the relations between the two Services, the general situation had worsened. Elliot himself was torn by a private dilemma that brought him increasing embarrassment and worry. The Fates had trapped and fettered him. There can be no doubt of his intensifying hatred of the opium traffic that

[34] See Maitland to Wood, *Wellesley* at sea, 9 Oct. 1838 (No. 60), encl. Elliot to Palmerston, 10 Aug. 1838, and Maitland to the Chinese Admiral at the Bogue, 29 Aug. 1838, Adm. 1/219.

'was rapidly staining the British character with deep disgrace', sentiments which were cordially echoed by the Viceroy. But warnings and injunctions to his erring countrymen in the opium ships had no effect, any more than the presence of the diminutive British squadron had intimidated the Chinese into abandoning their relentless crusade. Constant arrests, fines, tortures, imprisonments, and strangulations indicated the unbending determination of the Imperial government to eradicate the evil among its own subjects. In Canton, by December 1838, it was estimated that at least two thousand opium dealers, brokers, and smokers had been gaoled. Executions were taking place every day. The export trade, chiefly in British tea, naturally suffered. Chinese Factory servants or their associates were ready scapegoats of viceregal displeasure; and when on 26 February 1839, a Chinese retainer was strangled on the Factory quay for his presumed connection with the drug traffic, British, American, Dutch, and French flags were hauled down in unison. They were not to be re-hoisted until 22 March 1842.

IV

THE FLASHPOINT OF ANGLO-CHINESE RELATIONS 1839

Towards the end of 1838, the new Emperor of China sum-moned to his capital a man who was to become as famous in London as in Macao and Canton, Commissioner Tse-haü Lin, the Governor-General of Hunan and Hupeh. On 31 December, Lin was told by his master that he needed a strong and an honest agent to eradicate the opium evil once and for all.[1] If Lin had been as sensible and wise as he was tough and trustworthy, a war might have been averted. The new Imperial Commissioner arrived at Canton by boat during the early morning of 10 March 1839, accompanied by a retinue of red- and blue-button mandarins. Contemporaries speak of him as rather corpulent, aged about fifty-four, with a heavy black moustache and a long beard. In his train came a flotilla of local craft, beflagged and decorated in gold, containing the principal officers of the city, civil and military, from the Viceroy to the Superintendent of the Salt Department. The walls of the Red Fort on the Honam shore were lined with soldiers, as were those of the Dutch Folly, a mile or more eastward of the Factories. Only two or three foreigners were visible among the vast assemblage, and 'a universal silence prevailed' as the Commissioner stepped ashore.[2]

On March 1839 this 'Celestial Robespierre' as the *United Service Magazine* called him,[3] issued his first proclamation to

[1] For the past three years, Lin had been one of the strongest supporters of outright suppression. According to reports from Canton, the Emperor, with tears in his eyes, had besought his help: 'How, alas! can I die and go to the shades of my imperial father and ancestors, until these direful evils are removed!' S. Wells Williams, *The Middle Kingdom*, ii. 498.

[2] William C. Hunter, *The 'Fan Kwae' at Canton before Treaty Days, 1825–1844* (2nd edn., Shanghai, 1911), pp. 136–7. Hunter was an American merchant who had been living in Macao and Canton since 1824. The first edition was published in 1882 under the author's pseudonym, 'An Old Resident'.

[3] Vol. II, May 1844, p. 43.

the Hong merchants and to the 'barbarian' traders. The former were charged with conniving in the opium trade, and threatened with strangulation at the stake if they failed to insist on the surrender by foreign dealers of all the opium in the store-ships. Four days later, Elliot, then at Macao, notified the Viceroy of his willingness to meet the Chinese authorities, and, in all sincerity, to discuss what measures might be taken 'to fulfil the pleasure of the great Emperor'. On the 24th, pushing his way in the *Larne*'s gig past jostling and obviously hostile boatmen, he arrived at Canton in full naval uniform, without the customary detachment of marines. Almost immediately he found himself, along with some 275 foreign residents, a prisoner of the Chinese.

Behind the Factories, hundreds of soldiers filled the lanes and streets; others guarded the quay, while a triple cordon of boats blocked the river approaches for some six miles in the direction of Whampoa. Bereft of their Chinese servants, who had been ordered to quit the premises on pain of death, and under constant pressure from the frightened Hong inter-mediaries, the merchants looked to the Superintendent as guarantee of their personal safety. To improve morale, Elliot ordered his boat's ensign to be tied to the broken flagstaff on the Factory roof; '. . . for I well know, my Lord', he wrote to Palmerston, 'that there is a sense of support in the sight of that honoured Flag, fly where it will, that none can feel but men who look upon it in some such dismal streight as ours'.[4]

At the moment, the only substantial guardian of British in-terests in China waters was the sloop *Larne*. Goaded no doubt by merchant appeals for armed support,[5] Elliot instructed her captain to stay in the neighbourhood (rather than return to India) until the situation cleared. Once he appreciated the Superintendent's desperate plight, Captain Blake found him-self in a quandary. Without undue difficulty, he could prob-ably make his way up river to Whampoa, but once there, he could only take action at the risk of endangering the lives of his fellow Europeans in the beleaguered city. 'The [merchant] Ships at Whampoa,' he wrote to Admiral Maitland, 'are all in

[4] Canton, 30 Mar. 1839 (No. 16), F.O. 17/31.
[5] See Bell & Co. and others to A.R. Johnston, Deputy Superintendent, Canton, 2 Mar. 1839, F.O. 17/31.

a state of defence and ready for sea. I am informed that they could muster 250 men and 28 boats of all Sorts, leaving sufficient on board to look after the Ships, but they have been most earnestly and urgently enjoined by advice from Canton to attempt nothing. . . .' In brief, a rash effort, which almost inevitably with so scanty a force would fail, seemed more than likely to invite retribution on the Europeans living precariously in Canton.[6] So Captain Blake held his hand.

Elliot himself had weighed the risks of an armed rescue attempt, and had decided against intervention. Once he had reached the conclusion that his position was hopeless, there was no alternative to capitulation. On 27 March, he agreed to surrender some 20,000 chests of opium.[7] On 3 April, the Deputy Superintendent, A. R. Johnson, was given permission to leave Canton to arrange for the delivery. Slowly, the storeships moved up from Lintin as far as the Bogue. On 21 May, the opium cargoes were handed over to the Commissioner's officers, and, shortly after, destroyed in deep trenches on the heights of Chuenpi. Lin had triumphed. In aggressively gaining the upper hand, and humiliating his opponents without a fight, Lin assumed that he had solved the problem of opium smuggling. By the end of the month, all British subjects had departed for Macao; of other foreigners, only some 25 Americans remained, and these were intent on picking up cargoes that had been left behind. 'Cap^tn Elliot says that when he leaves Canton,' wrote James Matheson to his correspondent in Bombay on 3 May, 'which he proposes doing as soon as released from durance, he will make the place too hot for the foreigners of any other nation to remain here, but I question if he can manage this until he has a squadron to blockade the port. . . .' Meanwhile, he continued, although the Canton River system was under official blockade, 'unless open hostilities take place, we trust we shall be able to devise means of unloading and realizing your consignments'.[8]

[6] Blake to Maitland, *Larne* at Macao, 31 Mar. 1839, Foreign Dept., Consultation No. 124, 5 June 1839 (N.A.I.).

[7] See 'Public Notice to British Subjects' (to be copied in the Press) announcing the arrangements made for the delivery of the opium. Canton Register Office, 3 Apr. 1839, ibid.

[8] Canton, 3 May 1839, Private Letter Books (B9), J. Matheson, vol. 4, 1939 (J.M.A.).

In the early days of his anguished confinement, Elliot had been able to write to Palmerston a cool and balanced dispatch, which, judging by the subsequent Treaty of 1842, must have carried some weight with the Foreign Office. 'This is the first intercourse of a sure kind with our countrymen and families outside for twelve days,' wrote the unhappy Superintendent on 3 April. 'I crave your Lordship's excuse for my bad hand writing, but I consider it my duty not to divulge this despatch.' Elliot began by stating his conviction that further negotiations, even if supported by arms, could not restore confidence in future trade relations. 'All sense of security has been broken in pieces.' Recent events had strikingly demonstrated 'that a separation from the Ships of our Country on the mainland of China is wholly unsafe. The movement of a few hours has placed the lives, liberty and property of the foreign community, with all the vast interests, commercial and financial, contingent upon our Security at the mercy of this Government.'

He implored the Foreign Secretary to set out, at the earliest possible moment, a course of action that would forever extinguish 'this defiance of every obligation of truth and right toward the whole Christian World'. The Chinese had not acted in ignorance of the evils they committed, 'but in ignorance of the Power of His Majesty's Government to resent them'. To provide proper enlightenment, Elliot recommended the immediate occupation of the Chusan Islands, along with the simultaneous blockade of Canton, Ningpo, and the Yangtse River from the estuary to its junction with the Imperial Canal. Such action might then be followed by an ultimatum to the Court in Peking demanding the disgrace and punishment of the Commissioner, Lin, and the Viceroy, Tang. In addition, the Imperial government should be asked to pay a fixed sum of money in satisfaction of the heavy losses incurred by their outrageous proceedings, and they must be made to accept the formal cession to Britain of the Chusan Islands.

Elliot doubted if an indemnity of five millions sterling would do more than cover the merchant's losses. But even should this be true, it would be sensible to commute part of such a sum in return for the free entrance, during a stated number of years, of British ships and cargoes into the ports of

Canton, Ningpo, Amoy, and Nanking. But such a settlement could only be achieved by means of 'a swift and heavy blow'. Further negotiations and conciliatory compromises would merely mislead the Emperor, and make inevitable the dispatch of a large-scale military action at a later date. This might have drastic consequences; a prolonged war would 'probably break up the fabric of society in this portion of the globe'.[9] But Elliot looked not only to England. Urgent appeals for aid went out, not only to the Governor-General of India, Lord Auckland, but to the governors of Macao and Manilla. Obviously, Portuguese Macao lay under the thumb of Canton, and the authorities could scarcely guarantee the safety of British lives and property. On the other hand, with British financial help, the Typa anchorage, which had long harboured British ships, could be put in an immediate state of defence, and from this protected base small armed craft could be used to seek out enemy junks.[10]

The Governor of Macao, Dom Adrias da Silveira Pinto, was excessively cordial in his acknowledgement of the British government's beneficence. Unhappily, owing to the 'very peculiar situation' imposed upon him, he was unable at the moment to accept so generous an offer, feeling it 'his bounden duty to observe a strict neutrality, so long as powerful reasons shall not constrain him to a different line of conduct, or until there shall be evidence of the imminent peril which the Superintendent seems to fear as being about to happen'. In such an event, he would, of course, 'frankly take advantage of the generous facilities presented to him'. Meanwhile, he was prepared to protect 'as far as within his reach' the lives and property of British subjects in Macao, excluding only (at Elliot's suggestion) persons engaged in the opium trade.[11]

[9] Canton, 3 Apr. 1839, Foreign Dept., Consultation No. 74, 26 June 1839 (N.A.I.).
On 6 April, Elliot sent Palmerston a summary of events over the past two months, including a day by day record of his detention in Canton. 'I feel assured', he wrote, 'that the single mode of saving the Coasts of the Empire from a shocking character of warfare, both foreign and domestic, will be the very prompt and powerful interference of Her Majesty's Government for the just vindication of all wrongs and the effectual prevention of crime and wretchedness, by permanent settlement', No. 18, F.O. 17/31.
[10] See letter to the Governor-General of India, Canton, 16 Apr. 1839, Foreign Dept., Consultation No. 74, 26 June 1839 (N.A.I.).
[11] Encl. in No. 74, doc. cit., above.

The Governor of Macao was undoubtedly in a ticklish position. He had already forwarded to Manilla stores of Portuguese opium for safe keeping there, but a highly suspicious Lin was insisting that he find 3,000 chests and surrender them, without further delay, to his officers. As a guarantee of delivery and continued good behaviour, the Commissioner also proposed that Chinese troops should occupy the Portuguese boundary forts which separated the peninsula from the mainland. In such an event, there was little the *Larne* could do but watch events, and make certain that the settlement was provisioned. But even if rations sufficed, a garrison of some 400 mediocre troops, and 500 Kaffir slaves, 'by far the best part of the force', were scarcely capable of holding the place against a resolute Chinese attack. On the other hand, there was talk that the Americans might feel obliged to come to the rescue. Their frigates *Columbia* (60) and *John Adams* (24) had recently arrived at Macao. So long as they remained in the offing, the safety of the settlement was probably assured, but there could be no certainty. Warships directed to 'show the flag' on 'round the world' cruises were likely to be chary of taking on the responsibilities of 'station ships', especially under British auspices.[12]

In existing circumstances, there could be only one answer. Unless Portugal provided facilities for adequate British defence—say, a thousand troops, principally artillery, and a few gunboats—the compulsory purchase of the Macao lease might be imperative. If Macao were declared a free port under the British flag, and sufficiently garrisoned against Chinese attack, 'it would soon pay every expence, and place the whole foreign trade with this part of the Empire on a firm footing'.[13]

Fantasy and fact, optimism and despair, mingled as the unhappy prisoner 'on parole' inscribed his visions in letter after letter to London, Calcutta, and Macao. On 24 May, after issuing an order that no British ships should enter the Whampoa anchorage in view of the danger to life and property, Elliot left Canton for Macao.

---

[12] See in this connection, Joshua Henshaw, *Around the World: Narrative of a Voyage in the East India Squadron under Commodore George C. Read* (2 vols., New York and Boston, 1840), and Fitch W. Taylor, *A Voyage Round the World . . . in the United States Frigate Columbia . . .* (2 vols., 5th edn., New Haven and New York, 1846).
[13] Elliot to Palmerston, 6 May 1839 (No. 19), F.O. 17/31.

Not until the end of May, did news of Elliot's predicament reach India. The source was a copy of the *Singapore Free Press Chronicle* (Friday, 26 April 1839) which informed the startled members of Council that the lives and liberties of all the foreigners in Canton had won reprieve only by the surrender of more than 20,000 chests of opium, estimated to be worth more than 2m. pounds sterling. Personal accounts of the event, which followed shortly, confirmed the printed word. After prolonged discussions, somewhat snarled as a result of competing troubles in Rangoon, the President in Council (since the Governor-General was absent) addressed a circumspect, if not entirely tepid, letter to Admiral Maitland at Trincomalee.[14] The Government of India had no power to instruct—that was London's concern; nor did the Council wish 'to interfere with the free exercise of yr. Excellency's judgment'. But, assuming that the Admiral, like the Council, had received no official news of the recent emergency from the Superintendent, he might feel the need to hasten to China, and see for himself what was going on. In which case, he must regard himself as free to take the battleship *Wellesley*, and any other ships of the East Indies squadron. At the moment, there was no urgent demand for the services of the navy in the Bay of Bengal. So it was up to the Admiral to decide whether 'important interests at stake on the other side of India' might make such a withdrawal a risky one.[15]

Quite naturally, Maitland was reluctant to act in a vacuum. Apart from press clippings, he received no communications in regard to the Canton imbroglio until the morning of 13 June. This was chiefly owing to bad luck. China dispatches, sent in care of his agents, had reached Madras shortly before mid-May, whence they were forwarded to Bombay, and thence, on

[14] Maitland had left Bombay on 15 May, arriving at Trincomalee on the 28th.

[15] President in Council to Maitland, Fort William, 31 May 1839, Foreign Dept., Consultation No. 126, 5 June 1839 (N.A.I.) and Extract of Proceedings of the Honble. President in Council, 29 May 1839, No. 125, ibid. See also, Maitland to Wood (Admiralty), Trincomalee, 30 May 1839 (No. 49), Adm. 1/220.

On 5 June, the Council (W. Morrison, T. C. Robertson and W. W. Bird) informed the Secret Committee of the Court of Directors in London of their dispatch to the commander-in-chief, in which they 'cautiously avoided expressing any opinion as to the nature of the exigency, and left His Excellency quite free to act under his own judgment as to whether the case was such as to require his presence. . . .' Fort William, 5 June 1839, Foreign Dept., Consultation No. 12, 5 June 1839 (N.A.I.).

to Trincomalee. At least a month overdue, such information as was contained in this mail was obviously too stale to provide anything of value for an assessment of the existing situation. Like so many of his predecessors, Maitland faced the eternal dilemma that was a consequence of the time-lag. Assuming that affairs in Canton had returned to normal, precipitate action might have the effect of injuring both the merchants and their trade. Before coming to a decision, he felt he needed more light on a problem which, barring an emergency that would call for automatic action, 'must be most delicate to handle, without instructions from Her Majesty's Government'. On the other hand, he made bold to confess that had the *Wellesley* been present in the Canton River at the time of the threatening ultimatum, he would, in his own words, have 'taken upon Myself the responsibility of even waging War against the Chinese authorities had I considered such a measure necessary for the protection and safety of my countrymen placed in a state of restraint, contrary to the usages of civilized nations'. But for the time being, unless further bad news was forthcoming, Maitland thought it best to wait on events. Procrastination, as the Government of India had implied in their advice, remained the better part of valour until Whitehall had pondered the evidence and decided what coercive measures might be required by way of redress.[16]

But the long delayed dispatches from the Superintendent in Canton, when they did eventually reach India on 24 June, did little to enlighten either Admiral or Governor-General. The Supreme Government sympathized with Captain Elliot in his painful predicament, but saw no need to modify their policy of *laissez-faire*. Maitland was still free to make up his mind, and if he judged an emergency warranted quick action, he was welcome to remove either the *Wellesley* or the *Conway* (28) from the Bay of Bengal, despite worsening relations with the Burmese Court.[17] Two weeks later, however, Elliot was told that Calcutta 'would gladly learn' that the release of the European

[16] To the President in Council, *Wellesley* at Trincomalee, 13 June 1839, Foreign Dept., Consulatation No. [indecipherable], 5 July 1839 (N.A.I.).

[17] Fort William, 24 June 1839, Foreign Dept., Consultation No. 75, 26 June 1839 (N.A.I.).

By the first Burman War (1824–6) the British had secured the right to send a Resident to the Court of Ava, but this concession was abandoned in 1837, and

population could remove any need for the presence of the *Wellesley*.[18] In the end, Maitland did not take his flagship to the China Sea, but, once again, feeling the need to offer encouragement, he dispatched the *Volage* (28) with instructions to show the flag, but not to flaunt it. Provided 'the lives and liberties of H.M. subjects' were not in jeopardy, the frigate was to return, via Singapore, to Trincomalee during the early days of the north-east monsoon. Regardless of possible demands for naval assistance in Burma, Maitland was still convinced that too imposing a force in the Canton River would handicap rather than help the Superintendent, pending negotiations for a new trade agreement. Moreover, like Elliot, he hoped that the presence of two American warships (assuming their captains could be prevailed upon to delay departure) would secure the safety of the European settlement.[19] Heretofore, the little *Larne*, in response to Elliot's pleadings, had postponed her sailing, and remained the only active assurance of peaceful existence in Macao.[20] But Captain Blake was getting restive, and, despite the plaintive appeals of the Canton merchants (for the moment resident in Macao) and the urgent promptings of the Superintendent, he refused to delay his departure for more than a day. He saw no reason why a visiting vessel of the Royal Navy should occupy itself with police work, especially when the presence of such a protector seemed to have so little effect in easing a static situation. On 30 May, the *Larne* set off with dispatches, reaching Trincomalee on 29 August after a passage of 92 days.[21]

The commander-in-chief's reaction, when informed of the pressures to which Blake was subjected, one again demonstrates the traditional determination of the navy to reject civilian interference even at high government level, unless an

---

thereafter relations continued to deteriorate, amid conditions of constant friction that were to lead to the second Burma War of 1852–3.

[18] See draft of 8 July, and letter of 11 July 1839 ibid., Nos. 74 and 75 respectively.

[19] Maitland to Wood, Trincomalee, 15 June (No. 59) and 15 July (No. 80) 1839, Adm. 1/220.

[20] See Elliot to Palmerston, 4 June 1839 (No. 25) F.O. 17/32.

[21] Ibid., enclosing Elliot to Blake, 28 May, and Blake's reply of the same date. See also, Maitland to Wood, Trincomalee, 10 Sept. 1839 (No. 105), with encl., Blake to Maitland, 30 May 1839, Adm. 1/220.

emergency was clearly proven.[22] In a letter to the Admiralty, which was subsequently passed on to Palmerston, Maitland strenuously rejected 'any assumption that the Captain of one of H.M. Ships of War is bound under every circumstance to comply with the requisition of one of H.M. Consuls or other Functionaries, when such requisition is opposed to his own judgment, and probably at variance with his orders'.[23]

Meanwhile, British trade with Canton continued under foreign flags, chiefly American. A large share of the tea exports fell to Russell & Co., who, along with other American houses, were determined to continue their business, much to the relief of their former British competitors. Three years earlier, William Jardine had delivered a stinging rebuke to the captain of the brig *Governor Findlay*. 'On what principle did you Salute the American ship of war? Were every Merchant vessel arriving in the Cumsingmoon to salute Commodore Kennedy, he would, in less than a month, have no powder to return the Compliment with. The Commodore would have felt more obliged to you had you not put his civility to the test. Reserve your powder for more useful purposes.'[24] Although British merchants showed concern over the high freight charges involved in transhipment outside the River, they were, on the whole, content that so many Americans were co-operating cheerfully, if not entirely unselfishly, in keeping a mutually profitable business afloat. 'My dear Forbes', said Elliot, when he encountered the American trader in Macao during the summer of 1839, 'the Queen owes you many thanks for not taking my advice as to leaving Canton. We have got in all our goods, and got out a full supply of teas and silk. If the American houses had not remained at their post, the English would have gone in. I had no power to prevent them from going'.[25] This was only too true. Yet not a few British skippers were to be tempted by Commissioner Lin's invitation to ignore the Superintendent's embargo, and to bring their ships to Whampoa. Continued frustration might well drive them to

[22] See in this connection, G. S. Graham, *Great Britain in the Indian Ocean 1810–1850* (Oxford, 1967), p. 63.

[23] Maitland to Wood, Trincomalee, 10 Sept. 1839 (No. 104), Adm. 1/220.

[24] To Capt. Mackenzie, Canton, 5 June 1836, Private Letter Books (B9), William Jardine, vol. 5, 1836–7 (J.M.A.).

[25] Quoted, Chang, op. cit., p. 208.

desperation, James Matheson remarked to William Jardine. Most of them would risk almost any hazard on the journey, rather than sit quietly off Lintin 'while foreigners were fattening on their ruin'.[26] As it happened, expediency triumphed over accumulating national resentments until, in the spring of 1840, an anomalous situation was resolved by the threat of impending war. In June of that year the American community, 35 in number, left Canton for Macao.

Meanwhile, Anglo-Chinese relations showed no signs of improvement; only another incident, involving bloodshed or 'face', was required to break the uneasy statement. In July 1839, during a drunken affray in Hong Kong involving some English sailors, an innocent Chinese, Lin Wei-hi was killed. As customary, the surrender of a murderer, real or symbolic, was demanded by the Cantonese authorities. Elliot immediately empanelled a court of criminal and admiralty jurisdiction to try the arrested seamen, and advanced $2,000 to relatives of the deceased as a gesture of compensation for their loss. The actual perpetrator of the deed was never discovered, but a few sailors were convicted of riotous behaviour and sent to England under arrest. (They were liberated shortly after arrival). Failing to obtain a victim, Lin prepared to punish the whole British community in Macao for the Superintendent's biased and incompetent conduct of the case.

On 15 August, he forbad the delivery of all supplies, including foodstuffs, to British merchants and their families either in Macao or on shipboard, and ordered the withdrawal of all Chinese servants attached to British households or business establishments. Moreover, he directed the Governor of Macao to expel all British residents from the colony.[27] A crisis was at hand which could easily have blown into war had sufficient British forces been available. But the *Larne* had departed, and the *Volage* had yet to arrive. Hence, Elliot was quite incapable of putting up a proper resistance. On the 26th, the entire British community embarked for Hong Kong in every available ship or boat that bore the British flag. The weather was

[26] Letter of 25 June 1839, Private Letter Books (B9), J. Matheson, vol. 4, 1839 (J.M.A.).
[27] J. H. Anstell to Elliot, Macao, 25 Aug., encl. No. 1, in Elliot to Palmerston (No. 34), F.O. 17/32.

foul, and several of the small craft did not reach their destination until the beginning of September.[28] The transfer meant suffering, or at least considerable discomfort, for the refugees, especially for the more 'delicate females in the last stage of pregnancy'. However, the loss of the base had little effect on enterprising opium dealers, whose trade in consequence of Elliot's heavy surrender became more profitable than ever. Fast boats simply took their supplies to less exposed ports further up the coast, where they received higher prices to compensate for shrunken stocks and increased labour. Such encouragement seemed too good to last. Anticipating a further campaign of suppression, James Matheson begged his colleague Jardine not to lose heart. Even if forced out of Macao, they could all live and do business afloat; 'on no account' would they desert their post.[29]

The *Volage* dropped anchor in Hong Kong harbour on 21 August, where she was joined shortly after by the *Hyacinth* (18). Thus armoured, Elliot immediately renewed his efforts to oust the British opium carriers from Lintin and other coastal anchorages. But without the exercise of force, his order of 11 September demanding their withdrawal from the area had little more effect than his previous injunction.[30] However, he could tackle the illegal trade, and arrangements were made for

[28] A brief account of the expulsion is contained in the *Bombay Times Extraordinary*, 25 November 1839, based on a Hong Kong report, dated 9 September. The newspaper also outlined the sequence of events in China up to 6 September, and concluded that 'war has actually commenced in China. Whatever may be the merits of the case which has actually given rise to it, there can be no longer any question of the course which it is now imperative on the British nation to pursue towards China'.

Also included in the same edition is a lengthy memorial addressed to Lord Palmerston by twenty six merchant firms, formerly residing in Canton, and lately (following three months in Macao) refugees on board their ships at Hong Kong. Admiral Maitland enclosed a copy of this particular *Bombay Times* in his dispatch to the Admiralty of 26 Nov. 1839, No. 125, Adm. 1/5496. See also, James Matheson to John Abel Smith, M.P., Hong Kong, 9 Sept. 1839, Private Letter Books (B9), J. Matheson, vol. 4, 1839 (J.M.A.).

[29] Letter of 13 May 1839, ibid.

[30] Although it was (as he so often expressed it) contrary to the wishes of government that any countenance or protection should be given to opium smugglers, Palmerston insisted that Captain Elliot had no authority to demand, as he had done by public notice on 11 September 1839, that all British vessels engaged in the trade should depart from the coast of China. Palmerston to Elliot, 20 Feb. 1840, (draft copy sent to Admiralty in a letter of 18 Mar. 1840) Adm. 1/5499.

the hire of armed boats from the *Volage*, at $1,000 a month, to hunt down the smugglers.[31]

More immediately in need of attention was the problem of food supply in Hong Kong. Fortunately, it was more amenable to solution. With the fire-power of two warships now at his disposal, Elliot was able to arrange for regular shipments of provisions from the local peasantry in and around Kowloon. As it happened, this tactical success resulted in the first naval collision between Chinese and British warships, a trifling engagement, which, as after-events were to demonstrate, was the prelude to the first act in a drama, generally known as the Opium War.

On 4 September 1839, when a number of war junks attempted to interfere with the delivery of supplies from Kowloon, shots were exchanged, and a few Chinese vessels were driven ashore. British ships suffered no real damage, and there were no casualties among the crews.[32] On the following day, near Macao, the Chinese attacked again, and mistakenly seized and burned the Spanish brig, *Bilbianco*. On the 18th, a few desultory shots were fired in the direction of a small English schooner, but no effort was made to close.[33] Despite these significant brushes with the enemy, Elliot still hoped to reach some kind of settlement with Lin; and for his own sake as well

---

[31] Elliot to Palmerston, 9 Sept. 1839, F.O. 17/32.

[32] Lin did not inform the Emperor about the battle until 18 September, and, according to Arthur Waley, his accounts then and later tended to read more like passages from a contemporary heroic ballad or play rather than pieces of sober reporting. Both Chinese and British of the time regarded Lin as a man of unusual integrity, and it was, therefore, the more surprising that he should send out dispatches on military engagements which twisted the truth out of recognition. Waley is probably more competent than any other European scholar in explaining the curious contradiction. 'Any action', he writes, 'whether successful or unsuccessful, was immediately followed by a wild scramble to get mentioned in the official report on the battle. . . . The claims were usually based on alleged casualties inflicted on the enemy, and as the authorities at Peking had no way of checking up on enemy losses, the figures given were determined by what officers thought would entitle them to the reward they had in mind. . . . Naval warfare lent itself particularly well to fictitious claims of this kind. No officer who claimed to have sunk a foreign ship was expected to give its name or identify it in any way, except perhaps by mentioning how many masts it had.' It the long run, of course, this customary system of delivering false information eroded any genuine confidence between the Emperor and his senior provincial officers. See Arthur Waley, *The Opium War through Chinese Eyes* (London, 1958), pp. 70–2, 84–5.

[33] See Captain Smith (*Volage*) to Maitland, 14 Oct. 1839, Adm. 1/5496.

as Lin's (for he had a considerable respect of his opponent), he was determined in his efforts to rid the coast of British smugglers and their loathsome store-ships. Scarcely a week after the encounter off Kowloon, he issued his most severe and uncompromising order to the commanders of all British merchant ships, requiring them within forty-eight hours to report to him, and take oath that they harboured no opium aboard. He then repeated his previous demand (which was similarly unenforceable) that any vessel shown to have been engaged in the drug traffic should depart forthwith from the China coast.

James Matheson viewed the events of 1839 with increasing perturbation, as he watched his opium business gradually dwindle to a point of stagnation. He himself was frequently 'on the run', sometimes afloat south of Lantau, which '. . . being beyond the inner waters of China' was assumed to be 'less objectionable'.[34] Whatever the lamentations of the humanitarians, it was, in his view, clearly up to the Chinese government alone to enforce prohibition. Unfortunately, Elliot 'had adopted the novel course of assisting the Government in this, against his own Countrymen.' The result was certain to be detrimental to the East India Company's opium revenue. Napier had been blamed by Palmerston for having provoked the severity of the Chinese; Elliot, on the contrary, seemed determined to steer clear of such an accusation 'by doing their will in all things'. To any thoughtful observer, Matheson concluded, it must seem as if Elliot's whole career 'was expressly designed to lead on the Chinese to commit themselves and produce a collision.'[35]

Hence, the various private firms like Jardine's prepared to play hide-and-seek in neighbouring waters. As Matheson phrased it a little ironically, 'the abnoxious rebels' could avoid the ban by disappearing for a time, waiting to return when

[34] At the worst, they could all take refuge in Manilla, Matheson told William Jardine in a letter of 24 August. Private Letter Books (B9), J. Matheson, vol. 4, 1839 (J.M.A.). Two months later, he informed J. W. Henderson of Bombay that owing to the insistence of the authorities 'I go to sea in the *Good Success* as if bound for Manilla, but I shall tranship myself to another vessel outside'. He planned to 'hover on the coast', and with any luck reappear in two weeks or so. Hong Kong, 18 Oct. 1839, ibid.

[35] Matheson to William Jardine, 1 May 1839, ibid.; and Matheson to the Rt. Hon. Stewart Mackenzie, Governor of Ceylon, 26 Jan. 1839, Private Letter Books (B9), J. Matheson, vol. 3, 1836–9 (J.M.A.).

circumstances made life less uncomfortable; 'and none will be more ready to welcome them back than the Mandarins themselves, on account of the fertile source of emolument derived to them from conniving at the prohibited trade'.[36] Less inhibited in their sympathies were friends of the 'abnoxious rebels'. Shortly before his departure for England, William Jardine found himself fêted by the commercial community of Canton, and presented with a service of plate worth 1,000 guineas.[37]

Elliot was well aware that conciliation was no longer the prelude to negotiation; the Chinese Imperial Commissioner was not to be appeased by gestures of co-operation. But what Lin could scarcely have realized was the Superintendent's personal commitment. For Elliot, the enforcement of a ban on opium store-ships had become a matter of principle as well as one of policy. In his view, British officials on the spot could not cast a blind eye on a noxious traffic (very largely in British hands) which was being carried on against the orders of the Chinese government. Elliot's greatest mistake, which he was painfully slow to recognize, had been his assumption that the import of opium would soon be officially regulated by Peking, and the smuggler put out of business. This confidence had died hard. Indeed, some months before Lin arrived in Canton, the Imperial Court had dismissed the prospect with scorn. Not until his incarceration in Canton did the scales drop from the Superintendent's eyes.

When it finally dawned on him that Lin was staking his office and possibly his life on the outcome of the crusade, Elliot knew that the time for a show-down was close at hand. In the event, he himself made the first challenge. On learning that a boat from one of the Country schooners had been found missing on 11 September and, so it was assumed, was being held by the Chinese, he rashly declared a blockade of the river and port of Canton. As it happened, the boat turned up within three days, having been swept ahead of the convoy by strong

---

[36] Howqua, the head of the Hong merchants for nearly forty years until his death in September 1843, was deeply involved in the illicit trade, which doubtless accounted for the fact that he was a millionaire many times over. See Matheson to Rt. Hon. Stewart Mackenzie, 26 Jan. 1839, and successive letters concluding with the end of February, ibid.

[37] Matheson to Thos. Chas. Smith, 29 Jan. 1839, ibid.

tides. The blockade was annulled, probably a wise move in any circumstance, with only the 28-gun *Volage* available to enforce Her Britannic Majesty's authority.[38]

Meanwhile, the Superintendent had left his temporary refuge in Hong Kong for Macao, where he hoped, preferably with the help of the Portuguese, to try once more to resolve the deadlock and bring about a resumption of British trade in British ships. With the sword of China dangling by a thread above his settlement, the Governor of Macao had been, as previously noted, impelled to declare a policy of strict neutrality. He was in no position either to influence the Chinese by force, or by good works to conciliate the British. Nevertheless, Elliot continued to press him to reopen the doors to British merchant families and to permit the storage of legitimate British cargoes on payment of the usual duties. Such actions, the Superintendent pointed out, involved no breach of neutrality. Macao was not blockaded; it was, correctly, open to both states, China and Britain. But entirely apart from legality, such a wise and friendly act, Elliot reminded the Governor, would not be forgotten by the government of Great Britain.[39]

Commissioner Lin was also eager to see a resumption of direct trade in British bottoms, but on his own terms. In brief, these involved the signing of a bond by the masters of British merchantmen *en route* to Whampoa that their vessels carried no opium. Should opium subsequently be discovered on board, the penalty was death and confiscation of the cargo. To Elliot, sympathetic to Lin's aims but increasingly weary of his arrogant dictation, such demands were presumptuous and offensive. Acceptance of such terms, he wrote to the captain of the *Volage*, meant consent to barbarous Chinese penal legislation, 'involving capital punishment by Chinese forms of trial'. It was an arrangement he could neither sanction, nor 'fail to prevent by all lawful means in my power, till I am differently instructed from England'.[40]

. .

[38] Elliot to Palmerston, Hong Kong, 23 Sept. 1839, Adm. 1/5499; and James Matheson to John Abel Smith, M.P., Hong Kong, 24 Sept. 1839, Private Letter Books (B9), J. Matheson, vol. 4, 1839 (J.M.A.).

[39] To Dom A.A. da Silveira Pinto, Hong Kong, 12 Sept. 1839, Adm. 1/5496.

[40] Elliot to Captain Smith, Macao, 27 Oct. 1839, Adm. 1/5496.
At this time, and subsequently, Elliot was accused by the Chinese of favouring the

Not until September, nearly six months after the event, was the Company's Court of Directors in possession of the facts concerning the opium surrender, and in a position to ponder the Superintendent's dramatic and uncompromising letter of 3 April, which had been sent to them at Palmerston's recommendation. The Court was scarcely prepared for vengeance in the shape of 'a swift and heavy blow', unprefaced by any written ultimatum; nor could they legitimately consider the forcible occupation of various Chinese ports or islands.[41] Such a violent course of action, they considered, was entirely a Foreign Office concern. Admittedly, India was closely involved with 'the Chinese question': 'if the Chinese will not eat opium, the Indian revenue must materially suffer; but it is presumed that it is quite out of the question to suppose that the British Govt. would be justified in compelling the Chinese to eat opium'.[42]

British merchant organizations thought otherwise, and during the months of September and October they bombarded the Foreign Office with resolutions in favour of a firm stand against Chinese pretensions and injustices. The London East India and China merchant association wanted some positive statement on the opium traffic through Canton, unrelated to general trade considerations. Other agencies demanded settlement of claims for property losses; all asked for positive action, and almost all hopefully protested their trust in the British government to remedy obvious wrongs.[43] Energized

---

trade, if not promoting it under the protection of his country's flag. Lin certainly believed that he gave protection at times to guilty participants; but Lin failed to take into account how scanty was the force available to police wide waters with innumerable island and coastal hideouts. Moreover, lacking (as Elliot put it) 'some simple but efficacious civil jurisdiction at this remote Commercial Station', he had to steer, however clumsily, between Scylla and Charybdis. To Palmerston, Canton, 14 Feb. 1839 (No. 100) F.O. 17/30.

[41] p. 89.

[42] Memorandum on Mr. Strangeway's letters of 20 Sept. 1839 (signed T.N.W.). 21 Sept. 1839, L/P & S/9/1 (I.O.A.).

[43] A large assortment of petitions is contained in F.O. 17/31, 35 and 36. Note also, William Jardine's letter to Palmerston, 26 Oct. 1839, recommending the opening of additional ports ('as many as can be obtained') to foreign shipping. 'Should it be deemed necessary to possess ourselves of an Island or Harbour near Canton,' Jardine added, 'the island of Hong Kong might be taken. It commands a very safe and extensive anchorage, with an abundant supply of water, and would be easily defended. . . .' L/P & S/9/1 (I.O.A.).

(and outraged) by news of the Factories siege, and much resulting parliamentary rhetoric, the Foreign Office did (as a Lancashire manufacturer's association was informed in early October) have the matter of retribution 'under serious consideration'.[44] A draft of proposals for consideration by Elliot was completed on 18 October, the argument following fairly closely along the lines suggested by the Superintendent of Trade in his letter of 3 April, and generally sustained by the marshalled evidence of Mr. Secretary Barrow of the Admiralty, whose spirited, if not pungent, style doubtless helped to animate the mind and pen of his opposite number in the Foreign Office—John Backhouse.[45]

'We feel', Palmerston informed Elliot in a personal letter of the same date, 'that it is impossible for Gt. Britain not to resent the outrages which have been committed by the Chinese upon British subjects & upon the Queen's officer; and we are of opinion that it is absolutely necessary that our future relations with China should be placed upon a definite secure footing.' For this purpose, the government proposed sending a naval, '& probably a small Military Force', to arrive, he hoped, in the following March. By that time the trade for the year would be nearly over, and the monsoon winds would shortly blow fair to the northward. The first object of the expedition would be the establishment of a blockade of the Canton and Peking approaches, and such intermediary points as seemed expedient. Accompanying troops would also seize and occupy one of the islands of the Chusan archipelago, or the town of Amoy, 'or any other Insular Position which might serve as a Rendezvous and Basis of operations . . . and afterwards as a Secure Basis for our Commercial Establishments'. It was the government's aim, he emphasized, 'to retain permanent possession of some such Station'. During the course of the proceedings the Admiral would be asked to go to the mouth of the Peiho with a letter addressed to the government at Peking, informing them, 'Why we have adopted these Proceedings & what are our demands . . .'.

This outline of proposals was, the Foreign Secretary reiter-

<hr />

[44] See Backhouse's (F.O.) reply to memorials, 14 Oct. 1839 (draft), F.O. 17/35.
[45] Palmerston to Elliot, 18 Oct. 1839, (No. 15) draft, F.O. 17/29. See also Barrow to Backhouse, 17 Nov. 1839, F.O. 17/36.

ated, subject to modifications, and he hoped that the Superintendent, as well as the Governor-General of India and the Admiral at the China station, would ponder on the difficulties and make suggestions in regard to the wisdom and, if needs be, the practical execution of the plan. The merchants in England, he added, were crying out for vigorous measures, but only after the present trading season had ended. Meanwhile, as March [1840] approached, it might be well to advise all Britons to withdraw themselves and their property as quietly as possible from Canton.[46] This withdrawal had, of course, already taken place during the summer, and from Macao too, but the news had not yet reached London. The British government intended, in the Chinese manner, to strike suddenly, and give explanations afterwards. A sharp, brief lesson in European military power and efficiency would, it was to be hoped, tempt the Emperor to receive the British government's letter from the hands of Admiral Maitland, and to accept the stated fact that unless British demands were satisfied, hostilities would continue with increasing vigour.

Apart from the long-sought equality of diplomatic status, it is clear from the correspondence that Palmerston's objectives had not crystallized. A proper commercial treaty and the opening of additional Chinese ports to British trade had long been subjects of discussion, but on the question of whether or not an island or some such permanent base should be acquired, Palmerston was still wavering. As for the opium question—the Chinese demand that British ships should cease to bring the drug to the coast of China for delivery as contraband—this scarcely entered into any British official discussion of war aims and a post-war settlement. Yet Palmerston had no more love for the profitable but nefarious traffic than had Elliot, and he would have regarded as sinful any effort to force 'the detested drug' on the Chinese people in order to find the silver to pay for the Briton's daily tea.[47]

[46] Palmerston to Elliot, F.O., 18 Oct. 1839, Broadlands MSS., GC/EL/28/2. This draft provided the substance of dispatches sent to Elliot and to the Admiralty on 4 November. See Palmerston to Elliot, 4 Nov. 1839, F.O. 17/29; same to Admiralty, same date, F.O. 17/36.

[47] James Matheson apparently believed that the need for tea justified the sin. In February 1840, he wrote to his friend John Abel Smith, M.P.: 'It is worthy of consideration whether, as Tea is such a necessary of life in England, the British Govt.

But by the end of 1839, moral strictures and moral judge-ments on the opium trade, like official prohibitions, were to be no longer crucial to the main issue of whether or not Britain should go to war with China. The question of whether 'the detested drug' should continue to be a preserve of the smug-gler, or become, as both Elliot and Palmerston continued to hope, a government-controlled legal import, could be left until the war was won. Meanwhile, it was sufficient to concen-trate on bringing home to Peking some knowledge of the overwhelming power of the Royal Navy. A naval, or at least an amphibious, war it had to be; no large British armies would attempt to penetrate the Chinese mainland. The occupation of one or more islands would present little difficulty, but the suggestion that more than 1,500 miles of coastline could be successfully blockaded was out of the question. Such a task, according to the Admiralty, would require the services of the whole British fleet, and as for moving up the Peiho towards Peking, it was from all accounts too shallow for any but small craft which might with difficulty navigate as far as Tientsin but no further. Even with 'an imposing force' such as Palmer-ston had promised, Barrow, speaking for their Lordships of the Admiralty, was convinced that

it would be prudent, in the first instance, to confine the operations to Canton, to take possession of the island of Hong Kong which is outside the Bocca Tigris, has a good road-stead for the anchorage of a multitude of ships, and plenty of fresh water. Here a few guns mounted and men to work them, with a ship of war, would afford protection to the merchant shipping while the Naval Force was employed in blockading the mouth of the Canton River, in taking possession of Wampoa [sic], which commands the inner as well as the main branch of the river, and in opening an immediate com-munication with the Viceroy of Canton. . . .[48]

Meanwhile, as Palmerston pondered on the collective advice of the Superintendent, the Admiralty, and William

---

will not, even in the event of hostilities with China, prefer to connive [at] the export of Teas, as now thro' foreigners, rather than by establishing a blockade, cut off the supplies to the distress and discontent of our trobulent [turbulent] home popula-tion. . . . I incline to think that the British Government will not under any circums-tances, consent to be long without supplies of tea.' Macao, 29 Feb. 1840, Private Letter Books (B9), J. Matheson, vol. 5, 1840 (J.M.A.).

[48] Barrow to Backhouse (F.O.), 17 Nov. 1839, F.O. 17/36.

Jardine and his associates, Lin had been proclaiming death and disaster to the 'criminal barbarians' who refused to surrender a token offender to be tried for the murder of Lin Wei-hi. By mid-October, a considerable force had been assembled at the entrance to the Bocca Tigris, which, in Elliot's opinion, suggested 'some early attempt upon the merchant fleet' under pretence of looking for the assassin.[49] With the guns of the *Volage* and the *Hyacinth* in support, the Superintendent was certain that any Chinese assault could be repulsed, but it gave him no pleasure to realize that Lin was living in 'a fool's paradise'. The Commissioner's 'unwavering confidence', whether genuine or pretended, in the superiority of Chinese over Western arms was bound to lead to 'sudden and fatal disaster', involving the death and mutilation of hundreds, if not thousands, a bloody denouement which Elliot despairingly knew could now hardly be avoided.

On 27 October the *Volage* and the *Hyacinth* were moved to an anchorage some distance below Chuenpi, where they had been practically under the noses of the watchful Commissioner and his eager gunners. They were now a little closer to the British merchant fleet, lying at anchor near Hong Kong. These vessels carried not only large cargoes of goods and stores, but a goodly portion of the British community that had fled from Macao. Elliot was not worried by the prospect of an attack by Chinese war junks, but he did fear 'a stealthy and treacherous approach' in the night. Even in less confined waters, fire-ships represented a hazard difficult to counter, if sufficiently numerous and intelligently directed.[50]

The tension was aggravated by the recklessness of the captain of the merchantman *Thomas Coutts*, who, against Elliot's rigid instructions, signed the anti-opium bond, and sailed boldly to Whampoa. Almost certainly this breach in the Superintendent's embargo encouraged the self-assured Lin to increase the pressure by threat of outright war.[51] Hardly had the two British warships withdrawn from the neighbourhood

---

[49] Elliot to Captain Smith (*Volage*), Macao, 27 Oct. 1839, Adm. 1/5496.

[50] 27 Oct. 1839, ibid.

[51] See Captain Smith to Elliot, Macao, 28 Oct. 1839, Adm. 1/5496; see also Smith to Maitland, Chuenpi, 6 Nov. 1839, Adm. 1/5496 and Broadlands MSS. MM/CH/1–9. In December too a second ship, the *Royal Saxon*, sailed for Whampoa after executing the bond.

of Chuenpi, when Lin, over the head of the Superintendent, publicly invited all the British merchant ships, hovering idly near Hong Kong, to follow the *Thomas Coutts* into the River and make sail for Whampoa under bond. Otherwise, announced Lin, unless they left the China Sea within three days they would be destroyed.

On 28 October, accompanied by the *Hyacinth*, Elliot set sail in the *Volage* with his own ultimatum in hand. Strong northerly winds delayed arrival off Chuenpi until the morning of 2 November, at which time the two vessels anchored about a mile below the first battery, and nearly the same distance from a large fleet of war junks and fire-ships. Elliot's dispatch, addressed to the Viceroy, requested the withdrawal of Lin's ultimatum, and the right of British merchants and their families to live in Macao without further molestation. It was received with due civility by Admiral Kuan, who at the same time suggested that the two British ships of war move further away from the river entrance. This request was acted upon. Late the next morning, however, some 29 of the war junks weighed anchor and stood towards the British ships, who immediately prepared to meet them. Less than 500 yards away, the Chinese force dropped anchor. Thereupon, a dispatch boat from the *Volage* carried the peremptory message that the Chinese fleet should retire immediately above Chuenpi. When this demand was, as expected, turned down, both Elliot and Captain Smith realized that there was no alternative to an immediate engagement. Unless the junks were destroyed or scattered, detachments might well infiltrate during the night and attack merchant vessels at the Hong Kong anchorage. Consequently, shortly after noon Smith gave the signal to attack.[52]

Moving to windward of the well-ordered line of junks, the starboard guns of the *Volage* and *Hyacinth* swept the decks, one after another, and a similar execution from the port side guns followed the turn-about. One junk blew up, three were sunk, and two or three others appeared to be waterlogged, later

---

[52] Smith's account of the battle is contained in his dispatch to Admiral Maitland, 6 Nov. 1839, Adm. 1/5496, and in Broadlands MSS. above. See also, H. Hamilton Lindsay ['A Resident in China'], *Remarks on Occurrences in China . . .* (London, 1840), pp. 45–6.

beached.[53] The remainder retreated unharassed to their original anchorage off Chuenpi. At the end of the engagement, which lasted only an hour, the two British ships turned their heads towards Macao. The honour of the flag had been vindicated, and Elliot no doubt assumed that this modest chastisement would be sufficient to moderate Lin's bellicose ambitions. It seemed that the whole Chinese squadron could have been wiped out and the land batteries at Chuenpi effectively silenced. But in defending the British withdrawal, Elliot maintained that Captain Smith had acted correctly: '. . . to repel onwards movements was the limit to which he was justified in proceeding'. Indeed, he was convinced that the most obtuse observer could no longer deceive either himself or his masters: surely, the Canton authorities were bound to confess how hopelessly unprepared was China to cope with the armaments of the West. So easy and devastating a victory, Elliot concluded, was bound to 'impress the [Chinese] government wholesomely';[54] and in the future, he was to reiterate with increasing emphasis his determination to avoid shedding blood unless extreme provocation gave him no other alternative.

[53] According to Maitland's report to the Admiralty (Bombay, 31 Dec. 1839), five were sunk and one blown up. Adm. 1/5496.
[54] To Maitland, 8 Nov. 1839, Broadlands MSS., MM/CH/1–9.

V

EXCURSION TO THE PEIHO 1840

In 1839, the suppression of the opium trade was a substantial issue, but it represented no more than a fraction of Peking's imperial design. Even if Britain had been capable of expropriating all the opium ships and expelling the dealers, such a surrender would not have altered Chinese policy, which was primarily concerned with controlling, on Chinese terms, the lives as well as the 'baggage' of the hated foreigner. Peking was not interested in re-establishing a commerce on a 'liberal and satisfactory footing' with full reparation for injuries received. By the end of the year this stark fact had finally been absorbed by the authorities in Whitehall. Barring a miracle, it appeared that military operations were inevitable. Latest reports confirmed earlier advice from Canton and Macao that further negotiations for removal of grievances and for equality of treatment, whether in matters of commerce or normal diplomatic intercourse, had not the slightest chance of success unless backed by preponderant force.

At the same time, since trade not conquest was the end in view, it was important that hostilities should be limited to blockade and possibly the temporary seizure of a few coastal bases. Such demonstrations of naval power might, it was hoped, impress the Emperor and tempt him to open northerly ports for trade. What had to be avoided was a mainland war of attrition and the death or demoralization of thousands of innocent fisherfolk and peasants. British diplomats, believing that the majority of the coastal Chinese were thirsting for European trade, liked to assume that the common man was at heart a friendly fellow who might even be enlisted on the side of the 'big battalions'. In fact, an effectual blockade of the coast (and with the help of the entire Royal Navy it was scarcely possible), while undoubtedly embarrassing to Peking, would have certainly embittered, and conceivably impoverished, the very people whom the British government aimed to placate.

Since he had received advance information that an expedition would shortly be on its way to the Far East, Elliot continued to ponder the problem of finding a suitable base, preferably an island, where, once a settled peace had been secured, trade could be carried on officially and safely with Canton and, one day perhaps, with other ports. Although the merchants themselves opposed the permanent seizure of Macao on the grounds that the inner harbour was neither large enough nor sufficiently secure against the weather and Chinese land forces, Elliot had no wish to desert a position within easy reach of Canton.[1] As things stood, the Portuguese, for all their official neutrality, were friendly and sometimes bravely hospitable despite their dependence on the watchful mandarins. But a British entrepôt for 'the most flourishing trade on earth' had to be free of intimidation from the Chinese mainland. Macao was vulnerable, as events had recently demonstrated.

On 4 February 1840, on the orders of Captain Smith of the *Volage*, the *Hyacinth* entered the inner harbour of Macao to bolster Portuguese morale and, in the process, test the response of Canton. Chinese troops and war-boats scattered in hasty retreat. Unfortunately, the Portuguese became equally alarmed, especially when the Chinese began to trickle back in force, and, rather than embarrass the Macao government further, the *Hyacinth* withdrew on the following morning, with orders not to retaliate even should the Portuguese harbour fortress fire aimless, placatory shots in the interest of Chinese amity.[2]

The incident of the *Hyacinth*, illustrating the ease with which the Chinese could roll over the peninsula should they so decide, forced Elliot to reconsider the value of Macao. He wavered between its occupation as a short-term expedient and the choice of one of the Chusan Islands as a permanent base. Amoy he shrugged off as too dependent on its heavily populated hinterland. By 21 February he plumped for Chusan Island, 'for every reason', political, naval, and commercial. In a long and enthusiastic letter to Admiral Maitland (of whose

[1] Elliot to Palmerston, Macao, 19 Jan. 1840, F.O. 17/38.
[2] Elliot to Palmerston, Macao, 11 Feb. 1840, Adm. 1/5500. Captain Smith's conduct was subsequently approved by the Admiralty (although *not* commented on by Palmerston), Barrow to Elliot, 30 June 1840, Adm. 2/1597.

death at sea on 30 December 1839 he had not yet heard), he pointed out the importance of an 'insular situation' neither too far from nor too near the mainland: '. . . with our feet upon the threshold of their inner Chambers, they will be ready to compound with us'. There was, moreover, the additional attraction of possessing a naval station which was bound to become within ten years or so the pivotal point in a flourishing trade with Japan.

It is obvious that Elliot was not certain in his own mind what should be held, but he was in no doubt that before any bargain could be struck, Peking would have to learn the weight of British power. A blockade of that 'seething water-way', the Yangtse-kiang, by cutting off the capital's food supply should help to bring the Emperor to reason; but, first of all, Canton would have to be taught a lesson. A few well-placed shells were essential in order to expose 'the utter help-lessness of the Chinese against a naval argument'. The forts at the Bocca Tigris would have to be destroyed, and a flotilla pushed at least within gunshot of Canton. Such action could be undertaken without fear of retaliation, because, thanks to the anti-opium 'bond', no British merchants remained above the Bocca narrows. As a demonstration of military strength it would ensure the uninterrupted navigation of the Canton River for years to come, and, if needs be, the occupation of Macao.[3]

A year before Palmerston would have agreed with Elliot in favouring Chusan Island as a permanent acquisition, but by February 1840 he had changed his mind. Since trade security was the important thing, it might be wiser to abstain from territorial acquisitions and concentrate on winning commercial guarantees in certain ports. 'We want to obtain certain things from the Chinese, & we know that it is force & not persuasion by which we can obtain them.' The force was available. On the other hand, the best arrangement

would be no Islands, but Commercial Security in certain Towns, and by Towns, of course we mean the liberty of walking and riding a few miles out of the Town for Health and Recreation. . . . Such an

[3] Elliot to Palmerston, Macao, 16 Feb. 1840, Elliot to Maitland, 21 Feb. 1840, F.O. 17/38. See also, Elliot to Auckland, Macao, 24 Feb. 1840, Adm. 125/94 and 28 Feb. 1840, F.O. 17/43.

arrangement would make our people safer in some cases than if we had an island, because if we went to war with France or the United States our enemy might send a force to surprise our island, whereas they could not meddle with our people in a town on the mainland of China.[4]

This curious shift in his thinking, implying as it did an extra-ordinary belittling of the role of the leading sea power, need not be taken too seriously. Palmerston was obviously fearful, at least for the moment, of using force in a manner that might damage the prospects of achieving the longed-for commercial treaty.

The titular commander-in-chief of the projected expedit-ionary force to China was the Governor-General of India, George Eden, first Earl of Auckland. Auckland had been given his peerage as a reward for a successful Afghan cam-paign in 1839, which saw the reinstatement of the Shah Shuja as Amir. Two years later, he was to be recalled by Peel, following the annihilation of the British force at the hands of Dost Muhammed. Although be no means entirely responsible for the disaster at Kabul, Auckland had certainly misread the politics of the North-West Frontier, and had shown defective judgement to the point of downright stupidity.[5] On Chinese affairs, however, he was to show considerably more acumen and balance.

On the grounds that British relations with China had 'a more special bearing upon the interests of Her Majesty's Indian Provinces', the Governor-General was given charge of all military arrangements, in co-operation with the Admiral commanding the East Indies station. In preparation for this new and rather frightening responsibility, Auckland was sen-sible enough to brief himself thoroughly by reading not only the dispatches of Captain Charles Elliot, but the letters from visiting R.N. and merchantman captains. He also waded through a plethora of petitions and reports from Company and private merchants in Canton and Calcutta. Subsequently,

[4] Palmerston to Admiral George Elliot, 20 Feb. 1840, Broadlands MSS. GC/EL/37.

[5] His biographer found him only *in part* to blame for the tragedy, but guilty of 'half-measures and ill-timed economies'. L. J. Trotter, *The Earl of Auckland* (Oxford, 1893), p. 166. Auckland lived down the disgrace to become First Lord of the Admir-alty in 1846, an office which he had previously held in 1834. He became Governor-General of India in 1835.

he was happy to discover that the main substance of his recommendations on the conduct of the China expedition accorded fairly closely with Palmerston's instructions, which reached him precisely two months later.

If there was to be a war, and preferably a short, sharp one, Auckland wanted no better end to it than 'the establishment of a secure rendezvous for China and European Commerce under the protection of the British flag at a station apart from the mainland of China. . . .'. He felt that the Foreign Office was too much interested in 'the aquisition [sic] of pecuniary reparations as well as of Commercial facilities by the Capture of private property and by direct concession from the Court at Pekin. . . .'. Nor was he as optimistic as the government about the impression that a powerful British squadron would have on Peking, and the concessions that must inevitably be offered by a subdued and compliant Emperor.[6] The recent orders from England, he wrote to Commodore Bremer, the acting commander-in-chief of the East Indies station, were 'too confident'.[7] The government was anticipating greater results from the expedition than could reasonably be hoped: '. . . if greater enterprises are expected from us than the maintaining of a blockade, and the occupation of one or two islands,' he wrote to Maitland's successor, Admiral George Elliot, 'the first Campaign must be spent in forming a basis from thence they may be conducted. . . .'[8]

But he had in mind, not only the need for a base of operations, but one that could be used at the end of hostilities as a permanent trading rendezvous. Obviously Macao was worth

---

[6] To Admiral George Elliot, Calcutta, 30 Apr. 1840, Auckland Papers, China Book, Vol. 1, Add. MS. 37715. Auckland sent a copy of this letter to Hobhouse (President, Board of (Control) on 8 May 1840, Broughton Papers, Add. MS. 36474; he had also written privately to Hobhouse: 'You will see . . . that I do not anticipate our being easily able to bring the Emperor of China to accede to terms of humiliation, or make him directly repair the injuries which his officers have committed towards us. . . .' On the other hand, Auckland pays tribute to the Superintendent's quality as a teacher: 'Chas. Elliot seems to think that a strong effort on our part will lead to concession, and he should be a better authority than any with whom I have been able to communicate on the subject here. . . .' Auckland to Hobhouse, 19 Apr. 1840, Broughton Papers, Add. MS. 36474.

[7] 17 Apr. 1840, Auckland Papers, China Book, Vol. 1, Add. MS. 37715. For Bremer's part in the establishment of a settlement at Port Essington in north-east Australia, see Graham, *Great Britain in the Indian Ocean*, pp. 408–10, 428–30, 439.

[8] 20 May 1840, Auckland Papers, doc. cit.

considering. Sovereignty belonged to the Chinese, not the Portuguese, and in the event of war, it would be quite proper to sail in and take it. Yet, like everyone else who thought about the problem, he knew that the peninsula was vulnerable. The Chinese needed no ships to invade Macao; a close adjunct of the mainland, it lay under the thumb of Canton. All in all, Auckland inclined to throw his weight in favour of Chusan. The principal island in the Chusan archipelago, some 55 miles in circumference and nicely situated to command the estuary of the Yangtse (about 85 miles to the north), would be a manageable base. The population was estimated at nearly a million, and a fairly large garrison would be required, but given proper naval support, Chusan, he felt, could be held against the whole Chinese Empire.[9]

Meanwhile, on 20 February 1840, Palmerston had issued instructions for the organization of an expeditionary force should the Chinese, as was expected, refuse to negotiate. In essentials, they differed little in substance from the recommendations embodied in his dispatch of 4 November 1839.[10] A highly expensive punitive exercise was intended simply to bring an obtuse Peking government to the conference table. The Superintendent, Captain Charles Elliot, and the newly appointed commander-in-chief, Rear-Admiral George Elliot, the younger brother of the First Lord of the Admiralty, were endowed with full plenipotentiary power.[11] The Admiral in particular was given 'latitude of discretion', although, what-

[9] Auckland estimated the annual expenditure for troops, transports, and stores at approximately £500,000. See the elaborate Minute on the purposes and conduct of the expedition (printed for the Cabinet only), 7 Apr. 1840, sent by India Board to Foreign Office, 22 June 1840, F.O. 17/43.

Auckland's political adviser on far eastern affairs, H. W. Parker, was strongly opposed to any territorial acquisitions and, especially, to the occupation of Chusan. The cession of Chusan, if forced on the Imperial Government, would in his view be comparable to a compulsory British surrender of the Isle of Wight. Formosa was a far more sensible choice, chiefly because it was only half under Chinese control. See '2nd Memo on Chinese Affairs', 7 Apr. 1840, Ellenborough Papers (P.R.O.) 30/12/31/13. The contents of the first memorandum are summarized at the beginning of the second.

[10] To Admiralty, F.O. 17/36.

[11] Elliot had been commander-in-chief on the Cape station, 1837–40. He was the second son of Sir Gilbert Elliot, the first Earl of Minto; the second Earl was First Lord from 1835 to 1841. The importance of family networks in all branches of the establishment, whether naval, military, or political, can scarcely be exaggerated.

ever might be the modifications deemed necessary, he was warned to keep 'the spirit' of his instructions in mind.[12] As it happened, nearly a year later, both the Elliots were severely upbraided for failing to do just that.[13]

In the House of Commons, it was admitted that the government was organizing a naval and military expedition to obtain reparations from China for 'insults and injuries', securities for the future protection of persons and property of traders on the coast, and indemnification for the confiscated opium. No mention was made of the fact that the Chinese would be asked to pay the cost of any necessary military operations, nor that, despite Palmerston's denial of any wish to seize territory, the cession of a strategic trading and naval base was now being seriously considered. In the spring of 1840, Chusan was as familiar a name in Whitehall as Macao.

In fairness to Palmerston, while he had at one time talked of Chusan, he was still far from committed to the acquisition of any base on the China coast. The vital thing was trade security, and he was not yet convinced that another addition to the British Empire was a necessity. Prestige and custom demanded that the government support their Superintendent and the British merchants; at the same time, Captain Elliot, whose sensitivity had been sharpened by the humiliations and violence of the past four years, needed watching. In moments of crisis, temperamental explosions could be damaging to the British position, which had to be carefully guarded in terms of British politics and the *jus gentium*. Send the commander-in-chief a copy of 'The Law and Practice of Nations', Palmerston told the Admiralty. It was important tht Admiral Elliot should have knowledge of the 'extreme rights' of Great Britain, 'although as a matter of choice and discretion, Her Majesty's government may not think it advisable in the first instance to enforce them'.[14]

[12] F.O., 20 Feb. 1840, Broadland MSS. GC/EL/37.
[13] See Letter of 9 Jan. 1841, L/P & S/9/2 (I.O.A.).
[14] 29 July, 1840, Adm. 1/5500. As a matter of fact, if war broke out, it was intended that the junk trade should be largely ignored in the interest of good public relations. It would not be politic, as Palmerston had previously informed the Admiralty, 'to do anything, which should permanently indispose towards England, the people of China'. 20 Feb. 1840, Adm. 1/5499. Subsequently, the Foreign Office was to inform the Admiralty of Palmerston's satisfaction that Admiral Elliot had exercised (under

Originally, it had been hoped that both naval and military units would be ready to sail from Singapore, the base of assembly, at the end of April, by which time the Canton trading season would have ended and the south-west monsoon gathered strength. In fact, the expedition did not get under way until 30 May. The first objective was the Canton River, where every effort was to be made to establish an effective blockade. At the same time, Palmerston made it quite clear to the Admiralty that no military operations should be attempted beyond what might be necessary for the purpose of blockade. Having established such a closure, and having made it publicly known that the Canton River was barred to trade, the Admiral was instructed to proceed, northward

taking measures as he goes, to cut off communication between Amoy and Formosa: He should also blockade the Estuary opposite the Tchusan Islands leading up to Hang-Tchoo-Fow: He should also blockade the mouth of the Yang-Tse, and that of the Yellow River; and he should take military possession of such of the Tchusan Islands as may appear to him to be best adapted to become a Head Quarter Station for a prolonged occupation; and he should, as in the Canton River, seize and detain all Chinese Vessels he may meet with.

Thereafter, assuming all went well, he was expected to open communication with the Chinese government. If Peking should 'come to terms' and a satisfactory convention be concluded and ratified by the Emperor, the Admiral would then raise the blockades, releasing all detained vessels and cargoes belonging to private individuals. Those belonging to the Chinese government were to be kept in pledge until a part of the compensation (ultimately to be demanded) were paid. Occupied islands were to be held until all engagements had been executed. After that, there was to be a complete restoration of Chinese territory, except such part as might be voluntarily ceded to Great Britain under the settlement.

However, if negotiations failed to get started or were broken off, 'active hostilities' must begin immediately. Palmerston realized that an operation against Canton alone

---

the order-in-council of 3 April) 'a sound distinction in abstaining in the outset from detaining Chinese Vessels belonging to private Individuals, and in confining his detentions to Vessels belonging to the Government'. Leveson (F.O.) to Barrow, 17 Sept. 1840, Adm. 1/5501; also, Barrow to Admiral Elliot, 19 Dec. 1840, Adm. 2/1598.

would have no decisive effect on peace terms; it was too remote from Peking. To be effectual a blow would have to be struck nearer the capital, and he suggested sending a force up the Yellow River to the point where it joined the Grand Canal; in this manner inland communication between the northern and southern provinces could be cut. Or, after weighing the evidence, it might be preferable to send a force up the Yangtse as far as its intersection with the Grand Canal. There were two large towns on the river, which supported heavy traffic for most of the year. In addition, if he thought he had the means, the Admiral might like to take Amoy. In short, the commander-in-chief was given complete latitude to carry on operations as he saw fit, provided preliminary action was reasonably restrained. Drastic measures would only be employed if the Chinese government refused to accept British demands. Since the Chinese naval force was small and inefficient, it could be assumed that a British squadron of no more than two line-of-battleships, three or four frigates, and two or three steamers (provided the Company could make them available) would suffice. Arrangements would be made by the Government of India to send a suitable military force.[15]

During this time, the Indian government (working through an *ad hoc* presidential committee for marine affairs) was busily engaged in recruiting ships and men, not only from England, but from the Cape, South America, and New South Wales. As newly-appointed leader of the combined expeditionary force, Rear-Admiral Elliot, Maitland's successor, was ordered to leave his station at the Cape as soon as possible and proceed to Singapore. But neither Admiralty nor Governor-General knew when or where he might receive notice of his appointment—station commanders were in the habit of taking

[15] Palmerston to Lords Commissioners of Admiralty, 20 Feb. 1840, Adm. 1/5499, and F.O. 17/41. A draft memorandum to the Admiralty on measures to be taken against China is contained in the Broadland MSS., MM/CH/1–9. See also, Palmerston to the Elliots (Admiral and Captain), 20 Feb. 1840, in which the Foreign Secretary remarked that Britain had no wish to retain permanent occupation of any island, so long as a treaty guaranteed 'freedom and security of commerce' to British residents in China. On the other hand, such security for the future might be provided by the cession of an island, 'if the Chinese should prefer such an arrangement. . . .' L/P & S/9/1 (I.O.A.).

periodic cruises—and it seemed unlikely that he would reach
Singapore before the end of May, by which time the expedition should have been well on its way to the China Sea.[16] In the
circumstances, it was decided that should Admiral Elliot not
arrive before the 20th—at the very outside limit, the 25th of
May—his second in command, Commodore Sir John Gordon
Bremer, should take charge. Meanwhile, until Bremer took
over from Maitland (which he did, in March), the Senior
Officer in the Indian Ocean, Captain Drinkwater Bethune was
responsible, in consultation with the Governor-General, for
assembling and equipping the fleet, making plans for the
embarkation of the troops, and, of equal importance, setting
up fuelling depots in Chinese waters to supply at least four
steamers from the Indian Navy. It was estimated that 3,000
tons of coal would suffice for two months or more, and the
Supreme Government was insistent that the best English coal
should be substituted for the available but inferior Indian
product.[17]

Auckland had already made up his mind that one vessel,
preferably a small frigate, would be sufficient to watch the
Burmese coast. But within the next six months, he was to
become increasingly cautious about denuding Indian waters
in view of strained relations with both Persia and Burma:
'. . . when you have made your impression', he wrote a trifle
sardonically to Admiral Elliot, 'and find that Line of Battle
Ships are not adapted to the Chinese Coasts, you may send us
one of yours'.[18] Although he knew full well that he could
scarcely expect any such reinforcement before the end of the
year, or the beginning of the next, none the less, Auckland was
prepared to take the risk. Along with troops and artillery from
the three Presidencies, he sent Elliot four Company armed
steamers. By the end of 1842, this number had been increased
to seven. Transports were hired from private firms by the

[16] See Minute on China Affairs, by Lord Auckland, Calcutta, 7 Apr. 1840, Adm.
1/5496.
[17] See President in Council to Court of Directors, 18 Jan. 1840 (No. 6) and Auckland
to Court of Directors, 15 Feb. 1840 (No. 13), L/P & S/5/9; also, Admiralty to Senior
Officer on East Indies station, 15 Feb. 1840, Adm. 2/1597; and Sir John Hobhouse
(President of the Board of Control, 1835–41, raised to the peerage as Baron Broughton in 1851) to Palmerston, 14 Mar. 1840, F.O. 17/41.
[18] 17 July 1840, Auckland Papers, China Book, Vol. 1, Add. MS. 37715.

month, at what Bremer regarded as exhorbitant rates, Bengal alone providing 12,000 tons of shipping.

Meanwhile, warships were raked in from stations around the globe. New South Wales contributed the *Druid* (44), the first of the expedition to reach China waters; the *Blenheim* (74), the *Blonde* (44), the *Pylades* (20), and the *Nimrod* (20) were on their way from the Cape, and, failing a junction with the fleet at Singapore, would proceed independently to China. Trincomalee too played its last important role as a base until the coming of World War II. It became the rear supply depot for the operational areas in the China Sea. Trincomalee was a more convenient base than Madras, and to save time Madras stores destined for Singapore went first to Ceylon. In addition to provisions—four months' supply for warships and six months' supply for transports—ships' masters took on as much Ceylon arrack as they could safely stow among the sails, rope, canvas, and blocks, of which the Yard surrendered nearly its entire store.[19] In India, Auckland made arrangements for the dispatch of 10 lackhs of rupees divided into dollars, rupees, and sycee silver, a substantial portion of which was to be delivered personally to Captain Elliot, presumably aboard ship near the mouth of the Canton River.

Admiral Elliot was reported to have returned to the Cape on 22 March; but even with favouring winds it was unlikely that he would arrive by 25 May. In the circumstances, Bremer had no choice but to take over the command. He knew that July, August, and September were typhoon months. To hold off departure until June (assuming the Admiral was able to reach Singapore early in that month) could be dangerous, especially for the transports. A hurricane, or even a severe gale, might literally wreck the projected operation.[20]

[19] The Supreme Government had been requested to supply 16,000 gallons of rum or arrack for use in H.M. ships on the China coast. See Bremer's Journal, 26 Feb. and 5 Mar. 1840, Adm. 50/262; also, Bremer to R. M. O'Ferrall (Admiralty) 9 and 13 Apr, 22 and 24 May 1840, Adm. 1/5496.

[20] To R. M. O'Ferrall (Admiralty) 26 May 1840 (No. 35), ibid. Obviously, Bremer had the support of the Governor-General. Two weeks earlier, after consulting with Bremer, Auckland warned Hobhouse that winds and seasons were 'not to be carelessly dealt with in these latitudes, and the delay of a few weeks might lead to little less than the delay for a whole year'. Calcutta, 11/12 May 1840, Broughton Papers, Add. MS. 36474. It is also worth noting that stores from Trincomalee, ordered in April 1841, were eventually shipped in late June. The transports ran into a hurricane off the

After three confused weeks of hurried preparation, the expedition finally got under way on 30 May. It consisted of the *Wellesley*, *Conway* (28), *Alligator* (28), *Cruiser* (18), *Larne*, *Algerine*, the *Rattlesnake* troop-ship, and two Company steamers, the *Atalanta* and *Madagascar*. The warships were accompanied by 26 transports and store-ships, bringing the 18th (Royal Irish), 26th (Cameronians), and 49th (later Royal Berkshires) regiments of foot, a battalion of Bengal Volunteers, two companies of artillery with 9-pounder field pieces and 12-pounder howitzers, and two companies of sappers and miners from Madras. Colonel, subsequently Brigadier, Burrell of the 18th was in command of the troops; Colonel Oglander of the 26th was second in command.[21]

The bulk of the fleet arrived off the Ladrones on 21 June, by which time the vanguard of Bremer's little armada had reached Macao Roads. They were all together by the 28th, including the commander-in-chief's flagship *Melville* (74) and the frigate *Blonde*.[22] In the meantime, Captain Elliot had been sticking to his policy of 'cold war', refraining from any form of 'aggressive hostilities' unless 'mischievous dispositions' should force him into action. In March, he had been joined by the *Druid*,[23] and, with the *Volage* and the *Hyacinth*, Elliot now felt he could take on, if needs be, the batteries at the Bocca Tigris, destroy them, and then move on to Whampoa.[24]

Hence his surprise when Commodore Bremer, instead of preparing for the anticipated attack on Canton, publicly announced, in pursuance of orders, that a blockade of the river and port would be established as from 28 June. Instead of a quick hard blow, there was to be a bloodless gesture, and subsequent events revealed how hollow such gestures could

China coast, and were severely damaged. Bremer to Admiralty, 28 July 1841, Adm. 50/262.

[21] Oglander died at sea on the way to Chusan.

[22] Admiral Elliot had left Simon's Bay (Cape station) on 30 April, proceeding by way of Singapore. Senior Officer Cape station to O'Ferrall (Admiralty), 12 May 1840, Adm. 1/5495. He sailed for Singapore on 18 June, making unusually good time on the journey to Macao. Auckland to Court of Directors, 10 Aug. 1840, L/P & S/5/9 (I.O.A.).

[23] The *Druid*'s captain, Lord John Churchill, fourth son of the Duke of Marlborough, died of dysentery on 2 June and was buried in Macao where his tombstone is still to be seen with those of other officers of the R.N.

[24] To Palmerston, 6 June 1840 (No. 14), F.O. 17/40.

be. Blocking the passage through the narrows of the Bocca Tigris was easy, but Chinese 'fast boats' could still smuggle teas and silks to Macao and elsewhere along back-door routes that led circuitously, by way of the Broadway or Hong-Shan river, through to the inner harbour, west of the Macao Peninsula. As the dramatic story of the *Nemesis* was to show, this route was barely navigable for vessels drawing five feet of water. The Chinese 'fast boats' drew less than four.

But worse was to come. The main fleet, which was waiting outside the Ladrones, was apparently never expected to invade the river should the embargo fail to bring the Canton authorities to the negotiating table. On 23 June, the order was given to make ready to proceed northwards to Chusan. Bremer was obviously acting under Whitehall instructions, but the Superintendent of Trade was shocked by the sudden unheralded reversal of his own recommendation, and the ships' companies, pining for action after weeks of boredom, soon showed themselves as scarcely less depressed. As the signal flags were hoisted, in the words of a young lieutenant, 'a gloom fell upon all; and those who had been rejoicing in the expectation of the laurels to be gathered on the battlements of the Bogue, now walked the decks listlessly, unwilling and unable to conceal their disappointment'.[25]

Despite Palmerston's instructions of 20 February to avoid military operations in the Canton River area, beyond what was necessary for securing the blockade, Captain Elliot had continued to assume that any sensible naval commander, or his superiors in Whitehall, would recognize the strategic importance of first seizing the Canton River. Not until the Chinese learned that the Bogue was not impregnable, would Britain obtain any secure and reasonable trading terms. 'Whilst they believe that Canton is unapproachable, there will be no steady Trade for us anywhere else.'[26] Sooner or later, he wrote to Palmerston shortly after the fleet had departed for the

[25] Lord Robert Jocelyn, *Six Months with the Chinese Expedition* . . . (London, 1841), p. 42. Jocelyn, who was military secretary to the mission, records that: 'All were on the tiptoe of expectation, as it was anticipated that the taking of the Bogue forts would be the prelude to active hostilities. To this, however, the opinions from England were averse.' Ibid.

[26] To Auckland, 9 Apr. 1840, L/P & S/9/10 (I.O.A.); to Palmerston, 10 June 1840 (No. 20), F.O. 17/40.

north, 'I am greatly afraid that a blow at the Bocca Tigris will be indispensable.'[27]

Such certainly was the view of British merchants, captains, and supercargoes in or about Macao, who found it difficult to believe that an expedition, sent to relieve an intolerable situation, should suddenly sail away. To them, it was incomprehensible that a city where British Factories had been raided, British flags torn down, and British merchants and officials mistreated or imprisoned should not have been the first objective of His Majesty's forces. After all, the declared aim of the expedition was to obtain redress and indemnity for past injuries.

Bremer had given the order five days before the commander-in-chief arrived at Macao, to avoid, as he had explained in Singapore more than once the dangers of the typhoon season. But even had Admiral Elliot arrived before the transports had set out for Chusan, it was hardly likely that he, in view of the adverse opinion of the British Cabinet (as summarized by Palmerston in his February dispatch), any more than Bremer, would have asked the advice of the Superintendent of Trade and postponed the northward tour until Canton had been chastised. 'At present,' the Admiral wrote to Palmerston,

my anxious wish is to get on to deliver your letter at the mouth of the Pei Ho—that we may be able to judge what the disposition of the Peking Govt. is.—You will see that there was a strong disposition here to take the forts at the Bocca Tigris in the first instance, but I do not quite come into that plan, not only because it is against your Instructions, but it would be rather a violent act as a precursor to asking for reparation from the Emperor, and thirdly, because when it is done it ought to be by a force which is fully equal to do it effectually, and in a way to let them see our Power—Captain Smith tells me they have he supposes above one hundred guns mounted there.[28]

On 24 June the warships weighed anchor, the *Conway* (28, Captain Bethune) in the lead. The assembly point, in the event of separation, was Buffaloes Nose, a rocky islet of the Chusan archipelago. Fortunately, the weather was serene and the wind

[27] 30 June 1840 (No. 24), F.O. 17/40.
[28] Admiral Elliot to Palmerston, *Melville*, Macao Roads, 29 June 1840, Broadlands MSS. GC/EL/34/2.

steady; the fleet kept well together, anchoring on 2 July to the leeward of their rendezvous.[29] By this time, Admiral Elliot had arrived at Macao, bearing commissions for himself and the Superintendent as first and second plenipotentiaries respectively. On 1 July they set sail for Chusan. Captain Elliot, so it was reported, remained dispirited and full of foreboding. Five days later, they had reached Tinghae.[30] There, the forces were reminded by circular that the object of the projected blockade was to obtain satisfaction, not from the people, but from the government, and both soldiers and sailors were exhorted to do all in their power to cultivate the goodwill of the local populations with whom they made contact.

The Foreign Office still believed that various discontents with ruling authority would eventually make the common man of China amenable to friendly approaches. In Kwangtung province, even in Canton and around the adjacent coast, according to rumour, vast numbers were irked by the restrictions and consequent trade stagnation which Commissioner Lin's actions had provoked. In the opinion of Arthur Waley (who read and translated Lin's diary), there was much more indignation against the government's opium policy than against the foreigner. In any event, making war on the Chinese people, as Palmerston had repeatedly urged in public and in official dispatch, was not the object of the expedition, provided the ends could be secured by other means.[31] Unfortu-

[29] Admiral Elliot to O'Ferrall, *Melville*, Lamma Passage, 30 June 1840, Adm. 1/5496. See also Lt. John Ouchterlony, *The Chinese War: An Account* . . . (London, 1844; Praeger reprint, 1970), pp. 41–3.

[30] Capital of the island of Chusan, and of the Chusan archipelago, which consisted of nearly 100 islands and islets.

[31] In Waley's view, it was not until British troops assaulted and looted the towns and villages north of Canton in 1841 that hatred of the 'barbarian' English began to grow; *The Opium War through Chinese Eyes*, p. 87. Palmerston seems to have been influenced too by the widespread notion that the southerly peoples of Fukien and Chekiang were essentially hostile to their Tartar rulers, could be cultivated, and conceivably won over as friends. In this opinion, which ran counter to growing evidence, he had the support of the Governor-General of India. Long before news of the dismal conclusion of the northern expedition reached him, Lord Auckland wrote to Charles Elliot with ponderous assurance: 'I earnestly hope that in regard to a conciliatory policy towards the people and to Commercial objects and Navigations this will have been the construction and decision of you and the Admiral. More particularly with regard to the Southern Coast of China. What you do further North is of much less importance.' 9 Sept. 1840. China Book, Vol. 1, Auckland Papers, Add. MS. 37715.

nately, 'other means', involving a stoppage of trade through the principal Chinese sea ports, was bound, if it worked with reasonable effectiveness, to cause a good deal of general distress, as Palmerston should have known, and insolvent or hungry people were more likely to blame the enemy rather than the Peking government for their predicament.

The first effort at close blockade was planned for the port of Amoy, at this time the most important entrepôt on the coast for overseas carriers. Some 300 miles from Hong Kong, the island of Amoy lies within a spacious bay which includes numerous islands, one of the largest to the eastward being Quemoy, and one of the smallest and strategically the most important, Koolangsu. Separated from Amoy by a narrow corridor, at the most 600 yards wide, Koolangsu commanded the port's main harbour, as well as the surrounding suburbs of the thriving town. Into this harbour, when the south-west monsoon blew, hundreds of junks from Japan, Singapore, Borneo, and the islands of the East Indies archipelago, brought their cargoes of spices, dyewoods, and ivory to exchange for tea, silk, and other indigenous products of the country. A more suitable point at which to apply a trial blockade seemed unlikely to be found on the entire coast.

However, as a courteous preliminary, Admiral Elliot, *en route* to Chusan, dispatched the *Blonde* (Captain Bourchier) with orders to deliver to 'the imperial-appointed admiral of the Chinese nation' Palmerston's letter of greeting, along with an explanation of the British presence. This communication, it was hoped, would be forwarded to Peking. Unhappily, it *was* a letter, not the customary humble petition demanded by Viceroy and Emperor. In consequence, the reception accorded to the visitors by the local mandarins was frigid and eventually hostile. As the unarmed messenger-boat bore him within a few yards of the shore, the interpreter. Robert Thom, pointed in vain at the white flag, prominently displayed above his head, alongside a notice of peaceful intentions printed in Chinese on a piece of calico. Despite such obvious entreaties, the assembled crowd of spectators and troops replied with threats and curses 'making signs of decapitation'. 'At this time', Thom later recorded, we were scarce two yards from the beach, and the boatmen called my attention to some soldiers wading in the water to seize the boat; upon this we pulled to eight or ten yards, when, standing up in the boat, I said in a loud voice, 'I now ask for the last time, will you receive it, or not?' 'No!' they all roared simultaneously, 'we fear you not'; and other expressions of defiance. Seeing all hopes of delivering it gone, I desired the men to pull back to the ship, the force of the oars pulling jerked the boat. I lost my balance and fell, and a lucky fall it proved; as, just at that very moment, a well-directed arrow flew over the spot I had quitted, and struck on the bottom of the boat with such force as to shiver its head to pieces: one moment sooner it had passed through my body. A bullet hit the stern a few inches from the coxwain's seat, several more passed over our heads; a couple of field-pieces were getting ready to fire a general discharge at us, when a circumstance took place which completely turned the tables in our favour, and most justly punished the offenders for their cold-blooded cruelty. Two thirty-two pound shot from the guns of the frigate, sent officers, soldiers, and spectators wildly scampering for their lives, leaving the lifeless bodies of some ten or a dozen behind.[32]

For a few minutes more, the *Blonde*'s guns raked the forts and walls until all sounds of resistance ceased. With no troops on board to parade before the town's frightened inhabitants, or such of them as had not fled into the surrounding hills, Captain Bourchier had to content himself with an impromptu and not altogether dignified ceremony. On the beach in front of the city walls, a bamboo pole was erected to which was tied a proclamation explaining the objects of the visit, along with a copy of Lord Palmerston's rejected letter. It was to be regretted, wrote the ruffled interpreter, 'that we had not had a steamer which by being lashed to the *Blonde* might have taken her up in front of the town, when, selecting the different public offices, we might have battered them down one by one or blown them up. This would have served still more strongly to show the people, that our quarrel was with the rulers *alone* and not with them.'[33]

Originally, the task of blockading Amoy had been assigned to the *Blenheim*. Unfortunately, Admiral Elliot's flagship,

---

[32] Quoted in F. E. Forbes (Lieutenant, R.N.), *Five Years in China; from 1842 to 1847* (London, 1848), pp. 213–16.

[33] *Chinese Repository*, ix. Aug. 1840, p. 227. For an account of the attack see ibid., pp. 222–7; also Ouchterlony, pp. 51–2.

Melville, had struck a reef as she was nearing Chusan, and since the *Blenheim* was the only vessel in harbour by which a 74 could be hove down, she was forced to surrender her role as a man-of-war, and remain for some weeks as a kind of floating dockyard. The squadron had lost two of their three most imposing ships, leaving the tasks of blockade to the *Alligator* (28) in company with two armed transports. But the *Alligator*'s brass 12-pounders, which lacked power and range, were hardly likely to dent the defences of Amoy. Within a week after the *Blonde*'s first unproductive visit, while trying to pass the batteries flanking the passage between Koolangsu and the harbour, she ran into a storm of shot to which she could make no effective reply. Such painful punishment clearly revealed the futility of hanging about a well-defended harbour entrance. Following a less hazardous reconnaissance, she returned to Chusan, where Commodore Bremer and his squadron had been lying at anchor off Buffaloes Nose.

Separated from the mainland by a narrow strait, the island of Chusan was the largest of the thickly scattered group of that name. Like many another traveller before him, Lord Elgin found it 'a most charming island'. 'How any people, in their senses,' he wrote in 1858, 'could have preferred Hong Kong to it, seems incredible.'[34] After the flat and ugly banks of the Yangtse, Colonel Garnet Wolseley was captivated by its 'undulating beauty. . . . The eye wanders from hill to plain, now resting on the dark green foliage of the cedars, then on the pink and white of peach blossoms. The old, dull grey of the steep rocks, partly in shadow, gave distance to the surrounding objects.'[35]

Tinghae, the picturesque capital, overlooked the principal harbour, a broad bay accessible from the sea by a narrow channel (or more correctly, in the view of seamen, a sluice), through which the compressed tidal waters, rising and falling between six and twelve feet, raced and twisted. However, the steamer *Madagascar* managed after a struggle to reach sheltered water, whence she was able to reconnoitre the defences. Her

---

[34] Theodore Walrond (ed.), *Letters and Journals of James Eighth Earl of Elgin* (London, 1872), p. 233.
[35] Lt.-Col. G. J. Wolseley, *Narrative of the War with China in 1860* (London, 1862), p. 31.

movements were leisurely and seemingly casual. Although a few fiercely adorned war junks lay at anchor, the steamer's boats pursued their investigations without opposition, wandering freely even close to the shore, sounding for suitable anchorages. The Chinese, so the *Madagascar*'s captain reported, seemed little prepared for an attack. Along the waterfront soldiers without apparent haste erected makeshift parapets, consisting, so it appeared from the deck, of cloth bags filled with grain.

On the early morning of 4 July the main squadron which had been lying quietly at anchor waiting for survey reports prepared to move. As the tide ebbed with the first dawn light, surprised ships' companies rubbed their eyes at the fantastic marine wilderness that had risen wraith-like overnight from the depths. For miles around, forests of fishermens' nets emerged in grotesque patterns above the surface. It was as though a vast spider's web had been woven on the sea by the guardians of Chusan in mysterious and silent protest against the foreign outrage that was about to be committed. Towed by the *Atalanta*, the battleship *Wellesley* made devious passage through the nets in the direction of the harbour, followed by the rest of the force. Only after long and torturous endeavours did most of the main armament, with the help of the steamers, conquer the convulsive channel currents and take up position abreast of the town. Retreating before these strange intruders were the war junks, ten or eleven in number (each of which carried about 50 men) with flaunting streamers and red-muzzled guns. These eventually formed up in front of the merchant junks. All of them had gorgeous painted poops, the most lavishly decorated being the Admiral's with its lines of coloured pennons ascending high above the heads of three tigers, which glared in lacquered ferocity from the stern.

In the evening, a deputation of high Chinese officials boarded the *Wellesley*, and were received by the Commodore in the great cabin. They confessed their inability to defend the capital, but maintained with stoic dignity that duty and honour made abject surrender out of the question. Bremer appreciated their delicate situation, and respected their soldierly decision, but in the faint hope of avoiding bloodshed, he promised that, perchance the gallant defenders found

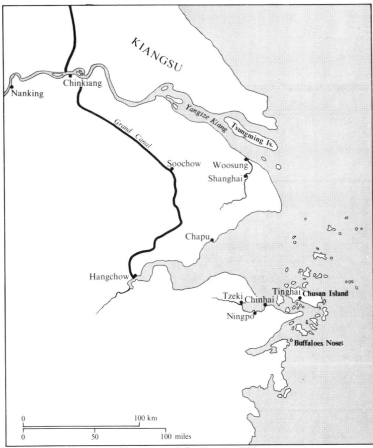

KIANGSU

Chinkiang

Nanking

Grand Canal

Yangtze Kiang

Tsungming Is.

Soochow   Woosung

Shanghai

Chapu

Hangchow

Tzeki Chinhai   Tinghai Chusan Island

Ningpo

Buffaloes Nose

0   100 km

0   50   100 miles

MAP 2   The Chusan Archipelago, and the Yangtse Kiang

reason to change their minds, no attack would be made until 2.00 p.m. on the following day. By that time, no answer having been received, a single shot was fired as a warning gesture in the direction of the shore-line. It was immediately returned by the Chinese Admiral's junk, and shortly thereafter the engagement became general. When the smoke finally cleared away, the junks had all but disappeared; the trifling shore defences had been breached and abandoned. Within minutes following the brief bombardment, the troops, already in the boats, had formed up on their assigned landing places. By 2.50 p.m. the British flag was hoisted on a hill above the harbour, 'the first Military Position in the Chinese Empire captured by Her Majesty's Forces'.[36] British casualties were negligible; probably 25 Chinese were killed or wounded. Comfortably bivouacked beyond and above the walls of the town, British troops prepared to wait for a new day before making formal entrance.

As darkness fell and the clamours of the day gradually dwindled into the pitch-black night, restless officers of the watch on the *Wellesley* witnessed their first dramatic Chinese spectacle. Far off, the black mass of surrounding hills and suburbs was suddenly broken by tiny flashes of yellow light that quickly extended into thin, wavering lines of fire as frightened inhabitants fled from their homes. Carried by hand, or on a short bamboo, the painted lanterns bobbed and twinkled in eccentric dance along the curving mountain tracks. Across the bay, merchant junks were faintly visible, stealing phantom-like along the shore-line, decks crowded with women and children and laden half-way to the mast-head with merchandise. A few daring British captains steered unmolested through the middle of this merchant fleet. By daylight, when the vanguard of the invaders entered the town, they found it almost deserted, apart from handfuls of anxious shopkeepers and their families, who had shut themselves in their abodes or taken refuge in joss-houses, where they were to be seen on their knees burning incense to their gods.[37]

The two Elliots, the Admiral and the Superintendent, arrived the following day, 6 July. On the 9th, after arranging for the administration of the island, Captain Elliot accompanied a small force to Chinhai at the mouth of the Ningpo river to deliver still another copy of Lord Palmerston's letter; this was intended, like the Amoy communication, for the perusal of the Emperor and his ministers at Peking. Perhaps the affair at Amoy had been reported. In any event, for the first time in the history of Anglo-Chinese official exchanges, the conversations carried no hint of unequal status; no mention of petitions. The 'barbarians' had become 'Honorable Officers of the English nation'. The letter was received by a mandarin, and presumably transcribed before it was finally returned with an intimation that 'the style and subject of the communication

---

[36] Bremer to O'Ferrall, 6 July 1840, Adm. 1/5496; Ouchterlony, pp. 43–6.
[37] See Jocelyn, *Six Months . . .*, pp. 53–9.

were not such as they could venture to expose to the glance of the imperial eye. . . .'[38]

In consequence, on 15 July a blockade of the coast was established from Chinhai northward to the mouth of the Yangtse, the most frequented and commercially important section of the entire Chinese seaboard. A closure of this focal trading area was likely, in the Admiral's view, to make a deeper impression on the Emperor's mind than guns or diplomats.[39] The Yangtse was the main artery of the Chinese Empire. Originating in north-east Tibet, and fed by innumerable and far-flung tributaries, it wound its way over some 3,200 miles into the broad waters of the Yellow Sea. Linked to the northern provinces by the Grand Canal, it provided a sheltered passageway for thousands of junks that annually ascended the combined river and canal system to within forty miles of Peking.

On 28 July the squadron, consisting of the *Wellesley*, to which Admiral Elliot had transferred his flag, *Pylades*, *Blonde*, *Volage*, and *Modeste*, the steamer *Madagascar*, and ten transports, set sail in hopes of reaching the mouth of the Peiho, before the strength of the southerly monsoon had subsided. Commodore Bremer was left in command of the remaining ships, including the stricken *Melville* which, as has been noticed, was being heaved down for repairs and refit.[40]

---

[38] Ouchterlony, p. 51.

[39] Admiral Elliot to O'Ferrall, 17 July 1840, Adm. 1/5496; also note Ouchterlony, p. 51.

[40] The total British force in Chinese waters in July and August 1840 was as follows:

Melville (74), bearing the flag of Rear-Admiral the hon. George Elliot, C.B.; Capt. the hon. R. S. Dundas.

Wellesley (74), bearing the broad pennant of Commodore Sir J. J. Gordon Bremer, C.B.; Capt. Thomas Maitland.

Blenheim (74), Sir H. S. Fleming Senhouse, K.C.B.

Druid (44), Capt. H. Smith.

Blonde (44), Capt. F. Bourchier.

Conway (28), Capt. C. D. Bethune.

Volage (28), Capt. Geo. Elliot.

Alligator (28), Capt. H. Kuper.

Larne (20), Capt. J. P. Blake.

Hyacinth (20), Capt. W. Warren.

Modeste (20), Capt. H. Eyres.

Pylades (20), Capt. T. V. Anson.

Nimrod (20), Capt. C. A. Barlow.

Cruiser (18), Capt. H. W. Gifford.

Columbine (18), Capt. T. J. Clarke.

Algerine (10), Capt. T. S. Musson.

Rattlesnake troop-ship, Brodie.

Hon. Company's Armed Steamers *Queen*, *Atalanta*, *Madagascar*, and *Enterprise*; and 27 transports.

Three regiments, the 18th (Royal Irish), the 26th (Cameronians), and the 49th Bengal

Between 5 and 6 August the squadron passed the Shantung promontory, sufficiently close to land to excite the appetites of hungry sailors who saw the hilltops astir with the gentle movements of grazing cattle. On the slopes below, flocks of sheep and goats cropped patches of rough pasture. Indeed, there was little change from the rugged, mountainous scenery to which they had become accustomed on the voyage from Chusan. But the shadow-line of the north was evident in stunted trees and the absence of the rich foliage, so characteristic of more southerly latitudes. On the 10th the squadron anchored in the Gulf of Pecheli, eleven miles off the mouth of the Peiho (Pei River). A nearer approach would have involved risk; at low tide the anchorage provided only six fathoms. Even at that distance from land, the water was turbid and yellow, the consequence of steady outpourings of earthy silt from the Peiho. In the far distance, near the entrance, long stretches of mud banks were vaguely visible from the maintop of the flagship. A closer approach on the following day revealed a substantial bar of mud and sand crossing the mouth almost from bank to bank. Fortunately, the expedition had arrived at the time of spring tides, when the water on the bar ranged from two to fourteen feet. Consequently, the *Madagascar*, which drew 11 feet, was able to make a safe crossing into the river with about six inches to spare. She anchored off one of the low forts on the south bank guarding the approaches to the little town of Taku, some 35 miles from the provincial capital, Tientsin. From a high bank, four miles up-river, the pagoda pinnacles of Tientsin were faintly visible to the naked eye.

The British approach was cautious but determined. The Admiral's letter to the local authorities expressed the amicable sentiments of the sender, while requesting with courteous firmness the submission to the Emperor of the Foreign Secretary's letter, so rudely returned at Amoy and Chinhai.[41] For

---

volunteers; a corps of Bengal engineers, and a corps of Madras sappers and miners—say, about 4,000 fighting men comprised the land force. *Chinese Repository*, ix. August 1840, p. 221. The list of warships is also contained in *Nemesis*, p. 71.

[41] Admiral Elliot to 'Governor of Pechele', *Wellesley*, off Pei-ho, 11 Aug. 1840, encl. (with sixteen other letters) in Elliot to Palmerston, 20 Sept. 1840, L/P & S/9/10 (I.O.A.).

a moment of time the presence of a small but powerful squadron, scarcely a hundred miles from the capital of the Chinese Empire, seems to have had a galvanizing effect on the Imperial government. The twice-rejected Palmerston letter was received and the tone of official correspondence issuing from Peking became, of a sudden, polite, if not positively, ingratiating. It is possible that the occupation of Chusan helped to loosen the scales from Celestial eyes; in any event, it appeared that the Viceroy of the province of Chihli, Ch'i-shan (or Keshen, as spelt by most British officers), had taken up residence in Taku, where, on orders from the Emperor, he had been patiently awaiting the arrival of the expedition.

In his reply of 15 August to the request of the plenipotentiaries, Ch'i-shan agreed to receive the letter on behalf of the Emperor, but, as might have been expected, declined to discuss the problem of a settlement until given authority by the Court at Peking. He asked for ten days' grace from 18 August, which was granted. During this interval, the squadron separated, one detachment following the Pecheli coastline, the other moving directly northwards to the Manchu provinces. Shore leaves were frequent, and ships' companies found refreshment and sport at various points along the shores. From the marshes of the interior, snipe and wild-fowl of various sorts rose by the thousand to their guns.

Lieutenant Lord Jocelyn found the country in physical appearance not unlike parts of the west coast of Scotland. The homes were much the same as in southern China, but a harsher land meant more laborious cultivation. The hills were terraced to the summit to circumvent devastating rains, capable of sweeping entire hillsides into the valleys below. The inhabitants appeared to live chiefly on vegetables, varied at times by puppies flesh. In many of the peasant domiciles, he found 'these little creatures fattening for their fate; for although they have plenty of bullocks, they employ them only for agricultural purposes; and all through China and along this coast, milk, the principal article of diet among European peasantry, is not used.'[42]

Without accident, the various units of the squadron reassembled at the mouth of the Peiho in time for the promised

[42] Jocelyn, *Six Months . . .*, pp. 104–5.

Imperial response to Palmerston's demands. On the afternoon of the 28th three mandarin junks pushed off from shore, and came alongside the flagship, bringing the hoped-for letter, along with gifts of beef and fruit. Ch'i-shan declared his willingness to talk to the second plenipotentiary, Captain Elliot, and arrangements were made for the reception of the Superintendent and his advisers at Taku on the 30th. Two miles from the town, the ships' delegation in six boats, privately armed in case of trouble, were met by two mandarins of high rank, who joined the British party and expressed their government's friendly intentions by passing around the snuff bottles. Ch'i-shan received them in his encampment, especially constructed for the occasion, with a courtesy which would have done credit 'to the most polished court in Europe'.

Although in his late fifties, Ch'i-shan gave the appearance of a vigorous man of forty. In toughness of character and intellectual quality he was probably the equal of Lin; indeed, he had thrown his weight against Lin in the course of the opium debate which had shaken Court circles since 1836.[43] His physical appearance was impressive, with a pig-tail as remarkable for its length as for its careful grooming. On that late August afternoon, he was dressed in a blue silk robe, with an embroidered girdle; his legs were encased in white satin boots; his head was covered by a mandarin summer cap made of fine straw, to which was attached the deep-red coral button indicating rank, and the equally impressive peacock's feather which drooped languidly between his shoulders.[44]

Following a breakfast of bird's nest soup, sea-slugs, sharks' fins, hard-boiled eggs, and dressed fish (aspects of Chinese hospitality which nineteenth-century travellers loved to dwell on), the conference got down to business. At the end of six hours' talk, it was clear that further communication with Peking was necessary. Little doubt was left in the minds of the British delegates that the Emperor was determined to stop the opium traffic, but of injuries suffered by British merchants in the course of government action, he appeared to have been left in complete ignorance.[45] In consequence, rather than mark

[43] Waley, p. 21.
[44] Jocelyn, *Six Months . . .*, p. 111.
[45] See Admiral Elliot to O'Ferrall, *Wellesley*, 12 and 22 Sept. 1840, Adm. 1/5506.

time in the offing, the squadron prepared once again to sail on a tour of discovery up the coast to the point where the Great Wall ran into the sea.

For officers and men, especially those who had been serving in the Indian Ocean, the change in temperature from semi-tropical to semi-Arctic was painful, the more so because of sharp winds that cut across the desolate coast. But the better clothed or the more romantic could afford to ignore the elements, and contemplate the grandeur of the Great Wall—the story-book wonder which climbed precipices and breasted the summits of craggy hills before descending, not abruptly into the sea as Lord Macartney had described it, but gradually to a low flat some miles from the foot of the mountain chain before entering a small town, which stood upon the water's edge.

On 12 September the squadron returned again to the mouth of the Peiho where Captain Elliot may have been comforted to learn that Ch'i-shan would shortly proceed to Canton as High Commissioner to investigate the conduct of Lin and the claims for reparations made by the plenipotentiaries. Since Ch'i-shan seemed both visibly impressed by the power of the barbarian invaders and intent on pulling down Lin, further negotiation in Canton with so agreeable and influential a representative of the Emperor appeared to be not without promise. But even if trust in Chinese intentions proved to be without foundation, would it have been possible to bring Peking to terms on the spot by means of a close blockade?

Admiral Elliot and his captains must have pondered the problem at length. They were aware of Palmerston's objectives; they were equally aware of the difficulties and the risks. Sand and mud shut out all but the light-draught vessels from the Peiho, even in periods of high tide. Moreover, the weather was beginning to change. Winter was on the way and the Admiral was anxious, as he later confessed, to seek a less vulnerable harbour for his ships and a less frigid climate for his men.

In retrospect, the two British Plenipotentiaries did appear to have been unduly trusting and unnecessarily timid. This was certainly Palmerston's view of the proceedings. The Foreign Secretary had been mistaken in refusing to accept Charles Elliot's advice to begin the campaign by taking the Bogue forts. Canton, the source of the troubles, was not to be wooed with words. On the other hand, Palmerston correctly saw that Peking held the keys to a final settlement. Canton was a painful thorn in the flesh; yet it was little more than a satellite of Empire—an Empire which an alien authority in Peking still managed to control indirectly with phenomenal success. In his opinion, to get at the root of trouble a British force must block the main communications to Peking, destroy the fleets of carrier junks, starve the capital, and thereby 'strike terror to the very foot of the throne'.

He was bound to acknowledge that the Admiral had the right to decide a course of action in the light of conditions of the moment. None the less, when four months later he learned of the decision to break off discussions at Taku and return to Canton, a distressed and very angry Foreign Secretary roundly condemned the failure of his commanders to use the military and naval force with proper resolution. Admittedly, the entrance to the river was partially blocked by shoals; the north-east monsoon was about to break and winter was coming on. Nevertheless, had the leaders of the expedition acted promptly, they would not, he contended, have lacked for time. During August and September in periods of high tide, it would have been possible (as the Admiral's dispatches confessed) for steamers and sloops with draughts less than 12 feet to cross the bar. Such vessels could easily have knocked out the hastily prepared forts at Taku. In a matter of eight hours or so they could have penetrated to Tientsin, blocking off the Grand Canal at the point where it joined the Peiho, and thus, by cutting off supplies from Peking, might have brought the Emperor to his senses.[46] By agreeing to go back to the extremity of China, the Foreign Secretary told Admiral Elliot, 'and apparently in deference to the orders of the Emperor, and by allowing the Question of our Demands to be mixed up with and in any degree to depend upon the Result of a Chinese Enquiry, I fear you have much weakened your position, and rendered much Delay certain, and partial Failure possible'.[47]

It is possible that the Admiral's developing coronary illness

[46] Palmerston to Plenipotentiaries, 9 Jan. 1841, F.O. 17/45. See also, Palmerston to Admiralty, 3 Feb. 1841, Adm. 1/5509.
[47] 16 Jan. 1841, Broadlands MSS. GC/EL/38/1.

was responsible for gloomy forebodings and unseamanlike hesitations. For him, the China seas were no fit areas for ships so far removed from a dockyard. Apart from severe winters in the north which made blockade an impossible task for a relatively small force, the muddy and shallow waters near the coast were full of unseen dangers, 'violent tides, eddies and ripplings, being as frequent in clear ground as in foul'. At one time or another, half the squadron had been aground; the process was continual. Moreover, as he pointed out to Palmerston with justifiable bitterness, the accompanying troops had been badly trained. The military commander, old, infirm, and utterly inept, had spent two vital summer months either in bed or confined to his house on the ground that the climate did not agree with him.[48]

Obviously Elliot was not a well man, but even in good health he would have been out of his depth in dealing with the Chinese. 'I am', he once confessed to the Admiralty, 'from being a stranger to the Character and Habits of the Chinese, but ill calculated to form an opinion. . . .'[49] His fellow-plenipotentiary, Charles Elliot, was an unhappy man, blinkered, perhaps inevitably, by long and almost total absorption in the affairs of Canton. His own attitude to the Peiho expedition had been, at the best, half-hearted. Some hesitations were no doubt understandable, but through lack of initiative and aggressiveness much time had been wasted. After a month of dawdling, Ch'i-shan had offered an easy way out. Less than two years later, history was to confirm that Palmerston, some 6,000 miles away, was, in his general conjectures, nearer the mark than the men who were on the spot. The Imperial Court would not—indeed, could not—yield to British demands unless compelled by *force majeure*.

Realizing that they lacked the strength to reject outright

[48] H.M.S. *Wellesley*, Chusan, 30 Sept. 1840, Broadlands MSS. GC/EL/35/1. See also, Elliot to Palmerston, Chusan, 21 Oct. 1840, doc. cit., GC/EL/36/2.

Palmerston was already aware of 'the utter Incapacity of the Military Commander', and he could only pray that Lord Auckland would soon get rid of him. 'Col. Burrell,' he informed the Admiral, 'is well known at Home as a very worthy and brave, but most dull and stupid man and totally unfit therefore to be placed in the situation in which he finds himself.' How could the authorities in India, he ruminated, have appointed such an idiot! 16 Jan. 1841, doc. cit., GC/EL/38/1.

[49] 15 Sept. 1840 (No. 26), including enclosures from Captain Charles Elliot, Adm. 1/5506.

British terms for a final settlement so long as British squadrons were in a position to ravage their coastline, the Emperor's representatives could do little more than talk and procrastinate, postponing the day of possible reckoning with promises and quaint confessions of sorrowful repentance. But once the ships had left the estuary of the Peiho, confidence returned in flood-tide; protestations of eternal friendship dwindled into murmurs that soon rose to choruses of vilification. Long before the mast-heads had vanished over the horizon, any prospect of an agreement 'lasting peace' had dissolved.

On 15 September the squadron weighed anchor, and set sail for Chusan. They arrived on the 28th to find a broken garrison barely recovering from an epidemic that swept the island. Out of the 4,000 troops who had come ashore in July, some 1,300 were invalids; nearly 150 were dead, and the number of victims continued to grow. To Lord Auckland, when the news reached India in December, the whole expedition appeared as little more than a futile and disastrous parade. The choice of Chusan as a permanent base should be postponed, he urged, until medical authorities reported on the various climatic factors affecting health and food supply.[50]

Like Charles Elliot, Auckland had always been more interested in an independent island base than in trying to squeeze indemnities from a reluctant government, and at one time (as has been noted) he had favoured Chusan.[51] But his doubts had multiplied as the months went by, not only on grounds of high mortality, but because of the island's proximity to the mainland and its exposure to Chinese influence. Moreover, to the Chinese, a British Chusan might represent a dagger pointed towards the Yangtse valley and the heart of China. This they would never be prepared to accept, even at the risk of years of war.[52]

Unfortunately for the Governor-General, he could never be certain, at any moment of cogitation, what stage operations or

---

[50] To Admiral Elliot, Fort William, 28 Dec. 1840, L/P & S/9/10 (I.O.A.).

[51] 'If we can but hold the place,' Elliot wrote to the Foreign Office in July, 'we will make a second Havanneh [*sic*] of it in three years.' To G. L. Conyngham (F.O.), Chusan, 20 July 1840, F.O. 17/40.

[52] See Auckland to Plenipotentiaries, 20 Nov. 1840, F.O. 17/49, and L/P & S/9/10 (I.O.A.); also, Auckland to Plenipotentiaries, 26 Oct. 1840, ibid.

negotiations had reached; and often for weeks at a time there was little he could do but restlessly pace the sidelines, waiting for specific information on events, which, as he informed Admiral Elliot a little bitterly, he had a right to possess, assuming Sir George had been properly instructed.[53] Meanwhile, he continued to fire advice at both plenipotentiaries, who were still in Chusan negotiating during the greater part of October with the Viceroy of the region, I-li-pu.

Most of the conversations were concerned with the release of a dozen or more British subjects captured or kidnapped during the previous three months. Although I-li-pu was anxious to exchange the captives for Tinghae, a *modus vivendi* was eventually reached on 6 November whereby Chusan and the islands immediately adjacent would continue under British protection until negotiations were resumed in Canton.[54]

Both Elliots were back in Macao by 20 November. Shortly after, the Admiral resigned for reasons of health, leaving Captain Elliot as sole plenipotentiary to conduct negotiations with Ch'i-shan, who had succeeded the disgraced Lin as Imperial Commissioner and chief negotiator at the end of September.[55] Momentarily, Elliot's confidence in the prospect of a final agreement took an upward turn. Ch'i-shan appeared to have the ear of the Imperial Court, and he had declared his ability to arrange a new and more equal system of trade relations. None the less, although the conversations continued in a relatively friendly fashion, they were marked by a growing Chinese reserve that was anything but encouraging. And as his optimism waned, increasingly Captain Elliot regretted that the Bogue narrows had not been forced in the previous July, a miscalculation that bothered him the more, as further details reached him of recent Chinese aggressive actions in the neighbourhood of Macao. For, no sooner had the expedition

---

[53] See Auckland to Admiral Elliot, Calcutta, 27 Nov. 1840, F.O. 17/49.

[54] See General Memorandum issued by Admiral Elliot, *Melville*, Chusan, 6 Nov. 1840, quoted in Bingham, *Narrative*, II, pp. 13–14. In the interim, arrangements were to be made for the release of the long-suffering prisoners.

[55] Lin Tse-hsu was dismissed on 28 September 1840 and ordered to return to Peking to await punishment. Following a brief exile, he was restored to favour, and subsequently held important administrative posts. He died in 1850, honoured as one of China's eminent statesmen. In 1929, a monument to his memory was erected at the Bogue, and 3 June designated as a National Opium Prohibition Day.

departed for Chusan near the end of June, than it was discovered that a battery mounting 17 guns was being erected near the barrier wall on the narrow neck of land which separated Macao from Chinese territory. Troops movements on the hills and the appearance of war junks within the Inner Harbour indicated that an assault was being planned. The crisis was precipitated on 6 August when the Reverend Mr. Staunton, while enjoying his early morning bathe in Casilha Bay, was seized by armed Chinese, bound, and taken to Canton. The senior naval officer in the south, Captain H. Smith of the *Druid*, was immediately notified; at the same time he was informed of the troop concentrations around the shores of the inner harbour and close to the barrier, and was given a copy of the Viceroy of Kwangtung's most recent proclamation offering substantial rewards for the seizure or assassination of British subjects. Despite the friendly disposition of the Portuguese, the British community appeared to be in peril.

Representations to Canton failed, and since all the signs pointed to a renewal of the harassments which in the preceding year had caused the expulsion of British personnel from Macao, Captain Smith prepared to act. Collecting all the marines that were available (a total of twelve), 80 seamen from the *Druid*, and 180 of the Bengal Volunteers, he loaded as many as possible on board the *Enterprise* and the remainder in long-boats to be towed astern. On the morning of 19 August the steamer with its streaming tail of assault troops pushed northward up the inner harbour in readiness for a landing on the flank. The *Druid*, in company with the *Hyacinth*, the *Larne*, and the *Louisa* cutter (6) stood across in the direction of the battery near the barrier gate. Following a bombardment of junks and shore installations—some 600 thirty-two pounder shot were fired—the troops swept up the Chinese positions at a cost of only four men wounded. Seventeen guns were spiked, and tents, magazines, and stores were destroyed.[56] It was unfortunate that Commissioner Lin, who had glorified Chinese successes at the 'battle of Kowloon', should have, in one of his last dispatches, informed his receptive, but unper-

---

[56] See Admiral Elliot to O'Ferrall, encl. report of Captain H. Smith on proceedings at Macao, 6 Oct. 1840 (No. 38), Adm. 1/5506; *Nemesis*, pp. 75–6; Ouchterlony, pp. 76–7.

ceptive, Emperor, that the British withdrawal represented a further victory.

Meanwhile, negotiations continued uneasily and increasingly spasmodically through December. But time was running out, and to the once trusting Superintendent the chances of any satisfactory conclusion seemed to crumble steadily as the days went by. Elliot was still impressed by Ch'i-shan's apparently genuine wish for a peaceful settlement, but he had become more and more doubtful of his authority and status as a representative of Court policy. Whatever might be the Imperial Commissioner's personal views—and he was reluctant to find him false—Elliot was no longer hopeful that Peking, however much shaken by the fall of Chusan, had been taught the folly of further resistance.

VI

THE *NEMESIS* AND THE CAMPAIGN OF 1841

In August 1840, the China squadron had been strengthened by the arrival at Macao of the *Calliope* (28) and the *Samarang* (28); both had made the long journey from the west coast of South America.[1] But far more significant in the history of naval operations in the China seas was the arrival in November of 'the incredible *Nemesis*', the first iron steamer to demonstrate the ruggedness of that type of ship by sailing half-way round the world, confronting in the course of the voyage the winter gales of the Cape, the capricious currents and hurricanes of the Indian Ocean as well as innumerable uncharted sand banks and reefs that were strewn along her way.[2]

Although quite heavily armed, and commanded by an officer of the Royal Navy, she began her career as a unit of the Bengal Marine.[3] Her captain, William H. Hall, bore the ambiguous title—'Master-Commanding', R.N.; and but for the extraordinary distinction he earned during nearly three years of operations, he would never have obtained a post captain's commission, as he did in 1844. Hall had joined the Royal Navy as a first-class volunteer in 1811, obtaining his master's warrant in 1822. After various assignments, includ-

[1] For sending these reinforcements to China without instructions, Rear Admiral Ross received an Admirality 'rocket'. Recent events in the Rio de la Plata, he was told, had made it impossible to send replacements from the Brazil station. Barrow to Ross at Callao, 5 Dec. 1840, Adm. 2/1598. The *Calliope* was ordered to return to Valparaiso in March 1841, but owing to the renewal of hostilities, Commodore Bremer felt unable to dispense with her 'valuable assistance', and Ross was bold enough to ask the Admiralty to send another vessel in her stead. To R. M. O'Ferrall, Valparaiso, 10 Aug. 1841, Adm. 1/5505.

[2] See *Nemesis*, pp. 4–14.

[3] During the first two years of active war in China, all armed steamers (i.e. *Queen*, *Enterprise*, *Madagascar*, *Atalanta*, and the *Nemesis*) were under the control of the Indian government, and their commanders as well as crews found themselves in a highly anomalous position, having no commission or rank, and the men not subject to martial law. The navy, in fact, had no love for foul-smoking steamers and dirtier men. The engineers and mechanics of steam were almost social outcasts.

ing a period of steam-boating on the Hudson and Delaware rivers, he was invalided out of the service, certified as unfit for further sea duties. Thereafter, a remarkable restoration must have occurred; even allowing for the low status of steamship commands, he would scarcely have been given the command of the *Nemesis* had there been serious doubts about his health. Indeed, the succeeding years of gruelling toil and bloody battles in vicious climates were to demonstrate that he was as tough and durable as the metal of his ship.[4]

Officially cleared for Odessa, the *Nemesis* left Portsmouth on 28 March 1840. For reasons difficult to fathom, her destination was kept secret. Some thought she was intended as a patrol vessel to fight the slavers; others suggested that she might be employed in the Liverpool slave trade, thus adding to its efficiency. By the 30th she had passed the Lizard, advancing nonchalantly into the swell of the Bay of Biscay under steam at seven or eight knots. On 6 April, only nine days out, Madeira came in sight. On the 11th she passed the Canaries entirely under canvas, moving under the north-east trades between Cape Verde and the coast of Africa, returning to steam only during periods of calm. For an almost flat-bottomed vessel, she sailed remarkably well, either under sail or engine-power, but tending to make slightly more leeway under canvas.

On 14 May she anchored at Princes's Island, not far from Fernando Po (forty-four days from England), where 70 tons of wood were taken on board. It was extremely good hardwood, but, since it had been recently cut, small quantities of coal had to be added. In this manner, half a ton of wood an hour fed to six fires was sufficient to keep up full steam pressure.[5] Being an uncoppered iron ship, the *Nemesis* was peculiarly susceptible to attack by barnacles, and at Princes's Island, as elsewhere along the route, a small army of native divers armed with broomsticks and iron bars was employed scraping from her bottom immense accretions of the tenacious cirripeds.

[4] Following service in the Baltic during the Crimean War, he rose progressively to full admiral's rank, and died, probably at the age of 80, in 1878 a K.C.B., and a Fellow of the Royal Society. Vice-Admiral Augustus Phillimore, *The Life of Admiral of the Fleet Sir William Parker, Bart. G.C.B.* . . . (3 vols., London, 1876–80), ii. 445, 447–8; see also, *D.N.B.*

[5] About 1,000 logs were estimated to make up twenty-two-and-a-half tons of firewood.

On 1 July, after a southerly voyage in the most unfavourable season of the year, to the astonishment of Cape Town's welcoming citizenry, she steamed quietly into Table Bay. Exposed in winter-time to the full fury of north-west gales, Table Bay was no place of refuge for the ordinary merchant ship or man-of-war; these normally took shelter in the secure but less convenient Simon's Bay on the opposite side of the Cape. But the *Nemesis*, drawing little over five feet, was able to anchor snugly in a small cove near the new stone jetty—almost the only inhabitant of the huge and wind-swept bay.

Bound for Singapore, although, for some mysterious reason, the publicized destination was now Port Essington on the north-east coast of Australia, she left Table Bay on 11 July, proceeding up the Mozambique Channel between the African coast and Madagascar. Six days later with Algoa Bay well in the rear, she ran into a gale that came close to destroying her. On the night of the 17th she was struck by a tremendous sea that broke the starboard paddle-wheel and fractured the iron hull amidships. The plates began to open on both sides, extending gradually and ominously downwards for more than three and a half feet. Although, by immense good fortune, the engines continued to work the pumps, the storm continued, producing a pitching cross-sea that threatened to split the ship in two. Within the next few days, the fracture spread to seven feet on each side, leaving only about two-thirds of the hull intact. Despite the frantic efforts of officers and men to patch the tear, the ship seemed doomed. Yet she survived. For reasons inexplicable in retrospect to the ships' company, the *Nemesis* continued to float in one piece.

On 27 July she steamed painfully into the English River which runs into Delagoa Bay. The repairs took time, but the work was expertly accomplished. Large timbers were riveted to the sides by foot-long bolts, new plates were fixed and so effective was the construction that the vessel was able to continue, apparently stronger than ever, for some two and a half years of strenuous and uninterrupted service.

On 17 August, just twenty days after reaching safety, she headed for the Comoro Islands, near the middle of the Channel, stopping briefly at Mozambique on the way. Johanna, one of the four Comoro islands, was left behind on 5 September, but owing to contrary winds and currents progress in the direction of Ceylon was slow until, some 200 miles to the northward, the benefits of the south-west monsoon began to be felt. But the elements were erratic, and despite the expected 'favourable season', strong head winds and much stronger southerly currents were encountered than could have been anticipated. Captain Hall would have been wiser to have followed Horsburgh's printed directions, and proceeded eastward of Madagascar.

On 1 October the Maldives were sighted where, thanks to the surveying skill and meticulous care of Captains Moresby and Powell, the *Nemesis* could thread her way through the islands, trusting to charts that were as easy to read as a modern road map. After a month of almost continuous steaming from Johanna, Point de Galle was reached on 5 October; by that time all the wood had been consumed, and only eight tons of coal remained in the bunkers.

In Ceylon, the mystery of the *Nemesis'* intentions was at long last unveiled. The dispatch delivered to Captain Hall from the Governor-General of India requested him to complete necessary repairs, take in coal and provisions, and then make sail for the mouth of the Canton River, there to join the main squadron. On 14 October Hall set a course for Penang (a journey of about ten days), where the ship was again debarnacled and painted; thence the short passage down the Straits of Malacca to Singapore, when more fuel was taken aboard. The north-east monsoon had already set in, and since head winds were likely to be met all the way to China, every spare foot of deck space was packed with coal bags, sufficient, it was hoped, to provide a full fifteen days of steaming. On the morning of the 17 November the *Nemesis* passed close to Manilla, and although short of fuel in consequence of the buffeting head winds, Captain Hall preferred not to extend an already protracted voyage. Somewhat reluctantly he passed by the inviting port, and steered for Macao. Not until seven days later was land sighted which, for some curious reason, Hall described as the Lieu-chew Islands, islands he had visited many years earlier in his youth.[6] In all probability, however, he was referring to the Tung Sha group (Tung Sha Chun Tao)

[6] The Liu-Chiu or Loochoo Islands form a long arc between Taiwan and Japan.

which in view of the strength of the monsoon must have been almost directly on his course.[7]

At daylight on the 25th the long and eventful odyssey came to an end. The *Nemesis* steamed through the Typa anchorage outside Macao, moving close in to the town, where only shallow-draught trading vessels had hitherto ventured. A booming salute to the Portuguese flag was sufficient to bring the population of the town pell-mell down to the Praya Grande to gaze at the first iron steamer they had seen anchor practically under the windows of the Governor's palace.[8] A few hours later, in Tong-ku Roads (Urmston Bay) to the west of Castle Peak, the *Nemesis* joined the squadron, recently returned from the ill-fated Peiho expedition and now commanded by Commodore Sir Gordon Bremer. There she was saluted by the flagship as a veteran man-of-war. After nearly eight months on the way, the dishevelled iron duckling found herself the honoured member of a company that included three line-of-battleships, *Wellesley*, *Melville*, and *Blenheim*—all 74's—as well as lesser breeds like the *Druid*, *Herald* (26), *Modeste*, and *Hyacinth*. Such exaltation invited anticlimax. Next day the *Nemesis* got down to the filthy and tedious process of coaling.

By this time, Charles Elliot's patience was wearing thin. When it was apparent that Chinese guarantees of fair trading and adequate compensation for opium losses were not forthcoming, the Superintendent had no other recourse than to go ahead with his original plan of river invasion. Ch'i-shan's reply to his last appeal of 29 December appeared to be 'conclusive of the intention of the Court to force us back to Canton upon the old System'. And he warned the Imperial Commissioner on 5 January that if no favourable response was made within forty-eight hours, Commodore Bremer would demolish the forts guarding the Bocca Tigris, and move his ships in the direction of Canton.[9]

[7] Less likely as a landfall (although sometimes suggested) were the Paracels, a small archipelago lying nearly 200 miles to the south-west.

[8] Captain Hall must have had some recollection of Macao Roads. He had served as a midshipman on board the *Lyra* during Lord Amherst's embassy to China in 1816.

[9] Elliot to Palmerston, 5 Jan. 1841, including copies of the correspondence between himself and Ch'i-shan during December, L/P & S/9/10 (I.O.A.).

No reply being forthcoming, on 8 January the squadron proceeded up the estuary. Guarding the entrance to the narrows, and nearly double that distance from Macao, lay the two well-defended islands—Tycocktow on the west and Chuenpi, a compressed lump of small hills, on the east. Most important as a bastion of defence was Anunghoy, separated from Chuenpi on the east side by the picturesque Anson's Bay.

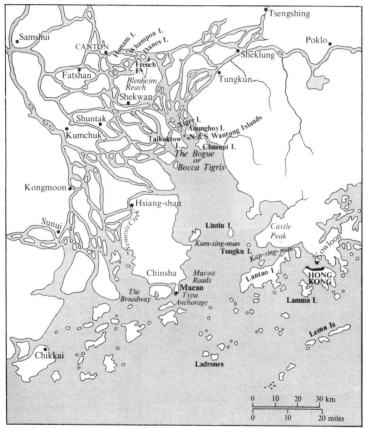

MAP 3   The Canton Delta and Hong Kong

Anunghoy, to the navy's complete surprise, was, in the course of operations, discovered to be an island.[10] The fortifications

[10] Had this been known in time, light-draught vessels might have gone up-river to the rear of Anunghoy.

had been strongly reinforced, with two heavy batteries on granite foundations protected in the rear by stout semicircular walls. Here, the river is barely two miles wide and divided in the middle by two rocky islands, North and South Wantung. The eastern channel (the Bocca Tigris, or Bogue), about three-quarters of a mile wide, and overlooked by Anunghoy, had been the only route used by foreign shipping. Not until hostilities were well underway was it discovered that the western passage was navigable. North Wantung, lying directly opposite Anunghoy, was strongly fortified; South Wantung, the smaller of the two and lower down the river, had been left undefended. Consequently, when occupied by British troops without opposition, it provided a perfect plat-form for the shelling of the northern island. As a further aid to barring the passage up the Bogue, a heavy double chain had been strung between Anunghoy and a high rock slightly north of South Wantung Island. To the Canton authorities, who had no notion of the devastating power of the shell gun, the Bogue defences were impregnable.[11]

Nearly two miles above North Wantung lies Tiger Island, at one time fortified on the east side but sensibly abandoned by the Chinese in view of the increasing width of the river. Ten miles further, the channel narrowed at what was called the Second Bar, a large sandy shoal extending from the right bank. About seven miles higher up on the opposite side of the river, the First Bar led to a further contraction, providing the most tenable defensive position in advance of Canton. Five miles or so on lies Whampoa, the largest of the several islands blocking the main course of the river. Narrow channels run on either side, but only light-draught vessels could navigate them

---

[11] Shortly after his arrival in Canton in March 1839, Commissioner Lin reported on the defences of the Bocca Tigris:

'Should any unauthorized foreign ships attempt to enter, even if the wind and the tide are in their favour, and the ships are sailing as if flying, they will find it impossible to go further than the chained timbers. Granted that the strong foreign boats can break the first line of iron chains, they will be stopped by the second line. Supposing all the chains and lines of timber can be broken it will take a long time for them to accomplish the task. Meanwhile guns from all the forts will fire on them, and the foreign ships may easily become ashes.' A translation from 'The Commissioner's Memorial's' in Gideon Chen, *Lin Tsê-hsü, Pioneer Promoter of the Adoption of Western Means of Maritime Defense in China* (Peiping, 1934; reprint, New York, 1961). See also, *Chinese Repository*, x. Jan. 1841, p. 37.

safely. Hence the majority of merchant vessels anchored towards the lower end of the island in Whampoa Reach, and, less frequently, round the opposite north-east corner, close to a long narrow strip called Junk Island. Smaller vessels occasionally sailed past Whampoa village on the south side into the narrow channel called Fiddler's Reach, while the heavier found safe anchorage in Blenheim Reach, southward of Danes' Island.

Shortly after 8.00 on the morning of 7 January 1841 the *Calliope*, *Hyacinth*, and *Larne* moved up river towards Chuenpi, supported (and occasionally towed) by the steamers *Queen* and *Nemesis*. The *Samarang*, *Druid*, *Modeste*, and *Columbine* steered for Tycocktow. The *Wellesley* and the other heavy ships moved into mid-channel and proceeded above the two forts preparatory to bombarding Anunghoy and North Wantung. At 11.30, by the time the latter came to anchor, the battle was over. The thick-walled forts and deep entrenchments had fallen within an hour and a half to superior gunnery and disciplined troops. Most of the Chinese fought with the desperate gallantry of the hopeless, if one may accept the repeated tributes of ships' captains and army officers; but they had had no experience of modern explosives. Within minutes, forts were breached and entrenchments, batteries, and magazines beaten into rubble. Of the British forces, not one was killed; thirty-eight were wounded, most of them slightly. There was one brief pause in the course of the morning engagement when, the Chinese Admiral Kuan lost his cap and, more important, his red button of status, which he begged might be returned to him. Following the return of both cap and button, action was resumed.

The most impressive display of energy and versatility was provided by the *Nemesis*. She carried troops, towed boats, and threw shells with devastating effect on the hill forts of Chuenpi; grape and cannister were reserved for batteries and entrenchments. Pushing into the shallow waters of Anson's Bay, her Congreve rockets destroyed eleven war junks; thence she moved up a twisting creek, grappling and towing away two more junks without giving or receiving a single shot.[12]

[12] See Bremer to O'Ferrall, *Wellesley*, 7 and 8 Jan. 1841, Adm. 1/5506; *Chinese Repository*, x, Jan. 1841. pp. 37–43; Captain Sir Edward Belcher, R.N., *Narrative of a*

Convinced of the folly of further resistance, Ch'i-shan resumed negotiations, and a preliminary settlement was concluded on 20 January. Under the agreement, the Convention of Chuenpi, an indemnity of $6m. [Spanish dollars] was to be paid, and the island of Hong Kong was to be ceded to Great Britain. Without instruction, Elliot had insisted on the surrender of what he regarded as an indispensable base. In return, he pledged that there should be no demands for further acquisitions in the future, and promised the evacuation of Chusan as soon as the Convention was ratified. As it happened, three days after the signing of the agreement, a 'fast brig' was on her way to Chusan with orders for immediate withdrawal, a task that was completed on 24 February. Hong Kong was formally occupied on 26 January, with a fanfare of salutes from harbour shipping.

There seems to be little doubt that a personal rapport with Ch'i-shan had made Elliot over-optimistic. Certainly he had shown himself vulnerable to the Commissioner's frankness and warmth. It may not have occurred to him that, in agreeing to the Chuenpi Convention, Ch'i-shan, whatever his private feelings, might have been acting under some duress from the Court and hence was playing for time—bridging the interval before the arrival of reinforcements from the provinces. On the other hand, for a man of his experience in dealing with Chinese officials, it is curious that Elliot should have almost naïvely ignored Peking's well-advertised aversion to any form of territorial concession. With Britain in possession of all the trumps, Peking was bound to submit to British demands in the long run; but the Superintendent overestimated Peking's grasp of realities. To Elliot, the cession of Hong Kong, even as a paper transaction, provided a sensible basis for a settlement that would bring lasting peace. It was an important achievement that could be made to stick.

In a letter to Palmerston, the day after the Convention had been accepted by Ch'i-shan, he tried to explain briefly why he had followed the 'spirit' rather than the 'letter' of his instructions. Rather than adopting a policy of 'fire and sword', leav-

Voyage Round the World, performed in Her Majesty's Ship Sulphur, during the years 1836–1842, including details of the Naval Operations in China, from Dec. 1840 to Nov. 1841 (2 vols., London, 1843), pp. 140–6; *Nemesis*, pp. 84–97.

ing a heritage of smouldering resentment, he had wished to avoid further 'destructive hostilities', secure in the knowledge that in possessing Hong Kong Britain could dominate the commerce of the entire Chinese coast. There was 'not a nobler Harbour, nor a more valuable position, in every point of view, in the Queen's Possessions'. In short, what had been achieved by the cession of Hong Kong outweighed the advantages to be gained by protracted hostilities for the sake of additional trade pickings.[13]

That his unsolicited *coup* would be acceptable in both Peking and Whitehall, Elliot seems to have taken for granted. On 23 January he wrote to Palmerston a second letter, advising him rather pontifically that 'the more the subject is considered the more will it appear that we have reached an honorable and most advantageous conclusion; advantageous in an incalculable degree. Hong Kong, my Lord, will very soon be one of the most important possessions of the British Crown. Of that result I am well convinced.' Even should the amiable Ch'ishan ('a man of remarkable capacity') be succeeded by perverse and stupid administrators, the trading community could now seek refuge under the British flag, and he hoped that some form of provisional government for the new colony might be set up as soon as possible. The Superintendent was properly reluctant to suggest himself as first governor, but diffidence did not prevent him from remarking that despite his own deficiencies, of which he was only too conscious, 'Your Lordship will not need to be told that my humblest abilities are always at the Command of The Queen's Government, without reference to my inclinations one way or another.'[14]

In order to avoid jealousy by foreign powers, Elliot suggested that Hong Kong be made a free port. Foreign representatives in London should be informed publicly or privately 'that in the event of a war with Great Britain, Hong Kong should be considered a neutral port *for commercial purposes*; and that all property deposited there should be respected, and all ships allowed free egress and ingress, with reasonable latitude respecting capture by British Cruizers'.

[13] Macao, 21 Jan. 1841 (No. 5), F.O. 17/47.
[14] Macao, 23 Jan. 1841, Broadlands MSS., GC/EL/27/1. The letter arrived at Whitehall on 9 April.

Perhaps Elliot did have some qualms in regard to his independent and precipitate action. He expressed gratitude for
unvarying help and kindness. 'I was unknown to you, and
much of my public conduct must have been hard to understand. But the feeling that I have always acted for the public
interest in trying circumstances according to the best of my
judgment, without thought of personal risk or responsibility,
has always been enough to secure to me Your Lordship's
public spirited and kindest support.' He concluded, 'I repeat
the offer of my respectful thanks, not only in your high station
as a Minister of the Crown, but far more deeply as between
man and man.'

On 27 January Elliot left Hong Kong and, accompanied by
his staff, proceeded up the Canton River in the *Nemesis*. Some
twelve miles below Whampoa, at the Second Bar, a pavilion
had been set up, and the substance of a permanent treaty
discussed with the Chinese with all gravity and without bitterness. Throughout the conference, the British guests were
treated with every mark of respect and warmth, and entertained at a banquet with (so it was assumed in retrospect)
'honeyed and wily' speeches, sufficient to put to flight any
suspicion of double-dealing. Further discussions were held on
13 February, by which time the river, under the terms of the
Convention, should have been open to trade. But in Canton
there was no resumption of business; at Whampoa there was
no loading and unloading of cargoes. No explanation of the
delay was forthcoming. Meanwhile, rumours continued to
circulate which suggested that what appeared to be a peace
settlement was merely another truce. There were reports of
troops pouring into Canton, of new fortifications along the
river banks, of new entrenchments, new magazines and additional guns, particularly on Anunghoy and Wantung.

It was obvious that the Chinese were preparing to renew
hostilities, even before news of the Emperor's 'extermination'
order of 27 January reached Macao. 'The rebellious dispositions of these foreigners being now plainly manifested', read
the edict—'there remains no other course than, without
remorse, to destroy and wash them clean away, and thus
display the majesty of the empire.'[15] By way of encourage-

[15] *Chinese Repository*, x. Feb. 1841, p. 113; see also, Wells Williams, op. cit., p. 519.

ment, rewards of $50,000 were offered for the heads of Elliot, Bremer, and John Robert Morrison (who had succeeded his deceased father as interpreter). When the last effort to secure ratification of the Chuenpi agreement failed, Captain Elliot reluctantly ordered the resumption of hostilities. By 26 February, the partly repaired Bogue forts had once again succumbed to shell fire, the indomitable Admirable Kwan dying at his post. At nightfall, the *Blenheim* fired a salute of minute-guns to honour a brave and respected enemy. Five of the attackers were slightly wounded; none were killed. Chinese losses were probably about 500 killed and wounded.

On the following day the small ships moved up river towards the Second Bar to confront fortified entrenchments bristling with cannon and protected by a strong raft of well-secured timbers across the river. The raft was easily shifted by the steamers; the recently purchased *Cambridge* (with an admiral's flag at the main) was blown up and the fortifications destroyed.[16]

The Canton River, along which the steamers were feeling their way, was but one of a network of twisting streams that meandered through the swampy rice-ground of the great Canton delta. In the distant past, so it appeared to the first European explorers, the main channel must, at various times, have overflowed its banks and flooded the surrounding country. Numerous new channels were thus created, and these in turn divided into distinct but smaller branches. In some instances, the minor courses, wandering off for short distances, returned again to the main stream, creating in their innumerable convolutions various picturesque islands and islets. It was a remarkable fact, in the opinion of the captain of the *Nemesis*, that over the years no foreign visitor had been curious enough to investigate the more obvious passages that

[16] The *Cambridge*, previously known as the *Chesapeake*, had been bought from the American firm, Russell and Company, at Canton. Fitted as a guard-ship in defence of the raft, she was more imposing as a festive show-boat than as a dangerous man-of-war. Two great eyes had been painted on her bows, long streamers hung from the masts, and various flags of all shapes and colours were strung around the taffrail. Cannon and ammunition were arranged about the two decks, but unfortunately for her new owners, she was moored head and stern in such a way that only her bow guns could be brought to bear in defence of the raft. *Nemesis*, pp. 125–9; see also W. C. Hunter, *The Fan Kwae at Canton*, pp. 147–9, which gives a highly colourful but exaggerated account of the loss of the ship.

led into the main channel. It needed a war to stimulate discovery and to reveal, as the Chinese Imperial Commissioner Ch'i-shan drily observed, that no ordinary blockade could prevent small vessels from reaching Canton circuitously without need to use the main river.[17]

For the steamer crews, the exploration of the labyrinth of rivers, canals, and creeks leading eventually in mystifying fashion to the capital was undoubtedly the most exciting part of the desultory and one-sided campaign. A glance at a detailed map is sufficient to indicate the amount of navigational 'trial and error' involved. Captain Eyres was not the only officer to lose his way amid the tangled branches of the Canton River. Returning to the *Modeste* in his galley, he found himself, with an ebbing tide, high and dry in the middle of a paddy-field, where he and his boat's crew spent the night, 'the more uncomfortable owing to a paucity of Hodgson's. . . .'[18]

Chinese pilots, like interpreters, were rarely available, and when, on occasion they were impressed, they were not always trustworthy. 'Going aground' became a daily occurrence for the larger ships; only the steamers escaped this routine fate—unless, of course, they happened to be nudging and scraping their way through shallow creeks. Unlike sailing vessels, the movements of the steamer could be almost precisely regulated. The paddle-wheeler could usually back off on touching bottom, and it was capable of changing direction in an instant. Consequently, it proved the perfect reconnaissance cruiser, always in the van pioneering new routes, towing boats, pulling frigates and 74s off mud banks, or, when opposition was encountered, raking forts and entrenchments, sometimes, like the iron *Nemesis*, sheltering under the very muzzles of fortress guns that could be depressed no further. No vessel was so suited to combined operations than the light-draught iron steamer, wrote Captain Elliot to the Governor-General of India. 'With three vessels of that class, I should feel that we were strong indeed . . .' If the *Nemesis* had

[17] *Nemesis*, p. 123. n.

[18] Bingham, p. 163. The captain craved an unusual medicine for a night out, although its tonic qualities were recommended in doggerel verse by Charles Stuart Calverley:

> O Beer! O Hodgson, Guinness, Allsopp, Bass.
> Names that should be on every infant's tongue.

been with the squadron at the mouth of the Peiho, he concluded, it was 'highly probable we should have concluded our
Treaty at Tientsin'.[19]

It may be proper at this point to say something about the
construction and armament of this unique vessel. Iron had
already proved its value in the construction of shallow-
draught sailing-ships, but its use for steamship hulls had not
been fully tested. Consequently, the *Nemesis*, built in 1839 at
the Birkenhead Iron Works, was very much an experimental
craft. In length, 184 feet, in breadth, 29, and in depth, 11, and
nearly 700 tons burden, she was capable of developing 120
horsepower. Without a fixed keel, she was almost flat-
bottomed, but to compensate for this disadvantage at sea, two
sliding keels had been fitted which could be lowered to a depth
of five feet below the bottom. Made of wood, $4\frac{1}{2}$ inches thick,
one before and one abaft the engine-room, they could be raised
by a chain attached to a small winch when the ship entered
shallow waters. When fully loaded with coal, stores, and
armament, her mean-draught was only six feet. In actual
service on Canton rivers, she drew little more than five feet,
and on one or two occasions during her explorations of
unknown channels she managed to slide along soft mud bottoms at four and a half. The problem of steering while at sea
was solved by the addition of a false or movable rudder,
attached to the true or fixed rudder, which, if need be, could be
lowered to the same depth as the two false keels, and, like the
keels, could be raised for shallow river work. Unlike the fixed
rudder which was made of wood, the movable was forged
from iron.

The gun-power of the *Nemesis* varied, depending on the task
in hand, whether, for example, she was to be used as a tug to
pull heavy ships into action, as a transport for assault landing
parties, or as an armed cruiser. Generally, the *Nemesis* carried
two 32-pounder guns, mounted on pivot or traversing carriages, one forward, the other aft. Some time after her arrival
in Chinese waters, five long brass 6-pounders were added, two

---

[19] Macao, 24 Mar. 1841, F.O. 17/48. Included in this volume, dated 20 May, is a plan
of the city of Canton and surrounding water-ways. The various obstacles encountered
en route are marked.

on each side, and one on the bridge. She also carried Congreve rockets which could be fired from a platform in the centre of the ship.

Perhaps the most novel feature of the vessel was the division of the hull into seven watertight compartments by means of iron bulkheads. Such an arrangement proved itself abundantly during the first three years of active service; indeed, the life of the *Nemesis* would have been a short one had such safety devices not been provided, for on her first trials she struck heavily on rocks near the entrance to St. Ives Bay, and similar accidents were to recur on the China coast. It is possible she might have escaped some of these misfortunes had her compasses been free of error. In England, correctors had been fitted to counteract the local attraction of the iron hull, but despite continued alterations 'according to the most approved principles', they were never to be trusted.[20]

But navigation by compass was not important in river work, when even experienced pilots felt their way by sight, smell, and instinct. Unhappily, pilots were hard to come by, and the vital task of finding safe channels in ever-changing river-beds had to be left to the more manoeuvrable shallow-draught craft. In other words, the conquest of the Canton River system was the result of a long series of explorations, which demonstrated beyond quibble how indispensable was the steamer in promoting tactical detours around and behind enemy fixed defences. In the most boldly executed operation of the whole campaign, the *Nemesis* forced her way up the uncharted Inner Passage from the Broadway, as the main entrance to the backwaters of the delta was called. Beginning her journey a few miles to the north-west of Macao, she followed a devious route which hitherto had been frequented only by native boats. Indeed, it could hardly be called a distinct river. The Inner Passage was simply a name for one of the larger of the many streams forming the fluid network of the

[20] The corrector devised by Sir George Airy, the Astronomer Royal, proved to be completely inadequate to compensate for compass variations. See in this connection, 'Evans and the Importance of Magnetism', Chapter 21, in Rear-Admiral G. S. Richie's *The Admiralty Chart, British Naval Hydrography in The Nineteenth Century* (London, 1967).

delta, 'dividing and then re-uniting, sometimes receiving large branches, sometimes throwing them off, here communicating with other rivers, and there traversing them'.[21]

Leaving Macao before sunrise on 13 March, with the boats of the *Atalanta* and *Samarang* in tow and a reluctant pilot in the bows, the *Nemesis* steamed northward, pressing aggressively through the sedge grass, or, in broader channels, puffing below the verandas of prosperous traders who quite sensibly took to their heels as the smoking devil-ship moved by. Surprisingly, the passage was defended at odd places, which suggests that the Chinese had pondered the prospect, however unlikely, of an advance around and to the rear of the Bogue forts. In any event, she had little or no difficulty in capturing or destroying every fortification, raft, junk, battery, or stockade that stood in the way of her triumphant progress. But it was never plain sailing; navigation was a far greater hazard than enemy fire. In some parts, so shallow was the course that there was scarcely an inch to spare, and on these occasions, the *Nemesis* practically slithered along the muddy river bed. Sometimes, the stream narrowed to little more than the vessel's length, making it necessary at sharp bends to force her bow into the bank and bushes on one side, in order to clear her heel of the dry ground on the opposite bank. Late on 15 March the *Nemesis* broke through into the main river, close to the Second Bar, and shortly after took her place in the van of the squadron, along with her consort, the *Madagascar*.[22]

Meanwhile a light, reconnoitring detachment was within five or six miles of Canton, and had this surprise approach been followed up immediately the city must have been at the mercy of the navy's guns. But Elliot, although he had recently learned that his co-negotiator Ch'i-shan had been degraded and sent to Peking in chains, was still anxious to spare an obstinate foe a futile struggle, involving next to no casualties on the British side, and a heavy death toll among the Chinese.[23] Once again he accepted the Canton government's

[21] *Nemesis*, p. 138.

[22] See *Nemesis*, pp. 139–48; Ouchterlony, pp. 122–5; Belcher, pp. 159–67.

[23] See Elliot to Palmerston, Canton, 21 Mar. 1841 F.O. 17/47. During the final engagements not one British serviceman had been killed, and only one had died of wounds.

proposal for a truce, although he might have realized that this form of procrastination was simply a cover for deception. At any rate, after an interlude of three days, the general advance was continued, and one by one the defence works that dotted the banks of river and tributaries were silenced and sometimes demolished.

On 18 March the last fortified bastion near the Factories, the Dutch Folly, surrendered. Two days later hostilities were . again suspended, and this time the disillusioned Canton authorities meant business. Hastening to the scene of action in the *Hyacinth*'s gig, Commodore Bremer was just in time to see the British colours hoisted above the Company's Factory.[24] 'Thus, for the first time in the history of China,' Bremer informed the Admiralty, 'have ships been brought under the Walls of Canton, and by Channels and branches on which a foreign ship never before floated.'[25] Obviously, concluded the Commodore, the Chinese were not acquainted with 'the capabilities of their splendid river'.[26] The second city in the Celestial Empire had been revealed as vulnerable to assault from the sea; but to the dismay of the Service chiefs, it was left unharmed and unrepentant. Under the terms of the armistice of 20 March, trade was to be reopened, but the gates of Canton remained closed to the foreigner. Only one distasteful concession was forced on the reluctant defenders. As a guarantee of good behaviour, British warships were to stay on guard below

---

[24] *Nemesis*, p. 157. Elliot's 'stop–go' tactics were not to the liking of Major-General Gough, who had arrived early in March from Madras to take command of the land forces. Gough had no firsthand knowledge of China, but he had won distinction during the Peninsular War, and the Governor-General, Lord Auckland, believed him to be politically astute as well as soldierly. He was made a Field-Marshal in 1862.

[25] The vessels engaged in the expedition to Canton were: *Modeste* (18), Com. Harry Eyres; *Algerine* (10), Lieut. Mason; *Starling* (surveying schooner), Lieut. Kellett; *Herald* (26), Capt. Joseph Nias; *Hebe* (schooner), and *Louisa* (cutter), Tenders Mr. R. R. Quin and Mr. T. Carmichael respectively; and steamers: *Nemesis*, master-commanding, W. H. Hall, R.N. and *Madagascar*, master-commanding, J. Dicey.

A large flotilla of boats, about 40 in number, was placed under the command of Captain T. Bourchier, assisted by Captain C. R. Drinkwater Bethune. *Nemesis*, p. 152. For a list of ships and vessels on the coast of China, 1 Jan. 1841, see *Chinese Repository*, x. 1841, p. 57.

[26] Bremer to O'Ferrall, off British Factory, Canton, 19 Mar. 1841 (No. 21), Adm. 1/5506. His letter, No. 19, of 15 March describes the attack on the approaches to Canton. See also, *Nemesis*, pp. 112–59, and James Matheson to Wm. Jardine, 27 Feb. 1841, and 19 Mar. 1841, Private Letter Books (B9), vol. 6, pp. 85–6, 107–9 (J.M.A.).

the city to ensure, for the time being, the safety and comfort of the Factory personnel.

Whatever Palmerston and the Cabinet were to feel about Elliot's repeated and clearly premature truce agreements, the Admiralty, when they got the news of the successful advance up-river, were more than satisfied with the performance of the steamers. 'The zeal and perseverance exhibited by them in forcing their way through intricate River navigation, the greatest part of which was little known, and some of which had never been navigated by an European Vessel, rendered still more difficult by artificial obstructions, deserve the highest commendation. . . .'[27] All the captains were valiant, but William H. Hall had hitched his steam wagon to a star. The *Nemesis* added glamour to an otherwise dismal colonial war.

Meanwhile, on 1 April Commodore Bremer, taking advantage of what he believed would be no more than a lull, sailed for Calcutta hoping to seek reinforcements of troops, and especially of steamers for river operations. During his absence, the Senior Naval Officer, Sir Humphrey Le Fleming Senhouse, who had just reached the age of sixty, took over the command. Bremer counted on an armistice of about six weeks, by which time the north-east monsoon should have blown itself out. If 'the folly of the Court of China' were then to lead to a resumption of hostilities, he hoped (with the concurrence of the Governor-General) to continue his command in the China Sea and, with any luck, supervise the siege and occupation of Canton.[28]

Shortly after Bremer's departure, Elliot returned to Canton. Although outwardly professing no fears for life and property in the Factories, he was quickly aware that some sort of renewed military action was pending. The tense faces of Chinese entrepreneurs and servants, the growing timidity of local shopkeepers who were beginning to withdraw their merchandise from open shelves, the whirl of rumours that pene-

[27] Barrow to Admiral Parker, 11 June 1841, Adm. 2/1598. The Governor-General of India was so impressed that he ordered two more iron steamers, *Phlegethon* and *Proserpine*, to join the force at Canton. Auckland to the Chairman of Directors, 12 May 1841 (No. 40), L/P & S/5/10 (I.O.A.).

[28] Bremer to O'Ferrall, *Wellesley Galley* at sea, 16 Apr. 1841 (No. 24), Adm. 1/5506. See also, Senhouse to Bremer, *Blenheim*, Macao Passage, 28 May 1841, ibid.

trated bolted doors in Canton and jarred the ears of supercargoes from Whampoa to Macao, all gave warning of the storm, which merchants like Jardine and naval officers like Bremer had predicted.[29] On one occasion, Elliot had an unpleasant encounter with the 'exterminating General' Chi'i-shan, recently arrived with more troops from the north. This mighty soldier, Elliot sensed, bore the imprint of Peking's philosophy of 'war to the death'.

None the less, British merchant vessels continued to move up-river, and until mid-May trade went on without interruption. Whatever the weaknesses of Elliot's policy in the light of larger strategy—'ill-timed mercies' as S. Wells Williams called them—such interludes allowed the tea to flow out of the warehouses into the ships anchored at Whampoa. By sparing Canton, 20,000 tons of shipping left the river, carrying some 30m. pounds of tea.[30]

In view of the impending crisis, preparations for a second expedition to the north and the occupation of Amoy and Chusan were temporarily suspended. On 10 May Elliot, who could never be said to lack courage or audacity, made a personal visit to Canton in company with his wife, and interviewed the embarrassed provincial governor, whose evasive answers confirmed the Superintendent's worst fears. On the 12th he returned to Hong Kong and there arranged that all the men-of-war and transports, with troops on board, should make ready to sail up the Canton River.

Once more he returned to Canton where it was clear that the situation had worsened. The only armed vessel at hand was the *Nemesis* which moved close up to the Factories on the 20th, cleared for action, with steam up and guns loaded, ready to slip

[29] Judging by his letters to Bombay written from his base in Macao, James Matheson had communication through the grape-vine telegraph which occasionally carried advance information on Chinese actions and British official responses. For some time, he had opposed punitive action as likely to fail through lack of sufficient force, and anyway as dangerous to the trade connection. But delays in negotiation were to convince him that Elliot might well be taken in by placatory gestures. 'You know how slippery and plastic the Chinese are,' he wrote to William Jardine in London. On the other hand, Matheson was in a position to give warning. 'I have favourable opportunities for impressing my views on E[Elliot]', he added, and, since his audience appeared receptive, he hoped he had 'done some good'. 4 Jan. 1841, Private Letter Books (B9), vol. 6, p. 37 (J.M.A.). Further letters from Macao referring to military and commercial operations are contained in the same volume (Nov. 1840-May 1841).

[30] Elliot to Auckland, Macao, 21 June 1841, L/P & S/9/10 (I.O.A.).

her cable at a moment's notice. Tartar troops,[31] it was discovered, were pouring into the city in great numbers; new batteries had been erected above and below the town while anxious citizens, like confused ants, rushed hither and thither with goods and chattels which they obviously hoped to hide or remove before the onslaught. Meanwhile, the force from Hong Kong had passed the Bogue and moved steadily towards Whampoa. The Chinese were well aware of the fleet's progress, and it could be assumed that they would act before relief arrived.

Yet Captain Elliot held his hand almost to the last moment. Not until the morning of the 21st did he recommend (it was really an order) that all foreigners should leave the Canton Factories before sunset. The margin of safety was perilously narrow. Most of the merchants were already in Whampoa. The remainder, with the exception of two Americans, got away in boats. The Superintendent and a small party of marines remained just long enough to see, before sunset, the final lowering of the flag. By this time, the *Pylades* and the *Modeste* together with the *Algerine* had moved up, close to the town. The *Nemesis* kept position a short distance above the Factories.

The sun set gloomily, and Captain Hall smelt danger lurking in the black reaches beyond the furthest anchorage. The tight alertness of seamen and marines reflected the ominous silence that had descended on shore and river. About 11.00 a sentry on the *Modeste* thought he saw dark-looking masses moving down stream. In reply to a hail, a sudden burst of flame split the darkness; an over-anxious Chinese officer had set fire to the first of a hundred or more combustible rafts.[32] This error in timing upset a highly-organized effort to destroy or damage the British detachment. Perhaps a dozen blazing rafts were towed away by ships' boats before they reached

[31] It is unlikely that British observers knew whether or not these troops came from Tartary. A good many may have been regular Chinese militia. Reinforcements from the north were usually (and uncritically) labelled, 'Tartars'.

[32] These rafts were composed of boats, filled with all kinds of combustible materials, chained together in two's and three's. When allowed to drift down stream, it could be assumed that a good many would catch on the bows of intervening ships, swinging the fiery contents alongside. For Hall's narrative of the action and its aftermath, see *Nemesis*, pp. 162–73.

their target near the Factories. Further down river, off How-qua's Fort, the *Alligator* faced a similar attack. Fortunately, she had time to raise anchors and escape without hurt. A few rafts burned themselves up in mid-river or drifted ashore, setting fire to suburban structures on the bank. The majority were deserted, unignited, by their confused and frightened crews.

But Chinese plans were not limited to fire-rafts. On the following morning a fleet of war junks and armed fishing boats, a few of which contained combustible stuffs, was dis-covered hidden in the bend of a large creek above the city. These were soon destroyed, in company with the newly-erected batteries at Shameen. During the next two days, the navy sank 71 war junks, and smashed or disabled every battery along the waterfront. On the 23rd the *Nemesis* moved upstream to investigate possible landing spots, dropping anchor close to shore and to the rear of the land defences. By this time, the combined military and naval force under General Gough and Captain Le Fleming Senhouse was concentrated below Whampoa, preparatory to an advance on the city. The stage was set for the final assault, scheduled for the following day.

As it happened, there was a dramatic, if not slightly comic, interlude. Gough was anxious to begin operations 'on so auspicious an epoch as the anniversary of Your Majesty's birth'.[33] Consequently, a boat from the *Hyacinth* was sent on a visiting shore mission at 6.00 a.m., distributing notices to the effect that Her Majesty's birthday would shortly be celebrated by gun-fire *without shot*, and there was, therefore, no need for public panic. Following this sympathetic warning, precisely at noon a royal salute was fired by the whole fleet, 'for the first time in the inner waters of 'the Central Flowery Land' ''. Captain Elliot noted that it was two years to a day since he had left the Factory, behind whose bolted doors he and his mer-chant companions had been incarcerated. An hour or so later, the *Nemesis* began the delicate task of towing some seventy or eighty ships' boats, jammed to the gunwales with men, arms, and accoutrements, in the direction of the upper shore which curved below the hills round the north and north-east sides of

[33] See Lord Ellenborough to the Queen, 7 Oct. 1841, Lord Charles Colchester (ed.), *History of the Indian Administration of Lord Ellenborough* (London, 1874), pp. 12–13.

the city. Here, at a little place called Tsingpoo, reconnaissance boats directed by Captain Belcher of the *Sulphur* had discovered the perfect landing spot for the troops, whose objective was the heights above.[34] From that eminence, they could oversee the fortifications around and below.

The city and suburbs of Canton lie on a plain, bounded on two sides by the river, and not far from the foot of a mountain called the White Cloud. Immediately to the rear are three or four hills of no great height, but sufficiently elevated to command the city. On these hills forts had been built, and around them were encamped large bodies of Imperial troops. The city proper was surrounded by a high wall, 25 feet thick at the base and about seven miles in circumference, with twelve entrance gates. The top of the wall, protected on its outer side by a parapet, formed an unbroken highway of communication around the entire metropolis. The south face of the wall ran east and west, parallel with the Canton River. The eastern and western sides extended at right angles from the neighbourhood of the river; the northern face formed a rough crescent below the brow of the hills. The Old City, separated from the more modern conglomeration by a dividing wall, was traversed by one main avenue running east and west between two imposing gates, the Chung-hsi and the Chung-tung. From this thoroughfare there branched small streets, rarely more than 20 feet wide, the intervening spaces being crisscrossed by innumerable narrow lanes. Within the Old City was the government arsenal and the residences of the Viceroy, the Governor, the Tartar general, and various other high officials.

Not until the morning of 25 May was the total assault force, a mixture of Indian and British troops with detachments of artillery, put ashore. Against sporadic resistance, they marched eastward across the paddy-fields and climbed the slopes of the adjacent hill, scattering the undisciplined ranks of

---

[34] Edward Belcher, who gained his post-captaincy in 1841, had joined the navy in 1812 at the age of thirteen. Despite a quarrelsome, if not turbulent, nature which made him an almost impossible colleague, he proved to be a superb surveyor, and, with Hall in the *Nemesis*, led the victorious squadron to and past the Bogue forts, and subsequently upstream to Whampoa. As captain of the *Sulphur*, he took part in the operations leading to the capitulation of Canton; but he is probably best known for his bracing *Narrative of a Voyage Round the World*. . . .

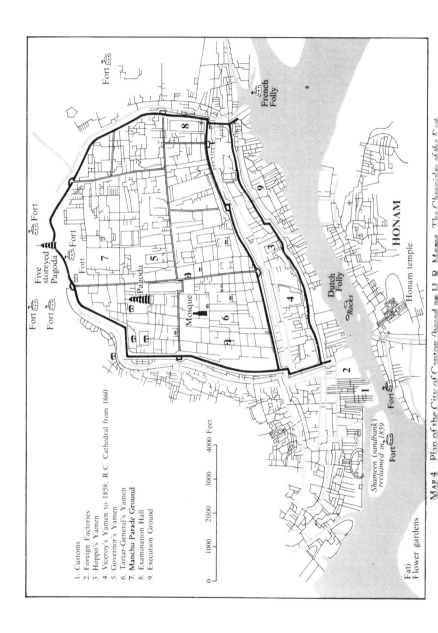

1. Customs
2. Foreign Factories
3. Hoppo's Yamen
4. Viceroy's Yamen to 1858; R.C. Cathedral from 1860
5. Governor's Yamen
6. Tartar-General's Yamen
7. **Manchu Parade Ground**
8. Examination Hall
9. Execution Ground

0   1000   2000   3000   4000 Feet

MAP 4   Plan of the City of Canton (based on H.B. Morse, *The Chronicles of the East*

an enemy as yet unaccustomed to the concentrated fire of ship and rifleman.[35] From this modest height they looked down, not without awe, on an ancient city with its labyrinth of alleys, creeks, and canals, and the shambling accretions of shops and dwelling-houses that extended into sprawling suburbs beyond the walls. Far away, beyond the city, the low-lying plain gave the appearance of being rich and well-watered, divided as it was by canals and little streams, between which lay rice-fields and small gardens. Every few miles small circles of trees marked the boundaries of tiny villages.

By the evening of the 26th all the forts on the encircling hills above Canton, as well as the river defences, were in British hands, and Gough's eager battalions were poised for the final assault. So far the British losses had been 15 killed and 112 wounded. In the view of almost every officer, naval or military, 'a treacherous, deceitful and arrogant people' were about to be, and deserved to be, properly humbled. It was at this moment that Elliot arranged yet another truce.[36]

Against the protests of the General, who complained that his troops remained in a highly precarious situation, on 27 May Elliot made immediate arrangements with the three Imperial Commissioners—the general of the Tartar garrison, the Viceroy, and the Governor of Kwangtung—for the withdrawal of all Imperial troops (some 45,000) to a distance of at least sixty miles. Six million dollars indemnity was to be paid within a week.[37]

General Gough's explosive anger at Elliot's unexpected intervention was shared by troops and seamen. For the plenipotentiary's judgement that it would be inexpedient, as well as sinful, to harm 'the vast and rich city before us, and its immense unoffending population',[38] Gough had nothing but

[35] See E. H. Parker, *Chinese Account of the Opium War* (Shanghai, 1888), pp. 31–2; Frederic Wakeman, Jr., *Strangers at the Gate: Social Disorder in South China, 1839—1861* (Berkeley, 1966), pp. 12–13; and *Nemesis*, pp. 177–84.

[36] Details of the attack and capture of Canton are contained in Elliot to Palmerston, Macao, 8 June 1841, R. 10/5 Miscel. (I.O.A.). A printed and corrected (in ink) account of the May operations in the Canton River is contained in the *London Gazette Extraordinary*, Fri. 8 Oct. 1841, Adm. 1/5508; see also, *Nemesis*, pp. 182–96.

[37] See Elliot to Gough, *Hyacinth* off Canton, 27 May 1841, Adm. 1/5506. On receipt of these sums, British forces would be withdrawn from Wantung and the Bocca Tigris.

[38] See Elliot to Gough (encl. 3), 24 May 1841, F.O. 17/48.

contempt. As a commander, this junior captain of the Royal Navy was as 'whimsical as a shuttlecock', more concerned with trade returns than with national honour. Captain Le Fleming Senhouse was equally outraged. But there is no evidence to support Alexander Michie's charges that his death, shortly after his return to Macao, was hastened by the physical upset occasioned by Elliot's act of mercy.[39] *The Times* correspondent, G. W. Cooke, viewed the episode in retrospect more phlegmatically. 'That gallant, wrong-headed little man' was temperamentally opposed to the traditional, and perhaps the least expensive, policy of 'making omelettes by breaking eggs'.[40]

But Elliot was too much of an idealist to base his approach entirely on commercial need and, least of all, on merchant cupidity. Whether he was influenced substantially by fears for the cherished English tea trade may be doubted. Of course, he was anxious to keep the commercial channels open; tea had become an indispensable article of consumption, the merits of which had been advertised for all time by the Boston radicals who had held their tea-party in 1773. But like Palmerston, he viewed the political as the more important issue; in the long run, a lasting trade agreement depended upon a satisfactory political settlement. Admittedly, the treaty terms applied only to the city and river of Canton; but, as Captain Le Fleming Senhouse wrote bitterly to Elliot, the arrangement seemed intended 'for a general pacification which would appear a very poor compensation for all the insults and injuries we have received. . . .'[41]

This feeling of bitter resentment is understandable. Once again a British victory was incomplete; the British flag had not been planted on the ramparts of the 'inviolate city'.[42] But the problem remains more than one of emotional response.

---

[39] Alexander Michie, *The Englishman in China during the Victorian Era: The Career of Sir Rutherford Alcock* (2 vols., London, 1900), i. 69. Some of the correspondence of that period suggests, however, that Senhouse was an ill man who should never have been given command during Bremer's absence in Calcutta. See, for example, Bremer to Admiralty, *Wellesley* at Hong Kong, Adm. 1/5506.

[40] George Wingrove Cooke, *China: being 'The Times' special correspondence from China in the years 1857–58* (London, 1859), pp. 76–7.

[41] 28 May 1841, Adm. 1/5506.

[42] Ouchterlony, p. 148.

Would a complete victory, which certainly would have been the result of a combined assault, have obtained the objectives which Palmerston and Elliot sought? The question is of course unanswerable; but as after events were to reveal so emphatically, the failure to raise the flag over a beaten and broken city saved Chinese 'face' and turned defeat into triumph. In customary fashion, the Emperor was informed that the 'barbarians' had once again been repulsed from the outskirts of the invincible City. Admittedly, the Imperial troops had been forced to leave, but the thousands of villagers who watched from surrounding hills the withdrawal of British troops and, from the shore lines, the retreat of British ships down to the Bogue and beyond, were soon spinning the legend of Chinese valour and invincibility. They *had* beaten the British, despite the treachery and pusillanimity of merchants and city administrators who had been willing to come to terms with the enemy.

This belief probably provides the most significant single motive of the later anti-foreign movement, when ' . . . any official who thereafter adopted a moderate policy towards the barbarians could be accused of collaboration and treason'.[43] Consequently, Elliot's assumption that war could be waged against Cantonese officialdom without unduly antagonizing the rural population turned out to be a grotesque miscalculation. Whatever the resentments harboured by the rural Cantonese against affluent city folk who appeared willing to come to terms with the enemy, hatred of the foreigner became, after the end of the war and the signing of the Treaty of Nanking, gradually a shared regional emotion that dwarfed any civil antipathies. The period after 1846 was to be marked not so much be incidents as by serious and prolonged crises.[44]

In brief, the combination of stick and carrot, gun-fire and conciliation, had no chance of success, even before xenophobia hardened into adamant. Although Elliot had declared more than once that a northern campaign might be necessary to convince Peking that British treaty terms had to be accepted,

---

[43] Wakeman, p. 53.

[44] On the question of Cantonese xenophobia following the war, see John J. Nolde, 'The "False Edict" of 1849', *Journal of Asian Studies*, xx, No. 3, 1961, and 'Xenophobia in Canton, 1842–1849', *Journal of Oriental Studies*, xiii, No. 1, 1075 (Hong Kong University Press), especially 3–5, 20–2.

he seems to have been convinced that a short cut was possible, that the essential ends of British policy could be attained in Canton. Hence, his honest grief that the Bogue forts had not been assaulted in the first campaign, and his successive and absurd peace efforts thereafter to come to terms with the Cantonese provincial government. Just as he believed the provincial governing class might be detached from 'the populace', with equal lack of perception he seems to have assumed that Canton might be isolated from the Imperial central government without civil war and consequent anarchy. 'In a practical point of view,' he wrote to Lord Auckland, 'it is no exaggeration to say, that peaceful commercial relations with the Government and people of Canton are more important to us, than Treaty of peace with the Emperor.'[45]

In retrospect, Elliot might well be accused of *naïveté* and, according to Palmerston's interpretation, crass stupidity. The man who had been close to Chinese affairs for seven years was less astute in his judgement of events than a soldier who had served in the country less than three months or a Foreign Secretary who had never seen it. But such an indictment, however reasonable, would be an over-simplification. Elliot was wrong in his interpretation of the Chinese reaction to conciliatory diplomacy following local and limited gunboat operations, but, curiously enough, he was right (and General Gough was wrong) in estimating the danger of leaving a small British garrison locked up within the closeted spaces of an unconquered walled city. The victorious British force on 27 May was less than 2,200 men of all ranks; within Canton were probably 20,000 or more troops and probably close to a million angry citizens—here was a vast murmuring wasps' nest, needing only to be stirred before releasing its excited occupants from the innumerable crooked lanes and narrow streets. Outside in the villages, watching and waiting, was a raucous and rancorous population, yearning for revenge and loot. A little more than a year later the perils of garrison life behind high walls that overlooked a hostile countryside were to be revealed in Ningpo.

[45] Macao, 21 June 1841, L/P & S/9/10 (I.O.A.). This letter was in reply to Auckland's of 12 May. A copy was enclosed with a letter to Palmerston (No. 27) of the same date, China Records, Miscel. vol. 5, R/10 (I.O.A.).

Morale was another matter, and scarcely less significant, as history has repeatedly confirmed. Sickness, disease, all the ills that accompany a cloistered garrison existence in alien lands, with unfamiliar weather conditions, were probably as inevitable in Canton as in Hong Kong or Chusan. Less to be dreaded, but nevertheless to be feared, were the customary temptations offered to bored and frustrated men—liquor, plunder, and sex.

Elliot had spared Canton in return for a ransom. Whether bombardment, assault, fire and sword would have brought Peking rulers to the council table may be doubted. Conceivably, Elliot's action served to strengthen the Imperial Court's confidence in their heaven-sent invulnerability; but even had this important southern capital city been sacked, and its walls demolished, it was scarcely likely that such a catastrophe would have been accepted as a heavenly sign that the end of the Ch'ing dynasty was at hand. A British expedition would still have to sail northward to assert its power over the heartland.

VII

EAST COAST OPERATIONS: EN ROUTE TO THE YANGTSE

IT was late in April when Palmerston received Elliot's letter of 23 January with news of the acquisition of Hong Kong. He was deeply shocked by what he regarded as blatant insubordination, and remained quite unmoved by the plenipotentiary's arguments. In a reply which was unsparing in its accusations of perverseness and stupidity, Elliot was told bluntly that his appointment in China was at an end. 'You have disobeyed and neglected your Instructions; you have deliberately abstained from employing as you might have done, the Force placed at your disposal, and you have without sufficient necessity accepted Terms which fell far short of those which you were instructed to obtain.'[1] Palmerston had become increasingly suspicious of Elliot's judgement. He was 'a clever man', he wrote to Admiral Elliot with not a little bitterness,' and has much knowledge of the Chinese character, but he wants Firmness, Decision, Boldness and Enterprise, I mean in Negotiation. He is too fond of Refinements and of getting, by Roundabout ways, and by Finesse, at Results which can better & more speedily and certainly be arrived at by Straightforward Energy & Determination.'[2]

News of the abortive negotiations at the Peiho had reached the Foreign Secretary in mid-January, and had served to confirm his worst fears. The man whom he had once judged to be tough, shrewd, and resolute, had turned out to be soft and gullible. He particularly resented Elliot's apparent acceptance of 'the pretentious superiority' implied in much of the correspondence issuing from Peking. In dealing with the Chinese, Palmerston had warned him,

the best way to carry points with a half civilized People, as well as with wholly civilized People, is to be steady, firm, persevering and

---

[1] 21 Apr. 1841, Broadlands MSS. GC/EL/30/3.
[2] 16 Jan. 1841, ibid. GC/EL/38/1.

unyielding. Go straight and fixedly to your Point, and do not fall into the Mistake of supposing that when you are speaking for a great Power like England, and are backed by a naval and military Force, it is either useful or becoming to play at follow my Leader with the Chinese, and to let them draw you after them through the windings and Intracacies [sic] of their own Diplomacy.

To be tempted away 'to the further Extremity of the Chinese Empire' appeared to him prima facie to be a mistake, and certainly at variance with instructions.[3]

Palmerston had no doubt in his own mind that Peking was deftly setting up a peace table to suit Chinese convenience and purposes. Both sides would meet far away from the seat of Imperial power, and in accepting postponement of negotiations under such terms, the British emissaries had lost the initiative and, equally important, had lost 'face'. The presence of a British force so close to the capital 'had produced a great and most useful impression upon the Government of China', and negotiations could have been carried on with advantage, at a time when Peking was obviously suffering 'the most apprehension'.[4] In short, the two British plenipotentiaries had been unduly trusting and unnecessarily timid. The Chinese delegates should have been given a stiff ultimatum: accept our terms in a given number of days, or full-scale operations will be launched on the Yangtse River.[5] As things stood, however, there was no alternative but to go ahead with the utmost resolution in order to achieve a complete and final settlement, 'because we should not again for so small a Quarrel send a similar force to the China Sea; and we ought to settle all our matters, now that we have on the Coast a Force which is sufficient to compel concession to all we ask'.[6] And once again, Palmerston reminded Charles Elliot of the instructions that had been sent him in February of the previous year.

Three months after writing this warning letter came the second blow. Chusan had been surrendered without reciprocal benefit, and the Foreign Secretary was at a loss to under-

---

[3] Palmerston to Captain Elliot, 24 Jan. [1841], not 1840 as inscribed on the document, ibid. GC/EL/29/2.

[4] Palmerston to Plenipotentiaries, 9 Jan. 1841, encl. in Leveson (F.O.) to Barrow, 25 Feb. 1841, Adm. 1/5509.

[5] To Admiral Elliot, 16 Jan. 1841, Broadlands MSS. GC/EL/38/1.

[6] To Captain Charles Elliot, 24 Jan. [1841], doc. cit.

stand what he regarded as a lamentable climb down. British arms had been everywhere successful. Chusan had been taken without loss, and held without difficulty. At Amoy and with the lower forts on the Canton River, the 'irresistible Navy' had shown how efficiently they could demolish defences and vanquish such enemy forces they could get at. 'The Presence of our Squadron at the mouth of the Peiho had evidently produced a deep impression on the Govt. at Peking.'

In the circumstances, why was the British force not employed for the purpose for which it was sent. Why, Palmerston wrote bitingly, 'did you accept inadequate Conditions without at least trying whether your Means would not enable you to obtain the full Extent demanded?' The power was available, but he, Charles Elliot, seemed to have regarded his instructions as so much waste paper. The interests of the country were merely matters to be dealt with 'according to your own Fancy'. Palmerston then tabled the list of errors. Full compensation had been demanded for the opium chests confiscated by Lin, and Elliot had accepted 'a sum much smaller than the amount due'. Moreover, the total amount spread over yearly instalments would be paid, not by the Chinese government, but by British merchants in the shape of additional duties on their own goods. He had failed to present bills covering the cost of the punitive expedition, as well as the debts owed by Hong merchants to British firms. He had been ordered to retain Chusan until the whole of the pecuniary indemnity had been paid; instead, he had evacuated the Island precipitately. Admittedly, he had obtained Hong Kong, 'a barren island with hardly a House upon it', but without the Emperor's signature their could be no cession of sovereignty. All he had acquired was the right of settlement, on the same legal footing as the Portuguese at Macao. Finally, by abruptly surrendering Chusan, he had failed to win openings for British trade to the northward, with access to the vast, untapped markets of the interior.[7]

Her Majesty's government, Palmerston informed the newly appointed plenipotentiary, Sir Henry Pottinger, in

---

[7] F.O., 21 Apr. 1841, Broadlands MSS. GC/EL/30/3. A draft of this letter, and a second, addressed to both Bremer and Elliot, 3 May 1841 (No. 12), are contained in F.O. 17/45.

May, 'apprehend that Hong Kong could not for a great length of Time afford to our Merchants any new Facilities for Trade with the northern Ports and consequently the Possession of Hong Kong should not supersede the necessity of obtaining either another Insular Possession on the Eastern Coast, or Permission for British Subjects to reside in some of the principal Cities on that Coast'.[8]

Elliot had never had much sympathy with Palmerston's design to acquire trade privileges in northern ports. He did not share the constantly recurring visions of many merchants and some ministers that great, untapped markets lay waiting in the vast hinterland of the Middle Kingdom. Even if true, such objectives could only be promoted at a cost of untold blood and money. He felt that the British government, and especially Palmerston, had succumbed to fantasies woven by ambitious and avaricious industrialists and traders who had never set foot in the courts of Kubla Khan, but who dreamed dreams of opulent cities with streets of gold, and of vast hinterlands, carpeted with tea plantations stretching to far horizons. With Hong Kong in British hands, there was no need in his view for further permanent acquisitions; that island held the keys to profitable commercial intercourse with the mainland.[9] And even if the occupation of Chusan should subsequently show comparable merit as a 'seat of commerce', such a settlement could 'only be productive of an indefinite protraction of hostilities in China, at an enormous cost. . . .' Because he hated bloodshed, and because he had little but contempt for the greedy merchant princes (whom, he believed, were indirectly responsible for the war), Elliot was determined to negotiate at every opportunity, in the hope of restoring friendly relations with a people who, after all, were the 'source of trade'.[10]

[8] Palmerston to Pottinger, 31 May 1841 (No. 16, corrected draft), F.O. 17/53.
[9] Writing to Palmerston on 25 March, Elliot reiterated his conviction that Hong Kong should be kept as a base of operations, both civil and military. 'I hold that position to be in every respect best suited for such purposes, and I cannot but think that no time should be lost in our firm establishment there, not merely with intentions of temporary settlement, but with the deliberate object of fixing the chief seat of our commercial intercourse with the Empire at that place. . . .' Macao, 25 Mar. 1841, F.O. 17/48. See also, Auckland to Hobhouse, 21 Apr. 1841, following receipt of a similar dispatch from Elliot, dated 24 March, L/P & S/9/10 (I.O.A.).
[10] See Elliot's defence of his conduct in long memorandum addressed to Aberdeen, 25 Jan. 1842, F.O.17/61. This document which was circulated to members of the

Unfortunately for himself, in challenging the official Whitehall policy, Elliot was guilty of one fundamental error of judgement. He had assumed, at least until his retirement, that the government's view would be influenced by, if not based on, the advice of their representative on the spot. If these views changed, so should the British government consider a change of policy. Since most people in Whitehall were ignorant of the inhabitants, the geography, and the climate of China, they should the more readily accept the recommendations of their appointed agents. The argument was not without its logic, but as Palmerston had shrewdly noted, self-confidence combined with an idiosyncratic doggedness had induced in Elliot a strain of perversity. He was absorbed by Canton; solve the problem of Cantonese intransigence and bloody-mindedness, and all could be well. He simply would not recognize the wholeness of China, the incredible illogical unity of an Empire, capable in the long run of withstanding or outliving regional differences and conflicts that could breed civil wars. In 1841 there *was* a Middle Kingdom, and a Manchu Emperor who really ruled, and whose powerful arms reached without effort to Canton, as various Imperial Commissioners and envoys knew to their cost. Treating with provincial governments or Imperial agents far removed from the capital got one nowhere. Elliot failed to understand the extent to which the Emperor and his advisers were Peking-minded. As long as there was one China, only a threat to Peking could have any effect on their policy. So, '. . . to hammer away at Canton was a mere waste of time'.[11]

On 3 May, the day on which Elliot was notified of his recall, Palmerston instructed the Admiralty to order Commodore Bremer to retake Chusan, withdrawing troops if necessary for that purpose from Hong Kong. A small naval force could be

Cabinet is summarized in W. C. Costin, *Great Britain and China 1833–1860* (Oxford, 1937; Reprint 1968), pp. 93–5. As an officer who had in circumstances of extreme difficulty tried to do his duty, and as a British plenipotentiary who had been abused by Palmerston, Elliot won the support of the Duke. Wellington had personally, so he informed Lord Stanley in his famous letter on 'guarding the Constitution' (19 Feb. 1846), 'protected the servant of the Government, Captain Elliot in China. . . .' Quoted, Richard Aldington, *Wellington*, Being an account of the Life & Achievements of Arthur Wellesley, 1st Duke of Wellington (London, 1946), p. 336.
[11] Waley, *The Opium War . . .* , p. 156.

left behind to protect British interests in the Canton River.[12] By the end of May, his projected programme had begun to crystallize, although certain options were left open for consideration by the men on the spot. The occupation of Chusan would provide, he believed, opportunity for the resumption of negotiations, which could take place either in Chusan or on the banks of the Peiho, but *not* at Canton. A naval force should accompany the plenipotentiary to the mouth of the Peiho (assuming this rendezvous to be preferable to Chusan) where 'the Chinese Plenipotentiary would have before his eyes greater and more manifest evidences of the Power of Great Britain'. But on no account was Chusan to be evacuated until compensation had been paid in full for the destroyed opium and the cost of two expeditions. Less than £3 m. would not cover expenses.[13] Recollecting, however, that his instructions could not possibly reach the China coast before weather conditions made an expedition to the Peiho out of the question, he informed the Admiralty that the new commander-in-chief, Admiral Sir William Parker, should be instructed (in pursuance of British efforts to bring about a final settlement) to penetrate the Yangtse-Kiang to the point of its junction with the Grand Canal, occupy the neighbouring island, and destroy all locks and sluices. Precise plans for such operations were to be worked out in co-operation with the Governor-General of India.[14]

In fact, the general strategy which Palmerston recommended had already been advanced by Charles Elliot, with, of course, the additional exhortation that Hong Kong should be retained as a permanent base. Elliot was now less certain that the Canton imbroglio could be resolved in Canton, and already in March he had advocated the ascent of the Yangtse as far as the Grand Canal, and the occupation of an island in or by the estuary as a base. For this purpose, he would need at least one ship of the line, two heavy frigates, and two sloops. He was by no means opposed to a demonstration off the Peiho,

---

[12] Palmerston to Admiralty, 3 May 1841; Palmerston to Bremer and Elliot, same date (No. 12, copy), L/P & S/9/2 (I.O.A.) and F.O. 17/45.

[13] Palmerston to Pottinger, 31 May 1841 (No. 16, draft) L/P & S/9/2, and F.O. 17/53.

[14] 2 June 1841, F.O. 17/51.

but even if time allowed, he was doubtful if a sufficient force was available.[15]

It is clear that the summer campaign was based on Elliot's proposals rather than Palmerston's, since, even with vastly improved communications with London—the overland route had cut almost two months off the time taken to circumnavigate the Cape—the Foreign Secretary's directions to Admiral Parker would have reached the China Sea only to confirm plans already in progress. Indeed, on 10 May Commodore Bremer forwarded to the Admiralty his plan of operations for the approaching campaign on the East and North East coasts of China'. Having established a garrison of some 1,500 troops at Hong Kong, and four ships, including one or two steamers, to watch the entrance to the Bocca Tigris at Wangtung, he proposed to take a combined force of about 3,000 soldiers, seamen, and marines northward to the Yangtse, with the object of blocking the Grand Canal, or (preferably) pushing on to the mouth of the Peiho, forcing the entrance and establishing a base as close as possible to the Imperial capital. But Bremer admitted that time was limited; the strong north winds that set in at the beginning of October precluded any operations in the Gulf of Pecheli that could not be completed by September.[16]

Lord Auckland had already taken for granted that the proposed expedition would not go beyond the Yangtse even if a sufficient force were available. He personally could see no alternative to a return to the Peiho and a confrontation with the Imperial Court in Peking. Half-way measures—the original Elliot policy of forbearance—would simply prolong an expensive war.[17] Unfortunately, it was too late to take the decisive step. It was clear to Auckland that by the time a British squadron reached the Gulf of Pecheli in, say, early autumn, it would have to contend with the monsoon that would soon blow hard and bitterly from the north-east. It was,

---

[15] Elliot to Palmerston, 25 Mar. 1841 (No. 13, copy), enclosing Elliot to Auckland, 24 Mar. 1841, China Records, Miscel. vol. 5, R/10 (I.O.A.). Elliot to Auckland, 24 Mar. 1841, is also contained in F.O. 17/48.

[16] See Bremer to O'Ferrall, 10 May 1841 (No. 27), Adm. 1/5506.

[17] Aware that he was under censure from the Foreign Office, Elliot had written to Auckland on 1 May: 'Force was requisite, but forbearance was indispensable.' Encl. in Elliot to Palmerston, 1 May 1841, F.O. 17/48.

therefore, absurd even to consider a plan of campaign directed towards the Imperial capital until the spring of 1842.[18]

But the Governor-General did whole-heartedly agree with Elliot on the importance of hanging on to Hong Kong. Such an island base was, in his view, essential for the effective conduct of any substantial campaign, and Auckland urged Elliot's successor to insist on the permanent settlement and organization of Hong Kong, 'not upon the promise alone of commercial advantages . . . but *because in the prospect of a protracted war*, it has seemed to me absolutely necessary, that we should have in advance of Singapore, a secure position for Magazines, Hospitals, and reserves, and a Harbour in which Naval repairs to some extent may be effected'.[19]

Auckland's discreet recommendation scarcely disguised his disapproval of what he believed to be Palmerston's preference for 'Treaty ports' as an alternative to acquiring territory. The Foreign Secretary seemed to be wedded to the notion that getting permission for British subjects 'to reside and to trade under declared privileges, in some of the principle Cities on that coast' was equivalent to acquiring a permanent base. The Governor-General attached 'very far greater value' to the possession of an island, 'provided one can be found accessible to Shipping, healthy in Climate, and secure in Military tenure'.[20] He was still heavily prejudiced against Chusan; and as fate would have it, he left India before learning that the reoccupying forces on that once stricken island were leading a far healthier existence than the garrison of Hong Kong.

Palmerston had hoped that the steam frigate *Sesostris* which was carrying the new plenipotentiary, Sir Henry Pottinger, to Bombay would call at Calcutta to permit useful discussions with the Governor-General. But fearful that his prospective guest would lose good sailing weather, and anxious to speed up the organization of the northern campaign, Auckland

---

[18] Auckland to Hobhouse (President of the Board of Control), 11 Aug. 1841, Auckland Papers, China Book, Vol. 1, Add. MS. 37715; also, L/P & S/9/10 (I.O.A.).

[19] Auckland to Pottinger (private), 24 June 1841, Auckland Papers, China Book, I; and Auckland to Hobhouse, 11 Aug. 1841, ibid. See also, summary of this advice enclosed in Ellenborough to Aberdeen, 9 Oct. 1841, F.O. 17/52.

[20] Auckland to Hobhouse, 11 Aug. 1841, doc. cit.

directed that the frigate should proceed non-stop to the China coast.[21] As it happened, his decision made possible a record run from London to Hong Kong of sixty-seven days, ten of which had been spent in Bombay.

Pottinger arrived in China with the reputation of a distinguished and large-minded soldier and diplomat of initiative and adventurous spirit. Joining the Indian army in 1804 as a cadet, he obtained leave in 1809, and spent the next two years exploring the country between Persia and India disguised as a native. He served with credit during the Mahratta War, and between 1836 and 1840 acted as political agent in Sind. Shortly before leaving for China in the late spring of 1841, he was made a baronet in recognition of his versatility and talent. Although utterly unlike Elliot in temperament and character, his administrative career, like Elliot's, was to be tarnished by human error. Incredibly stuffy in his relations with equals—and with the merchant community he could be ham-handed—he at least won the respect, if not the affection, of his junior staff. In May 1841, Palmerston had congratulated himself on finding precisely the man for the job.

Pottinger was accompanied on the voyage by Rear-Admiral William Parker, who was to take over command of the China squadron from Commodore Bremer.[22] Parker, a first cousin of John Jervis, the first Earl of St. Vincent, was regarded as a first-rate seaman, and, moreover, one with a heart. The new plenipotentiary and the Admiral were likely to get on well, Alexander Matheson informed his associate in Singapore.[23] Certainly, in a Victorian navy that bulged with prickles, the Admiral had never been called 'difficult'. For the final effort to bring Peking to the peace table, the government obviously needed an officer of discretion and balance—a natural diplomat as well as an efficient commander. Parker was perfectly

[21] Admiral Parker to Admiralty, Bombay, 12 July 1841, Adm. 1/5506.

[22] A summary of Parker's instructions is contained in Palmerston to Parker, 6 May 1841, Phillimore, ii. 449.

[23] To John Purvis, Macao, 17 Aug. 1841, Private Letter Books (B9), Vol. 1, Aug. 1841–Feb. 1842 (J.M.A.). 'It is reported', the letter went on, 'that the expedition for the northward will start this week, in two divisions, one direct to the mouth of the Peiho, with Sir H. Pottinger, and the other to retake Chusan. The long talked of attack on Amoy has been abandoned owing to the lateness of the season.' Rumours, as reported in Jardine–Matheson correspondence, very often had sound foundations.

suited for the dual role, a strict but not a harsh disciplinarian, a deeply religious man whose faith augmented exceptional will-power. Apart from a strong aversion to tobacco—no smoking was permitted on his flagship—he was a reasonably patient and tolerant man who recognized the need, especially in viciously hot climates, of preserving the social amenities. In times to come, he was to resent Pottinger's interference with the movements of his ships, but his biting criticisms were confined to Admiralty correspondence. An honest zeal for the service buttressed his remarkable self-control, enabling him to suppress the occasional violent outburst which, however justified, would have jeopardized relations with his shrewd but eccentric and obstinate team-mate.[24]

With the arrival of Pottinger and Parker at Macao on 9 August 1841, the days of frustrating 'stop and go' hostilities, when iron fists alternated with velvet gloves, were over. For the moment, a patchwork truce allowed a full resumption of trade at Canton, but Peking remained rigidly antipathetic to all overtures. Palmerston, with new brooms at hand, was intent on forcing a confrontation and a settlement, eventually if needs be, at the very gates of the Imperial capital. How fortunate, the Foreign Secretary wrote to Pottinger, 'that the Emperor has given us such a good cause of Quarrel, and thus enabled us to begin Hostilities at the Commencement of the favourable season. . . .'—in other words, *after* the beginning of the south-west monsoon.[25] At that time, the Yangtse would be readily accessible to even the heavier ships. No one could foretell the results of so dramatic as incursion into the Chinese interior, but, assuming success forced the Emperor to reconsider British terms, it was up to the plenipotentiary to decide the best place for negotiating a final peace.[26]

[24] Parker was made a Vice-Admiral in November, 1841, and Baronet three years later. He served as c.-in-c. of the Mediterranean squadron, and, in 1863, ten years after his retirement, became an Admiral of the Fleet. He died in 1866 at the age of 85.

[25] 5 June 1841, encl. in Palmerston to Admiralty, 5 June 1841, Adm. 1/5509.

[26] 'I may add', wrote James Matheson to William Jardine in London, 'that the unpopularity of our cause in England, the smallness of our forces, & the inefficiency of its heads were so many reasons that moderated my expectations of a favourable result, and led me to put up with almost any sort of settlement, were it only for the sake of its furnishing us with a better *Casus belly* on some future occasion. If Sir Henry Pottinger can obviate this by making a *good* settlement at once, it will, of course, be

The projected expedition, which Elliot had limited to the Yangtse, and which Palmerston's subsequent instructions confirmed, was intended to be no less powerful than that of the previous year, but far more mobile. 'We have endeavoured to make you as strong as possible in steamers,' Auckland wrote to Parker.[27] The Admiral could count on keeping the two Company frigates *Queen* and *Sesostris*, and two smaller steamers, the well-tried *Madagascar* and the *Hooghly*. In addition, there were the iron-hulled *Nemesis* and the *Phlegethon*, already regarded as indispensable for river work, because unlike the heavier, wooden paddle-wheelers, which drew ten feet or more of water, they could move in as little as four or five. Another of the same class, the *Prosperpine*, was already on her way from the shipbuilders in England, and Auckland promised to send her to the China station immediately on her arrival in India.[28]

Parker had scarcely taken over command of the squadron on 10 August when sickness of epidemic proportions swept through the assembled troops and prostrated a good part of the fleet. As long as the men had remained on the heights above Canton, there had been little or no illness, despite the savage rains; but on their return to Hong Kong, fever, ague, and dysentry spread with alarming rapidity. At one time 1,100 men were in hospital; regiments were reduced to skeleton strength. Out of 560 men of the 37th Madras native infantry, only 60 were capable of fixing bayonets. The ships suffered equally. The *Modeste* and *Herald* could barely find fifteen men each for active duty; the *Conway* was turned into a floating hospital. So long as this situation lasted, it was impossible to move northward. The day before the expedition got under way, the seamen's sickness roll showed: fever—128, dysentry—57, other ailments—159. If the last summer's campaign offered a precedent, Admiral Parker was bound to need reinforcements before the New Year.[29]

---

infinitely better.' Macao, 23 Aug. 1841, Private Letter Books (B9), Vol. 7, 1841 (J.M.A.).

[27] See in this connection, a detailed survey on the use of steamboats on Chinese interior waters by Palmerston's correspondent, John Copling, 16 June 1841, contained in Palmerston to Hobhouse, 31 Aug. 1841, L/P & S/9/2 (I.O.A.).

[28] Auckland to Parker, 24 June 1841, Philimore, ii. 444–5.

[29] Parker to Auckland, 20 Aug. 1841, L/P & S/9/10 (I.O.A.). See also, *Chinese*

It seemed equally certain that the fleet would be in dire need of provisions. The bread and salt meat obtained in India had mouldered and decayed *en route*. Only by cutting rations, or by tempting substantial supplies from Chinese peasants, was the commissariat likely to meet the needs of a long winter season. Moreover, an unusually severe typhoon had swept Hong Kong on 21 July, followed by one of less extreme violence on the 26th. Sails had suffered more than superstructures, but all told the damage was serious, and more than a week had to be spent on crucial repairs.[30]

Shortage of crews for ships, and particularly for transports, remained a chronic problem that only a revolution of medical practice could solve. Equally serious, when one considers the lethal typhoons that could develop of a sudden in eastern waters, was the ignorance or imperfect knowledge of the Chinese coastline, which Admiralty charts did little to remedy. As the chronicler of the *Nemesis* wrote:

When we remember what a large number of hired transports and store-ships passed up and down along the coast of China . . . many of which had frequently part of their crew sick, we cannot but be surprised that so few accidents happened. The inaccuracies of the surveys of the coast which had been then made; the wrong position on the charts of most of the numerous islands which stand out as bulwarks at very uncertain distances from the shore; the strength and unknown irregularities of the currents, and the heavy squalls which frequently burst suddenly over that part of China, rendered the navigation precarious, and frequently caused the utmost anxiety. Occasionally the captains found themselves inside of islands when they believed they were some distance outside. . . .[31]

In fact, it was not uncommon to find islands marked on the charts ten to twenty miles from their rightful latitudes. 'The China seas north and south are narrow seas', wrote Joseph Conrad, more than half a century later, in a short story called

---

Repository, x. Nov. 1841, p. 169; also, Bingham, *Narrative of the Expedition . . .* , p. 245. A hospital in Macao was leased to look after the worst cases.

[30] During the morning of the first outburst, the military hospital collapsed, crushing under its ruins the majority of the bed-ridden patients. Although many sustained serious injuries, only one soldier was killed, 'a poor helpless maniac'. *Chinese Repository*, x. Nov. 1841, p. 619; see also, *Nemesis*, pp. 211–18. During the course of the storm, Captain Elliot nearly lost his life, and owed survival to his own brilliant initiative and courage.

[31] *Nemesis*, p. 241.

Typhoon. 'They are seas full of everyday eloquent facts, such as islands, sand-banks, reefs, swift and changeable currents —tangled facts that nevertheless speak to a seaman in clear and definite language.'

The task of getting a shattered squadron fit for sea and on the way north before the north-east monsoon put an end to operations, almost overwhelmed a distracted Admiral.[32] The northern expedition was not to be a mere exhibition on the part of the navy—a 'showing the flag' parade, with occasional assaults on poorly defended Chinese towns. Both army and navy expected to encounter strong opposition from an enemy that had learned the destructive power of modern guns. Hence Parker was grateful that the steam reinforcements, promised by the Governor-General, had arrived in time. Meanwhile, the Admiralty had requested Rear-Admiral King of the South American station (Brazil) to send two cruisers to the Canton River (*Pearl* or the *Clio*, and the *Camelion*); at the same time, the *Pelican* was ordered to quit Lisbon, and make all haste to join the squadron. It seemed unlikely, however, that the last three vessels could beat the monsoon, in which case they were expected to sojourn in Singapore until the weather pendulum reversed.[33]

Early on the morning of 21 August the fleet got underway. It consisted of 36 sail: 21 hired transports and store-ships, two line-of-battleships, *Wellesley* and *Blenheim*, seven frigates and sloops from 44 to 10 guns, *Modeste, Druid, Columbine, Blonde, Pylades, Cruiser*, and *Algerine*, the troop-ship *Rattlesnake*, the *Bentinck* (renamed *Plover*) surveying vessel, and the four Company steamers, the *Queen, Phlegethon, Nemesis*, and *Sesostris*. The weather was unusually favourable, and the first objective, some 300 miles distant, was reached on 25 August. 'Amoy will be punished by our squadron *en passant*' wrote James Matheson, 'but probably no other place in the vicinity', and he saw no reason why Canton should be upset and roused to violence by the attack.[34]

---

[32] Parker to Auckland, Hong Kong, 20 Aug. 1841, L/P & S/9/10 (I.O.A.); also Bremer to O'Ferrall, *Wellesley*, 28 July 1841, Adm. 1/5506.

[33] Barrow to King, 8 June 1841, Adm. 2/1598.

[34] To Joseph Coolidge, Macao, 28 Aug. 1841, Private Letter Books (B9), Vol. 7, p. 127. (J.M.A.).

The outer defences of the town had been heavily fortified since the visit of the *Alligator* in the previous summer. The little islands which stretched across the mouth of the bay were pocked with gun emplacements. Koolangsu, the key to Amoy, guarding the eastern entrance to the harbour, had been hewn into one vast fortress. 'Green as an emerald', this oval shaped island, about one and a half miles long and half a mile in breadth was in substance little more than a mass of granite rock chiselled by centuries of weather into fantastic shapes. Seen from a distance, Koolangsu looked to be another 'Seychelles fairyland', a cool and luxurious retreat for weak and weary seamen. But to the British garrison, who occupied it a few months later, it became a prison, secured by high walls of scorching granite, rank vegetation, and malarial air. Remittent and intermittent fevers, as well as cholera, yellow fever, and dysentry were almost endemic between the end of June and the middle of November. Its unhealthiness, according to an officer of the occupying force, had 'scarcely a parallel on the deadly shores of Western Africa . . .'[34a] whence came that ominous warning, which he had doubtless heeded:

> Beware! beware! of the Bight of Benin
> Where few come out,
> Though many go in.

Fixed firmly on the island's granite foundations, numerous strong and well-designed works mounting around 76 guns had been built. In addition to the solid mass of masonry which formed the parapets, banks of earth bound with sods reinforced the outer face, leaving only narrow openings for the guns. The subsequent engagement revealed that such batteries could withstand any amount of horizontal fire, even from the

---

[34a] W. Tyrone, D. A. C. G., *Recollections of a Three Years' Residence in China* . . . (London, 1853), pp. 127 et seq. 'Much as I suffered at Koo Lung Soo from sickness and isolation and hope deferred', wrote Tyrone Power, 'I can never forget how richly nature was arrayed, how temptingly and Circe-like she donned her most bewitching robes, making one sometimes forget that every air which rippled the lake-like water and impelled the fleet of boats in ever-changing groups, was infected and poisonous.' p. 131. First-Lieutenant Bingham of the *Modeste* must have visited the island after the rainy season, for he found it barren and desolate, apart from a few shade trees in squalid villages. Bingham, pp. 317–18.

32-pounders of the battleships. The 74s fired for a full two hours, something like 12,000 rounds, with no effect whatsoever. Not a gun was disabled; the furthest penetration of shot was later found to be 16 inches. Amoy itself was a walled town almost equally well accoutred, and the local authorities seemed to have believed the defences to be impregnable. Earth and stone entrenchments commanded the area in front of the beach, in the rear of which strong, high castellated walls climbed the steep slopes above the harbour. In addition, flanking the eastern entrance to the harbour, a number of war junks were moored, but these were easy prey for the guns of the agile steamers.

The capture of Amoy was essentially a naval operation; the army—in this case—the 18th Royal Irish—did the necessary mopping up. On the morning of the 26th, following an exchange of protests and challenges under a flag of truce, the *Wellesley* and the *Bleinheim* laid alongside the main shore batteries to pave the way for the troops' landing. The frigates, *Druid* and *Blonde*, accompanied by the light-draught vessels, engaged the batteries on Kulangsu, while the steamers cruised about, transporting troops to the beaches, or running down and destroying junks and gunboats. By 3.00 p.m. General Gough and his staff were able to step ashore, gratefully surprised at the rapidity of the operation. Once again it was clear that had the efficiently constructed works and batteries been manned by skilled gunners with modern weapons, Amoy would never have been taken from the sea. That night the troops bivouacked on or near the shore, and next morning took possession of the near-empty city.

To the occupying force, the prospect was inviting, especially to soldiers who had little taste for shipboard life. Built on an island that was almost a part of the mainland, Amoy with its panorama of trees and gardens seemed a smaller edition of Chusan. All the two-storey houses on the curving waterside had 'rooms with a view'. Large balconies overlooked the harbour which glittered with the painted emblems, flags, and the coloured awnings of junks and fishing craft wafted in by the south-west monsoon. Heedless of the unceasing din below, here the elder occupants had reclined in slippered ease, smoking, reading, or gazing nostalgically at swooping kites strung by highly competitive urchins from neighbouring windows and verandas.

By the afternoon of 27 August the noise and excitement of harbour life had been extinguished. The streets so recently filled with jostling porters, pedlars, barbers, merchants, soldiers, idlers, and mandarins in sedan chairs, were almost silent. Most of the inhabitants had fled, and during the night the pillagers had come in to ransack government offices as well as private homes. There were few pickings left for the British soldier in search of souvenirs. On the other hand, a vast quantity of military stores remained untouched, and these the invaders destroyed. In the dockyard naval officers were astonished to find the near-perfect model of a British two-decker, carrying thirty guns, and ready for sea. The skeletons of others were on the stocks.[35]

After leaving garrison detachments of foot and artillery at Koolangsu, along with a small blockading force consisting of the *Druid*, *Pylades*, and *Algerine*, on 6 September the expedition got underway for Chusan with orders to rendezvous at Buffaloes Nose. Unhappily, soon after leaving the Formosa Channel, a boisterous gale combined with strong and uncertain currents scattered the sailing ships in all directions. The transports were blown far down to leeward, and many of them did not catch up with the squadron until the evening of the 25th. The steamers, lucky enough to pick up sufficient wood fuel on one of the outlying islands, managed to reach the appointed rendezvous a week earlier. Not until the 29th were the strays reunited and the squadron able to assemble for action outside the harbour of Chusan. During the interval, the steamers once again bested the tidal channel to reconnoitre the bay defences which, as anticipated, had been greatly extended and strengthened.

At mast-head, even with the naked eye, one change in the face of the city since the previous occupation was obvious. The whole sea front extending for some two miles was now one continuous line of fortifications. But beyond the defence rim, nothing had altered. Behind rose the steep hills, cultivated to the summit in geometric ridges—a chequer-board of gardens in shimmering colours. Below in the valleys, neat and tiny

[35] *Chinese Repository*, x. Nov. 1841, pp. 621–3; see also, Ouchterlony, pp. 173–4.

villages were visible at every bend in the coast, seemingly suspended in the swampy terrain that had been laid out in irrigated rice fields. In 1840, it may be doubted if the Emperor knew of the existence of this fertile and picturesque island, with its walled capital. Two months after its first capitulation it had become one of his 'most valuable possessions'; and rumour had it that he read the account of its fall 'with fast running tears'.[36]

Against the channel mill-race, even with the assistance of the steamers, neither the 74s nor the heavy frigates could make the inner harbour. Eventually, on 1 October shallow-draught vessels like the *Modeste* were able to ferry the troops ashore at the western extremity of the inner harbour. Despite heavy fire from the shore batteries, the right flank of the long shore entrenchments was turned, and a way opened to the encampments on the hills above. While the heavy ships shelled embankments and troop concentrations on the summits, the advancing troops swept up the hill, and against gallant resistance captured the batteries at a cost of 20 dead and wounded. Pushing across country to the heights immediately above the city, a combined British and Indian force, aided by a detachment of artillery with guns and rockets, soon cleared the way to the city walls, which were scaled without loss. For the second time, Chusan had fallen to the 'barbarian' host. With traditional pride, the Chinese commander sought death, and his officers who stayed with him to the last fell by his side. This self-immolation—death rather than surrender—left an abiding impression on British officers and men. Such fearlessness of the unknown expressed a strange and awesome nobility, uncharacteristic of the European battlefield.[37]

As soon as Tinghai was fully occupied, on 6 October a military government was established, supported by a garrison of 400 troops. By this time the first blasts heralding the beginning of the north-east monsoon had dwindled, and the fleet moved across the strait to the mainland some 36 miles away. But cold weather was not far away, and General Gough believed that Ningpo, the second city in the province of

---

[36] *Nemesis*, p. 243.
[37] The best description of the attack and capture of Chusan is contained in *Nemesis*, pp. 243–51.

Chekiang, would provide a useful winter quarters, an ostentatious 'digging in' that would, it was assumed, impress
Peking.

Ningpo is situated on the extremity of a tongue of land at
the junction of two rivers, which unite below the town to
form the Ningpo river that flows some twelve miles to the
sea. Next to Hangchow, the capital of Chekiang, Ningpo was
the largest and wealthiest city of the province, and, being so
easily accessible by water, it had once been the site of an
English Factory. At the mouth of the river, on the projecting
left bank, lay the small town of Chinhai, encircled by two and
a half miles of castellated wall, 37 feet thick and 27 feet high; at
one point this wall joined a stone embankment that ran up the
coast for nearly three miles. But the main strength of the
position, regarded as the key to Ningpo, lay in the precipitous
rocky spur rising abruptly close behind the town which completely commanded the estuary. On the summit a citadel had
been erected, connected by loop-holed walls with flanking
batteries. The river below was effectively barred by stakes
extending across the entrance, and these obstructions were
covered by batteries mounting more than thirty guns.

The morning of the attack (10 October) dawned gently and
sleepily. There was not a breath of wind, and the sea lay
smooth as a mirror. The big 74s, the *Blenheim* and the *Wellesley*, were towed into position in little more than their own
draught of water, and remained throughout the engagement
nearly as steady as batteries on land. Assisted by the frigates
which concentrated on the entrenchments below, the battleships, with almost rifle-like precision, directed their heavy
shells against the citadel, gradually pulverizing it. Once the
batteries on the slopes had been neutralized, the steamers
ferried the troops to the shore, a service for which the light-
iron vessels were particularly well adapted, since the men were
usually able to jump on land without the aid of boats. By two
o'clock the town and all the defences on both sides of the river
were in British possession.

Once he saw the day was lost, the Imperial Commissioner
walked quietly to the river bank, performed the kowtow in the
direction of the Imperial city, and threw himself into the
rushing water. By this time most of the defenders had fled;

those who allowed themselves to be captured had their pigtails cut off, and were then set at liberty.[38] All told, British casualties at Tinghai and Chinhai had been unusually heavy in comparison with previous actions, namely, 17 killed and 36 wounded. The Chinese losses were very roughly estimated at 3,500 or more. Ninety iron and 67 brass guns were taken, the latter, as was customary, being shifted on board one of the transports, along with a large quantity of metal discovered in a near-by cannon foundry.[39]

Two days after the capture of Chinhai, Admiral Parker boarded the *Nemesis* and proceeded up river to reconnoitre the defences of Ningpo, and to see if the larger steamers and the sloops could be navigated as far as the city walls. With nearly 18 feet of water available all the way, neither wooden steamers nor sailing vessels had any difficulty in making a journey, which, in the earlier stages at least, offered striking scenery. As they moved up the bending river between high, conical hills, distant mountains suddenly burst into view, a vision which lasted until the city came in sight. Ningpo was an imposing, and for its area—about five miles in circumference—a densely populated metropolis. No opposition was encountered; an intervening bridge of boats barred the way, but this was easily removed. By 3.00 p.m. on 13 October the whole force amounting to 750 troops, besides artillery and sappers, had disembarked. Thousands of onlookers lined the banks, impassive, uncomprehending, yet curious as the band of the 18th Royal Irish played 'God Save the Queen'.

It was a victory obtained without firing a shot. Judging by the absence of fixed defences, the Chinese had apparently counted on the supposedly indestructible fortifications of Chinhai. The shock sustained by the high command must have been considerable. After Chinhai, so it was remarked at the time, British troops 'might have marched the whole length and breadth of the land, so great was the effect of the panic'.[40] The city mandarins had deserted; none of the ordinarily

---

[38] *Chinese Repository*, X. Nov. 1841, p. 629.
[39] For accounts of the operations see, *Nemesis*, pp. 256–60; Parker to Auckland, *Modeste*, 11 Oct. 1841, in Phillimore, ii. 452–8; and John F. Davis, *China during the War and since the Peace*, (2 Vols., London, 1852), i. 199–200.
[40] Davis, op. cit., i. 207–8.

staunch Tartar troops were to be seen, and the few inhabitants who remained, shut themselves in their houses, marking their doors with the Chinese characters—'Submissive People'.[41] As Parker wrote to Lord Auckland on 14 October, they evinced 'much less apprehension at the presence of the English than was exhibited either at Amoy or Chusan'.[42] The air was clear but cold, for it was the end of autumn. Here was an accessible, and seemingly not inhospitable, asylum for British troops during the coming winter, when icy Siberian winds would block the further progress of the expedition northward.

Apparently Sir Henry Pottinger, who accompanied the expedition throughout the operations, had been prepared for a stiff fight. Indeed, he had looked forward, so he confessed, to sacking Ningpo not only as an act of retribution, but as an example and warning to other places. Happily for the future peace of mind of the new Foreign Secretary, Lord Aberdeen, who would have been deeply shocked by any suggestion of Cromwellian terrorism, more humane principles prevailed. A certain amount of government property was confiscated, including about £90,000 in sycee silver and quantities of silk goods, but very little was destroyed.[43]

By mid-December, the garrison at Ningpo had settled down a little nervously in the midst of an unfriendly and uncowed country population, to face temperatures which might well have reminded a Canadian of his native land. While the summers are exceedingly hot, some winter days can be bitterly cold. In July the thermometer may reach 90° or higher, and a few months later drop to 10°F. above zero, or even lower when the north winds developed 'a Siberian edge'. Braced by the cold, it was by no means a boring season for the garrisons at Ningpo and Chusan. Especially during the Christmas season, officers amused themselves with shooting-parties in the neighbouring snow-covered hills, where wild geese, duck, woodcock, snipe, quail, partridge, and pheasant abounded. Nowhere, except perhaps in India,

[41] *Chinese Repository* x. Nov. 1841, p. 630.
[42] Phillimore, ii. 459.
[43] See Memorandum submitted at a conference with Admiral Parker and General Gough, 14 Oct. 1841, L/P & S/9/10 (I.O.A.).

were such excursions conducted with so much luxury and in so much comfort.

Sometimes, as at Chusan where there was less to fear from troublesome guerrillas, a houseboat was fitted up with sleeping apartment and sitting-room, the latter often furnished with rich Chinese draperies, armchairs, tables, stove, and various other amenities reminiscent of a good London club. A second boat, accommodating servants and kitchen apparatus, followed astern, except at meal times when it was drawn alongside, and the innumerable hot dishes passed through a hatch into the dining-room. The meal finished, the hatch was closed, and the tender dropped back, leaving the gentlemen to enjoy their cigars and brandy.

But the true aristocrat of sport, who scorned the soft life of the river-boat, trudged to the shooting ground before daybreak, accompanied by bearers carrying a complete breakfast service, several changes of clothing, blankets, towels, sponges, bath salts, and writing materials and books. When the game-bag was filled, he headed for the pre-arranged rendezvous, possibly a small temple, in which his servants had prepared fires, boiling pots of water, and a bath, which had been carefully transported on the shoulders of willing bearers, along with embroidered curtains to ensure privacy. After the bath came a breakfast of game and curry, interrupted not infrequently by the courtesy visits of aged priests or local mandarins.[44]

Equally diverting, particularly for the garrison at Ningpo, were the armed excursions to spy out the surrounding land, and possibly uncover the lairs of enemy troops, or the haunts of combustible fire-boats and rafts. Perhaps the most valuable discovery was a stud of Ningpo ponies, used exclusively for saddle, and ridden only by the more exalted mandarins. More than forty of these ponies were commandeered to pull artillery, and, of equal importance in the eyes of young subalterns, to provide mounts for staff messenger work and, above all, for recreation.

Pottinger's 'scorched earth' proposal, if such it can be called, reflects the extent to which Elliot's policy of conciliation had

[44] Tyrone Power, op. cit., pp. 250–2.

been deliberately reversed. Hitherto hostilities, as has been noted, were carried out on a 'stop, go, stop' basis—a phase of destructive advance followed by an interval for negotiation. Such a policy of stick and carrot had made no impression whatsoever on Peking, whose ministers assumed, but for the wrong reasons, that the enemy would sooner or later be consumed by Celestial fire or fever. The Chinese policy of hanging on, playing for time, negotiating and re-negotiating, was obviously a sensible approach to an enemy in possession of overwhelming armaments, but it was sheer folly—the folly of ignorance or vanity—to have sacrificed so many thousands of men and so much property once the vast superiority of the 'barbarians' had been recognized. Commissioner Lin was wiser than he knew when he tactlessly advised his Emperor to cease using physical force to expel the enemy; what expense did not ruin, disease would destroy.[45] As has been remarked, British casualties on the battlefield had been negligible by European standards, but dysentry and malaria ('capricious in its action and unsearchable in its nature') came close at times to annihilating regiments and ships' companies. The Emperor, not Pottinger, should have pursued the 'scorched earth' policy. China was vast enough to swallow up, not only the mere 2,000 who sailed for Chusan and Ningpo, but the 10,000 who would be shortly on their way from Britain and India. As with the Napoleonic legions who marched to Moscow, the Empire of China might well have become their burial ground.

While the Court in Peking seemed to have been taught little of the truth, and learned less, Pottinger, representing the new school of disillusioned diplomats, appreciated the absurdity of calling the conflict *a war with Chinese governments*. Two years of futile campaigning had convinced him (as Palmerston had been somewhat earlier convinced) that the Cantonese were at least as obstinate and truculent as their rulers, and that direct official communication with Peking was the only solution to the problem of a lasting settlement. Assuming it was true that the Emperor was living in a 'fool's paradise', cut off from reality by the misrepresentations of his regional administrators, he was still the ruler of the Chinese Empire. The subjugation of Canton would never suffice to bring Peking to

[45] *Chinese Repository* x. Nov. 1841, p. 633.

the conference table; Peking, not Canton, could decide the future of Anglo-Chinese relations.

The second Melbourne government had lasted, with the inevitable shiftings of personnel, from April 1835 to the summer of 1841. It was succeeded in September by the second Peel government, which continued in office until the crisis over the Corn Laws in 1846 split the party, paving the way for the return of the Whigs under Lord John Russell. Lord Aberdeen succeeded Palmerston as Foreign Secretary, and the ninth Earl of Haddington followed Minto at the Admiralty. Counting on an easy and fruitful relationship with the commander-in-chief of the China station, the Earl reminded Parker that he could claim a family connection with him through his marriage to Lord Macclesfield's daughter.[46] No doubt, so indirect a personal connection was a help when it was a matter of putting bitter thoughts to official paper, but even in his subsequent dispute with Sir Henry Pottinger, Parker needed no privileged support at the Admiralty.

Meanwhile, Lord Auckland was preparing to leave Calcutta, 'not sorry to be about to return to England'. He had not forgotten his promise to the Admiral, and had already made arrangements for the delivery of more steamers—'about thirteen at the beginning, and fifteen at the end of the season', provided, of course, that all remained quiet in the Persian Gulf and 'towards the Red Sea'. But in a private letter to Lord Ellenborough, his appointed successor, he stressed the folly of spreading limited British forces in China too thin. Lines of communication, in his opinion, had been over-extended. Instead of concentrating in the Canton River area, and preparing assiduously for the campaign in 1842, the Gough-Parker expedition had unwisely occupied itself in northern escapades.[47] However, if the next year's operations were begun 'at the opening of the favourable season, and if the naval and military forces allotted to the expedition shall have been well collected', he trusted that the effect would be decisive. 'I will

---

[46] Sir Thomas Parker, first Earl of Macclesfield, had been appointed Lord Chief Justice of England in 1710, and had filled the office of Lord Chancellor for six years under George I.

[47] 20 Dec. 1841, Auckland Papers, China Book, Vol. III, Add. MS. 37717.

not speculate', he told Admiral Parker, 'upon what will be the course of your proceedings in another year, for the plan of your campaign will be prepared in England. . . .'[48]

In view of the varied political and diplomatic issues at stake, general strategy had, obviously, to be decided in Whitehall. What happened in Afghanistan or in the Mediterranean could have a very direct bearing on the use of soldiers and sailors in far eastern areas. None the less, the formal responsibility for directing the war in China remained with the Governor-General of India. He was essentially a chief of staff for joint military and naval affairs, but he was also in the slightly embarrassing position of being supreme middle man, too far away from Whitehall to shape policy, too far away from the field of action to direct events. He could organize the expeditions—get the transports, the steamers, the troops, stores and fuel, and see that the fleet left Singapore in time to find the best weather in the China seas; but after that, intervention in regard to the use of the forces required courage, great self-confidence, and possibly the quality of clairvoyance. Once broad policy had been settled in London, only an incredibly self-assured and articulate Governor-General (especially with Palmerston at the helm) was likely to oppose ministerial decisions; and once the commander-in-chief on the station had received his instructions regarding the objectives settled by Whitehall, only in abnormally altered circumstances was it likely that he could demand radical changes in those instructions, such as would affect the conduct of operations. Clearly, any drastic modification could only be the prerogative of the commander-in-chief, who in an emergency was entitled, indeed, might be impelled, to act on his own account without waiting for instructions from London or India.[49]

With Palmerston in charge of foreign affairs, a man of Ellenborough's stamp might have found it difficult to throw his weight about; with Lord Aberdeen, an energetic role was possible without too much interference. Moreover, a situation greatly favouring Ellenborough's influence in policy-making developed almost overnight following his appointment as President of the Board of Control. In September, responsibil-

---

[48] Auckland to Parker, Calcutta, 6 Dec. 1841; Phillimore, ii, 465–7.
[49] See Admiralty to Parker, 4 and 14 Nov. 1841, Adm. 2/1599.

ity for the conduct of the war in China was transferred from the Foreign Secretary to the Secretary for War and Colonies. The transfer was a consequence of the steadily accumulating pressures on one ministry; it betokened in no way the imminent acquisition of Hong Kong as a colony. Europe and the Middle East alone provided sufficiently complex problems of power-balancing to absorb the energies of any but the toughest and most resilient diplomatic conjurer.

The untried Lord Stanley had no hesitation in confessing his ignorance of far eastern affairs, and it seemed highly likely that the over-all strategy advocated by Ellenborough at the India Office would be implemented by Ellenborough, the Governor-General of India.[50] Inevitably the new Colonial Secretary would be subject to the persuasive arguments of his erstwhile colleague, a specialist in eastern affairs—and the more so, if the Governor-General had the backing of the legendary Duke of Wellington.

Admiral Parker learned of the realignments of Whitehall jurisdictions late in November, and, as was customary, he was instructed to act on such general operational orders as the Governor-General should enjoin. Fortunately, the Secretary for War and Colonies had the good sense to inform the Admiralty that, since the movement of troops and supplies depended so much on capricious tides and weather, it was 'absolutely necessary' that the final responsibility for directing particular operations 'should be left to the Admiral or Officer Commanding the Naval Forces'.[51]

Seventeen years earlier, engaged in what was regarded as a local operation on the Rangoon River with the assistance of the Royal Navy, the Indian government had failed to ponder the hazards inseparable from a one-sided partnership. During the Burma campaign of 1824–6, a single naval division, including transports, had been placed under the orders of the army. Not until the end of the campaign did the Admiralty comprehend the importance of small ships of war, and especially the steamship, in river fighting, and the British government

---

[50] On his appointment in October 1841, he was replaced at the Board of Control by Lord Fitzgerald who held office until May 1843, when he was succeeded by the Earl of Ripon.

[51] Stanley to Canning, 4 Nov. 1841, F.O. 17/52.

recognize the folly of leaving to the Governor-General of India untrammelled command of an expedition in which ships of the Royal Navy served.[52] In 1841, the Governor-General still retained his overall command, but in practice only as adviser and contributor to strategy-making. Like the first Burma war, the first China war may have been properly regarded as a side-show; none the less, it was essentially a war directed in the interests of Great Britain as well as India, and, moreover, because of its amphibious nature—because, as the Duke of Wellington put it, the army was dependent on the Royal Navy at all times—it was only sensible that the final responsibility during the course of hostilities should rest with the Admiral.[53]

This policy of erosion—of gradually eliminating the middle man—was strongly supported by the Duke of Wellington, a Cabinet member without portfolio in Peel's government, an Olympian figure whose immense prestige as a soldier continued to give him political power and influence both in and behind the scenes. Indeed, he was made commander-in-chief of the British army in 1842 at the considerable age of 73. Although increasingly deaf, he remained in reasonably good health, despite a series of attacks over the previous few years, which may have been minor strokes or epilepsy.[54] Some of the old agility was missing, but he was still capable of concentrating on, and analysing, strategical problems, and ordering his conclusions in clear and simple English for the benefit of his ministerial colleagues. It is possible, however, to suspect a normal human bias against Palmerston and the Whigs, particularly evident when he opposed the plans of the previous government.

Wellington's memorandum on 'Joint Commands', dated 16 October, had obviously been read by his friend, Lord Ellen-

[52] See Graham, *Great Britain in the Indian Ocean . . .,* pp. 353–5.

[53] As Lord Auckland remarked in a minute of April 1840: 'It [the expedition to China] is a naval operation, undertaken by the Crown, to which some assistance in troops has been required, and the chief command will be executed by the Admiral, or officer holding his authority, on his own responsibility. . . .' He acknowledged, however, the right of the army commander to deal with 'what relates exclusively to the land forces'. See Phillimore, ii. 443, 481.

[54] My colleague, Professor Neville Thompson of the University of Western Ontario, tells me that the Duke suffered a major attack in 1839 which doubtless affected his well-being and judgement over the last ten years of his life. According to the doctor who attended him, epilepsy was the ultimate cause of death.

borough, then President of the Board of Control. The Duke accepted the fact of supreme civilian control; in short, the general direction of operations in the China seas should continue to rest with the Governor-General. But in the planning and conduct of particular amphibious operations, the judgements of the naval commander-in-chief had to be paramount. An intelligent admiral would naturally communicate freely with his opposite number in the army, and have regard for his views. But the Duke emphasized: 'If they should differ in opinion, each is to put his opinion in writing, and that of the admiral is to be the rule of conduct.' It was more than a matter of genteel service co-operation; moving from port to port on the long coast of China, the army's dependence on secure communication for military stores, provisions, and ammunition enforced, as the Duke said, even a 'union with the fleet'.[55]

Auckland's successor, Lord Ellenborough, was bound, as has been noted, to feel more at home in the Orient than the Secretary for War and Colonies. From 1828 to 1830 he had been a member of the Board of Control, and until his appointment as Governor-General of India on 20 October, he had been for more than a month its President. A stiff and unbending Tory, Ellenborough's rather chilly aloofness in relations with the public inevitably suggested conceit. He never compromised with his convictions. Scorning the politician's arts, he showed little but contempt for the clamours of the crowd, whether in or outside Parliament, a form of self-indulgence which helps to explain his recall in 1844. Often brash, sometimes intemperate, and all too frequently lacking in discretion, he possessed administrative gifts of a very high order.[56] It was not a little owing to his energy and skill that the tide of disaster was halted following the destruction of a British army at Kabul, and the morale of the Indian army gradually restored. In the opinion of his biographer, Ellen-

---

[55] Memorandum on Joint Commands, Walmer Castle, 16 Oct. 1841, Colchester, *Ellenborough*, App., pp. 454–6.

[56] In making the appointment, the Prime Minister took account of 'his knowledge of Indian affairs, his industry & general ability', and hence regarded him as 'preferable to Lord Wharncliffe. . . .' The only drawback appeared to be 'a tendency to precipitation & over-activity. . . .' Peel to Wellington, 6 Oct. 1841, Wellington Papers.

borough's Governor-Generalship found him 'at his best'.[57]

In one of his last letters before leaving India, Lord Auckland had commented with scarcely muffled astringency on Palmerston's instructions to Sir Henry Pottinger, and begged for an early and definite expression of the government's intentions in regard to 'the precise ends to which future operations against China are to be directed'. Was it still the intention to reach Peking? As President of the Board of Control, Ellenborough had been naturally concerned with the projected expedition of 1842 which was being organized under the aegis of the government of India. But he had no wish to see any 'precise' plan of campaign given Cabinet approval until more information had been received on the course of operations, presumably still in progress. He had, however, no hesitation in rejecting the fundamental Palmerston objective: ' . . . in no case will it be proposed that any operation should be directed against Peking—the danger of any such operation being of too grave a character to justify the attempt. . . .'[58] In Ellenborough's view, the cutting of the Grand Canal where it crossed the Yangtse would produce results equally decisive without incurring the risks inherent in an assault up the Peiho. Such an operation would disrupt the whole internal communications of the Empire. Admittedly, the occupation of Tientsin would provide more stringent leverage, but even if successful, the chances of remaining there until peace was negotiated were remote. (Lord Macartney's embassy had seen 60,000 warriors assembled in the neighbourhood of Peking!) The navy could do little to help. The ships could not arrive before June, and would be ice-bound by late autumn. Moreover, the river route—almost 80 miles from the sea to Tientsin—was winding and, in the summer season, shallow. The distance by land was little over 40 miles, but pack animals were non-existent in that part of the country, and supplies that could not be sent by water would have to be carried by bearers on foot. In addition, such a campaign would have to be conducted in the hottest and most unhealthy part of the year, when even the ranks of seamen afloat were decimated through illness.[59]

---

[57] A. H. Imlah, *Lord Ellenborough* (Cambridge, Mass., 1939), ix.

[58] To the Queen, 9 Oct. 1841, Colchester, *Ellenborough*, pp. 14–15.

[59] Memorandum from Ellenborough to the Duke of Wellington, on the proposed

It is not surprising that Ellenborough's strongly expressed views on the original Palmerston strategy bear a striking resemblance to those of his friend, the Duke, with whom he was in almost constant correspondence. It was absolutely impossible, according to Wellington, whose advice had been asked, 'that an army can be landed with a view to an operation upon the city of Peking itself, unless in daily communication with, and supported by the fleet'. British warships would be unable to enter any of the rivers by which the capital could be reached; whereas 'the whole fleet might anchor with safety' in the Yangtse river.[60] On the other hand, if the Palmerston proposal 'to carry the operations of the War nearer to Pekin' was not rejected, it would be advisable, Wellington told the Cabinet, to subject the whole coast from Canton northward to a 'belligerent blockade'; and, to make doubly sure that the sea communications were always intact, two or three strategic islands with good harbours might well be occupied. But the first objective had to be the blocking of the Yangtse at its junction with the Grand Imperial Canal. Only then should the commander-in-chief reconsider the possibility of reaching towards Peking—with the assistance of the steamers.[61] Peking was not, like Canton, at the mercy of the light-draught war vessel, but if the government were determined to negotiate in strength at the gates of Peking, success 'depended upon the strength of the means of navigation by steam'. The armed steamer had proved itself a useful asset on the Rangoon river; on the China coast it was indispensable.[62]

Meanwhile, within little over a week after accepting appointment as Governor-General, Ellenborough confessed his whole-hearted distaste for Palmerston's plans for 1842. He had already expressed his opposition to the Peiho–Tientsin operation and, again following in Auckland's footsteps, he preferred the actual possession of a few offshore islands to the acquisition of trading rights in four or five coastal towns. 'I

operations against China, undated (probably early October 1841), Wellington Papers, also printed in Colchester, op. cit., pp. 145–52.

[60] Memorandum by the Duke on the War with China, 30 Sept. 1841, Colchester, p. 141.

[61] Memorandum re Military Operations on the China Coast, 28 Oct. 1841, Aberdeen Papers, vol. xxii, Add. MS. 43060.

[62] Wellington to Ellenborough, 29 Dec. 1841, Wellington Papers.

have always thought that our Trade could thenceforward be best conducted from Insular Possessions held by us on the Coast of China, to which the Chinese might and would come to trade.'[63]

But Ellenborough's condemnation of Palmerston's China plans should not be judged in isolation. He was, first of all, Governor-General of India, and a few Chinese ports were small potatoes compared with the future of the Indian Empire. Auckland had underestimated the threat to the British raj on the Afghan and Burmese frontiers; not so Ellenborough, who had earlier been cautioned by the Duke against draining further European forces from Bengal and Bombay in order to strengthen General Gough's contingent.[64] And, when still a minister, he warned the Cabinet that he might have to recall ships and men from the China coast.[65] At the same time, Ellenborough realized that most of the China information available in London might be four to five months old, and in the circumstances he claimed the right to change his own mind. Once installed as Governor-General of India he would be in receipt of earlier intelligence which might justify even a radical change of course—intelligence which the Colonial Secretary would not see until nearly two months later![66]

For the moment, therefore, Ellenborough held a tactical advantage over his titular superior, the very able Lord Stanley, who, as he himself admitted, was much more at home with Irish than with Oriental affairs.[67] Yet the final decision had to be made by the responsible Secretary of State. Stanley would have preferred to wait and learn, but there was little time for contemplation. Plans for the next season's campaign had to be

[63] Memorandum on Modifications, in Instructions to Pottinger, 29 Oct. 1841, Ellenborough Papers, 30/12/26/3.

[64] Memorandum on the War with China, 30 Sept. 1841, Colchester, *Ellenborough* p. 139.

[65] Cabinet Minute, 29 Oct. 1841, Ellenborough Papers, doc. cit. Not until he reached Calcutta in February 1842, did Ellenborough learn from Wellington that Auckland, driven by events in Burma, had been forced to curb his generous impulses, and hold back two of the steam vessels which had been earmarked for service in the China Sea. Wellington to Ellenborough, 29 Dec. 1841, Colchester, *Ellenborough*, p. 199.

[66] Cabinet Minute, 29 Oct. 1841, Ellenborough Papers, doc. cit.

[67] He became fourteenth Earl of Derby in 1851, and was Prime Minister for a few months in 1852 and again in 1858–9.

settled by December at the latest, and it would be difficult, if not unwise, to reverse the machinery of war set in motion by his predecessor-in-charge, the Foreign Secretary. Contrary to Auckland's private admonition, he had no option but to carry forward Palmerston's plans, which meant, of course, carrying the war 'to the gates of Peking'. Yet Stanley hesitated to confirm Palmerston's last instructions to Pottinger until the government had received and digested reports on the results of autumn operations.[68] It might, after all, be sensible to wait on events, and learn.

Meanwhile, maps and charts, précis and abstracts, memoranda on Chinese life and customs, notes on water communications and weather, personal advice on future strategy from merchants, retired naval officers, and former East India Company officials, kept pouring into Whitehall. It was a period of nervous tension for those who must 'swot up' their geography and recent history, and speak 'their lines' with confidence. Although the political props and stage scenery remained the same, the cast, as has been noticed, had almost completely altered. With the resignation of Melbourne's second Cabinet, Aberdeen had relieved Palmerston at the Foreign Office; at the Admiralty, the Earl of Minto (another Elliot) had given way to the Earl of Haddington; Lord Stanley had been given a new role as Secretary of State for War and Colonies, and the illustrious Duke had been added as a Minister without portfolio. Across the seas, Auckland's viceregal part had been taken by the knowlegeable and flamboyant Lord Ellenborough; on the coast of China, Charles Elliot had been replaced by an actor of enormous vigour and decisive manner, Sir Henry Pottinger, while Admiral Parker had assumed command of a China squadron, which, for the past eight months, had been directed by the capable Commodore Bremer. These were the men who would determine whether the year 1842 would see a final settlement of the China question.

[68] Stanley to President, Board of Control, 31 Dec. 1841, L/P & S/9/7 (I.O.A.).

VIII

FROM SHANGHAI TO NANKING
1842

By the end of the year (1841), the British government were still ignorant of the previous summer's events. Had the expedition which set sail on 21 August managed to take Amoy and recapture Chusan? Had there been time to demonstrate British power at the mouth of the Yangtse, and possibly penetrate that river? For more than four months (an exceptional length of time considering the steam links on either side of the Suez isthmus) they were without means of judging what impression had been made on Peking as a result of the operations at Canton.[1] It could be assumed, however, that no matter how successful the amphibious attacks, such pinpricks would not be sufficiently decisive to bring hostilities to an end. British forces, wrote a correspondent of the *Chinese Repository*, should cease reposing after battle, amid the scattered, but unvanquished, multitudes of the enemy. 'Blow must succeed rapidly to blow, if final success is to be hoped for. It was by the windmills in active motion that the redoubtable Don Quixote was worsted: he might have come off scatheless . . . in the calm and idle rest of a breathless summer's day.'[2]

The fiery correspondent might well have been a spokesman for the Cabinet. Whatever the strategy, one simple political consideration was now accepted without question. Something like overwhelming power was necessary if the Court in Pek-

[1] On 31 December 1841, Stanley informed Lord Fitzgerald, the President of the Board of Control, that the latest intelligence in the possession of the Cabinet did not extend beyond 22 August, 'at which period the expedition had just sailed to the Northward', and because of the lateness of the season 'its operations were necessarily liable to great uncertainty'. The government had no news of the intended attack on Amoy, or of any activity on the Yangtse. They assumed Chusan Island had been reoccupied, but they had 'no means of judging what impression may have been made upon the authorities of China by the manifestation of the power of the British Arms at Canton, and by subsequent operations'. Secret Dispatches from Secretary of State, Foreign Dept., Consultation No. 815, 4 Jan. 1842 (N.A.I.).

[2] Art. IV, xi. May 1842, p. 293.

ing were to be suitably impressed, and, if necessary, beaten into submission on the field. In other words, more ships and far more troops should be made available so that 'the war with China could be conducted on an enlarged scale'.[3]

In a New Year's message to Lord Fitzgerald, Ellenborough's successor at the Board of Control, Lord Stanley, explained that the projected campaign involved no pursuit of territorial ambitions. Britain wanted no more than satisfaction for injuries and insults received, and, at the earliest opportunity, the establishment of friendly and secure commercial relations. Such objectives, the Cabinet assumed, could be obtained by striking at the heart of China, thus enabling the occupying force 'to control the internal commerce of the Chinese Empire, and thus render the moral pressure upon the Court of Pekin irresistible'. Hence, the proposed ascent of the Yangtse 'to take and retain possession of the Island [Kinshan] which lies at the intersection of that River with the Grand Canal of China' was to be the principal campaign effort of 1842.[4]

For this purpose, some 10,000 men were to be made available—a total which allowed for garrisons in Hong Kong, Kulangsu, and Chusan. Of these, five regiments (approximately 4,000 men) and a company of artillery would be British; the remainder Indian troops. Both in pay and provisions, the Sepoy was less expensive than the European soldier. As for the navy, three ships of the line would be available in all probability. Despite Lord Ellenborough's doubts, they offered the best means of destroying the forts and batteries.[5] In addition, the Admiralty hoped to send four or five frigates, some twenty sloops and brigs, and, most important of all, thirteen or fourteen steamers for use on the Yangtse.

The single, as compared with a two-pronged strategy, was based simply on the oft-stated assumption that Peking, with its near-barren hinterland, depended for its existence on the Grand Canal, and that this vital artery could easily be severed

[3] Ellenborough to the Queen, 2 Oct. 1841, Colchester, *Ellenborough*, pp. 11–12.

[4] Downing Street, 31 Dec. 1841, Secret Dispatches from Secretary of State, doc. cit.

[5] Ellenborough contended that unless 'some large American or French ships should appear there to dispute the blockade, battleships in the shape of 72's were not essential'. Memorandum on the Campaign of 1842, Colchester, *Ellenborough*, pp. 146–9. See also, Ellenborough to Herbert, 2 Oct. 1841, Ellenborough Papers 30/12/26/1.

by the navy. Starting from the city of Hangchow, the canal passed through some of the most fertile and densely populated regions of China, crossing in its course the Yangtse and the Yellow rivers, and continuing northward as far as the outskirts of Peking. The necessaries of life came from the southerly provinces, and if communications could be broken, Chinese trade and industry would, it was generally assumed, suffer heavily; discontents would multiply, and the impoverished Manchu capital would have to cry for mercy. Palmerston had never been opposed to this operation, but he seriously doubted whether such a blockade would be sufficient of itself to break what he regarded as the adamantine heart of Peking. In addition to blocking the Grand Canal, he wanted to see an advance up the Peiho in adequate force to threaten, and, if needs be, to take the capital, and thereby bring the Emperor and his Court to their knees.

Although he was anxious not to undo plans of campaign that had already been set in motion, Stanley was suspicious of Palmerston's two-pronged strategy, and particularly of his confident prediction that the navy could without undue risk land a substantial force at the entrance of the Peiho, and go on from there. In 1841, the government's knowledge of contours and climates in the north of China was, in Stanley's own language of understatement, 'very imperfect'. General features like mountains, plains, and the size and source of rivers had been fixed with fair accuracy, the consequence, no doubt, of the early work of the Jesuits. Indeed, as that astute critic of events, Captain Sherard Osborn once remarked, 'the old Jesuit map of China, compiled two centuries ago' was still the only guide.[6] It is true that hydrographic knowledge was negligible, and seasonal climatic conditions were based largely on hearsay, but parts of the east coast and areas adjoining the Peiho estuary in the Gulf of Pecheli had been surveyed in 1816 during the course of the Amherst mission,[7] and this work, though cursory, had made possible the expedition of 1840. Moreover,

---

[6] Captain Sherard Osborn, C.B., R.N., *The Past and Present of British Relations in China* (Edinburgh and London, 1860), p. 128.

[7] Surveyors included Captain Daniel Ross of H.E.I.C. *Discovery*, who had been working for the Company since 1806, Captain Sir Murray Maxwell of the *Alceste*, and Captain Basil Hall of the *Lyra*.

in the course of this fruitless foray into the Gulf, while the two Elliots wrestled with their slippery opponents, the Master of H.M.S. *Plyades*, George Nosworthy, and Captain Bourchier of the *Blonde*, had found time to check and comment on some of these earlier surveys.

This knowledge must have been available to the Admiralty by the middle of 1841, but there is no evidence that the Cabinet was enlightened in consequence, which suggests that either the Admiralty were dilatory in passing on the information, or that Whitehall and Calcutta were incredibly slow in digesting it. 'The weather is so dark,' wrote the Duke of Wellington to his friend Lord Ellenborough in January 1842, 'and the maps and plans of the country so imperfect, and the topography accounts of the country so scanty, that I cannot venture to do more from hence than to suggest for consideration this plan, in case it should be found that the adoption of the other will not attain our true object.'[8]

In the Duke's opinion—and his advice on strategical problems was always welcomed in Cabinet—the blockade of the Grand Canal off the island of Kinshan was the correct procedure; it would 'settle the business for us, particularly if no disaster occurs'. But if disaster did occur, if the blockade did not produce the expected result, and if a drive on Peking by way of Peiho still appeared sufficiently risky as to be impracticable, then the occupation of Hangchow should be seriously considered. The seizure of that city, at no great distance from the Yangtse, 'would be considered in China a most severe blow, and must have the effect of giving us peace if our position at Kinshan should not'. The Duke brushed off Palmerston's proposed 'march on Peking' as the recommendation of a civilian, obviously unaware of the difficulties of bringing men-of-war and transports over the bar into the Peiho: '. . . the Sea must be our magazine for Stores, Ammunition and Provisions . . . we must keep our Communications with the sea; go where we will; and draw from the sea what we may require'.[9]

Less than two weeks later, however, in the course of a conversation with the First Sea Lord, Admiral Sir George Cockburn, which he summarized for the benefit of Lord Stan-

---

[8] London, 19 Jan. 1842, Wellington Papers.   [9] Ibid.

ley, Wellington learned to his surprise that it quite possible to find safe anchorage for both warships and transports not far from the mouth of the Peiho. The navy had made rough but reliable surveys of the area. Likewise it appeared possible

to carry into and up the Peiho (that is to say, across the bar of that river and up the stream) that part of the fleet propelled by steam and the men-of-war of the fleet having the least draught of water; and that this part of the fleet, and the army on board, might take possession of Peiho River, keeping its communication with the large ships and transports anchored as above described.[10]

Trusting this latest testimony to be well-founded, Wellington abruptly changed his mind. The absolute minimum force should be used against Kinshan, and 'the whole of the disposable military force' sent to the Peiho. But he insisted—and the word *insist* was used—that the fleet should not be exposed at anchor, or even under weigh, to storm risks in unfavourable seasons. Secondly (and here he may have had Lord Cornwallis and Yorktown in mind), the army should not be permitted 'to act alone in the interior of the country unsupported as a military body by a sufficient military force of the fleet'. In brief, the army must maintain constant communication with 'the great body of the fleet'. Given the acceptance of this standard principle, the Duke was prepared to leave the conduct of operations in the hands of the two commanders-in-chief.

By 3 February Wellington's conversion to the Peiho plan seemed to be complete.

There can be no doubt [he wrote to Lord Stanley] that the line of attack by the Peiho is the preferable one, if with the principles on which we originally determined to act, or any reasonable modification of them such as is now proposed; and I do not doubt that that line would have been adopted in September instead of that by Yangtse, if we had then had the information of anchorage facilities, of ingress and egress from the Peiho, which we have at present. Indeed, I cannot tell how it happened that we had it not. It is unfortunate that we had not. I at least should have been spared a good deal of labour.[11]

[10] Memorandum, 1 Feb. 1842, encl. in Wellington to Ellenborough, 2 Feb. 1842, Wellington Papers.
[11] 3 Feb. 1842, Colchester, *Ellenborough*, p. 212.

Perhaps the Duke was reluctanct to confess his sudden volte-face to Ellenborough, for whom he had indeed laboured, providing him, as President of the Board of Control, with the professional judgements which may have influenced his rejection of the Peiho plan. Now, with convictions already cemented, the Governor-General of India, as supreme military commander, was preparing for an advance up the Yangtse into 'the heart of China', and Wellington was afraid to tell him that recent intelligence (which should have been available to him much earlier) had forced him to change his mind.[12] Despite his unqualified assertion to Stanley, 'There can be no doubt', did he have doubts which he was unwilling to expose to the Cabinet? Otherwise, why should he, when writing privately to Ellenborough on 2 February in regard to the revised scheme of operations, have concluded with the extraordinary caution-ary observation that the Peiho scheme was all right provided the anchorage was safe, and ingress and egress from the river assured. 'But I think that in order to effect this operation we are about to give up a practicability of success for a possible failure.'"[13]

Possibly because time was short, Wellington was leaving the final decision to Lord Ellenborough's discretion, but any such rationalization scarcely justifies what appears on the sur-face as a curious waffling, if not double-dealing. In any event, the revised instructions read by Peel and thence forwarded to the Governor-General and the commanders-in-chief, made no bones about the Cabinet's reliance on the emphatic judgement of Britain's greatest soldier. A draft was sent to the Duke with the humble expression of hope that the content would corres-pond to his personal views, by which, Lord Stanley added, 'I need not say, we are most anxious to be guided'.[14]

Assuming decent weather conditions, the first step, the blockade of the Yangtse and the cutting of the north–south

[12] It is difficult to believe that Ellenborough was not, at least on arrival in India, in full possession of the facts in regard to the prospects of landing a force on the Peiho. The survey work done in 1841 would normally have been reported to the Governor-General's office.

[13] Wellington to Ellenborough, 2 Feb. 1842, Wellington Papers. The incorrect printed version of the letter in Colchester, *Ellenborough*, reads 'probability of success for a probable failure' (p. 211).

[14] Stanley to Wellington, 3 Feb. 1842, Colchester, *Ellenborough*, p. 211.

canal system would not be difficult. With Chinkiang in British possession, Kinshan island, close by the entrance to the Grand Canal, could be garrisoned, and two or three small vessels left as guard-ships. Thence the expedition could return down river, proceeding with all available troops and ships to and across the Gulf of Pecheli, where light-draught steamers could ascend the winding Peiho to Tientsin, thus bringing 'British power' close to the walls of Peking. Between May and the end of August, the monsoon was at its most favourable; the outer anchorage, five or six miles from the estuary of the Peiho, was, according to recent evidence, safe in all winds and seasons, and there the big ships might rest, while the smaller craft, sloops and steamers and armed boats, ferried troops across the mud bar at high water.

The main problem would be that of maintaining close communication between the landing force and the ships outside the bar. The means for an easy and unobstructed retreat, as the Duke had emphasized, had to be secured in the improbable event of a reverse. This involved continuous and exclusive possession of the river, which, in turn, meant that the steamers would have to carry sufficient, and sufficiently heavy, guns not only to protect themselves, but also to clear the banks and cover the landings at such points as the army commander assigned. Provided Admiral Parker and General Gough gave their blessing, the ascent of the Peiho, Stanley informed the Admiralty in February, 'must be made the primary object of the Campaign, and the sufficiency of the force for that object secured before any other operation is contemplated.' If, on the other hand, the Admiral and the General were opposed, they should ascend the Yangtse in all strength, seize Kinshan with the suggestion of 'a permanent occupation', and thus 'seek to counter-balance by the imposing nature of the force . . . the comparative disadvantage resulting from the increased distance from the seat of government'.[15]

Since the Admiralty, in the persons of Sir George Cockburn and the Secretary, Sir John Barrow, had been responsible for the change of plan, Stanley's letter to the Admiralty was

[15] Downing Street, 4 Feb. 1841; Adm. 1/5523. Duplicate of same in Foreign Dept. Secret Despatch from Secretary of State, Consultation No. 821, 4 Feb 1841 (N.A.I.). A copy is also contained in L/P & S/9/5.

essentially a repetition of their arguments. But the task of informing, not to say convincing, the indomitable Governor-General was bound to be far more difficult and hazardous. 'You will observe,' wrote the Colonial Secretary disarmingly, 'that we leave a large discretion to Parker and Gough, but liable to be contracted by you, who are left, in point of fact, absolutely to control our proceedings.' In these circumstances, with final authority surrendered, Stanley could only plead, with the support of the Admiralty, that the Governor-General should weight carefully the latest information. The Yangtse project might fail in its purpose: '. . . there are seventy miles of it of which we know nothing, and it is *possible* that our whole force directed thither might meet with some unexpected obstruction, which would render nugatory the whole year's operations.' Moreover, even if successful, the occupation of Kinshan might not have the anticipated effect. The persistent and obstinate Chinese might well find means of turning the British position by constructing detours, leaving the British garrison with 'undisputed but unprofitable sovereignty over a rocky island'. On the whole, an assault up the Peiho offered the better opportunity of ending the war. Following a close inspection of Admiralty charts 'with the assistance of Captain Beaufort',[16] it was clear that a secure anchorage for the larger vessels was available 'much nearer the mouth of the Peiho than we had any idea that ships of any size could lie'. Further, not only the steamers, but light-draught sailing vessels like the 18-gun *Modeste* could cross the bar into the river, and accompany the army's advance upon Tientsin, where the headwaters of the Great Canal enter into the Peiho. . .'. In this manner, an effective blockade could be established close to the heart of the Chinese Empire. Finally, Stanley made what he must have hoped would be his most telling point. In company with Sir George Cockburn, he had, so he informed Ellenborough, called on the Duke of Wellington. 'The new point about the safe anchorage produced the greatest effect on the Duke, who at once said that he adopted Kinshan only as a *pis aller*, on the supposition that the Peiho was impracticable.'[17]

But Lord Ellenborough would have none of it. Indeed, the

[16] Hydrographer to the Royal Navy, 1829–55.
[17] St. James's Square, 3 Feb. 1842, Colchester, *Ellenborough*, pp. 214–17.

newly arrived but supremely self-confident Governor-General took immediate advantage of his authority as supreme commander, and without the qualifications and provisos customarily inserted by more cautious men far from the field of combat, came out flatly against the Peiho proposal. In a letter to Sir Hugh Gough describing the instruction of 4 February (which Gough had yet to receive), he wrote: 'I entertain so strong an opinion of the extreme danger of the proposed advance of the troops . . . by the Pei-ho River . . . I do not hesitate at once to direct your Excellency not to undertake that operation.'[18]

Ellenborough had sent Gough copies of Wellington's letter of 2 February, with the accompanying memorandum of the 1st, as well as Lord Stanley's letter to the Admiralty of 4 February, 'in order that he might have before him all the materials of which I was myself in possession'. 'I told him', he wrote to the Duke, 'that if he agreed with me upon that point [the danger of marching on Peking via the Peiho] & was in want of the aid of my authority I *directed* him not to move upon the Peiho.' And he added, 'I trust he will not.'[19]

Ellenborough was rightly concerned that any military force moving on or alongside the Peiho would, as a result of weakening links with the main naval force, be vulnerable (as the Duke's warning had implied) to potentially overwhelming Chinese land forces. During the hottest season of the year, they would be navigating in open boats a winding river, bestrewn with innumerable shoals, dependent for supplies on ships five or six miles from the point of landing, and nearly 90 miles from their objective, the terminus of navigation. In the event of repulse, the consequences for India would be incalculable. The impact on Indian opinion, particularly on the Indian army, of his predecessor's failure to hold Kabul, had not dwindled. Any great military disaster, any severe loss of men, in China might further alienate the native troops, and deal an even more damaging blow to British arms.[20] Already certain

[18] Ellenborough to Gough, 25 Mar. 1842, encl. in James Stephen to H. U. Addington (F.O.), 2 July 1842, F.O. 17/63.

[19] Ellenborough to Wellington, Calcutta, 6 Apr. 1842, Wellington Papers.

[20] To Gough, 25 Mar. 1842, contained in James Stephen to H. U. Addington (F.O.), 2 July 1842, F.O. 17/63.

Madras regiments showed a reluctance to embark for overseas service, and not entirely for religious reasons. A general unease seemed to be affecting the whole Indian army, and this was undoubtedly a reflection of the Afghan calamity.[21]

The stability of China, he advised the Duke, was also a consideration of importance when it came to deciding how best to terminate a war, 'if war it can be properly called which is carried on in the midst of the transactions of commerce'. And Ellenborough added: 'My only fear is that the pressure of our force will lead to the overthrow of the Government. I shall by the next ship caution the Commanders [Gough and Parker] against doing anything which can lead to Territorial acquisition on the mainland.'[22] India might have been occupied in 'a fit of absence of mind', but the continual accretions of unwanted territory seemed to follow with remarkable consistency the destruction of native governments. Four days after writing to Wellington, he ordered Admiral Parker in rather peremptory terms to abstain from supporting, for temporary benefits, any insurrection against the Emperor of China, and any measures that might indirectly lead to permanent territorial acquisitions on the mainland.[23]

Since appeals from Whitehall in regard to campaign strategy had no effect—the Governor-General refusing to budge —Lord Stanley acceded.as gracefully as he could under the circumstances to the dismissal of his revised proposals. Fortified by Wellington's original doubts, Ellenborough kept on reciting his fears about the safety of a British expeditionary

[21] Ellenborough to Wellington, Calcutta, 21 Mar. 1842, Wellington Papers. The Duke himself was concerned with the effect of the defeat on British power and influence 'throughout the whole Extent of Asia. . . . There is not a Moslem Heart from Peking to Constantinople, which will not vibrate when reflecting upon the fact that the European Ladies and other Females attached to the troops at Cabul, were made over to the tender mercies of the Moslem Chief, who had with his own hand murdered Sir William Macnaghten, the Representative of the British Govt. at the Court of Afghanistan.' Wellington to Ellenborough, 31 Mar. 1842, ibid.

Six months later, equally fearful of French intervention at a time of apparent British weakness, he warned Lord Fitzgerald (who had succeeded Ellenborough as President of the Board of Control in the previous year) that the Admiralty should be made to understand 'the necessity of keeping in strength our Naval force in the East, so as to provide for the Maritime Defence of the mouths of the Indus, as well as of other points. . . .' 11 Oct. 1842, ibid.

[22] Ellenborough to Wellington, 21 Mar. 1842, doc. cit.

[23] 25 Mar. 1842, L/P & S/9/3 (I.O.A.).

force moving far from its sea base up river to Peking. He told the Queen that he had 'strongly expressed his opinion to that effect in a letter to Sir Hugh Gough', and he felt it to be his duty 'to give the full support of his authority to Sir Hugh Gough should that officer coincide in the opinion so expressed'.[24]

Not until late in June did Ellenborough receive Wellington's second, and equally well-guarded letter of advice, hedged almost to the point of ambiguity. The instructions sent to Sir Hugh Gough by the Governor-General on 6 March were 'quite right', since they 'were founded upon what was settled previous to your leaving England, and remained settled up to the dispatch of the Overland Despatch of 4th Feby.' This revised instruction had been the consequence of the discovery of new facts in regard to invasion by way of the Peiho. Assuming, therefore, that Sir George Cockburn and the Admiralty had not been misinformed and had not misled Lord Stanley, and if the information in regard to the Peiho anchorage was still regarded as correct, it should not be difficult 'to alter these Instructions in conformity with those from England last mentioned. . . .'[25]

Whether Ellenborough would have been influenced by this curiously delayed and cautious letter may be doubted. In any event (as the Duke might well have known), the message came far too late to affect operations already in motion. The reluctance of Wellington to support the recommendations of the Admiralty in his correspondence with the Governor-General is as difficult to explain as is his apparent acceptance of the revised Peiho strategy contained in his letter to Stanley.

Whatever their inmost thoughts and reactions to the Ellenborough strategy, both Gough and Parker remained dutifully silent. On the main issue of strategy, their own discretionary power had been negated by the Governor-General's superior discretionary power, although it seems likely that the Admiral was fully in agreement with Ellenborough's decision.[26] But

---

[24] April 1842, Colchester, *Ellenborough*, p. 26.

[25] Wellington to Ellenborough, 5 May 1842, Wellington Papers.

[26] A year later, Admiral Parker justified his acquiescence in a letter to Lord Auckland: 'I never entertained a doubt that a descent in the Peiho with our whole force must have produced the same decisive end that was effected in the Yang-tse-kiang, but looking to the disadvantage of a shoal bar at the entrance of the river, and the almost impracticability of landing a single soldier outside the Peiho; the distance from which

the Secretary for War and Colonies was suspicious of such obliging acquiescence. He was 'prepared to learn', he wrote to General Gough, not without irony,

that the strong opinion expressed by the Governor-General against the latter scheme has decided you and Sir William Parker against making the attempt, and whatever may be your determination, you may be assured that Her Majesty's Government will be prepared to put upon it the most favourable construction, and will be perfectly satisfied that it has been the result of a well-considered calculation of the means at your disposal, and the prospects of probable failure or of success upon knowledge of facts which was not at the Command of Her Majesty's Government.[27]

Meanwhile, the British garrison in Ningpo had been living a far from comfortable existence. 'Infernal machines' exploded in unexpected quarters, fire-rafts were used in an attempt to destroy shipping at Chinhai, and kidnapping was fast becoming a skilled art. A few shops remained open in the centre of the city, but a host of gangsters had imbedded themselves in the suburbs, issuing forth, as occasion suited, to burn, rob, and murder. In a sense, the garrison was under siege; the enemy's aim was to demoralize, and then strike. 'We are in an extraordinary position here,' General Gough wrote to Alexander Matheson in Macao, 'one which the home or Indian Gov't. never contemplated, & which may make it necessary to change the line of policy hitherto pursued. The Emperor, it would appear, is prepared to set his Kingdom on the issue. Never was gamester more certain of defeat.'[28]

It needed only a serious attack to demonstrate the risks of

our supplies were to be drawn; the strong works erected by the Chinese within the bar; the impossibility of getting any of the large ships to co-operate with the army; and the probable increase of sickness, I could not but prefer the Yang-tse-kiang as the scene of first operations, intending if the blockade of the Grand Canal, and occupation of their cities in that river had not equalled our hopes, to have sent a squadron immediately to the northward with steamers, to seal up the Peiho mouth, and establish ourselves (for the earliest movements in 1843) at the Miatan Islands. Everything, however, favoured the course we adopted, and I trust the advantages anticipated will be fully realized to the country.' Parker to Auckland, *Cornwallis*, Hong Kong, 9 Apr. 1843, Phillimore, ii. 546–7.

[27] 6 Sept. 1842 (No. 36), F.O. 17/63.
[28] Matheson to Jardine, 7 Feb. 1842, Private Letter Books (B9), vol. 2, Jan.–June 1842 (J.M.A.).

occupying large cities in the midst of hostile populations. Until British forces had shown themselves strong enough to advance on the Imperial capital itself, it was a mistake to isolate garrisons under what amounted to siege conditions. Moreover, as Pottinger argued in a letter to Gough:

Our occupation of them is, to lay aside other serious considerations, beyond all doubt the greatest evil we can inflict on their inhabitants, and unavoidably most opposed to kindness and humanity; for, both from the natural course of events inseparable from a state of warfare, and more especially from the peculiar constitution of the Government of the Chinese Empire, they must, like Ningpo, become 'a wilderness', and a focus for strife and anarchy, which no measures that we can adopt can possibly ward off.[29]

The garrison in Ningpo had been forewarned that an attack was imminent, but no definite intelligence in regard to the day or hour had been received. This warning was not ignored, but there was a lack of alertness. Certainly no plans had been made for the sudden onrush of several thousand Chinese troops, many of them in civilian dress, who climbed over the walls and by daybreak on 10 March had penetrated to the very centre of the city.[30] The signal for the general attack was to have been the lighting of fire-rafts shortly before they made contact with the English shipping on the river. But, as happened at Canton, the Chinese commandos' nerves gave way as they approached within range of the warships' guns; and the rafts were ignited nearly three miles away from the targets. In consequence, ships' boats were able to tow them ashore long before they reached the anchorage.[31]

Once the garrison recovered from the initial shock of finding the enemy within the gates, field guns were rapidly produced, and these opened fire with grape and canister at less than a hundred yards on the undisciplined mass that spewed from narrow streets into the market-place. It was all over in

[29] 12 Apr. 1842, quoted Phillimore, ii. 471.

[30] Chinese accounts gave the number of attackers as less than 3,000; British guesses ranged from over 5,000 to 15,000.

[31] It had apparently been proposed that inflammatory fire-crackers should be tied to the backs of a number of monkeys, who would at the right moment be tossed on board English vessels. According to a Chinese source, 19 monkeys were actually bought for this purpose, but since no one volunteered to carry out the operation, the plan was never put into effect. Waley, *The Opium War . . .*, pp. 169–72.

minutes, and the survivors who managed to find their way over the walls were pursued far into the countryside.[32] Five days later, the steamers, *Nemesis*, *Phlegethon*, and *Queen*, carried a raiding force of 1,200 troops, seamen, and marines, sixteen miles up river. A march of five miles brought them to a village, called by the British, Sykee, where an entrenched camp, defended by probably 8,000 Chinese, was demolished, with a loss of six killed and 37 wounded.

But such successes did little to reduce the precarious position of a British garrison isolated in an alien and hostile land; nor were siege conditions likely to impress Peking with 'the terror of the invader'. In the end, it was decided to evacuate the garrison and add their numbers to the expeditionary force already assembling at Chinhai. On 7 May the troops embarked in three steamers, with bands playing and colours flying, to join the fleet at the Chinhai anchorage. The withdrawal was a simple and sensible retreat, heralding the start of a new campaign; but, as interpreted for the benefit of Peking, it was an ignominious defeat. The official report to the Emperor contained the news of another great victory.

With the arrival of Admiral Parker in the *Cornwallis* (74), royal salutes were fired in belated honour of the Prince of Wales,[33] to which (unable to use their arms on shipboard) the army responded with successive cheers. During this time, reinforcements of infantry and artillery from India had been gathering at the anchorage, along with the necessary horses for the guns. With them came several Company steamers,[34] all well armed, and some of them peculiarly adapted for river navigation.[35] 'What a power is England!' wrote a field officer on board one of the transports. 'Here in this distant quarter of the globe, a few thousands of her sons—sailors and soldiers—are inspiring terror in a great empire, and insuring future respect for their queen and her infant heir from 300 millions of souls. The English will henceforth be respected in China as elsewhere, and they will never again deem it neces-

---

[32] See report by Pottinger, 1 Apr. 1842, in *Chinese Repository*, xi. Apr. 1842, pp. 233–4; and *Nemesis*, pp. 287–93.

[33] Albert Edward, subsequently Edward VII, was born on 9 November 1841.

[34] *Vixen*, *Tenasserim*, *Hooghly*, *Auckland*, *Ariadne*, and the iron *Medusa*.

[35] *Nemesis*, p. 299.

sary to admit to degradation or ill treatment to obtain the highest commercial advantages.'[36]

The expedition now prepared to attack Chapu, north-west of Chinhai and about 50 miles distant by sea, an operation that had been delayed owing to doubts about the navigability of the Hangchow estuary and river. However, reconnaissance in January by the surveyors, Collinson and Kellett, had shown Chapu to be readily accessible, and easily reduceable. From the estuary onwards, not only a broad river, four miles wide at high water, but a good causeway, ran fairly directly to Hangchow, some 50 miles away.[37] Unfortunately, later reports emphasized the risks from unusually heavy and rapid tides. It was possible to ascend the river with favouring tide, but against a furious ebb even steamers would have difficulty in making headway. Moreover, neither paddle-wheeler nor sailing vessel could, like the Chinese junk, lie serenely on the mud until refloated many hours later.[38] In addition, the harbour, although well protected against the north-east monsoon, was less than 400 yards across, and scarcely likely to contain comfortably the entire squadron. More space was available in the bay, a mile and a half to the north of the town, but with considerably less shelter. Exposed to all the gales that blew, any ship having to slip anchors during a hurricane would have to run for the western islands of the Chusan archipelago.[39]

As it happened, the agile steamers solved the problem on 17 May by quickly and effortlessly shuttling the troops ashore within musket-shot of the town. Like so many Chinese towns, Chapu was enclosed by ancient walls about three miles in circumference, and these in turn were encircled by a shallow canal or ditch. But the combination was scarcely defensible, since the ramparts of the north-east angle were closely overlooked by unguarded hills, whence guns, once they had been dragged to the top, could open fire at 500 yards. The town itself was shaped in the form of a square, about a fourth of the space being occupied by the Tartar garrison, numbering, with

[36] 'A Field Officer', *The Last Year in China* ... (London, 1843), Letter XXII, p. 157.
[37] *Nemesis*, pp. 283–4.
[38] Parker to Pottinger, in Pottinger to Aberdeen, 22 Mar. 1842 (No. 11), F.O. 17/56.
[39] Ouchterlony, op. cit., p. 284.

families, between seven and eight thousand.[40] As in other fortified towns or cities, they lived apart from the Chinese in walled enclaves usually called 'Tartar Cities'.

The short and bloody encounter at Chapu saw the first meeting of British troops with the soldiers of the Manchu; and for the former it was a traumatic experience. The dreadful, in some respects heroic, story of 'No-Surrender' has been told a hundred times. Whether it was the pride of the erstwhile conquerors, or fear of the foreign barbarian invader, or a combination of the two, suffice it to say both naval and army sources testify to the horror of the average British serviceman before the holocaust of self-destruction: '. . . the women destroying their children, drowning them in wells, and throwing themselves in afterwards; the husbands hanging and poisoning their wives, and deliberately cutting their own throats . . .'[41]

Chapu fell on the 18th, and that night, still shaken by the ghastly immolations, a British officer made his bed 'on the high altar of a temple, before a fierce-looking god, whom the Hindoo followers had disencumbered of his silken attire. He looked very terrible by moonlight!' Some 1,500 dead were buried after the battle, of which more than half were Tartar soldiers. British losses were 9 killed and 54 wounded.

From Chapu the expedition, on 28 May, again proceeded northward to the mouth of the Yangtse, finally anchoring on 13 June off Woosung, less than a 100 miles away. The town of Woosung lies on the south bank of the Yangtse, opposite the large island of Tsung-ming which divides the estuary (about 40 miles in breadth) into two channels. Over the years the changing contours of Tsung-ming reveal the influence of perpetual alluvial deposits. Bordering the town, the Whangpu River, flowing north-eastward, joins the Yangtse some 12 miles from Shanghai. According to reports reaching the flagship, a branch of the Whangpu provided another vital channel

[40] The British called them 'Tartar garrisons', the term *Tartar* being frequently used by foreigners as a general name for the non-Chinese tribes. The regional garrisons usually contained Chinese as well as Mongol and Manchu subdivisions.

[41] The assault and its consequences are vividly described in *Nemesis*, pp. 308–17.

of commerce through the province of Kiangsu, passing the manufacturing town of Soochow, and subsequently linking with the Grand Canal.

Woosung was well defended by strong batteries at the river entrance, but elsewhere the fortifications had not been built with the same skill and thoroughness as at Amoy, Chusan, or Chinhai. Mud ramparts, topping the sea-wall chiefly as protection against inundations, flanked every winding turn of the channel, which was scarcely more than 300 yards wide. Stone gun-emplacements extended at intervals for a good three miles along the western bank, as far as the village of Paoshan. Opposite, on the eastern bank, more elaborate works, especially near the river's mouth, were defended by the pick of the Tartar army. On the morning of 16 June, both tide and weather being favourable, the squadron got under way. The *Cornwallis* and *Blonde* being the heaviest ships took up positions just below the village of Woosung, opposite the batteries. The lighter war vessels—*Modeste*, *Columbine*, and *Clio* —proceeded up river to attack the village and the battery at the mouth of the creek above it, as well as the battery on the opposite or east side of the river. The channel had been buoyed off during the previous night, and ships had little difficulty in reaching their appointed stations under the guidance of the five attending steamers. Rather than acting in advance as tow for the lighter craft and troop transports, the steamer was lashed alongside, an arrangement so admirably suited to the twists and turns of the river passage that it was later employed in similar operations. It was the first naval action in which ships-of-war were *all* brought into position by the steamer.

That Chinese gunnery had improved was soon evident. Long before the *Blonde* and *Cornwallis* had anchored, some 250 guns opened fire. The *Blonde* received at least 14 shots in her hull before effective broadsides silenced the Chinese batteries. Up river, the *Nemesis*, towing the *Modeste*, suffered repeated hits as she entered the creek above the village. The *Columbine* and *Clio* followed, in company of steamers *Phlegethon* and *Pluto*. In the course of the operation, 14 war junks were captured, as well as 5 recently built wheel-boats (each with two wooden paddles on either side). The latter carried newly-cast brass guns and large gingalls, and were commanded by mandarins of high rank, a testimony to the importance the Chinese attached to their new invention.

Clearly the Chinese did not anticipate so quick and devastating a defeat, and certainly the end would have been far less immediate had they constructed effective flanking defences. As it happened, once a man-of-war took position beyond the arc of the enemy's fixed guns, she was immune from heavy fire.[42] Indeed, the battle was over before the troops and marines got ashore; the ramparts were occupied without incident. Chinese losses in the course of this brief encounter were probably less than 200 killed and wounded; British casualties were 27. With the exception of one Bombay artillery man, all were seamen or marines.[43] The way was now open to Shanghai by land and sea.

Since no serious resistance was expected, only one Madras regiment and detachments of artillery, sappers, and miners were grouped for this attack. Gough formed the force in two divisions, one to march on Shanghai by the left bank; the other to make the journey aboard steamer. The marching column encountered no obstacles. Inhabitants lined the roads through the villages to gaze wide-eyed at the novel sight of heavy field-pieces, drawn by horses of a size and strength regarded as fabulous in provinces where nothing larger than the stunted Tartar pony was ever seen. 'We saw crowds of peasantry in every direction,' wrote Captain Granville Loch, R.N., 'they climbed the trees and little knolls to obtain a good view of us from a distance; but when a long survey convinced them that we were not "frantically" disposed, they approached with confidence. Our handful of men would not have been a mouthful apiece to the multitudes around us.'[44]

Once again, there was curiosity rather than fear or hostility. The column that trudged along the flattened tops of earthen

[42] According to Morse, the British assault on the flank where most of the guns were fixed for a frontal attack was regarded by the Chinese as 'treacherously' unfair. H. B. Morse, *The International Relations of the Chinese Empire* (3 vols., Shanghai, 1910), i. 295.

[43] See Ouchterlony, pp. 294–8; *Nemesis*, pp. 325–30.

[44] Loch, *The Closing Events of the Campaign in China* . . ., p. 58. Captain Loch travelled to China in H.M.S. *Dido* early in 1842 as a guest of the ship's captain, the Hon. Henry Keppel, 'my old and esteemed friend', transferring in the Yangtse to Admiral Parker's flagship. He also acted as an extra aide to General Gough. The book was based on his journals.

dikes (which were the only roads) was scarcely two miles beyond the town when scaling ladders were resting on the shoulders of willing, or at least not resentful, natives. When the occasional deep ditch stopped the progress of the artillery, equally happy conscripts unyoked the horses, and manned the drag-ropes that pulled the guns across. The derisive laughter when one of their number chanced to slip and fall flat on his back, wrote Lieutenant Ouchterlony, sounded 'as careless and joyous, as if they were amusing themselves with their fellows of the village, instead of aiding in dragging against the city of their rulers those terrible engines from which . . . ruin and death to all they held most dear would be poured forth.'[45]

On the river route each of the four warships—the *North Star* (26), *Modeste* (18), *Clio* (16), and *Columbine* (16)—was towed by a steamer. Although the course was not an easy one, the detachment arrived unscathed within half a mile of Shanghai. Such good fortune was hardly deserved. Not infrequently the British flotilla offered as tempting a target as a covey of 'sitting ducks'. Just below the town, at a sharp, right-angled bend in the river, the Chinese had mounted 18 guns behind an earthen parapet. Reasonably skilful gunners could have raked the approaching vessels fore and aft, especially the steamers whose soldier-passengers were crowded on deck like sheep in a pen. As it happened, nearly all the shots missed, and then two well directed broadsides from the *North Star* and the *Modeste* scattered the defenders. On 19 June the troops were disembarked without opposition, the *Nemesis* landing the 55th directly on a small jetty without the need for boats, 'another instance of the great utility of flat-bottomed iron steamers'.[46]

Thus did the vanguard of Admiral Parker's fleet 'burst upon the Chinese quiet of [Shanghai's] existence'. Although supposedly ranking second to Canton in commercial importance, the town was a disappointment to Captain Loch who found the houses 'generally shabby and insignificant, built of wood, the upper stories projecting over the narrow streets'.[47] Young Sherard Osborn, a future Rear-Admiral, then a midshipman in charge of one of the boats, was equally depressed by the

---

[45] Ouchterlony, p. 301.
[46] *Nemesis*, p. 332.
[47] Loch, op. cit., p. 59.

squalid Chinese abodes rising from the midst of 'a low, unhealthy marsh'. Sixteen years later, he was to find that city 'Queen of Central China', with handsome houses and gardens, and busy quays 'as would put those who live on the banks of Father Thames to the blush!'[48]

By the time the steamers had arrived, the infantry, which had advanced overland without opposition, were already in possession without a shot being fired. News of the unexpected defeat at Woosung had obviously weakened morale in an ancient town which was not nearly so defensible. Although the ramparts, about four miles in circumference, were reasonably well built, they were not high, and at many points could have been escalated without great difficulty. The four gateways, contained in bastions which projected clear of the main rampart, had double entrances. Any frontal attack would obviously have been costly, but all of them could have been overrun by troops climbing the walls in the rear. Although Shanghai proved comparatively weak in gun-power as compared with Woosung, the invaders were interested to find 16 copper carronades, exact copies of a modern 18-pounder carronade.[49]

On the 21st Admiral Parker shifted his flag to the *Nemesis* and, accompanied by a survey party, set out with the other iron steamers *Phlegethon* and *Medusa* to reconnoitre the river, hoping to reach Soochow, of whose whereabouts no one was entirely certain. Some 45 miles above Shanghai, finding almost continual shoal water and no indications of a town or its approaches, the flotilla turned back.[50] It was subsequently discovered to the chagrin of Captain Hall that the smoke of the steamer had been clearly visible, a few miles away, from the walls of Soochow.

Meanwhile, towards the end of June, ships of the squadron

[48] Osborn, op. cit., pp. 13–14.

[49] This model of a ship's gun was exactly imitated, with the sight cast on the piece, and the vent pierced for a flint lock. The carriages were equally modern, four wooden trucks with iron axles. They were, Ouchterlony noted, 'the most serviceable engine of war that British seamen had yet found in the hands of the Chinese'. Ouchterlony, pp. 307–8.

[50] The *Medusa* which drew a foot to eighteen inches less water than the *Nemesis* or *Phlegethon* did manage to get eight or nine miles further, but was eventually stopped by shallow water. *Nemesis*, p. 338.

began to assemble at Woosung, making ready for the long
and, it was presumed, hazardous journey to the old capital of
the Chinese Empire, Nanking, some 170 miles away. Rising in
the Tangla mountains in north-east Tibet, the Yangtse flows
some 3,200 miles into the silt-laden estuary that gave access to
Woosung and Shanghai. Bending north and south in giant
coils, the river traverses the whole of central China from west
to east. Cutting through successive ranges of mountains, its
waters pour through formidable gorges which, during the
rainy season, compress the flow into surging rapids. Oxen-
like in patience and stamina, generations of boatmen had
fought the currents, towing the junks with long bamboo ropes
over or around projecting ledges and pinnacles, sometimes
150 feet above the river. Shortly above Ichang, the tumult
ceases as the mountains recede and the country begins to open.
From Wuhu, running roughly north-east to Nanking, the
river expands from one to five miles in width, with innumerable shoals, sandbanks, and islands. At Chinkiang, it eventually emerges from the hills, and thenceforward thrusts eastward, a central corridor through the broadening delta that
reaches the sea some 70 miles away.

A good deal of information on the Yangtse was available
to the squadron. In the 1830s the Woosung River as far as
Shanghai had been surveyed by a Captain Rees (who may well
be John Rees, one of Jardine's most experienced captains). In
August 1840, during the fitful Peiho negotiations, Captain
Drinkwater Bethune in the *Conway*, assisted by the *Algerine*
and *Kite*, had pressed some 60 miles up-river, sounding and
marking the more conspicuous banks and shoals. Their
rough-and-ready charts indicated a twisting, but comparatively safe, passage for frigates and even ships of the line. This
work was to be continued by Lieutenant Richard Collinson
who had arrived at Chusan late in 1840 with instructions from
the Admiralty to take charge of all surveying operations.[51] On
5 July Collinson, accompanied by Lieutenant Kellett, returned

---

[51] This appointment provoked the wrath of the skilled but temperamental Captain
Belcher, who had expected to be given the job in appreciation of his services on the
Canton River, the more so when he learned that his erstwhile assistant, Lieutenant
Henry Kellett (who had been with him for five years on the west coasts of Central and
North America), had been sent in 1841 to join Collinson.

to Woosung after an exacting trip that took them almost as far as Kinshan Island, [Golden Island] close to the entrance of the Grand Canal. Their reports confirmed Bethune's earlier intelligence. Close guidance would be necessary all the way; pilot boats would have to lead, sounding, marking, and buoying, but the 74s could get through.

At daylight on the 6th the fleet, consisting of 72 vessels, including transports, ten steamers, and two ships of the line, weighed anchor. It was not easy, wrote Captain Loch, 'to describe the feeling of exultation which more or less animated all at the prospect of entering as invaders into the heart of an immense empire. . . .'[52] Two French warships, the *Erigone* (44) and the *Favourite* (18), showed some anxiety to share the excitement. Their captains asked for the use of a towing-steamer so that they might accompany the fleet up the river, a request which was courteously refused on the grounds that every paddle-wheeler was required by the transports in view of the strength of adverse currents.[53]

Mile upon mile the land continued low and flat, although extremely fertile, with plenty of wood fuel for the ever active steamers. On the fifth day, ranges of hills took shape in the distance to the south-west, following as though by design the meandering line of the river. By 13 July, the speed of the current increased as the channel narrowed. Steep spits and shoals jutted from deepening water which sometimes shoaled in a ship's breadth from seven fathoms to a few feet. Two small steamers kept guard position about four points upon the bows of the flagship. A half-mile ahead, the *Modeste* led the way, signalling the soundings as reported by surveying boats in the van. Care was taken to maintain communication with the bases at Woosung and Chusan, as Wellington would have wished, but the line of supply (and of retreat) was never even threatened.

During the first few days, no resistance was encountered. Scantily protected by primitive emplacements, the small

[52] Loch, op. cit., p. 65. There are numerous accounts and observations on the expedition's progress. Perhaps the most useful is contained in *Nemesis*, pp. 321–72. A lively narrative is Captain Arthur Cunynghame's *The Opium War, Being Recollections of Service in China* (London, 1844), pp. 67–135.

[53] *Nemesis*, p. 340. Above Woosung, the main stream, five miles broad in places, is fed by countless creeks and canals; the leads showed depths of from 12 to 20 fathoms.

towns or villages on the river banks kept silence to avoid damage or destruction. Not until 15 July, when the fleet reached a point about 15 miles below Chinkiang, did any opposition show itself. At the base of a hill rising some 400 feet above the river, a small number of fixed guns and gingalls challenged the leading steamers, but a few 32-pounders soon routed the handful of defenders. Having spiked the guns and destroyed the fortifications, Captain Loch climbed the precipitous slope of the hill and, despite the extreme heat, managed to make the summit. Like the Breton seaman, Jacques Cartier, who, in 1534, gazed with some emotion on the vast, beckoning St. Lawrence River from the top of Montreal's mountain, so was the English captain moved by the prospect that opened before him.

Inland, towards the S.E., this detached cluster of hills broke into undulating country clothed with verdure, and fir plantations bordered small lakes confined in natural basins. Extending my view beyond, I saw the windings of the vast river we had ascended; our ships were still scattered over its broad surface, the sternmost divisions of the fleet coming up under all sail. To the other side I turned with yet greater interest; there the land in the foreground continued a low and swampy flat, leaving it difficult at a little distance to determine which of the several broad waters, winding in serpentine channels through the country, was the main branch. . . . Beyond this again, towards the west, the pagoda of Chin-kiang-foo was observable; it is built on a slight eminence eight or ten miles in advance, by the river's course, from where I stood. The sun had set some time; the mists rose from the marshes, until it became the only object in the distant view.[54]

Close on Chinkiang, the current doubled in force as the waters were suddenly squeezed between the left bank and the island of Seung-shan (Silver Island) which blocked half the width of the river. Only after several attempts did the lighter sailing ships make the passage. Whirlpools caught two of the

---

[54] Loch, pp. 74–5. Nearly 75 years after Cartier had broken the curtain that concealed Canada from the West, the founder of Quebec, Samuel de Champlain, had dreamed of following the St. Lawrence and its tributaries to the fabulous Cathay that Captain Loch had sought as an eager tourist more than three centuries later. And tradition has it that Champlain's fellow explorer, Jean Nicolet, as he moved slowly up the lakes in 1612, carried a mandarin's robe, that he might be respectably attired when he entered the court of the great Khan.

sloops half-way along, turning them around and tossing them down stream like toys. Priests seemed to be the only occupants of Seung-shan. They emerged like startled gnomes from miniature temples, perched on sloping granite terraces and half-concealed by ornamental trees and flowering shrubs.

Once past the strait, the tumult ceased; in the far distance across the valleys, the high walls and bastions of Chinkiang were visible in silhouette against the surrounding plain. High above a turreted gateway a red and yellow flag waved; there was no other movement. Not a man was to be seen along the long line of the ramparts. The place appeared to be as deserted and silent as a city of the dead.

By 15 July, the fleet was abreast the island of Kinshan, opposite the southern entrance of the Grand Canal, which ran directly through the suburbs of Chinkiang. It was smaller than Seung-shan, but not less enchanted. Ranged about a tall, golden-tipped pagoda were clusters of temples and pavilions roofed with yellow and green porcelain tiles that glittered like fairy-tale palaces in the sun.

On the following day, both Admiral Parker and General Gough reconnoitred the approaches by steamer, passing above the city without opposition. Judging by experience of the previous nine days, little or no resistance was anticipated. On the 19th the *Cornwallis* took up position within a 1,000 yards of the city walls on the right or south bank of the river, near the southern entrance to the Canal. Not a gun was fired to break the ominous stillness; from all appearances the garrison had departed. On the 20th the rest of the squadron dropped anchor beside the flagship. A second reconnaissance made from the top of the pagoda on Kinshan revealed three encampments on hill slopes, slightly south-west of the city, a discovery seeming to confirm the impression that the troops had moved out of the town. For this reason, there was no preliminary bombardment; no trial shells to test the presence of the enemy.

Apart from providing boats which were employed in landing men on the banks of surrounding canal branches, the navy played little part in the breaching of the gates nor in the street fighting that had hardly been anticipated following the assault on 21 July. As events were shortly to reveal, about 2,600 Chinese were concealed behind the walls, of whom some 1,200 were Manchu Bannermen; and these fought with the superb tenacity and desperate courage characteristic of the race. On the ramparts, as on the ground, they disputed every advance inch by inch. By midday the massive western and southern gates had been blown in by British sappers, and the fighting, often hand-to-hand, continued in the compounds and narrow streets. The heat was intense, and almost as many British soldiers dropped from exhaustion as from enemy lances and gingalls.

Once the Tartars realized that defeat was inevitable, the same terrible scenes of agony and self-immolation that had shocked even the least sensitive of British soldiers at Chapu were re-enacted once more. The dead bodies, principally women and children, lay in heaps in courtyard and hall; others had been thrown into wells, either strangled or with their throats cut by their own people. The Tartar general in command deliberately put himself to death on an extemporized funeral pyre in his own house. 'The hardest heart of the oldest man who ever lived a life of rapine and slaughter could not have gazed on this scene of woe unchanged,' wrote the horror-struck Captain Loch.[55]

Out of a Manchu population estimated to be at least 4,000, scarcely more than 500 survived; the great majority had perished by their own hands. This desperate and heroic stand, wrote Hosea Ballou Morse in his classic chronicle of scenes and events, 'was the last expiring flash from the old-time valour of the all-conquering Manchu bowmen; their prestige was broken, and from this time on they never again conquered in battle'.[56] Shortly before sunset, the commander-in-chief, General Gough, moved two regiments into the blood-stained Tartar quarter. The quiet of death, Captain Loch noted in his diary, 'seemed to reign paramount' in the still evening air, while 'the fragrance of the flowers surrounding almost every

[55] Loch, p. 110.

[56] Morse, op. cit., p. 296. See also, Ouchterlony, (1844 ed.) pp. 350–406; Nemesis, pp. 355–7; 'A Field Officer', op. cit., pp. 176–7; Loch, op. cit., pp. 102–13; Wells Williams, The Middle Kingdom, pp. 542–3. Sir William Parker's dispatch to the Admiralty (26 July 1842) on the course of the operation is contained in Chinese Repository, xi. July–Aug. 1842, pp. 464–8.

house calmed the strong excitement' that had possessed the
day.

On 2 August preparations for the advance to Nanking were
completed; the surveying vessels were already on the way.
The chief problem was still the current, and without the
steamers it is doubtful whether the majority of the ships could
have reached the old capital. By the 9th, after many tricky feats
of towing, they reached their goal and took station. The *Cornwallis*, the *Blonde*, and the heavy steamers anchored in range of
the walls which stretched some 700 to 1,000 yards from the
river bank. The assault was timed to begin on the morning of
the 15th. Meanwhile, however, messages had been travelling
back and forth between local government officials and the
Court in Peking. On the night of the 14th, scarcely three hours
before the bombardment was to begin, an official communication was delivered to the *Cornwallis* announcing the
Emperor's decision to treat for peace. Undoubtedly, the fall of
Chinkiang, the spreading panic throughout the countryside,
and the almost complete suspension of trade following on the
seizure of several hundred junks,[57] helped to convince Peking
that, for the time being, so one-sided a struggle must end.
Following ceremonial visits on shipboard and ashore, Sir
Henry Pottinger and his suite, including the three interpreters,
Messrs. Morrison, Thom, and Gutzlaff, met with the Imperial
Commissioners and the Viceroy.[58] On this occasion, 26
August, the thirteen articles of the proposed treaty were put
forward, and, in the course of two or three hours of courteous
discussion, accepted. 'How unlike the 26th of August, 1839,
when Lin expelled the English from Macao!', exclaimed the
jubilant editor of the *Chinese Repository*.

On the 26th of August, 1840, the British plenipotentiaries returned

[57] It had been hoped to intercept the substantial fleet of grain-junks, which at that
time of year carried up food supplies to the capital, as well as tribute for the Imperial
treasury. Subsequently it was discovered that these vessels had crossed the river from
the southern to the northern branch of the canal about three weeks before the
vanguard of the British squadron reached this vital intersection close by Kinshan.

[58] Apparently, the Chinese Commissioners were struck with the fact that mere
boys, in the uniform of midshipmen, were learning the art of war so young. The aged
I-li-pu, so it is related, said something to the effect that they would be much better off
in school, imbibing the 'doctrines of pure reason', than learning to fight on board a
man-of-war. *Nemesis*, p. 371n.

to the mouth of the Peiho, to seek an interview with Kishen. In 1841, August 26th, the British forces expelled the Chinese from the batteries of Amoy. And on the same day, 1842, they win the three years' game, and enter in triumph the old capital of the empire, Lin and Kishen [Ch'i-Shan] both being in exile.[59]

On 29 August, authority having been received from the Imperial Court, the treaty was signed on board the *Cornwallis* and on the same day forwarded to Peking for ratification.[60] The participants then sat down to 'a grand tiffin' in the aftercabin. Toasts were drunk to the Queen and the Emperor; a yellow flag for China and the Union Jack for the United Kingdom were hoisted at the main and mizzen, while 21 guns announced to fleet and army and hundreds of curious spectators, the happy consummation of a war that still lies heavily on the British conscience. The Emperor's ratification was received on 15 September. On that same day Major Malcolm, Pottinger's secretary, began his record journey to England by the overland Suez route, carrying with him the precious treaty and news that the first instalment of $6m. in sycee had been received, and that H.M. ships *Blonde*, *Herald*, *Modeste*, and

[59] *Chinese Repository, Journal of Occurrences*, xi. Oct. 1842, p. 575.

[60] The Treaty of Nanking, which concluded what is often called the 'Opium War', made no mention of the opium traffic. It contained seven stipulations:
1. Hong Kong was to be ceded in perpetuity to Britain.
2. Five ports—Canton, Foochow, Ningpo, Shanghai, and Nanking—were to be opened to trade. (Canton was opened on 27 July 1843; Amoy and Shanghai in November; Ningpo in January 1844 and Foochow in June.)
3. Resident British consuls could be appointed to each of the treaty ports.
4. An indemnity of $21m. was to be paid by China for losses and expenses.
5. The Chinese merchant monopoly system, known as the Cohong, was to be abolished.
6. A uniform and moderate tariff was to be established on imports and exports.
7. There was to be equality between Chinese and British officials of corresponding rank.

The three subsequent treaties were the British Supplementary Treaty of the Bogue, signed on 8 Oct. 1843; the American Treaty of Wang-hsia, 3 July 1844; and the French Treaty of Whampoa, 24 Oct. 1844. These agreements involved the grant of two important concessions: one provided for a 'most-favoured-nation clause', automatically extended to each treaty power the concessions any other power might obtain from China. The other, involving 'extraterritoriality', provided that foreigners should be subject only to the legal jurisdiction of their own country's representative in China. On the final operations, see Parker to Secretary of Admiralty, 24 Aug. 1842, *Cornwallis*, off Nanking; and same to same, on renewal of Chinese trade and 'friendly intercourse', 30 Aug. 1842, Adm. 1/5514. See also, *Chinese Repository*, xi. Oct. 1842, pp. 569–75.

Columbine, to whom the bullion had been entrusted, had already sailed.[61]

For the first time in the history of China, a 'treaty of defeat' had been imposed by a European power, whose battleships, frigates, sloops, steamers, and transports lay at anchor close by the walls of the old capital of the Ming Empire. Not only was the right to direct and equal diplomatic relations acknowledged, but Hong Kong had been definitely ceded, and four ports, in addition to Canton, were to be thrown open to the commerce of Britain and, indirectly, to the world. For the Chinese it was a catastrophic revolution, and some Western optimists foresaw, as a consequence, the opening up of the whole of 'the Flowery Land' to European enterprise and civilization.[62]

Subsequently, however, it was to be argued that failure to follow London's advice and advance on Peking had been a fateful omission. No doubt, during the negotiations at Nanking, some of the ancient barriers of exclusiveness had been broken down, but the inner sanctum of Imperial authority remained untouched and unyielding. No steamers had thrust up the Peiho as far as Tientsin; no troops had marched against the capital, and torn away the cobwebbed curtain that hid so much of the truth from an ignorant Court. Without the leverage provided by direct representation in Peking, the way was still open for continued and harassing interference with British trading interests, leading to further crises and, conceivably, further armed conflict.[63]

.   .   .

[61] See Admiral Parker to Cmdr. Ethersey, Indian Navy, 15 Sept. 1842, directing him to receive Major Malcolm on board H.C. Steam Frigate *Auckland*, and to proceed 'with all possible expedition' to Bombay, and thence either to Aden or Suez, 'as far as circumstances may admit for accelerating his arrival in England'. Foreign Dept., Consultation No. 21–3, 15 Mar. 1843 (N.A.I.).

[62] Unhappily, as Professor John Fairbank has made clear, the Chinese version of the treaty was not quite the same as that signed on the *Cornwallis*. National equality was not made explicit; and, without the right of direct representation in Peking, any claim to equality of diplomatic status was likely to prove illusory. John Fairbank, *Trade and Diplomacy on the China Coast. The Opening of the Treaty Ports 1842–1854* (vols. i and ii, Cambridge, Mass., 1953), i. 102–3.

[63] Too late, declared the *Quarterly Review*, Peking had recognized that 'under the mask of trade, western nations had . . . inveigled it into political intercourse. A powerful fleet at Nanking, and the Grand Canal in our hands, the Emperor and his councillors were fain to submit; but the hatred they must have entertained towards those who had inflicted the humiliation can only be understood by persons acquainted with the Asiatic character.' Vol. 107 (1860), p. 94.

Following ratification of the Treaty on 15 September, war-ships and transports began to move down stream. In some respects the return trip was more hazardous than the ascent, partly because the Chinese had removed the buoys with which the squadron's pilots had marked the channel. Every effort was made to keep in the middle of the river, but appearances remained deceitful to the last and, although survey vessels and boats went ahead to signal their soundings, ship after ship had to be unstuck by the steamers. Luckily, experiments with Nanking coal had been entirely successful, and these indis-pensable tugs filled their bunkers to the limit from large stores conveniently placed on the river bank. With her insignificant draught, the *Nemesis* ranged everywhere like a well-trained sheep-dog. 'She is very beautiful', wrote young Harry Parkes, 'but nearly knocked to pieces, having seen a great deal of service.' Inevitably the line-of-battleships lived precariously in shoal and shallow waters of less than five fathoms. On the voyage upstream, the Admiral's flagship had gone aground and stuck fast almost every day.[64] Fortunately, the river bot-tom was softly cushioned, and not a ship was lost. 'Mud, mud, beautiful mud' was the salvation of the fleet. All told, the long and laborious journey in unsettled and hazy weather was a triumph of navigation by the nose. By the end of October the whole fleet was quit of the Yangtse, and had begun to reassemble at Tinghai and neighbouring harbours and anchor-ages of Chusan. It had been a carefully planned and nicely executed operation. In the words of the chronicler of the *Nemesis*, '. . . if it were required to point to any one circums-tance which redounded more than another to the honour of the British service, it would be that of having carried a fleet of nearly 80 sail to the walls of Nanking and brought it safely back again'.[65]

Nevertheless, when the time came to move south, most of the transports and many of the warships were scarcely man-ageable for lack of hands. Once again, disease had proved a far

[64] 'Everybody', wrote Parkes, 'seems much dissatisfied at these large ships coming up, especially at the Admiral leading the way in that monster the *Cornwallis*, because if he gets ashore, all the fleet would have to stay for him, even if it were a week. . . .' Lane-Poole, *Life of Sir Harry Parkes*, i. p. 29.

[65] *Nemesis*, p. 344.

more formidable foe than the enemy. During the sojourn at Nanking, and on the passage down river, cholera and 'a low marsh fever' spread like wildfire. Newcomers to the China seas, especially Indian troops, suffered most severely. Every ship was full of invalids; on average, at least a third were incapacitated, officers as well as men. The Bengal Volunteers suffered most, partly from confinement on transports, but chiefly owing to dietary prejudices. Most of them being high-caste Hindus were prohibited from eating any food cooked on board a ship, and their staple rations of dried rice and shrivelled pease were insufficient to ward off dysentry. The Bengal Volunteers had reached Hong Kong 900 strong; less than 300 appeared on the parade-ground at Barrackpore when they were reviewed for the last time by Sir Hugh Gough. The majority had preferred death to the violation of their religious feelings. The Muslims, it is interesting to note, escaped almost without serious illness. Only with the coming of cooler weather did the sickness begin to abate. By the time the last ships had arrived in Hong Kong harbour in mid-November, the total death toll was more than a thousand.

In December, most of the transports and warships not needed for further service in China sailed away, either for home ports or to stations in India or at the Cape. To the average observer, who had shared the excitements and tribulations of a triumphant punitive expedition against a 'bows and arrows' foe, there appeared no reasonable grounds for anticipating, at least in the forseeable future, another collision with the Chinese, 'to whose moderation and good faith, since the terms of peace have been settled, [so spoke the captain of the Nemesis] too much justice cannot be done'.[66] None the less,

---

[66] Nemesis, p. 382. The Nemesis, still as 'tight as a bottle', continued to serve as an anti-pirate cruiser in Borneo and Chinese waters until withdrawn from Canton in 1852, when she was ordered for service in the second Burma War. (W. A. B. Hamilton to Rear-Admiral Austin, 19 Aug. 1852, Adm. 2/1610.) Her name appears in the lists of the Bengal Marine until the time of the Indian Mutiny, but drops out of sight during the general reorganization of the Indian marine services after 1858. However, it is clear that the Nemesis was still in service in 1872, for the Mends Report of that year recommended the disposal of the ship, then apparently stationed in Burma. According to the Report, the engines were 33 years old, but the hull only 15, which would indicate that sometime between 1857 and 1858 the old Nemesis had been scrapped and her engines installed in a new hull. Regrettably, her last days are hidden in the mists; the reborn Nemesis makes no further appearance in the India Office records, and one

Admiral Parker warned his countrymen against the danger of dozing passively; he believed in 'showing the flag' with guns attached. It was his recommendation that one heavy frigate, a sloop, a steamer, and two troopships should be retained at Chusan; at Koolangsu, a 5th-rate frigate, a sloop and a troopship; and at Hong Kong, one battleship (at least for the winter), along with a small frigate, a sloop, a steamer, and a communications' vessel.[67]

---

can only assume that she ended up as a woebegone coal hulk, or more probably and more ignominiously, as a victim of the breakers' yard.

[67] To Pottinger, *Cornwallis*, off Woosung, 11 Oct. 1842, encl. Pottinger to Aberdeen, 16 Oct. 1842, F.O. 17/58.

IX

UNEASY LULL: HONG KONG
AND CANTON 1843–1848

WITH the ratification of the Treaty of Nanking on 26 June
1843, the British government found itself in reluctant possession of a rugged, near barren, wind-swept island, which not a
few British politicians as well as merchants continued to contrast unfavourably with the rich and inviting island of Chusan
to the northward, where an industrious population cultivated
their fields high up the hillsides and down to the water's edge.
Approximately eleven miles in length and from two to five
miles broad, Hong Kong lies nearly 90 miles to the south-east
of Canton. Although almost completely land-locked, Victoria
Bay, its much prized deep-water harbour, was then, and
remains, exposed to the full fury of typhoons, comparable at
their worst to the hurricanes that periodically strike Mauritius
and the West Indies.[1] But a more severe handicap, as labouring
Colonial Office servants were soon to discover, was the baking heat of June, July, and August. Rising more than 1,200 feet
above the harbour, Victoria Peak can be properly described as
majestic; yet it is but one of a barrier of hills stretching across
the longest part of the island, shutting out the cooling south-
west breezes that might otherwise have made bearable the
long, oppressive summer. Alcohol has never proved a satisfactory antidote to heat and ennui. 'From this arid rock,' wrote
one of Britain's most distinguished colonial officers, not long
after settlement had taken root, 'many go home sick every
year, with spleens much larger than their fortunes; and not a
few remain, to have their bones laid in six feet of Chinese
earth, in the "Happy Valley", where an English cemetery has
been located'.[2]

[1] The typhoons of 21 and 26 July 1841, which threatened the existence of the
expeditionary force of that year (see p. 179) were among the most savage in the
island's history.

[2] Sir Rutherford Alcock, *The Capital of the Tycoon: A Narrative of a Three Years'
Residence in Japan* (2 vols., London, 1863), i. 17.

In retrospect, the permanent occupation of Hong Kong appears as something pre-ordained by the Fates. But the official correspondence offers no cumulative, step-by-step advance to a final settlement. The events leading to ultimate cession were confused and extremely complex, and, until the final ratification of the Treaty of Nanking, cannot be described in terms of purposeful statecraft.[3] On the other hand, there can be little doubt that Sir Henry Pottinger's determination, supported by a natural stubbornness, if not plain perversity, proved to be a principal factor in the ultimate and seemingly inevitable decision. As with Raffles and the taking of Singapore, the actions of the man on the spot were of major significance. Once a toe-hold had been obtained—once, as in the case of Newfoundland in the eighteenth century, rudimentary community and commercial life had taken root even against stern prohibitions—it was difficult, especially from a great distance, to annul existing arrangements, and extinguish the *fait accompli*.

When Pottinger replaced Elliot in the summer of 1841, Victoria had already taken on the appearance of a 'shack town' with its mat and bamboo sheds and huts. Almost immediately after his arrival, the Superintendent began encouraging merchants to build warehouses for the storage of cottons and other manufactured goods.[4] Scarcely a year later, streets had been laid out, bazaars and dwellings, and wharves and jetties were in course of construction, and a firm road had begun to wind its way along the foot of the hills. By the beginning of 1842, Pottinger, whose fervent hopes stimulated his imagination, estimated the population of Victoria to be nearly 25,000, many of them 'highly respectable and affluent Chinese merchants', who had migrated from Canton and Macao. Full of enthusiasm for the settlement, which he regarded as his own creation, he pressed forward with plans that called for ever rapid expansion.[5]

[3] See in this connection E. S. Taylor, 'Hong Kong as a Factor in British Relations with China, 1834–1860' (Univ. of London M.A. thesis 1967), pp. 165–70.

[4] See Commodore Bremer to Admiralty, 29 Sept. 1841 (No. 61); also, Admiral Parker to Admiralty, *Wellesley* at Hong Kong, 20 Aug. 1841 (No. 38), encl. Parker to Bremer, 17 Aug. 1841, Adm. 1/5506.

[5] See G. B. Endacott, *An Eastern Entrepot; A Collection of documents illustrating the history of Hong Kong* (H.M.S.O., London, 1964), pp. 96–7.

But the Governor-to-be was in for a rude awakening, which would have cowed a less fanatical believer. Lord Aberdeen, the Foreign Secretary, saw no need for permanent occupation. Possession would involve heavy expense, and, as history had repeatedly demonstrated, such action was bound to lead to further friction with China, and quite possibly to open hostility.[6] Moreover, like the new Colonial Secretary, Lord Stanley, he felt that progressive settlement would draw speculators, both foreign and British, to the scene of potential pickings, as well as encouraging would-be Chinese refugees to cross the narrow straits. These, at a later date, might well have to be 'abandoned to no doubtful fate'.[7] At the end of January 1842 he ordered all building operations, other than temporary, to be suspended. For the time being, he warned Pottinger, Hong Kong was to be regarded as 'a place militarily occupied, and liable to be restored to the Chinese Govt. on the attainment of the objects which H.M.'s Govt. seek from China. . . .'[8] Not only commercial establishments, but the necessary permanent garrison, whether in Hong Kong or Chusan, would be a constant provocation and temptation to unfriendly hordes on the mainland. Consequently, construction must be limited to the bare minimum, viz., such offices and dwellings as were indispensable for carrying out the business of the day. It was a firm, unambiguous instruction, but the astute first secretary to the Admiralty, reading between the lines, observed that the message held good only until it was finally determined whether the island should be permanently acquired.[9]

[6] Aberdeen to Pottinger, 4 Nov. 1841, F.O. 17/53.

[7] While the situation was still *sub judice*, Stanley believed in deliberate indecision; there were advantages in leaving options open. On the other hand, failing ratification of the Treaty of Nanking, it was clearly his hope that Hong Kong should be retained permanently, along with perhaps three or four other ports, 'to carry on an essentially smuggling trade with the empire'. See Stanley to Ellenborough, 3 Feb. 1842, Colchester, *Ellenborough*, p. 218. It appears likely that Stanley was influenced in his strange 'smuggling' recommendation by Ellenborough himself, who had suggested in his memorandum of October 1841, that should operations fail to produce a satisfactory peace, 'we must content ourselves with the occupation of points on the Coast, & with an illicit trade. . . .' Memorandum on Operations against China, doc. cit., Wellington Papers.

[8] 31 Jan. 1842 (No. 4), L/P & S/9/3 (I.O.A.). See also, James Stephen to Baring (C.O.), 2 Feb. 1842, L/P & S/9/5.

[9] Barrow to Parker, 3 Feb. 1842, Adm. 2/1599; see also Fitzgerald (President of the Board of Control) to Ellenborough, 26 Feb. 1842, L/P & S/9/8.

Although he was aware by the end of February that the Foreign Secretary was opposed to any territorial acquisitions, and would apparently have been happy to renounce Hong Kong, not until April did Pottinger receive the ultimatum suspending further building construction. Aberdeen had said nothing about surrendering the island, which could be interpreted as evidence of continued Cabinet indecision. Such being the case, the Superintendent made up his mind to cast a blind eye on any instructions which suggested future withdrawal. In fact, the command to stop building operations merely hardened his resolve and stimulated him to combative action. He had inherited, so he wrote to Lord Aberdeen in March, a going concern, and it was simply impossible to undo suddenly what Captain Elliot had begun.[10] With several thousand miles of water between himself and Whitehall, Pottinger hoped that by a process of protracted stalling and pleading he might postpone any sudden decision to forsake the island until saner thoughts crystallized. 'I have done as much as I could', he wrote to the Governor-General in May 1842, 'to retard, without injuring this Settlement, but the disposition to colonize under our protection is so strong that I behold a large and wealthy City springing up under my temporizing measures, and the chief difficulty I now have is the provision of locations for respectable and opulent Chinese Traders who are flocking to this Island.'[11]

Pottinger stuck to his guns, and he won. In transmitting the terms of the Treaty of Nanking to Lord Aberdeen, he confessed that the retention of Hong Kong was 'the only single point on which I intentionally exceeded my modified instructions'. And he tried to justify his insubordination on the ground that 'every hour I have passed in this superb country has convinced me of the necessity and desirability of our possessing such a settlement as an Emporium for our trade and a place from which Her Majesty's subjects in China may be

---

[10] 20 Mar. 1842 (No. 8), F.O. 17/60.
[11] 3 May 1842, enclosure 4 in Pottinger to Aberdeen, Macao, 14 May 1842, F.O. 17/56. Ellenborough strongly supported the case for Hong Kong. It made sense to hold one or more bases permanently as security against Chinese misbehaviour. The Chinese 'should come to us to trade, not we to them. . . .' and Chusan was much too large to administer efficiently. To Lord Stanley, 7 June 1842, Ellenborough Papers 30/12/36/1.

alike protected and controlled'.[12] For this cavalier performance, the bold Sir Henry was not rebuked. Neither in speech nor in writing did the Foreign Secretary give any indication that he disapproved of such singular behaviour. Although concrete evidence is lacking, it is likely that Aberdeen had succumbed to the pressures of opinion within the Cabinet, a reversal of attitudes that was influenced, if not engineered, by the Colonial Secretary. Lord Stanley had come to the conclusion that, regardless of arguments pro and con, it was too late to back out; largely as a consequence of Pottinger's development and immigration schemes, Hong Kong had become irrevocably British, and already before the Treaty had been signed, he was drawing up plans for the administration of the island.[13]

Early in June 1843, Stanley transmitted general instructions for the benefit of the Superintendent, who was shortly to become first Governor of Hong Kong under the Colonial Office.[14] One section, a piquant and revealing commentary on policy-making, bears the stamp of Mr. Under-Secretary James Stephen.

. . . there is no case which forms so remarkable an exception to ordinary rules as that of the Island of Hong Kong. . . . It is occupied not with a view to Colonization, but for Diplomatic, Commercial and Military purposes. And it is governed by an Officer who is at once to negociate with the Emperor of China or his Officers; to superintend the Trade of the Queen's subjects in the Seas, Rivers and Coasts of the Empire and to regulate all the internal economy of the Settlement itself. Hence, it follows, that methods of proceeding unknown in other British Colonies must be followed in Hong Kong, and that the Rules and Regulations . . . must, in many regards, bend to exigencies beyond the contemplation of the framers of them.[15]

---

[12] 29 Aug. 1842; see also, 3 Sept. 1842, Steam Frigate *Queen*, off Nanking, F.O. 17/57.
[13] See W. P. Morrell, *British Colonial Policy in the Age of Peel and Russell* (Oxford, 1930), p. 32; also, Taylor, op. cit., pp. 162–3.
[14] After 26 June 1843, the date of ratification, Pottinger held, in addition, the two offices of Chief Superintendent of Trade, and Plenipotentiary and Minister Extraordinary under the Foreign Office.
[15] James Stephen to H. U. Addington, 3 June 1843, enclosing a copy of Stanley to Pottinger, same date (No. 8), F.O. 17/75. A draft of the enclosure is contained in C.O. 129/2.

Not all the British merchants felt happy about the new acquisition as supplementary to, if not a substitute for, Canton. Pottinger had assumed that the majority could be induced to transfer their principal business to Hong Kong, and he had reminded the Factory community that the future was bound to be as uncertain as the past. For more than a decade, Canton had represented the red-hot core of Anglo-Chinese friction, and the Treaty of Nanking, which appeared to permit 'barbarian' access to the city, was hardly likely to cool the passions of the inflammable citizenry. Those who chose to remain in Canton did so at their own peril. All this was understood by firms such as Jardine, Matheson, who had no illusions about the long-term prospects of a quiet life. None the less, they were determined to maintain their trading headquarters at the 'fountain-head' as long as they could. They had grown accustomed to doing business in what had been for so many decades the sole, authorized entrepôt for trade with the West.[16]

This was more or less Whitehall's conclusion. The Foreign Office was resolved not to be unjustifiably shifted from an entrepôt, the possession of which was confirmed by tradition and guaranteed by treaty. The maintenance of amity and order was a matter for Canton. Optimistically, they counted on limiting their efforts to a cautious reminder; the City authorities were to be told the full extent of their responsibility, and (an argument that would have amused Commissioner Lin) 'the danger which they will incur from the Emperor's displeasure . . . ' should they ignore their obligations.[17]

By Article II of the Treaty of Nanking, it was the duty of the Imperial High Commissioner residing at Canton to protect British subjects, their families, and establishments in the five Treaty ports. In four of the ports, the British Consul could take up residence 'within the city', but, as it turned out, *not* in Canton; neither he, nor any other foreigner, not even Her Majesty's Plenipotentiary, was allowed within the gates. The

---

[16] Alexander Jardine to R. W. Crawford of Bombay, Macao, 14 Feb. 1842, Private Letter Books, (B9) vol. 2, Jan.–June 1842 (J.M.A.). None the less, most merchants favoured territorial extensions in the shape of island bases. Hong Kong, wrote Alexander Matheson in May 1842, would be 'indispensable for the extension of British trade in China', and the sooner it was declared a colony, the better. To John Abel Smith, 25 May 1842, ibid.

[17] F.O. to Davis, 5 Oct. 1844 (No. 78), F.O. 17/86.

Factories were outside the walls, close to the river bank, and the European community was practically restricted to the narrow limits of a garden in the forefront of the buildings.

But enforced isolation by the river was no guarantee of safety from periodic invasions by thugs and hooligans. Factory residents faced 'the inconvenience and calamities of a state of warfare from the plundering and violence of native Robbers, against whose nightly excesses . . . our very small Force can affect but little'. So wrote Her Majesty's Plenipotentiary in 1841, and the coming of peace did little to alter this situation.[18] Indeed, the Canton authorities had proved quite incapable of protecting foreigners against sudden mob violence beyond the City walls in the suburbs, or, in moments of high fever, even within the gates of Factory areas. In no time at all, minor scuffles could turn into mass fulminations, which boiled up to explosion point with incredible rapidity. Early in 1844, when a series of provocations leading to civil disorder threatened to attract armed intervention, the Foreign Office warned the Governor that it would be unwise for British marines to interfere, even at consular request, 'except in cases of such great emergency as it is almost impossible to define beforehand'. Canton had become a law unto itself. While station ships might figuratively watch over the consulates at Shanghai, Ningpo, and Amoy, and at Foochow 'as near as the river will admit', Canton possessed no such symbolic protection.

The new Governor of Hong Kong was inclined to agree.[19] With Pottinger's retirement in the spring of 1844, the problem of dealing with the ever recalcitrant Canton fell to a highly experienced 'Old China Hand', John Francis Davis. At the age of eighteen, Davis had come to Canton as a Company employee, and three years later had accompanied the unfortunate Amherst Mission to Peking. Entering on a business career with the Company, he eventually became second Superintendent during Lord Napier's embarrassing internment at Canton in 1834, and he continued as acting Superintendent of

Trade for three months following Napier's death in October of the same year. Davis knew a good deal more about China than most officials of the time; indeed, he was one of the first of a new generation of governors and consuls who had learned the language, and made use of it.[20]

But despite his considerable erudition, and his openly acknowledged contempt for the 'free traders', Davis remained at heart a merchant of the old school. He had little of his predecessor's paternalistic attitude towards the Chinese, but he had far greater patience in dealing with the failings, follies, or adventurings of his Service colleagues and subordinates. Even under stress, he never lost his temper, but he could be doggedly persistent. Within recent months, he had done his best to press on his superiors the righteousness of the British claim to enter Canton freely; access to Canton was one means of removing the 'old and degrading distinction between Chinese and Foreigners'. Like Lord Aberdeen, he would have preferred to settle the matter before surrendering Chusan. Unfortunately, the eleventh article of the Supplementary Treaty of October 1843 had clearly stipulated that British troops were to be withdrawn once the full indemnity had been paid. If the British government now insisted that the restitution of Chusan was part of a *quid pro quo* deal involving the opening of Canton, they ran the risk of being charged with a breach of faith. In the opinion of the Foreign Secretary, such an accusation had to be avoided at all costs. Britain was playing for higher stakes than the Open Door to the City. Moreover, immediate demands for acccss under pressure of naval guns would certainly rekindle the flames of 'an over-excited Canton populace', and Britain's friendly ally, the Imperial Commissioner, Ch'i-ying, would very likely be made the

---

[20] Sir Rutherford Alcock, who began his diplomatic career in the East under Davis, dedicated his Japanese memoirs *The Capital of the Tycoon* to 'the author of the best and only popular work we possess on the Chinese Empire; and the first who succeeded in making the subject familiar to readers in general'.

Apart from the scholarly Davis, Governors Bonham and Bowring were linguists of merit, and at the new consulates, Lay, Parkes, Thom, and Wade were proficient, as were missionaries such as the Medhursts, and a new breed of interpreters such as T. T. and his brother, J. A. T. Meadows. The upsurge of Chinese studies at this time when determined efforts were being made to make the Treaty and its Supplementary provisions work is significant in its bearing on the British policy of furthering conciliation with understanding.

scapegoat, and suffer dismissal.[21] At the moment, in Davis's opinion, the Emperor was impressed by British fair-play, and realized he was committed to settling the Canton question, but before conventional obligations could be satisfied, 'the turbulent population of that place' had to be brought under control.[22]

But would the permanent stationing of a warship opposite the Factories—a police guard in fact—help to reduce the threat of turbulence? As incidents of violence mounted, the merchants quite naturally clamoured for protection. They contended that a city whose trade usually exceeded that of all the other Treaty ports put together should not be ignored, and its British community left comparatively helpless.[23] On the other hand, the Consul at Canton was certain that such action would excite unrest, and thus encourage the Cantonese authorities to spurn their responsibility under the Treaty for the safeguarding of the foreign trader. In any event, one relatively small warship could scarcely intimidate a multitude of vandals bent on destruction ashore. Davis accepted this argument.

There was probably an element of 'pretend' in his optimistic assumption that, with proper nourishment, the 'flower of conciliation' might bloom in the shape of an amicable Anglo-Chinese relationship. Indeed, one of the significant features of the period is the ingenuous manner with which British official representatives in Hong Kong and at Canton dealt with the authorities of an Empire whose coasts had so recently been savagely assaulted. It is curious that they should have assumed that the wounds of war could be so quickly healed; that the truculent Cantonese, so conspicuous for their hatred of the foreigner, should have forgiven the blood-letting in response to the sincere but nervous advances of the late enemy.

[21] See Aberdeen to Davis, 17 Apr. (No. 17), 25 May (No. 25), and 24 June 1846 (No. 30), F.O. 17/108. Copies of drafts of these three dispatches, probably requested by Palmerston after his resumption of office in July 1846, are contained in Broadlands MSS. BD/CH/4–6.

[22] Davis to Aberdeen, 19 May 1846 (No. 67), Foreign Dept., Consultation No. 1467–68, 26 Dec. 1846 (N.A.I.).

[23] See A. R. Johnston (secretary to the Governor of Hong Kong) to H. U. Addington, 24 July 1846, enclosing No. 10, an address of 62 merchants to the Consul at Canton (F. C. MacGregor), 10 July 1846; also, a similar petition to Lord Aberdeen, 22 July 1846, encl. No. 2, in secretary's letter of 25 July 1846, F.O. 17/113.

In fact, the gap produced by a deep, smarting antipathy was unbridgeable, but this condition seems not to have been recognized either in Hong Kong or Whitehall. Hope that the Canton problem would one day solve itself with the help of purposeful effort and wishful thinking was no doubt responsible for the Foreign Office entreaty that not only British officials on the spot, but the British merchant community at Canton, should practise the 'utmost patience and forbearance' in dealing with the Chinese authorities. This meant in practice that while the privilege of anchoring H.M. ships in the neighbourhood of the Factories would not be abandoned, for the time being it was clearly unwise to take advantage of the privilege. A British war vessel stationed opposite the City would be the source of more harm than good.[24]

It was a sadly weakened navy that presumed to rule the waves when the Russell Ministry took office in July 1846. Shorn estimates were chiefly responsible for the decline of the China squadron. At one time (admittedly owing to the late arrival of reliefs), it had been reduced to one frigate and three brigs:[25] and the First Lord of the Admiralty warned that the conduct of British foreign policy, not only in Chinese waters, but around the world, would be severely hampered, if not hamstrung, as a consequence of shrinking naval power.[26] '. . . I see that even now we have not a stout frigate to protect our interests at Canton,' the new Prime Minister confided to Lord Auckland in September 1846.[27] A few days later, Governor Davis was told that, whatever the past practice, whatever the restraints in the interest of amity and order, recent riots had made it imperative that a British warship should take up station, at least temporarily, opposite the City, and beside the

[24] See Davis to Aberdeen, Hong Kong, 7 Aug. 1846 (No. 91), F.O. 17/113. Four months later, Davis was speculating as to whether the presence of a cruiser at Canton was not contrary to the provisions of the Treaty. After all, the port of Canton was actually Whampoa. Davis to Palmerston, 5 Dec. 1846 (No. 172), F.O. 17/115.
[25] See Davis to Aberdeen, 24 May 1846, and Davis to F.O., 23 June 1846, F.O. 17/112.
[26] See Auckland to Russell, 8 Sept. 1846; also, Minto to Russell, 10 Sept. 1846, Russell Papers, 30/22/5 (P.R.O.). Lord Auckland joined the Russell administration as First Lord of the Admiralty, being succeeded on his death in January 1849, by F. T. Baring.
[27] 23 Sept., ibid.

Factories. Palmerston hoped that such an arrangement would not have to be permanent.[28]

Palmerston had succeeded the gentler Aberdeen as Foreign Secretary at a moment when 'patience and forbearance' were under increasing strain as maxims of British policy. He was a firm believer in operating, if needs be audaciously, from strength. It is understandable, therefore, that a newly energized Board of Admiralty should have pressed for reinforcements. Their recommendation, supported, and probably directed, by the Foreign Secretary, called for a minimum force of one frigate, six sloops, and a steamer in the South China Sea.[29] Even if this modest total meant a weakening of Commodore Blackwood's division in East Indian waters, the recently appointed commander-in-chief of the station, Rear-Admiral Samuel Hood Inglefield, was told to keep his squadron up to this limit, and preferably beyond.[30]

Unaware of this sudden hardening of British policy, Davis, with the backing of Admiral Cochrane, had continued to support the British Consul in Canton in his efforts to achieve calm by kindness. Sporadic rioting, and in particular the savage outbreak in the previous July, he told Palmerston, was of the merchants' own making. Their behaviour had been notoriously offensive and aggressive. 'I am not the first', he wrote, 'who has been compelled to remark that it is more difficult to deal with our own Countrymen at Canton than with the Chinese government. . . .'[31]

Late in November, Davis ordered the *Nemesis*, after less than a month's visit to Whampoa and Canton, to return to Hong Kong on the grounds that 'her remaining under present circumstances would only foster the insolent and aggressive spirit of the ill-disposed among our merchant residents'. The citizens of other nations, he informed Palmerston, had never

[28] See Palmerston to Davis, 3 and 24 Oct. 1846 (Nos. 25 and 29), F.O. 17/108.

[29] See Palmerston to Davis, 12 Jan. 1847 (No. 3 draft), F.O. 17/121; and Davis to Palmerston, 28 Feb. 1847 (No. 29), F.O. 17/123.

[30] Admiralty to Inglefield, 30 Apr. 1847 (No. 94) and 6 July 1847 (No. 136), Adm. 2/1605. Inglefield had been appointed to succeed Cochrane in August 1846. Blackwood's division then consisted of a frigate, two sloops, and one steamer.

[31] Davis to Palmerston, 12 Nov. 1846 (No. 158), F.O. 17/115. In regard to the riot at Canton in July, merchants' requests for naval protection, and the objections of Davis, Cochrane, and Consul MacGregor, see printed and documentary reports in F.O. 17/120.

demanded such protection from their governments, no doubt because 'their better conduct' rendered them 'less desirous to seek it'.[32] Two weeks later, he was unwise enough to write again, acquainting a less than patient Foreign Secretary that the peevish merchant residents could scarcely expect Her Majesty's government to listen to their pleas for the 'visible presence' of so intimidating a contrivance as a British war-ship.[33]

Admiral Cochrane followed the same line of argument. A sloop, or a steamship—occasionally a frigate—was nearly always on station at Whampoa, only twelve miles from Canton. Light-draught steamers like the *Nemesis* or *Pluto* could reach the Factory area within two or three hours; but even in the event of serious trouble, would it be wise for them to appear on the scene? Rather than aid in suppression, they would be more likely to add fuel to the flames. If hostile demonstrations of a dangerous nature developed, the sensible and dignified course was to get out, leaving redress to the British government; it would be absurd 'to contest the point with a small steam ship'. Basing his conclusion apparently on an uninterrupted six-hour walk which he had taken, presum-ably outside the walls of the City, he maintained that the Cantonese were a peaceable people, unless needled to breaking point by devil-may-care merchants. A naval vessel in front of the Factories would merely encourage those British subjects 'prone to domineering and aggression', indicating that they could, in extremity, take shelter under the ship's guns. Ameri-cans, French, Dutch, and other foreign nationals seemed to be able to live in peace and harmony with the Chinese; Cochrane saw no reason why Britons should not be capable of doing the same.[34]

But long before these apologias reached Whitehall, Palmer-ston had thundered, and Davis and Cochrane were to hear the

[32] Davis to Palmerston, 21 Nov. 1846 (No. 163), F.O. 17/115.

[33] Davis to Palmerston, 5 Dec. 1846 (No. 172), ibid. Early in the New Year, he listed examples of 'the wanton provocation given by the English Residents at Canton to the native Chinese', and he specifically named the firm of Messrs. Ellis and Dunlop, whose 'aggressive propensities' would only be encouraged by 'the unnecessary pres-ence of a war steamer'. Davis to Palmerston, 13 Jan. 1847 (No. 5), F.O. 17/123.

[34] Cochrane to Admiralty, *Agincourt* at Penang, 21 Jan. 1847 (No. 9), enclosing copies of two letters, written to Davis in Hong Kong, 20 Nov. and 3 Dec. 1846, Adm. 1/5575.

distant echoes of *Civis Romanus sum*. Even were the merchants at Canton the scum of the earth masquerading as its salt, 'I have only to say that wherever British subjects are placed in danger, in a situation which is accessible to a British Ship of War, thither a British Ship of War ought to be, and will be ordered not only to go, but to remain as long as its presence may be required for the protection of British interests.'[35] It might be desirable, the Foreign Secretary informed Davis, to impress upon Mr. F. C. MacGregor the fact that Her Majesty's government counted on their Consul at Canton having sufficient 'energy and determination' to maintain his authority over British subjects, and sufficient firmness to hold the Chinese authorities to their duty.[36] 'I do not see why', he wrote in March 1847, 'the occasional presence of a Ship of War at Canton should prevent the British Consul from repressing by the legal means within his power any tendency to violence or provocation on the part of the British residents. . . .' The doctrine of Cantonese responsibility for maintaining order obviously could not rule out uncontrollable explosions. Such emergencies were of frequent occurrence all over the world, and it had been the practice of British governments to send ships of war to areas where local disturbances appeared likely to threaten the lives or endanger the property of British subjects.[37]

Davis had argued that the fundamental problem of Anglo-Chinese relations was not how to contain unrest and violence by shows of force, but how to divert or retard 'the onward progress of that European ascendancy which acts with the pressure of a constant spring'.[38] Palmerston was willing to admit that European ascendancy might well be 'the constant spring' behind belligerent Chinese nationalism. But chronic xenophopia in no way justified the constant harassment of

[35] Palmerston to Davis, 10 Dec. 1846 (No. 37), F.O. 17/108.
[36] Palmerston to Davis (draft), 12 Jan. 1847; also, 25 Mar. 1847, Broadlands MSS., BD/CH/1–22. Prolonged visits by warships, he insisted two weeks later, provided a useful restraint on Chinese ebullience, and 'by inspiring the British with a feeling of protection renders them less disposed to take their defence into their own hands'. To Davis, 25 Jan. 1847 (No. 14), and 14 Apr. 1847 (No. 52), F.O. 17/121. See also in this connection, Admiralty to commander-in-chief or Senior Naval Officer, 16 Apr. 1847, Adm. 2/1605.
[37] To Davis, 25 Mar. 1847 (No. 49), F.O. 17/121.
[38] To Palmerston, 26 Jan. 1847 (No. 10), F.O. 17/123.

traders who pursued their business under agreed Treaty terms.[39] A sympthetic understanding of Chinese attitudes solved no problems. Patient acquiescence in the interests of peace and goodwill was bound to be mistaken for submissiveness. 'We shall lose all the vantageground we have gained by our victories in China', he wrote to Davis, 'if we take a low tone.'

We must especially care not to descend from the relative position which we have acquired. If we maintain that position morally, by the tone of our intercourse, we shall not be obliged to recover it by forcible acts; but if we permit the Chinese either at Canton or elsewhere, to resume, as they will no doubt always be endeavouring to do, their former tone of superiority, we shall very soon be compelied to blows with them again.

The Chinese, as he had somewhat mistakenly reminded a previous plenipotentiary, Captain Elliot, were not in the least different from the rest of mankind;[40] and the best way to keep tiresome men quiet was to let them see that force would be used with determination to repel force. The Chinese had to learn that if they attacked either persons or buildings they would be shot, that if they ill-treated innocent Englishmen, who might be out for a peaceful walk, they would be punished. These sentiments were repeated in letter after letter to the Governor and plenipotentiary in Hong Kong, whence they were forwarded, sometimes tactfully abbreviated, to the Imperial Commissioner in Canton.[41]

Both Davis and Admiral Cochrane underestimated the deep-seated illwill of the Cantonese for the British community. They were equally slow to realize that the Imperial Commissioner, Ch'i-ying, and his fellow administrators, whatever their personal views, were powerless to pacify the mob element and carry into practice the stipulations of the Treaty, in particular, that clause concerned with the free entry of British subjects through the city gates. Not until the spring of 1847

[39] See Palmerston to Davis, 11 Mar. 1847, F.O. 17/121.
[40] p. 9.
[41] See Palmerston to Davis, 9 Jan. 1847, F.O. 17/121; also contained in Correspondence relative to the Operations in the Canton River, April 1847, Parliamentary Papers, vol. xl, 1847, p. 467.

did accumulating violence finally shatter Davis's faith and policy. Early in March, following a series of minor incidents, six Englishmen were attacked, chiefly with stones, in the course of an excursion to Fatshan, some fifteen miles from Canton. This apparently unprovoked assault could scarcely be explained as a consequence of merchant meddlesomeness, and immediately on receiving the news, the Governor sent out a call for help, urging Admiral Inglefield to hasten back from the Malacca Straits where he had been on tour. In view of his prolonged and verbose efforts to convince Palmerston of the need for the 'velvet glove', there is irony and some comedy in Davis's belated effort to show the iron fist. The records of the Foreign Office, he wrote to Palmerston, 'will convince your Lordship that during the last three years I have been rigidly tied down by my instructions to the most forbearing policy. . . . The time has in my opinion certainly arrived when decision becomes necessary, and further forbearance impolitic.' To the Admiral, he justified his proposed sudden and drastic reprisals on the ground that the Foreign Secretary had demanded redress for outrages 'in a tone so decided, as to render desirable that it [redress] should be backed by a force on the spot'.[42]

The 'reprisals raid' which took place in early April 1847, was chiefly a military operation with which the navy co-operated. Within thirty-six hours, Major-General G. C. D'Aquilar, the commander of the Hong Kong garrison,[43] managed to assemble a force of 900 men, which was transported to the Canton estuary by steamer, sloop, and lorcha. The Bogue forts were once again captured without much difficulty, over 800 cannon were spiked, and the way opened to Canton, where the Factories were occupied with negligible resistance, with no British casualties. A hastily gathered collection of troops, Davis wrote triumphantly to Palmerston, had made themselves

[42] Davis to Palmerston, 27 Mar. 1847, with encl. No. 4, Davis to Inglefield, same date (No. 35), F.O. 17/124.

[43] For a summary of his distinguished military career, see 'D'Aguilar of Hong Kong', *Library Notes*, New Series, No. 80, August 1963 (The Royal Commonwealth Society, Northumberland Avenue, London, W.C. 2). Drawing on his diaries, letters, and memories, General D'Aguilar wrote an account of his command in Hong Kong (1843–8), *Pencillings on the Rock*, a manuscript volume of 137 pages preserved in the Society's library.

'absolute masters of the river from Hong Kong to Canton'.[44] The surrender was complete; all British demands were met, including, in particular, the long-sought right of British subjects to enter the city gates unconditionally within two years' time. Provision was also made for additional warehouse and residential space on the south bank of the Canton River.

Palmerston was pleased with the result. Davis had followed his bidding, and he hoped that the Chinese authorities had learned a lesson, and would thenceforth abide by Treaty terms. If not, they knew what to expect. At the same time, however, he warned Davis to keep a sharp eye on the Canton merchant community, and suppress rigorously any manifestations of arrogance and aggressiveness.[45] Since all was serene along the waterfront, the *Pluto* was withdrawn from Canton in October, but Ch'i-ying was informed that a warship would continue to be maintained at Whampoa.[46] The April raid seemed likely to have a salutary effect, but Chinese memories were certain to be short-lived, and Palmerston surmised that the day for renewed action would come again, and soon. Hence, he was happy to support an Admiralty proposal for the addition of a number of shallow-draught mortar-boats, especially for use in the Canton River.[47] Meanwhile, should another crisis arise, Davis (who in August had asked to be relieved of his post before the onset of his fifth hot season) was urged not to leave the negotiating table hastily. He should 'go the limit' in talk before considering the use of force.[48]

Nevertheless, the Russell Ministry was disturbed by the April *coup*. At a time when British naval strength had been cut to the bone, and when inflammatory situations were developing on the continent of Europe, they were alarmed by the

---

[44] 5 Apr. 1847 (No. 53); in a second letter of 6 April (No. 54), Davis reported that Ch'i-ying had agreed to all his demands. Ibid. See also, Major-General D'Aquilar to Earl Grey, Hong Kong, 15 Apr. 1847, Foreign Dept., Consultation No. 35–40, 29 May 1847 (N.A.I.); and Inglefield to Admiralty, Penang, 8 May 1847 (No. 23) encl. Captain M. Dougall (S.N.O.) to Inglefield, 9 Apr. 1847, Adm. 1/5575.

[45] Palmerston to Davis, 24 June 1847 (No. 68), and 5 July 1847 (No. 79), F.O. 17/121 and 122 respectively.

[46] Davis to Palmerston, 25 Aug. 1847 (No. 158), F.O. 17/129, 23 Sept. 1847 (No. 174), and 2 Oct. 1847 (No. 180), enclosing No. 2, Davis to Ch'i-ying, notifying the latter of the withdrawal of the *Pluto*, F.O. 17/130.

[47] See F.O. to C.O., 6 Nov. 1847, F.O. 17/137.

[48] Palmerston to Davis, 12 Oct. 1847 (No. 123), F.O. 17/122.

thought that a single individual, acting on his own responsibility, could set in motion events that might lead to a full-scale war.[49] Supported by the rest of the Cabinet, the Colonial Secretary, Earl Grey, was not loath to hobble over-zealous servants of the Crown, and in November the Governor of Hong Kong was informed that henceforth no offensive operations against the Chinese should take place without Cabinet sanction. The British government was satisfied that 'although the later operations in the Canton River were attended with immediate success, the risk of a second attempt of the same kind would far overbalance any advantage to be derived from such a step. . . .'[50]

It was a command which was undoubtedly influenced by general naval weakness, and Davis, on receiving it, could not forbear reminding the government of Pottinger's advice to Lord Aberdeen, namely, if the British position was to be really secure and unassailable, the China squadron would have to be kept at a minimum of fifteen ships, viz., four frigates, seven sloops, and four steamers.[51]

As it happened, before the end of the year, owing to 'the greatly improved relations with the Chinese government', even Whampoa could be left without a steamer, and Indian troops, summoned at the time of the emergency, were already on their way back to the homeland.[52] On 4 December the Governor wrote his customary letter of thanks to the Governor-General of India for generous help which, he trusted, was not likely to be needed again. One day later, on a Sunday, a small party of Englishmen were hiking through the countryside near Canton, when they were suddenly attacked, and two Chinese were either killed or badly wounded in the course of the affray. Although Davis might have been able to scrape together 700 men or thereabouts to repeat the operations of the preceding April (and, at the time, two steamers were available), he had not forgotten his instructions. Negotiations for redress must come first, and even if negotiations

[49] See Lane-Poole, op. cit. i. 133.
[50] Grey to Major-General D'Aquilar, 24 Nov. 1847, L/P & S/9/9 (I.O.A.).
[51] Davis to Palmerston, 26 Feb. 1848 (No. 38), F.O. 17/140.
[52] Davis to Viscount Hardinge, Governor-General of India, Victoria, Hong Kong, 4 Dec. 1847, Foreign Dept., Consultation No. 17, 25 Feb. 1848 (N.A.I.).

broke down, he was forbidden to undertake offensive operations in the Canton River without permission of the British government. The British government, as he was well aware, was determined that there should be no more armed interventions unless there was convincing evidence that gun-fire could achieve something lasting. Grey had already refused to replace the Indian contingent with a regiment from Ceylon, and Davis's request of 29 December to the Governor-General for the loan of a British regiment, in view of the tension following the December 'incident', was countermanded by Whitehall only a few hours after the troops had embarked at Madras.[53]

Despite Davis's fear that the celebration of the Chinese New Year might be accompanied by anti-foreign agitations, negotiations proceeded with caution and hope during January 1848. By the middle of the month he was able to tell the garrison commander and the Senior Naval Officer that hostile measures might not be necessary. In view of the improved atmosphere, the steam frigate *Vulture*, already under Admiralty orders to return to England, was released, and a second request for reinforcements from India was cancelled. Ch'i-ying was apparently 'doing everything in his power to bring negotiation to a satisfactory termination. . . .' Such a prospect was the more fortunate, since one week later the British mails brought the reiterated injunction from Whitehall not to take any aggressive measures against the Chinese government without orders from home.[54]

Davis accepted the government's latest admonition without demur. He fully appreciated the argument that repeated invasions of the Canton River, and the slaughter of thousands of Chinese had proved of little or no political value. At the same

[53] Davis to Palmerston, 28 Dec. 1847 (No. 219), 29 Dec. 1847 (No. 220), F.O. 17/132, and also, 10 Jan. 1848 (No. 5), with encl. No. 1, relating to preparations for an attack on the defences of the Canton River should negotiations fail, and 28 Jan. 1848 (No. 15), with encl. No. 2, Grey to Davis, 24 Nov. 1847, F.O. 17/140. Note in addition, Dalhousie to Secret Committee, Court of Directors, 19 Feb. 1848 (No. 16), and 22 Mar. 1848 (No. 24), with encls. L/P & S/5/14 (I.O.A.).

[54] See S.N.O. to Inglefield, Hong Kong, 21 and 26 Jan. 1848; Davis to S.N.O., 26 Jan. 1848, enclosed in Capt. J. H. Plumridge to S.N.O., *Cambrian*, Bombay, 24 Feb. 1848, Foreign Dept., Consultation Nos. 18–20, 31 Mar. 1848; also, Governor-in-Council to the Governor of the Straits Settlements, Fort William, 6 Mar. 1848 (No. 95), Foreign Dept., Consultation No. 21, 31 Mar. 1848 (N.A.I.).

time, he no longer counted on Chinese good faith as representing anything more than meeting the needs of the day as they
came, and he was aware that this fragile basis was likely to
deteriorate in view of Ch'i-ying's decline as a paramount
influence at Court. In the circumstances, as long as British
trade continued to be centred on Canton, Davis was 'not
willing to reduce the Naval Force in China at present, beyond
what the most urgent necessity in other quarters may
require'.[55] Early in February, although the number of sloops
was below customary strength, he gave orders for the stationing of a steamer at the Factory anchorage [Whampoa] 'whatever the force on the China station'. Three months later,
despite the opposition of some members of the Cabinet who
regarded such a course as dangerously defiant, Palmerston
informed Davis's successor, George Bonham, of his complete
approval.[56]

The addition was scarcely impressive, but in the 1840s
excisions in the name of economy were more common than
additions. The joint East Indies and China station now ranked
second to the Mediterranean squadron in numbers of vessels,
viz., a total of eleven. The Treaty ports were normally given a
brig each, with the exception of Whampoa (now accepted as
the port of Canton) which usually had a steamer. A frigate
and a steamer were normally stationed at or near Hong
Kong.[57] Once occupation had been formally decided in 1843,
Hong Kong had grown steadily in general effectiveness
as a naval base. Because the Island lies in a typhoon
area, lack of a dockyard remained a particular handicap;
but reasonable careening facilities, along with an adequate
quota of skilled artificers, meant that, barring major repairs,
ships need no longer return to Bombay for refit. Similarly,
the establishment of a stores depot reduced reliance on
Trincomalee.[58]

.   .   .

[55] To S.N.O., 26 Jan. 1848, doc. cit. Also, Davis to Palmerston, 8 Feb. 1848 (No. 23), F.O. 17/140.

[56] Davis to Palmerston, 12 Feb. 1848 (No. 27), F.O. 17/140, and Palmerston to Bonham, 11 May 1848 (No. 36 draft), F.O. 17/138.

[57] See Comparative Table of Station Strengths Overseas, Admiralty, 1849, Adm. 2/1607.

[58] See Admiralty Minute of 6 Aug. 1849, Adm. 2/1608; also Cochrane to Admiralty, 17 June 1847 (No. 82), Adm. 1/5575.

Apart from piratical activity, which increased somewhat beyond normal during the next five years, the China seas were at peace. For the time being, too, French adventures in pursuit of empire had ceased, and all was quiet in the Pacific. Partly as a consequence of unsettled political alignments in Britain, and partly as a reflection of the personality of Davis's successor, George Bonham, it was also a period of diplomatic calm.[59]

Bonham's father had been captain of an East Indiaman, and as a youngster, the new Governor had inevitably soaked up something of the ethos of oriental trade. In 1830, while still in his twenties, he became resident councillor of Singapore, succeeding seven years later to a governorship of Penang, Singapore, and Malacca. Singapore was an outpost of the China station, and during his tenure, Bonham had studied the Chinese language and, in so far as it was possible, the Chinese way of life. Palmerston later confessed that Sir George's 'practical common sense' was the main reason for his appointment to Hong Kong. Certainly, his sympathy for the mercantile community, whose interests he was constantly to uphold, made him a far more popular leader of Hong Kong society than the austere and somewhat suspicious Davis.[60]

Bonham, who took office in March 1848, was reasonably happy with the situation, and prepared to 'let sleeping dogs lie'.[61] After long, and, on the whole uneventful, experience of Indian and Malayan affairs, he had become accustomed to a peaceful life, and he continued to seek tranquil ways with wary deliberation. Towards the end of his appointment, he confessed to his colleague, the French Plenipotentiary, M. de Bourboulon, that despite the frustrations and painful 'inci-

[59] See J. J. Gerson, *Horatio Nelson Lay and Sino-British Relations 1854–1864* (Cambridge, Mass., 1972), pp. 24 ff.; and Earl Swisher, *China's Management of the American Barbarians . . . 1841–1861* (New Haven, Conn. 1951), chap. 5, *passim*. Bonham was to be knighted in 1851.

[60] See Fairbank, op. cit. i. 276–7.

[61] As it happened, Bonham had scarcely arrived at Hong Kong when he was faced with a typical 'incident'—an assault on three missionaries some 30 miles outside Shanghai. Rutherford Alcock was the vigorous and knowledgeable Consul in the city. Spared the interference of that consular bugbear of the future, the telegraph, he stopped the Chinese grain ships from entering the Grand Canal, and ordered a warship up the Yangtse to threaten Nanking. As a newcomer to the scene, Bonham was reluctant to intervene, and it was perhaps fortunate for his peace of mind that after 15 days' blockade Alcock managed to settle the affair before he himself would have been compelled to take a hand as arbitrator.

dents', British policy simply had to be gentle and pacific. Trade with China was bringing India an annual revenue of £3m., and Britain, some £6m. He had no wish to tamper unduly with so valuable an asset. No doubt the Chinese had scant reason for loving the British, but 'if they often oppose us by duplicity and bad faith, is not that the natural defence of the weak?'[62]

In the interests of this flourishing trade, Bonham was, therefore, content with the bare necessities of naval strength. The China allotment, he told Lord Grey, was quite ample for the purposes proposed. An armed brig lay at anchor at each of four Treaty ports; a steamer was once again at Whampoa, in position to visit the Canton Factory when called upon, while two additional steamers were temporarily attached to the Hong Kong base.[63] Without a station ship at Whampoa, Bonham informed Palmerston, it would have been quite impossible to have kept order. At the moment, the anchorage contained upwards of 1,200 high-spirited merchant seamen.[64] Henceforward, it became a standing Admiralty injunction that the Canton approaches were never to be left without at least one warship, preferably a steamer.[65]

Yet the Canton 'City question' remained the focus of popular Chinese feeling and unresolved diplomatic conflict.[66] The Factories were still at the mercy of the amorphous mob, which, not infrequently stirred to hysteria by disaffected leaders, could spring up savagely from the streets like dragons' teeth. Such outbreaks could be mastered only by armed force on the spot; Whampoa was too far distant. Early in 1849, impatient of what they regarded as undue governmental procrastination, the merchants hired their own 'stationed' ship, the steamer *Corsair*, to police the Factory river front, a trucul-

[62] De Bourboulon to Ministère des Affaires Étrangères, 28 Dec. 1852, quoted, Costin, op. cit., p. 152.

[63] Bonham to Palmerston, 24 May 1848 (No. 35), F.O. 17/143.

[64] 29 Nov. 1848 (No. 132), F.O. 17/146.

[65] Admiralty to the commander-in-chief (Admiral Collier), 25 Nov. 1848, Adm. 2/1607.

[66] Fairbank, op. cit. i. 267. The right of entrance into Canton was deferred in 1849, again in 1854 (at the time when Treaty terms were due for revision), and once again in 1855. On this occasion, the subject was dropped, according to Consul Harry Parkes, for lack of naval support. See Lane-Poole, i. 222–3. The gates of Canton remained closed until January 1858.

ent show of independence of which Palmerston strongly disapproved.[67]

Until late in September 1850, Palmerston had clung to the hope that he could leap-frog the 'Canton question', and deal directly with Peking. Unfortunately such sanguine daydreams had no chance of realization. The young Emperor, who had ascended the throne in March 1850, was under the influence, not of 'barbarian conciliators', but of hard-shell, xenophobic nationalists. Consequently, the quest for direct communication was a complete failure. The ensuing rebuffs were the more painful in view of the British government's wish to exchange Ningpo and Foochow for mainland ports better situated for attracting trade. Since the Chinese were refusing to stick either to the spirit or the letter of the Treaty of Nanking in respect to the opening of Canton, Palmerston saw no reason why a British cruiser should be stuck in the river Min, below Foochow, to watch over a trade which scarcely existed.

Economy dictated the abandonment of the port. But the British government was reluctant to take any hasty step which might suggest a willingness to relinquish advantages assumed to have been conceded by the Treaty. If the Governor of Hong Kong could think of two other ports which might be substituted as trading rendezvous, the Foreign Office would propose such an exchange to the Chinese government.[68] Bonham agreed that if a 'swop' could be arranged, Hangchow and Soochow would be ideal substitutes, and in addition, if a strategic base like Chinkiang (where the Yangtse intersected the Grand Canal) could be secured, the political leverage so obtained would be as valuable an asset as the commerce. But negotiation for such ends, he sensibly concluded, would be a waste of time; only a naval demonstration before Chinkiang would induce the Chinese to listen, much less to agree to such a proposal.[69]

Palmerston accepted Bonham's suggestions for the pro-

---

[67] Palmerston to Bonham, 31 Oct. 1849, F.O. 17/152.

[68] Palmerston to Bonham, 10 Apr. 1849 (No. 28), in reply to Bonham's of 8 Jan. 1849, F.O. 17/152. See also Palmerston to Bonham, 14 Sept. 1849 (No. 89, in rough draft), Broadlands MSS., BD/CH/23–33.

[69] Bonham to Palmerston, 15 Apr. 1850, F.O. 17/166.

posed exchange, but made it quite clear that there should be no naval demonstrations. The approach was to take the form of an exercise in tactful diplomacy. The grounds for such an exchange were quite simple. Ningpo and Foochow had not fulfilled the hopes of the two governments who had concluded the Treaty of Nanking. Consequently, it was now proposed that the consuls at both ports should be transferred to three more favourably sited areas.[70] But Bonham failed to make contact with Peking, and in his opinion there was now no alternative to the use of force, namely, the occupation of Chinkiang and the blockade of the Grand Canal. An exchange of ports was obviously out of the question. None the less, Palmerston was still anxious to withdraw from Foochow and Ningpo; the consulates could be reconstituted should commerce improve in the future. Meanwhile, the Chinese would no doubt rejoice at the British retreat.

But the chief clerk in the Foreign Office, Edmund Hammond, a former Fellow of University College, Oxford, who was to become Permanent Under-Secretary in 1854, showed himself to be more decided in his recommendations than the more astute bureaucrat of later days.[71] Hammond minuted Palmerston's own minute with five terse arguments in favour of retention: (1) if abandoned, the two ports would be difficult to reoccupy; (2) because Canton was vulnerable and its trade precarious, it was the more to be regretted that Foochow should go; (3) personnel at the two ports could, of course, be reduced; but (4), it was important to remember that both Ningpo and Foochow were useful ports of call for ships in need of refreshment and medical care. Finally, (5), Hammond emphasized the fact that British trade in China was entirely dependent on the consular agency. Addington, who had become under-secretary in the Foreign Office in 1842 (and

[70] Palmerston to Bonham, 3 Sept. 1850, F.O. 17/164; see also, Fairbank, i. 379–80; cf. Costin, *Great Britain and China* . . ., pp. 149–50.

[71] Some years later, Hammond acknowledged that an under-secretary had no business to give a decision on any point; he was merely the channel, a 'ministerial officer' bound to advise and to recommend, but without power of independent action. Actually, Hammond was as assertive in his advice and recommendations in later years, as he had been in earlier times. But he had learned the folly of trying, as a senior civil servant, to impose his views by frontal attack. By practising something like diplomatic *finesse* in preference to logical bludgeoning he continued to exercise a very effective influence on government policy until his retirement in 1873.

who claimed China as his preserve) agreed entirely with this assessment. He added his own minute: 'I would rather keep a man of straw at each place than withdraw entirely.' If the British Consuls were retired, in his view the loss of prestige would have to be counteracted by an increased naval force.[72]

Palmerston acquiesced without audible murmur, but he remained disturbed by the failure of his diplomacy to penetrate the walls of Peking. Further efforts at negotiation were obviously futile, and the British stood uncertainly at a crossroad, hesitating to make the choice between further conciliation or coercion. But in his own mind, the choice was narrowing. For three years he had shown great restraint; like Bonham, he was reluctant to upset the prosperous calm, however precarious, by some impulsive action that, it might be said, occasionally characterized his demeanour and often his conduct on certain European questions. There had certainly been no blustering jingoism in his recent handling of the Canton question. Even when the Chinese had broken an explicit promise to open the City gates in 1849, he had advised Bonham not to press the issue for the moment. A better occasion was bound to present itself. But as incident followed incident, his patience began to show signs of wear, and more and more, he was coming to the conclusion that there was no alternative but to combine new diplomatic overtures with a display of armed strength.

In a memorandum of 29 September 1850, which was more a soliloquy than a statement of policy, he wrote:

. . . the Time is fast coming when we shall be obliged to strike another blow in China, and that Blow must be the occupation of a Position in the Yang tse Kiang to cut off communication by the Great Canal. But it would not be advisable to give the Chinese any Intimation that such would be our measure. They should be left to reflect upon it when and after it was done.[73]

[72] See minutes by Palmerston, 24 Sept. 1850, Hammond, n.d. and Addington, 26 Sept. 1850 on Bonham's dispatches, Nos. 65, 67, 72, F.O. 17/173.
[73] F.O. 17/173, quoted in Fairbank, i. 380, and Costin, pp. 149–50.

X

THE CHINA STATION:
THE PROBLEM OF DIVIDED
AUTHORITY

IN the nineteenth century, rivalry between civilian administrator and naval commander was an almost constant element
in British colonial life overseas. Before the advent of the
telegraph, British representatives abroad—governors, consuls, district commissioners—invariably enjoyed weeks, if not
months, of luxurious freedom from interference by higher
authority at home. Regardless of the views of a commodore or
commander-in-chief, their decisions, when circumstances
seemed to call for drastic action, could affect the movements of
a ship, a detachment, or a squadron. The captain of a sloop
could be, and often was, given special tasks to perform in
civilian authority, presumably in the national interest; and on
occasion, the plans of a naval commander-in-chief might be
overruled by a governor or a visiting plenipotentiary. And the
more sensitive or aggressive the governor or the plenipotentiary, the more likely it was that political considerations of the
moment would dominate his thinking. He was not always
willing to recognize the competing needs of other theatres, or
the squadron's limitations in ships and men. Indeed, the very
presence of a war vessel within harbour reach could encourage
individual initiative and precipitate action, in a manner not
possible for one of Her Majesty's servants in London, answer-
able for his actions to Parliament.

On the China station, this contest was sharpened by day-
to-day existence which was politically unsettled, frequently
uncomfortable, and sometimes feverish. The naval command
resented and protested against civilian interference in much
the same way that merchants in the Treaty ports were to chafe
under the meddling attentions of a British consul, bound by
the red tape of regulations from which Americans, French, and
other foreigners were happily free. But no amount of appeals

to the Admiralty could alter the fundamental fact that the navy remained essentially the handmaiden of the Foreign Office, responsible to their Lordships in Whitehall, but in practice the tool of an overseas administration, owing its authority in matters of Anglo-Chinese relations to the Foreign Secretary.[1] 'Being itinerant and birds of passage, and in no manner connected with Colonial matters,' wrote one commander-in-chief a little sorrowfully, 'they [the navy] are viewed simply in the light of strangers, or guests—and treated accordingly. . . .' Except on the high seas, where he was monarch of all he surveyed, the naval captain lacked status.[2]

On the other hand, a harassed Governor, John Francis Davis, had been pained to discover that officers in the Royal Navy did not 'look very far beyond their own profession, nor attach much importance in general to the civil objects to which Her Majesty's ships may be made available'.[3] It appeared to him that the navy resented civilian advice because they failed to understand the political implications of independent action on their part, and Davis begged that the Foreign Office persuade the Admiralty to listen more carefully to suggestions or recommendations from Her Majesty's civil authority.[4]

In time of war, of course, friction was likely to be at a minimum. Both naval and military services had clearly defined tasks to perform. The Governor-General of India, as supreme commander-in-chief had authority over the planning of operations; but in practice, as has been noted, a wise governor-general, aware of his distance from changing patterns of events on the China coast, appreciated his dependence on the decisions of professionals on the spot.[5] As it happened,

---

[1] In 1849, apparently without a qualm, Palmerston ordered the Governor of Hong Kong (which, incidentally, was in the care of the Secretary for War and Colonies) to arrange for the delivery of a letter to the authorities in the Loochoo Islands by a warship of the Royal Navy. It was a bold but sensible official of the Foreign Office who scribbled a minute at the end of the instruction, questioning whether such a request (which could only be satisfied by the commander-in-chief of the China station) should not have gone through the Admiralty. Palmerston to Bonham, 10 Aug. 1849 (No. 63), Broadlands MSS., BD/CH/23–33.

[2] Admiral Cochrane to Admiralty, 4 Apr. 1845, Adm. 1/5548.

[3] To Lord Aberdeen, 3 Mar. 1845, F.O. 17/98.

[4] Davis to Palmerston, 7 Dec. 1847 (No. 207), F.O. 17/132.

[5] On paper, however, his powers as supreme commander remained unaffected, even when the war was over. See Aberdeen to Pottinger, 4 Jan. 1843, F.O. 17/64.

unfortunately, interludes of peace were the seed-time producing the thorniest problems of liaison. This was chiefly owing to the fact that the administrative authorities frequently found it necessary to influence the course of political negotiations by 'showing the flag' or by more belligerent gestures, that did not necessarily involve a 'threat of grape'. 'Gunboat diplomacy' was intended in theory to be the bloodless method of hastening a decision, and in such circumstances, as Lord Aberdeen pointed out more than once, the superior authority of Her Majesty's governor of plenipotentiary had to be accepted.[6] The Foreign Secretary was not unmindful of what might happen should an overwrought captain, by precipitate action, unlock China's Pandora Box of ills.

So sound a philosophy of action was scarcely likely to reduce the rigid barriers that separated civilian plenipotentiary or Superintendent of Trade from the naval commander-in-chief. On grounds of political necessity, Sir Henry Pottinger was determined to exert his authority over the operations of such squadron units as were engaged in the never-ending struggle against pirates, opium smugglers, or Cantonese, the latter of which he now felt bound to conciliate. Inevitably, the truculent effort to impose his will on the conduct of the squadron was to lead to almost continuous and damaging in-fighting. One particularly publicized example serves to illustrate the perplexing nature of divided authority.

It so happened that in April 1843 one of Jardine, Matheson's schooners, the *Vixen*, set sail from Chusan, ostensibly for Koolangsu. Captain Hope, the senior officer at Chusan, believed that the vessel, like others of her kind, was engaged in the opium traffic, and that she was heading for Shanghai before the port had been legally declared open for trade. He therefore ordered the *Vixen* to be detained, and sent the sloop *Childers* and the steamer *Medusa* to Shanghai with orders to chase all British merchant ships out of the river within twenty-four hours. Thereafter, the Yangtse was to be blockaded against their further intrusions. Hitherto, the 'opium gentlemen' had been allowed to move along the coast between Chusan and Macao with no questions asked. 'As the higher power allowed them to do this I never interfered,' said Hope.

[6] Aberdeen to Pottinger, 3 June 1842 (No. 18), L/P & S/9/3 (I.O.A.).

But when they began to visit Shanghai, it seemed high time to put a stop to such proceedings, 'more especially as those vessels are manned and armed more like men of war than merchantmen, and are well known to commit all kinds of irregularities, and to[o] often great excesses to promote their own selfish ends. . . .'[7]

Captain Hope's emissaries failed to catch the *Vixen* (which eventually returned to Hong Kong), but they did, on 20 April, find four other British vessels at the mouth of the Yangtse which they encouraged to leave within the twenty-four-hour limit. On learning of the incident, merchant houses in Macao and Hong Kong raised shrill voices against presumptuous proceedings that threatened the profitable sale of the drug, hitherto warmly welcomed by Chinese officials as well as populace up and down the coast. Pottinger's response was more measured since he found himself uncomfortably placed on the horns of a dilemma. He believed that the 'pernicious and baleful effects of opium' had been grossly exaggerated; on the other hand, he was properly fearful of giving the impression that he approved of the trade. He was, however, saved from an awkward predicament when official investigation failed to prove that the *Vixen* was carrying opium. Hence, the Superintendent of Trade was able to reprimand the over-zealous Hope, without incurring the risk of being charged as a supporter of illegal trade.[8]

None the less, Pottinger was well aware that smuggling was on the increase, especially around Woosung, and, as he reported to Lord Aberdeen, he was in no position to disavow publicly Hope's action, because the Captain was clearly attempting to stop what he believed to be an illegal trader.[9] On the other hand, the Imperial Commissioner had to be placated, for the simple reason that a British warship had invaded Chinese territorial waters. Ch'i-ying himself seems to have believed that the episode belied the British contention that the China station was badly undermanned. Obviously, more warships were roving the China seas than were required for peaceful purposes. '. . . I am afraid', Pottinger informed Aberdeen a

---

[7] Quoted, Fairbank, *Trade and Diplomacy . . .*, i. 139.
[8] See Pottinger to Aberdeen, 21 and 29 Apr. 1843 (Nos. 39 and 40), F.O. 17/67.
[9] 9 June 1843 (No. 56), ibid.

little archly, 'that the idea to which Keying [Ch'i-ying] alluded as to there being so many Ships of War to the Northward has originated in ourselves, for I observed in one of Captain Hope's letters to the Admiral, that he had inconsiderately made use of that very expression as one of the reasons for his proceedings.' But to the Imperial Commissioner, the Governor declared with hand on heart that rumours in regard to the number of ships in and around Chusan were positively untrue. Apart from merchant vessels, only one large warship, two sloops, and two small steamers remained in that area. Moreover, Hope's efforts to interrupt trade on the Yangtse had been condemned, and the Captain posted to a distant station.[10]

Indeed, Hope had been peremptorily recalled. On 14 June he left Hong Kong for Singapore, but not before issuing a vigorous defence of his conduct. He had simply followed Pottinger's own ruling against illegal trade issued on 14 November 1842, and, he added, so sensible a regulation deserved continued and whole-hearted support. The First Lord was not unimpressed by such candour: '. . . about his fiery and unfortunate warfare agst opium,' he wrote to Lord Aberdeen, 'he may have acted illegally—but certainly he has not acted inequitably'.[11]

Although Pottinger, with some suavity, informed Aberdeen that the incident had in no way altered friendly relations between himself and the Admiral, Parker was incensed by what he regarded as the political manœuvring of the Superintendent of Trade, and more particularly by his efforts to circumscribe the movement of Her Majesty's ships. He was clearly trying 'to reduce the position of the Naval Commander in chief in these seas to a mere cypher'. In brief, he aimed at placing Parker's officers under his own orders.[12] Pottinger's justification for his conduct was based on a rather finely drawn interpretation of official instructions, which gave him, so he maintained, sole authority over any activities ashore or afloat

---

[10] Pottinger to Aberdeen, 5 July 1843 (No. 74), encl. Pottinger to Ch'i-ying, 1 July 1843, F.O. 17/68.

[11] Haddington to Aberdeen, 12 Aug. 1843, F.O. 17/75.

[12] Parker to Secretary of Admiralty, *Cornwallis* at Hong Kong, 26 July 1843, Adm. 1/553.

that might have political implications. 'With these Instructions in my possession,' he wrote to Parker a little ponderously, 'it may seem strange and unaccountable for me to say that I do not happen officially to know where a single ship, except your Excellency's Flag Ship, of Her Majesty's Vessels in the China Seas is at the moment . . .; numbers of Her Majesty's Ships have repeatedly sailed from Hong Kong without my even hearing of it until they were gone.' And he concluded: 'The impression I have is, that the Naval Commander and Squadron is precisely placed on the same footing as far as I am concerned, as the Military Commander of the Land Forces. It is clear that your Excellency does not subscribe to that impression, and it is surely clear, that one of us must be in error.'[13]

The Board of Admiralty quite naturally scorned such bureaucratic logic as spurious and offensive. Resentful of Pottinger's search for an over-all supremacy, they supported Parker, and in a candid minute, chiefly for the benefit of Lord Aberdeen, they professed unqualified approval of the commander-in-chief's 'discretion' and 'the temperate tone' of his correspondence.[14] But for all the cautionary admonitions from the Foreign Office, Pottinger continued to throw his weight about, ordering R.N. captains to take instructions from his civilian or military subordinates should political considerations, in his view, be involved. On one occasion, he went so far as to order the flogging of merchant seamen on board ship, an outrageous inflation of authority which drew the ire of the Admiralty and a reprimand from Lord Aberdeen. His request that a special flag be displayed when he, as Governor of Hong Kong, was aboard one of Her Majesty's ships merely amused the Admiral, who observed that such personal distinctions were forbidden by Queen's regulations.[15] So terse and conclusive a response pleased their Lordships, who complimented the Admiral on keeping his temper.

Despite the efforts of both Admiralty and Foreign Office to restore harmony on the China station, 'cold war' rather than

[13] Pottinger to Aberdeen, 18 July 1843 (No. 84), encl. No. 3, Pottinger to Parker, same date, F.O. 17/68.

[14] Minute of 1 Nov. 1843, attached to Parker to Secretary of Admiralty, 26 July 1843, Adm. 1/5530.

[15] Parker to Secretary of Admiralty, 14 and 24 Oct. 1843, Adm. 1/5530; see also, Phillimore, *Life of Parker*, ii. 388–9.

co-operation continued to mark the relations of plenipoteni-
ary and Admiral. Throughout the controversy, both
Whitehall offices had intervened on occasion, praying that the
antagonists seek the national rather than private interest. For
the sake of tranquillity and efficiency on the station, Lord
Aberdeen hoped that the Admiral would consider Pottinger's
more extreme or unreasonable demands 'in spirit rather than
in letter'. At the same time, he should remember that, because
of the precarious nature of Anglo-Chinese relations, it would
be unwise for him to 'move in force on any part of the Coast of
China without the concurrence of the Plenipotentiary',[16] and
he should not undertake operations, such as Captain Hope had
authorized 'with great zeal, but under an error of judgment
. . . without previously ascertaining how such an operation
would be viewed by the Plenipotentiary, and guiding himself
accordingly'. It was of course the prerogative of the Admiral
to assign and command the ships required for particular objectives 'having regard to demands . . . from other portions of the
station', but the coast of China was the special care of the
Superintendent of Trade, and had to be given first priority. In
turn, Pottinger was advised to adopt a more friendly and
considerate attitude towards his naval colleague, and any plans
which might involve the use of H.M.'s ships should be made
known to the Admiral before action was taken.[17]

But the doctrine of civilian authority was bound to be open
to abuse, especially when interpreted by a trinitarian—governor, plenipotentiary, and superintendent of trade—of Pottinger's peculiar sensitivity and vanity. The more demands
that were made on the squadron, the greater the strain on the
commander-in-chief in his efforts to make ends meet. With
the signing of the Supplementary Treaty on 8 October 1843,
the call on resources was more than doubled, and tension
between civilian and naval authority mounted correspondingly. Article X of the Supplementary Treaty bears the stamp
of Pottinger's own thinking. Within the Article, it was laid

[16] After 26 June 1843 when Hong Kong was declared a British colony, Pottinger
held the three offices of Plenipotentiary and Minister Extraordinary, Chief Superintendent of Trade, and Governor of Hong Kong. The last office, as has been noted, was
placed under the Colonial Office, the first two remaining under the Foreign Office.
[17] Aberdeen to Haddington (First Lord of the Admiralty), 24 Aug. 1843, F.O.
17/75. See also, F.O. to Pottinger, same date, F.O. 17/65.

down that at each of the five Treaty ports to be opened to British trade, one cruiser was to be stationed 'to enforce good order and discipline amongst the Crews of Merchant Shipping', and to support the authority of the consul over British subjects.

The obligation to place a warship at every Treaty port put the commander-in-chief in an embarrassing quandary. Admiral Parker lacked the disposable units to comply with such an agreement. Were he to provide the required harbour force, he would be without ships to carry out necessary anti-pirate patrol and convoy duties. The recall of vessels for refit before their reliefs appeared added to the problem. In the event of an emergency, he might have to release a cruiser for punitive operations on the Borneo coast, or to rescue a missionary in distant New Zealand. In addition, he was called upon to transport homeward, or at least as far as India, successive instalments of the Chinese indemnity. All told, he was working on a very tight string, and he made it clear to the Superintendent that the maintenance of secure communications along a largely uncharted and pirate-ridden coast was for the moment beyond the capacity of his squadron. The difficulty could, of course, be ameliorated if station vessels could be released for special services; and he made the further point that both ships and crews tended to deteriorate when tied to civilian jetties over long periods. If such a solution were out of the question, he saw no reason why the occasional troop-ship could not be used for station duties, alternating, when opportunity offered, with the visiting frigate, sloop, or steamer.

The Admiralty accepted the fact that the navy's hands were tied by Article X; none the less, they supported Parker in his opposition to a rigid interpretation which would put trade security at risk and turn at least five warships into decaying police stations. The Foreign Office was equally concerned, and Lord Aberdeen hoped that the Chinese could be made to recognize the obvious, presuming the British point of view was presented convincingly. It would be sheer nonsense to interpret the offending Article literally. Surely, periodic visits would fulfil the spirit of the agreement, in which case the formal prescription could be safely ignored and eventually forgotten. In the meantime, Her Majesty's consuls should be

warned not to ask for naval assistance except in case of dire
need, when, for example, they found 'their own powers insufficient to maintain order among the crews of British vessels'.[18]

But Pottinger remained intent on keeping scrupulously to
the terms of the Treaty and its Supplementary provisions in
the interest of improved Anglo-Chinese relations. He insisted
that he was chiefly concerned with the 'spirit and intention',
but all the evidence suggests that he was an obstinate stickler
for the 'letter' of the law. Because China was not like any
European nation, she could only learn the meaning of European conventions if she were treated with punctilious correct-
ness; '. . . it grieves me to remark', he wrote to Lord Aberdeen
some five months after the Supplementary agreement on
stationed ships had been signed, 'that I think there is a certain
carelessness . . . as to infringing it [the Treaty]. I mean, that
things are often done, or attempted to be done, which though
not expressly prohibited by the Treaty, I do not believe would
be considered admissible with regard to independent states in
Europe.'[19]

Pottinger was intent on bending over backwards, if needs
be, to avoid rousing sensitive prickles in Peking.[20] Admiral
Parker had already been warned not to 'show the flag' outside
the projected Treaty ports. Flaunting even a meagre naval
strength might rouse fears and suspicion, and for this reason he
had asked the commander-in-chief to cancel a northern cruise
which had been planned for the flagship *Agincourt*.[21] To sustain the present fragile harmony, the hatchet must not only be
buried; it must be seen to be buried. No line-of-battleship
should approach the coast of China without first obtaining

[18] Aberdeen to Pottinger, 15 Nov. 1843 (No. 88, draft), F.O. 17/65.

[19] 1 Mar. 1844 (No. 41), F.O. 17/80.

[20] For example, he refused to sanction the appointment of Captain Sir Edward
Belcher who had been given command of the *Samarang* with orders to survey the new
Treaty ports. Belcher's pugnacious ways were well known, and the substitution of
Lieutenant William Bate was wise. See Parker to Admiralty, 16 Nov. 1843, enclosing
instructions, Parker to Belcher, 28 Oct. 1843, Adm. 1/5530; also, Ritchie, *The Admir-
alty Chart* p. 235.
After many useful years surveying the coasts of China, Bate was killed in the course
of operations against Canton in December 1857.

[21] Pottinger to Parker (encl. No. 3), 31 Mar. 1843, F.O. 17/67. See also, Pottinger to
Aberdeen, 17 Apr. 1843, enclosing a letter from the Imperial Commission, praying
that British ships, including trading vessels, should stick to 'Outer Waters' to avoid
frightening the coastal inhabitants. Ibid.

permission from the Superintendent of Trade.[22] And scarcely two weeks after the Supplementary Treaty had been signed, Pottinger was responsible for a proclamation forbidding all vessels carrying British colours from passing northward of the 32° of latitude (which meant the mouth of the Yangtse) unless under stress of weather.[23] The squadron was reduced 'to the lowest possible scale', he wrote to the Imperial Commissioner, Ch'i-ying, shortly after the Supplementary Treaty had been ratified. 'Indeed, the Government of England has no object now that Peace and Goodwill is so firmly established, in keeping ships of War in China, beyond what are absolutely required for duty. These ships will be occasionally relieved and will return to England when others come to take their duties, but there will be no permanent increase.'[24]

Until his recall in the early spring of 1844, Pottinger remained determinedly opposed to 'the indiscriminate visits' of British warships. Fearful of endangering the brittle *entente*, he contended (quite unreasonably) that any show of strength and flag beyond the requirements listed in Article X would constitute a flagrant violation of Treaty. Even a new face and a fresh effort at amicable co-operation failed to dent the hard shell of obduracy. When Rear-Admiral Sir Thomas Cochrane, who took over the command from Parker in December 1843, asked permission to move his flagship into the Canton River at Blenheim Reach where fresh water would release a two years' accumulation of barnacles from her hull, Pottinger abruptly refused. He saw 'the strongest political objections' to such a proposal. The Chinese had recently shown resistance even to the presence of large merchant ships within the river. He had, he thought, calmed their fears; but the entry of a line-of-battleship could easily blow his carefully wrought diplomacy to bits. 'I am quite convinced', he wrote to Lord Aberdeen, 'that the Government of China would consider the *Agincourt*'s entering the River—whatever reason might be assigned for her doing so—to be an infraction of the Treaty, and that the

[22] Barrow (Admiralty) to Parker, 29 Aug. 1843, Adm. 2/1601.
[23] See General Memorandum (printed) issued by Vice-Admiral Parker, 7 Nov. 1843, Adm. 125/94.
[24] 26 Oct. 1843 (No. 23), encl. in Pottinger to Aberdeen, 3 Nov. 1843 (No. 142), F.O. 17/70. The letter to Ch'i-ying contained an enumeration of British warships and surveying vessels in the South China Sea.

local authorities would instantly call on me to have her removed.'[25]

Pottinger may be found guilty of *naïveté*, but not knavery. His effort at appeasement was honest, and to interested members of the Peel Cabinet his argument was not unreasonable. In his dealings with Ch'i-ying, for whom he developed a considerable affection (which seems to have been reciprocated), he was at his best, although it is probable that the relationship helped to blur his sense of realities. A man of high principle and tremendous industry, he found himself gradually borne down by tides of trivia that often assumed mammoth shape in his imagination. And as his physical strength and morale declined, prickliness and aggressiveness, so often the accompaniment of isolation and loneliness, grew correspondingly. In the manner of an over-wrought destroyer captain in a submarine-infested sea, he felt obliged to watch, superintend, and amend the work of almost every subordinate within range. The resulting fatigue and nervous strain eroded judgement, and put in jeopardy the work of conciliation and co-operation on which he had set his heart.

Acting on his own 'unassisted judgment', so he wrote to Lord Stanley shortly before his departure from Hong Kong, he had been made the scapegoat for 'all public mistakes and oversights'. Certainly there was not much governmental business that escaped his attention, or failed to attract his interference. In consequence, he was destined to quarrel with everyone up to the end—not only the navy, but the army, his administrative colleagues, and most of the directors of merchant firms. Admiral Cochrane, not ordinarily given to rancour, described him an 'impossible'. Pottinger, he informed the Admiralty, was vain, vengeful, and impudent.[26] Like Ishmael's, his hand seemed to be against every man. And when at long last, amid scarcely concealed sighs of relief, he made ready to leave Hong Kong for Bombay, he suddenly refused to embark because a Spanish officer had been given a guest

[25] Pottinger to Aberdeen, 1 Mar. 1844 (No. 41), encl. letter from Admiral Cochrane, 29 Feb. 1844, and his reply, 1 Mar. (No. 65), F.O. 17/80. See also, Cochrane to Admiralty, Hong Kong, 13 June 1844, Adm. 1/5539, and Auckland to Russell, 23 Feb. 1848, Russell Papers, 36/22/7A. On the same point, see Phillimore, ii. 641–7.

[26] *Agincourt* at Hong Kong, 20 June 1844 (No. 21), Adm. 1/5539.

cabin on the very steamer that had been promised for his sole accommodation.

Overwork possibly accounted for a neurotic querulousness, sometimes approaching hysteria, that clouded his latter days in Hong Kong. The establishment of a new colony demanded Herculean labours; the local problems of government had been complex. But Pottinger was not only Governor; he was also Her Majesty's Plenipotentiary and Superintendent of Trade, offices which involved the exasperating task of organizing a new pattern of relationships with China. It was all too much for a man of his scrupulous intensity.[27] Although no medical evidence is available to support the thesis, it is conceivable that Pottinger was a sick man.[28] In any event, his enormous industry and his exacting sense of duty had not gone unobserved in Whitehall. With all his weaknesses, the home government was not unsympathetic to their harassed and weary servant, and as long as Lord Aberdeen remained at the Foreign Office, his philosophy of conciliation was accepted in rough by the Admiralty. From midsummer 1844, all naval officers on the station were earnestly bidden to respect Chinese usages and institutions, and to study the wishes and feelings of authorities and people.[29] On return to England, Pottinger was given a pension, and after a short leave was appointed Governor of the Cape of Good Hope, subsequently obtaining the post he most desired, the governorship of Madras.

Meanwhile, back from a spring tour of the northern Treaty ports, where he was treated with customary courtesy and

[27] See G. B. Endacott, *A History of Hong Kong* (London, 1958), p. 40.

[28] Admittedly, given the conditions of the service, and the chronic conflict between civilian and naval authority, anyone, during periods of stress, might well be diagnosed as 'sick'. The distinguished ex-army surgeon, Rutherford Alcock, Consul at Foochow in 1841 and later at Shanghai (1846), could write feelingly and accurately about a diplomat's life in the East. 'With the thermometer at 97° in bedroom, mosquitos swarming outside the curtains, and too often within, sleep is a blessing which comes but seldom, and is never sound and refreshing. . . . The heat itself, enervating and exhausting as it is, would be ten times more endurable, but for the winged plagues. . . . It is hardly fair then, in Eastern travellers, to suppress, as they almost invariably do, any reference to this greatest of small miseries. With the exception of enlarged livers and sudden death, no more grievous drawbacks to an eastern climate can be conceived.' Alcock, i, 6–7.

[29] Barrow to Cochrane, 8 July 1844, Adm. 2/1602.

kindness, Admiral Cochrane could see no reason why the required harbour protection as guaranteed by Supplementary Treaty, could not be effectively provided by visiting patrol cruisers.[30] Hence, he was the more ready to acclaim his predecessor's victory against civilian domination in Hong Kong. Wearied of the acrimonious exchanges between Admiral Parker and Sir Henry Pottinger, the Foreign Office had finally consulted their legal advisers on the role of the navy in support of British consular authority. The Attorney- and Solicitor-Generals' joint report, which was approved by the Cabinet on 6 February 1844, affirmed the government's faith in the judgement of the senior service, and offered the opinion that the Treaty pledge under Article X could be fully sustained by alternating available ships as opportunity offered.[31] In short, it was neither sensible nor possible 'to keep a ship constantly at each of the five places of trade on the Chinese coast as had been requested by Sir H. Pottinger'.[32]

But even with this welcome concession, it was going to be difficult findings ships to carry home the indemnity silver and other bullion, not to speak of providing escorts for British merchant ships at a time when the whole south-east coastal area was swarming with pirates.[33] One or two small steamers were obviously required to watch Canton, but if the more northerly Treaty ports were to be visited regularly during the period of the north-east monsoon, only steamers could provide anything like scheduled passages. In other words, regular supervision of the Treaty ports would require two more large steamers, possible a third. In a pinch, the Admiral could make do, as had his predecessors, with *ad hoc* arrangements. He was aware, he confessed, that naval estimates were to be further reduced, and he was not prepared to make urgent requisitions, out of 'duty to HMG's purse'.[34]

[30] Cochrane to Secretary to the Admiralty, 13 June 1844 (No. 6), Adm. 1/5539.

[31] Aberdeen to Pottinger, 6 Feb. 1844 (No. 14), F.O. 17/77. See also, Addington (F.O.) to Barrow, same date, encl. No. 14, Adm. 1/5544.

[32] Barrow to Parker at Trincomalee, 3 Feb. 1844, Adm. 2/1330; also, Haddington to Cochrane, same date, ibid.

[33] See Davis to Aberdeen, 28 May 1844 (No. 10), encl. in Addington to Herbert, 23 Sept. 1844; and same to same, 1 June 1844 (No. 13), encl. Davis to Parker, 30 May 1844 (No. 22), Adm. 1/5544.

[34] Cochrane to Admiralty, 13 June 1844 (No. 6), encl. with Barrow to Addington (F.O.), 23 Sept. 1844, F.O. 17/95. See also, Cochrane to Admiralty, 12 Aug. 1844 (No.

Had it not been for the national addiction to tea, and the pressures exerted by the East India interest in parliament, the China squadron (alleged defender of the notorious opium traffic) might, like the Mediterranean squadron, have suffered substantial reductions at the hands of an economizing House of Commons.[35] In the view of radicals like Hume, Bright, and Gladstone, even the elimination of Malayan or Borneo pirates, or the sinking of Arab slavers, represented a needless expenditure to satisfy the blood-lust of the Royal Navy. In the circumstances of the time, Cochrane was fortunate to command a by no means inconsiderable force in an area, which, before 1840, had been almost entirely neglected.

Early in 1844, the far-flung East Indies station had been divided, and a China station established as a separate entity with headquarters at Hong Kong. The East Indies division became, in consequence, a subordinate command under a captain, who was given the rank of commodore, second class. His station was restricted to the area between the Red Sea and Achin Head at the north-west tip of Sumatra. In charge of both divisions was the commander-in-chief, usually a rear-admiral, who was, however, instructed, barring an emergency, to stay away from the Indian Ocean in order to ensure 'the more effective performance of the important duties connected with China and that portion of the station'.[36] The dual squadron, China and East Indies, now consisted of one battleship, the *Agincourt*, two fifth-rates, *Cambrian* and *Castor*, four sixth-rates, five sloops, and three steamships.[37] Of the fifteen vessels (not counting two surveying ships), only four, a frigate, two sloops, and one steamer, were assigned to the Indian Ocean. Cochrane was given the rest.

·   ·   ·

52), encl. with Barrow to Addington, 14 Dec. 1844, ibid. As it happened, between 1846 and 1848, despite the pirate menace, six warships were withdrawn without immediate relief, and when the gaps were filled, not infrequently a brig replaced a sloop, and on one occasion, a frigate.

[35] The hitherto powerful Mediterranean squadron, second in importance to the Home fleet, had been reduced to one battleship of the second or third rate, one fourth-rate, two sixth-rates and three sloops, exclusive of steamships. Admiralty to Admiral Sir Edward Owen, 26 Jan. 1844 (draft), Adm. 1/5543.

[36] See Appendix B.

[37] Admiralty Instruction, Barrow to Vice-Admiral Parker at Trincomalee, 3 Feb. 1844, Adm. 2/1330. See also, Parker to Barrow, 10 Apr. 1844 (No. 67), Adm. 1/5539.

But a dozen or so sloops and steamers—indeed, the whole Royal Navy—was hardly sufficient to patrol effectively a thousand miles of coast, remarkable for its innumerable shoals, tiny islands, rocky headlands, and capricious currents, the perfect environment for the piratical adventurer. In the early years of the China station, when it had been a subordinate branch of the East Indies squadron, little attention was paid to a scourge which was endemic, and therefore taken for granted by both British and Chinese authorities. Although British involvement in the coastal trade was steadily increasing, the problem was either ignored, as in the Persian Gulf, or tackled piecemeal, with short-lived ardency that sometimes seemed to reflect Chinese approval. For most of the time, the pirates had a free run. The Chinese had no navy equipped to deal with well-organized bands of marauders; in times of urgency, they could do little more than try to appease, and submit to expensive blackmail.

Like the south-west coast of the Persian Gulf, the southern coast of China, with its fringes of islands and shallow channels, provided snug anchorages that were difficult to reach. By the end of the 1840s, Captains Collinson and Kellett had surveyed the greater part of the shore-line, but it was not their task to penetrate the labyrinths and locate pirate settlements that infested the whole coast, from well below the Canton estuary and above Amoy. The pirates were not all professionals in the sense that they had, as in the Persian Gulf, or on the outskirts of northern Borneo, adopted buccaneering as a career. Possibly in consequence of a bad catch at the end of a fishing season, whole villages might sally out on cruises, ready if necessary to fight to the death, even with neighbouring villagers, for the rich freights of passing junks.[38] As he left Macao for the last time in December 1842, Captain Hall of the *Nemesis* observed that the fishermen along the whole coast as far as Macao were 'rogues, pirates and smugglers. . . . They will perhaps appear quite friendly at first; and if they then find that a vessel is not prepared to resist or if they think that they could overpower her, the chances are that they would not hesitate to make the attempt when least expected.'[39]

[38] See Parkes's Journal for 1844, in Lane-Poole, i. 74–5.
[39] *Nemesis*, p. 385. As the Admiralty informed the Foreign Office with cautious

Under international law, the Royal Navy could claim the right to attack pirates anywhere on the high seas, but not within three miles of foreign coasts. In short, British warships were not justified in penetrating Chinese coastal waters without Chinese consent; and since this boundary limitation had been written into the Treaty of Nanking, any pursuit into estuaries and up rivers could be regarded as a breach of agreement. Pottinger had declared his whole-hearted acceptance of this ruling, and maintained that the Chinese authorities were perfectly able 'to curb their own subjects', whether as pirates, smugglers, or petty thieves. They had declined Britain's proffered assistance, he told Lord Aberdeen, and any attempt to put on pressure would damage a happily developing *entente*. Anglo-Chinese relations had settled down 'into a state of the most friendly and confidential alliance'. Preventive action, he warned Admiral Cochrane, should be confined strictly to the high seas, and then, only when the offenders were caught 'red-handed', or offered positive proof of ill-doing such as would satisfy a Court of Admiralty in Great Britain.[40]

This conception of a mixed moral and legal responsibility he was happy to demonstrate early in 1844. When, in the course of offshore surveying operations, Captain Collinson of H.M.S. *Plover* laid hold of what was clearly a pirate junk, Pottinger peremptorily reminded the commander-in-chief that such assaults were in breach of standing orders. Admiral Cochrane was bound to accept the complaint, and obliged to reprimand Collinson. Such aggressions, he was told, were only justified in the case of self-defence, or if a European vessel was under attack.[41]

In years to come, Cochrane was unfairly to bear much of the blame for what the British merchant community regarded as a 'pussyfooting' attitude to ruffianism and murder.[42] His suc-

understatement, 'the distinction between the fair trader and the pirate is not always marked in the East, and strong general measures for the suppression of piracy are subject to abuse and must be regulated with caution'. 27 Oct. 1848, Adm. 2/1665.

[40] 16 Mar. 1844 (No. 50), encl. Pottinger to Cochrane, 15 Mar. 1844, F.O. 17/80.

[41] Pottinger to Aberdeen, 16 Mar. 1844 (No. 50), encl. correspondence between Pottinger and Cochrane, F.O. 17/80. Cf. encl. No. 2, in Pottinger to Admiral Parker, 20 Mar. 1843 (No. 18), F.O. 17/66.

[42] An obituary in the Hong Kong *Register* the day following the death of Admiral Sir Francis Collier on 28 October 1849, reflects the resentment of the merchant community towards a frustrated squadron commander whose hands were tied by

cessors, Admirals Inglefield and Collier, were pledged to equal restraint,[43] and the same instruction was repeated again and again, even into the 1850s. The presumed pirate must have been caught at sea in the act; if not, positive and convincing evidence had to be provided, proving beyong legal quibble that a felony had been committed.

The question of establishing proof beyond doubt was bound to remain, with or without Chinese co-operation, an exceedingly sensitive one. Unless an attack was actually in progress, the problem of distinguishing the true pirate at sea from the apparently innocent Chinese trader or fisherman was practically insoluble. It was naturally assumed in Hong Kong that the Chinese authorities would have no difficulty in separating the sheep from the wolves; only to a European did one Chinese look like every other Chinese![44] It stood to reason, therefore, that the vexing problem of recognition would be enormously simplified if Peking would agree to co-operate. As a matter of fact, even the local mandarins, with the advantage of language and local experience, often found it difficult to distinguish the good from the bad.[45]

With the growth of the opium trade, the impact of piracy made itself particularly felt among the growing European trading fleets, especially British and American. The list of

---

government instruction. 'One of the last acts of this lamented officer . . . was to repeal the . . . mischievous memorandum of Sir Thomas Cochrane, on the subject of Piracy in these seas. A memorandum which, in tying up the hands of the commanders of Her Majesty's ships, has cost thousands of innocent lives, and brought the murderer, who knows no mercy, into the very harbour of Hong Kong.'

[43] See instructions to Collier of 16 June 1848; Adm. 13/3/267–88. See also in this connection, Grace Fox, *British Admirals and Chinese Pirates 1832–1869* (London, 1940), pp. 97–100, and Endacott, *A History of Hong Kong*, p. 76.

[44] The Chinese seem to have distinguished between 'pirates at sea' and banditti who plundered on river and land. Obviously, a neat line is impossible to draw between the two, although it would appear that the truly professional pirate was less affected in his career by famine or prosperity, while the ordinary coastal fisherman was much more likely to be tempted to smuggling and violence by hunger and want of employment. Both Dr. Gutzlaff, who was well acquainted with the coast of the Canton delta and of Fukien, and Admiral Sir James Stirling, commander-in-chief, 1854–6, believed that both amateur and professional pirates plundered and killed less in times of abundance. But each region produced its own type, and it seems to have been generally agreed that the whole of the maritime population of the southerly coast possessed a toughness and guile, and perhaps a ferocity, that marked them off from the usually mild and peace-loving Chinese of the interior.

[45] See Fox, op. cit., pp. 97–8.

casualties mounted yearly. The cession of Hong Kong, it had been hoped, would greatly relieve an unhealthy and increasingly embarrassing situation, but, as it happened, not only did Hong Kong become the principal opium distributing centre (and therefore a kind of aggrandized thieves' kitchen), it seemed to be developing as a prolific breeding ground. With agents and spies in every gambling den—even in the police force—it was possible to learn the prospective movements not only of merchant vessels, but of British warships. Occasionally, the pirate ranks were reinforced by American and European adventurers, drawn to the new colony by easy pickings. By 1844, underground organizations controlled fleets, so it was estimated, of around 150 war vessels, and it could be assumed that some of them had been registered as peaceful traders in Hong Kong and carried the British flag.

It was hoped that the worst attentions of the pirates might be avoided by arranging convoys that would be escorted by Portuguese lorchas from Macao.[46] These officially appointed escorts were well armed, and their masters knew the coasts. Yet it was in the nature of things that acquisitive captains should abuse their power. In not a few instances, convoy fees became another form of blackmail. To Palmerston, not only was such a system open to grave abuse, it was harmful to British prestige that foreigners should be called in to help safeguard British trade. It was the Royal Navy's job to deal with pirates, and to press for the co-operation of the Chinese who were the worst sufferers.[47]

In October 1848, the Admiralty recommended that a colonial 'floating police' should be organized to take over responsibility for the Hong Kong area, to be aided in time of stress by available ships from the China squadron—possibly 'stationed' ships at present rusting at anchor. Despite severely limited means, considerable successes had already been recorded.

[46] See Bonham to Palmerston, 9 June 1848, F.O. 17/143.

[47] A part of the price of co-operation was the surrender of Chinese pirates to the local authorities, an arrangement which worried Governor Davis because of the indiscriminate severity with which the authorities dealt with such captives. Palmerston recommended that 'at least for the present' they should be handed over; but if the Chinese government were to persevere 'in such sweeping executions as they have hitherto inflicted upon such criminals' the prisoners would have to be tried in Hong Kong, 'whatever the inconvenience of doing so may be'. Palmerston to Davis, 9 Nov. 1847 (No. 138), Broadlands MSS., BD/CH/1–22.

Within a few months of their assignment to an anti-piracy role, the cruisers *Scout* and *Espiègle* had been serving in convoys, or, with proven effectiveness, helping to ferret out pirate nests along the coast. Provided such reinforcements could be trebled, there would be no need to call on the Portuguese for assistance.[48] Palmerston had already discussed the plan of a 'floating police' with Earl Grey. He liked the idea, but in his view such a force, organized under the auspices of the Governor of Hong Kong, was clearly the responsibility of the Colonial Secretary.[49] But Grey was reluctant to take the initiative. In his opinion, the control and operation of armed ships was the responsibility of the Admiralty; but even if this were not so, the expense of such an undertaking would be more than the Colonial exchequer could bear.[50]

For the moment, the only alternative to official British naval protection was the issuance of licences or 'sailing letters' to suitably armed private craft, acting as escorts under British colours. Unfortunately, piracy was just as capable of prospering under 'the honoured flag'. The masters of these registered coastal escorts proved scarcely less corruptible than their predecessors, although their interests were more likely to be concentrated on opium smuggling than on violent blackmail. The system seemed to breed more abuses than it prevented, and in the end, chiefly as a result of the Governor's bitter criticisms, Palmerston at long last felt compelled to call for strong action. 'Vague and imperfect' safeguards were to be replaced by punitive pursuits, and the first serious assault on organized piracy was planned for the spring of 1849.

Chasing the individual pirate vessel was a matter of 'hit and miss'; catching him in the course of an attack was pure luck. Paradoxically as it may appear, pirate organization simplified the task of suppression. A fleet of enemy ships was easier to trace, and much easier to identify, for their bloody trails of destruction along the coast were only too obvious. Moreover, the assembly haunts, usually in lagoons well guarded by reefs

---

[48] See W. A. B. Hamilton (Admiralty) to Addington (F.O.), 27 Oct. 1848, Adm. 2/1665. These recommendations were sent to Admiral Collier for consideration. Admiralty to Collier, 16 Nov. 1848, Adm. 2/1607.

[49] Palmerston to Grey, 19 Sept. 1848, F.O. 17/151.

[50] See Fred. Elliot (C.O.) to Addington, 7 Oct. 1848, ibid.

and shallows, could sooner or later be established as the suffering victims, often village fisherfolk, spread their tales of woe on the grape-vine telegraph.

The Henry Morgan of the most important and dangerous confederacy was Shap-ng-tsai, who frequently worked in consort with his scarcely less enterprising partner, Chui-apoo. Following a series of sweeps along the south-east seaboard, Chui-apoo's fleet was practically destroyed following an encounter off Ty-sa-mi Inlet [Great Sand Spit], nearly midway between Hong Kong and Swatow, and finally, on 1 October 1849, in Bias Bay, an inlet some forty miles to the north-eastward of Hong Kong. Assisted by the P. & O. steamer *Canton*, the sloops *Columbine* and *Fury*, along with boats from H.M.S. *Hastings*, not only demolished 23 armed junks, averaging 500 tons, but captured 200 guns and large stores of ammunition. All told, 500 pirates were killed; the British losses were four killed and six wounded.[51]

Some days later, the squadron turned southward in the direction of Hainan Island, where it was reported that Shap-ng-tsai had taken refuge. Captain Hay's little force (which now included the Company steamer *Phlegethon*) left Hainan on 14 October, reinforced by eight Chinese junks carrying a 100 native soldiers under the command of a fighting mandarin, Hwáng. After a close search along the coast, good intelligence led them six days later to the shallows of the Bay of Tonquin. The fleet found there numbered 64 vessels, carrying, so it was subsequently estimated, 1,200 guns and 3,000 men, with Shap-ng-tsai's large junk alone mounting at least 42 guns. For nine hours the British cruisers hunted for a channel in the manner, as Hay's dispatch expressed it, of 'terriers at a rat hole'. In the end, a native pilot who managed to escape from the shore took the squadron over the mud bar, where Shap-ng-tsai awaited the attackers with his heaviest junks moored in line. The fighting was sharp, and might have been prolonged for hours had not a lucky shell from the *Phlegethon*

[51] See Captain (subsequently Admiral Sir John) Hay's account in *The Suppression of Piracy in the China Sea, 1849* (London, 1889), pp. 28–31, and Beresford Scott (Paymaster and Purser of H.M.S. *Columbine*), *An Account of the Destruction of the Fleets of the Celebrated Pirate Chieftains Chui-Apoo and Shap-ng-Tsai, on the Coast of China, in September and October, 1849* (London 1881, dedication inscribed *1851*), pp. 88–92.

entered the magazine of the 'flagship'. The resulting explosion left only the poop afloat, the pirate's flag of defiance still flying at the top of the railing until engulfed by the spreading fire. Shap-ng-tsai had the good fortune to escape in a small boat, risking on shore the vengeance of an infuriated populace, ready with spears and knives to dispatch any survivors.

The engagement was resumed next day with some difficulty, since the lighter junks had fled up the Tonquin River, wiggling through shoals and shallows into creeks and crannies, accessible only to boats. In the end, 24 junks were taken, and most of them burned, bringing the total, after two days' fighting, to 58, without any British loss of life.[52] At least 1,700 pirates had been killed, a collective execution which, so the navy assumed, would jar Mr. Gladstone and the Peace Society into further agitation for the protection of 'these innocent fishermen'. Such action, wrote the purser of the *Columbine*, would be quite as reasonable as 'an appeal to the Society for Preventing Cruelty to Animals on behalf of the now ravenous wolves in the Pyrenees'. *The Times* (21 Jan. 1850) hoped that the expedition would teach the Chinese 'to respect and fear British arms; for their own war-junks have been actually afraid to encounter the pirates'. Unhappily, so devastating a victory did little to diminish individual enterprise elsewhere. Hundreds of ruthless and ingenious adventurers and rascals remained committed to their professional calling. Echoes from the guns that blew fleets apart in Bias Bay and Tonquin had scarcely died down before a concentration of trading junks was boarded and plundered almost within hailing distance of H.M.S. *Hastings* in Hong Kong harbour.

The elimination in Tonquin Bay of the best organized pirate fleet in the China seas had been essentially a victory for Chinese intelligence. The discovery of the whereabouts of the enemy had by itself demonstrated how basic was Chinese co-operation in any policy of suppression. As it happened, it was not long after Shap-ng-tsai's humiliating defeat that

---

[52] Hay to Rear-Admiral Sir Francis Collier, *Columbine*, Chokeum, Cochin-China, 23 Oct. 1849, contained in Beresford Scott, op. cit., pp. 160–5. See also, Secretary to H.M.'s Plenipotentiary in China, to Secretary, Government of India, Victoria, Hong Kong, 22 Nov. 1849 (No. 123), Foreign Dept., Political, Consultation No. 28, 18 Jan. 1850 (N.A.I.).

requests began to come in from Chinese coast officials and provincial admirals asking for assistance. This was almost always provided, and following such instances of joint endeavour (which were usually successful), the captured pirates were turned over to Chinese courts for trial.[53] Unfortunately for the immediate future of Anglo-Chinese co-operation, Rear-Admiral Collier, who had worked hard to establish an effective association with the Chinese authorities, died from apoplexy on 28 October 1849. His successor, Rear-Admiral Charles Austin, who acted as stop-gap, did not put in an appearance until the summer of 1850. Austin was not opposed to dealing with the Chinese in an effort to co-ordinate operations, even on a small scale; but like Cochrane he was not prepared to risk his neck by bending standing orders. Individual demonstrations of zeal outside the rules had not won favour with either Hong Kong or the Admiralty, chiefly owing to fear of Chinese displeasure. The awkward problem of recognition and identification still stood in the way of aggressive action, and Austin's 'copy-book' instructions followed the official path of caution and restraint. Like his predecessors, he was expected to display a 'benevolent blindness' to the ugly spectre of piracy, unless revealed physically in 'predatory and violent acts at sea'.

[53] Fox, op. cit., p. 119.

XI

REBELS, PIRATES, AND RUSSIANS: THE CRIMEAN WAR

PALMERSTON went out of office following the accession of the short-lived Derby Ministry in February 1852, and when he returned in December of that year, it was as Home Secretary in Lord Aberdeen's Cabinet. But even had he, instead of Lord Clarendon, succeeded to the Foreign Office in February 1853, it is unlikely that he could have maintained an increasingly rigid attitude towards a China in turmoil.[1] By that time, the Taiping rebels were advancing headlong down the Yangtse valley, capturing Nanking in March, and threatening to reach the sea. Although the trade of Shanghai suffered severely, Governor Bonham had turned down Peking's request for intervention on the side of the Imperial government. Cautious by nature, he was fearful of mixing in a civil war and conceivably helping to prolong it. In a letter to the Foreign Secretary, he strongly urged a policy of non-interference, except when injury to British subjects or British trade was threatened, as shortly proved to be the case in Shanghai. Bonham himself had a brush with the insurgents when he visited Ningpo in April 1853; but in Shanghai, where a jittery population awaited the gathering storm, he found comfort in the presence of a French and an American frigate, and considerable relief on learning that British reinforcements were on the way to join in the task of safeguarding the European community.[2]

The British government was naturally uneasy in a situation which threatened trade prospects and might well endanger the northern Treaty ports. No one in Whitehall knew precisely what the war was about, and Lord Clarendon was loath to lay

[1] Lord Clarendon replaced Lord John Russell as Foreign Secretary, Russell remaining in the Cabinet as Minister without portfolio.

[2] See Bonham to Russell, Shanghai, 22 Mar. 1853. The visit to Ningpo and the engagement with the rebels is described in two letters addressed to the Earl of Clarendon, one of 6 May (No. 109) and the other, 11 May (No. 110), India Proceedings, vol. 183, Consultation No. 107, 29 July 1853 (N.A.I.).

down specific rules of conduct 'at a distance'. He could do little more for the moment than enjoin strict neutrality. Foreign participants on either side forfeited any claim to British protection. On the other hand, he saw no reason why the navy should not adopt a protective role where British interests were at stake. If the rebels attempted to occupy Shanghai, they should, if possible, be repelled, and Bonham was given full authority in co-operation with the newly appointed commander-in-chief, Vice-Admiral Sir Fleetwood Pellew, to conscribe, if necessary, available British merchantmen in the neighbourhood, and arm them. Meanwhile, with the second Burma War at an end, all war vessels that could be spared from Indian waters were ordered to China. The first and paramount duty of the augmented squadron, the Admiralty informed Pellew, was 'to provide adequately for the protection of British subjects and property in Canton, Amoy and Shanghai'.[3]

Sir Fleetwood Broughton Reynolds Pellew, second son of the famous Admiral, Viscount Exmouth, was nominated to succeed Rear-Admiral Charles Austin in December 1852. It was an unfortunate appointment, and therefore a short-lived one. Even at the time, doubts were expressed on the wisdom of sending a highly-strung man of sixty-four to command a squadron mainly concerned with river operations in a hot and often unhealthy climate. Pellew reached Rangoon in April 1853, where he hoisted his flag on the *Winchester*, examined the latest Chinese intelligence, and then set forth to give an anxious Governor of Hong Kong 'all necessary assistance'. Perhaps his very keenness, his zeal for efficiency, was responsible for an excessive imperiousness in dealing with subordinates. In any event, he was ruthlessly intent on carrying out his instructions, and when in September after prolonged cruising the *Winchester* dropped anchor in Hong Kong harbour, her

---

[3] 9 May 1853 (No. 53), Adm. 2/1611. By July, there was only one warship, the *Fox* (42), in Indian waters, and her captain was preparing to refit at Trincomalee in readiness for the expected summons to China. Cmdr. Lambert to Secretary, Government of India, 4 July 1853, India Proc., vol. 183, Consultation No. 1, 26 Aug. 1853; and receipt of such instructions acknowledged No. 2, 21 July 1853, ibid. (N.A.I.).

See also, Dalhousie to Secret Committee, Court of Directors, 5 Aug. 1853 (No. 53), L/P & S/5/16 (I.O.A.); and Foreign Dept. (Fort William), Consultation No. 44, 16 June, Consultation No. 85, 24 June, with Minute by the Governor-General, 15 June 1853, and Consultation No. 86, 24 June, relating advice from Whitehall on the assembly of a naval squadron in China waters (N.A.I.).

weary crew, fretting under the broiling sun, the humidity, and the boredom of a confined existence, were already restive, impatiently awaiting their long-deserved shore leave.

Carefully weighing the problem of health and discipline in an ebullient Chinese town of low grog shops, brothels, filthy alleys, and damp heat, Pellew decided against 'leave', at least until the weather became cooler. But, like a fool, he failed to give any explanation of his purpose. At this further postponement, there were bitter murmurings from a sorely disappointed crew, and some of them spoke their minds with a fluency and pungency that, to Pellew, savoured of mutiny. Whereupon, he ordered the drummer to 'beat to quarters', and when this dramatic command was ignored, officers with drawn swords were sent to the lower deck to enforce obedience. In the course of the disturbance, three or four men were wounded, and the so-called mutiny was quelled.

Eventually the news reached England, and *The Times* in biting leading articles drew attention to the fact that this was Pellew's third mutiny. But even without pressure from *The Times*, it seems likely that the Admiralty would have acted. In January 1854, he was relieved of his command on the simplified ground that he had inflicted unauthorized corporal punishment upon six seamen. He was ordered to sail for Trincomalee, where his successor, Rear-Admiral Sir James Stirling, founder in 1826 of the settlement in Raffles Bay, north Australia, and subsequently the first Governor of Western Australia (1829–39), would take command.[4] Six weeks later, however, because of worsening relations with Russia, Stirling was told to bypass Trincomalee, and head directly for Hong Kong. Once past Pointe de Galle, he was to regard himself as commander-in-chief of the East Indies and China station.[5]

Stirling arrived in the China Sea just in time to learn that Shanghai had been practically under siege by insurgent forces, and that Consul Rutherford Alcock had authorized a sortie across the international settlement boundaries in the hope of safeguarding the various foreign communities. Early in April,

---

[4] Admiralty to Pellew, 9 Jan. 1854, Adm. 2/1611. See also, Graham, *Great Britain in the Indian Ocean*, pp. 415–17, 421. Pellew was 'beached', but not dismissed. He became a full admiral in February 1858, and died at Marseilles in July 1861.

[5] Admiralty to Stirling, 21 Feb. 1854 (No. 7), Adm. 2/1611.

in co-operation with the commander of the U.S. sloop
Plymouth, and assisted by civilian volunteers from the Factories, Captain O'Callaghan, in charge of the local stationed
ship, had rushed the Chinese encampments.

While offering the British captain congratulations on his
gallantry and success, Stirling, as a newcomer, was naturally
nervous of the consequences that might follow this unexpected stroke. He was well aware that Admiralty instructions
forbade independent acts of hostility. On the other hand, he
was prepared to accept the argument for the defence that
continued provocative gestures by insurgent soldiery could
very easily have turned into lethal encounters had steps not
been taken to extinguish the threat of armed trespass.[6] In the
end, a non-interference agreement was worked out with the
help of the Americans, to the apparent satisfaction of the
Imperial Authorities in Shanghai. If the self-denying scheme
worked, Admiral Stirling informed the Admiralty, henceforth
British, French, and American subjects could live in peace, and
their ships would move freely and safely to and fro from the
port to the open sea.[7]

Lacking Alcock's experience in Chinese diplomacy, Stirling
was content to be 'Treaty-minded'. There can be no doubt,
however, of his concern that units of his small force should
not be tied up in safe-guarding a foreign enclave, and that he
was looking for a suitable means of escape. The defence of
Shanghai against either rebels or Imperial troops was not, he
argued, a duty that his squadron was 'intended, qualified and
authorized to perform'.[8] For a very different reason, the
British Consul was in complete agreement with the Admiral's
interpretation of his responsibility. He had no faith in the
assurances of 'bandit soldiery' that the neutrality of foreign
settlements, so recently under siege, would be respected, but
he resented outside interference with his own plans for
defence. Not that he blamed Stirling, who was obviously
anxious to be free of the place. Like himself, the Admiral was

---

[6] Stirling to Admiralty, Hong Kong, 19 May (No. 35), Adm 1/5629. See also, same
to same, Singapore, 26 and 29 Apr. 1854 (Nos. 23 and 26, with encls., ibid.

[7] 13 July 1854 (No. 47), ibid.

[8] R. Osborne (Admiralty) to E. Hammond (F.O.), 19 Dec. 1854, encl. Stirling to
Admiralty, 19 June 1854, F.O. 17/223.

bound by injunctions formulated thousands of miles from the scene of crisis. 'The whole tenor of the instructions received from Her Majesty's Government', Alcock protested to the Senior Naval Officer at Shanghai,

has been to enforce on Her Majesty's Civil Servants, and upon all British subjects, the obligation of maintaining a strict neutrality, so far as this could be effected with a due regard to the existing Treaty obligations, and the security of life and property in the Foreign Settlement. To carry out the spirit of these instructions has not been an easy task from the beginning, for the two objects to be secured have often been more or less irreconcilable.[9]

Although scarcely perceptible at the beginning of the fifties, the growing confusion in China, consequent on expanding Taiping successes, was helping to shape a common Western front. Especially in areas devastated or threatened by the rebels which lay close to foreign trading communities, close association became almost inevitable in view of the pressing need for self-defence. This partnership of rivals had been earlier promoted by the gradual hardening of the Chinese official attitude towards all foreigners. Britain no longer stood alone as the arch-invader and would-be despoiler of the Middle Kingdom. Peking policy remained essentially one of avoiding any suggestion of equality in international dealings, and this continued rough assertion of the double standard had been steadily pushing the Treaty powers of Britain, France, and the United States—hitherto both jealous and suspicious of each other—into various forms of collaboration.

This provocative policy was undoubtedly accelerated by the succession to the Imperial throne in 1850 of a highly militant young man. Attributing the defeats and humiliations suffered during his father's rule to weak and incompetent officials, the new Hsien-feng Emperor, still in his twenties, showed himself anxious to regain lost dignity by supporting whole-heartedly

[9] John Bowring (the new Governor of Hong Kong) to Clarendon, 28 Nov. 1854 (No. 197), encl. No. 2, Alcock to Cmdr. Keane, 31 Oct. 1854, F.O. 17/217.

In April 1855, the law officers of the Crown were asked by Lord Clarendon in what circumstances British naval or military forces might intervene to protect British subjects and property at the Treaty ports. Since banditry was not likely to be affected by a legal approach, no positive instruction in regard to naval action was offered. The decision to intervene, it was submitted, had to be left to the Consul and service officers on the spot. See F.O. to Admiralty, 16 Apr. 1855, Adm. 1/5662.

an anti-foreign administration. In 1852, he appointed as director of a more aggressively nationalist strategy, Yeh Ming-ch'en, who had been Governor in Canton since 1848. This outwardly mild but fiercely determined man, as Viceroy and Imperial Commissioner in charge of 'barbarian affairs', was to rule his *regnum in regno* with an iron hand until 1858.

But regardless of stiffening Chinese attitudes, the Crimean War was to put an end to any hopes that Britain might at long last force China to acquiesce in her demands for Treaty revision, which, so it was understood, had been promised for 1852. Indeed, until the end of the war, it was only too clear to the authorities in Hong Kong that questions so remote as freedom of entry into Canton city had best be postponed until the Muscovite threat had been removed. Accordingly, Foreign Office instructions to the new Governor of Hong Kong, Sir John Bowring, over the next two years were to contain earnest prayers for restraint. Within the Treaty ports, consuls were warned to conduct themselves with patience, and, especially on the outskirts of Canton, with deliberate forbearance.

John Bowring, who bore the main weight of responsibility for implementing a détente with Peking, was sixty-two years of age at the time of his appointment in 1854. He was a curious, if not fantastic, mixture of the *littérateur*, linguist, and would-be man of action. That he had a penetrating mind was generally admitted, but his judgement could be capricious, and his actions were too often vitiated by downright arrogance. Unfortunately, this overweening sense of his own importance never gave him quite the confidence to steer to conclusion the various projects he was so happy to launch. He was not 'a lath painted to look like iron', but this outwardly fortress-like figure could crumble under pressure.

Like so many British pro-consuls in China, Bowring was a man of parts. A youthful disciple of Jeremy Bentham, he had helped to found the *Westminster Review* in 1824, and had subsequently edited Bentham's *Life and Works* in eleven volumes. While rebutting with some pungency many of the arguments of the anti-opium campaigners, he was capable, with apparently genuine religious fervour, of writing hymns,[10] the best known being 'In the Cross of Christ I glory.' As a linguist, he had a deservedly international reputation, being gener-ally credited with a command of six European languages and a reasonable knowledge of seven others, in addition to Arabic and Chinese. His *Autobiographical Recollections* (Lon-don, 1877) throw useful sidelights on the career of this versa-tile, scholarly, vain, and flamboyant agent of Her Majesty's government.

Bowring was a member of parliament from 1833 to 1837, and from 1841 to 1849. During the latter period, he served on a parliamentary commission inquiring into the commercial relations with China. This experience, plus the fact that his finances were at low ebb owing to a business collapse, helps to explain Palmerston's intervention on his behalf. He was appointed Consul at Canton, and took over his new duties in March 1849. In 1852, following Bonham's absence on leave, he acted temporarily as Superintendent of Trade at Hong Kong,[11] but not as Governor, a function which devolved automatically on the Lieutenant-Governor, Major-General Jervois.[12] He returned to England in 1853, and in the following year was appointed to Bonham's post, with a knighthood presented just before his departure in April. As Plenipotenti-ary, in addition to his normal duties as Governor and Superin-tendent of Trade, he had authority to negotiate commercial treaties with China, Siam, Cochin-China, and Japan, being accredited, he loftily remarked, to 'a greater number of human beings . . . than any individual . . . before him'.[13]

As Consul, and later, in 1852, as *locum tenens* for Bonham, he had resented the latter's efforts to conciliate the Cantonese. He

---

[10] In Hastings, overlooking the cricket ground and the sea, stands the Unitarian Free Christian Church. The foundation stone (cemented into the face) was, as in-scribed, 'laid by Sir John Bowring LLD FRS October 2, 1867'. The situation may v.ell have reminded him of the cricket field in Hong Kong which overlooked Victoria harbour.

[11] In a long letter to Lord Clarendon of 19 April 1852, Bowring gave a useful critique of Chinese policy towards the foreigner covering the preceding ten years. See Parliamentary Papers, vol. xii, 1857, Correspondence as to Entrance into Canton, 1850–55.

[12] On the peculiar nature of this, and subsequent appointments, see Endacott, *A History of Hong Kong*, pp. 87–90.

[13] Bowring, *Autobiographical Recollections* . . . (London, 1877), p. 216.

was equally loath to accept Foreign Office instructions forbidding him to engage in 'irritating discussions with the Chinese', and to 'abstain from mooting the question of the right of British subjects to enter into the city of Canton'.[14] And when at last he took over the combined post of Governor and Superintendent, even before he boarded ship for China, he was rash enough to hope that 'the maritime powers' might profit from the embarrassment of the Tartar dynasty as a consequence of the civil war.[15]

But questions involving the Taiping rebellion, and even the safety of Shanghai in the face of rebel advances, were soon to be shelved. The possibility of a Russian descent into the South China Sea provided sufficient substance for worry; and Bowring could only pray, as his ship laboriously ploughed its way toward Hong Kong, that European demands would not weaken the dispersed and vulnerable China squadron. Although much stronger than it had been over the previous five years, it was highly stretched. The *Barracouta*, flagship of the commander-in-chief, Admiral Stirling, was still on her way, although shortly expected; likewise the *Winchester* bringing Bowring to his new post. On arrival, she had been ordered to stay close to Hong Kong. The *Sparrow* and the *Rattler* had already left Singapore for the China Sea, and it was expected that they would be followed shortly by the *Sybilla*, *Lily*, and *Rapid*.[16] Following the April clashes with Taiping rebels at Shanghai, the *Encounter*, *Grecian*, and *Styx* had taken up station in the Yangtse estuary. Meanwhile, the station ships had been ordered to leave the Treaty ports, not to confront, as might have been anticipated, Russian raiders, but re-energized pirates, anxious to take advantage of Hong Kong's apparent extremity.[17]

. . .

[14] Instructions from Lord Malmesbury [Foreign Secretary in the Derby Ministry of 1852], Parliamentary Papers, xii, 1857, Correspondence as to Entrance into Canton, 1850–55.

[15] See Cady, *Roots of French Imperialism*, p. 121.

[16] Stirling to Admiralty, Singapore, 30 Apr. 1854 (No. 28), Adm. 1/5629. See also, Bowring to the Gov.-Gen. of India (Lord Dalhousie), 3 May 1854, Foreign Dept., Consultation No. 15, 21 July 1854 (N.A.I.).

[17] Secretary to the Governor of Hong Kong, to Secretary of the Government of India, Shanghai, 19 July 1854, Foreign Dept., Consultation Nos. 26–28, 22 Dec. 1854 (N.A.I.).

By the end of 1854, piratical assaults had brought British trade to a veritable standstill.[18] Even well-manned P. & O. ships had ceased to carry passengers, a precaution against surprise, which was understandable in view of recent calamities. Two out of five passenger vessels had been taken by surprise assault, and all on board put to death.[19] Even the possibility of an attack on Hong Kong could not be ignored. It was no secret that the vagabond elements on the Island had close ties with piratical organizations. It was equally common knowledge that the pirates drew supplies of every kind from the colony. Looking out over Victoria Harbour, the correspondent of *The Times* could count more than two hundred junks at anchor, every one of them armed with at least two heavy guns. Probably one quarter of them, he mused, were pirates who adopted the coasting trade as cover for their real profession.[20] With a mixed assembly of junks from every seaport and island between Shantung and Singapore and the Philippines, and with a population of around 50,000 Chinese, as well as a mixed Portuguese element from Macao, it was impossible for the authorities to lay hands on the pirates, who took shelter under the protection of the British flag.[21] Consequently, when Admiral Stirling sailed away to forestall a possible Russian surprise invasion from the north, it was generally assumed that Victoria might expect a midnight raid by as many as 2,000 of the miscreants. With only one colonial gunboat immediately available, untold damage could be done before troops and police could be assembled to dislodge them. By that time, the elusive marauders, whose movements were always well planned, might be miles away at sea.[22]

No China squadron, had it been treble its normal strength, could have coped with an undeclared war of such extent. One

[18] See Costin, *Great Britain and China* . . ., p. 177; Fox, *British Admirals* . . ., p. 123, and Endacott, *History of Hong Kong*, p. 90.

[19] Cooke, *China* . . ., p. 67. According to this *Times* correspondent, one of the American ships had an iron cage on deck, in which all Chinese passengers were locked up for the voyage as a security precaution.

[20] Ibid., p. 69.

[21] Alcock, *Tycoon*, pp. 15–16. Stirling believed that nearly 5,000 people in Victoria lived by piracy. Stirling to Bowring, *Winchester*, at Hong Kong, 16 Nov. 1855, encl. No. 1 in Bowring to Clarendon, 20 Nov. 1855 (No. 370), F.O. 17/235.

[22] See Admiral Pellew to Admiralty, *Winchester*, Hong Kong, 17 Jan. 1854 (No. 9), Adm. 1/5629; same to same, 21 Feb. 1854 (No. 27), ibid.

stationed gunboat, however zealous her commander, was completely useless in checking forays within the neighbouring waters of Hong Kong. Yet, with a full-scale European war on their hands, the Admiralty felt in no position to add appreciably to anti-pirate patrols, and it is conceivable that the Foreign Secretary, Lord Clarendon, had his tongue in his cheek when in December 1854 he asked their Lordships to provide additional protection for 'respectable Chinese merchants' using the Canton River.[23]

Curiously enough, the Americans did little to help, and the Indian government, always in the past a generous source of ships and men in times of emergency, had early in the year to refuse a request for reinforcements 'owing to the urgent wants of the Indian service'. All Calcutta had done was to see that Port Clearance surveillance in Singapore was tightened. Such a precaution was aimed to prevent piratical vessels from setting out for China under false or falsely obtained registers, and the Indian government was prepared to legislate to this effect, 'if the object in view could be more effectually attained'.[24]

Admiral Stirling was not long in appreciating that the pirate raider was a far greater danger to trade and settlement than the Russian cruiser. One of his first acts, as noted, was to unlock the station ships in view of the emergency, and make them available for patrol duties. Within a year, he hoped to have the unextinguishable menace under some sort of control. The navy, he was confident, 'would give the requisite protection in the most effectual manner, simply by affording convoy at periods to be arranged and from place to place as fixed upon. . . .'[25] In the meantime, however, Governor Bowring had sought the blessing and aid of the Chinese. 'The general outline which I have suggested to the local mandarins at the 5 Ports', he informed the Foreign Secretary, 'is that an authorized Chinese Junk shd. form a part of any expedition of British ships engaged against the Pirates—or that, at all events, some Mandarin of adequate rank shd. accompany our naval

[23] To Admiralty, 21 Dec. 1854, in reply to Consul Robertson's dispatch, 29 Oct. 1854, F.O. 17/223.

[24] Secretary, Government of India, Fort William, 18 Mar. 1854, Foreign Dept., Consultation No. 30, 18 Mar. 1854 (N.A.I.).

[25] Stirling to Bowring, 16 Nov. 1855, encl. in Bowring to Clarendon, 20 Nov. 1855 (No. 370), F.O. 17/235.

authorities on such expeditions.'[26] Stirling insisted that responsibility for naval operations clearly rested with the Royal Navy, but he too saw the immense advantages to be gained if the Chinese chose to co-operate.[27] Indeed, on his own initiative, he wrote a personal letter to the Viceroy at Canton asking his help. Somewhat to his surprise, the appeal was successful.[28] No doubt, Bowring's plea reinforced the Admiral's statement of need. In any event, the Viceroy made prompt arrangements to send a red-button mandarin and a war junk to Hong Kong to help in the task of visiting and examining 'every port and Place upon the coast known or suspected to be the Haunts of Pirates, and every vessel of a suspicious character'. In addition, the Governor of Macao contributed a lorcha, the American Commodore chartered a steamer, which was quickly armed, and the leading merchants, including Chinese firms, contributed money.

Meanwhile, augmented by two hired P. & O. vessels and a Chinese junk, a strong squadron detachment attacked a pirate stronghold up the Broadway behind Macao, burning 50 junks and destroying 27 guns.[29] With the occasional assistance of the Chinese, the crusade was continued, and thanks to the absence of Russian warships, by the end of 1855 the pirate stranglehold on main trade routes had been shaken, if not broken. During the next four years, even during periods of active hostilities in the north, mandarins of the coastal towns contributed information, and sometimes junks and men.[30]

But there were never enough warships to make the convoy system work as Admiral Stirling had anticipated. Tougher restrictions were placed on the issuance of Sailing Letters to

---

[26] To Lord Clarendon, 30 Nov. 1854 (No. 205), encl. in Hammond (F.O.) to Admiralty, 29 Jan. 1855, Adm. 1/5661.

[27] See A. B. Robertson (Consul at Canton) to Hammond (F.O.), 10 Nov. 1854, F.O. 17/217. This communication reached London in the remarkable time of seven weeks.

[28] Stirling to Admiralty, Hong Kong, 25 Nov. 1854, with printed enclosures 'On the Repression of Piracy', Adm. 1/5657.

[29] See Captain O'Callaghan to Stirling, 17 Nov. 1854, encl. in Stirling to Admiralty, 25 Nov. 1854, Adm. 1/5657. The British detachment included H.M.S. *Encounter*, *Barracouta*, and *Styx*, the launch of the *Winchester*, and the pinnace of the *Spartan*.

[30] See Vansittart to Admiral Seymour, 20 Oct. 1858, encl. in Seymour to Admiralty, 23 Oct. 1858 (No. 362), Adm. 1/5693; and Colville to Seymour, 16 Mar. 1859, encl. in Seymour to Admiralty, 29 Mar. 1859 (No. 144), Adm. 1/5712.

traders suspected of using the British flag for illegal purposes, but such action hardly affected the operations of the pirate, parading as a Taiping loyalist. 'Scarcely a day passes', wrote Bowring early in 1855, 'in which the so-called rebels do not stop Ships and boats bearing the British flag, many of which they pillage, and the whole movement seems merging into such undoubted and palpable piracy that a collision can hardly be avoided if our trade is to receive protection.' A blend of patriotism and piracy, he told Lord Clarendon, was 'disturbing all our peaceful and honourable commercial relations. . . .'[31] The China squadron was reinforced early in 1855, but six additional cruisers were not capable of producing a *Pax Britannica* in the South China Sea. Long after the Crimean War was over, the Admiralty could do little more than proclaim its moral support of 'rigorous measures for the effectual suppression of Pirates infesting the neighbourhood of Hong Kong'.

Meanwhile, news of the outbreak of war with Russia reached Hong Kong in May 1854. Shortly after, came reports that detachments of the Russian Far Eastern fleet had been discovered more than a thousand miles to the north in De Castries Bay. The mere rumour of a projected attack (which momentarily produced near panic in Hong Kong) was sufficiently arousing to stimulate flurried efforts in defence. Battery points and signal stations were hastily constructed on various headlands or hills. A European volunteer corps drilled and practised exhausting manœuvres, often in company with the auxiliary police.[32]

In fact, as was later revealed, Russian warships in the month of April had been little more than six hundred miles from Hong Kong. Intelligence reports from the British Consul in Manilla intimated that a squadron, consisting of a frigate (50), the flagship of Admiral, Count Poutiatine, a sloop of twenty

[31] Bowring to Clarendon, 22 Feb. 1855 (No. 96); see also, same to same, 26 Feb. 1855 (No. 108), F.O. 17/227 and 228 respectively.

[32] On 25 May, when news of the official declaration of war was officially confirmed, a special issue of the government's *Gazette* provided general and some technical information on how best to contribute to the Island's safety. Lieutenant-Governor W. Caine to Newcastle (Secretary for War and Colonies), 5 June 1854 (No. 21), encl. Bowring to Caine, *Winchester* at sea, 25 May 1854, F.O. 17/214.

guns, another of six, and a steamer of four, had put in for repairs. These had been refused. Admiral Pellew (who in mid-April was still awaiting transport at Pointe de Galle) was certain that the ships were making for Java, despite the Russian Admiral's public assertion that he was bound for Kamchatka.

Before the outbreak of the Crimean War, Britain had visualized Russia as 'a swollen militarist power based on slavery, combatting Liberal ideas both at home and abroad; swallowing region after region within her frontiers . . . covering India, bringing disaster in Afghanistan . . . designing the subjugation of Turkey'.[33] Admittedly, that 'great grim shadowy power' which brooded darkly over two continents could no longer be described, in Prince Albert's words, as 'complete master of Europe'. Russia no longer controlled the destinies of the Ottoman Empire. On the other hand, her navy was strongly represented in both the Black and Baltic Seas, and a small squadron was now operating within striking distance of the northern coast of China.

Her purpose, so it appeared, was to extend and consolidate a chain of communications southward through Manchuria. Of all the powers, Russia alone was in a position to operate directly from home territory and bring pressure to bear on China without fear of outside intervention. Unlike India, China had no protective mountain barriers on her Manchurian frontier.[34] Consequently, as Admiral Stirling reported to the Admiralty, Russia could advance, step by step, towards the heartland of the Chinese Empire.

Signs of that intended progression had been long evident. Since the end of the seventeenth century, both Cossacks and merchants had made occasional appearances on the left bank of the Amur River; now, and without licence from China, the mouth of that river was being fortified. Two steam vessels had been launched, and from inland trading posts fleets of barges were being towed down to the sea.[35] Moreover, a Russian

---

[33] Sir Adolphus Ward and G. P. Gooch (eds.), *Cambridge History of British Foreign Policy*, 1783–1919, ii. 1815–1866 (London and New York, 1923), p. 393.

[34] On the other hand, the trans-Siberian railway had not yet been built, and communication with the Russian industrial and military centres presented a difficult problem of logistics, by no means solved even when the railway had been completed.

[35] George Hamilton Seymour to Clarendon, Saint Petersburg, 21 Feb. 1854 (No. 177) L/P & S/9/4 (I.O.A.). The first barges made the journey in May and June of 1854,

squadron had taken refuge on the Siberian coast in De Castries Bay, opposite Sakhalin Island in the upper reaches of the Gulf of Tartary. The acquisition of this strategic harbour threatened an advance still further southward in the direction of the Yellow Sea. Recent intelligence reports also suggested that plans were on foot to set up a Russian naval base on the Bonin Islands, some 600 miles to the south-east of Japan. Such a base could be linked with the estuary of the Amur (more than 1,600 miles distant), thus providing in the rather curious judgement of the Admiralty, a 'great highway of traffic with Central Asia', especially if and when Japan were opened to trade.[36]

All told, in the eyes of suspicious denizens of Whitehall, Russia was preparing to take a stranglehold on Manchuria. Already, it was assumed, she could command the Sea of Japan, and, according to Foreign Office report, by consolidating a foothold on the Gulf of Tartary she was in process of establishing a base from which she could control the whole of the North Pacific. 'By what tenure they [the Russians] hold De Castries Bay is scarcely known; it may be that of right or that of might; report says the latter; but under any circumstance, we find them holding a most formidable and threatening position and one that may hereafter give us grave cause of anxiety.'[37] In addition, the Russians, according to Admiralty intelligence, had by the beginning of 1855 established some 30,000 men in and around their forts on the north bank of the Amur River. Should Russian armies larger than those of Attila or Genghis Khan overrun the 'Turkey of the Eastern Seas', wrote Admiral Stirling, British maritime supremacy would be endangered and British trade extinguished. A precarious hold

a second fleet in May 1855, and a third in January 1856. See Cady, op. cit., p. 137, n.3. See also, F.O. to Admiralty, 14 Mar. 1856, transmitting information received on Russian movements on the banks of the Amur in the latter part of 1856, encl. in Admiralty to Admiral Seymour, 3 Mar. 1856, Adm. 125/1.

[36] W. A. B. Hamilton to E. Hammond, 20 Oct. 1854, F.O. 17/223. See also, Hamilton to Stirling, 24 Feb. 1855 (No. 62), with encl., Adm. 125/96.

Neither Britain nor the United States had ever claimed sovereignty over the Bonins, although it was rumoured that Commodore Perry had privately purchased a section of land for an American coal depot. See F.O. Minute, appended to Hamilton's letter to Hammond, 20 Oct. 1854, above. On the history of British interest in the Bonins as a possible base, see W. G. Beasley, *Great Britain and the Opening of Japan* (London, 1951), pp. 15–20.

[37] F.O. to Admiralty, 12 Mar. 1856, encl. extract of a dispatch from H.M. Consul in Shanghai, to Governor Bowring of Hong Kong, 31 Dec. 1855, Adm. 1/5477.

on five Chinese ports was hardly a guarantee of British trade expansion within the great Chinese Empire. Patrolling Chinese coasts was not enough. There was urgent need for a better understanding with Peking and the Chinese people. 'I am prepared to admit,' Stirling went on, 'that something must be left to time, but if China be not electrified & organized by British energy & management; or brought under the influence which a more extended Commerce will give us, she will soon fall within the Dominion of Russia. . . .'[38]

Admiral Stirling wanted the Royal Navy to play the same paternal role in shaping Chinese destinies, as the British army had played in India. But in his fears as with his hopes, he was out of touch with reality. Before the Mutiny, Britain counted on getting out of India as soon as it were decently possible; and, as has been noted elsewhere in this book, British policy, regardless of party, was utterly set against a project as frightening in its dimensions as another India. Stirling's memorandum, at least in its planning for the future, represented a wild chimera, whose corporeal manifestation vanished into the dusty pigeon-hole of Admiralty archives. His kind of imperialism was out of date.

Meanwhile, on hearing that the Russian squadron had been seen off the coast of Japan, Admiral Pellew, on his way home, seized on the reports, whether true or false, as offering a unique opportunity for Britain to press negotiations with Japan, already threatened by Commodore Perry of the United States. Perry, so it was said, had taken possession of the Loochoo Islands, and American competition, now adroitly centred between Japan and the Chinese mainland, could well prove a considerable barrier to British trade prospects.[39] Pellew's successor, Admiral Stirling, without waiting for instructions, had no hesitation in grasping the nettle. For the moment, Britain and the United States had nothing to quarrel about, and in circumstances (which could so easily have provoked suspicion and bad feeling) Stirling could only thank his

[38] 'Memoir on the Maritime Policy of England in the Eastern Seas', written from the *Winchester*, Hong Kong, encl. in Stirling to Wood (Admiralty), Hong Kong, 15 Nov. 1855, Adm. 1/5660.

[39] Pellew to Admiralty, *Barracouta*, Pointe de Galle, 15 Apr. 1854, Adm. 1/5629; see also, Bowring to Dalhousie, 3 May 1854, Foreign Dept., Consultation No. 15, 21 July 1854, doc. cit. (N.A.I.).

lucky stars that the most cordial relations existed between their two services. Indeed, he was far from unhappy when Perry arranged to leave three of his squadron for a spell on the China coast.[40]

On 29 August, in company with the *Encounter*, *Barracouta*, and *Styx*, the flagship *Winchester* with Stirling aboard set sail for Nagasaki. His objectives were twofold: one, to seek out a Russian squadron reported over the past month to be moving about mysteriously in nearby waters; and, two, to make certain that no Japanese ports were being used by the Russians for supply and refitting. Since no enemy ships were sighted in the course of a few desultory sweeps, Stirling prepared to tackle the political side of his mission, namely, the winning of access to certain Japanese ports, if not for trade, at least as convenient sources of wood and water and as temporary repair bases. On 14 October negotiations were concluded, and while he failed to achieve satisfactory trading privileges, the Admiral did obtain promise of the 'naval' use of two important harbours, Nagasaki and Hakodade, along with a useful refreshment resort, Simoda.[41] With a little more pressure, the Russians might well have been excluded from such benefits, but sufficient diplomatic leverage was obviously wanting. Very similar privileges were granted to Russia in February of the following year. The Foreign Office was pleased with 'the remarkable discretion and ability evinced by Sir J. Stirling in this matter'. Largely on his own initiative, he had achieved the opening of hitherto closely barred Japanese ports.[42]

Confirmation of this *coup* was not immediate. Not until the end of September 1855 did the final ceremony take place, an exhibition of flag and force which Stirling thought to be 'not without advantage'. Almost the entire China squadron, along with two French warships, gathered off Nagasaki, as an expression of European naval power.[43] Prolonged discussions

---

[40] Stirling to Admiralty, *Encounter*, Shanghai, 30 June 1854 (No. 44), Adm. 1/5629.

[41] Stirling to Admiralty, 26 Oct. 1854 (No. 71), Adm. 1/5629. This dispatch was printed, along with other material relating to the negotiations (49 pp.) for the Foreign Office, 23 Dec. 1854, Adm. 1/5640.

[42] Hammond (F.O.) to Admiralty, 18 Jan. 1855, Adm. 1/5661; see also, same to same, 21 Jan. 1856, Adm. 1/5677.

[43] Stirling to Admiralty, 1 Oct. 1855 (No. 74), Adm. 1/5657; also Beasley, *Great Britain and the Opening of China*, p. 136.

during the next few days removed ambiguities, and (so it was hoped) rectified muddled translations. On the morning of 9 October the revised texts of the previous year's convention were given formal and final approval.

Stirling had no doubt that the key to success lay in predominance at sea. Although by the terms of the Treaty, Britain had no advantages that were not shared equally with the United States and Russia, in reality, by reason of her naval superiority, she was in a far stronger position to exploit the Treaty privileges. 'For instance,' as the Admiral pointed out, 'in the last summer [1855] the Ports and resources of Japan were at the disposal of any Cruiser for support, refreshments and communication, and in these respects Japan was as useful to us as a British Colony in that locality, but holding as we did the superiority in force, these Ports and resources were not available for Russian ships, and thus in the first year of its existence we were enabled to turn the Treaty to account in our own favour and against the Enemy.'[44]

But even without Japanese supply bases, it was clear by midsummer 1855 that British interests in the China seas had nothing to fear from the Russians. Indeed, during the whole course of the war, there had been no battles, not even contacts. The cruisers, *Bittern* and *Hornet*, had, like their frustrated predecessors, done their best to trace the phantom enemy, but discovered little but stale rumours. The Russians, their captains were told, had been observed in various areas, but almost immediately had escaped into the thick fogs of northern waters for 'unknown destinations'.[45] Some reports, unverified, described a squadron consisting of a frigate (46), two sloops, a steamer, and a store-ship, that had taken refuge in De Castries Bay. The British cruiser captain was inclined to accept the information as valid, but sensibly refused to risk his ships in unknown and constricted waters against an enemy who

---

[44] Stirling to Admiralty, *Winchester*, Hong Kong, 8 Nov. 1855 (No. 75), Adm. 1/125. Further official correspondence (Jan. to Feb. 1856) in the same volume indicates favourable Admiralty assessment of Stirling's procedure and achievement.

[45] Most of the scouting had been done by sailing vessels, which were not easily adaptable to frost and fog, as well as monsoon weather. Future activity off the Manchurian and Siberian coasts should, it was recommended, be left to steamers only. Bowring to Clarendon, 8 Dec. 1855 (No. 393), encl. Commodore Elliot to Bowring, 25 Nov. 1855, F.O. 17/235.

could probably outmanœuvre and certainly outgun his diminutive force.[46]

In retrospect, it is clear that the Russians never intended active naval operations in the Far East. Even had resources permitted, they had no interest in winning paramountcy in the China seas; the traditional practice had been aggrandizement by land, and in the west their progress had been stopped. The Congress of Paris which met between 25 February and 30 March produced a European settlement. Russia was forced to back away from the shores of the Danube and the Straits. On the other hand, this retreat in the west served to encourage rather than retard her subsequent advances into Manchuria. At a time when the Peking government needed every available man to fight the Taiping rebels, Russia was in process of scooping up a large portion of Tartary. Well might Admiral Stirling envisage the day when the hosts of Muscovy would roll relentlessly southward to control the heartland of the Chinese Empire.

Indeed, two years after the end of the Crimean War, Russia was to acquire, by the Treaty of Aigun, the huge area north of the Amur River, with uncontested control of the left bank and the right of free navigation to the coast. On the banks of the estuary, a dockyard and an arsenal were already taking shape, and British surveying ships were warned not to enter any bays or harbours where the Russian flag was in evidence.[47]

For centuries, Russian connections with China had been maintained by land through Siberia. By 1860, with port facilities nearing completion and a squadron from all accounts worthy of 'showing the flag' in the Gulf of Tartary and beyond, Russian diplomatic leverage *vis-à-vis* the Chinese Empire was to be enhanced beyond all previous reckoning. 'Compelled by an unexpected combination of two powerful States to recede a few steps in Europe,' declared the *Quarterly Review*,

Russia has since made one of her gigantic strides in Asia, adding to her previously enormous empire a territory equal to the combined

---

[46] See W. Woodgate (Secretary to Governor of Hong Kong) to C. Readon (Secretary to Government of India), 10 Aug. 1855, in reference to a letter from Admiral Stirling, 23 July 1855, India Proc., vol. 193, Consultation No. 128, 30 Nov. 1855 (I.O.A.).

[47] Corry (Admiralty) to Admiral Seymour, 19 Nov. 1858 (No. 538), Adm. 2/1616.

areas of France and Italy. She has obtained an extensive seaboard on the North Pacific, access by one of the noblest rivers in Asia to the centre of her dominions, a considerable increase in population, and a position in Central Asia in dangerous proximity to the weakened and distracted empire of China, from the capital of which her frontier is now less than 600 miles.[48]

A new commander-in-chief, Rear-Admiral Sir Michael Seymour, arrived in the early spring of 1856. He had instructions to keep an eye on the Russians, and to support the Governor in a renewed effort to obtain revision of the Nanking Treaty terms. An officer of more than forty years' experience—and one whose father had distinguished himself during the Napoleonic War—Seymour had recently served in the Baltic under Sir Charles Napier. Translation to this far-flung command represented promotion to an operational area that had steadily grown in international significance. Despite the recall of reinforcements as the Crimean War faltered to a close, he inherited a China squadron of sixteen ships, of which two were screw steamers, and one a paddle-wheeler.[49]

The problem of Russian encroachments on the Manchurian coast obviously deserved attention. British nervousness of Russian ambitions had not dissolved as a result of the Treaty of Paris (30 March 1856), and British cruisers continued to keep an eye out for signs of aggressive activity in and about the Gulf of Tartary. Admiral Seymour was told to lose no time in adding to the surveying detachment already working as far north as the 49th parallel.[50]

But for the moment, the eastward thrust of Russia involved no urgency. The Foreign Office in particular could now afford to concentrate their attentions on the unyielding wall of Chinese non-co-operation. As already recounted, by insisting

[48] Vol. 110 (1861), p. 180. See also in connection with Russian eastern expansion, Romaine to Seymour in Hong Kong, 23 Mar. 1858 (No. 147); same to same, 22 May 1858 (No. 151), Adm. 2/1615; and Corry to Seymour, 9 Sept. 1858 (No. 306), Adm. 2/1616.

[49] Within little more than a year (viz., by December 1857), the total for the East Indies and China station had reached 64, of which 42 were screw steamers. See Admiralty to Foreign Office, 10 Sept. 1856, F.O. 17/258; also, D. Bonner-Smith and E. W. B. Lumby, *The Second China War 1856–1860*, Navy Records Society, vol. 95 (London, 1954), p. xxii.

[50] Admiralty to Seymour, 3 Mar. 1856, with encls. Adm. 125/1; and same to same, 18 Nov. 1856 (No. 195), Adm. 2/1613.

upon the narrowest interpretation of the Treaty contracts, Peking, acting chiefly through its provincial agency in Canton, had managed to frustrate any effort by Britain (who was supported on occasion by France and the United States) to promote the diplomatic dialogue of equals. The fact that certain of the articles were lacking in precision, or might be rendered ambiguous in translation, naturally encouraged Chinese intransigence.[51] In consequence, the machinery of the Treaty system of 1842–4, which had been creaking ominously for more than ten years, was clearly reaching a point of total breakdown.[52]

Heartened by reports of American support for an advance to Peking, even to the Emperor's palace, influential members of the British government were more willing to listen to Bowring's bold, but scarcely original pronouncement that only a show of force could breach the walls of the 'forbidden city' of the south, Canton. Moreover, close collaboration in the late war suggested that a less edgy France might lend her weight to the joint task of opening a door that stood barely ajar. Hitherto, French interest in the Far East had been largely concerned with missionary activity. Consequently, when news of the murder of Father Chapdelaine in February 1856 reached Paris, Napoleon III was not unhappy to join the Anglo-American partnership aimed at opening a road to Peking.[53]

The American objective, an accessible China, was based not on Christian missionary interest, but on trade. The American President, Franklin Pierce (1853–57) was determined, with the help of Britain, to obtain a revision of the commercial agreements, and he appointed as his diplomatic agent an ex-medical missionary, Dr. Peter Parker.[54] Parker had had some experi-

---

[51] As far back as 1846, Yeh's predecessor, the amiable Ch'i-ying, had resisted the introduction of steamships to the Canton River on the ground that such vessels were not mentioned in any treaty. Moreover, in his view, they created a danger to shipping. See Davis to Aberdeen, 22 Apr. 1846 F.O. 17/112.

[52] See Fairbank, op. cit., p. 368.

[53] See Clarendon to Bowring, 29 Sept. 1856, confirming that the French government would demand ample reparation for the murder of their missionary. F.O. 17/243.

[54] See V. Gulick, *Peter Parker and the opening of China* (Cambridge, Mass., 1974), *passim*.

ence in Chinese legation work; he was undoubtedly intelligent, but his capacity as a plenipotentiary was unfortunately reduced by a *naïveté* that would have been pathetic had it not been wedded to an exceptional conceit. In January 1856, Parker was for a short time the guest of Government House in Hong Kong, and he and Bowring discussed the prospect of sending a fleet to the Gulf of Pecheli in June. They also talked about the prospect of establishing foreign embassies in Peking, a procedure which, hopefully, might ease the task of unlocking further doors of trade. Bowring had few doubts about his own abilities as a diplomat, and he also shared with Parker rather grandiose dreams of success in dealing with the inscrutable Oriental. But unlike the American, who wanted all Chinese ports open to trade, Bowring was opposed to an 'unlimited' expansion. Moreover, he was sceptical of his colleague's faith in the benefits to be obtained by exerting moral influence on the Chinese as a major part of negotiating technique.[55]

Bowring's particular concern about having a British mission established in Peking had much to do with counteracting Russian influence. At this time, the Crimean War had not yet ended, and alone among the foreign powers Russia maintained a strategic listening-post in the Imperial capital, designated as an Ecclesiastical Mission. By means of this neatly camouflaged agency, her emissaries, so it was assumed, were able to communicate directly with the Court, and, if needs be, express privately their opposition to British and French plans, and advise as to how they might be circumvented. Whether or not the Mission was a cover for diplomatic intrigue, it was not unnatural for British officials in Hong Kong to be suspicious of a rival in possession of such an exclusive foothold. Apart from any other advantages, the Russians were in a position to garner more information about China than any other Western power.[56]

In May 1856, Bowring begged that the China squadron should be allowed to strengthen the British position by doing

---

[55] Bowring to Clarendon, 5 Jan. 1856 (No. 11), F.O. 17/244; and same to same, 6 Feb. 1856, F.O. 17/245. It is worth noting that both letters took only two months to reach Whitehall.

[56] Dating back more than 150 years, this establishment, properly called a seminary, seems to have been principally the home of a few orthodox priests, half a dozen

something more tangible than 'showing the flag'. On this particular dispatch, Clarendon had scribbled a minute recommending action, but action in company with France and the United States.[57] On 22 July, on the assumption that 'showing the guns' might be the master key to a successful mission, the Foreign Office requested that Admiral Seymour be ordered to convey Sir John Bowring northward 'for the purpose of revising certain Treaty provisions'.[58] In the meantime, taking it for granted that consent would be forthcoming, Bowring hoped to take advantage of prevailing June winds and sail northward with such British and American ships as were available. Co-operation with France was not possible, because at the time no French warships were serving in Chinese waters. Unfortunately, Seymour refused to budge without instructions from the Admiralty; and when these orders did eventually arrive in Hong Kong, it was too late in the year to set off.

Bowring felt that he had been let down, and querulously complained to Clarendon about the Admiral's lack of imagination. Lacking the written authority, Seymour had refused, in an excess of pedantry, to employ the force under his command in furtherance of the Governor's political objectives. But even had he agreed to the request, Bowring went on, an inadequate China squadron was scarcely in a position to impress the ruling authorities in Peking with the might of British arms; even the Taiping rebels near Shanghai were

---

language students, and occasional visiting caravan merchants and official envoys. Bowring maintained that there 'never was an instance known of a young man being sent from Moscow to the Russian College at Peking who could speak any other language than his native Russ. . . .' In this manner, other Europeans were debarred from gaining information acquired by the residents of the seminary. This assertion was subsequently denied by a Russian visitor to the Royal Asiatic Society, who insisted that while Sir John Bowring's observation had been once valid, for at least twenty years students from various ecclesiastical academies and universities had been admitted, and all of them could read and write several European languages. In reply to this intervention, the Governor of Hong Kong gracefully allowed 'that important changes had no doubt taken place since he had resided in Russia'. Minutes of 8 Aug. 1855, *Transactions of the China Branch of the Royal Asiatic Society*, Part V, Hong Kong, 1855, pp. 155–6.

[57] Bowring to Clarendon, 16 May 1856 (No. 166), with Minute by Clarendon, 17 July 1856, F.O. 17/247. See also, Hammond (F.O.) to Admiralty, 22 Feb. 1856, with encls. from Bowring, Nos. 379, 382, 393, and 405, Adm. 1/5677.

[58] Hammond to Admiralty, 22 July 1856, Adm. 125/1.

showing contempt of British efforts to maintain neutrality. The Admiralty had no hesitation in brushing aside both Bowring's grumbles and his nonsensical fears.[59] In their view, Admiral Seymour had shown common sense in refusing to commit his force to a forlorn venture, presumably to be shared by an impulsive American whose comprehension of strategy derived from dreams. As for the inadequacy of the China squadron, it was well for the Foreign Office to remember that Seymour had under his command the largest naval force ever to be assembled in peace time in the China seas. In brief, the Governor's grievances were completely without foundation.[60] Roughly translated from the stately language of Whitehall, Bowring, like Dogberry, could be 'writ down an ass!'

However, the British government did accept Bowring's statement in regard to the increased *tempo* of agitation in and around Canton, and on 10 September Admiral Seymour was told that he might dispatch such reinforcements to Canton as would be sufficient to protect endangered British interests.[61] Two weeks later, activated by news of the Chapdelaine tragedy, the French agreed in principle to Clarendon's proposal that, with or without the Americans, the two powers should approach Peking and demand a revision of the treaties. The time had come, Clarendon insisted, 'when either the Emperor . . . must be made to adopt a more liberal system in his intercourse with foreign nations or some other combination must be acceded to by which the humiliating position in which foreigners still continued to be placed in China must be improved and the vast resources of that vast Empire opened up to the industrial enterprise of foreign nations'.[62] By December 1856, a French squadron consisting of one frigate, two corvettes, four gunboats, and two transports carrying a contingent of marines, was ready to join the Royal Navy in the China seas.

[59] See Hammond to Admiralty, 8 Sept. 1856, Adm. 1/5678.
[60] See Minute by 'CW' [Sir Charles Wood] 10 Sept. 1856, inscribed on Hammond to Admiralty, 8 Sept. 1856, Adm. 1/5678.
[61] Admiralty to Seymour, 10 Sept 1856, Adm. 125/1.
[62] Clarendon to British Ambassador in Paris, 24 Sept. 1856, and same to Bowring on the same day, F.O. 17/261, quoted in Cady, op. cit., p. 167.

XII

'A WRETCHED BLUNDER': THE ASSAULT ON CANTON 1856–1857

THE origins of the 'Arrow affair', on which Bowring hastened to capitalize, can be traced indirectly to the Taiping rebellion, and the consequent dislocation of trade that gave such an immense impetus to piracy. Frequently professing allegiance to the rebel banners of Taiping, swarms of junks and lorchas[1] issued from narrow inlets and swampy estuaries to seek their prey along the coast. Lack of sufficient light-draught gunboats made the task of pursuit through twisting channels between innumerable islands an impossible one. Admiral Stirling, as has been noticed, had introduced a limited convoy system, but the arrangements had failed chiefly because sufficient escorts were not available. Consequently, Chinese owners in particular preferred to safeguard their ships and cargoes by paying 'protection' or 'blackmail' money to pirate agents.

Beginning on 1 January 1856, however, the system was reorganized, with the institution of scheduled sailings. Each month between 1 November and 1 April, a convoy, accompanied by a man-of-war, would leave Woosung (the main port of Shanghai) with the north-east monsoon, and proceed successively to Ningpo, Foochow, Amoy, Hong Kong, and Whampoa. Similarly, on the first day of every month of the south-west monsoon, between 1 April and 1 October, a British warship would escort the trade from Whampoa, calling at the same ports on the way to the terminus, Woosung.[2] The new arrangements were chiefly concerned with safeguarding European shipping, but Bowring hit upon the notion of giving the protection of the British flag to the ships

---

[1] A lorcha was a vessel with a hull of European shape, and Chinese rig.

[2] See Bowring to Clarendon, 1 Jan. 1856 (No. 3), encl. Stirling's official public notification, F.O. 17/244. See also, Admiralty to Seymour, 3 Mar. 1856 (No. 1), encl. Stirling to Bowring, 30 Dec. 1855, Bowring to Stirling, 9 Jan. 1856, Stirling to Admiralty, 9 Jan. 1856, along with a copy of Stirling's convoy draft, and Seymour to Admiralty, 9 May 1856, Adm. 125/1.

of Chinese merchants who were inhabitants of Hong Kong. Assuming the vessel was properly registered in Hong Kong, and carried a certificate to that effect, there was no abuse of British colours (provided, of course, that pirates did not counterfeit the sacrosanct document, as they frequently did). Accordingly, Ordinance No. 4 of 1855 had been passed by the Legislative Council, and subsequently approved by the law officers of the Crown, permitting the transfer to British registry of Chinese vessels belonging to Hong Kong residents. Under the Ordinance, Hong Kong Chinese owners became British Chinese, and while such a paper safeguard was no guarantee against piratical attack, it placed such ships and their crews in a privileged position *vis-à-vis* Chinese authority on the mainland.[3]

On 8 October 1856 the *Arrow*, owned by a Chinese resident of Hong Kong, registered under the Colonial Ordinance of 1855, and flying the British flag, was suddenly boarded by Chinese police officers, while lying at anchor off the Dutch Folly, not far from the British Factory at Canton. Twelve of her Chinese crew were arrested, and witnesses, including her British captain, testified that her colours were unceremoniously hauled down. The British Consul, Harry Parkes, as soon as he learned of the incident, demanded of the Imperial Commissioner, Yeh Ming-ch'ên, the return of the crew, and an immediate apology for the insult to the flag. Although he did order the return of nine of the men, Yeh refused to make full amends, denying both that the British flag was flying and that the ship itself was of British register. He further maintained that at least one crew member was a notorious pirate.[4] As it turned out, the *Arrow*'s register had expired eleven days before the assault took place, but that was a pure technicality. When Chinese officers boarded what was under British law a British vessel, they had no knowledge that the registry had lapsed.

Faced with an emergency, and alert to its implications for

---

[3] See Instructions based on the Act of 18/19 Vict., cap. 104, 'For the Regulation of Chinese Passenger Ships' [14 Aug. 1855], in Admiralty to C.-in-C., China Station [printed], 12 June 1856, Adm. 125/1.

[4] The story of the *Arrow* incident has been told many times, and with particular thoroughness by Costin, *Great Britain and China*, v, 206–30. Yeh was subsequently to protest the right of any foreign state to transfer registries to Chinese vessels.

the future, Bowring rose majestically, if not prudently, to the occasion. Between the 14th and 16th of October, he consulted with Admiral Seymour and the aggressive representative at Canton, as to 'the most appropriate means of obtaining redress'. In his own opinion, this was a God-sent opportunity to settle the 'City question', the right of foreign entry through the gates of Canton. If the Admiral agreed, he would happily see the China squadron ascend the River, and decide the matter finally.[5]

Bowring had long been spoiling for a fight with the Canton authorities, and in particular with Commissioner Yeh, who so obviously underestimated his importance and the strength of the fleet at his disposal. It must be remembered that Bowring was a political appointee—a newcomer to high-powered diplomacy—and Hong Kong was providing him with his first experience in the role of imperial pro-consul. His ambition to 'show the flag' at Peking had been frustrated by cautious politicians at home. Now, the occasion seemed to have arrived when idle ships could be used effectively to produce final results. Yeh could be discredited in the eyes of his masters, and the 'City question' at long last permanently settled. Although he must have known that plans were on foot to send an expedition to the China Sea, Bowring had no authority to undertake the violent action he proposed. His instructions had dealt simply with the need to work for a general Treaty revision in concert with the Americans and the French. In this instance, he was to have the approval of both, but not their active support.

The Admiral was less than exuberant about the project, but seemed for the moment willing to be led by the impetuous Governor. He appeared to have no reservations about the lack of official orders, but he did have serious doubts as to whether the force at his disposal was sufficient for the task. He could batter the city with shells, assuming the Imperial Commissioner proved recalcitrant, but occupying and garrisoning Canton was another matter. Yeh was not so easily browbeaten or subject to shell-shock as the Governor seemed to believe. On the other hand, a severely threatening gesture had to be made; this was not the time to back down, and Seymour

---

[5] See Lane-Poole, *Parkes*, i, 237.

could only pray that a 'whiff of grape' would suffice to bring the obstinate Yeh to his senses.[6] In short, the sword was to be drawn, but only half-way from the scabbard.

First of all, the Senior Naval Officer, Commodore C. G. J. B. Elliot, was ordered to take a detachment, which included the *Sybille*, the *Barracouta*, and the tender, *Coromandel*, up-river, as evidence that hostile action was being meditated. In the course of the operation, what appeared to be an Imperial war junk was seized. Unhappily, the hostage turned out to be a private merchantman. Two steam frigates, *Encounter* and *Sampson*, were then sent to join the Commodore, in the hope that so imposing a force would bend the Commissioner in the direction of prudence. The ships' guns were ostentatiously trained on the city, but Yeh refused to budge.

In view of this annoying stalemate, on 20 October Parkes took ship to Hong Kong, where, in consultation with the Governor and the Admiral, it was decided that, failing a second ultimatum, the navy supported by reinforcements of manpower from the heavier ships, would seize the outer defences of Canton. Yeh responded to the challenge by attempting to return all twelve members of the *Arrow*'s crew, but since this surrender was not accompanied by an apology, the poor fellows were restored to their keepers, and negotiations came to an abrupt end. '. . . [E]xperience of the Chinese

---

[6] An account of the ensuing operations, and of the negotiations with the Imperial Commissioner between 8 October and 14 November, is contained in fifteen day-by-day reports forwarded by Admiral Seymour to Ralph Osborne, Secretary to the Admiralty on 14 November 1856 (Dispatch No. 103). These reports were accompanied by 45 enclosures, comprising the correspondence between Bowring, Parkes, Seymour, and Yeh. This very substantial collection, addressed by Seymour from the *Niger* at Canton, is contained in Adm. 1/5683. See also Seymour to Admiralty, 24 Nov. 1856 (No. 106), 'Operations at Canton', encl. No. 1, Yeh to Bowring, trans. by Thomas Wade, Chinese Secretary [received 12 Nov.]; same to same, 14 Dec. 1856 (No. 116), 'Proceedings before Canton', with enclosures; and same to same, 29 Dec. 1856, ibid.

Most of the letters included in Seymour's dispatch of 14 November are printed in Bonner-Smith and Lumby's volume of documents, *The Second China War 1856–1860* vol. 95. Unfortunately there is no citation of sources, apart from the general statement that the majority of the documents are to be found in the Foreign Office correspondence (Series F.O. 17) in the Public Record Office. Although marred by a somewhat jingoistic slant as well as by errors of fact, a largely first-hand account of the operations in 1856, based on Admiral Seymour's dispatches, is (despite the strange omission of 1856 in the title) George Wingrove Cooke's *China: 1857–58*, already cited.

character having proved that moderation is considered by the officials as an evidence of weakness', Admiral Seymour proceeded to assault the four barrier forts, some five miles below the city. Carrying Royal Marines and the boats' crews of the *Calcutta*, *Winchester*, and *Bittern*, the *Sampson* and the *Barracouta*, accompanied by the boats of the *Sybille* under Commodore Elliot, set out from Whampoa. Arriving at Blenheim Reach on 23 October, the two steam sloops, *Sampson* and *Barracouta*, ascended the Macao Passage in order to block the alternative backwater channel. Blenheim Fort capitulated quickly, as did Macao Fort, a well-sited bastion on an island in mid-river, mounting 86 guns. This latter stronghold, Seymour prepared to hold and garrison.

By the 24th, the British detachment was in possession of all the outer forts, including Dutch Folly and Shameen at the head of the Macao Passage. Despite the presence of more than 150 enemy guns, varying from one-foot bore to four-pounders, resistance had been meagre. Chinese casualties numbered five killed; British, nil. With the exception of Dutch Folly, which overlooked the south wall of the city, and which was therefore retained and garrisoned, the remaining forts, apart from the Macao fort, were dismantled, the guns spiked and all ammunition destroyed. By the 25th, a combined force of marines and seamen had taken up quarters in the Factories, erected makeshift defences, and successfully repelled an ill-organized Chinese attack.

This unexacting success gave Bowring his opportunity to press the long-festering complaint: refusal of access within the walls as promised by Treaty. Hitherto, as has been noticed more than once, the claim had rested in abeyance. On this occasion, with Canton apparently at his mercy, Bowring was able to pose as the magnanimous victor. He prepared to hold out an olive twig, to the extent that he demanded only official access. His argument was expounded succinctly by Admiral Seymour in a letter to Commissioner Yeh: 'To prevent the recurrence of evils like the present, which have been occasioned by the disregard paid by the Imperial Commissioner to the repeated application for redress and satisfaction made to him by letter in the matter of the *Arrow* . . .,' Her Majesty's Plenipotentiary simply requested 'for all foreign representatives the same free access to the authorities and city of Canton (where all the Chinese high officials reside) as is enjoyed under Treaty at the other four ports, and denied to us at Canton alone.'[7]

Hitherto the point at issue had turned upon the right of the Chinese authorities to seize a vessel presumed to be protected by British registry. Apparently the point was taken. Judging by his efforts to restore the captured crew, Yeh seemed to have developed doubts about the wisdom of his summary police action. In any event, the evidence suggests that he was disposed to concede a minor point of principle for the sake of patching up the peace. But now, all of a sudden, Bowring had presented him with a far more serious problem of principle—the failure of the government to fulfil their long-evaded treaty obligations, a vexatious issue from the past which Yeh had assumed, or at least fervently hoped, had been laid to rest. Quite naturally, he resented the reintroduction of such a painful subject under the pretence that it was linked to the affair of the lorscha *Arrow*, and he retorted somewhat tartly that the original claim had been long abandoned.

In the face of so flat a rejection of his demands, which must have been anticipated, Bowring was happy to carry on. Doubtless in the prayerful hope that Yeh might be pressed into a more receptive frame of mind, he proposed lobbing one or two shells into his official residence or *Yamen*. Shortly after noon on 27 October, a single 10-inch gun on the *Encounter* fired a few bursts into the sky by way of warning. On the following day, after the inhabitants had been told (presumably by sign language, for no translated announcements were distributed) firing was resumed more seriously by two 32-pounders from Dutch Folly. The city wall was breached and one gateway partially shattered. Enraged rather than intimidated by such bullying, Yeh issued a proclamation, which was placarded on every conceivable vantage point, commanding the citizens to exterminate the barbarians, and offering a bonus of thirty dollars, later increased to a hundred, for every English head taken. Lacking the opportunities to practise such profit-

[7] Contained in Seymour to Admiralty, 14 Nov. 1856 (No. 103), Adm. 1/5683.

able surgery, the townsfolk were little tempted. Beyond a certain amount of wild sniping from the walls, their more deadly efforts were confined to floating fire-ships down river towards the British anchorage.

Meanwhile, on the 29th, a detachment of seamen and marines, against negligible opposition, scrambled through the gap in the wall which the guns had opened, and made their way into the Commissioner's *yamen*. Admiral Seymour and the Consul, Harry Parkes, followed close behind, the latter proclaiming from the height of the entrance steps to a handful of wondering spectators the right of free entry into the city. According to French accounts, a good deal of looting took place within the Commissioner's private apartments, as well as in the harem, a brutal pillaging in which local inhabitants as well as Americans and French joined. In his own report, Seymour testified to the restrained behaviour of the British force; none the less, the whole untidy affair was bound to confirm Yeh in his determination to get the uncivilized foreigner out of Canton, and to keep him out.

Following more futile efforts to persuade the Commissioner to accede to British demands (with which, despite their declared neutrality, both American and French representatives showed sympathy) sporadic shelling began again on 3 November, and continued for three days. Government buildings were the chief targets. On the 6th, fearing the attentions of 23 war junks anchored down river, close to French Folly, Seymour sent the steam tender, *Coromandel*, and the *Barracouta*, with accompanying boats, to disperse them. This was accomplished against unusually stout resistance, and the fort itself was captured with a loss of one killed and four wounded. A week later, with still no response from the inflexible Yeh, a fresh demonstration of naval power was provided. The order was given to retake the Bogue forts which had been intermittently strengthened since their first capture in 1841. The two Wantung forts fell after an hour's stiff fighting, with similarly negligible casualties.[8] On the 13th the Anunghoy forts were seized without loss, despite the formidable presence of 210 guns. Brave defenders and sound matériel were not wanting,

[8] Captain R. Stewart to Admiralty, 14 Nov. 1856, encl. list of casualties, Adm. 1/5683.

but bad discipline and careless training meant much mis-
directed fire.[9]

The navy now possessed an over-all command of the Canton waterways, and for the time being there was little else to
do beyond blowing up such forts as had been reoccupied by
the Chinese. But such exhibitions of power had no obvious
effect on Yeh. Incensed, impatient, and perplexed, Bowring
journeyed to Canton on 16 November, but in spite of a further
shelling of government buildings, the Commissioner refused
to receive him. Clearly, Yeh was neither frightened nor
humbled, and certainly in no mood to discuss anything with
foreign gunmen. As a result, Bowring had no choice but to
retreat with as much dignity as he could muster. 'I must leave
to His Excellency the Naval Commander in Chief', the disillusioned Governor wrote to Yeh, shortly before his departure,
'the measures which a painful necessity may compel him to
take, and to Your Excellency all the responsibility which
belongs to those who disregard Treaties and visit upon a
people the unhappy consequence of their own obstinacy.' A
little naïvely, he added by way of warning that he would
advise Peking of its representative's wicked intransigence.[10]
To this rebuke, penned 'more in sorrow than in anger', Yeh
replied with customary blandness, disclaiming responsibility,
repudiating the unjust British claims, and expressing shocked
surprise that Admiral Seymour had been allowed to go to such
devastating lengths. As regards telling tales to the Emperor, he
assured Bowring that Peking had been receiving full reports of
the proceedings ever since the troubles began.[11]

By 22 November, the snubbed but scarcely humbled
crusader was back in Hong Kong, only to face more problems
in the shape of a domestic crisis. The *Arrow* affair leading to the

[9] Admiral Seymour's report on operations between 12 and 21 November is
embodied chiefly in ten letters between himself, Bowring, and Yeh. See Seymour to
Admiralty, *Niger* at Canton, 24 Nov. 1856 (No. 106), Adm. 1/5683. Sir John Bowring
published the official correspondence between himself, Seymour, and the Imperial
Commissioner for the period October–November, in *The Hong Kong Government
Gazette Extraordinary*, Victoria, 28 November 1856. A copy is to be found in Foreign
Dept., Consultation No. 126, 30 Jan. 1857 (N.A.I.).

[10] 20 Nov. 1856, encl. in Seymour to Admiralty, *Niger* at Canton, 24 Nov. 1856
(No. 106), Adm. 1/5683.

[11] Yeh to Bowring, 21 Nov. 1856, encl. in Seymour to Admiralty, 24 Nov. 1856,
ibid.

assault on Canton had inevitably excited the recently settled Chinese population, and various incidents suggested strong and malign influences at work within an island that was but thinly policed. Actually, the Governor could have called on sufficient marines and seamen from the squadron to quash any riotous disturbance, but nervously apprehensive of the evil spirits that his adversary in Canton might generate, he called to India for help. Another six months were to elapse before the outbreak of the Mutiny, but Calcutta found it impossible to spare the troops. However, in the event of extreme urgency, the Straits Settlements could be asked to provide 500 sepoys and thirty European artillery men with six guns.[12]

But long before this 'cold comfort' reached Hong Kong, the Canton situation had gone from bad to worse. Even before Bowring had started on his mournful return journey, the French were preparing to vacate their Factory. Although the Chargé d'Affaires, the Count de Courcy, himself favoured a policy of sticking with the British, Admiral Guérin, recently arrived with the frigate *Virginie* to look after French interests, ordered the withdrawal of all French vessels from the River and the striking of the Consulate flag. The American Commissioner, Dr. Peter Parker, while outwardly reluctant to follow suit, decided after talks with Commodore Armstrong, the commander of the American squadron, to urge the withdrawal of all nationals, along with the naval detachment recently provided for the defence of the American Factory. Unhappily, a dignified retirement was interrupted when one of the boats of the U.S. corvette *Portsmouth*, *en route* from Whampoa to Canton, was subjected to desultory but unusually accurate fire from river-bank forts, regarrisoned since their dismantlement on 23 October. Although well soaked by the water thrown up by the round shot, the occupants escaped unhurt.[13] Angered by this unexpected insult to the Flag (which in all probability, the heedless Chinese gunners did not recognize), on the following day Armstrong's flotilla bombarded the gun-emplacements for nearly three hours. Between 20 and

---

[12] Secretary, Government of India, to Secret Committee, 22 Dec. 1856, Foreign Dept., Secret Dispatch to Secretary of State, Consultation No. 63, 22 Dec. 1856 (N.A.I.).
[13] Parkes to Bowring, Canton, 16 Nov. 1856, Bonner-Smith, pp. 109–11.

22 November, four forts were taken by assault, and despite strenuous resistance which cost a good many Chinese lives, Armstrong's instant retaliation, wrote Parker to the American Secretary of State on 22 November, was 'the first blow that has ever been struck by our navy in China', an exercise in *force majeure* necessitated by the 'quite inscrutable obstinacy' of the Imperial Commissioner.[14]

Yeh did not apologize for his gunners' temerity, and since no such satisfaction was likely to be forthcoming, as a demonstration of displeasure it was decided to blow up the forts.[15] With the powder available, it proved to be a task hardly simpler than the destruction of Hamburg's U-boat pens nearly ninety years later. Just as British sappers had been impressed by the sturdiness of the Bogue forts, the Americans were surprised by the solidity of the upper-river batteries, as well as by the weight of armament. The granite walls were from nine to ten feet thick, and many of the guns must have weighed between seven and eight tons. One brass $8\frac{1}{2}$ inch gun—a particularly attractive trophy—was more than twenty-one feet long. Admiral Seymour was interested to note that heavy cannon were mounted in the same manner as ships' guns, with the breachings secured across the outside of the embrasures, which suggested to him that some of the Chinese artillerymen may have had previous service in European warships, or at least been given the opportunity to observe European methods. By 6 December, the work of demolition was completed, and the American force dropped down to Whampoa.[16]

During this time, although the river was kept open, with a chain-boom across the Factory creek as protection against fire-ships, traffic had almost ceased and, ashore, business had come to a standstill. With very few exceptions, all neutral foreigners had left Canton. Only twenty British subjects remained, but these had sensibly sent their furniture and other effects to Hong Kong or Macao. On the river bank, the European Factories presented a desolate sight, more nearly

[14] Quoted in Costin, p. 213.
[15] See Dr. Peter Parker to O. H. Perry, U.S. Consul in Canton, 25 Nov. 1856, encl. No. 1, in Seymour to Admiralty, 24 Dec. 1856 (No. 116), Adm. 1/5683.
[16] Letter of Peter Parker, Macao, 9 Dec. 1856, encl. No. 6 in Seymour to Admiralty (No. 116), ibid.

resembling untidy and neglected barracks than prosperous emporiums of trade. Visits were sometimes made to Chinese merchants whose warehouses could be approached by water, but for both communities such contacts were a monopoly of the daring few.[17]

Despite desultory shelling, usually directed against the crumbled administrative buildings in the city, Chinese resistance persisted. Indeed, the badly ravaged French Folly, which had suffered two British assaults, had been reoccupied, and partly repaired, with additional flanking batteries set in semicircular fashion in the foreground. Such a strategically placed snipers' nest could be a nuisance to ships in the river, and on the morning of 4 December the *Encounter* and the *Barracouta*, accompanied by about 350 small-arms men in boats, made ready to retake the fort. The two vessels anchored some 850 yards from the fort, and, covered by a battery on Dutch Folly, the assault force pushed under the muzzles of the enemy's guns, and got ashore.[18] Twice the Chinese defenders attempted to rally, but despite desperate hand-to-hand fighting, they were driven back. The whole affair was over within an hour of the first shot being fired, and, as customary, the flag was raised on the highest point of the battered fort. Chinese gunnery had improved considerably, but casualties were few: one marine was killed and one seaman wounded. Before nightfall, a party of Royal Artillery fixed mines under the works, and laid the whole massive structure in ruins.

Reprisal was not long on the way, and when it came, it was devastating. On 14 December the Chinese set fire to houses close to the Factory area. Many of the buildings had been demolished more than a month earlier as a precaution against arson, but time and labour had been insufficient to permit a complete clearance. The flames spread with incredible rapidity, and despite the efforts of officers and men, by the morning of the 16th, with the exception of one house, all that remained of Factories, banks, consulates, dwellings, and contiguous suburbs, was a heap of smoking ruins.

Although the seizure of Canton was still believed to be

[17] See [John Scarth], *Twelve Years in China. The People, the Rebels and the Mandarins* (Edinburgh, 1860), p. 283.
[18] Seymour to Admiralty, 24 Dec. 1856 (No. 116), doc. cit.

beyond the resources of the British force, the Admiral had no intention of removing his ships, 'the great importance of holding our position at Canton being evident. . .'.[19] An *ad hoc* garrison of some 300 marines, seamen, and soldiers, with zeal appropriate to their hazardous situation, dug entrenchments across the Factory gardens, built breastworks, and set up field-pieces. But apart from the watchful sloops on the river, the principal protection was provided by the guns of the Dutch Folly, with its garrison of 140 seamen. Only 400 yards from the city wall, it was well placed to restrain would-be attackers, or to assist, when the time came, appropriate offensive operations.

It was now Christmas 1856. Within the city, Yeh sat tight, surrounded by his militia 'braves'—some 20,000 in number. Against an enemy amounting to less than 1,000, he prepared to bide his time, unwilling to counter-attack against the lethal fire of European ships that sheltered in the water, but certain that he could hold at bay such foes as were 'visible to the eye'. Distant horizons were beyond the reach of his imagination. Like the Emperor, his mind did not begin to grasp the certainty of ultimate defeat. Amid the ruins of his Yamen, he would sit, stubborn and defiant, clothed in viceregal majesty, unconcerned with the prospect of barbarian hordes that might one day come over the sea to wreak their revenge and seize his capital.

Meanwhile, Bowring had become increasingly worried about the safety of Hong Kong. Since early December, rumblings of discontent among the Chinese population had grown in volume, punctuated by the lurid activities of incendiarists. The Governor suspected some deep-seated plan to overthrow the constitution, supported by Cantonese interventionists on the mainland. Lacking an effectual police force, he was anxious to restore the garrison to its normal complement. In the previous November, Admiral Seymour had borrowed a detachment from the 50th Regiment of foot (later the Queen's Own Royal West Kents)—about 100 men—to assist in the defence of the Factories, a reinforcement badly needed following the withdrawal of the American guard force on 17 November,

---

[19] Seymour to Admiralty, 29 Dec. 1856, ibid.

and that of the French five days later.[20] Since British control of the river, and especially the vital shore-line between Whampoa and Canton, was becoming increasingly precarious, Seymour was in no haste to return so useful a contingent, and said so. None the less, the Executive Council backed Bowring, resolving that, in view of the 'imperfectly protected condition of the Colony', the naval force for its protection should be augmented, and the troops that had been withdrawn for the defence of the Factories should be sent back.[21]

Although his appeal to the Government of India for one British regiment had been turned down, the unabashed Governor had no hesitation in returning to the offensive.[22] One hundred and fifty native troops and a few European sappers would be warmly welcomed, he told the Hon. E. A. Blundell, Governor of the Straits Settlements. It was of consummate importance, he wrote on 8 January 1857, 'not only that the Colony should be placed in a state of security, but that the positions occupied by our Naval forces at Canton should be maintained. A withdrawal from that locality would in my judgment greatly augment the perils in which the Colony is exposed.'[23] And a little later, he repeated his request to the Governor-General for 5,000 troops, along with a detachment of artillery. Pin-pricking Canton with insufficient forces had merely served to make the Viceroy's conduct 'the more inveterate and unmanageable'.[24]

On the Malayan peninsula, and particularly in Singapore, the situation was scarcely one of internal tranquillity. Nevertheless, Blundell arranged for the dispatch from Penang of two companies of native Indian infantry, and a detachment of British artillery. Although obviously affected by Bowring's

---

[20] See Bowring to Clarendon, 20 Nov. 1856, Bonner-Smith, p. 122.

[21] In support of this resolution, Bowring was delighted to confront Seymour with a letter addressed to Sir Henry Pottinger by the Colonial Secretary, Lord Stanley, in 1843. In regard to the defence of Hong Kong, Stanley observed that 'Her Majesty's Government concur generally with you in opinion that we must depend on our Naval Superiority for the Complete Security of our future commercial Establishments in that Island'. Bowring to Seymour, 3 Jan. 1857, encl. Minutes of the Executive Council for that day, all of which are included as No. 2, in Seymour to Admiralty, 14 Jan. 1857, No. 6, Foreign Dept., Consultation Nos. 63–64, 27 Mar. 1857 (N.A.I.).

[22] See Bowring to Canning, Hong Kong, 14 Jan. 1857, Foreign Dept., Consultation No. 61–62, ibid.

[23] Ibid., No. 29–30.

[24] 10 Mar., ibid., No. 54–58.

plea of urgency, he could afford no more. The reinforcement could have been sent in the Company's steam frigate *Auckland*, via Labuan, a journey of about 16 days. But this would have meant bedding the troops on deck, and exposing them to the prevailing north-east monsoon. So, in the end, the Governor hired a private steamer, the *Sir James Brooke*, at a cost of 12,000 Spanish dollars. And to ensure that all 340 officers and men arrived in good condition, plenty of blankets were provided, and each of the sepoys was presented with two Guernsey frocks.[25]

The *Sir James Brooke* sailed on 21 January 1857, dropping anchor off Victoria ten days later.[26] By that time, morale in Hong Kong had improved, partly owing to the presence in harbour of the French Admiral and the American Commodore, and partly to the arrival of a newly-fitted and well-armed guard ship, whose nightly patrols were intended to frighten off intruders from the mainland. In addition, H.M. sloops *Elk* and *Camille* along with the Company's *Auckland* were on call in the offing. As yet untouched, and for the time being unchallenged by pirates, Hong Kong had ceased to be a major 'worry centre'.[27]

The arrival of good news from Hong Kong must have brought considerable relief to the Governor-General of India, who had clearly suffered embarrassment as a result of the constant insatiable demands of Governor Bowring. 'It is not

[25] Governor of the Straits Settlements (Prince of Wales Island, Singapore, and Malacca) to Secretary of the Government of India, 6 Jan. 1857; reply of the Secretary, 16 Jan. 1857; Governor's second letter to the Secretary, 19 Jan. 1857; Foreign Dept., Consultation No. 32–35, ibid.

[26] On 20 January, a number of merchants representing established Singapore firms protested to Blundell that the dispatch of detachments to China was 'highly injudicious', in view of their valuable property holdings, which might be in jeopardy in the event of a Chinese uprising. 'Respectfully' (although the word scarcely concealed an impertinence) they gave notice that the Honourable East India Company would be held responsible for any losses suffered in consequence of the weakening of the Singapore garrison. The snub which the Governor administered in response to this 'injudicious' advice was entirely approved by the Governor-General of India. See Governor of Straits Settlements to Secretary of the Government of India, 20 and 27 Jan. 1857; reply of the Governor-General, 27 Feb., Foreign Dept., Consultation No. 37–39, 51–52, and 53, ibid.

[27] See Governor of Straits Settlements to Secretary, Government of India, 22 Jan. 1857, Foreign Dept., Consultation No. 41; also Seymour to Canning, 15 Feb. 1857, encl. Seymour to Admiralty, 15 Feb. (No. 30), Consultation No. 134–136; and Seymour to Canning, 30 Jan. 1857 (No. 18), Consultation No. 68–71, ibid.

an agreeable duty', Lord Canning noted in a long minute, 'to answer so earnest an appeal in the negative; but the case is one on which there is no choice before the Govt. of India. To send away from India at this moment Five thousand men of whom a considerable portion should be Europeans is simply impossible.' He then went on, in ruminating fashion, to explain his problem, at a time, it should be observed, when no shadow of mutiny fell over the northern landscape. Britain was already engaged in war with Persia, and only one European regiment was available, should General Outram needed reinforcements.[28] In his view, it would be madness to denude the Lower Provinces of their scanty strength in English troops. 'Even in peaceful Bengal we are not safe without them.'

I give the answer [he continued] with regret, but the answer must be that not a European can be spared, and that the Force asked by Sir John Bowring for the subjugation of Canton cannot be supplied. I say this without taking into account the Bengal Division for the Army in Persia, which must be in readiness by the close of the Monsoon.

All that the Govt. of India can attempt is to [encourage] the authorities in Hong Kong to maintain the Colony in safety. To aid in this the Govt. of Singapore has already despatched a force of nearly 500 men which will by this time have reached its destination. To replace this force at Singapore, and to put further means at the disposal of the Governor, a Regiment of N[ative] Infantry left Madras for the Straits on the very day on which these Despatches were received here. . . .

Canning hoped that the addition in the near future of five or six hundred sepoys and some artillery would at least 'place the Colony in security for the present against any attack from within or without'.[29]

In fact, the colony of Hong Kong, despite the Governor's apprehension, was amply secured by two or three sloops. However, far up the Canton River system, the badly mauled Factory area was once again undergoing savage raids from the

---

[28] Britain declared war against Persia late in 1856, and the dispatch of Outram's expedition had the ultimate effect of checking Persian interventions in India, while at the same time forcing recognition of Afghan independence.

[29] Minute by the Governor-General, 20 Feb. 1857, Foreign Dept., Consultation No. 65, 27 Mar. 1857 (N.A.I.).

city. Concentrated attacks were made on the quays, and on visiting vessels, sometimes by fleets of war junks, but more frequently by fire-rafts, shore-based rockets, stinkpots, and various incendiary devices.[30] To safeguard anchored ships as well as to preserve the protective boom behind which they were moored, Seymour felt obliged to clear the suburbs on each side of the Factory gardens. In the end, as a result of combined Chinese and British efforts, the entire shore area lay in ruins—not a house remained intact—as far as Dutch Folly and some two hundred yards beyond.

But it was wasted effort. With so few reserves, the British position continued to be highly precarious; a surprise attack by land and river might well submerge the weary defenders. In the circumstances, there was no alternative to withdrawal, not only from the devastated Factory site but from Dutch Folly fort. Under Seymour's direction this was accomplished with disciplined precision and without casualties, thus releasing the two steamers, *Niger* and *Encounter*, from their confined anchorage close to the left bank, where they had suffered nightly showers of rockets and fireworks. They were now freed for emergency services, chief of which was to battle with the phalanxes of war junks, rowing-boats, and various piratical craft that continued to harass British shipping above and below Whampoa. At the same time, to preserve a *point d'appui* for future operations against Canton, Seymour needed a base not too far removed from the Factory shore. He chose Macao Fort near the south-west corner of Honam Island, and this erstwhile Chinese stronghold became the sole British post on the upper river. Meanwhile, in Canton, as news of the British retirement spread throughout the lanes and alleys, a grateful populace raised triumphal arches in Yeh's honour.[31]

For the next two or three months, on instructions from the Admiralty, the commander-in-chief confined himself to 'present undertakings'.[32] There was, in fact, little to do, apart from keeping an eye on Hong Kong, but organize hunts for

[30] Seymour to Admiralty, 14 Jan. 1857 (No. 6), Adm. 1/5583. See also, Bonner-Smith, pp. 163–7.

[31] Seymour to Admiralty, *Calcutta* at Hong Kong, 30 Jan. 1857 (No. 18), and encl. No. 1, Bowring to Seymour, 24 Jan. 1857 (No. 24), Adm. 1/5583. Admiralty approval of Seymour's action was forwarded on 8 April 1857 (No. 133), Adm. 2/1613.

[32] See Clarendon to Admiralty, 9 Mar. 1857, Adm. 1/5687.

the increasing number of war junks that sheltered in the surrounding network of creeks. Lack of shallow-draught craft made the task of burning out the infestations a difficult one. Moreover, the Chinese had the habit of slipping out at night to sink ballast-laden boats in the narrower parts of the approach channels to Canton. Nevertheless, the patrolling continued in so far as resources permitted, but the health of skeleton crews deteriorated as the hot season advanced.[33] Equally under strain, the garrison in Macao Fort stood firm against nightly attacks, sometimes from rowing-boats firing scrap-iron as well as round shot. But the men stayed fit, arms and ammunition were plentiful, and Seymour had no fears for their safety.[34]

Thanks chiefly to the generosity of the Governor of the Straits Settlements, the first of a series of operations meriting the name of 'campaign' took place in May and June. It was river war at its most exciting and dramatic; cutlass and bayonet and fireworks galore! Had they preceded an attack on Canton, the ensuing commando raids might have been regarded as the effective softening up of the defences. In fact, the opposition was not only softened, but largely broken; yet more than six months were to elapse before the final assault was undertaken. Both sides shared the valorous display—the mad dashes of British boats through storms of fire, the scaling of junk walls, the desperate resistance of 'the pig-tailed defenders'—all of this provided the stuff which much later was to enthrall a generation nourished on Henty's yarns, *Chums*, and the *Boy's Own Paper*.

The first operation began on 25 May against a large fleet of 'mandarin' junks—sometimes called snake boats—that had moved about five or six miles up Escape Creek, one of the four streams running eastward from the Canton River. The British force, commanded by Commodore Elliot, consisted of small steam gunboats—the hired *Hong Kong*, *Bustard*, *Starling*, *Staunch*, and *Sir Charles Forbes*; these towed the boats and crews of the *Inflexible*, *Hornet*, and *Tribune*. The navigational

---

[33] See Seymour to Admiralty, 2 Mar. 1857 (No. 52), Adm. 1/5583; and same to same, 10 July 1857 (No. 155), Adm. 125/96.

[34] Seymour to Admiralty, 26 Apr. 1857 (No. 86), 'Operations in Canton River' file, Adm. 1/5683.

range of the gunboats was limited. Drawing from seven to seven and a half feet of water, they were apt to ground in the shallows, or, on more than one occasion, break down through lack of skilled repairs. Being flat-bottomed, the junks were spared this inconvenience, but they were far from manœuvrable with sail. However, since most of them carried forty or more oars, they had almost as much agility as steamers. Their armament usually consisted of one heavy gun in the bow, a 24- or a 32-pounder, and from four to six lighter guns further along the deck, most of them 9-pounders.

On this occasion, they waited in the shallows until the leading gunboats came into full view, fired more or less in concert from the bows, and then took to flight up the creeks, pursued by sweating seamen in rowing-boats. It was a chase that demanded 'boat race' fitness. The men stuck to their oars, the Commodore wrote to Admiral Seymour, 'through a harder day's work than I have ever before witnessed under a tropical sun'. For two days the hunt continued through the maze of twisting channels with temperatures often over 100°F. By the evening of 27 July, probably forty junks had been disabled or destroyed.[35]

The second expedition up Fatshan Creek on 1 June was more closely fought. After capturing two small forts at the entrance, Seymour in the *Coromandel* (a small, light-draught paddle-steamer), accompanied by his second-in-command, Commodore Henry Keppel, in the *Hong Kong*, engaged the main Chinese fleet.[36] Since the British vessels continued to run aground, the brunt of the battle had to be borne by storming parties in barges, gigs, and pinnaces, and launches.[37] After an unusually prolonged and bloody action, the Chinese gave way, and were pursued about seven miles, as far as Fatshan. Earlier on, Keppel had left his ship to lead the attack by boat, and, according to *The Times* war correspondent, seems to have thoroughly enjoyed the excitement of the chase, as did George Wingrove Cooke himself. But neither participated in the

[35] *Sybille*, 2nd Bar, Canton River, 29 May 1857, Bonner-Smith, p. 199.

[36] Keppel's flagship, the 50-gun sailing frigate *Raleigh* had wrecked herself on a reef some weeks earlier, and the Commodore was still awaiting the formality of a court-martial, which customarily followed such accidents.

[37] Only the *Haughty* and *Plover* were able to see action throughout; the *Opposum* and *Forester* were fast aground.

costly boarding operations which took a heavy toll. One in every ten men suffered some form of injury, a fairly large percentage even in terms of European warfare. On deck too, there was fierce hand-to-hand fighting, until finally aware that the day was lost, the defenders slipped overboard, wading or swimming to the shore, and thence across the paddy-fields to safety.

Between seventy and eighty war junks were captured, and most of them were burned in a kind of 'Glorious First of June' display of pyrotechnics. The bulk of the Chinese navy had been wiped out. All told, British casualties amounted to 84 killed or badly wounded. Seymour, who had been present at the earlier stages of the battle, was surprised that the losses were not greater. He was even more surprised at the quality of Chinese resistance; at times a British victory seemed to sway precariously in the balance. The Chinese were learning not only the art of fleet manœuvre, but of gunnery—concentration of fire and disciplined gun-laying for accuracy. The second engagement in particular had, in his view, opened 'a new era in Chinese naval warfare'. Considerable judgement had been shown in disposing the fleet for battle, and the last division especially when attacked by Keppel had defended their ships 'with skill, courage and effect'.[38]

But triumph in the creeks in no way simplified the problem of holding Canton, assuming its fall under superior gun power. Macao Fort represented a continuing British presence in the neighbourhood of the city; yet as fruitless bombardments had demonstrated, a substantial land force would be necessary for its effective occupation and retention against the defiant resistance of a population seething with hatred of the foreigner. The citizenry of Canton had little means of judging Britain's naval and military resources. In their eyes, Yeh's tenacity and courage had prevailed; a humiliated enemy had turned tail and retreated down river, abandoning all but one of their captured forts, and leaving behind little but smouldering ruins, symbols of a vanquished Western interloper. Yeh himself seems to have been confident that he could, with his mixed

---

[38] Seymour to Admiralty, *Calcutta* at Hong Kong, 10 June 1857 (No. 133), Adm. 1/5583; Bonner-Smith, pp. 204–8. See also, a graphic account of the engagement in Holt, *The Opium Wars*, pp. 205–10.

force of 'Braves' and professional Tartar soldiers, eventually exterminate the barbarians. Dismissing the prospect of vast reinforcements which the Governor of Hong Kong had threatened to bring to bear on his defences, he chose to demonstrate his contempt of the invader by stopping all trade with Canton, and by forbidding all intercourse with Hong Kong on the assumption that the colony could be starved out.

Back in England, it had been expected that the destruction of the River forts and the intermittent bombardment of Canton, however distasteful the operation to many observers in Westminster, would have convinced the Chinese authorities that a settlement was inevitable. But the only result had been increased malevolence and intransigence. 'Everything that could be fairly hoped for, from the prudence, enterprise and valour of H.M. Naval forces has been accomplished,' wrote Bowring in January 1857, 'but,' he added in a manner reminiscent of Captain Charles Elliot, 'they are not able to take the City of Canton, and deem its capture absolutely necessary for our final triumph.' The British government, he went on, had been slow to realize that diplomatic approaches to Peking were wasted until a subjugated city could be, so to speak, exhibited on a platter before the Emperor. The gate of China was Canton, and unless the resistance could be broken, and entrance obtained by force, he believed that the difficulties of obtaining 'an improved position' would be 'almost invincible'.[39]

This argument the British government was prepared to accept. But a restive Opposition, weary of Palmerston's 'mad adventuring', was anxious to bring him to book. For over a month, legal and moral judgements on the matter of the lorcha *Arrow* had been angrily tossed about in Parliament, and by March the Prime Minister found himself with his back against the wall, fighting for existence against an incongruous alliance that included Lords Derby, Russell, and Lyndhurst, Bishop Wilberforce, Gladstone, Graham, Cobden, Bright, and Disraeli, all of whom were banded together in 'unanimosity' to his Ministry. Sir John Bowring was the obvious scape-

---

[39] Bowring to Clarendon, Hong Kong, 10 Jan. 1857; see also, Bowring to Governor-General of India, same date, Bonner-Smith, pp. 161–3.

goat—an overbearing bully, who, according to the ex-Lord Chancellor, Lyndhurst, suffered from a mania about securing entrance to Canton. His was 'the mischievous policy of a most mischievous man dressed in a little brief authority'. In the same vein, Cobden damned the pretensions of British merchants abroad, who continually sought to benefit from the overwhelming force of the Royal Navy. It was, in his opinion, a mistake to persevere in the demand for free access to a city where nothing but turbulence, insubordination, and hostility could be expected. Canton was not worth fighting for; outside lay the great empire of China, and nowhere in the world was trade so free as in this vast country. Characteristically, Gladstone denounced the whole of British policy and practice in China on moral grounds. Britain had broken her solemn treaty obligations by encouraging a contraband trade in opium, largely under the British flag. Originally a port where British ships might careen and refit. Hong Kong had become the base for 'a pernicious, demoralizing, and destructive trade'.[40] Beaten by sixteen votes in the Commons on 20 March 1857, Palmerston dissolved parliament, and in the general election that followed came back with an increased majority. The country obviously wanted lusty, and, if needs be, domineering leadership. It is also conceivable that the British electorate was less impressed by the importance of Canton as the chief European trading entrepôt, than by the startling report of a Chinese attempt to poison the foreign community of Hong Kong by seasoning the bread from the Pottinger Street bakery with arsenic. Wholesale carnage was averted only because the zealous miscreant over-did the dose, causing much uncomfortable vomiting, but no deaths. Yeh indignantly rejected the charges of complicity, declaring with sardonic courtesy that such actions did smack of barbarism—indeed, it was as loathsome a crime as throwing high explosive shells into the midst of populous Canton. On the other hand, he did *not* withdraw his offer of a hundred dollars for every English head.

[40] *Hansard* (3rd Series), cxliv, cols. 1212–20, 1391–1421, 1787–1809, quoted in William Page, *Commerce and Industry* (2 vols., London, 1919), i. 200–1. See also Rt. Hon. Sir Herbert Maxwell, *The Life and Letters of George William Frederick, Fourth Earl of Clarendon* (2 vols., London, 1913), ii. 138.

Palmerston's victory over the formidable, if not always well-informed, Manchester liberals and Peelites meant stepping up plans for the dispatch of a naval force to the Far East. It also led to the organization of a special mission to study the China problem at first hand. In charge of the mission was a distinguished proconsul, known for his judgement and restraint in circumstances that called for the highest diplomatic talent. James Bruce, the eighth Earl of Elgin, had been a successful governor of Jamaica, but had become better known as Governor-General of British North America (1847–54). The victory of responsible government in Canada was, in a sense, won by a conciliator. His opponents charged that he had a soft centre; that he was lacking in toughness as a defender of imperial values. Forty-six years of age on his arrival in China—a rather youthful looking middle-aged man—Elgin was resentfully intent on disproving the allegation of weakness. This determination was not likely to be expressed in any positive or ostentatious show of strength. He remained always the sensitive and cultured aristocrat, a lonely man with few friends apart from his brother Frederick, and his able secretary, Laurence Oliphant. He treated his subordinates very much *de haut en bas*, and they in their turn disliked his cold cautiousness and apparent superciliousness.[41] Outwardly controlled and impassive, he could, under extreme pressure, suddenly burst out viciously like a volcano. Such brief spells of temperament were usually the consequence of tension, of long weeks of fierce tropical heat in rooms that knew no air-conditioning. Added to climatic discomfort was the strain of dealing with prickly, contumacious, and equally weary allies like the French or Americans, and, more especially, with the highly provocative Yeh, who could write letter after repetitive letter with the imperturbable, but maddening, self-assurance of Chinese diplomacy. Yet, the 'little fat man with white hair and smooth face' (as a British army officer described him)[42] soon came to recognize and appreciate the achievements, social and cultural, of Chinese civilization. Certainly, he was to make no bones about his aversion to avaricious foreign merchants who

[41] See Lane-Poole, p. 339.
[42] Col. R. H. Vetch (ed.) *Life, Letters, and Diaries of Lieut.-General Sir Gerald Graham V.C.* (Edinburgh and London, 1901), p. 147.

seemed oblivious to the sensitivities of their unwilling hosts. Likewise, he hated bloodshed, and was capable of castigating military commanders when, as it appeared to him, they had indulged in needless violence. Elgin regarded the *Arrow* affair as a wretched blunder, and his sympathies (in the view of his immediate associates) seemed to be with the Cantonese rather than with his fellow-countrymen.

Steaming slowly up to Canton with the expeditionary force in December 1857, he was to record his shame at the destruction British men-of-war were about to wreak on an ancient civilization. And in the course of operations to come, he was constantly to take credit for inducing commanding officers to employ methods of common humanity in dealing with a brave but ill-equipped enemy. Naturally such expressions of nobility did not endear him either to the military, or to the Old China Hands, who, since he treated their opinions in cavalier fashion, were none too sure that he understood situations about which he showed so little inclination to learn. 'We admire his wit . . . ,' wrote the editor of the *North China Herald* on behalf of the Shanghai British community, 'but of China in general, and of the past and present state of affairs between the English and the Chinese, he exhibits a deficiency of information, which is greatly to be wondered at, and much to be deplored.'[43]

In undertaking the Chinese mission as Envoy Extraordinary, Lord Elgin was informed that he would assume on arrival in Hong Kong the military and diplomatic functions of H.M.'s High Commissioner and Plenipotentiary, leaving to Sir John Bowring little beyond the routine duties of Governor.[44] By this time, there was little arrogance and a good deal less bombast attaching to the Governor, who three or four years earlier had been set on cutting a figure and making a name for himself. Bowring had grown with the job, and in the course of this development, defeat and humiliation had acted as a powerful astringent. He had learned much, and some of his later correspondence reveals the extent to which he had

---

[43] Quoted in C. Y. Hsü, *China's Entrance into the Family of Nations, The Diplomatic Phase 1858–1880* (Cambridge, Mass., 1960), p. 84.

[44] Clarendon to Bowring, 25 Mar. 1857, Bonner-Smith, pp. 190–1. See also, F.O. to Elgin, 20 Apr. 1857, F.O. 17/274.

ceased to be a moralist and a doctrinaire. Yet the House of Commons was bound to be his undoing. Following a series of violent attacks on his methods and manner, retirement was inevitable. Many of his oldest friends saw him as the betrayer of moral principles he had once so staunchly upheld. To them, the once courageous conciliator had become a war-monger. Equally significant of popular distaste (although be no means decisive) was Elgin's ill-concealed antipathy. Indeed, the more that Elgin saw of Bowring, the less was he willing to believe that anything the Governor recommended should be taken seriously.[45]

Before leaving England, Elgin had been told that a force of some 1,500 infantry and artillery had been dispatched to the transit depot at Singapore, which could be drawn on for reinforcements in case of need. By the time of his arrival in Hong Kong, in addition to the garrison force, he could expect to find the 5th Regiment (later the Northumberland Fusiliers) of about 750 men from Mauritius, as well as detachments of native troops from the Straits Settlements. Having familiarized himself with local affairs, he was instructed, in association with the French and American authorities (with whom it was hoped arrangements for a joint effort could be made), to 'proceed to the mouth of the Peiho River with as considerable a naval force as can be spared from the neighbourhood of Canton. From past experience it was clear that shallow-draught steam vessels and gunboats would be the key to success in the event of serious opposition, and reinforcements of such craft were promised by early August.

It was taken for granted that Elgin would communicate 'freely and unreservedly' with the respective commanders-in-chief, army and navy, but it was left to his sole discretion to decide what naval and military operations might be necessary in the light of his instructions. The United States had certain trade interests at stake, but Britain and France had more particular complaints, viz., the outrage committed on the British flag at Canton, and the barbarous murder of a French missionary in the interior. In the first instance, therefore, Elgin felt almost bound to make contact with Peking. He was, in fact, told to do his very best to meet representatives of the Imperial

[45] Gerson, *Horatio Nelson Lay . . .*, p. 75.

Court at some convenient point, preferably near the entrance of the Peiho, and there demand: first, reparations for injuries to British subjects, the complete fulfilment of stipulations promised by treaty, and compensation to British subjects for losses incurred in the course of past disturbances; second, the assent of the Chinese government to diplomatic representation in Peking, or, at the least, periodic visits to the capital by an accredited minister of the Crown, along with the right of the British plenipotentiary and chief superintendent of trade to communicate directly with the Court; and finally, a revision of the commercial treaties with China that would permit 'access to cities on the great rivers', as well as permission for Chinese vessels to resort to Hong Kong for purposes of trade. Should the Chinese government refuse to accept the first demands, namely, reparation for injuries, compensation for losses, and the implementation of treaties formerly agreed, Elgin was told he would be justified in taking immediate coercive measures. It would then rest with Admiral Seymour to determine where and how the forces at his disposal should be employed. In the view of the Foreign Office, punitive operations would be chiefly the responsibility of the navy, an advice which introduced some ambiguity into the respective jurisdictions of Admiral and Envoy Extraordinary. No troops were to be moved further from the shore than would allow of ready communication with the ships. 'It is not', read the official instruction, 'the intention of Her Majesty's government to undertake any land operations in the interior of the country.'[46]

On 21 April Elgin left London for Paris, where he conferred with Napoleon III and his ministers. Here it was agreed that France would undertake a similar mission, to be led by a plenipotentiary whose stature should not be unequal to that of the British. Baron Gros, an older man of long diplomatic experience, was subsequently chosen. After an uneventful voyage from the Red Sea, Elgin reached Pointe de Galle on the

---

[46] Clarendon to Elgin, 20 Apr. 1857, Bonner-Smith, op. cit., pp. 191–7. The Foreign Office directive on arrangements to be concerted between Elgin, General Ashburnham, and Admiral Seymour in the event of hostilities was sent to Admiral Seymour. See Admiralty to Seymour, 22 Apr. 1857 (N. 158), Adm. 2/1613.

southern tip of Ceylon towards the end of May, where he was joined by Major-General Thomas Ashburnham, commander of the land force, who brought him first intelligence of an Indian mutiny. Penang provided no further bulletins, but on reaching Singapore on 3 June, he was presented with the stunning news that scattered agitations had developed into widespread rebellion, which threatened to extinguish the British raj. In a message of almost emotional urgency, Lord Canning pleaded that any European regiments intended for the China theatre should be diverted to Calcutta. There was no mention of naval reinforcements, although marines and seamen were subsequently conscripted for service.[47]

Elgin acted quickly. The 5th Regiment from Mauritius and the 90th (Cameronians) from England were already on their way to China, but one or both might be caught in the Straits of Sunda, or stopped at Singapore. These, he ordered, should turn back, and proceed forthwith to Calcutta.[48] Admittedly, the situation in China might well go from bad to worse; this was a risk that Elgin had to take, and he could not forbear telling the Governor-General that, in ordering the diversion of troops intended for China, he was 'incurring a heavy responsibility and making a great sacrifice'. Assuming the emergency was short-lived, he hoped that the 'full amount of the allotted force' would be restored at the earliest possible moment, in view of the fact that it was 'by no means more than adequate to the work we have in hand'.[49]

Three weeks later, Canning replied that the situation had worsened, that a great part of the North-West Provinces was in a state of anarchy, and that there had been risings in other parts of the interior 'attended with horrible atrocities'. Every European soldier *en route* to China that could be spared should be sent immediately to Calcutta. Reinforcements requested from England would be a long time coming, and the survival of British communities in danger of extinction depended on speedy action. Of course, if events perchance took a sudden

[47] See Canning to Elgin, 19 May 1857, L/P & S/5/149 (I.O.A.).

[48] See Elgin to Clarendon, Singapore, 3 June 1857, Foreign Dept., Consultation No. 32-32A, 26 June 1857 (N.A.I.). The troopship *Simoom* carrying the 5th Regiment reached Singapore on 19 June, and was immediately diverted to Calcutta. Elgin to Canning, 20 June 1857, ibid., No. 34.

[49] Elgin to Canning, Singapore, 4 June 1857, ibid.

turn, and the mutiny fizzled out, he would send a regiment or
two on to China at the earliest opportunity.[50]

The *Shannon* bearing the new plenipotentiary and his suite
reached Hong Kong on 2 July. Within a half-hour of the
arrival, Admiral Seymour was on board to acquaint Lord
Elgin with news of the successful operations in Escape and
Fatshan creeks. Elgin's first impulse was to take immediate
advantage of so favourable a situation and set out with an
appropriate naval detachment for the Peiho. Seymour was
perfectly willing to accompany him, but pointed out that
Canton was more than a local problem; the whole question of
achieving a settlement with Peking depended first of all on the
reduction of Canton and the humiliation of the 'Braves';
'. . . any attempt to settle the question by negotiation elsewhere would excite uneasiness in those parts of China where
trade is flourishing, and confirm the Chinese in their belief of
the impregnability of Canton, on which, as it is alleged, rests
the whole system of their exclusiveness and arrogance
towards strangers'.[51]

Provided the navy performed as effectively as in recent
operations, Seymour believed that Canton could be taken
with 5,000 troops. General Ashburnham thought 4,000 would
suffice, but ruefully admitted that climate could play havoc
with numbers; in other words, 5,000 at any given time within
the next few months could in reality mean 4,000 or even fewer
men, fit for active service. At the moment (July) Ashburnham's command amounted only to 1,484, of whom 244 were
on the sick list. Clearly, the occupation of Canton was still out
of the question; the choice lay between inaction on the Canton
River, or 'showing the flag' in the estuary of the Peiho. But, as
Seymour pointed out, what effect would an approach to the
Court of Peking have, if the Emperor could assume that
Canton was impregnable and the 'Braves' invincible? Little
could be expected beyond a rebuff and loss of face. Elgin was
impressed by the argument, supported as it was by the Governor and other experienced officials in Hong Kong. He admit-

[50] Canning to Elgin, Government House, Calcutta, 24 June 1857, Foreign Dept.,
Consultation No. 33, 26 June 1857 (N.A.I.).
[51] See Seymour to Admiralty, 10 July 1857 (No. 189), Adm. 1/5583; Bonner-Smith,
pp. 214–15.

ted the impossibility of penetrating the mysterious workings of the Peking mind, and of being certain of the type of operation that would be most influential in bringing the Emperor's delegates to the council table. But common sense suggested that 'unless overwhelming considerations of public policy' forbade it, the main force should be brought to bear 'on that portion of the population of China by which we have been aggrieved, [rather] than on those whose conduct in their relations with us has been altogether irreproachable'.[52]

Unfortunately, at the moment, the mighty military lever was not available to provide the needful pressure on Canton. The leisurely-moving Baron Gros had not yet put in an appearance with the French contingent. So far, only an advance naval detachment had arrived with Admiral Rigault de Genouilly. Moreover, the situation in India had worsened, and promised reinforcements might be held back for many months to come. In the circumstances, Elgin, unwilling to twiddle his thumbs in Hong Kong, made ready to escape frustration by collecting whatever marines and seamen that could be spared, and sailing for Calcutta, 'the centre of military interest and activity'. He counted on an absence of no more than seven weeks. He was assured, he told Bowring, 'by persons well acquainted with India' that his presence at the head of a small reinforcement (which popular imagination might well suppose to be the harbinger of an armada) would produce a powerful moral effect.[53]

So for the time being, both projected expeditions—to Canton and to the Peiho—were shelved. On 18 July 'Peel's Naval Brigade', consisting of 300 marines, in company with the Plenipotentiary, set off for Calcutta in two ships, the corvette *Pearl*, and the *Shannon* (Captain Peel), the latter carrying sixty 68-pounders. At Singapore, Elgin was shocked to learn of the massacre of Cawnpore and of the desperate state of isolated British garrisons. By the time the *Shannon* dropped anchor off Fort William on 8 August, latest intelligence reports indicated that savage disaffection had spread throughout the entire north-west. In view of the emergency, no one, least of all, Lord Canning, was likely to question the wisdom of his

[52] Elgin to Clarendon, Hong Kong, 9 July 1857, Bonner-Smith, pp. 208–14.
[53] Elgin to Bowring, Hong Kong, 16 July 1857, ibid., pp. 216–17.

impulsive action. In British India's extremity, every man, whether soldier, sailor, or marine, counted. None of the reinforcements requested from England had arrived, nor could they be expected to arrive for another two months.

Unfortunately, the boredom and frustration which he had anticipated in Hong Kong soon clouded Elgin's days in Calcutta. Innumerable parties and other social engagements did little to take his mind off the tragedies that were being enacted a few days' journey away. He had hoped in conversation with the Governor-General to get some idea of the amount and kind of military assistance which Canning might make available for winter operations in China, but very understandably at this time of crisis no one in Calcutta took China very seriously.

Rather crude notions respecting the Chinese expedition [he wrote to his wife] prevail in India. The popular belief seems to be that by some lucky chance a large military force was despatched from England this spring to these Eastern Seas, and that the Indian Government have conferred a favour upon us by providing something for it to do. I tried when in Calcutta to persuade Canning that this was a mistake, and to convince him that a contest between English pretensions and Chinese prejudices and millions, with all the nations of the earth summoned as spectators or backers, was something more than a bad pleasantry. He used to listen to my declarations on this subject with admirable patience, but with something of the benevolence which a kind-hearted man accords to a maniac.[54]

With the arrival of British reinforcements, Elgin apparently counted on a quick suppression of the revolt, following which the forces originally consigned to China could be released for service, and dispatched to Hong Kong. In this instance, his judgement was faulty.

During Elgin's absence, little had happened to disturb British patrols on the Canton River, or to excite the highly-strung inhabitants of Hong Kong. British trade remained at a standstill, but impatient and acquisitive foreigners were hanging about the river entrance, and obviously making profitable contact with night-runners from Canton. To Seymour, it seemed unjust that rival merchants, many of whom had

[54] Quoted in Douglas Hurd, *The Arrow War 1856–1860* (London, 1967), pp. 106–7.

escaped the unpleasantries in the Factories' area, should take advantage of the embargo, and in clandestine fashion load teas and other accumulating Chinese produce at Whampoa and in the estuary for their own markets. For this reason, on 3 August he declared a naval blockade of the river and port of Canton.[55] At the same time, to prevent counter-operations by the Chinese, the new screw line-of-battleship, *Sans Pareil*, which had arrived at Hong Kong ten days after the departure of the *Shannon*, was sent to the Bogue.[56] On 3 and 4 August, Captain Cooper Key, the commander of the *Sans Pareil*, landed marines to tighten British control of the Chuenpi forts.[57]

Seymour's effort to cut off trade to Canton by naval blockade was based more on bluff than brute force. Previous attempts during the first Anglo-Chinese war had failed utterly to stop the agile smuggler from reaching the coast by one or other of the innumerable rivers or creeks that led through the back-door of the Canton delta. Notice of intention was not good enough. It was futile to declare a blockade, when all the evidence clearly showed that it could not be effective.[58]

By 20 September, Elgin was back in Hong Kong, living on board the P. & O. steamer *Ava* which had brought him from Calcutta. Neither of the allied plenipotentiaries had put in an appearance. Baron Gros, preferring the unhurried Cape route to the Overland short-cut by way of Suez, did not take up his anchorage in Castle Peak Bay until mid-October, barely preceding the first French contingent of marines. The newly

[55] Seymour to Admiralty, *Calcutta* at Hong Kong, 8 Aug. 1857, Adm. 1/5683 encl. *Hong Kong Gazette Extraordinary* of 4 Aug. 1857. See also, F.O. to Admiralty, 10 Oct. 1857, transmitting Seymour's notice of the blockade.

[56] The *Sans Pareil*, of 3,000 tons displacement, carried a complement of 40 officers, 455 seamen and boys, and 125 marines, 'not a very large complement for a battleship of those days'. But there was no economy of armament, viz., 28 32-pounders on her lower deck; six 8-inch and 24 32-pounders on her main deck; four 32-pounders on her quarterdeck, and eight 32-pounders on her forecastle. Vice-Admiral P. H. Colomb, *Memoirs of Admiral the Right Honble. Sir Astley Cooper Key* (London, 1898), pp. 267–8.

[57] Less than two weeks later, he was being towed to sea by the *Sampson*, *en route* to India. With only about 140 tons coal capacity, the *Sans Pareil* lacked the fuel to steam against the south-west monsoon, and the *Sampson* was unable to drop her for a week. Ibid., p. 275.

[58] See in this connection, Admiralty to Seymour, 6 Aug. 1857 (No. 317), and 10 Oct. 1857 (No. 407), Adm. 2/1614. During the period between December 1856 and October 1857, a series of 'progress reports' on the surveying and charting of river and shore-line, inlets, creeks, and other channels through the delta from Canton to Macao, were forwarded by Seymour to the Admiralty. All are contained in Adm. 1/5583.

appointed American Minister, William B. Reed did not reach
Macao until three weeks later, to be followed shortly by the
Russian diplomatic agent, Admiral, Count Poutiatine, still
smarting from the rebuffs of his mission to Peking. Little did
Elgin realize that nearly three years of exhausting co-operation
with men as weary and sensitive as himself lay ahead. During
that period, mutual distrust was to flourish on mutual
fears—fears of competitive trade exploitation, of possible territorial gains, even to the frightening thought of partition.
'Few people,' he wrote to his wife months later, 'have ever
been in a position which required greater tact—four ambassadors, two admirals, a general and Sir John Bowring, and
notwithstanding this luxury of colleagues, no sufficient
force.'[59] Meanwhile, in the loosely translated language of
Commissioner Yeh: 'Elgin passes day after day at Hong
Kong, stamping his foot and sighing. His anxiety is increased
by the non-arrival of despatches from his government.'[60] The
British Commissioner, wrote the boisterous correspondent of
The Times, even with the navy of England behind him,

must dance attendance in a sea of winter tempests while the petty
mandarin at the mouth of the Pekin river is calculating how long he
can keep up the exhibition of the humiliation of the 'barbarians'. Oh!
that narrow blue ribband of the Foreign Office. It is harder, and
tougher, and stiffer than the red tape of the Circumlocution Office; it
swathes the energies of nations, while the red tape only cripples a
clerk. . . . Oh for one three months of the elder Pitt! He would have
telegraphed—'Take Canton and hold it with your present force.'
And it would have been done. . . . With Canton taken, and some
gunboats at Tien-sing, we might write our own treaty and have it
signed in three months. But no; years and millions, and perhaps
fleets, certainly human lives, must be sacrificed to the pedantry of
diplomacy. Somehow or other those six black rams who are reputed
to be the genii of Canton city seem to have obtained seats in our
House of Commons.[61]

[59] Quoted, Hurd, p. 114.
[60] *Edinburgh Review*, Jan. 1860, p. 100.
[61] Shanghai, 20 Sept. 1857, Cooke, op. cit., p. 154.

XIII

MILITARY TRIUMPHS AND POLITICAL DECEPTION: THE TREATY OF TIENTSIN 1858

LORD Elgin had not long to worry about obsolete instructions, advising a direct approach to Peking. Clarendon's dispatch of 26 August reached him on 14 October, just one day before the arrival of Baron Gros. On the assumption that he had not been able to reach the Peiho, the Foreign Office authorized him, first, 'to use force at Canton', provided the naval and military commanders agreed that sufficient means lay at their disposal.[1] The projected visit to Peking had been sensibly abandoned, and, happily for Elgin's peace of mind, he was able to persuade Gros to accept the 'local engagement', which he had earlier disparaged, and which was shortly to have the blessing of the French Foreign Ministry.

Neither plenipotentiary had any appetite for the mission he was destined to pursue to the bitter end. It would be easy, Gros ruminated, 'to destroy Canton, or to reduce it to ashes; but such a deed, entailing suffering on so many innocent persons, would bring no practical result, and would be, in short, an act of barbarism which would stamp the two flags of France and England with an indelible stain'.[2] Lord Elgin felt equally strongly. He hated the thought of using ships' guns to demolish Canton with 'much consequent discredit to the British name'. Moreover, pulverizing cities from a safe distance could never mean the conquest of China. Artillery demonstrations would scarcely persuade the Chinese either within the pro-

---

[1] Subject to the approval of Elgin and General Ashburnham, Seymour had already been told that he might begin operations at Canton. Admiralty to Seymour, 9 July 1857 (No. 283), Adm. 2/1614.

[2] Memorandum written on board the *Audacieuse*, Castle Peak Bay, 18 Nov. 1857, Bonner-Smith, *The Second China War. . . .*, p. 244.

vince or far away in Peking that British troops were capable of defeating Cantonese 'Braves' in the field.[3]

Unhappily, neither the shame nor the sacrifice was to be fully shared by the interested powers. Obviously, the main brunt of the assault would fall on the French and British, both of whom had specific claims to assert and implement. Neither the American nor the Russian envoys had authority to join in military operations, although both were clearly anxious that their respective countries should benefit from any coercive measures that led to treaty revision. In fact, the Russian government began to develop a deep interest in the protection of Christians, as well as the opening of treaty ports. All four powers sought the establishment of permanent legations in Peking.[4]

Meanwhile, Elgin, in company with his military associates, had to ponder the problem of action against Canton, assuming 'sufficient means' lay at his disposal. The assessment was by no means heartening. The diversion to Calcutta of all the troops destined for China left only the garrison of Hong Kong, consisting, by the late summer of 1857, of one company of Royal Artillery, one infantry regiment, and seven companies of native infantry. The total amounted to about 1,150 men. But statistics of manpower, as has been noted, carried little validity—probably less in China than in India. On an annual average, about 20 per cent were on the sick list, and many more so weakened by disease as to be unfit for prolonged or exacting operations in the field. Assuming that at least 350 men would have to remain in Hong Kong to secure the depots and magazines, about 800 of all ranks remained for service outside the colony. But allowing for probable casualties through sickness, the total was much more likely to be around 650.[5]

Almost equally disquieting was the total absence of engineers from the projected assault force. After all, the con-

[3] Elgin to Canning, 12 Oct. 1857, Foreign Dept., Consultation No. 60–65, 27 Nov. 1857 (N.A.I.).

[4] See Masataka Banno, *China and the West 1858–1861, The Origins of the Tsungli Yamen* (Cambridge, Mass., 1964), p. 12.

[5] See Deputy Quarter-Master-General to Lt. Gen. Ashburnham, 11 Oct. 1857, encl. with Elgin to Canning, 12 Oct. 1857, Foreign Dept., Consultation No. 60–65, 27 Nov. 1857 (N.A.I.).

quest of Canton would be essentially a siege operation. The 23rd Company of Royal Engineers had originally been attached to General Ashburnham's force, but had been transferred to India. Ashburnham appreciated the motive behind the shift—he had himself served in India—but he doubted very much whether the sappers would find in Bengal such stout walls and such strong forts as Canton possessed. Admittedly, the expected reinforcement of 1,500 marines from England should ensure the capture of the city; in the general's view, it would be hazardous to attempt the task with less.[6] Generally speaking, however, none of the commanders was worried about taking Canton; the main problem would be to hold Canton during the anticipated period of negotiation and after. Experience of the last occupation in 1841 had shown the painful difficulty of controlling a turbulent population with a limited garrison continually eroded in numbers by disease. England was far away; only the restoration of the troops and guns that had been diverted to India could make the subjugation of the city an enduring accomplishment.

This was Lord Elgin's view, which was supported wholeheartedly by his military advisers: '. . . in the interests of the extension of trade, of the establishment of peace on a solid and enduring foundation, and, above all, in those of humanity and civilization', he hoped he would not have to assault Canton with inadequate manpower. Despite Lord Canning's long, if somewhat ambiguous, efforts at enlightenment, Elgin failed to recognize the real gravity of the situation in India; he could not comprehend that an emergency still existed. In a thirty-five-page letter, obviously by his own hand and distinguished for prolixity if not always by its logic, he attempted to explain to the Governor-General that the projected attack on Canton was more than a local affair; an all-out war with China could not be excluded from 'the category of possible contingencies'. Those who dreamed that once the Braves were defeated, Canton captured, and the legend of its impregnability destroyed, Yeh's anti-Western policy, as well as that of his Emperor, would collapse, were playing with chimeras.

In short, Britain was not engaged in a mere river war of

[6] Ashburnham to Elgin, Hong Kong, 11 Oct. 1857, encl. with Elgin to Canning, 12 Oct. 1857, ibid.

'limited hostilities'. Troops, guns, ships, and supplies were
necessary if, as seemed likely, a British expedition would be
obliged to penetrate to the heart of the Chinese Empire. And
to make certain that Canning appreciated the seriousness of
the situation in China, Elgin laboriously summarized his original instructions. Parts of the exegesis are worth quoting in
explanation of his loyalty to his Westminster instructors, but,
more particularly, as expressing a personal conviction that
Palmerston was right to order 'the bearding of the Emperor' in
his celestial capital, provided the means were sufficient to
make the effort more than a gamble.

... I was directed on my arrival in China, to proceed to the mouth of
the Peiho with the view of opening at once, if possible, a communication with the Court of Peking. There was of course a bare possibility that if I had been able to take this step at the head of a powerful
Fleet, in company with the Representatives of other treaty Powers,
and at a time when troops were daily arriving at Hong Kong, it
might have led to the immediate and satisfactory settlement of all our
differences with China. I am bound however to state that in my
opinion it is rather to be desired than expected that, with Canton still
untaken, an appeal to the Emperor would, even under the most
favourable circumstances, have been attended with this result.

I was instructed as your Lordship knows to insist on the unqualified concession of the demands of the British Government on the
Canton question, and the Emperor could hardly, without humiliation, have, on a point of so much importance yielded to menace at the
mouth of the Peiho, what we were (for such no doubt was the tenor
of the representations of Commissioner Yeh to the Imperial Court)
vainly endeavouring to extort by force from His Vice Roy on the
spot.

His Majesty's Government accordingly made provision against
the very probable contingency of failure in these first diplomatic
overtures. A military force somewhat similar to that which supported Sir H. Pottinger in his negotiation, was put under orders for
China. Ample evidence of their determination that his Force should
be thoroughly efficient is afforded in the excellent Staff and abundant
supplies of every description which are now accumulated at Hong
Kong.

Elgin went on to say that he had not as yet made ready to sail
to the Peiho: '. . . if I had obeyed the letter of my Instructions in
this particular, I should in all probability have provoked a War

with the Emperor of China at a time when we had neither the troops to fight our Battles, nor allies to fight them for us'. Even as things stood at the moment, a war with China was not inconceivable, but with any luck, hostilities could be confined to Canton. All depended on the character of the force committed to the assault. If there were to be any chance of bringing Peking to its senses, the attack on Canton had to be more than a naval raid. Many ships and many men would be required, not simply to take the city, but to hold it and dominate it. Far more ships and far more men would be needed to carry the flag to the mouth of the Peiho, should the Emperor not bow before the fate of Canton.

I am most unquestionably of opinion that if, after capturing the city, we are able to rout and disperse any armies, whether of regulars or Braves who may attempt to retake it—and if, after achieving these objects, we can keep it in our hands, maintaining order and discipline, until the terms of the treaty with China are definitely settled, these proceedings will powerfully contribute to the success of the negotiation upon which I am commanded to enter with the Chinese Government.[7]

Elgin's lengthy dispatch reached Calcutta sixteen days later, and, shortly after, Canning was able to report that the *Sans Pareil* was on her way back to China, and that H.M. steamer *Assistance* was preparing to sail with one company of the 59th (later East Lancs.) Regiment, originally destined for garrison duty in Hong Kong, and the three hundred marines which had accompanied Elgin in the *Shannon* the previous July. But in regard to other European detachments that had been diverted to Indian ports, the Governor-General could see no prospect of releasing them within 'any assignable time'. True, Delhi had been saved, but the rescuers of Lucknow, Outram and Havelock, were now themselves under siege, along with the garrison and the numerous women and children they had attempted to save. Rebel bands were still running amuck in the countryside, especially in areas denuded of British troops.

In the circumstances, Canning could only state quite bluntly that 'Not one European Soldier can be spared; and when all is done the number will be small for the work which lies before

[7] Elgin to Canning, Hong Kong, 12 Oct. 1857, Foreign Dept., Consultation No. 60–65, 27 Nov. 1857 (N.A.I.).

them.' And he went on to warn Elgin in 'strict truth' that 'when every Regiment promised from England shall have arrived, there will be work in India for every man of them'. At the same time, he chided Elgin on his suspicions that he, the Governor-General, underestimated the tasks facing the expeditionary force in China, and ignored the possibility of outright war.

Your Excellency may be certain that the Government of India is very sensible of the urgent need of a Land Force in China, and of the obligation which lies upon it to supply at the earliest possible opportunity the deficiency caused by the imperious necessities of India to which in anticipation of the views of Her Majesty's Government your Excellency and Lieutenant-General Ashburnham have extended so liberal a consideration.[8]

Elgin had lost almost his entire expeditionary force in the effort to stem the tide of catastrophe in India, and naturally he had lamented his inability to carry out instructions. Once again, however, it becomes evident from the quality and number of his appeals for aid that neither he nor his colleagues appreciated the desperate position of the British raj in India. Indeed, not until the end of the year was he finally convinced that substantial reinforcements would not be available in the near future, despite the advice of his naval commander-in-chief, who wrote on 23 November: 'Until the crisis in India shall have passed, I consider it uncertain that the Governor-General will be able to spare any European troops for service in China.'[9] In Seymour's view, it was thus best, for the moment, to forget about the Peiho and to concentrate on the capture of Canton. Whatever present deficiencies, the accumulating military force in the neighbourhood of the estuary was certainly capable of taking the city, and of holding it against counter-attack. Two battalions of marines had already arrived from England, and the remainder of the brigade was expected within a few weeks. There were also 'the three hundred' graciously returned by Lord Canning from Calcutta. Moreover, the Admiral was no longer in command of a

---

[8] Canning to Elgin, 3 Nov. 1857, ibid.
[9] Seymour to Elgin, Calcutta, Tiger Island, 23 Nov. 1857, Bonner-Smith, pp. 248–9.

starved and despairing squadron. The *Sans Pareil* was on her way back; the *Adelaide* and *Assistance* were expected any day, as were the *Princess Charlotte* and *Fury*. All told, in addition to a French naval division, he had at his disposal, including auxiliary vessels, some thirty ships. Marines, artillerymen, infantry, and seamen amounted to more than 5,500 men, a sufficient force, as Seymour remarked, for all required purposes.[10]

Impatient for action, and confident that the manpower was fully adequate, Admiral Seymour proposed to reoccupy Honam Point, across the river from Canton, as a base of operations. But Elgin demurred; he was opposed to any form of hostile action until Commissioner Yeh had been presented with an ultimatum, demanding compensation for personal and property injuries, and the right of entrance to the City. Moreover, he was wary of taking any aggressive step unless both French and British commanders were absolutely certain they had the power not merely to seize, but to control and administer the city. Happily, on 10 December Admiral Genouilly, with three frigates, two corvettes, and four gunboats, at long last passed the Bogue to join Seymour near the British anchorage at Whampoa. In the opinion of General Sir C. T. van Straubenzee, who had succeeded Ashburnham, there could now be no doubt of the outcome; only disease and loss of morale stood in the way of a secure occupation. Two days later came the heartening news—just at the moment when the allied terms were finally delivered to Yeh—that Lucknow had been relieved.

As was anticipated, Yeh turned down the French and British ultimatum. On 15 December 1857 Honam Point was occupied without resistance, and the Commissioner was informed that naval and military operations would be undertaken in view of his unacceptable response. Unless the garrison, assumed to be about 30,000, was seen to withdraw outside the walls within forty-eight hours, the attack would be launched.

On 20 December Elgin boarded a gunboat, and moved up river, past the barrier forts destroyed by the Americans the previous winter, as far as the Factory quays, within pistol shot of the city walls. In mid-stream lay the British squadron, moored stem to stern, broadside to the shore—*Nimrod*,

[10] Ibid. See also, Colomb, *Life of Cooper Key*, p. 276.

Hornet, Cruiser, Bittern, Actaeon, Acorn. In a diary annotation of the 22nd, His Excellency recorded his fears and his shame:

There we were accumulating the means of destruction under the very eyes, and within reach, of a population of about 1,000,000 people, against whom these means of destruction were to be employed. 'Yes', I said to Commodore Elliot, 'I am sad, because when I look at that town, I feel that I am earning for myself a place in the litany, immediately after plague, pestilence and famine.'[11]

Meanwhile, gigs, cutters, and dinghies shuttled about the placid surface of the river like water bugs, carrying messages, reconnoitring the shore, or stopping occasionally to bring aboard oranges and bananas from the innumerable Chinese boats that plied their trade under the shadow of enemy guns. Beyond the south bank, however, the prospect held little of the picturesque; there were no domes, no temples, no pagodas. In the foreground lay the rectangular warehouses, interspersed with shabby waterside dwellings, 'almost hovels', generally built on piles. Beyond, there was little to break the vast city level of grey roofs, except diminutive watch-boxes, erected on bamboo scaffoldings and looking rather like large dovecots. Behind this drab urban perspective lay rising fields of nearly barren uplands, marked now and then at summit level by hill forts. The reddish tint of the soil reminded Lord Elgin of heather slopes in the Highlands. Beyond these again, stood the White Cloud mountain range, bold and blue in the clear sunshine.

At daylight, on the morning of 28 December, a deliberately slow bombardment, intended to be intimidating rather than lethal, was begun by British and French ships and from two mortar batteries established on the Dutch Folly. It continued steadily all day and the next night, no more than sixty rounds being fired during the first twenty-four hours. The shelling of the city walls, in the vicinity of the Viceroy's *yamen*, fell to the French *Mitraille* and *Fusée*, assisted by the *Hornet* and the gunboats *Niger* and *Avalanche*. The south-west wall was the responsibility of the *Actaeon, Phlegethon* and assigned gunboats. A spasmodic bombardment of the city from the

[11] Walrond (ed.), *Letters and Journals*, p. 212.

south-west was the task of the *Nimrod, Surprise,* and the French *Dragonne* and *Marceau*.[12]

Against so considerable a superiority in numbers, the allied landings and advance under uneven fire-cover was remarkably unexacting. All told, about 800 British troops and less than 5,000 French and British marines and seamen were able to gain footholds about a mile from the south-east corner of the city, and push back the Chinese outposts. On the following day, with a total of 96 British and 34 French killed or wounded, the walls were scaled, the over-looking forts captured, and the defenders routed.[13] Flags of truce began to make their appearance on the 30th, and on the last day of the year Lord Elgin, after clambering up a scaling-ladder at the southeast angle of the City wall, descended (as the *Edinburgh Review* put it) into streets never before trodden by a European.[14]

Within the next few days, a concentrated effort was made to winkle out the notables from their secret retreats. The Tartar General and the Governor, Pih-kwei, were the first to fall into the searchers' net, along with fifty-two boxes of dollars, and sixty-eight of sycee silver. Commissioner Yeh was a much more difficult catch, and his capture on 5 January 1858 was not without its share of drama. Forcing the doors of a rather frowzy *yamen* which appeared to be closed and deserted, blue jackets discovered 'pink button' mandarins rushing about like ants amid piles of hastily packed baggage. After a few minutes, one of the mardarins approached the invaders, offering to surrender himself as Commissioner Yeh, the Viceroy. But he was not sufficiently rotund to fool the British Consul, Harry Parkes, who had arrived on the scene accompanied by Captain

---

[12] Admiral Seymour's flag flew in the *Coromandel*. His flagship, the *Calcutta*, along with the *Sans Pareil* and other ships whose size prevented them from ascending as far as Canton, were left at Tycocktow, some forty miles below the city. But such ships provided boats' crews, carrying scaling ladders, and three days' provisions.

[13] For a summary of the operation, see Seymour to Admiralty, 13 Jan. 1858, Bonner-Smith, op. cit., pp. 273–81; see also a condensed French version in Marquis de Moges, *Recollections of Baron Gros Embassy to China in 1857–58* (London and Glasgow, 1860), pp. 97–116. By the end of the day, the American Plenipotentiary, William Reed, with what might be called poetical licence, congratulated Elgin on a bloodless victory. Waldron (ed.), p. 222. Elgin himself recorded in his diary as he was leaving Canton (which he hoped never to see again) that 'There never was a Chinese town which suffered so little by the occupation of a hostile force. ...', 20 Feb. 1859, ibid., pp. 224–5.

[14] January 1860, p. 100.

Cooper Key. Pushing him aside, they crossed the court, just in time to see a tall and bulky man making strenuous but unavailing efforts to get over the wall at the extreme rear of the *yamen*. Cooper Key took the gentleman around the waist, and the coxswain, who had turned up at this opportune moment, grabbed the pigtail. There was no mistake; it was Yeh.[15]

Once the Imperial Commissioner was lodged in H.M. steam sloop *Inflexible*, the problem of administering a city with upwards of a million inhabitants lapsed into the reluctant hands of France and Britain. Both Elgin and Gros had been concerned about the prospect well before the capitulation; neither trained officials, nor police were available in sufficient number to guarantee peace and order over a long period. A joint force of French and British soldiers, seamen, and marines naturally stayed behind to enforce martial law, but both Elgin and Gros intended that civil rule should gradually devolve on the Chinese. Pih-kwei was reinstated as Governor, and in the absence of Yeh, became acting Viceroy of the two Kwang provinces, assisted by an allied control commission, which for the next three years prospered under the resolute leadership of Consul Harry Parkes.[16]

This *ad hoc* system worked. The Tartar troops were allowed to stay in the city, where they could be watched, but they were forbidden to carry arms. Looting was stopped, shops were reopened, violent disturbances became increasingly rare. Canton enjoyed what might have been termed an 'Indian Summer' of content. To ensure that Yeh would not by his very presence in the neighbourhood intimidate nervous Cantonese officials, it was arranged that he should be removed in comfort and with dignity to a far country. By 20 February, the former Imperial Commissioner, appropriately enough still a guest of the *Inflexible*, departed for Calcutta, never to return.[17] He was given a pleasant villa outside Calcutta, where he remained until his death.

[15] See Cooke, *China*, pp. 341–2; Colomb, pp. 268–70; also, Commodore Elliot to Major-General van Straubenzee, H.Q., Naval Brigade, Canton, 5 Jan. 1858, Bonner-Smith, pp. 271–2.

[16] See Elgin to Clarendon, *Furious* at Canton, 14 Jan. 1858, Bonner-Smith, pp. 281–7. See also, Wells Williams, *The Middle Kingdom*, pp. 644–8.

[17] Elgin to Seymour, *Furious*, 11 Feb. 1858; Seymour to Elgin, *Calcutta* at Hong Kong, 15 Feb. 1858, Bonner-Smith, pp. 289–90.

Their Lordships of the Admiralty were happy to learn of the expeditious capture of Canton, and so informed Admiral Seymour.[18] News of the official degradation of Yeh as Viceroy and the apparent willingness of his acting successor, Pih-kwei, to negotiate a new treaty seemed to promise an early settlement of the Canton question. Meanwhile, the allied defences were strengthened as far as possible against sudden attack. Magazine Hill, whose batteries commanded the city, was ditched, scarped, and stockaded. Six hundred Royal Marines took up headquarters in the former General's *yamen*, in close touch with a neighbouring division of the French brigade. A select Chinese force was gradually enlisted, and these in company with garrison troops (the total garrison numbered around 4,000 officers and men) were able to provide night and day patrols of the principal streets which were renamed in French and English.[19] As regards naval protection, a good deal of discretion was left to the commander-in-chief, who was told to retain, beyond their allotted duty periods, any vessels that seemed essential to the squadron's needs. A chastened Admiralty was determined that the China station should never again be reduced to the skeleton strength existing prior to the Crimean War. At least three gunboats were assigned to patrol the Canton River, and to support with arms and men, in the event of an emergency, the isolated Canton garrison.[20]

After Canton, Peking was intended to be the next objective. But before starting on this long journey northward, Elgin, with the support of his allied associates and the apparent blessing of Pih-kwei, thought it obligatory to make one more diplomatic approach. He proposed to bring pressure to bear 'at some point near the capital', and Shanghai was chosen as a convenient rendezvous for negotiation. Admiral Seymour was asked to dispatch by the end of March or the beginning of April as large a force, 'more especially of gunboats drawing little water,' as could be spared from service elsewhere. The Admiral seemed to have anticipated some such plan, for two

[18] W. G. Romaine to Seymour, 23 Feb. 1858 (No. 93), Adm. 2/1614.
[19] See Seymour to Admiralty, *Calcutta*, Hong Kong, 15 Mar. 1858, Bonner-Smith, p. 305.
[20] See Romaine to Seymour, 19 May 1858 (No. 256), Adm. 2/1615.

gunboats were already on their way to Shanghai, and others, he reported, would follow in due course.[21]

The most northerly of the Treaty ports, Shanghai had been named 'the most flourishing stronghold of European influence and civilization then existing in China'.[22] When Rutherford Alcock first arrived there as consul in 1846, the foreign settlement consisted of three or four tawdry houses on the banks of a broad stream running into the Yangtse. Behind the Bund, as the river-front came to be called, a missionary settlement was very slowly taking shape in the midst of corn fields, interspersed with squalid Chinese hamlets. Twelve years later, the Bund itself extended in a continuous line for nearly two miles towards the south gates of the city. In front of the houses ('more like palaces than anything else') ran the long quay which provided a useful promenade for the isolated inhabitants, and behind the quay were pretty gardens, which, as Lieutenant-Colonel Garnet Wolseley put it, indicated that mercantile operations in China paid well.[23]

The city itself could scarcely have been attractive to the exile, with its labyrinth of streets and alleys, crowded with Jews and Christians, Buddhists and Parsees, Chinese and Europeans. Adding to the tumult were the endless gangs of coolies pressing onward relentlessly beneath their burdens of tea-chests, silk bales, and long cloth, and swerving only before the mad rush of sedan chairs with their mandarin or mercantile occupants.[24] For a man without serious employment, Wolseley thought it a 'dreadful station'. 'Nothing but a desire to grow rich could induce men to reside there; one racket court, no club, a stifling hot room, surrounded by book shelves, called by the inhabitants a library, a dismal-looking race-course enclosed by deep and unwholesome-looking ditches, are the places of public amusement.' Admittedly, in times of peace (which were rare so long as the Taiping rebels were about) excursions into the country offered relief, if not salvation. Some six miles beyond the city, an attractive pagoda

[21] Elgin to Seymour, Hong Kong, 2 Mar. 1858; and Seymour to Elgin, same date, Bonner-Smith, p. 304.

[22] Walrond (ed.), pp. 257–8.

[23] Wolseley, *Narrative of the War* . . . p. 62.

[24] See Alcock, *Tycoon* 14, p. 35.

of six storeys offered a panoramic view of the surrounding landscape. 'There is no part of the world', added the future General, and without irony, 'to which distance lends more enchantment than in China.'[25]

Seymour had counted on sailing for Shanghai with the main squadron in late March, but not until 3 April, by which time Elgin had himself reached the city, did Elgin learn that the departure of the commander-in-chief had been postponed for ten or more days. Meanwhile, the advance agents of the allies, Viscount de Contades and Elgin's secretary, Laurence Oliphant, who were to deliver the notes requesting negotiation, had been at Shanghai since 20 February. Unfortunately for them, Chinese New Year celebrations were still in progress, and all the high officials were absent from duty. Hence, there was no alternative to travelling, not without considerable discomfort, to the provincial capital Soochow, where the allied notes were actually delivered to the Kiangsu Governor. The only positive result of this tiring adventure was a terse communication from Peking suggesting that the British Commissioner, on his arrival in Shanghai, should do a prompt turn-about, and negotiate with Yeh's successor in Canton.

In the circumstances, it was clear to Elgin that the allied expedition had no alternative but to move with all speed northwards. Elgin rightly believed, as did Gros, that they should act immediately, partly because any appearance of wavering would suggest weakness, partly because the best season for operations would be over by the end of May, and finally, in the hope of blocking the grain fleet, which now, owing to partial disruption of the Canal traffic, made the circuitous route by sea from Shanghai and other ports on the Yangtse.[26]

At daylight, on the morning of 10 April, after leaving a letter for the procrastinating Admiral urging the speedy dispatch of shallow-draught gunboats, Elgin set sail aboard the *Furious* (Captain Sherard Osborn), in tow of the steam gunboat

[25] Wolseley, pp. 64–5.

[26] Hitherto, the Imperial Grand Canal had been the great artery of internal commerce, but when the Yellow River (which had a southern mouth, by way of the Huai River, in the Yellow Sea) burst its banks in 1853, it not only destroyed a large section of the canal, it confined that river to a single mouth in the Gulf of Pecheli, nearly a 100 miles south of the estuary of the Peiho.

Slaney. He was confident that nothing was so likely to bring the Imperial government to terms 'as the appearance of vessels of war within the bar of the Peiho river'. The British Commissioner was accompanied by the *Pique* (40), *Nimrod* (6), and *Cormorant* (4). The Russian steamer *Amerika*, carrying the flag of Admiral, Count Poutiatine, had left a day or so earlier; the French *Audacieuse* and the U.S.S. *Minnesota* were to follow shortly.

From all accounts, the voyage was a tourist's delight. From the estuary of the Yangtse and northward through the Yellow Sea as far as the Shantung promontory, 400 miles up the coast, there was good weather and smooth water. A gentle south wind sometimes brought a low white mist, through which the strange hulls and sails of Chinese junks appeared like quaint fantasies of a picture-book world. Rounding the peninsula, the little squadron entered the Yellow Sea, whose waters impressed Captain Sherard Osborn of the *Furious* as 'of a purer pale sea-green than those of the region we had left behind us, or those of the Gulf of Pecheli, which we afterwards entered'.[27] By 13 April, the *Furious* stood off Alceste Island, steering westward past Liu-kun Island and Wei-hai-wei into the Gulf of Pecheli. On the following day she dropped anchor about eight and a half miles off shore, near the entrance to the Peiho, with twenty-two feet of water under her keel at low tide. The Admiralty chart of the area, compiled in 1840 by Mr. Nosworthy of H.M.A. *Pylades*, had proved to be surprisingly correct in almost every detail.

To the westward, the low, swampy shores of the mainland danced in the reflected rays of the setting sun. A few bamboo poles, marking the edge of the bar, were barely visible. To the more optimistic readers of the chart, even the frigates, with a bit of luck, could traverse that mud barrier at high tide. The captain of the *Furious* did not share this exuberance; the lead, not the 'lucky star', had been his principle guide at sea. 'It has seldom been my fate', he wrote a few days after arrival, 'to anchor in a more dreary spot than that off the bar of the Peiho River, or one more unpromising as a secure place for a ship.' There was no scope for any form of amusement, wrote the attaché of the French mission, the Marquis de Moges. 'We

[27] Osborn, *The Past and Future of British Relations in China*, pp. 15–19.

have no compradores, nor any communication with the Chinese villages. We live entirely on the ships stores . . . and . . . begin to feel the want of fruit and vegetables. A country more parched, desolate and miserable it is impossible to imagine. Nothing to be seen but mud, slime, salt-pans and a few sand-hills.'[28]

Ten or twelve years earlier, the appearance of this mixed, but imposing, fleet, with its twisting pillars of smoke rising high into the quiet sky, would have aroused the Imperial Court and sent nervous emissaries scurrying the 120 miles or so to the coast. By now, however, China was becoming accustomed to the sight and sound of Western machinery and Western weapons. The apparitions no longer induced either awe or fright. The authorities in Peking were perfectly willing to wait on events, trusting to Fate and the arts of oriental diplomacy. In far less congenial surroundings, their bored and frustrated visitors waited too. Fortunately, despite recurrent fogs and 'minute blinding dust' that floated about like the North African harmattan, the anchorage proved to be less hazardous than first supposed. Indeed, despite sudden heavy squalls that broke the monotony of eleven weeks of inaction (for the Gulf is on the outer typhoon belt), steamers with good anchors and cables were able to keep their positions without any great risk. As later events were to reveal, not till the winter ice began to form did they have to seek safer berths. The heaviest gales came from the south-east, but at no time was it necessary to lower topgallant masts. On the other hand, boat-work—inter-communication between ships, and between ships and shore—was often hazardous and sometimes impossible. Despite much initial optimism, the task of crossing the Peiho bar, especially during stiff gales, was left to the gunboats, and even these had to confine their activities to periods of high tide. Curiously enough, the only precise survey of the bar had been made by officers of the U.S.S. *John Hancock* some years earlier. For reasons unexplained, a copy of the American chart had fallen into the hands of Count Poutiatine, who (since no copy had been forwarded by the Hydrographic Bureau in Washington) had shown it to the astonished captain of the *Minnesota*. The chart was subse-

[28] Moges, pp. 203, 206.

quently made available to Captain Osborn of the *Furious*. The Americans had also put down a good deal of information on tides. They had slightly overestimated the depth of water over the bar at low tide, but otherwise, judging by the daily measurements taken by British crews, their reckonings proved substantially valid.

The bar, which extended in a giant arc for about six miles, was composed principally of clay, with occasional patches of shingle, overlaid with nine or ten inches of alluvial deposit from the river. At low water, the greatest depth might be only two feet; with a stiff offshore breeze, scarcely a foot. The deepest recording in calm weather at spring tide was slightly over eleven feet. According to Chinese informants, the largest junks trading to Tientsin—around 300 to 500 tons burden —crossed without difficulty at high water during spring tides. Obviously, the season of the year as well as the force and direction of winds could raise or retard the height of water over the bar by as much as a foot to eighteen inches. The Chinese bamboo markers had been noted on the American chart. However, since many of these had been removed, the area had to be resurveyed, and buoys fixed alongside the deepest part of the channel entrance.

During the period from 14 April to 5 May, Elgin paced the deck with mounting impatience and resentment. Since only two vessels were capable of crossing the bar in safety, he found himself with little to do but direct reconnaissances of a desolate shore-line. The anxiously awaited Admiral Seymour did not arrive until 24 April, and then without the essential light-draught gunboats, eighteen of which had been promised in March.[29]

Over the next three weeks, they began to arrive in driblets. All told, as Elgin put it with some bitterness, there had been

[29] By 24 April, the British force consisted of the *Calcutta* (84), which drew twenty-five feet of water and was, therefore, unable to sail within several miles of the Peiho bar, the steam frigate *Furious*, the frigate *Pique* (40), *Sampson* (6), *Cormorant* (4), *Slaney* (3), and *Coromandel* (5). Seymour hoped that the *Fury* (6), a steam sloop, the *Hesper*, a steam store-ship with coal, and five gunboats, would be available by 4 May. Elgin made no effort to conceal his irritation at the delay, and at his request the *Sampson*, a paddle-wheeler, was sent back to help speed up the delinquents, if necessary by towing some of them. See Seymour to Admiralty, *Calcutta*, Gulf of Pecheli, 29 Apr. 1858, Bonner-Smith, pp. 316–17.

five weeks of 'deplorable inaction', during which time the Chinese had been busily constructing stockades and abattis around the Taku forts that overlooked the entrance to the Peiho. During the same interval, probably nine hundred or more grain junks had entered the river without hindrance. It was obviously impossible to establish a blockade with the object of starving the capital into submission while negotiations were still in progress. It was similarly impossible to close the negotiations until sufficient gunboats could cross the bar and take the guardian forts. In retrospect, it is clear that had the allies disembarked during the first few days after arrival, and transported their joint forces across the bar in boats, in all likelihood they could have done so without opposition; indeed, had they wished to risk their communication lines with the sea, the way was clear to Tientsin, only some twenty-five miles away by land but at least twice that distance when traversing the twisting river.

Meanwhile, the main French squadron under the command of Admiral Rigault de Genouilly had arrived, along with the French plenipotentiary, Baron Gros.[30] The voyage from Shanghai had begun in dense fog, but thanks largely to the skill of a Chinese pilot, all the vessels reached the mouth of the Yangtse within hours of each other. Thenceforward, as with Elgin, the journey had been uneventful. Although the captain of the *Furious* disdained such safeguards as 'crossing the fingers', luck was always a factor in the China seas. 'We have very imperfect information about the geography of these waters', Moges noted in his journal: 'the soundings and reefs are not known, and the charts are defective.' None the less, under a brilliant sun but in bitter cold, the French squadron had rounded Cape Shantung, and entered the Gulf of Pecheli not far behind the British commander-in-chief, Admiral Seymour.[31]

By 28 April, since no reply to allied demands for a top-level meeting had been forthcoming from Peking, the French gun-

---

[30] The French squadron consisted of the *Audacieuse, Phlégethon, Primoguet*, and three gunboats, *Avalanche, Dragonne,* and *Fusée*. Waiting on the side-lines as non-belligerents were the American *Mississippi, Minnesota,* and *Antelope,* as well as the Russian *Amerika*.

[31] Moges, pp. 176–7, 199.

boats were sent over the bar, followed the next day by the *Nimrod* and *Cormorant*. This, in itself a belligerent act, had little effect in accelerating negotiations, which, it was now clear, were being deliberately postponed. Happily, such diplomatic procrastination was by no means displeasing to the two admirals, who were still awaiting the arrival of the all-important gunboat reinforcements. They had no wish to proceed up-river to Tientsin without dismantling the Taku forts that would lie between them and the sea. Since no army units were available, there was no alternative to making the assault on the forts from the water.

When the allied commissioners at long last met with the acting Imperial Commissioner, the Governor-General of the province of Chihli, on 6 May, they were still playing for time. The remaining gunboats had not turned up; consequently, they offered the Imperial Commissioner with every appearance of generosity, another six days in which to obtain from the Emperor plenary powers equivalent to those granted to his predecessor at the time of the Treaty of Nanking. By the time Peking had responded—and the reply was not satisfactory—the last of the gunboat contingent had joined the main fleet. Nearly a month had elapsed since the *Furious* had dropped anchor off the Peiho estuary.

Because of the long and wearing delay, both Elgin and Gros wanted an immediate advance towards Tientsin, by passing the Taku forts. But both admirals, Seymour and de Genouilly, dug in their heels. Both were opposed to ascending the Peiho and occupying Tientsin with their supply route to the Gulf insecure. Seymour suggested as an alternative a combined forces' blockade not only of the Peiho, but of the Yangtse at its junction with the Grand Canal.[32] To Elgin such a proposal was nonsense. Apart from the fact that such a far-flung blockade would amount to a declaration of war against China—a hazardous ploy in view of limited allied resources—most of the grain-bearing junks coming by sea had already entered the Peiho. As for the Yangtse–Grand Canal route, which in former times the grain ships from the south followed as far as the capital, that inland passage had been abandoned for some years.

[32] Seymour to Elgin, *Calcutta*, 11 May 1858; same to same, 14 May 1858, Bonner-Smith, pp. 326–8.

For a moment Elgin hesitated; in the end he recognized the layman's ultimate dependence on the opinions of his professional advisers. On 18 May, following a discussion with the two admirals, it was finally agreed that the seizure of the Taku forts should precede any advance up the Peiho, the only operation, so it appeared, which would force Peking to do business.[33] At 8.00 a.m. on 20 May the Imperial Commissioner was formally summoned to surrender the forts within two hours, on the assurance that they would be returned as soon as the negotiations had been brought to a satisfactory solution. No reply being received by 10 o'clock, the gunboats moved in to the attack, led by the *Cormorant*.

The main Taku forts, three in number, stood upon natural and artificial ground elevations of ten to twelve feet on the banks of the Peiho, just above the entrance to the estuary. Even at high water, the guns pointed down on any vessels in the channel, an advantage obviously increased when the tide fell, often ten feet or more. The actual navigable passage facing the ports was rarely more than 300 feet at the widest, and the outward current running close to the right bank was estimated to be slightly more than three miles per hour. No part of the surrounding country was more than three or four feet above high water, and during the period of spring tides most of it was covered. The forts themselves were protected against flooding by high earthen parapets defended at strategic points by sandbag batteries, behind which a series of ditches had been dug, interspersed with rows of sharp-pointed stakes. In front of the earthen parapets, fully exposed at low tide, a deep mud flat sloped gently into the water.

The two southerly forts had a frontage of nearly 1,300 yards, and earlier reconnaissance had revealed twenty guns. Shielded on the river-side by a long covered-way containing sixteen guns *en barbette*, the north fort on the left bank mounted ten or twelve, some of them of heavy calibre. It was obvious even at a distance that considerable skill and labour had been expended in construction. When he inspected the forts after the battle, Admiral Seymour noted that the guns were 'much better cast, and not so unwieldy as those in the

---

[33] See Elgin to Seymour, *Furious*, 19 May 1858; also, Elgin to Malmesbury, 20 May 1858, Bonner-Smith, pp. 333–6.

Canton River. . . . They had good canister shot, and the hollow 8-inch shot appeared imitations from our own. There were several English guns in the batteries.'[34] It was impossible to do more than guess at the size of the garrisons, which did their flamboyant best to make a strong impression on the visitors. Almost every day, company after company—conceivably amounting in total to 4,000 men—paraded ostentatiously on or around the walls 'as gorgeous as a field of poppies' with flags for every four men.[35] Seymour did not anticipate a walk-over.

As it happened, the Chinese defences simply folded up shortly after the first shots were fired, and this entirely unexpected collapse undoubtedly saved the allied admirals from the embarrassments accompanying a long siege, and conceivably a stalemate. The gunboats, firing as they moved up channel, encountered little opposition from the forts. Indeed, the Chinese garrison troops fled their strongholds *en masse* before the assault forces reached the shore. By the end of an hour and a quarter, both north and south forts had been subdued and abandoned. A last effort to stop the invaders by sending down a score of junks aflame with burning straw failed when the vessels grounded and burned out harmlessly. The only losses occurred when, shortly after the forts capitulated, the accidental explosion of a magazine killed or wounded a French detachment.[36] British casualties amounted to one warrant officer and four men killed, and two officers and fifteen men wounded.

Moving up river, the gunboats destroyed flanking earthworks that ran for more than a mile on either side, and mopped up isolated batteries.[37] Towards evening, the little squadron droppped anchor close to the village of Taku, protected for the

[34] Seymour to Admiralty, *Coromandel* in the Peiho, 21 May 1858, Bonner-Smith, pp. 336–40. See also, Wolseley, op. cit., pp. 146–7.

[35] Capt. Sherard Osborn, *Queda, A Cruise in Japanese Waters* [which includes] *The Fight on the Peiho* [1859] (new edn., Edinburgh and London, 1865), pp. 30–7.

[36] Four officers and two men were killed; five officers and fifty-six men were wounded.

[37] The advance was led by the gunboats *Staunch* and *Bustard,* followed by Admiral Seymour in the *Coromandel,* and Admiral de Genouilly aboard the *Avalanche.* These were accompanied by the gunboats *Firm, Slaney, Opossum,* the French gunboat *Fusée,* and boats from the *Calcutta, Pique, Furious,* and *Fury* under, respectively, Captains Hall, Sir F. Nicholson, Sherard Osborn, and Commander C. Leckie.

night by the barrier of junks, conveniently chained together from shore to shore to block their own further progress. During the following morning, no serious artificial obstacles were encountered, once the junks had been removed. For nearly five miles the deeply scoured channel of the Peiho winds, at low tide between precipitous banks of mud, barely submerged at high tide, when the landscape changes to endless mud flats, dotted with patches of reed and rushes. The *Fusée* ran aground forty-two times.

Apart from great pyramids of salt, only clay-built hamlets broke the dead-level of the low-lying countryside that had barely raised itself on alluvial deposits above the water-line. Wretched and inhospitable as they appeared to be from the quarterdeck, the inhabitants proved on closer acquaintance to be lacking neither in gracious manners nor modest prosperity. Once they had recovered from their astonishment at seeing ships moving against wind and tide, they ranged along the banks, some performing kowtows as the gunboats passed; others offering for sale, fowl, vegetables and fruit. Seymour noted that much of the soil had been cultivated 'with a minuteness resembling a market garden'. Nearer to Tientsin, most of the European fruits and vegetables flourished in rich luxuriance, 'whilst waving fields of wheat and barley could be observed in the distance'.[38] Some villages were embosomed in fruit orchards, or managed to conceal their ugliness in groves of sheltering trees. Occasionally, the river expanded into reaches that were almost picturesque, but there was no background of grotesque temples or shining pagodas such as marked the China of the south.[39]

On the morning of 26 May the *Coromandel* with her consorts steamed up to the wharfs of Tientsin, the first foreign vessels, so it was assumed, ever to appear in the 'river of the north'. Tientsin was at this time a small walled city, composed chiefly of mud-built houses, fitted into the angle formed by the south bank of the Grand Canal and the Peiho. Sprawling suburbs extended on both sides of the river, as well as along the canal. Seymour estimated the population to be less than

[38] To Admiralty, *Coromandel*, at Tientsin, 4 June 1858, Bonner-Smith, p. 343. See also, Moges, pp. 206, 217.
[39] Osborn, *The Fight on the Peiho*, pp. 46–7.

half a million. In general, the inhabitants showed themselves as friendly as were the conciliatory invaders, but there was a melancholy inertia about the place—a lack of vigour that resembled apathy. Back in Hong Kong there had been talk of Tientsin's wealth and commercial liveliness, but both French and British visitors were struck by the outward appearance of poverty and dowdiness.[40] Lord Elgin was surprised by the austere, if not primitive, mode of existence, '. . . the absence of all luxurious habits, and even of ordinary comforts' which were so apparent elsewhere in China. Baron Gros found it difficult 'to conceive human abodes more comfortless than the yamouns where we were quartered; the occupants must freeze in them during the winter'. By comparison, Canton offered a *de luxe* standard of living.[41]

But the political results seemed to justify both the fatigue of the journey and the discomforts of ambassadorial quarters. Hardly had the engineers completed their task of demolishing, or at least neutralizing, the Taku forts, than two new Imperial Commissioners from Peking presented themselves, and after much temporizing, concluded separate negotiations with the three European powers and the United States. The Treaty of Tientsin between Great Britain and China was signed on 26 June. On 3 July it received the Emperor's approval; and on the 5th Elgin dispatched a copy to the Foreign Office. One day later he asked Admiral Seymour for 'a respectable naval force' to convey him to Japan.

The Treaty contained 56 clauses. Here, it is sufficient to give the gist of the more significant provisions. British ships of war were now permitted to visit all Chinese ports, and both countries were to co-operate in the suppression of piracy. Diplomatic representatives were to be exchanged on a footing of complete equality, and the British appointee might reside in Peking. British subjects, with proper passports, could travel into the interior, and British merchant ships could trade upon the Yangtse, allowing of course for the limitations imposed by rebel successes in that area. In addition to the original Treaty ports, five more cities were to be opened to British sea-borne

[40] Seymour to Admiralty, 4 June 1858, doc. cit.; and Osborn, *The Fight on the Peiho*, p. 53.
[41] Moges, p. 224.

commerce. It was further agreed that the tariff fixed by the Treaty of Nanking had been in parts excessive, and would be subsequently revised by a joint conference of experts meeting in Shanghai. A separate article provided for the payment of an indemnity by the authorities of Kwangtung province to cover the costs of the military expedition, and losses sustained by British subjects 'through the misconduct of the Chinese authorities at Canton'. Until the four million taels [more than a million pounds; £1 = Tls.3] were paid, British forces would continue in occupation of Canton.[42]

The opening of five more Treaty ports seemed to mean the final breaking of the giant oyster that was the Chinese Empire. British shipping could now penetrate the interior. The Yangtse was to be a free vestibule of trade as far as Hankow, and three river ports were to be established as soon as the rebels had been quashed or liquidated. These concessions, concerned essentially with water carriage, were simply a confirmation of Britain's traditional salt-water policy of limited liabilities. British factories must lie within reach of the Royal Navy. On the surface, the treaty represented a portentous diplomatic achievement. Even the Old China Hands appeared satisfied for the moment, although, as later events were to reveal, many saw little hope of sustained benefits 'unless the Treaties are carried into effect at the point of the bayonet'.[43]

In retrospect, it would appear that there was intentional deception. A fleet of gunboats, supported by a few frigates, controlled the gateway to the capital, and above all else, the Emperor and his advisers were anxious to rid themselves of the unwelcome visitors. Two systems of morality were involved. An agreement, which the Confucians had not the slightest intention of upholding, was the obvious means of removing the immediate threat. It was, said the perceptive Secretary for War, Sidney Herbert, 'a Treaty of peace with a

---

[42] A great deal has been written about the negotiations leading to the Treaty of Tientsin, and much is bound to be repetitive. Among many good books, see in particular, Hsü, *China's Entrance into the Family of Nations*, Chaps. II and III, *passim*.

[43] From a merchant's letter to Jardine, Matheson & Co., 15 Sept. 1859 (rec'd 16 Nov. answered 3 May 1860); Box 1859, No. 4741. (JMA). Some twenty letters dated 9 August 1858 related to this general theme are contained in the Jardine, Matheson Letter Book, 1858–59.

casus belli in every clause'.[44] It has been suggested more than once, that Elgin, in his ignorance of the Chinese character, was duped.[45] Even although lacking the support of an army, he should have pushed on to Peking, and demanded an audience of the Emperor. At the very least, he should have left an occupying force in Tientsin to guarantee the fulfilment of the Treaty, instead of retiring to the south with all his force.

Such an argument leaves out of account the fact that neither the French nor the British Admiral possessed the manpower to undertake a long occupation, especially with winter looming up; both would certainly have opposed such a risky advance. In the second place, Elgin seems to have sensed the danger to the Imperial dynasty, especially during a period of civil war, should an alien force have broken into the Chinese capital. If Britain were to maintain her traditional policy of trading from the sea, without the strain and drain of internal commitments, a strong central government was vital. Even had numbers made the operation practicable, a forward policy that led foreign legions to the gates of Peking could mean the disintegration of Imperial authority—the ejection of the Manchu dynasty as precipitately as that of their predecessors two hundred years earlier.[46]

It was largely for this reason that Lord Elgin, when he again met the Imperial Commissioners at Shanghai in October, was willing to concede in practice a modification of Article III of the Tientsin Treaty, which provided for residence within the Imperial capital of British diplomatic representatives. He was concerned, as he later confessed, to save 'the face' and probably the heads of the two Chinese Commissioners. But of more fundamental significance, he believed that there was little to lose, and much to gain by conceding 'a place of residence elsewhere than at Pekin'. British policy, in his view (and this view was accepted in Whitehall), should be directed towards aiding the reigning Emperor against the Taiping rebels. Diplomatic relations would still be conducted through Peking; to

---

[44] Speech on the navy estimates, 25 Feb. 1859, quoted in Lord Stanmore, *Sidney Herbert, Lord Herbert of Lea, A Memoir* (2 vols., London, 1906), ii. 294.

[45] See Lane-Poole, p. 310.

[46] See Nathan A. Pelcovits, *Old China Hands and the Foreign Office* (New York, 1958), pp. 17, 27–8; Wells Williams, *The Middle Kingdom*, p. 656; and *Edinburgh Review*, Jan. 1860, p. 104.

have insisted on a permanent *corps diplomatique* in China's capital could have been interpreted as a challenge to the dynasty, a victor's triumphant exaction, that would have been generally regarded as an outrage.

Meanwhile, the Foreign Office had been considering Elgin's accusations, contained in an imposing heap of April dispatches, that Admiral Seymour had put the whole Peiho expedition at hazard by his failure to ensure the prompt arrival of the vital gunboats.[47] It is 'indispensable', the British Commissioner told Lord Clarendon, 'that those who control the Material Force of Great Britain in this quarter should lend to those who direct its Diplomacy a vigorous and intelligent support', and he reminded the Foreign Secretary that as early as 2 March he had asked Seymour to assemble at Shanghai 'as large a Fleet, more especially of Gun Boats drawing little water, as you can spare from service elsewhere'. This request had not been complied with until too late.[48] 'The whole fleet reached this anchorage on the 25th Inst.,' he wrote at the end of April, 'and at the moment when I am writing this Despatch, the French flag is represented by two Gunboats within the bar of the Peiho, the English by two Despatch Boats aground on the top of it.' What Elgin could not understand was Seymour's acceptance of his request for gunboats, apparently without demur, and his subsequent failure to send them on the time agreed. Elgin's own conclusion was that most of the craft which Seymour had counted on were not fit for use, being 'unserviceable from the way in which they have been lately worked in the Canton River in the discharge of duties', which might just as well have been performed by 'ordinary passenger or other Merchant carrying craft . . .'. On which judgement, their Lordships of the Admiralty commented scornfully in a marginal minute: 'Not quite a question for Lord Elgin to determine.'[49]

Until the beginning of August, the Admiralty had no first-hand information to offer in regard to Seymour's conduct of operations. The Admiral had made no mention of a strained

---

[47] See Hammond (F.O.) to Admiralty, 16 July 1858, Adm 1/5699.

[48] 23 Apr. 1858 (No. 91), encl. in Hammond to Admiralty, ibid.

[49] See Elgin to Clarendon, 29 Apr. 1858 (No. 100), encl. in Hammond to Admiralty, ibid.

relationship, except to remark that he regretted not having had a talk with Lord Elgin before he left Shanghai.[50] Not until more than two weeks after Elgin's disturbing charges had been forwarded to them from the Foreign Office, was Seymour's report on the expedition received. Therein, the Admiral confessed that he had been somewhat late arriving at the Peiho (24 April), but the delay had in no way prejudiced allied strategy. In response to Elgin's plea for a rapid advance up-river, he had simply given his opinion (shared by the French Admiral) that the Taku forts had to be occupied first. This task required additional gunboats, which were already *en route* to the Gulf of Pecheli. Once the allied rear had been safeguarded, he had every intention (and had so spoken) of co-operating in the move towards Tientsin.[51]

But Seymour could not make a detailed reply to Elgin's accusations until the Admiralty had provided him with the particular charges and invited his defence. Not until 27 September did he finally complete a forty-seven-page refutation of the charges of procrastination and malingering, first raised by Elgin's dispatch of 29 April. Unfortunately, a good deal of the content was irrelevant. Apart from pointing out the dangers and delays involved in navigating China seas in monsoon weather, he offered little specific evidence to counter specific charges. There was no need to stress the obvious—and this was done rather lamely—namely, that diplomats did not understand the problems and preoccupations of naval commanders. As for the charge that many of the gunboats were unserviceable, he admitted that they had been overworked as transports in the Canton River. None the less, despite the long voyage from England, and the strain of constant employment in Chinese waters, they had made the long journey in stormy weather to the Gulf of Pecheli, and arrived intact. 'I do not believe', he told the Admiralty, 'that at any one time two gunboats out of the whole number were unequal to their work.'[52]

[50] F.O. to Admiralty, 28 July 1858, F.O. 17/305. For an Admiralty minute in comment, dated 27 July, see Adm. 1/5699.

[51] Seymour to Admiralty, 21 May 1858 (No. 172), encl. in W. G. Romaine (Adm.) to Hammond (F.O.), 3 Aug. 1858, F.O. 17/305.

[52] *Calcutta* at Hong Kong, 27 Sept. 1858, (No. 326), F.O. 17/307, Bonner-Smith, pp. 369–70.

But the gravamen of Elgin's complaint had concerned executive lethargy. A sufficient number of light-draught gunboats had failed to arrive in time to meet his expectations and intentions. The long weeks of compulsory idleness had been harmful, and conceivably might have been disastrous. Through lack of war vessels adapted to river operations, the allies were obliged to string out the negotiations. Consequently, their diplomacy took on a vacillating quality, suggesting to the Chinese a lack of confidence, if not positive military weakness. When the French gunboats went over the bar on 28 April, followed by the *Nimrod* and the *Cormorant* on the 29th, Peking had good grounds for believing that the threat of naval action was serious. But by the time the allied ultimatums had reached the capital, nothing had happened, and, albeit with soft words, the demands for a negotiated settlement were turned down. To the Court at Peking there could be only one of two interpretations. Either the foreigners lacked the strength to capture the forts, or men and ships were not available to undertake an advance up the Peiho, once the forts had succumbed.

Elgin had a good case, but he overstated it, and the reason is not clear. It may be that personal animosity gave an added thrust to his indictment of Seymour. Possibly, even probably, he was reacting to the caustic complaints about his own irresolute behaviour and the final decision to withdraw from Tientsin. Otherwise, it is hard to understand his accusation that the Admiral's tardy arrival on the scene was 'in highest degree' detrimental to the ultimate object of the expedition, namely, the reception of the allied delegation in Peking. The attack on Canton, followed by its occupation, and then, three months later, the approach of a naval expedition to the estuary of the Peiho, must certainly have been regarded by Peking as an act of war. That Elgin, even with many more gunboats and with the support of an army, could have ascended the river to Peking without hostile interruption was most improbable. Whether the odds were great or small, the Chinese would have resisted, however ineptly. Whether out of ignorance, natural courage, or despair, they were never cowed by the trappings of military might. The British Commissioner underestimated their determination and their tenacity.

On the other hand, Seymour made the fateful mistake, in the course of his rebuttal, of trying to vindicate a strategy of procrastination, as if the delays in bringing up the gunboats represented a subtle form of profound strategic thinking. The fact that the assault on the forts had been delayed for over a month, he argued, had been a blessing in disguise. Between the middle of April and the 20th of May, the Imperial army commanders had been given time 'to collect their military strength and resources to a degree that excited a confidence on their part so highly favourable to the ultimate estimate of our irresistible power'. Consequently, when, in little more than three hours, their defences were overthrown, the folly of resistance had been finally demonstrated, and the foundation for 'the successful fulfilment of Lord Elgin's mission to China' securely laid.[53] Subsequent events were to demonstrate the absurdity of this judgement.

But in a less significant context, Lord Elgin could be equally absurd, if not childish. Pride and pique would appear to be at the root of his further charge that Seymour's 'unjustifiable delay' had placed the British squadron in a position of humiliating contrast with that of her allies. Had the ten or twelve missing gunboats arrived at the Peiho in time, and made the necessary demonstrations (which presumably would have led immiediately to negotiation) 'the chief credit of this manœuvre . . . must have accrued to the British Navy. . . .'[54] To this charge, Seymour had no difficulty in finding adequate response. Whatever the embarrassment suffered by his Lordship during the interim, once operations had begun, any possible humiliation must have been obliterated. 'The French admiral hoisted his flag in an English gunboat; English gunboats took the French forces to the attack on the forts; an English gunboat led the attack; an English vessel received the French wounded; English gunboats led the way up the Tientsin River, and were the first foreign vessels ever off that city.'[55]

Nevertheless, the question remains: did Admiral Seymour ignore orders which apparently in the beginning he had

---

[53] Seymour to Admiralty, 27 Sept. 1858, ibid., p. 371.
[54] Elgin to Clarendon, *Furious*, Gulf of Pecheli, 23 Apr. 1858 (No. 91), Adm. 1/5699.
[55] The complete Seymour statement is contained in a file entitled 'Sir Michael Seymour's Reply to the Earl of Elgin's Charges', Adm. 1/5693.

accepted? His own effort at defence, when relevant, does not entirely satisfy; the explanation of prolonged delays is neither complete nor convincing.[56] There is little evidence to support Elgin's claim that most of the gunboats should have joined him before he left Shanghai on the journey north, but it is not easy to accept Seymour's assertion that once under way, the Royal Navy's gunboats could not keep within reasonable distance of the French detachment, which reached the Peiho on 25 April. On the other hand, the French vessels were probably in a better state of repair than the English, and better fitted to withstand rough weather. But can such advantages explain a time lag of nearly two weeks between the arrival of the French detachment and the last of the British gunboats? The Admiral did not attempt a specific answer. He simply contended that it was impossible to move a force of gunboats up a stormy coast with the precision of a railway train. 'My arrangements for getting the gunboats up to the north, were made with the view to see them arrive in an efficient state, and not torn to pieces by being towed against a head sea, an object I fully accomplished, by causing them to coast the shores and anchor in bad weather.'[57]

But whatever the logic of Seymour's defence, no amount of professional expertise can alter the fact that until all the gunboats were on the scene, the allied naval commanders refused to take the offensive. For this unanticipated delay, the Admiral must bear responsibility. Notwithstanding, the senior service stood by their man. On 23 November the Foreign Office was informed that their Lordships of the Admiralty 'think it due to the high character and long and distinguished service of Sir M. Seymour to state their opinion that such answer to the charges and imputations of Lord Elgin is complete and satisfactory'. And they added, that had Her Majesty's Plenipotentiary communicated the charges to the Admiral before sending

---

[56] Conceivably there were personal grounds that help to explain Seymour's apathy. Certainly, he resented Elgin's domineering manner of command. As late as 27 May, when the Commissioner suggested the advisability of bringing up additional forces from Hong Kong and the Canton River, Seymour ignored the counsel until formally ordered to act five days later. Seymour to Admiralty, 1 June 1858, encl. Elgin to Seymour, 1 June 1858, Adm. 50/281. See also, Gerson, pp. 86–7.

[57] Seymour to Admiralty, 27 Sept. 1858 (No. 326), F.O. 17/307; also, Bonner-Smith, pp. 367–8.

them to England he might have learned that he had no sufficient grounds of complaint.[58]

This judgement of the Board cannot be ignored, however influenced by a traditional sensitivity to civilian interference. But it was by no means acceptable to the press. Neither the *Edinburgh Review*, nor its deadly rival, the *Quarterly Review*, approved the official whitewash, and certainly neither was prepared to give the returning veteran a hero's welcome. It was not the first time, said the *Edinburgh Review* 'that the naval authorities at home have shown what we must consider a very culpable disposition to screen the shortcomings and misconduct of admirals employed on active service abroad; and more than one such officer has received a ribbon who would in former times have been arraigned before a court-martial'.[59]

One result of the easy victory at Taku, which was to have tragic consequences, was the fixed conviction, that however brave, the Chinese troops lacked training and discipline, and thus failed to make proper use of the weapons at their disposal. 'As soon as our men landed', wrote Lord Elgin, 'they abandoned the [Taku] forts and ran off in all directions. . . .' And he added: 'I fancy that we have got almost all the artillery which the Chinese Emperor possesses in this quarter.'[60] As a matter of fact, however farcical the defence of the forts, 'bolting like rabbits' was not characteristic of Manchu soldiery, and it is curious that Admiral Seymour should have shared the view that the Taku operation was the inevitable consequence of European superiority in morale, arms, and skills. 'At one blow . . .' he wrote, 'the whole of their guns were captured, and their army driven like a scattered rabble into the surrounding country, to spread everywhere the reports of our invincibility, and the destructive and terrific missiles we made use of.'[61]

Equally curious (as appears from the evidence acquired by scholars of a later generation) was the failure of Peking to

[58] Corry (Admiralty) to Hammond (F.O.), 23 Nov. 1858, F.O. 17/307.

[59] Review of Laurence Oliphant's, *Narrative of the Earl of Elgin's Mission to China and Japan* (2 vols., London, 1859), Jan. 1860, p. 102.

[60] To Lady Elgin, 21 May 1858, quoted J. L. Morison, *The Eighth Earl of Elgin. A Chapter in Nineteenth-Century Imperial History* (London, 1928), p. 222.

[61] Seymour to Admiralty, 27 Sept. 1858, doc. cit.

comprehend fully the causes of the successive and devastating victories of 1841–2 and 1857–8. Against European warships, they readily admitted their weakness, but against foreign armies fighting in alien territory, they refused to contemplate final defeat. The successful allied advance as far as Tientsin had pushed the Imperial Court into certain treaty obligations which it had no intention of carrying out. Obviously such evasion, once it was recognized by the enemy, could mean further and more serious invasions, in which case more troops, more guns, and stronger forts must be in readiness for the defence of Peking's frontier. But the 'barbarian' could be stopped, and once thoroughly defeated, he could be harried out of the land for ever.

Indeed, the task of bringing the Court of Peking to reason was to prove itself even more intractable than frustrated British officials had ever imagined; and the need to act in company with the French, and not infrequently with Americans and Russians, did not make it any easier. Moreover, the prestige supposedly accruing to an alliance of major powers seems to have made little impression; national divisions, jealousies, and trade rivalries were more manifest than any common European purpose. Perhaps the disaster at Taku should have opened Manchu eyes, but they remained tightly shut, and only one naval officer (who recorded his judgement more than a year after the attack) attempted to explain this apparent obtuseness. '. . .[T]he garrison of those forts', wrote Captain Sherard Osborn of the *Furious*, 'were not sufficiently punished to impress them with a due sense of the penalty of opposing Europeans'. The bulk of the defenders had run away unscathed without appreciating the enormous power of modern guns and explosives. Such benevolence had been misplaced; those who misunderstood forbearance regarded it as weakness. Consequently, mistaken forbearance could cost hundreds of lives and millions of pounds.[62]

The expedition up the Yangtse which Elgin had long anticipated, started on 9 November. This romantic adventure into the interior, along a river, which, beyond Nanking, had never previously been navigated by Europeans, has been vividly

---

[62] Osborn, *The Fight on the Peiho*, p. 43.

described by Laurence Oliphant.[63] Elgin remained aboard the *Furious*, still under the command of Captain Osborn, and was accompanied by the *Retribution* (Captain Barker, Senior Officer, commanding), the *Cruiser*, the gunboat *Lee*, and one surveying vessel, the *Dove*. For the greater part of the journey as far as Nanking, channel-hunting by the ships' boats became an almost daily exercise. Shifting sands and mud banks rendered the Admiralty charts, prepared with such care fifteen years earlier, almost worthless. A brisk cannonade was sufficient to scatter the rebels in possession of Nanking. After that came days of slow and cautious navigation through a devastated countryside, past the ruins and rubble of wasted cities, as far as the commercial metropolis of Hankow, at the junction of the Yangtse and the Han River.

After six days of pomp and increasingly friendly hospitality, reflected in the quality and amount of food provided, the flotilla began the return journey, with navigational embarrassments considerably augmented as the dry season reached its height. All went well for the first 140 miles, until the rapidly falling river made passage too hazardous for the larger vessels. Regretfully, Elgin and his staff were forced to leave their comfortable home in the frigate *Furious*, and transfer to the gunboat *Lee*.[64] The alternative was to spend the rest of the winter as prisoners of the capricious Yangtse. Only a crew member of a World War II corvette could visualize with any precision the life of 'twelve first-class passengers' in a gunboat's cabin, sleeping in fixed pattern 'like herrings in a barrel'. For eight days and nights over a distance of more than 450 miles Elgin and his companions adjusted themselves to the life of 'amphibious animals', their ordeal less distressing in conse-

---

[63] The Commissioner's private secretary, 'an exceptional figure in an age of exceptional Englishmen', kept a record of the Mission's activities, 'a classic account' in the words of a recent editor, Stephen Uhalley Jr., the result not only of the historical importance of Elgin's pilgrimage, 'but equally to the adventurous spirit, the observant eye, and the literary skill of its author'. *Narrative of the Earl of Elgin's Mission to China and Japan*, pp. v–ix. See also, Captain Barker to Seymour, Woosung, 5 Nov. 1858 (No. 20), announcing preparations to open the Yangtse under the Treaty terms, Adm. 1/5712. See also, reports on the expedition, encls. for 22 Nov., 8 Dec. 1858, and 5 Jan. 1859, in Seymour to Admiralty, 14 Jan. 1859 (No. 17), ibid. Their Lordships of the Admiralty thought the reports most interesting, and deserving of publication.

[64] The heavier steam frigate *Retribution* had already been left about 300 miles down river from Hankow.

quence of 'the obliging attentions of Lieutenant Jones', captain of the *Lee*.

The *Lee* reached Shanghai on New Year's Day, amid rumours that the rest of the expedition had suffered either shipwreck, or massacre by rebel bands.[65] Following a farewell ball at the Consulate, to the amazement of disbelievers in miracles, Elgin boarded the *Furious*. True to her name, she had taken advantage of a sudden rise in the river, and had charged over the impeding bars that had held her captive. On 25 January she was on her way to the sea.[66] On that day, Elgin recorded in his diary that an intuition bade him go directly to Hong Kong to take the Canton problem in hand personally.[67] '. . . a variety of circumstances lead me to the conclusion that the Court of Peking is out to play us false'.

Even before the capture of the Taku forts and the negotiations at Tientsin, highly disquieting news had been reaching the *Furious* from Canton. Violent disturbances in various parts of the city offered clear indications that the local Braves were preparing for guerrilla warfare both inside and outside the capital. More threatening, however, were the organized divisions of Taipings, which pressed heavily on surrounding districts. As early as May it had become clear that the rebels appreciated the advantages to be derived from a 'barbarians' war against Peking. The allied descent on the Gulf of Pecheli was, from their point of view, a most favourable diversion. At one time, a large Taiping army was reported to be within sixty miles of Canton, and, from all accounts had little trouble in defeating the badly led and ill-disposed Imperial troops. The allied garrison was still in possession of all the commanding positions in the city, and on the river three well-armed gunboats were in constant readiness to lend support. But the victorious Taipings crept ever closer, and Colonel Wolseley noted in his diary that the troops, however resolute in their behaviour, were experiencing 'a great feeling of insecurity'.[68]

---

[65] Seymour to Admiralty, 13 Jan. 1859 (No. 16), Adm. 1/5712. The *Lee* after facing gun-fire on the Yangtse and riding out a typhoon off the coast of Japan was to perish on the mud banks of the Peiho during the assualt on the Taku forts in the following June. Seventeen of her crew were killed or wounded before she sank.

[66] Oliphant, p. 607.

[67] Shanghai, 25 Jan. 1859, Walrond (ed), p. 307.

[68] Wolseley, pp. 54–5.

By July, it was clear that the restless Canton Braves had to be taught a lesson, and since news had arrived that the Treaty of Tientsin was about to be signed, ships could be made available for a combined punitive exercise. Acting on the excuse that a flag of truce had been fired upon, on 11 August Major-General van Straubenzee led a small commando force against the neighbouring walled town of Nantow, regarded as a seat of disaffection. Resistance was fierce, but within three hours the forts was captured and blown up. Two weeks later, visitors to Canton found the atmosphere almost tranquil. The scheming Governor-General of the two Kwang provinces had been informed about the Treaty of Tientsin, and his last communication to the allied commissioners, according to James Matheson, was said to be 'decidedly pacific and satisfactory'.[69]

Three months later, Admiral Seymour reported that he had walked the streets of the city, and the inhabitants had appeared peaceful and contented; the docks at Whampoa were busy with shipping, as trade resumed its normal routines.[70] By the end of the year, 'Canton affairs' had become 'most satisfactory'.[71] In mid-January 1859, however, the happy tranquillity was rudely broken by rebel invaders from the countryside. Fortunately, these ill-organized and perfunctory raids received little support within the walls, and the garrison had no difficulty in restoring order. But more important to the incarcerated allied force, the advancing Taiping army had retired, and from all accounts had dissolved. Everything pointed to a noisy but joyous Chinese New Year.[72] And so it proved to be. During the next few months, it was possible to make excursions into the neighbouring countryside, now patrolled regularly by garrison troops, whose friendly disposition was aimed

[69] To Messrs. Barbour & Bros., Hong Kong, 21 Aug. 1858; also, to Wm. P. Patton, 11 Sept. 1858, and same to same, 11 Oct. 1858, James Matheson Letter Book, B 6/23. Regarding developments in Canton, see Hammond (F.O.) to Admiralty, 14 Oct. 1858, encl. Parkes letter of 22 July, Adm. 1/5699; and Corry (Admiralty) to Seymour, 15 Oct. 1858, Adm. 2/1615. See also, van Straubenzee to Secretary of State for War, Canton, 21 Aug. 1858, Bonner-Smith, pp. 358–60.

[70] To Admiralty, Hong Kong, 15 Dec. 1858 (No. 440), Adm. 1/5712.

[71] To Admiralty, 30 Dec. 1858 (No. 463); see also, further letters of January 1859, on conditions in Canton, including proceedings against the Canton Braves by the Royal Marine brigade, ibid.

[72] Seymour to Admiralty, 14 (No. 24), 15 (Nos. 25 and 26), and 29 Jan. 1859 (No. 66), ibid.

at demonstrating the foreigner's peaceable intentions. Such immediate contact with the allied forces, Seymour noted, was 'producing a very beneficial effect'.[73] From bases on the river, the exploration of the delta maze was continued by gunboats and other light craft, and over a hundred miles of western branches was navigated and charted.[74]

But, as generally recognized at the beginning of the occupation by commanders of both services, garrison morale was likely to be the Achilles heel of the victors; and after two summers, the marines especially, despite some reliefs, had begun to show signs of fatigue and boredom. Although Canton was being held as a temporary hostage to ensure payment of the indemnity promised by the Treaty of Tientsin, by mid-summer of 1859 the Chinese had made no arrangements for its payment, and there were no signs that disbursements were likely to be forthcoming in the near future.[75] The auguries were not promising; yet the city was at peace, the garrison was in firm control, and Elgin rejoiced that no untoward disturbances prevented him from leaving the country he had so reluctantly consented to enter. On 3 March he set sail for England, but not before learning that his objectionable colleague, Admiral Seymour, had been given a eulogistic address by the merchants of Hong Kong, with the promise of £2,200 for a service of plate.[76]

[73] To Admiralty, 15 Feb. 1859 (No. 99), ibid.
[74] To Admiralty, 14 Mar. 1859 (No. 129), ibid.
[75] See Rear-Admiral Sir James Hope to Admiralty, 30 July 1859 (No. 91), ibid.
[76] See Seymour to Admiralty, *Calcutta* off Singapore, 28 Mar. 1859 (No. 142), ibid.

XIV

INGLORIOUS DEFEAT AND CHEERLESS VICTORY 1859-1860

THE Treaty of Tientsin had stipulated that ratifications were to be exchanged in Peking within a year of signature, and for Great Britain, the responsibility for formal endorsement was assigned to Lord Elgin's younger brother, the Honourable Frederick Bruce, who would assume the title of Minister Plenipotentiary, as well as taking over the duties of Chief Superintendent of Trade. The Government had accepted Elgin's advice not to insist on the immediate opening of an embassy in Peking. Bruce was to be accredited to the Emperor's Court, but, following exchange of ratifications, he was expected to bring the British mission back to Shanghai.

It was intended that his journey from Hong Kong to the estuary of the Peiho should be marked by a certain amount of pomp and military sinew. Elgin himself had suggested that the appearance of a substantial squadron would be an admirable means of impressing Peking. 'Showing the flag' under steam might well ease the doubts and hasten the signature of a squeamish Emperor. Backing down on engagements was 'by no means novel in Chinese diplomacy', and Admiral Seymour was, therefore, instructed to see that Bruce was accompanied on his voyage northward by 'an imposing naval force'.[1] The new Minister Plenipotentiary was well pleased with the recommended procedure. Personal experience of Chinese habits and character had shown him that 'the objects of this mission were most likely to be satisfactorily and peacefully attained if the British Minister were supported by a powerful demonstration of force at the mouth of the Peiho.[2]

---

[1] Corry (Admiralty) to Seymour, 9 Feb. 1859 (No. 57), Adm. 2/1616.
[2] Minute of Conference held at Government Offices, Hong Kong, attended by Bruce, Major-General van Straubenzee, and Rear-Admiral Hope, 28 Apr. 1859, Adm. 1/5720. A variety of Foreign Office papers and memoranda relating to the expedition is attached.

As it happened, Seymour had scarcely begun preparations for the odyssey, when he learned that he was to be succeeded by Rear-Admiral James Hope, the transfer to take place in Singapore. On 19 March he left Hong Kong, homeward bound in the *Calcutta*. In the same month, the newly appointed commander-in-chief set out from England, proceeding by the overland route to the Red Sea, and thence by steamer to Singapore. He reached Hong Kong on 21 April, just two days after Bruce had arrived in the *Magicienne*.[3] By this time, the unhappy Sir John Bowring had learned that once again his functions as Plenipotentiary and Chief Superintendent of Trade (resumed after Lord Elgin's departure) were to cease. He could, he was told, stay on as Governor of Hong Kong, provided the Colonial Secretary, Sir Edward Bulwer-Lytton, agreed.[4] Tired, exasperated, and disillusioned, Bowring was not tempted, and on 5 May, as (in his own words) 'a mere Colonial Governor', he took his departure.[5]

Bruce and the French Plenipotentiary, M. de Bourboulon, arrived at Shanghai in May for the preliminary meeting with the Chinese Commissioners, who, much to their surprise, were already waiting for them. (They proved to be the same representatives who had negotiated the Treaty of Tientsin). It was not long, however, before they realized that such punctuality was a consequence of Chinese anxiety to avoid, by one means or another, having the ratification ceremony take place in Peking. Indeed, according to rumours which filtered into official quarters, steps had been taken to obstruct the Peiho route to the capital, and to restore the Taku forts. In seeking to reopen negotiations, the Commissioners did their best to advance the claims of Shanghai as the most acceptable meeting ground for the exchange of final ratifications. Apparently less 'loss of face' was involved in using a commercial port already recognized as an international entrepôt. However, when it was made clear that the allied officials would not bend, Peking

---

[3] Hope was officially notified of his appointment on 28 February Adm. 13/4/461–3. One month later, he was informed of the Admiralty's decision to create an Australian station, independent of the East Indies and China station. See Instruction, 26 Mar. 1859, Adm. 13/4/469.

[4] See F.O. to C.O., 22 Nov. 1858, F.O. 17/307.

[5] At the end of his five-year appointment, Bowring had reached the age of 67. He died in 1872, aged 80.

reluctantly gave in, but with one significant reservation, of which the allied emissaries were not then informed. The mission could come to Peking, but not by way of the Peiho. Pehtang, some ten miles north of Taku as the crow flies, was designated as the port of entry; thence, the route to the capital would be almost entirely by land. But there was to be no cortège with waving banners, no escorting cavalcade to illustrate the power and prestige of Western arms—not even dignified transport in the comparative comfort of sedan chairs. No weapons of any sort were to be carried; an embassy required none of the tools of war! But of this plan, the British and French plenipotentiaries had little, if any, clear knowledge until they reached the Peiho and found the gates barred.

It was apparent that the Imperial Court was confident that even at this late date, the allies, including the Americans, could be diverted from their chosen route. But Bruce had been told to go to the mouth of the Peiho with 'a sufficient naval force', and whether in Peking, or on the journey there, he was directed to refuse compliance 'with any ceremony, or form of reception', which might 'be construed into an admission of inferiority on the part of Her Majesty in regard to the Emperor of China'.[6] But of these orders, the Imperial Court, it may be assumed, had no knowledge. They only knew that in June, a fleet of warships and transports carrying soldiers was on its way northward from Shanghai headed for the Gulf of Pecheli. Apparently still hopeful that their recommended procedures would be found acceptable, the authorities in the capital issued orders for the preparation of three large houses for the reception of the envoys 'after the fashion of the tributary practice'.[7]

The main British squadron sailed on 11 June; Bruce and de Bourboulon left four days later. Although Elgin had urged that no vessels from the augmented expedition of 1858 should be called home until ratifications had been completed, the Admiralty, in April, suddenly decided on a reduction. Since Shanghai rather than Peking was to be the seat of Her Majesty's representative in China, there was no need for a base near the Peiho, and no need, therefore, to reinforce the China

---

[6] See Banno, *China and the West*, pp. 30–1. The Russian Tientsin treaty, had been ratified in Peking on 24 April 1859.

[7] Hsü, *China's Entrance into the Family of Nations*, pp. 92–3.

squadron.[8] The instruction to reduce the strength of the China station did not reach Hong Kong until the expedition was well on its northward course. Even then, the British squadron could not be considered one of overwhelming force—one frigate (Admiral Hope's flagship, the *Chesapeake*), of 51 guns, four sloops, eleven gunboats, two troop-ships and a steam tender, nineteen vessels in all, carrying 154 guns and 2,068 men.[9] Nevertheless, this was clearly no flotilla on parade; here was a powerful instrument of war. As agreed with the French, responsibility for the final decision as to its use would rest with the British commander-in-chief, Rear-Admiral Hope.[10]

Hope, now fifty years old, had joined the Navy as a boy, but during the intervening period of service had seen relatively little action. In 1854, the Crimean War seemed likely to offer a break with professional routine, but the battleship *Majestic* (80), which he commanded in the Baltic, took no part in major operations. In brief, like the majority of his age-group, he had been taught few hard lessons under fire. Neither had he any knowledge of the Chinese official or military mind; nor was he in close touch with his French colleagues on the expedition, or for that matter the officers of his own service. Seymour had spent three years in the China Sea, and had learned a good deal about Chinese tactics, both diplomatic and martial. Yet, in accordance with naval etiquette, he was steaming home from Singapore in a P. & O. mail-boat less than forty-eight hours after Hope's arrival. A week of conversations might have been useful; but tradition bade the old commander-in-chief hasten away as soon as relieved by the new.

By 20 June the allied squadron had assembled at the appointed anchorage, fifteen miles off the entrance to the Peiho. Unfortunately, of the French detachment under Admiral Genouilly, not one vessel was capable of crossing the

[8] Corry to Hope, 6 Apr. 1859 (No. 58), Adm. 2/1616. The Distribution of Station Strength is contained in Hope to Admiralty, 19 April, encl. report by the Senior Officer, Hong Kong, 13 Apr. 1859, Adm. 1/5712. Correspondence concerning the need to hold the force intact includes Seymour to Admiralty, 12 Feb. (No. 86), same to same, 14 Mar. (No. 131), Seymour to Elgin (in reply to Elgin's letter of 2 March) 14 Mar., and Hope to Admiralty, 5 May (No. 20) 1859, ibid.

[9] Hope to Admiralty, Hong Kong, 21 May 1859 (No. 37), ibid.

[10] See Memorandum showing relative responsibilities of the Officers commanding H.M. Sea and Land Forces, encl. in F.O. folio on 'The Peiho Affair', 6 July 1859, Adm. 1/5720.

notorious bar into the river. Moreover, the continued occupation of Canton meant that Hope lost the services of the Royal
Regiment, a company of artillery, and number of marines. For
the moment, however, their presence seemed unnecessary.
Even if the Chinese repudiated their treaty obligations and
offered fight, they would surely crumble as quickly as they
had done in the past. All the evidence from 1840–1 onwards
seemed to confirm the view that they would respond ostentatiously, fire wildly, fight desperately for a short time, and
then run away. In the minds of officers and men in the ships
anchored off the Peiho, there was no thought that any serious
resistance would be encountered, should the Imperial Court
prove obdurate and hostile.

Almost immediately after his arrival, Admiral Hope had
boarded the gunboat *Plover*, and, escorted by the *Starling*, had
crossed the bar to reconnoitre the river entrance and, at the
same time, to inform any Chinese officials on the shore-line of
the pending arrival of the French and British plenipotentiaries.
It was soon clear from the nature of the river defences that
progress to the capital was not likely to be unopposed.
Moreover, even from a distance, it was obvious that the shattered Taku forts had been rebuilt and strengthened, apparently
in the modern European manner. To veterans of the 1858
campaign, it appeared curious that no soldiers showed themselves on battlements; very few guns were in evidence. There
was none of the martial display so characteristic of Chinese
behaviour before an engagement—no flaunting of valour, no
flags, no parades—only an ominous silence. On the other
hand, closer investigation showed that an immense complex
of river obstructions had rendered the Peiho route to the
capital all but impassable. Almost directly below the South
forts, where the channel was scarcely a hundred yards wide, a
triple series of timber booms and chains, interspersed with
iron stakes, had been firmly fixed in such a way as to force
oncoming vessels close to the right bank, and the more subject, therefore, to raking fire from the lower South batteries.
The stakes, about nine inches in circumference, with tripod
bases to hold them upright against the velocity of the stream,
had pointed tips, with nasty looking spurs protruding from
the sides. At high water, they were well below the surface.

Several nights of painstaking exploration revealed that a second barrier lay some five hundred yards further on, abreast the main South fort. It was composed of one eight-inch hemp and two heavy chain cables, strung across the river twelve feet or so from each other, and supported every thirty feet by well-embedded posts. The third barrier, higher upstream, below the main North fort, consisted of two massive timber rafts, moored on either side of the river, one slightly above the other, with more iron stakes so angled as to impale any gun-boats lucky enough to get so far.

Admiral Hope naturally demanded an explanation of this intimidating series of impediments to navigation, but his efforts to make personal contact with the Chinese commander failed. Communication with the ruler of fortress Taku proved as difficult as with the Court of Peking. His messenger was turned back at the beach, with the curt intimation that the defences were simply the rude work of local militia, designed as a precaution against the incursions of pirates and rebels. As for the fortifications, they had obviously been renovated, but the most careful scrutiny failed to provide even a rough esti-mate of apparently well-concealed batteries. It was, none the less, comforting for the allied commanders to realize that however malevolent in appearance, the forts were little more than impressive show-pieces, intended to frighten away the evil spirits personified by French and British seamen and marines. Of course, shots would be fired, and admittedly the gunboats would be 'sitting ducks', trapped in their onward progress by booms, stakes, and rafts, easy targets for the most agitated marksman. But only for the moment! Strong tackles would soon wrench out sufficient of the iron piles to make convenient gateways to open waters beyond. And one final consolation for the invaders, however threatening the fortress guns, and however impenetrable the walls, the simple-minded enemy knew nothing about the art of concentrated fire.

Between 18 and 20 June, the squadron moved from its distant anchorage to positions immediately off the bar of the Peiho. Three days later, the gunboats crossed the bar, where they were immune from the waves and winds of the Gulf. On the 21st the two plenipotentiaries, Bruce and de Bourboulon, assigned to the British Admiral the vital task of clearing the obstructions blocking the way to Tientsin and beyond. Four days later, they learned that arrangements were being made for their reception in Pehtang harbour, whence they might proceed across country to Tientsin with a small retinue, but without arms.[11] The message containing this advice reached Bruce at 9.00 a.m. on 25 June. Whether in any circumstances proceedings would have been delayed may be doubted. In any event, the proposal, which sounded more like a command than an invitation, arrived too late. Hope had already received orders to force a passage, and operations were about to begin.

On the night of the 24th, a pallid sun set over the broad, wet plains of Pecheli. Far up the river, the masts of countless trading junks traced an erratic pathway towards Tientsin until lost in a mirage. The outline of huge earthen mounds—the ramparts and bastions of the South forts—stood out in silhouette, screening the straggling village of Taku to the rear. As morning approached, the fortress mounds were still as silent as the graves they so deceptively resembled, inert and exposed, simple targets for the enthusiastic gun crews, who looked forward to a pleasant gunnery exercise. The only moving objects on the lifeless landscape were two black banners that flapped languidly from their staffs in a listless breeze. On the previous night, three boats' crews had made a final reconnaissance, exploding charges under the second barrier, and clearing a path wide enough for at least one vessel to pass through. In the course of their endeavours, they were obviously visible to Chinese look-outs. One or two guns were aimlessly fired, but no general alarm had been sounded. A bloodless victory could still be taken for granted.

At daybreak, with flood-tide running strong, eleven gunboats prepared to move into action stations off the first barrier. The *Plover* (flag), *Starling*, *Janus*, *Cormorant*, *Lee*, *Kestrel*, and *Banterer* lined up roughly parallel to the lower South fort. The *Opossum*, in advance, placed herself close to the stakes; the *Forester*, *Haughty*, and *Nimrod* remained in the rear; the *Forester* was under instruction to move up and take the *Plover*'s posi-

---

[11] After exchanging ratifications in Pehtang, the Americans did eventually reach Peking 'in rough, springless country carts', without, however, gaining an audience with the Emperor. See Lane-Poole, p. 315.

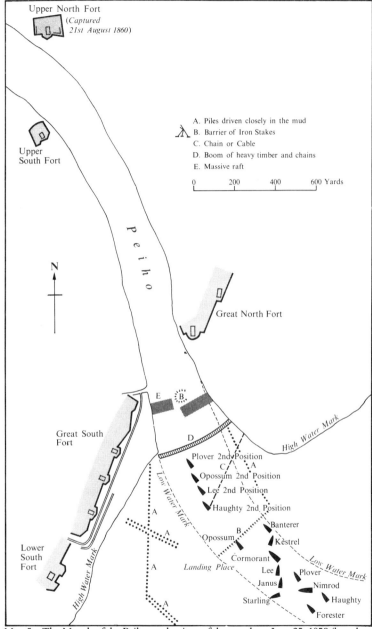

Upper North Fort
(*Captured 21st August 1860*)

Upper South Fort

A. Piles driven closely in the mud
B. Barrier of Iron Stakes
C. Chain or Cable
D. Boom of heavy timber and chains
E. Massive raft

0   200   400   600 Yards

P e i h o

N

Great North Fort

E

B.

Great South Fort

D

Plover 2nd Position

High Water Mark

C   A

Opossum 2nd Position

Lee 2nd Position

Haughty 2nd Position

Low Water Mark

A

A   Banterer

Opossum   B   Kestrel

Lower South Fort

A

Cormorant

Landing Place   Lee   Plover   *Low Water Mark*

Janus   Nimrod

A   Starling   Haughty

High Water Mark   Forester

MAP 5   The Mouth of the Peiho, at the time of the attack on June 25, 1859 (based on S. Wells Williams, *The Middle Kingdom* (rev. edn. 1883), II, p. 660).

tion should that vessel move in support of the *Opossum*.[12]
Slowly and relentlessly the waters of the Peiho crept over the
mud banks on either side, invading the borders of the plain,
and washing the bases of the huge earthworks that guarded the
forts of Taku. Before high water—between 11 o'clock and
noon—it would have been folly to have commenced an action.
The gunboats would either have grounded or been swept by
flood-tide directly beneath the fortress batteries. As it was, the
force of the current drove several of the waiting vessels into
the mud banks. By 1.00 p.m., when the ebb tide began to take
on strength, and the moment for attack had almost arrived, the
Banterer and *Starling* were still hopelessly stuck.

At 2.00 p.m., Admiral Hope from the *Plover* signalled the
Opossum to remove the iron pile to which she was secured, and
thus open a passage through the first barrier. This task was
accomplished in about thirty minutes, and both vessels headed
for the second barrier, which had been partially broken by
explosives. Hardly had the stem of the *Plover* struck one of the
under-water obstructions, when a single gun from the main
South fort sounded a signal. There were a few seconds of
ominous silence, and then, a storm of concentrated fire
descended on the little gunboat, severely wounding the
Admiral and killing or incapacitating all but nine of her crew
of forty. To the utter astonishment of the attacking squadron,
once they had recovered from the well-nigh paralysing shock,
the Chinese fire was as accurate as that of the British, and a
good deal more deadly. It was later estimated that between
thirty and forty fortress guns, some of them 32-pounders,
others of 8-inch calibre, were simultaneously engaged.

Hope transferred to the *Opossum*, and thence to the *Cormorant*, both of which suffered savage punishment, as did the *Lee*
and *Haughty* immediately astern of the *Opossum*. Soon the
whole squadron was involved, the more advanced vessels
firing at 150 yards range; the maximum distance was 800
yards. During the rest of the afternoon, the signal stayed:
'Engage the enemy', to which was added a red pendant: 'As
close as possible'. But all to no avail. The earthen mass of the
forts absorbed the pounding of shell and round shot like heavy

[12] Hope to Admiralty, *Chesapeake*, Gulf of Pecheli, 5 July 1859 (No. 77), Adm.
1/5712.

cushions. Occasionally guns and crews were knocked out but replacements took over almost immediately, actions which prompted Garnet Wolseley to comment, '. . . brave, indeed, must have been the men who served the guns for any length of time'.[13] When the tide fell, the Chinese tactical position improved still further. The fire from the forts became increasingly plunging, and for that reason the more destructive. By 6.00 p.m. it was clear that any chance of forcing the barriers was ended. The *Lee* and the *Haughty* had been smashed to pieces, the *Lee* managing to save herself from sinking completely by running on a mud bank. The *Kestrel* went aground, and the *Cormorant*, although surviving the first onslaught, eventually sank within range of the forts; the badly battered *Plover* succumbed by mid-afternoon. Held prisoners in the mud for most of the engagement, the *Banterer* and the *Starling* were even more vulnerable than 'sitting ducks', and, like the majority of their crews, were soon badly disabled, although the *Banterer* was ultimately able to pull clear and seek respite out of range.

Although twice seriously wounded, and repeatedly fainting from loss of blood, the Admiral refused to be carried to safety. Almost to the last, he was in the van, rowed hither and thither in his barge, urging his demoralized squadron to greater effort, until forced by his injuries to surrender the command to Captain C. F. A. Shadwell of the *Cormorant*. Although a non-combatant, the senior American naval officer in Chinese waters, Commodore Tatnall, on board the steamer *Toeywan*, continued throughout the action to tow boatloads of wounded to the big ships in the estuary, and on reverse course, detachments of marines and seamen to fill their places. His immortal apology for this technical breach of international law was apparently made to the wounded Admiral Hope: 'Blood is thicker than water.'[14]

There was to be one more desperate effort to save the day, which might be compared in its folly to 'The Charge of the

---

[13] Wolseley, *Narrative of the War with China*, p. 148.

[14] Official dispatches make no mention of this mighty aphorism, but whatever the basis, the legend is worth preserving. While rescuing Hope and others of the wounded, the crew of Tatnall's barge 'amused themselves by taking a turn at the guns, which were short-handed'. D. F. Rennie M.D., *The British Arms in North China and Japan* (London, 1864), p. 4.

Light Brigade' some four years earlier. Just as evening light began to fail, six hundred marines, sappers, and seamen were landed on the oozing mud bank leading to the lower South fort, where an attack could best be supported by the surviving gunboats. Even assuming (falsely, as it turned out) that many fortress guns had been silenced, it was a mad venture, involving a slow, occasionally frantic, plodding through a quagmire of deep, water-filled ditches under the pitiless fire of unsubdued cannon, gingalls, and rifles. A small detachment of French seamen took part under the command of Commandant Tricault, who had been attached during the earlier operation to Admiral Hope. In the course of the attempt to reach the fort (for which task Tricault had volunteered) he, along with three other Frenchmen, were killed, and ten were wounded.

A hundred and fifty of the British attackers reached the second ditch; about fifty struggled the three hundred yards to the fortress walls. All told, Admiral Hope informed the Admiralty with curious self-confidence, it was a force sufficient to have carried the place 'at the point of the bayonet', had the opposition been the sort usually encountered in Chinese warfare.[15] The retreat was as costly and more horrible than the advance. Many of the weary and wounded who could not pull themselves to safety were smothered in the relentless mud. Out of the 600, 64 were known to be dead, and 252 either badly wounded or missing. By 1.30 a.m. on a moonless night, the survivors embarked on the five remaining gunboats—*Nimrod*, *Banterer*, *Forester*, *Opossum*, and *Janus*.[16]

Young Jack Fisher took part in the battle from beginning to end, and in a letter written home three days afterwards he rightly laid claim to invulnerability. 'I am certain I am not born to be shot.' In a contemporary photograph, the face of the squat little midshipman with the surly mouth suggests the petulance, the arrogance, and the toughness that was to mark the later admiral. It can hardly be said that Fisher enjoyed his

[15] *Chesapeake*, 5 July 1859 (No. 77), Adm. 1/5712.

[16] The best account of the battle was written by Captain Sherard Osborn, *The Fight on the Peiho*, previously cited. See also, file entitled 'Forts, attack on, 1859', in Adm. 1/5712. This volume also includes a file on 'Reports and Plans of the Coast of the Gulf of Pecheli'. Further detailed information regarding the attack on the forts is contained in the file entitled, 'China: Foreign Office Papers—"Peiho Affair" [July–Dec. 1859]', Adm. 1/5720.

baptism of fire, but having lived through a disaster untouched, without losing his courage or his animal spirits, he could afford to show himself as a bit of a fire-eater, for whom death or mutilation held few terrors.

'28th [26th?] June.—Off the Peiho Forts' [he wrote from the *Banterer*:] My dear Mams,—By some wonderful means I have escaped unhurt, although my dear old Skipper has been very badly wounded in the foot, a large ball still being in it. I don't know whether I can give you a description of it; I feel in such a state of excitement. I will first tell you those who are killed or wounded that you know. Inglis, our Marine Officer, was smothered in the mud when we landed, being first wounded. Poor Huleatt was badly wounded in the groin; I don't think he will live. He fell close to me. Capt. Vansittart had his leg shot off, and Purvis is lightly wounded. There are very few wounded, I fancy, in comparison to those killed. In the *Plover*, the next gunboat to ours, twenty-six men were killed or wounded, the Admiral being one of them. Rase, her Commander, was smashed to atoms; so was McKenna, the Military Secretary, and all the Admiral's staff nearly. In the last part of the action I was the only one left to carry the orders about, the Flag Lieutenant having been sent to command the *Plover* with a fresh crew. We had a hard fight of it, but what could we do against such a fearful number of guns? and us poor little gunboats inclosed in such a small place, not much broader across than the length of our ship. . . .

The old Admiral behaved splendidly after he had part of his thigh and leg shot away. He had a cot swung to a pole and was carried about in a boat from the *Plover* to the *Cormorant* to encourage the men, and then was hoisted upon the bridge till he was hit again, and then they laid him down on the quarter-deck, where he remained till night. He won't be brought out to the *Chesapeake*, but will stop within range. My old Skipper keeps his pecker up. I was with him all day till he was wounded in the mud, and then I brought him out to the ship. . . . I had to fling all my arms away coming back from the forts, and was nearly smothered once, only one of the bluejackets was kind enough to heave me out. You sank up to your knees, *at least* every step, and just fancy the slaughter going 500 yards in the face of that fire of about thirty pieces of artillery right in front of you and on each flank. It was dreadful, horrible work, but thank God I came out all right. Broad, I hear, is slightly wounded, but it is only a rumour. Gallons Jones, I am afraid, has lost his gunboat. The *Kestrel* is gone down, and I am afraid the *Cormorant* will go too. They had horrid fire-balls firing at us when we landed. I saw one poor fellow with his eye and part of his face burnt right out. If a piece struck you, it stuck to you and regularly burnt you away until it was all gone. . . . It is a sad business, is it not, Mams? But they will be able to see by the return of killed that we fought hard for it. The Chinamen fought like anything. Some of our fellows solemnly swear they saw Russians quite distinctly when we got to the foot of the ditch. I believe they must have been Russians; no Chinaman ever fought like those fellows did yesterday. They had fearful advantages, no doubt. I expect the Admiral will either die or go home shortly.[17]

On the morning of 26 June, the sun rose on a shattered squadron, and on a shocked and bewildered Plenipotentiary. The losses had been heavy; the wonder is that they were not even greater. The eleven gunboats had lost 93 killed and 111 wounded; some of the latter were to die. Other British vessels that were engaged, *Chesapeake*, *Highflyer*, *Magicienne*, *Fury*, *Assistance*, and *Cruiser*, which contributed seamen and marines for the land assault, listed in total 426 killed and 345 wounded.[18] The battle for the forts had ended in humiliating catastrophe.

Perhaps the simplest, certainly the most succinct, explanation was the most accurate. 'The Admiral never expected the place was so strong,' observed Midshipman Fisher. 'They were never Chinamen who planned those forts.'[19] For one thing, no one had counted on the enormous thickness of the reconstructed mud parapets, or anticipated the resilience of the clay and timber embrasures, elevated some twenty-five feet in the European manner to provide a wide field of fire. In addition, as was later discovered, there were fifty to sixty more guns than in the previous year, and the batteries had been co-ordinated with professional skill. Indeed, the whole Chinese defence system had been reconstructed 'on a different principle'. Between July 1858 and June 1859, one might well visualize the Chinese commander-in-chief and his staff poring over available European material on fortifications, translated

[17] Sir Reginald S. Bacon, *Life of Lord Fisher of Kilverstone* (2 vols., London, 1920), i, 13–14.

The Russians would have been quite happy to embarrass both the French and the British, but the case against them has never been proven.

[18] Hope to Admiralty, *Chesapeake*, at Gulf of Pecheli, 5 July 1859 (No. 77), Adm. 1/5712.

Built as a steam sloop, known for a time as a steam frigate, by 1855 the *Highflyer* was designated a corvette. The *Magicienne* remained a paddle-frigate, the *Cruiser* a screw sloop, and the *Fury* a paddle-sloop. [19] Bacon, i. 15.

possibly by students from the mission schools! 'No ordinary tactician was behind those earthworks', wrote Captain Sherard Osborn, who, only a year before, had carried Lord Elgin to the Peiho in the *Furious*.[20]

News of the disaster reached England in September, and the reaction of Parliament and press was savage and unsparing. Frederick Bruce was condemned for planning to ride rough-shod into Peking regardless of the opposition. Admiral Hope was caustically censured for his ill-judged attack on the forts. Yet, as Colonel Wolseley mused at the time, '. . . how much more censure should we have heard if that gallant sailor . . . perceiving the difficulties to be overcome, and knowing his weakness in having no troops at his disposal—had announced to Mr. Bruce that his force was inadequate to capture the forts? England would have howled from one end of it to the other. . . .'[21] That may be. None the less, once the strength of the Chinese fortifications had been tested, Hope was wrong to send his seamen and marines against fixed defences, when a flanking movement from the land side had a far better chance of success. But even had the frontal defences been seriously weakened by bombardment from the water, it was madness to land an assault force on a bank of deep and treacly mud that immobilized the strong and engulfed the wounded like quick-sand. Hope's attempt was that of a determined, but foolhardy, seaman whose judgement may have been affected by physical agony and loss of blood. 'I suppose', Palmerston commented drily on 14 September, 'our officers were piqued to do some-thing desperate in the presence of France and America.'[22]

There was no Chinese treachery, as a few embittered critics were almost bound to suggest. The forts did not fire on the squadron without notice. The British commander-in-chief had been told quite plainly—and the river barriers confirmed the avowal—that a passage by the Peiho to Tientsin would be

[20] In the course of inspecting the South forts after the battle, Major Gerald Graham was astonished not only by the size of the brass guns, but by the strength of the high bastions which contained them. They were connected, he noted, by long 'curtains' with guns in casemates, and—a quaint medieval touch which amused him—at various intervals along the parapet, baskets of stones lay 'ready to be hurled at assailants'. Vetch (ed.), *Graham, Life, Letters and Diaries*, pp. 173–4.

[21] Wolseley, pp. 147–8.

[22] Quoted, Stanmore, *Sidney Herbert*, ii. 296.

resisted. But the warning had come very late in the day, after the British plan of operations had been finally determined. During the fruitless negotiations at Shanghai, nothing had been said about a detour through Pehtang, nor of the enormously strengthened defences at Taku. In retrospect, it was quite clear that the Chinese gunners, by constant practice, plotted the precise range of palisades and stakes, where the invading gunboats were certain to be stopped. In this sense, the defenders benefited from a prepared ambuscade. It must have been assumed that the navy would try to push through; but tactical surprise scarcely amounted to a betrayal.

It could, of course, be argued, that, like the Americans, Bruce should have accepted the proffered alternative—a journey, with a small unarmed escort to Peking by way of Pehtang (which the Foreign Secretary was surprised to learn was not on a branch of the Peiho). In view of the slights and humiliations subsequently suffered by the American delegation, he was probably wise in his refusal. Such an approach would almost certainly have failed to produce an unamended Treaty ratification. On the other hand, both the British Plenipotentiary and the commander-in-chief, Admiral Hope, had shown a remarkable lack of subtlety and imagination, once it was realized that the river defences were not only substantial, but conceivably impenetrable without considerable loss of life. Lord John Russell did not hesitate to tell Bruce that, in his opinion, he had shown an unjustified stubbornness, and an over-readiness to use physical force. 'Now, although the denial of a passage to the capital by the usual and most convenient route would have been evidence of an unfriendly disposition, yet it was a matter upon which you might have remonstrated and negotiated without having recourse to force to clear the passage.'[23]

The Cabinet condemned Bruce for his rashness, but he was not recalled to do penance for his sins, partly because he had the good sense to acknowledge his error of judgement by letter, and partly, perhaps, because his more generous critics must have known that they were being wise after the event.

[23] Draft of a dispatch from Lord J. Russell to Mr. Bruce (No. 2), Foreign Office, November 1859, printed for the use of the Foreign Office, 5 Nov. 1859, Broadlands MSS., MM/CH/9.

The Secretary of War, Sidney Herbert, delivered himself of a household truth when he told the Commons bluntly that had Admiral Hope succeeded in demolishing the forts, Bruce's judgement would not have been called in question.[24] Success would have bred its own logic.

Nevertheless, a defeat so damaging to British prestige in the East called for retribution. Whether by road or river, there was no debate about the necessity of hastening to Peking with an even more formidable armament. Possibly—and it was a faint prospect—ratification of the Treaty of Tientsin might still be obtained without fighting. Once the Chinese became aware of the size of the proposed French and British expeditionary force, might they not respond to allied demands, even though they included an apology and a substantial indemnity?[25] The threat of force did not necessarily mean war, but simply a determination to resort to war if redress could not be obtained by negotiation. However, such casuistry did not impress the French, who, to Russell's alarm, took the view that France was already at war with China. Meanwhile, as though in confirmation of British day-dreams, trade with the Treaty ports went on much as before, either openly or surreptitiously, and not only with the original five, but to a modest extent with those newly opened under the unratified Treaty of 1858.[26]

The appointment of Lord Elgin, once again to lead a British mission to China, was not made until early March 1860. The glamour surrounding his success as treaty-maker had not entirely faded. When he returned from China in the spring of 1859, he had been received with every honour. Palmerston had taken him into his newly-formed ministry as Post Master-General; Glasgow students had made him Lord Rector; London merchants and bankers had given him the Freedom of the City, and there was a grand dinner afterward in the Mansion

[24] See Hsü, pp. 94–5.

[25] See Instructions to Bruce, 10 and 29 Oct., 1859, F.O. 17/311.

[26] Lord Elgin commented on the curious fact that the Peking government was making no effort 'to molest us at the ports open to trade, and that, whatever responsibility attaches to it for recent occurrences at the mouth of the Peiho, it seems to be rather alarmed than elated by their result'. Memorandum in Operations against Peking, printed for the use of the Foreign Office, Oct. 19 1859, Broadlands MSS., MM/CH/8.

House.[27] Yet, within little more than a year of his departure from Hong Kong, he was off to the Far East to take over from his brother Frederick. Among British statesmen, obviously no one possessed Elgin's knowledge of this particular Chinese situation. In addition, he had the distinction, the authority, and (so Palmerston hoped), the toughness to stand up to the French as well as to the Old China Hands.[28] The French government was bound to appoint a plenipotentiary of comparable rank and stature, and happily they again chose Elgin's friendly colleague of 1858, Baron Gros.

Elgin undertook the mission with even less enthusiasm than on the first occasion. In accepting what was most likely to be a thankless task, he was sacrificing a seat in the Cabinet, and jeopardizing a career which could conceivably lead to the highest post in the land. An expedition to repair blunders and retrieve honour (which probably meant forcing a passage up the Peiho and exchanging ratifications at the point of the bayonet) held little attraction for one of his sensitive and essentially conciliatory nature. None the less, he knew that 'the mischievous consequences of the recent disaster' had to be expunged, and to that object a sufficient force was vital. It was hardly likely that the Chinese government would 'spontaneously, and without the excercise of any pressure on our part, tender to us terms of accommodation' which would satisfy the British government. Consequently, the Emperor's ministers should be informed of the British determination to carry out all the provisions of the Treaty of Tientsin, if necessary by arms. An ultimatum to this effect, Elgin was disposed to think, 'combined with moderation and tact in execution', would probably suffice to bring the Peking government to terms. Failing this approach, measures of coercion would obviously be required, but even then he felt that the wisest policy would be 'to endeavour to induce the Emperor to make peace before the army had advanced beyond Tientsin, or Tungchow, so as to avoid the necessity of a hostile entrance into the capital'.[29]

[27] See Walrond (ed.), *Letters and Journals*, pp. 314–15.
[28] See Stanmore, *Sidney Herbert*, ii. 298–301; and Cady, *The Roots of French Imperialism* . . ., pp. 239–40.
[29] Memorandum on Operations against Pekin, printed for the use of the Foreign Office, 19 Oct. 1859, Broadlands MSS., MM/CH/8.

The shock of shipwreck on the outward journey broke the fretful tedium, but scarcely served to relieve the despondency that clouded Elgin's mind during the long days at sea. Close by Point de Galle towards the end of May, a violent change of wind forced the *Malabar* off course, and she grounded heavily. Apart from a box of linen, some badly sea-stained decorations, and a few cases of champagne, most of his personal effects were lost overboard. There was much wishful thinking in one of his last diary entries recorded just before he disembarked at Hong Kong: 'What is desired is a speedy settlement on reasonable terms—as good terms as possible; but let the settlement be speedy.'[30]

Elgin had left England on 26 April with an unusually free hand. In view of the unexpected circumstances that had confronted his brother, the Foreign Secretary, Lord John Russell, offered 'suggestions rather than directions'. Her Majesty's Plenipotentiary was authorized to act as he saw fit, provided he did complete the journey to Peking, and come to terms with the ruling Manchu dynasty, whose foundations were not to be unduly shaken. The British government did not want to humiliate the Chinese more than the compulsion of arms made necessary. On the contrary, assuming quick military success, one fundamental concern was the continued stability of the existing Imperial throne; a state of turmoil would be fatal to British trading prospects. In a memorandum composed for the benefit of the Cabinet in the previous October, Elgin had pointed out that the occupation of Peking might well be followed by the subversion of the dynasty and a total disorganization of the Empire. Reverence for the Emperor's power was a bond which held together 'the vast population of the Empire'. If it was Britain's aim to carry on a favourable trade, and for that purpose, to make certain that the provisions of various treaties should be respected, it was in her interest to see that the bond should not be loosened.[31] At all costs, the threat of anarchy must be avoided, he wrote to Russell in July 1860. 'We might annex the Empire, if we were in humor to take a second India in hand—or we might change the Dynasty if we knew where to find a better. . . .' But since a satisfactory

---

[30] Walrond (ed.), p. 317.
[31] Memorandum on Operations against Pekin, doc. cit.

alternative was missing, the task of maintaining the *status quo* was going to require 'some delicacy of treatment'.[32] Above all else, the Emperor had to be treated with scrupulous care, but such solicitude in no way altered the fact that certain indispensable conditions would have to be met. One was an apology for the attack on the allied forces at the Peiho. Another, was the ratification of the Treaty of Tientsin, and a third, the payment of an additional indemnity for expenses incurred during the present naval and military preparations and in the course of prospective operations.

Palmerston believed that this simple formula could be submitted and accepted without shaking the Manchu throne. 'The occupation by a barbarian army of a capital into which even a barbarian diplomatist is not to be admitted, would go further to proclaim our power, and therefore to accomplish our ends, than any other military success, and I must own I have no belief whatever in the supposition that such an occupation would overthrow the Chinese Empire. Depend upon it, that occupation would bring the Emperor to reason.'[33] But the success of such 'shot-gun medicine' depended to a large extent on the speed of operations. Because of ice conditions, and the difficulty of transporting men and stores against the north-east monsoon, Peking was regarded as almost unattackable until the end of April. Then followed the fearfully hot weather of June and July, 'almost as powerful in its defence'. Mid-August to mid-October was the best campaigning season. For that reason, a brisk advance and a quick conclusion of business was imperative. Once winter set in, failing a settlement, the allied commanders would have to consider whether to 'stay put', with the loss of secure communications to the coast, or to retire southward with consequent loss of face.[34]

Although Lord Elgin (and the same consideration applied to Baron Gros) had no authority over either the naval or the military high command in the conduct of operations, the heads of mission might well have to intervene if, after the attainment of certain military objectives, the way seemed to be

[32] Elgin to Russell, 12 July 1860, Russell Papers 30/22/49.
[33] To Sidney Herbert, 20 Apr. 1860, Stanmore, *Sidney Herbert*, ii. 315.
[34] See Palmerston to Herbert, 27 Nov. 1859, ibid., 306; also, Herbert to Hope Grant, ibid., 203; and F.O. to Elgin, 17 Apr. 1860 (No. 1), F.O. 17/329.

open for serious negotiations and a possible peace. As the Minister of War explained in a memorandum for the benefit of his French ally: 'The whole object of these hostilities being the attainment of peace, if the Plenipotentiaries can obtain the latter, it would be absurd, and worse than absurd, to continue the former for the sake of barren military successes which can bring no prestige to our Armies, and which might materially impede the peace we seek.'[35]

Obviously no rule could be laid down to meet unanticipated situations, and equally obvious, everything depended on cordial joint action, not only between French and British plenipotentiaries, but between their military commanders. Hitherto, it had been generally accepted that when the operations of a British fleet and army were so interwoven that no definitive line could be drawn to mark the boundary between the two, then, in the manner of Wolfe and Saunders at Quebec, the only solution was close collaboration and mutual forbearance. However, in case of a deep division of opinion occurring, the Admiral's view prevailed. The French tradition was the reverse of the British, the military commander being ordinarily supreme over the naval in combined operations. However, in 1858–9, as has been noted, the French accepted a British admiral as commander-in-chief, once active operations had commenced, chiefly because in ships and men they were very much in a minority. But in 1860 the dispatch of a considerable army to the theatre of war was to increase immensely the difficulties of joint co-operation, and to make the appointment of a supreme commander-in-chief an impossibility.

When Elgin left England, it was still hoped that a substantial fleet, accompanied by an imposing army, would produce by its very presence in the Gulf of Pecheli a change of Chinese heart that would lead to an unopposed entry into Peking. The British expeditionary force consisted of slightly more than 13,000 troops of all arms under Elgin's brother-in-law, General Sir Hope Grant.[36] To this total, India contributed more

[35] Stanmore, *Sidney Herbert*, ii. 308–9.
[36] On 3 May 1860 Sidney Herbert told Lord Canning that he had wanted a compact force 'for a quick blow'. But instead of the expected 8,000, 13,225 were being sent. He was surprised at the large native force dispatched from India. 'Our agreement with

than half.[37] France provided nearly 7,000, under that sensitive and bull-headed product of the Third Empire, General Cousin de Montauban.[38] The Royal Navy's contribution of seventy ships, including gunboats, was not much larger than the squadron of the previous year, but on this occasion many transport vessels had to be added to carry the army. In all, there were more than two hundred transports, of which 120 had been hired; 33 were French. Of the fighting fleet, the French contingent consisted chiefly of gunboats under the command of Admiral Leonard Charner.[39]

From the middle of March, on through April into May, the troop transports and their escorts filtered into Hong Kong harbour. The greater part of the Bengal contingent had left Calcutta towards the end of February and early March. At that season of the year, a passage from India to the China coast usually took a full two months. As far as the Straits of Malacca, vessels coming from the Cape could count on favouring light breezes, but after that, strong head-winds were capricious and frequent. The sailing ships reached Singapore, the main rendezvous, in about twenty-eight days, but a good many, particularly the cavalry transports (thirteen in number), had to be towed in and out of Singapore harbour by steam warships, which found themselves assisting laggards all the way to Hong Kong. Kowloon, still part of the territory of Imperial China, was the principal assembly point.

Directly opposite Hong Kong, within three-quarters of a mile of Victoria, the promontory of Kowloon stretched out from the mainland. In the past, it had been the constant refuge of pirates, thieves, and smugglers, who preyed on the shipping entering the Bogue. During the first Anglo-Chinese war, the

---

France', he wrote Sir Hope Grant, 'included no more than 10,000 altogether, exclusive of the garrisons at Canton and Hong Kong.'

[37] Ibid., 318–19.

[38] On the eve of the third and final attack on the Taku forts, the General proclaimed his faith in the Napoleonic mission. 'France is a martial nation. The noise of battle intoxicates and enraptures it. . . . France goes to defend the great cause of civilization, and may God watch over the little army so far away from native soil.' Quoted, Cady, p. 250.

[39] They were relatively small, iron gunboats, fitted to carry one gun, and they were brought to China in pieces. When screwed together, each boat had three compartments, made watertight with layers of vulcanized rubber. See Wells Williams, *Middle Kingdom*, p. 672.

Chinese had set up batteries which, in theory at least, commanded the mile-wide harbour that separated the peninsula from the island of Hong Kong. After the war, the batteries had been dismantled, and, apart from a few settlers, Kowloon became a kind of no man's land, a smugglers' centre, and, in time of need, a typhoon refuge. Military engineers had long been exercised about the defences of Hong Kong, and Major-General van Straubenzee, in a dispatch to Lord Elgin, had had no hesitation in saying flatly that the occupation of the peninsula was absolutely essential to the security of the Island.[40]

An apparently healthy site for a barracks or camping ground, with plenty of water, and, unlike Victoria, open to the cooling south-west monsoon, Kowloon had the additional advantage of a large sandy plain to the rear, where cavalry horses could stretch their legs after the long voyage from India. Such amenities had not gone unnoticed by the French, who, so it was rumoured, were casting wistful eyes on so salubrious a transit base. Undoubtedly, fear of an uncertain ally, who might become a neighbour-within-gunshot, accelerated British action.[41] As it happened, to the considerable relief of Lord John Russell, on 25 April 1860 Admiral Hope was able to inform the Admiralty that the ingenious British Consul at Canton, Harry Parkes, had been able to arrange with the Governor-General of the two Kwang provinces for the perpetual lease of the Kowloon peninsula at a rent of £160 annually. According to Hope, the territory might have been ceded outright, had British relations with Peking been more amicable.[42]

Meanwhile, across the water in Hong Kong, all was bustle

[40] See Elgin to Clarendon, 7 Apr. 1858, encl. van Straubenzee's letter of 26 Mar. 1858, F.O. 17/287.

[41] See Admiralty to F.O., 27 May 1858, W.O. to F.O., 31 May and 14 June 1858, F.O. 17/304. See also, Captain Henry Knollys and General Sir Hope Grant, *Incidents in the China War of 1860* (Edinburgh and London, 1875), pp. 4–5; Wolseley, pp. 1–2; Lane-Poole, p. 322; Stanmore, *Sidney Herbert*, ii. 317–18.

[42] Hope to Paget (Admiralty), 25 Apr. 1860 (No. 149), Adm. 1/5735. The dénouement envisaged by Hope had to await the surrender of Peking in October 1860. In mid-January 1861 Lord Elgin was able to proclaim formally the annexation of the peninsula of Kowloon to the Crown in accordance with a provision in the new Treaty. See Hope to Admiralty, Hong Kong, 22 Jan. 1861 (No. 17), Adm. 1/5762; also, Lane-Poole, i. 406–7.

and chatter as the expedition prepared to start for the north. The streets swarmed with troops, discharged from the transports either at Kowloon or Hong Kong as late as May. Cantonese coolies were hired by the hundreds to carry the army's ammunition and stores. Apparently only 'the scum of the earth' enlisted; none the less, according to recruiting officers, one strong, good-natured coolie was more than the equal of two baggage mules.[43] Transport was always a major problem, especially in operational areas lacking good roads. All told, including the military train, about 1,800 horses, ponies, and mules were required by the artillery and cavalry units, and these, with difficulty and at great expense, were collected from India, Manila, and Japan. Not until mid-July was a General Order issued, sanctioning the private acquisition of horses for cash or by barter. In consequence, Canton, Amoy, and later on, the country to the north, was ransacked by the servants or agents of young officers. Large sums were paid, often for the most worthless animals, many of which, including the fit, had to be left behind because the transports were over-crowded.[44]

Generally speaking, infantry can survive the wildest weather at sea, but not horses. Indeed, a good many had already been lost or crippled during the 1,700-mile journey from Singapore. It was everywhere recognized that if there were to be a northern campaign, it had to begin and end before the frosts descended on the Peiho. Unfortunately, the northeast monsoon, blowing down the coast of China, only begins to die away towards the end of May, to be replaced by favouring winds from the south-west. In consequence, vessels transporting cavalry and horse artillery could not leave until the beginning of June, and even then, to shorten the time on board, many of them were towed by steamers in twos and threes. Towing in fitful weather is always a difficult operation, and during the first few days one accident followed another. Sailing ships ran foul of the steamers, and the latter ran into the ships. Bulwarks were smashed and rigging carried away. Not

[43] The absorption of so many of the rougher elements in Hong Kong into the army seems to have had a cleansing effect. Following the departure of the expedition, 'robbery had become a thing almost unknown on the island'. Robert Swinhoe, *Narrative of the North China Campaign of 1860 . . .* (London, 1861), pp. 1–2.

[44] Vetch (ed.), *Graham, Life, Letters and Diaries*, p. 149; also, Swinhoe, p. 8.

until 9 June, following a fresh start, did the expedition get under way.[45]

But the greater part of the French expeditionary force was absent; indeed, the main contingent did not appear until nearly a month later, a delay which grievously affected British tempers as well as operational arrangements. It was just as well, however, that the allies were not compelled to mingle in Kowloon and Hong Kong, 'broiling under a June sun, with nothing to do'. On S.S. *Granada* and its overflow consort, S.S. *Sirius*, the confined headquarters abodes of staff officers, boredom, and heat bred tension, and tension led to eruptions of temper. 'There was', wrote a fellow passenger, 'just that amount of disagreeableness that usually occurs among Englishmen who are strangers to one another, and yet are fully aware of the appointment and position each holds; in a word, there was no conviviality.'[46]

During this time, Admiral Hope had been mulling over plans for the anticipated operations in north China should Peking refuse the allies' proffered terms for a settlement.[47] Early in March, an ultimatum had been forwarded to the Imperial government through Shanghai demanding an apology for the Peiho incident, payment of an indemnity, and of course, ratification of the Tientsin Treaty. Thirty days was allowed for an answer. In the event of an unsatisfactory response, troops would be dispatched to Shanghai for the protection of British and French residents; Chusan would be occupied, and the Gulf of Pecheli blockaded as soon as a naval squadron could reach the area.[48]

The chances of success were viewed as increasingly dim in view of the prevailing mood of Peking, where posthumous honours had been bestowed on the fallen heroes of Taku, and

---

[45] Stanmore, *Sidney Herbert*, ii. 313–13, 316–17, 325–6; Wolseley, p. 58.

[46] Swinhoe, p. 9.

[47] Hope to Paget (Adm.), 28 Jan. 1860 (No. 35), and 15 Feb. 1860 (No. 67), Adm. 1/5735.

[48] Hope to Paget, 15 Mar. 1860 (No. 98), encl. Bruce to Hope, 6 Mar. 1860, Adm. 1/5735. It is worth noticing that the Admiralty's Secretary underlined heavily in pencil the recommendation for the blockade of the Gulf. Details of naval plans, should the ultimatum be rejected, are contained in Hope to Paget, Hong Kong, 30 Mar. 1860 (No. 123), ibid.

where high officials rejoiced at the discomfiture of enemies who had paid the penalty for slighting the martial dignity, and thus provoking the wrath of the Celestial Empire. However, when it eventually arrived, the Chinese answer was characteristically courteous, if slightly ambiguous, in its negative formality. Peking was prepared to complete the process of ratification, but on their own terms. 'If Mr. Bruce will come north without vessels of war and with but a moderate retinue, and will wait at Pehtang to exchange the treaties, China will not take him to task for what has gone by. But if he be resolved to bring up a number of war-vessels, and if he persist in proceeding by way of Taku, this will show that his true purpose is not the exchange of treaties.'[49]

It was only too clear that 'an imposing military display' would mean renewed war; that Peking was prepared to fight it out in the north, in the hope, as British strategists saw it, that any invading army would get bogged down on land, and eventually succumb to enveloping Chinese forces which would greatly outnumber them. 'The fact is', wrote the Minister of War in July, 'that Pekin is so placed that no European power can do much against it. We have lost the first half of the practicable season, and the rest is too short to do anything which shall have a permanent effect.'[50] But entirely apart from the hazards of land operations, Herbert believed—despite Palmerston's earlier objections—that a successful penetration inland might well throw an already disorganized Empire into a state of anarchy, 'fatal to the interests of commerce, because destructive of all production'.[51]

This reasoning helps to explain the proposed strategy of attempting to detach from Peking's influence and control the seafaring populations to the south of Shanghai. In a memorandum, dated 14 April 1860, Frederick Bruce pointed out that British policy should aim at winning at least the neutrality, if not the support, of the coastal junk traders who, in the manner of the New England coastal traders of 1812, knew that partici-

[49] Hope to Paget, 14 Apr. 1860 (No. 134), transmitting a copy of the ultimatum, and a translation of the reply from Peking, ibid. See also, Wells Williams, *Middle Kingdom*, p. 672, and Wolseley, pp. 11–14.
[50] Herbert to Lord Canning, 21 July 1860, Stanmore, *Sidney Herbert*, ii. 325.
[51] Herbert to Hope Grant, 26 Nov. 1859, ibid., 302–3.

pation in war was very bad for business. Britain should be careful not to antagonize by too comprehensive a blockade 'a class of men who are the best friends we have in this country . . .'. No doubt their ranks included a good many expert smugglers, but these were no different from the legitimate traders in their desire to maintain a profitable intercourse with Europeans regardless of political issues. A hundred thousand junk owners, if treated with sensible indulgence, might be saved from joining the frenzied elements whose aim was to oust Britain entirely from Chinese soil and sea.[52]

But a far more serious problem than the propitiation of southern Chinese junkmen and merchants was looming up, namely, the maintenance of a workable, if not an amicable, relationship with the French. Anything like close co-operation was, of course, out of the question in view of the persistent tension; the prospect of France as enemy rather than ally was never far from the thoughts of British military and naval commanders. The Crimean War had temporarily softened the tradition of hereditary hostility, but it established no lasting harmony. Indeed, following the conclusion of the Congress of Paris in 1856, the Franco-British alliance was subjected to strains which momentarily came close to breaking point. In January 1858, at a moment when British resources were stretched by mutiny in India, the Orsini bomb outrage had brought both countries to the verge of war. Censured for seemingly kowtowing to France, Palmerston resigned, and was succeeded by the Earl of Derby in February 1858.[53] Happily, Napoleon III, who had survived this assassination attempt, was anxious for peace, and by August both he and Queen Victoria were together in Cherbourg, celebrating with fireworks and music the newly established *bonne entente*.

But the gracious and probably sincere attentions of the Emperor could not console the British public for the secret and sudden manner with which he had entered on the Italian war

[52] See Hope to Paget, 25 Apr. 1860 (No. 143), encl. the Bruce Memorandum, Shanghai, 14 Apr. 1860, Adm. 1/5735. See also, in regard to this recommended policy of limited warfare, Russell to Admiralty, 5 Jan. 1860 [Confidential Print for the Foreign Office], F.O. 17/329.

[53] In June 1859, on the fall of the Derby Minister, Palmerston again became Prime Minister.

against Austria in May 1859. Not without reason did Lord John Russell regard this adventure 'in the name of Liberty' as the possible forerunner of other precipitate acts of aggression which might well end in a general war. In the minds of not a few Cabinet ministers, the weakened state of home defences might tempt Napoleon to make a sudden descent on Britain's thinly-guarded shore-line. From India too came warnings of dangers to come. In the event of war between France and England, wrote General Sir James Outram, 'naval prestige' was not enough to ensure the integrity of the British Empire in the East. In a memorandum stretching to fifteen foolscap pages, he argued that in view of vast 'defensive responsibilities', Britain simply did not have enough ships to cope with French squadrons that could range the Indian Ocean at will, and conceivably complete the task of swallowing Cochin-China. Moreover, both Indian and China shipping could suffer enormous losses at the hands of raiders capable of attacking Mauritius, Ceylon, Singapore, and Bombay at a time when some 28,000 Frenchmen were in a position to march through Egypt on the way to Aden and India.[54]

Although Cobden's commercial treaty of January 1860 had ameliorating effects, there was not much evidence of diminishing military ardour among the French populace. Moreover, the British public reacted with almost flamboyant bellicosity when, in March, came first reports of the French annexation of Nice and Savoy in the Italian Piedmont. The government was not unaffected by these successive waves of hostility; both suspicions and fears were shared. But despite the domestic anxieties, the Cabinet had not ignored the threat to British paramountcy in the China Seas. And forebodings of troubles to come seemed justified when it was learned that the French government proposed to send 15,000 troops on the punitive expedition to Peking. As it happened, because of shortage of transport, the French contingent was, as previously noted, limited to 7,000 men.[55]

[54] Memorandum of 4 Jan. 1860, contained in a dispatch to F.O., 7 Jan. 1860 (No. 1), L/P & S/5/175 (I.O.A.).

[55] In regard to Cabinet fears of French expansion, see Sidney Herbert's memoranda and letters in Stanmore, *Sidney Herbert*, ii. 211–16, 298, 301, 304, 310. Fortunately, for the precarious *entente*, Count Walewski retired from the Foreign Ministry in January 1860, and the expression of French policy assumed a less aggressive style.

It was doubly unfortunate that the spirit of *la gloire* extended
overseas, to be reflected in its less mellow tones by the commander of the French expeditionary force, General de Montauban. His first 'order of the day' following his appointment
proclaimed the honour and renown to be won in distant lands
'where immortal Rome at the time of its greatness never
thought to have its legions go'. Montauban was to prove a
singularly difficult partner for the highly competent and rather
astringent British commander, General Sir Hope Grant, who
found him a persistent 'drag upon our coach'. It is not unlikely
that the convention which finally brought an end to hostilities
might have been signed a month earlier had Grant been in sole
command of operations.[56] Grant was to find him 'a great
bore', a fragment of understatement that barely concealed the
torments he suffered in the cause of Anglo-French collaboration. But, personal difficulties apart, Grant was continually
irritated by French lack of organization. Deficiencies in
matériel and stores meant a dependence on British supply
services. He ignored the fact, which Admiral Hope was quick
to recognize, that France had no convenient assembly base in
India, or in intermediate ports like Singapore and Hong Kong.
For Britain, the problem of logistics was much simpler. As far
as shipping was concerned, repair facilities were nearly always
at hand, spaced along the route from the Cape eastward to the
China seas. Hope was less provoked to wrath than General
Grant, simply because he had learned to count on recurring
French delays.

But the differences between the two allies in China had a
more substantial foundation. Economic considerations had
little or nothing to do with French participation. They had no
serious commercial interest to pursue, and protection of
French missionaries was scarcely a complete justification for
military intervention on the mainland. Essentially, the differ-
ence was based on an antithesis of ideas. While British
enthusiasm for the China campaign declined amid a torrent of

[56] 'The business, I think, cannot be a long one, and . . . would in fact have been over
by this time, if the French had not been here,' wrote a highly articulate soldier from the
headquarters ship in Talien Bay. 'Nobody wanted them, and their presence only
serves as an encumbrance.' F. C. A. Stephenson, *At Home and on the Battlefield: Letters
from the Crimea, China and Egypt 1854–1888* (London, 1915), p. 261. The observation is
dated 12 July 1860.

parliamentary criticism, France saw it as an opportunity for increased prestige. While the British public were becoming much more interested in European politics than Empire-building, France, under the inspiration of glib and loquacious chauvinists, showed an eagerness for glamorous crusades abroad. In the Far East, Indo-China and the Empire of China offered fields for adventure and possible profit. Just as Napoleon III had been interested in Italian *pourboires* for help rendered, so was the Ministry of Marine, as well as the French Foreign Ministry, interested in a China base—but only if a suitable island or peninsula could be occupied without arousing British hostility beyond the crisis point. It was this reluctance to antagonize 'perfidious Albion' that the British Foreign Office had such difficulty in understanding and accepting. They simply could not believe that an informal *entente* held so much meaning in Paris; they could not believe that the French government of Napoleon III was capable of restricting its expansionist role anywhere in the world for the sake of preserving the brittle alliance forged during the Crimean War.

Hence, British worries over the future of Chusan, which had been assigned as a staging base for the joint expedition of 1860. Obviously any question of a permanent occupation could not be raised until the anticipated war was over, and Admirals Charner and Hope had both been instructed by their respective superiors to guard themselves in utterance, and extend themselves in tact. The greatest circumspection was necessary, wrote the French Minister of Marine to Admiral Charner in November 1859. 'You will easily understand how important it is to avoid with care any *démarche* likely to awaken [British] susceptibilities, before the Imperial Government, enlightened by your reports, has come to a definite decision on that important question.'[57]

The testing time came on 20 April when an advance detachment, combining French and British sail and steam, left the mouth of the Yangtse, and on the following day landed on Chusan Island without opposition. The colours of both nations were hoisted over the hilltop fort that had been so troublesome in 1842. Judging by outward appearances, the

[57] Quoted, Cady, pp. 235–6.

town fortifications were in the same state as at the time of the British withdrawal. Walls were clearly in disrepair, batteries had remained dismantled, and, while the Chinese commander laid claim to seven battalions of infantry, these appeared to exist only on paper.[58]

On the evening of the 21st, a merry party of French and British officers was held on board the headquarters ship, S.S. *Granada*. Friendly and uninhibited conversations 'over the cups' served to dissipate any fears that, perchance through a slip of the tongue, a crisis might be provoked. Whether it was the wine or 'the undulating beauty of the island under the stars', the guests were happily captive, and the *entente* suffered no strain.[59] But in Hong Kong and Shanghai, British officials continued to talk nostalgically about Chusan, and to stress its unique value. Well aware of the risks of rousing French sensitivities, nevertheless they found it difficult to refrain from pressing its advantages as a refreshment and coaling base. As a port for the new ocean steamers, observed D. B. Robertson, the British Consul at Shanghai, Chusan might become a second Malta.[60]

The naval meterologists had prophesied fair winds and a rapid passage to the Gulf of Pecheli, but dependence on the favour of the south-west monsoon proved unjustified. The passage took between twenty and thirty days instead of the expected ten or twelve. Half-way through the Formosa Channel, a gale from the north-east set in, and for several days transports were tossed between the Island and the mainland without sight of sun. At the end of a week, most of the vessels found themselves fifty miles nearer Hong Kong than when the storm began. 'The China Sea is always a nasty, capricious sea', Lieutenant Allgood, aboard the *Alfred*, wrote to his mother, when describing the painful progress of the fleet, 'and has not

---

[58] See Report on the capture of Chusan, in Hope to Paget, 28 Apr. 1860 (No. 150), Adm. 1/5735; also, Knollys and Grant, *Incidents in the China War of 1860*, pp. 10–11; and J. H. Dunne, *From Calcutta to Pekin: being notes taken from the Journal of an officer between those places* (London, 1861), p. 38.

[59] See Wolseley, p. 31; also, Swinhoe, pp. 6–7.

[60] Memoranda on the expediency of acquiring Chusan, 23 Jan. and 9 Feb. 1860, F.O. 17/343. Robertson had persistently advocated the annexation of Chusan, arguing in 1856 that a second island was necessary for the protection of European traders and missionaries on the mainland, and to neutralize Russian designs.

improved its reputation on this occasion. The wind hardly ever blows for more than a few hours at a time from the same direction, hence our course had been a very zigzag one.'[61]

Not until late June did the bulk of the British fleet assemble in Talien Bay, off the northern promontory at the entrance to the Gulf of Pecheli. Opening to the south-east, about ten miles in width, it offered a safe anchorage to the transports and their consorts from the Royal Navy.[62] Earlier in the year, despite almost constant bad weather, Admiral Hope's surveying teams had worked ceaselessly to find the ideal staging rendezvous. As a consequence of their efforts, the expedition possessed not only a good chart of Talien Bay, but also of the area within the Gulf where it was proposed the landings should take place.[63] Talien Bay may have provided the perfect harbour, but the promontory which gave it shelter was scarcely an enticing refreshment base for weary soldiers and sailors. The coast rises well above the sea in rocky precipitous hills as high as a thousand feet, to merge with rolling plains which at the time were dotted with cattle. Although surprised and sometimes frightened as hordes of redcoats emerged from transports and men-of-war, the Tartar inhabitants soon became friendly, and the various camps set up on shore were soon assured of abundant food supply—bullocks, sheep, poultry and eggs, as well as fish and fruit.[64] The only serious commissariat problem was water supply, and large parties, sent out daily to enlarge old wells and dig new, barely met the needs of 11,000 men. The story that inevitably went the rounds was founded on the characteristically rough logic of the service man: 'Admiral Hope knew deuced well there was no water here, and for that reason fixed on it as our rendezvous, knowing that we must commence operations without delay or die of thirst.'[65]

[61] Yellow Sea, 12 June 1860, letter XIV, in Major-General G. Allgood, *The China War, 1860: Letters and Journal* (London, 1901), pp. 30–1.

[62] This magnificent harbour includes four smaller bays, which subsequently, along with Port Arthur, became part of the Russian leasehold in China.

[63] See Hope to Admiralty, 27 Aug. 1860, Bonner-Smith, pp. 401–2.

[64] Vetch (ed.), *Graham, Life, Letters and Diaries*, p. 148.

[65] Allgood, *Letters and Journal*, letter XV, addressed to General Eyre, 20 June 1860, p. 32; see also, Swinhoe, pp. 14–20, *passim*. On the difficulties of provisioning the expedition, see Hope to Paget, 12 July 1860 (No. 244), Adm. 1/5735.

Lord Elgin, who had left Shanghai on 5 July, arrived after a fast voyage of only four days, 'the breath of Mars issuing from his nostils, much to the delight of the whole army'.[66] But Elgin's heavy breathing resulted more from impatience and irritation with the French than from any bellicose zeal to meet the Chinese. Some of the French contingent had arrived at the end of June, and had found good shelter across the strait, south of Talien, at Chefoo. But their commander refused to consider making a start until cavalry horses and baggage animals were on hand. A thoroughly roused Elgin threatened to act alone unless his ally speeded up his preparations. Happily, Sir Hope Grant on a visit to the French camp at Chefoo was able to sort things out with General de Montauban, and the plan of an exclusive British landing was dropped. It was finally agreed that the first assault should be made close by the river mouth at Pehtang, hardly more than eight miles overland to the mouth of the Peiho, whose muddy waters had claimed so many victims only a year ago.

Not until 20 July did the combined fleets of steam and sail, amounting to more than 200 vessels, including transports, set sail. Moving in parallel lines through smooth waters, this huge armada—far larger than the combined armanents of the previous two expeditions—offered 'a splendid sight, sufficiently terrifying', it was hoped, to bend the minds of obstinate 'Celestials'. On board S.S. *Imperatice* was Mr. Wirgman, artist for the *Illustrated London News*, who was expected to immortalize in colour the power and the glory. On 30 July the fleet anchored within eight to ten miles of Pehtang. Survivors of last year's campaign found little change of scenery. As far as the eye could see, the coastline remained monotonously unbroken, apart from a few flecks in the dim distance, which were thought to be the formidable Taku forts. It had been intended, on the following day, to move within range of two impressive-looking forts less than three miles from the entrance to the Pehtang River. But drizzling rain and troubled seas delayed the attempt for two days, by which time it was discovered that the larger vessels could scarcely edge their way over a bar which allowed thirteen feet at high water, but only three at low tide. Consequently, the assault had to be made

[66] Swinhoe, p. 33.

entirely by small craft, towed as close to the beach as possible by gunboats.

The morning of 1 August dawned darkly. The sea was calm, but torrents of rain poured ceaselessly, accompanied by occasional puffs of wind. At 9.00 a.m. the boats pulled off to the various transports, and by noon each was loaded with troops. The *Coromandel*, with General Grant and Admiral Hope on board, led the way, followed by the gunboats,[67] their decks crowded with redjackets, and each towing six launches jammed to the gunwales with men and gear. The French flotilla was close behind, their gunboats towing an even larger number of small craft, including some small Chinese junks. Whatever weaknesses in discipline were later to be exposed, the French troops set a notable example in *dressage*. Theirs was a regatta performance, conducted with all the precision and elegance of the Guards on a gloomy, drizzly day that smothered any prospect of glory. 'There were all the French officers in full dress', wrote a British soldier, who was much impressed by the ceremonial deportment, 'looking very smart, guns, Shanghai ponies, mules with pack-saddles on, etc.—everthing complete. I doubt if our arrangements are so good.'[68]

Four of five shells were fired at the forts, which proved to be constructed of mud and straw, but there was no reply. The landing was unopposed, but the gallant attackers were not to survive 'with their boots clean'. Shortly after 3.00 p.m. a vanguard of 400 men, about half of them French, made their way on foot towards the shore to reconnoitre a position so suspiciously quiet. It was nearly high water, but the advantage was negligible. For nearly half a mile, they floundered across a flat of oozing glue, never less than ankle deep, before reaching relatively hard ground. After wading across a moat that served as the town's sewer, the bedraggled troops, wet, filthy, and exhausted, sought dry quarters and rest, almost unobtainable except for the few officers who sought dry quarters in a decayed temple. An hour or so later, however, observant scouts discovered Pehtang's only communication with the

[67] *Leven, Janus, Clown, Woodcock, Drake, Watchful, Havoc, Forester, Opossum, Firm, Staunch, Banterer, Bustard, Flamer, Bouncer,* and *Snap.*
[68] Vetch (ed.), *Graham, Life, Letters and Diaries*, pp. 152–3.

outside world by land, and before midnight the main body of around 4,000 were stretched out on the causeway, fifteen feet broad that stretched across a salty swamp in the direction of Taku.[69]

Northern Chinese coastal towns were generally repulsive, and Pehtang was no exception. The dwellings, like the forts, were built of mud and chopped straw, the walls resting on layers of sorghum stalks spread over the foundations as damp courses against the persistent salt solutions. Because of the saline quality of the soil few trees and only occasional tufts of grass brightened either town or surrounding countryside. Yet more than 6,000 French and British troops, along with 4,000 horses, mules, and ponies, were compelled to stow themselves within this exceedingly unattractive area. The circumference of the camp settlement was little more than a mile. Even veterans attuned by experience to the horrors of war found the situation beyond description. 'The banks of the river', wrote Major Graham on 7 August, 'are one mass of filth and offal, behind which are mud cottages and narrow streets . . . crowded with a struggling mass of soldiers, coolies, guns, horses, kicking mules, stores of all descriptions, etc. etc., forming a babel of confusion, which, with the accompanying smells, far surpasses all I remember of Balaklava.'[70] However, shortly after this letter had been written, conditions were considerably eased when most of the inhabitants suddenly decided to evacuate their domiciles, departing in carts or boats with such goods as had been left them by the pillaging soldiery and coolies.[71]

By 12 August the allies prepared to move south-west overland with the object of outflanking the Taku forts. A frontal approach from the river, which had brought disaster the year before, seems to have been anticipated by the Chinese as part of decent military etiquette. Odd as it may appear, the Chinese continued to consider this kind of flanking movement as 'unethical' and contrary to the rules of 'civilized' warfare.

[69] See Lane-Poole, pp. 349–55; Swinhoe, pp. 46–56; Stephenson, *At Home and on the Battlefield*, p. 263.

[70] *Graham, Life, Letters and Diaries*, p. 156. See also, Sir Hope Grant to Herbert, 4 Aug. 1860, Stanmore, *Sidney Herbert*, ii. 330–1.

[71] See Knollys and Grant, op. cit., p. 57; Wells Williams, *The Middle Kingdom*, p. 673; Allgood, p. 73; Rennie, pp. 70–85.

Certainly, no serious effort had been made to obstruct or halt an invasion from the north-east. The causeway which extended for about three miles across the impassable terrain could easily have been blocked by three of four fixed guns had the enemy chosen to defend it. Even had the Chinese been able to anticipate such an overland operation, they might well have assumed that parleys leading to negotiation would bring a halt, or at least stall active hostilities.[72] Far too late in the day, a stand was made near Sinho.[73] There, the Mongol horsemen made a series of dashing attacks, but were put to flight by equally fearless Sikh cavalry supported by the new Armstrong guns.[74] The allied infantry moved slowly and cautiously, allowing plenty of time for the engineers to prepare pontoon trestles to bridge the wandering canals and waterways that intersected the country like a Chinese puzzle. Tang-ku village was occupied on the 14th; by the early morning of the 21st, the troops had crossed the Peiho near Taku village, and were shortly in position to bring their artillery to bear on the main North fort. Meanwhile, the gunboats, under the command of Rear-Admiral Lewis Tobias Jones, had moved into the Peiho with orders to distract the defenders, and, in particular, to muzzle the upper forts. Larger vessels, chiefly sloops of sufficiently light draught to keep position in high water, were kept in reserve to dampen any flanking fire from the main South fort should it prove embarrassing to the assault troops.

The bombardment of the main North fort began at daylight—a 'beautiful practice' that was carried out with 'Armstrong' precision.[75] Two hours later, the magazines exploded, demolishing the central structure of the fort; but not until

[72] See correspondence between Elgin and the Governor-General of Chihli, 10 Aug. 1860 (No. 270), Adm. 1/5735.

[73] See map of country around Pehtang and the Taku forts, Lane-Poole, opposite p. 348.

[74] It had been prophesied that the gun would be too delicate for rough campaign work and since it was untried, each piece had been accompanied by one of the old smooth-bore types, to be substituted in case of necessity. On 18 August Hope Grant reported that the Armstrong guns were a tremendous success. 'I never saw anything more beautiful than the precision of their fire at long ranges, and if the fuzes had only been good, the destruction of the enemy would have been greater.' To the Minister of War, Stanmore, *Sidney Herbert*, ii. 310; also ibid., pp. 335–6, 342, 355. Cf. Rennie, p. 103.

[75] See Vetch (ed.), *Graham, Life, Letters and Diaries*, pp. 167–9.

11.00 a.m. did the surviving occupants capitulate, and not until the evening sun had begun to set did the flags of truce appear on the upper North fort. British losses amounted to 17 killed and 183 wounded; French dead and wounded were around 130; Chinese casualties were later estimated to be at least 2,000. By noon of the following day, following the submission of the South forts, gunboat crews had removed the chained booms across the river, and, with much greater difficulty, pulled up two double rows of iron stakes that barred the passage to Tang-ku and Tientsin beyond.[76] In the official language of the conqueror: 'The tarnished honour of our arms was gloriously vindicated.'[77]

A search of the partly shattered defences provided few souvenirs. Three or four of the desirable brass cannon and two or three guns taken from British vessels, sunk during the June battle of the previous year, were recovered, but little else of any value or interest. But there was some comfort for the allied commanders, when they examined the construction of the walls, casemates, and external entrenchments, in the realization that the fortifications were wellnigh impregnable to frontal attack. Whether or not European, possibly Russian, advice had been available, the quality of engineering was distinguished. Unfortunately for the defenders, the Chinese commander-in-chief seems to have taken for granted that the futile assault of 1859 would be repeated. As a peculiarly maritime race, Britons, it may have been assumed, could handle guns efficiently only on shipboard. The bulk of the fortress guns faced the river.

On 23 August an advance detachment of French and British gunboats left for Tientsin—the *Havoc*, *Staunch*, *Opossum*, *Forester*, and *Algerine*. For vessels drawing up to ten or eleven

---

[76] See Hope to Admiralty, *Coromandel*, in the Peiho, 27 Aug. 1860 (No. 287), 'An Account of the Capture of the Taku forts on 21 August', Adm. 1/5735; also contained in Bonner-Smith, pp. 400–2. See also, Grant to Herbert, 23 Aug. 1860, Stanmore, *Sidney Herbert*, ii. 332–8. Notes on the part played by the marines is contained in Hope to Admiralty, 27 Aug. 1860 (No. 288), Adm. 1/5735. A bound folder entitled 'China, Combined (French & British) Operations leading up to the taking of the Peiho Forts' consists of Foreign Office correspondence with the Admiralty between January and December 1860, Adm. 1/5745.

[77] Quoted, Wells Williams, *Middle Kingdom*, p. 676. On Hope's dispatch (No. 287) above, the Admiralty minuted that no observations, apart from praise, could be offered at the moment.

feet, the twisting Peiho was safe as far as Tientsin, but when tidal aid ceased close to the city, boats of only very light draught could proceed further, and then for less than a dozen miles. Seamen who had served in the course of the 1858 expedition had not forgotten the tortuous angles, in many places so acute that the average-length steamer had to be pulled around by ropes. Sometimes the river would retreat, and a helmsman on one gunboat, looking backward to find his consort, occasionally to his astonishment saw her travelling in a diametrically opposite direction, although both were bound for the same destination. Obviously, then, it was sensible for most of the army to proceed on foot. The road from Taku followed the Peiho nearly all the way, but, by cutting off the incredible sinuosities, reduced the distance by half.

The river approach to Tientsin was covered by two small forts, one on each bank, about two miles below the city. Crenellated mud walls, approximately fifteen miles in length, encircled the city, broken in two parts by the course of the river. Nevertheless, had the walls been defended by the usual scores of gingalls, the allied vanguard might have experienced considerable annoyance, when it arrived on the morning of the 24th.[78]

Anxious to demonstrate their unconditional submission, the town fathers received the two Admirals, Charner and Hope, with the same amicable courtesy that had been shown the foreign visitors two years earlier. On the 25th the two plenipotentiaries, Elgin and Gros, arrived, and were welcomed shortly after by the Emperor's three Imperial Commissioners, one of whom was the venerable Kweiliang, chief negotiator of the Treaty of Tientsin. For the moment, conciliation was in the air, not to mention profit. Once recovered from initial fright and shyness, the inhabitants needed little exhortation to supply the new comers with sheep, oxen, apples, pears, grapes, and peaches, and, the greatest luxury of all, blocks of ice.[79] It was evident that the Chinese delegates wished to avoid further armed collision in the hope that they might retain at the

[78] It is possible, of course, that the powerful Armstrong guns had revealed the weakness of orthodox fortifications, intended, as these presumably were, to withstand assaults by enemy ships.

[79] Knollys and Grant, p. 94.

council table what might well be lost on the battlefield. Above all, they were anxious to establish some kind of settlement that would remove any danger of an allied advance on Peking.

By this time, however, Elgin's mood had hardened. The Bruce ultimatum of the previous March had been ignored; its terms must now be accepted, along with the demand for an additional £4m. indemnity. On 2 September the Imperial Commissioners agreed to all the claims, but when asked to sign the relevant convention, they raised doubts as to the manner of paying the indemnity, and asked for time to consult the authorities in Peking. Disgusted with what appeared to him to be deliberate trifling, Elgin terminated the palaver, and on 8 September (in company with the French) ordered preparations to be made for a march in the direction of Tung-chow, some twelve miles from the capital. It was hoped that such a challenge would bring an end to the shilly-shallying that had marked this and previous efforts at negotiation. Admiral Hope had already made arrangements for such an advance. The heavier guns making up the siege train were floated on pontoons, dragged by sailors or Chinese boatmen. Stores were carried in light-draught junks, accompanied along the banks by squads of infantry to fend off enemy raiders. Such protection, as it turned out, proved to be unnecessary, and was discontinued. No one knew how far above Tientsin the Peiho might be safely navigable; consequently Hope planned to keep on moving until his flotilla grounded, and at that point set up storage depots and a field hospital.[80]

The slow march to Peking and the diplomacy leading to the exchange of final ratifications has been described many times by Chinese, British, American, and French historians and journalists. Although an eventful progress, it provides little more than an epilogue to 'the naval side' of the Anglo–Chinese wars. While captains and lieutenants performed as traffic managers and baggage masters at Tientsin and Taku, further flurries of diplomatic notes led on 11 September to an arrangement whereby the advancing army should halt some eight miles short of Tung-chow. With no thought of treachery, an

---

[80] See report on the Peiho expedition, in Hope to Admiralty, 12 Sept. 1860 (No. 304), and Proceedings at the Peiho in, same to same, 20 Sept. (No. 309) and 12 Oct. (No. 326) 1860, Adm. 1/5735. See also, Wolseley, pp. 168–9.

allied mission with a small escort went ahead to discuss arrangements for further palaver. Of these, thirty-nine (of whom twenty-six were British) were ambushed and held as hostages, including Harry Parkes, the former Consul at Canton, who was acting as interpreter on Elgin's staff. He was one of the few to survive malnutrition and torture in the dungeons of Peking. This totally unexpected breach of faith naturally precipitated a battle, in which, once again, superior fire power and discipline triumphed. Badly beaten on the 18th, and again on the 21st of September close to the walls of Peking, the humiliated commander-in-chief, General Sêng-ko-lin-ch'in, withdrew from the city with the remnants of his dispirited army.

Slowing their advance in the hope that negotiations might secure the recovery of the captives, the allied force did not reach the city walls until 5 October. The main British approach was from the north; the French closed on the outskirts of the Summer Palace, whose priceless treasures they were soon to share out as plunder of war. Three days later, the surviving ill and bedraggled hostages were returned; thirteen British and seven Frenchmen had been either murdered, or died of ill-treatment. Not until the 13th, under threat of bombardment, was the majestic Anting Gate in British hands, and Peking for all intents and purposes, under allied control.[81] On 18 October the Summer Palace, already thoroughly looted,[82] was burned to the ground in expiation of the death of French and British prisoners. The tragic decision was taken by Elgin

[81] See letters of Hope Grant to Herbert, 9, 13, and 17 Oct. 1860, Stanmore, *Sidney Herbert*, ii. 343–8.

[82] Captain J. H. Dunne of the 99th Regiment (Wiltshire), who was present during the final stage of the plundering raid, later acknowledged with some shame that he had succumbed to mob hysteria. By way of extenuation, however, it had to be admitted that palaces were not open for looting every day. 'Imagine', he wrote, 'Christie's, Hunt and Roskell's, Howell and James's, half a dozen watch and clockmakers, two or three upholsterers, and that fine fan-shop in Regent Street, all being under the same roof; and then imagine, if you can, what would be your sensation when told that, without breaking the eighth commandment, you might have your run of the place for just ten minutes, and no more.' Dunne, *From Calcutta to Peking* . . ., p. 131.

Officers and men, wrote Garnet Wolseley, 'seem to have been seized with a temporary insanity; in body and soul they were absorbed in one pursuit, which was plunder, plunder.' Wolseley, p. 227. Soldiers of all nations tended to become looters following hard-won victories, but both Woleseley and Hope Grant were shocked by the excesses of the normally well-disciplined French troops.

against the advice of Baron Gros and General de Montauban, both of whom apparently feared that Britain wished to over- throw the Manchu dynasty, and that such drastic action would lead to anarchy.[83] Palmerston thought it 'absolutely necessary to stamp by some such permanent record our indignation at the treachery and brutality of these Tartars, for Chinese they are not'.[84] But the majority in the Cabinet, as well as service officers, while comprehending the black anger that led to an act of punitive destruction, were subsequently to lament the 'ruthless effacement' of the Summer capital, representing the splendour of an aged civilization.

One week after the holocaust, following the agreement to compensate the living victims and the relatives of the dead, two official ceremonies marked the signing of two separate conventions, British and French, and the exchange of ratifica- tions.[85] The double performance marked the end of an already thread-bare *entente*, and the conclusion of one of the best organized, shortest, most successful, and least glorious cam- paigns ever waged by French and British armies.

During the last days of the war, the Royal Navy had surren- dered its customary role as the predominant partner; none the less it had played a vital part in maintaining the long line of communications that stretched from Tientsin to the Gulf of Pecheli, and south to Chusan and Hong Kong. Food, extra clothing, and matériel for the sappers as well as heavy guns and ammunition for the breaching of Peking's walls were dis- patched will all speed from ship to river junk to land haulage teams. Admiral Hope, wrote General Hope Grant, was 'worth his weight in gold'. But only the army could reach Peking, and had the Chinese found the necessary troops to cut the Peiho river line below, or even at, Tientsin, the British advance to the capital might well have been placed in jeopardy. Such a des-

---

[83] One cannot help looking back a little ruefully to December 1857, when Elgin, from the deck of a gunboat, recorded his shame that the allied squadron was about to bombard Canton. He was sad at the thought of earning for himself 'a place in the litany, immediately after plague, pestilence and famine'. P. 337.

[84] To Herbert, 20 Dec. 1860, Stanmore, *Sidney Herbert*, ii. 350.

[85] The drama of the first ceremony (24 October) was somewhat marred by Elgin's rather inept effort to immortalize the scene by means of 'l'indiscret instrument du Photographe anglais'. At least, this was the opinion of a French observer, Paul Varin, in his *Expédition de Chine* (Paris, 1862), pp. 271-9.

perate relief operation was not attempted, and probably never considered.

Elgin was not anxious to see the allied forces withdrawn until all the provinces of the Empire had been informed of the peace settlement and, perhaps more significantly, until Bruce had asserted 'right of access' by personal appearance in Peking.[86] But the temperature had already dipped to a shivering 8°C., and both he and Gros were concerned lest the coming of winter weather should lead to snow-bound roads and a forced hibernation in the vicinity of Peking. According to Count Nikolai Ignatieff, the prospective Russian ambassador, who played an unfailing role as counsellor to both the Chinese and the allies, the Peiho would soon be frozen, and he warned Grant of the inconvenience of being immured in Peking until the spring. The British General needed no such warning. He wanted to be off the moment the treaty was signed, and positively declared he would not stay a day after 7 November, for fear a freeze-up would threaten the tidy embarkation of the army. He made his decision without consulting Admiral Hope, who would have risked waiting until December. But Grant's reasoning seems to have been convincing; on 9 November the entire British force, including diplomats and other civilians, left Peking. By 28 November, the Peiho was frozen solid, and departing staff officers in Tientsin faced blizzards as they rode thirty-five miles or more to the estuary, where they boarded ship. On 29 November the last of the fleet nudged its way through the ice-flows to begin the long journey south. A joint force of some 5,000 men, including three batteries of artillery, remained in Tientsin, and, by agreement with the Chinese, smaller garrisons were dropped off at Taku and north Shantung, as token guarantees of full indemnity payments.[87]

Lord Elgin was content that the long, frustrating, and bloody efforts to secure acceptance of the Treaty of Tientsin had at last succeeded, and he was warmed by the news that,

[86] While preparations were being made for his permanent residence in the capital, Bruce wintered in Tientsin.

[87] See Hope to Admiralty, Tientsin, 29 Oct. (No. 349), 4 Nov. (No. 354), and 12 Nov. (No. 361) 1860, Adm. 1/5735. See also, same to same, 3 Dec. 1860 (No. 372), ibid.

even while the fighting was going on, the Yangtse had been partially opened as a trading thoroughfare. General Hope Grant was happy that casualties had been so few; the rate of mortality had been lower than was usually expected of troops in tropical climates even in peacetime. Some lessons had evidently been learned from the Crimean War. The whole force, Grant told the Minister for War, had remained in excellent health, despite the intolerably hot weather. Scarcely one per cent of the troops went sick, and the all-important horses had survived in equally good fettle.[88]

And the British government was pleased, pleased that the Manchu Court had been preserved, and yet humbled, and that a permanent diplomatic mission in Peking could now watch over and safeguard the privileges won at such cost during the previous twenty years. By demonstrating, as the navy had done, the maritime power of England, Lord John Russell informed the Admiralty, the rulers and people of China were bound to be impressed 'with the conviction that their best policy is faithfully to fulfil their Treaty engagements, and to maintain friendly relations with a Power which has at its disposal such ample means for obtaining, in case of need, redress for injuries done to its subjects'.[89]

As it happened, Lord Elgin had achieved what he had set out to do, and Lord Russell's daring speculation turned out to be true prophesy. The long-sought Treaty, ratified in the Imperial capital itself, wrought no fundamental change of heart among the defeated, but it did produce between Britain and China an effective peace that lasted unbroken for forty years.

[88] To Herbert, Sinhoe, 18 Aug. 1860, Stanmore, *Sidney Herbert*, ii. 335.

Dr. D. F. Rennie, who was specially concerned with army hygiene, was not inclined to endorse the General's view that the expedition had been 'a remarkable sanitary success'. Although most of the troops had been well-seasoned in India, and the various companies weeded of the sick and weakly before the campaign got under way, none the less he maintained that the amount of illness and invaliding had been considerable. Malaria and 'ague' seem to have been the chief enemies. 'Sanitary science', in his opinion, 'proved totally unequal to coping with an epidemic constitution of the atmosphere which was not confined to Tient-sin, but was equally active at Peking, and which it is not unreasonable to suppose was in some way connected with the large comet that made its appearance in July, the more so as it was shortly after its advent that the serious sickness commenced.' Rennie, *The British Arms in North China* . . ., pp. vi–vii, 266.

[89] Russell to Admiralty, 10 Nov. 1860, Adm. 1/5745.

EPILOGUE

WHEN writing history with the object of making a book, one is always looking for a thread—and, if it concerns the activities of government, a policy—which will help to tie the narrative together. Long ago, it was clear to me that there never was such a thing as a *colonial* policy, and, as the years went by, it became increasingly evident that conscious thought played a very small part in moulding the British Empire. Certainly, during the course of operations in and about the China seas between 1830 and 1860, meeting the needs of the day seems to have been the first principle of British conduct; or, in view of the darkness which, in the eyes of the intruder, obscured so much of Chinese thought and action, meeting the needs of the night might be more appropriate.

The British gradually strengthened their foothold on the China coast in order to safeguard trade and promote it. The demand for equal treatment, commercial and diplomatic, was essential to these ends. Apart from this purpose, there were no general tenets governing British action, other than the purely negative resolve not to be drawn on to the mainland. Above all else, Britain must never risk the consequences that would follow the acquisition of a second India, in 'a fit of absence of mind'. Hence, it was quite natural that British policy decisions in regard to virtually unknown and uncharted areas should have been little more than reactions to specific incidents or issues.

As for the clearly defined positive element—the maintenance and expansion of trade—this, as circumstances revealed, remained a baffling pursuit for the men on the spot as well as for ministers in Whitehall. Should the trade be conducted through Macao, as in the past, with a seasonal entrepôt in operation at Canton, or, should there be a permanent base, say an island close to the mainland, like Chusan or Hong Kong, or, should there be a series of free ports open on equal terms to Britain's rivals?

Essentially, the choice was a matter for the Foreign Office, and the implementation of its decisions, where force seemed to be required, was the concern of the Royal Navy. The navy acted as the cutting edge of British diplomacy; and in the China seas its influence on events lay in the execution of policies, including plans of wartime strategy, which were formulated in London. Unfortunately, for many years, performance was blunted by the Ch'ing officials' unawareness of the consequences that resulted from enemy superiority at sea. British naval predominance in Chinese waters was, of course, admitted by Britain's competitors, France and the United States, who, for want of convenient bases, were hardly in a better position than Russia to challenge British hegemony. But not so the Chinese Imperial Court, which, despite the lessons provided during the war years 1839–42, was exceedingly slow to recognize the implications of 'command of the sea'.

The portentous fact of Chinese naval action between 1839–42 and 1857–60 was the decrepit state of their ships, weapons, and above all, training. Courage was a virtue rarely absent among captains and crews, but anything like a professional maritime spirit was missing. There was no Imperial navy, no national Board of Admiralty—only flotillas of local junks assembled at critical moments by provincial viceroys. Ill-armed and ill-organized, these awkward vessels were quite incapable of withstanding the shattering power of modern European warships. To commentators of the early nineteenth century, it was puzzling that a nation with an historic record of pioneering adventure in distant waters should have abandoned naval activity, and for more than two centuries have confined itself almost entirely to trading voyages in home waters. At the beginning of the fifteenth century, under the Ming dynasty, China was probably the strongest sea power in the world; her ships dominated south Asian waters.[1] Yet, by the beginning of the sixteenth century, with the arrival of the first Portuguese warships, a vigorous and inventive people, who had used the cross-staff and magnetic compass long before these were familiar objects in Europe, had lost interest in the sea.[2]

[1] See Ma Huan, Ying-yai Sheng-la, *The Overall Survey of the Ocean's Shores* [1433], trans. and ed. by J. V. G. Mills (Cambridge, for the Hakluyt Society, 1970), pp. 1–3, 8–34.

[2] K. M. Panikkar has suggested that in cutting Chinese trade connections, Portugal

By contrast with Chinese technical and administrative inep-
titude, all three British campaigns were superb examples of
navigational skill in difficult and largely unknown waters.
Whether to Canton, Chusan, up the Yangtse to Nanking, or
by the winding Peiho to Tientsin, the navy towed or carried
the troops, supported them with gun-fire, defended them
from counter-attack, and supplied them after they had landed.
Expeditious withdrawals were successfully accomplished,
such as the rescue of the garrison at Ningpo in 1841, and at
Peking in the autumn of 1860, when approaching winter
threatened to lock men, horses, and ships behind advancing ice
in the estuary.

The light-draught gunboats which led the way into the
interior held a position in the Royal Navy not unlike that of the
Irregular Service in the Indian army, giving young officers
opportunities of commanding, and frequently of acting on
their own responsibility.[3] These were the times when promotion was excessively slow, and when youth was in fact a
positive disqualification for advancement. The old guard, in
the interest of their own highly competitive order, were
assiduous in defending their monopoly against the challenging
tide of 'new blood'. To this generation, Nelson would have
been considered far too young for higher command. However, distant seas, like that of China, offering little in the way
of prize money (so long as piracy was not made the object of a
crusade) gave the young officer the chance to demonstrate his
capacity for independent action. The constant use of small
ships and boats offered one means of sorting out the best talent
from the over-crowded, stagnating wardrooms and gun-
rooms of the Victorian navy. River warfare uncovered for

---

inaugurated 'an effective blockade, which lasted to the middle of the nineteenth
century'. K. M. Panikkar, *Asia and Western Dominance* (London, 1953), pp. 13–14.
Admittedly, when the Portuguese first arrived in Malacca, they did encounter numbers of Chinese warships, but the rot had already set in before da Gama rounded the
Cape in 1498. In Sir George Sansom's opinion, the cessation of overseas activity
cannot be put down entirely to naval weakness. 'In view of the previous achievements
of the Chinese in the conduct of great land and sea expeditions, it cannot be supposed
that they lacked the capacity for such undertakings. One can only conclude that their
political constitution and their social order did not, in the period following the
Mongol conquest, afford the stimulus which sustained the contemporary European
effort to expand.' Sansom, *The Western World and Japan*, p. 46.
[3] See Wolseley, *Narrative of the War with China in 1860*, pp. 322–3.

future preferment, youngsters of initiative who might otherwise have remained midshipmen or lieutenants until retirement or death.[4]

The main peril in the South China Sea was not the national
enemy, whether Chinese, or during the Crimean War, Russian,
but the unknown reef, the constantly shifting mud and sand
banks, and the seasonal typhoons. Until 1842, when the
navy undertook careful surveys on the main sea and river
routes, these waters were virtually *Mare Incognita*. Of course, a
considerable body of knowledge had been assembled by trading captains, but only too often an unreliable chart proved far
more dangerous than no chart. Moreover, navigation of the
rivers, especially the route to Canton, was the more haphazard
owing to the silting up of old channels, and the formation of
new. Lack of pilots was another grave handicap, which
affected in particular the progress of the fleet to Nanking in
1842. But the shortage of skilled interpreters was, if anything,
even more troublesome. In the course of the advance on
Canton in 1841, not a single person in the leading squadron
detachment understood a word of the native language.[5] During the 1858–9 campaigns, the expeditions were dependent
throughout on no more than two persons who could speak the
appropriate Chinese dialect.[6]

But war played a relatively minor part in the lives of seamen
or civilians on the Chinese coast, and especially for the crews
on the station ships in the Treaty ports. Existence on a lonely
brig or in the semi-isolated consular dwelling could be just as
dreary, if physically more tolerable, than life in a baking,
sand-blown port in the Persian Gulf. Morale was bound to
suffer in consequence. The so-called Pellew mutiny serves to
illustrate the effects of the climate on men confined to shipboard over many months. Among officers, drunkenness was
widespread and as debilitating as dysentry or fever. Admiral

[4] During the fateful attack on the Taku forts in 1859, it was mainly the youngsters in
command of small craft who rescued the survivors from sinking vessels and treacherous mud banks.   [5] *Nemesis*, p. 151.

[6] In 1849, Palmerston was sufficiently concerned about the woeful situation to
instruct Governor Bonham that no young man was to be appointed to the Superin-
tendency or the Consulates who had not some knowledge of the Chinese language.
Those already in possession of posts should be told that want of a competent
knowledge of both language and country would be a bar to promotion. 4 June 1849
(No. 42, in rough draft), Broadlands MSS., BD/CH/23–33.

Cochrane mourned their lack of competence as seamen; they were, he once remarked, 'more of gentlemen and less of sailors'.[7] Obviously, in peacetime, the shore held greater inducements than the ship; self-discipline waned in consequence of endemic boredom. Moreover, because of the difficulty of collecting a court, it was next to impossible to bring officers to trial for flagrant misdeeds. *Ad hoc* courts martial on the spot might have had a useful astringent effect, but during the 1840s and 1850s such correctives were lacking.

It is important to keep in mind, however, that we are dealing, during the greater part of the period (1830–60), with a very small segment of the Royal Navy. Even after the establishment of a permanent China squadron in 1844, for many years scarcely more than half a dozen ships were on hand to threaten pirates or uphold treaty rights. Moreover, lack of a dockyard in a typhoon area inevitably affected ships' efficiency, although Hong Kong was eventually provided with a substantial stores depot, which meant less reliance on Tricomalee. As for the operational competence of ships' companies, gunnery continued to improve, particularly, as Admiral Cochrane modestly confessed, during his time of command after 1844. But despite frequent exercises, signalling remained a source of weakness, especially evident in joint manoeuvres.

In view of the vast distance that separated Whitehall from Macao or Hong Kong, it might easily be assumed that the commander-in-chief was in a position to exercise an almost unique independence; that whatever the occasion, he would have complete latitude in the manner and timing of his movements. As has been noticed previously, in the early 1840s four to six months might elapse before orders from London reached the China coast. Consequently, the weight of decision seemed bound to rest on the commander who was on the spot. Yet, unless safely at sea, the Admiral in charge of the China squadron was rarely monarch of all he surveyed beyond the quarterdeck. Rivalry between the civilian administrator and the naval chief was a constant factor in a chronically unsettled and sometimes tense existence, in which loss of sleep, contributing to bad health, played no small part in exciting a war

[7] Cochrane to Admiralty, *Agincourt*, 17 June 1847 (No. 82), Adm. 1/5575.

of nerves. In general, the civilian, whether superintendent of trade, governor, or sometimes even consul, held the upper hand. Her Majesty's representatives in China enjoyed, if they had the will, an almost unrestricted freedom of intervention in peacetime. The decision of Rutherford Alcock, Consul at Shanghai, to secure redress for local village attacks on British subjects is one well-known example. In 1848 he ordered the only available British warship, a ten-ton brig, to blockade more than a thousand grain junks which were preparing to sail for Peking; and because he was successful, not only the Governor of Hong Kong, but the commander-in-chief had to approve.[8]

In such instances, involving relations with the Ch'ing authorities, civilian judgement was clearly crucial. On the other hand, capricious local interventions could affect not only the movements of a ship, but a substantial detachment, even the whole squadron. In the circumstances, relations between the commander-in-chief and the government in Hong Kong remained chronically delicate; and the more prickly the governor or superintendent, the more likely it was that political considerations would dominate his thinking. Admiral Cochrane complained bitterly to the Admiralty, as had the long-suffering Admiral Parker before him, of Sir Henry Pottinger's clumsy efforts to interfere with his command. One of the most exasperating demonstrations of meddlesomeness occurred in 1844, when the Governor-cum-Superintendent, forbade the battleship *Agincourt* to enter the Canton River to rid her hull of accumulated barnacles. This was an operation much more easily accomplished in fresh water; the cirripeds simply dropped off, without the need for prolonged and violent scraping.[9]

The affair of the *Agincourt* was, of course, a very minor incident, but it underlined the endemic conflict between the political and the service chief that could involve issues of graver import. On grounds of emergency, Pottinger, or any of his successors, might, at almost any time, have jeopardized station strength by commandeering a sloop or a frigate, or both, to effect a particular purpose. Yet the gravity of political relations affecting Anglo-Chinese relations should not be

[8] See p. 249 n.   [9] See pp. 263–4.

underestimated. British civil representatives on the China coast were dealing with a vast Oriental empire, not with Buenos Aires or Fremantle, Aden or Muscat, Mauritius or the Comoros. Within the political context of China which knew no international law and admitted foreign traders only on sufferance, accumulating grievances leading to incidents and crises were bound to invite interventions beyond the normal obligations, and sometimes the capacities of a commander-in-chief.

Of course, this was true in other parts of the world. The Royal Navy, as an instrument of Empire-building, had been long accustomed to stretch its traditional functions over accepted limits. In many parts of the world, captains, junior officers, even midshipmen, had been forced at times to undertake the exceptional tasks of consul, judge, arbitrator, and even dictator. But on the China coast, the need for such versatility was never so pressing. An extensive panoply of civilian authority existed to deal with the most delicate or dangerous situations. After 1842, responsibilities for trade and government were divided between Foreign Office and Colonial Office. Admittedly, it was often difficult to distinguish the line between the governor, whose responsibilities as a Colonial Office appointee did not extend beyond the colony, and the superintendent of trade, whose Foreign Office responsibilities extended everywhere else, the more so because, until 1859, both offices were held by the same man. Under his authority as a Colonial Office servant, the governor might make demands on the squadron, or one of its units, relating to matters of island security; the same man, as superintendent (and occasionally as plenipotentiary) might order the squadron, or detachments of the squadron, to pass the Bocca Tigris, or to safeguard the foreign community at Shanghai against rebel assault.

Lack of co-operation between navy and civilian administration was never, therefore, simply a matter of the personalities involved. There were sometimes bitter policy differences which might concern, for example, the unequal treatment accorded both British officials and traders by the Chinese authorities. After 1842, the enforcement of the Treaty clauses became another contentious issue. The achievement of objectives by negotiation was, of course, part and parcel of a civilian art. But it was an art which, in practice, was often awkwardly and sometimes stupidly exercised. In Admiral Parker's view, the squadron was all too frequently placed 'in handcuffs', and the resulting frustrations of naval commanders could, without quibble, be put down to the blundering of inept diplomats.

To a certain extent this was true. Palmerston himself had admitted how easy it was for an otherwise intelligent representative of the Crown to be taken in by what appeared to be the high and sophisticated standards of the Chinese civil service. He had in mind superintendents of trade like Captain Charles Elliot, who had been naïve enough to believe that customary codes of conduct in England made common sense in China, and that if both sides could sit around a table and thrash out grievances, a mutually advantageous compromise would emerge. Once accepted, honourable gentlemen would abide by its provisions.

The process was no doubt logical, but the goal was sufficiently utopian to be ridiculous, as Major-General Gough declared with explosive epithets when on the verge of capturing Canton in May 1841. Such efforts to find a settlement assumed that it was possible to fix a working relationship on the basis of an established international practice of which the Chinese must have been totally unaware. British negotiators on the whole failed to appreciate the limits of Chinese horizons; China was not a modern European state. Yet only very gradually did it dawn on British officials, whether in Hong Kong or Whitehall, that Western rules or conventions meant little or nothing to the Oriental mind, and that the gap between European and Ch'ing conceptions of conduct, and between the systems within which they operated, was, for the time being at least, unbridgeable.

Under the shock of war, they learned to respect Chinese pertinacity and astuteness, but they continued to remain utterly perplexed and sometimes horrified by the Chinese capacity to ignore oral promises, written agreements, and, even more surprisingly, the obvious claims of political expediency. Successive reports from men in the field seemed to corroborate Palmerston's growing conviction that the Chinese were cunning and deceitful, yielding to nothing but necessity, and skilful at finding out the exact point at which the necessity of yielding ended.[10]

As long as British men-of-war remained in the offing, and garrisons held strategic ports or important cities, promises were likely to be, however unwillingly, carried out. But once troops were withdrawn, or the naval patrols reduced, treaty obligations were as far as possible spurned or ignored. In the Chinese view, since terms had been imposed by overwhelming force after a hostile invasion, accompanied by outrageously bad manners, the evils that followed in the wake of greedy trespass could properly be dissipated by guile. The Treaties represented humiliations that had to be erased by fair means or foul. John Stuart Mill tried to explain this point of view to the Foreign Office, while emphasizing the importance of the navy as an indispensable buttress for any diplomatic effort.

Probably a Chinese statesman thinks that when concessions galling to the national pride, or adverse to national policy, have been extorted by force of arms, and as it were under duress, he is doing no more than his duty in regarding the treaty as a nullity. Accordingly, the more extensive the concessions are which we think we have obtained, the more certain it is that they will be violated, and the less practical benefit shall we derive from them. . . . We find ourselves, therefore, in a vicious circle; for when one expedition has exacted and obtained certain concessions, another and more powerful expedition is required to enforce them; and our diplomacy stands for nothing when we have not a fleet to back it.[11]

During the greater part of the 1840s and '50s, British policy was largely in the hands of Palmerston, Aberdeen, Russell, and Clarendon, and, despite their differences (often exaggerated by some historians), their thinking on the China problem was not dissimilar to that of Mill. The supposedly more pacific Aberdeen, as Foreign Secretary in Peel's second Cabinet, was not backward in urging the need to advertise Britain's naval

[10] Palmerston to Admiral Elliot, 16 Jan. 1841, Broadlands MSS.,GC/EL/38/1. None the less, while the Imperial Court apparently failed to grasp the meaning of European power politics, undoubtedly, by the forties, there were a few literati in Canton, who were beginning to understand.

[11] *Edinburgh Review*, Jan. 1860, pp. 103–4.

muscularity by 'showing the flag' in periodic parades of strength, and he told Peel that he regarded China as an exception to his general rule of opposition to the use of force as a diplomatic lever. In his opinion, it was important to maintain in the China Sea 'a greater force than at first sight appeared necessary'. In view of the 'peculiarity' of Britain's position, the psychological impact on the uninformed mind of Peking could not be overestimated. The Chinese had received evidence of British power, and if a final settlement were to be reached, the Imperial Court must 'continue to see that we are superior to other nations. . . .' British ascendancy depended on constant and imposing demonstrations of force.[12] Even a governor as persistently cautious and peaceable as Sir John Davis saw the wisdom of wielding 'the big stick' on occasion. 'C'est ainsi', he wrote to the commander of the French squadron in 1847, 'qu'on est quelque fois obligé d'exiger le respect des peuples demi-sauvage envers les Nations civilisées de l'Occident. On commence par détruier à coups de Canon les barricades de la barbarie; puis s'ensuivent la Religion, le Commerce, avec leurs résultats.'[13]

Already, however, the colonial reformers'—the professional anti-militarists of their day—were preparing to excite themselves, not only as humanitarians, but as avowed exponents of peace and economic retrenchment, and as opponents of colonial exploitation. With cheerful self-assurance, members of the House of Commons like Gladstone, Bright, and Hume, were fully prepared to offer advice on matters of imperial concern of which they might be almost totally ignorant. No human being is more articulate or more ruthless than the self-righteous fanatic, the more so if he feels frustrated. On the opium question and on the question of punitive exactions which followed Chinese defeats, the reformers had much virtue on their side. They championed a cause which, judging by the amount of self-reproach reflected in subsequent English literature, weighed heavily for generations on the British conscience. Unfortunately, their fulminations were not always

---

[12] 16 Sept. 1844, Aberdeen Papers (B.L.) Add. MS. 43064. See also W. G. Beasley, *Great Britain and the Opening of Japan*, pp. 47–8.

[13] Davis to Captain La Pierre, Hong Kong, 26 Apr. 1847, F.O. 228/69, quoted, Beasley, p. 75.

supported by facts, although loaded with moral sentiments.
Yet one should not ask too much of well-intentioned zealots,
nor censure too confidently their often bitter outpourings.
Knowledge of China and Chinese affairs was limited, even
within the precincts of Whitehall where policies were shaped.
Despite the increasing knowledge and publicity produced in
part by travellers' tales, the reformers' ignorance was simply
one aspect of a wider darkness that hid China from the greater
part of the British people.[14]

On the other hand, while the struggle against the opium
trade could be made the subject of a crusade, the Chinese
themselves could scarcely be turned into objects of compassion in the manner of the African slaves who suffered the
tortures of the damned during, and sometimes after, the
Middle Passage. They might be regarded as victims of fearfully one-sided military campaigns, but the humblest and
meanest of them belonged to a great country that patronized,
bullied, and constantly insulted British plenipotentiaries and
British merchants. It was a weakness of Gladstone and his
allies that they ignored the ridiculous pretensions, the arrogance, the corruption, and the cruelty which were part of
nineteenth-century Manchu rule.

Not that the British public were particularly interested in
consular or merchant embarrassments, until the media took a
hand. When security of trade as well as security of life was
raised as an issue, and when broken treaties produced humiliations involving insults to the flag and affronts to 'the honour
and majesty of Britain', the multitude, stimulated by the press,
called for action. It was then, and only then, that ministers
could ignore the humanitarians and reformers and appeal to
the country to support a settlement by arms. 'If in the remotest
corner of the earth any Englishman gets a well-deserved, but
uncompensated black eye, the newspapers and parliament
immediately demand an enquiry into the conduct of the

[14] Whenever any effort was made to obtain sufficient facts on which to base a line of
action, wrote *The Times* correspondent, George Wingrove Cooke, in 1857, 'we were
brought up by the humiliating conviction that our ignorance of China is a darkness
that may be felt. Even of that great conglomerate of cities on the Yangtse, we know
little more than that it is the commercial emporium of central China . . . No one has
been there except native Chinamen and Jesuit missionaries.' Cooke, *China . . .*,
p. 273.

bloated sinecurist in Downing Street, who has no sense of British honour.'[15]

Black eyes or their equivalent provided 'a cause' which alone was capable of focusing public and parliamentary attention on China. If Gladstone enjoyed, and often profited by, his crusades, whether against Turks and opium smugglers, or in defence of Borneo pirates, similarly Palmerston enjoyed playing the *prima donna* in melodramas that not infrequently, in the name of patriotism, won the applause and votes of the man on the street. His oratory was never an instrument of persuasion to higher moral purpose; nevertheless, on matters like Italian unity, he could, in times of stress, be just as fanatical as Gladstone. And because of his concentration on the European scene—more especially the relations of France and Austria with Italy—he was slow to learn his eastern geography. In fact, until the first Opium War provided a challenge, he paid little attention to China, a neglect which is altogether understandable. To Russell, and Clarendon as well, the affairs of Europe were always more important than those of the Far East. Inevitably, Europe held the centre of parliamentary and public attention. In 1848, for example, a whole series of dramatic revolutions coincided with the beginning of the Italian War of Independence. Except in moments of extreme urgency, conflict in the China seas represented a mere side-show.

But outside Europe, there were many other distractions that helped to keep China in the background. The demands on British naval strength were world-wide and constant. Rivalry with France for maritime and overseas power extended from the Mediterranean to the Pacific, where competitive French annexations led to constant friction, complicated by a succession of race wars. Wary of American competition, modest detachments of the Royal Navy helped to pry open and hold open trading doors with Japan, and Lord Elgin's special visit served to indicate the importance attaching to Japanese relations. In central and South America, the navy was frequently on call to protect British lives and commercial interests. Troubles were always brewing in the Turkish Empire, and corvettes were needed on the east and west African coasts to

[15] Maxwell, *The Life and Letters of George William Frederick, Fourth Earl of Clarendon*, ii. 135–6.

suppress the slave trade. In addition, discontents festered in Burma, which ultimately led to a second Burmese conflict; a petty war had to be waged in Persia, and, to cap it all, the whole British Empire was temporarily shaken by the Indian Mutiny. It can scarcely be doubted that the course of British policy and British action in China would have been different had the problem of the Middle Kingdom not been over-shadowed by an almost ceaseless procession of critical events elsewhere.

But if, by the beginning of the 1840s, the attentions of British statesmen were increasingly diverted by European and other external crises, this was not true of the traders on the spot, and their influential patrons at home. The continent of Europe hardly entered into the thinking of men dominated by the vision of Eldorado, 'the next great arena for the develop-ment of British civilization', as that indefatigable publicist, R. M. Martin wrote in 1846. China, he contended, would provide ample compensation for the loss of the United States, and recompense for the inevitable departure of self-governing India.[16] To many Old China Hands, the war of 1839–42 was simply the first step in a programme of commercial expansion into the interior. To tap these vast, uncharted spaces guarded by secretive, dog-in-the-manger Chinese governments, mer-chant firms had no hesitation in demanding armed support for their endeavours. Actively backed by various chambers of commerce, they urged the British government in petition after petition to strengthen the China squadron, eliminate piracy, and insist on the long-sought equal diplomatic status, which should provide free access to Canton.

But all the appeals of mercantile interests, regardless of their merit, ignored the vital fact that the Chinese Empire could neither be subdued nor controlled from salt water. Admit-tedly, as in India, command of the sea could permit the elimi-nation of rivals and pave the way for advances inland. But conquering even a politically disunited subcontinent had been extremely expensive, and subsequent responsibilities for administration had been painfully heavy. In the middle of the nineteenth century, a time of scrupulous, if not penny-

---

[16] R. Montgomery Martin, *Reports, Minutes and Despatches on the British Position and Prospects in China* (London, 1846), p. 90.

pinching, book-keeping, these considerations had not been forgotten by Victorian statesmen. Long before the Mitchell Report of 1852 had been read and buried, and its myth-shattering conclusions could be confirmed in detail, no foreign secretary, Whig or Tory, was foolish enough to assert that prospects of a grand interior China market justified the cost of conquest, even if conquest were possible. Moreover, there was no Yellow Peril to justify a crusade in the interest of British Imperial security. Unlike Russia, China offered no 'back-door' threat to the security of India. The North-West Frontier would not be one whit the safer should the Manchu Emperor submit to British arms. In brief, any attempt to subdue three hundred million or more people, living on what was estimated to be a million and a third square miles, would have been—and was so regarded by Palmerston—an act of crazy bravado, not dissimilar to the dashing efforts of a small dog attempting to subdue an elephant by biting his heels.[17]

What did concern British governments was the danger of being drawn willy-nilly on to the Chinese mainland should the Manchu dynasty collapse and civil war ensue. The decay of the Mogul Empire in India had tempted Britain to undertake the task of salvage operations. Two centuries later, the first ominous symptoms of a similar decay had become apparent in the empire ruled from Peking. If the rickety throne of the Manchus toppled, Great Britain, jealously watched by Euro-pean rivals, might face the awful problem of restoring order, or, at the worst, joining in an indecent scramble for a share of the spoils. Admittedly, she could entrench herself in every important harbour on the coast, and control for many miles inland the principal rivers. But accessibility by sea in no way altered the fundamental fact that the navy was quite incapable of imposing British rule on the interior. Without a continental-type army, capable of providing endless contingents for the field, Britain was no better placed than Spain, who, a few years earlier, had tried in vain to maintain her vast South American empire. Any occupation policy was impracticable and ridicu-lous, even had it been desired.

It was, therefore, vital to British purposes that the Chinese

[17] See Robert Mudie, *China, and its Resources and Peculiarities, Physical, Political, Social and Commercial. . . .* (London, 1840), pp. vi, 25.

Empire should not, in the manner of the Sick Man of Europe, become the prey of hungry Western concession hunters. Foreign projects such as railways and telegraphs, for example, by providing footholds in the interior, could lead to serious complications. It was true that British naval and commercial hegemony based on India was unchallengeable. But no matter how formidable the numbers of the Royal Navy, a *Pax Britannica* required the friendship, or at least the forbearance, of European powers. Hence, during the course of three Anglo-Chinese campaigns, the reactions of France and Russia, whether as rivals, declared enemies, or allies of convenience, had to be carefully watched and weighed. The security of the British position in China depended upon a relatively constant balance of power. What happened in China might drastically affect a delicate equilibrium of forces on the other side of the world. A Chinese policy could never be entirely isolated from a European policy. Only Russia was in a position to conduct her foreign relations in two separate compartments, the Asiatic and the European, without one system of foreign relations seriously jeopardizing the other.

But not until the Treaty of Peking had been signed in October 1860, did Russia take full advantage of her unique situation in this respect. Within a few days of the departure of French and British troops from the capital, her plenipotentiary, Count Ignatieff, effected a supplementary treaty, which was to deprive China of some 400,000 square miles of territory. The annexation included a whole province south of the Amur River, and east of the Ussuri River which led to the sea and the future port of Vladivostock. Without firing a shot, Russia had become a Pacific power with a coastline that stretched as far south as the frontiers of Korea. A nation, whose warships had been confined by treaty to the Black Sea, and, for many months in the year, by ice in the Baltic, had acquired a maritime stake in the Far East. Not without apprehension did the Mistress of the Seas contemplate the future activities of an Asiatic power, so far removed from immediate European surveillance.

APPENDIX A

NOTE ON WARSHIPS' RATINGS

SAILING ships were rated *first* to *sixth* according to size and the number of guns carried. Most of the battleships involved in operations in the China seas were *third* rates, normally carrying between 60 and 74 guns. Eventually, as the 60s disappeared, this rate was applied to 80-gun ships. *Fifth* and *sixth* rates were frigates (and not infrequently *fourth* rates were so described) carrying generally from 50 downwards to 28 guns. Below these were sloops and brigs with around 20 and 10 guns respectively. The smaller ships, especially during the 1840s and 1850s are difficult to classify in terms of gun-power because the new steamer tended to have fewer but larger guns. Consequently, by the mid-forties, the Admiralty began to rate ships by complement as well as by guns.

Frigate has meant a great many things between the time of Noah and the beginning of World War II (when Canada suggested 'frigate' as the name for the large corvettes she was then building). Precise definition is almost impossible, and it is perhaps simpler to think of all frigates during the period under survey as full-rigged ships with quarterdeck and forecastle, commanded by post captains. *Corvette*, a French term used unofficially in the Royal Navy, was the name applied to a flush-decked ship, ordinarily commanded by a captain. *Sloop* may be considered as a commander's command, and by the early nineteenth century 'sloops rigged as ships' had become designated as a class, largely taking the place of small vessels like snows, brigs, and ketches. *Gunboat*, in origin, simply meant a boat with a gun on it. But with the coming of steam (and long before the popularization of the phrase 'gunboat diplomacy') the term was used to describe a miscellany of small steamers. These powerful, shallow-draught vessels were indispensable for river work, and were normally commanded by lieutenants. Not long after the Crimean War (which saw a considerable increase in numbers), larger gunboats began to be built, and these were officially designated as 'gun vessels'.

APPENDIX B

East India Station limits previous to 25 July 1844

ON the North by the Coast of Asia.
On the West by the coasts of Asia and Africa as far south as a line drawn from the coast of Africa along the Equator to 60° of E. longitude, thence along the meridian of the 60° E. longitude to the point where it intersects 10° S. latitude, thence by latitude 10° S. to 75° E. longitude, along which meridian it is to continue until it reaches the Antarctic Circle.
On the East by the meridian of 170° W. longitude.

East India Station limits from 25 July 1844

On the North by the shores of Asia.
On the West by Africa, north of the Equator, thence along the Equator to 66° E. longitude, thence by 66° E. longitude to latitude 10° S., thence by latitude 10° S. to longitude 75° E, thence by longitude 75° E. to the Antarctic Circle.
On the East by 170° W. longitude.
On the South by the Antarctic Circle.
(Admiralty to Rear-Admiral Sir Thomas Cochrane, 25 July, 1844 (No. 126); Adm. 1/5543; see also, Adm. 2/1330).

BIBLIOGRAPHY

The principal documentary and manuscript sources have been cited in the Preface.

I. PRINTED WORKS

Contemporary, including a few books of a later date containing source materials for the period, e.g. 'Life and Letters'.

ABEEL, DAVID, *Journal of a Residence in China and the Neighbouring Countries from 1830 to 1833*, London, 1835.

ALCOCK, SIR RUTHERFORD, *The Capital of the Tycoon: A Narrative of a Three Years' Residence in Japan* (2 vols.), London, 1863.

ALLEN, G. C. and DONNITHORNE, A. G., *Western Enterprise in Far Eastern Economic Development—China and Japan*, London, 1954.

ALLGOOD, MAJOR-GENERAL G., *China War, 1860: Letters and Journal*, London, 1901.

ANDERSON, CAPTAIN LINDSAY, *A Cruise in an Opium Clipper*, London, 1891.

AUBER, PETER, *China; an outline of its government, law and policy; and of the British and foreign embassies to, and intercourse with, that Empire*, London, 1834.

BELCHER, CAPTAIN SIR EDWARD, R. N., *Narrative of a Voyage Round the World, performed in Her Majesty's Ship Sulphur, during the years 1836–1842, including details of the Naval Operations in China, from Dec. 1840 to Nov. 1841* (2 vols.), London, 1843.
Narrative of the Voyage of H.M.S. Samarang during the years 1843–46 (2 vols.), London, 1848.

BERNARD, W. D., *Narrative of the Voyages and Services of the Nemesis from 1840 to 1843.* (2 vols.), London, 1844; Praeger reprint (1 vol.), New York, 1969.

BINGHAM, CMDR. J. ELLIOT, *Narrative of the Expedition to China from the Commencement of the War to the Present Period. . .* (2 vols.), London, 1842.

BONNER-SMITH, D. and LUMBY, E. W. B. (eds.), *The Second China War 1856–1860*, Navy Records Society, London, 1954.

BORGET, AUGUSTE, *La Chine et les Chinois . . .,* Paris, 1842.

BOWRING, SIR JOHN, *Autobiographical Recollections of*, with a brief memoir by Lewin B. Bowring, London, 1877.

COLCHESTER, LORD CHARLES (ed.), *History of the Indian Administration of Lord Ellenborough*, London, 1874.

COLOMB, VICE-ADMIRAL P. H., *Memoirs of Sir Astley Cooper Key*, London, 1898.

COOKE, GEORGE WINGROVE, *China: being 'The Times' special correspondence from China in the years 1857–58*, London, 1859.

CUNYNGHAME, CAPT. ARTHUR, *The Opium War, Being Recollections of Service in China*, London, 1844; Philadelphia, 1845.

DAVIDSON, G. F., *Trade and Travel in the Far East; or Recollections of Twenty One years passed in Java, Singapore, Australia & China*, London, 1846.

DAVIS, SIR JOHN, *The Chinese; A General Description of the Empire of China and its Inhabitants* (2 vols.), London, 1840.
China during the War and since the Peace (2 vols.), London, 1852.

DOWNING, C. TOOGOOD, *The Fan-Qui in China 1836–37*, London, 1838.

DUNNE, J. H., *From Calcutta to Pekin: being notes taken from the Journal of an officer between those places*, London, 1861.

EITEL, E. J., *Europe in China. The History of Hong Kong from the beginning to the year 1882*, London and Hong Kong, 1895.

ELLIOT, ADMIRAL SIR GEORGE, *Memoir of Admiral the Honourable Sir George Elliot*, London, 1863.

'A FIELD OFFICER', *The Last Year in China to the Peace of Nanking: as sketched in Letters to his Friends*, London, 1843.

FINLAY, JAMES AND CO. LTD., *Manufacturers and East India Merchants, 1750–1950*, Glasgow, 1951.

FISHBOURNE, CAPTAIN E. G. F., *Impressions of China, and the present Revolution: its Progress and Prospects*, London, 1855.

FORBES, LT F. E.,R.N., *Five Years in China; from 1842 to 1847*, London, 1848.

FORBES, ROBERT B., *Personal Reminiscences*, Boston, 1878; 3rd edn., Boston, 1892.

FORTUNE, ROBERT, *Three Years Wandering in the Northern Provinces of China*, 2nd edn., London, 1847.
A Journey to the Tea Countries of China, including Sung-Lo and the Bohen Hills, London, 1852.

GOOCH, G. P. (ed.), *The Later Correspondence of Lord John Russell, 1840–1878* (2 vols.), London, 1925.

GRANT, GENERAL SIR HOPE, and KNOLLYS, CAPT. HENRY, *Incidents in the China War of 1860*, Edinburgh and London, 1875.

GUTZLAFF, CHARLES, *Journal of Three Voyages along the Coast of China in 1831, 1832 and 1833*, London, 1834.

A Sketch of Chinese History, Ancient and Modern (2 vols.), London, 1834.

HALL, CAPTAIN BASIL, R.N., *Narrative of a Voyage to Java, China and the Great Loo-choo Island*, London, 1846.

HAY, ADMIRAL RT. HON. SIR JOHN C. D., *The Suppression of Piracy in the China Sea, 1849*, London, 1889.

HENSHAW, JOSHUA, *Around the World: Narrative of a Voyage in the East India Squadron under Commodore George C. Read* (2 vols.), New York and Boston, 1840.

HORSBURGH, JAMES, F.R.S., *The India Directory, or, Directions for Sailing to and from the East Indies, China, Australia, and the interjacent ports of Africa and South America* (2 vols.), seventh edn., London, 1855.

HUC, ABBÉ, *Travels in Tartary, Thibet, and China, 1844–5–6*, translated from the French by W. Hazlitt (2 vols.), London, 1852.

HUMMEL, ARTHUR W. (ed.), *Eminent Chinese of the Ch'ing Period,1644–1912* (2 vols.), Washington, D.C., 1943–4; reprint Taipei, Taiwan (1 vol.) 1972.

HUNTER, WILLIAM C., 'An Old Resident', *The 'Fan Kwae' at Canton before Treaty Days, 1825–1844*, London, 1882; Shanghai, 1911.

Jardine Matheson & Co. *An outline of the history of a China House for a hundred years, 1832–1932*, Hong Kong (privately printed), 1934.

JOCELYN, LORD ROBERT, *Six Months with the Chinese Expedition, or, Leaves from a Soldier's Note-Book*, London, 1841.

KNOLLYS, HENRY (CAPTAIN, ROYAL ARTILLERY), see under Grant, General Sir Hope.

LANE-POOLE, STANLEY, *The Life of Sir Harry Parkes* (vol. 1), *Consul in China*, London, 1894.

LAY, HORATIO NELSON, 'Our Interests in China'—a letter to the Rt. Hon. Earl Russell K.G. (H.M.'s Principal Secty. of State for Foreign Affairs), London, 1864.
Note on the Opium Question, and Brief Survey of our Relations with China, London, 1893.

LINDSAY, HUGH HAMILTON, *A Voyage to the Northern Ports of China in the Ship 'Lord Amherst'*, extracted from papers printed by order of the House of Commons relating to the Trade in China, London, 1833.
['A Resident in China'], *Remarks on Occurrences in China since the Opium Seizure in March, 1839 to the latest date*, London, 1840.

LOCH, CAPT. GRANVILLE G., R.N., *The Closing Events of the Campaign in China: The Operations in the Yang-Tse-Kiang; and Treaty of Nanking*, London, 1843.

LOCKHART, WILLIAM, *The Medical Missionary in China: A narrative of twenty years experience*, London, 1869.

LOW, C. R. *History of the Indian Navy* (2 vols.), London, 1877.

MACKENZIE, KEITH STEWART, *Narrative of the Second Campaign in China*, London, 1842.

MCLEOD, JOHN, (Surgeon), *Narrative of a Voyage in Her Majesty's late Ship Alceste to the Yellow Sea. . .*, London, 1817.

MCPHERSON, D. (M.D.), *Two Years in China: Narrative of the Chinese Expedition From its Formation in April 1840 till April, 1842*, London, 1842.
The War in China 1840–42, London, 1843.

MA HUAN, YING-YAI SHENG-LA, *The Overall Survey of the Ocean's Shores* [1433], trans. and ed. J. V. G. Mills, Cambridge (for the Hakluyt Society), 1970.

MARTIN, R. MONTGOMERY, *China; Political, Commercial and Social; in an Official Report to Her Majesty's Government*, London, 1847.
Reports, Minutes and Despatches on the British Position and Prospects in China, London, 1846.

MAXWELL, RT. HON. SIR HERBERT, *The Life and Letters of George William Frederick, Fourth Earl of Clarendon* (2 vols.), London, 1913.

MAYERS, W. F. (ed.), *Treaties between the Empire of China and Foreign Powers . . .*, 1st edn. 1877; 5th edn. Shanghai, 1906; Taipei, 1966.

MAYERS, W. F., DENNYS, N. B. and KING, CHAS., *The Treaty Ports of China and Japan, forming a Guide Book . . .*, London, 1867.

MEADOWS, THOMAS T., *The Chinese and their Rebellions, viewed in connection with their national Philosophy, Ethics, Legislation and Administration*, London, 1856.

MEDHURST, W. H., *China: Its State and Prospects . . .*, London, 1838.

MICHIE, ALEXANDER, *The Englishman in China during the Victorian Era: The Career of Sir Rutherford Alcock*, London, 1900.

MOGES, MARQUIS DE, *Recollections of Baron Gros' Embassy to China in 1857–8* (authorized translation), London and Glasgow, 1860.

MORSE, HOSEA BALLOU, *The Chronicles of the East India Company trading to China 1635–1843* (vol. iv), Oxford, 1926.
The International Relations of the Chinese Empire (3 vols), London and Shanghai, 1910.

MUDIE, ROBERT, *China, and its Resources and peculiarities, Physical, Political, Social and Commercial . . .*, London, 1840.

MUNDY, WALTER WILLIAM, *Canton and the Bogue, The Narrative of an eventful six months in China*, London, 1875.

MURRAY, LT. ALEXANDER, *Doings in China, being the Personal Narrative of an Officer engaged in the late Chinese Expedition*, London, 1843.

NAPIER, MAJOR-GENERAL SIR WILLIAM (ed.), *The Navy, Its Past and Present State, in a series of Letters by Rear-Admiral Sir Charles Napier, K.C.B.*, London, 1851.

NYE, GIDEON, *The Memorable Year* (privately printed), Macao, 1858.
The Morning of my Life in China, being lectures given to the Canton Community in 1873, Canton, 1873.

OLIPHANT, LAURENCE, *Narrative of the Earl of Elgin's Mission to China and Japan in the years 1857, '58, '59* (2 vols), London, 1859; Praeger reprint (one vol.), 1970.

OSBORN, CAPTAIN SHERARD, C.B., R.N., *Queda, A Cruise in Japanese Waters* [which includes] *The Fight on the Peiho* [1859] new ed., Edinburgh and London, 1865.
The Past and Future of British Relations in China, Edinburgh and London, 1860.

OUCHTERLONY, LT. JOHN, *The Chinese War: An Account of all the Operations of the British Forces from the Commencement to the Treaty of Nanking*, London, 1844; Praeger reprint, 1970.

PARKER, C. S., *Life and Letters of Sir James Graham* (2 vols), London, 1907.

PARKER, E. H., *Chinese Account of the Opium War*, a general translation by Wei Yüan of Shêng Wu-ki, or 'Military Operations of the present Dynasty', Shanghai, 1888.
China, Her History, Diplomacy and Commerce, from the Earliest Times to the Present Day, London 1901; New York, 1917.

PHILLIMORE, VICE-ADMIRAL AUGUSTUS, *The Life of Admiral of the Fleet Sir William Parker, Bart. G.C.B., from 1781 to 1866* (3 vols.), London, 1876–1880.

Parliamentary Papers, presented either to the House of Commons or the House of Lords, or both. Among many consulted, the most useful concerned naval operations leading to the capture of Canton; campaigns in the north associated with the Earl of Elgins 'Special Missions to China 1857 to 1859', and correspondence respecting affairs in China, 1859–60.

PLAYFAIR, G. M. H., *The Cities and Towns of China*, Shanghai, 1879; reprint, Taipei, 1968.

POWER, W. TYRONE, D. A. C. G., *Recollections of a Three Years' Residence in China*, London, 1853.

RAIT, ROBERT S., *The Life and Campaigns of Hugh, Field Marshal, Viscount Gough* (2 vols.), London, 1903.

RENNIE, D. F., M.D., *The British Arms in North China and Japan . . .*, London, 1864.

REYNOLDS, JOHN N., *Voyage of the United States Frigate Potomac under the command of Commodore John Downes, during the Circumnavigation of the Globe in the years 1831–34,* New York, 1835.

SANSOM, GEORGE B., *The Western World and Japan,* New York, 1950.

SCARTH, JOHN, *Twelve Years in China. The People, the Rebels and the Mandarins,* Edinburgh, 1860.

SCOTT, BERESFORD, *An Account of the Destruction of the Fleets of the celebrated Pirate Chieftains Chui-Apoo and Shap-ng-tsai, in September and October, 1849,* London, 1881.

STANMORE, A. H. GORDON, FIRST BARON, *Sidney Herbert, Lord Herbert of Lea, A Memoir* (2 vols.), London, 1906.

STAUNTON, SIR GEORGE, *Remarks on British Relations with China, and the Proposed Plans for Improving Them,* London, 1836.

STEPHENSON, F. C. A., *At Home and on the Battlefield: Letters from the Crimea, China and Egypt 1854–1888,* London, 1915.

SWINHOE, ROBERT, *Narrative of the North China Campaign of 1860 . . .,* London, 1861.

TAYLOR, FITCH W., *A Voyage Round the World . . . in the United States Frigate Columbia . . .* (2 vols., 5th edn.), New Haven and New York, 1846.

TAYLOR, SIR HENRY, *A Digest of the Despatches on China* (published anonymously), London, 1840.

TIMEWELL, H. C., *The First Reduction of the Taku Forts—1858* [based on the Public and Private Journal of Cmdr. Thomas Saumarez, *The Mariner's Mirror,* Vol. 63, No. 2 (May 1977), pp. 163–77].

VARIN, PAUL, *Expédition de Chine,* Paris, 1862.

VETCH, COL. R. H. (ed.), *Life Letters and Diaries of Lieut.-General Sir Gerald Graham, V.C.,* Edinburgh and London, 1901.

WALDROND, THEODORE (ed.), *The Letters and Journals of James, Eighth Earl of Elgin,* London, 1872.

WILLIAMS, S. WELLS, *The Middle Kingdom, A Survey of the Geography, Government, Literature, Social Life, Arts, Religion and History of the Chinese Empire and Its Inhabitants* (2 vols.), London, 1848; revised edn., New York, 1883.
The Chinese Commercial Guide . . . with an Appendix of Sailing Directions for those Seas and Coasts [reprinted from the *China Pilot*], Hong Kong, 1863; Taipei, 1966.

WOLSELEY, LT. COL. G. J., *Narrative of the War with China in 1860,* London, 1862.

WOOD, W. W., *Sketches of China,* Philadelphia, 1830.

I. LATER PRINTED WORKS

ALDINGTON, RICHARD, *Wellington, Being an account of the Life & Achievements of Arthur Wellesley, 1st Duke of Wellington*, London, 1946.

BACON, SIR REGINALD H. S., *Life of Lord Fisher of Kilverstone* (2 vols.), London 1929.

BANNO, MASATAKA, *China and the West 1858–1861, The Origins of the Tsungli Yamen*, Cambridge, Mass., 1964.

BEASLEY, W. G., *Great Britain and the Opening of Japan, 1834–1858*, London, 1951.

CADY, JOHN F., *The Roots of French Imperialism in Eastern Asia*, Ithaca, N.Y., 1954; new edn. 1967.

CHANG, HSIN-PAO, *Commissioner Lin and the Opium War*, Cambridge, Mass., 1964.

CHEN, GIDEON, *Lin Tsê-hsü, Pioneer Promoter of the Adoption of Western Means of Maritime Defense in China*, Peiping, 1934; reprint, New York, 1961.

CLARK, ARTHUR HAMILTON, *The Clipper Ship Era 1843–1869*, New York, 1910.

COSTIN, W. C., *Great Britain and China 1833–60*, Oxford, 1937; reprint, 1968.

DAWSON, RAYMOND, *The Chinese Chameleon: An Analysis of European Conceptions of Chinese Civilization*, Oxford, 1967.

ENDACOTT, G. B., *A History of Hong Kong*, London, 1958.
An Eastern Entrepot; A Collection of documents illustrating the history of Hong Kong, London (H.M.S.O.), 1964.

FAIRBANK, JOHN KING, *Trade and Diplomacy on the China Coast. The Opening of the Treaty Ports 1842–1854*, vols. i and ii (reference notes, Appendices, Bibliography and Glossary of Chinese Names and Terms), Cambridge, Mass., 1953.

FAY, PETER WARD, *The Opium War 1840–1842*, Chapel Hill, 1975.

FOX, GRACE, *British Admirals and Chinese Pirates 1832–1869*, London, 1940.

FRANKE, WOLFGANG, *A Century of Chinese Revolution 1851–1949*, Oxford (Blackwell), 1969.
China and the West, Oxford (Blackwell), 1969.

GERSON, JACK J., *Horatio Nelson Lay and Sino-British Relations 1854–1864*, Cambridge, Mass., 1972.

GRAHAM, GERALD S., *Great Britain in the Indian Ocean. A Study of Maritime Enterprise 1810–1850*, Oxford, 1967.

GREENBERG, MICHAEL, *British Trade and the Opening of China 1800–1842*, Cambridge, 1951; reprint, 1970.

GULICK, EDWARD V., *Peter Parker and the Opening of China,* Cambridge, Mass., 1974.

HSÜ, IMMANUEL C. Y., *China's Entrance into the Family of Nations The Diplomatic Phase 1858–1880,* Cambridge, Mass., 1960.

HOLT, EDGAR, *The Opium Wars in China,* London, 1964.

HURD, DOUGLAS, *The Arrow War 1856–1860,* London, 1967.

IMLAH, A. H., *Lord Ellenborough,* Cambridge, Mass., 1939.

KUO, P. C., *A Critical Study of the First Anglo–Chinese War, with Documents,* Shanghai, 1935; reprint, Taipei, 1970.

LUBBOCK, BASIL, *The Opium Clippers,* Glasgow, 1933.

MAO-YEE-HANG, *Les Relations politiques et économiques entre la Chine et les Puissances de 1842 à 1860* (Univ. of Paris, doctoral thesis), Lyon, 1923.

MANCALL, MARK, *Major-General Ignatieff's Mission to Peking 1859–1860* (Papers on China for the East Asian Regional Studies seminar, Harvard University), Cambridge, Mass., 1956.

MORISON, J. L., *The Eighth Earl of Elgin. A Chapter in Nineteenth-Century Imperial History,* London, 1928.

MORRELL, W. P., *British Colonial Policy in the Age of Peel and Russell,* Oxford, 1930.

NOLDE, JOHN J., 'The "False Edict" of 1849', *Journal of Asian Studies,* xx, No. 3, 1961.

'A Plea for a Regional Approach to Chinese History: The Case of the South China Coast', *The Journal of the Hong Kong Branch of the Royal Asiatic Society,* vol. 6, Oct. 1966.

'Xenophobia in Canton, 1842–1849', *Journal of Oriental Studies,* vol. xiii, No. 1, University of Hong Kong, 1975.

OWEN, DAVID E., *British Opium Policy in China and India,* New Haven, Conn., 1934.

PAGE, WILLIAM, *Commerce and Industry* . . . (2 vols.), London, 1913.

PANIKKAR, K. M., *Asia and Western Dominance,* London, 1953.

PELCOVITS, NATHAN A., *Old China Hands and the Foreign Office,* New York, 1958.

PLATT, D. C. M., *Finance, Trade and Politics in British Foreign Policy 1815–1914,* Oxford, 1968.

PRITCHARD, E. H., *The Critical Years of Early Anglo–Chinese Relations 1750–1800,* Pullman, Washington, 1936; reprint, 1970.

RITCHIE, G. S., *The Admiralty Chart, British Naval Hydrography in the Nineteenth Century,* London, 1967.

SARGENT, A. J., *Anglo–Chinese Commerce and Diplomacy (Mainly in the Nineteenth Century),* London, 1967.

SAYER, G. R., *Hong Kong, Birth, Adolescence, and Coming of Age,* Oxford, 1937.

SELBY, JOHN, *The Paper Dragon: A Account of the Chinese Wars, 1840–1900*, London, 1968.

SHEN, WEI-TAI, 'China's Foreign Policy 1839–1860' (Columbia Univ. Ph.D. thesis), New York, 1932.

SWISHER, EARL, *China's Management of the American Barbarians: A Study of Sino–American Relations 1841–1861, with Documents*, New Haven, Conn., 1951.

TAYLOR, E. S., 'Hong Kong as a Factor in British Relations with China, 1834–1860' (Univ. of London M.A. thesis, 1967).

TENG, SSU-YÜ, *Chang Hsi and the Treaty of Nanking 1842*, Chicago, 1944.

TROTTER, L. J., *The Earl of Auckland*, Oxford, 1893.

WAKEMAN, FREDERIC, JR., *Strangers at the Gate: Social Disorder in South China, 1839–1861*, Berkeley, 1966.

WALEY, ARTHUR, *The Opium War through Chinese Eyes*, London, 1958.

WARD, SIR ADOLPHUS, AND GOOCH, G. P. (eds.), *The Cambridge History of British Foreign Policy 1783–1919, Vol. II, 1815–1866*, London and New York, 1923.

WEBSTER, C. K., *The Foreign Policy of Palmerston, 1830–1841* (2 vols.), London, 1951.

WIETHOFF, BODO, *Chinas dritte Grenze. Der Traditionelle Chinesische Staat und der küstennahe Seeraum*, Wiesbaden, 1969.

WISSLER, ALBERT, *Zur Geschichte der Opium-frage*, Jena, 1930.

PERIODICALS

Including Hansard, *Parliamentary Debates,* Third Series, which has been consulted only for particular speeches on significant occasions (e.g. Palmerston, Russell, Gladstone). Useful material has been garnered from the *Asiatic Journal* (pamphlet reprints, J. L. Cox & Sons, London), the *Chinese Repository,* Canton [1832–51], the *Edinburgh Review,* the *Quarterly Review,* Transactions of the *China Branch of the Royal Asiatic Society,* the *United Service Journal* [1829–41], the *United Service Magazine* [1842–8], and the *Journal of the Royal United Service Institution,* Whitehall, S.W.1.

INDEX

Aberdeen, George Hamilton Gordon, fourth Earl of, humane principles of, 187; succeeds Palmerston as Foreign Secretary (1841), 190, 191; reaction to cession of Hong Kong, 233–4; argues superiority of civil power over naval, 256; prime minister (Dec. 1852), 276

Achin Head, 267

Aigun, Treaty of, 293

Alcock, Sir Rutherford (consul), ix, retaliates for assault on missionaries near Shanghai, 249, n. 61; on enervating climate of the East, 265, n. 28; his measures to protect foreign communities from Taipings, 278–9; emergency powers used (1848), 412

Amoy, recommended as anchorage by Matheson, 68; possible objective of expedition of 1840, 116; description of, and attack on (1840), 123–4; prospective occupation of, 158; projected punishment of, 180; capture of, 181

Amur River, 293, 421

Arrow 'affair', 300 *et seq*

Article X of Supplementary Treaty of Nanking (1843), 260; Navy's hands tied by, 261; 266

Ashburnham, Major-General Thomas (commander of land force (1857), 324, 325

Auckland, George Eden, Earl of, Governor-General of India in 1835, 111; views on need for a base in event of war, 112; his preparations for expedition of 1840, 117–18; opposes permanent occupation of Chusan, 136; on strategy, 174–5, 176, 193, n. 53; advises on danger of spreading forces too thin, 190–1

Austin, Rear-Admiral Charles (c. in c., China Station (1850) succeeding Collier), an ageing 'stop-gap' who stood by the rules, 275, 277

Barrow, Sir John (second secretary to Admiralty (1807–45), proposes operations off China coast (1839), 102, 104; supports advance to Peking by way of the Peiho (1842), 205

Bate, (Lt.) William, surveyor of Treaty ports, 262, n. 20

Belcher, Captain, Sir Edward, ix; directs landing at Canton (1841), 161 and n. 34; anger over Admiralty's failure to give him task of surveying the Yangtse, 219, n. 51; 262, n. 20

Bentinck, Lord William Cavendish (Governor-General of Bengal, first Governor-General of India, 1833), rebukes Select Committee (1830), 21–2; changes view, 27–8; aims at conciliation (1832), 42; lacking in power of decision, 69

Bethune, Captain Drinkwater (SNO in Indian Ocean), leads squadron towards Chusan, 121; survey of the Yangtse, 219

Bingham, Commander J. E., 2

Blackwood, Rear-Admiral Sir Henry (c. in c., East Indies Station, 1819–22), 15, 16–17

Blackwood, Captain P., assault on the Bocca Tigris forts (1834), 56–8; 60–1; commanding as Commodore, East Indies division (1847), 240

Blundell, Hon. E. A. (Governor of Straits Settlements), arranges despatch of Indian infantry to China, 311–12; 315

Bocca Tigris (the Bogue), Chinese regulations restricting entry of foreign ships into, 13–14; defences of, and destruction of forts (1834), 52, 56–8; 61, 66, 110, 144; reinforced defences of, 146–7

Bonham, Sir George (Governor of Hong Kong, 1848), character; content with bare naval necessities, 249–50; opposes Palmerston's policy of withdrawing from Foochow and